ELEMENTS OF ARGUMENT

SIXTH EDITION

ELEMENTS OF ARGUMENT
A Text and Reader

Annette T. Rottenberg

BEDFORD / ST. MARTIN'S   BOSTON   ◆   NEW YORK

For Alex and Anna

For Bedford/St. Martin's
Developmental Editor: Maura E. Shea
Production Editor: Deborah Baker
Production Supervisor: Catherine Hetmansky
Marketing Manager: Karen Melton
Editorial Assistant: Nicole Simonsen
Copyeditor: Rosemary Winfield
Text Design: Claire Seng-Niemoeller
Cover Design: Donna Lee Dennison
Cover Art: Balancing Act II by Scott Fraser. Courtesy of Gerold Wunderlich & Co., New York.
Composition: Pine Tree Composition, Inc.
Printing and Binding: Haddon Craftsmen, Inc.

President: Charles H. Christensen
Editorial Director: Joan E. Feinberg
Director of Editing, Design, and Production: Marcia Cohen
Managing Editor: Elizabeth M. Schaaf

Library of Congress Catalog Card Number: 99–62000

For information, write: Bedford/St. Martin's, 75 Arlington Street, Boston, MA 02116 (617–426–7440)

ISBN: 0–312–19576–1

ACKNOWLEDGMENTS

Stephen J. Adler. "Why Our Jury System Is in Trouble." Excerpted from *The Jury: Trial and Error in the American Courtroom* by Stephen J. Adler. Copyright © 1994 by Stephen J. Adler. Reprinted by permission of Time Books / Random House.
Gordon Allport. "The Nature of Prejudice." From the 17th Claremont Reading Conference Yearbook, 1952. Reprinted by permission of the Claremont Reading Conference.

Acknowledgments and copyrights are continued at the back of the book on pages 771–76, which constitute an extension of the copyright page. It is a violation of the law to reproduce these selections by any means whatsoever without the written permission of the copyright holder.

Preface
for Instructors

PURPOSE

Argumentation as the basis of a composition course should need no defense, especially at a time of renewed pedagogical interest in critical thinking. A course in argumentation encourages practice in close analysis, use of supporting materials, and logical organization. It encompasses all the modes of development around which composition courses are often built. It teaches students to read and to listen with more than ordinary care. Not least, argument can engage the interest of students who have been indifferent or even hostile to required writing courses. Because the subject matter of argument can be found in every human activity, from the most trivial to the most elevated, both students and teachers can choose the materials that appeal to them.

Composition courses using the materials of argument are, of course, not new. But the traditional methods of teaching argument through mastery of the formal processes of reasoning cannot account for the complexity of arguments in practice. Even more relevant to our purposes as teachers of composition is the tenuous relationship between learning about induction and deduction, however helpful in analysis, and the actual process of student composition. The challenge has been to find a method of teaching argument that assists students in defending their claims as directly and efficiently as possible, a method that reflects the way people actually go about organizing and developing claims outside the classroom.

One such method, first adapted to classroom instruction by teachers of rhetoric and speech, uses a model of argument advanced by Stephen Toulmin in *The Uses of Argument.* Toulmin was interested in producing a description of the real *process* of argument. His model was the law. "Arguments," he said, "can be compared with lawsuits, and the claims we make and argue for in extra-legal contexts with claims made in the courts."[1] Toulmin's model of argument was based on three principal elements: claim, evidence, and warrant. These elements answered the questions, "What are you trying to prove?" "What have you got to go on?" "How did you get from evidence to claim?" Needless to say, Toulmin's model of argument does not guarantee a classroom of skilled arguers, but his questions about the parts of an argument and their relationship are precisely the ones that students must ask and answer in writing their own essays and analyzing those of others. They lead students naturally into the formulation and development of their claims.

In this text I have adapted — and greatly simplified — some of Toulmin's concepts and terminology for first-year students. I have also introduced two elements of argument with which Toulmin is not directly concerned. Most rhetoricians consider them indispensable, however, to discussion of what actually happens in the defense or rejection of a claim. One is motivational appeals — warrants based on appeals to the needs and values of an audience, designed to evoke emotional responses. A distinction between logic and emotion may be useful as an analytical tool, but in producing or attacking arguments human beings find it difficult, if not impossible, to make such a separation. In this text, therefore, persuasion through appeals to needs and values is treated as a legitimate element in the argumentative process.

I have also stressed the significance of audience as a practical matter. In the rhetorical or audience-centered approach to argument, to which I subscribe in this text, success is defined as acceptance of the claim by an audience. Arguers in the real world recognize intuitively that their primary goal is not to demonstrate the purity of their logic, but to win the adherence of their audiences. To gain this adherence, students need to be reminded of the necessity for establishing themselves as credible sources for their readers.

I hope *Elements of Argument* will lead students to discover not only the practical and intellectual rewards of learning how to argue but the real excitement of engaging in civilized debate.

---

[1]*The Uses of Argument* (Cambridge: Cambridge University Press, 1958), p. 7.

ORGANIZATION

In Part One, after two introductory chapters, a chapter each is devoted to the chief elements of argument — the claims that students make in their arguments, the definitions and support they must supply for their claims, the warrants that underlie their arguments, the language that they use. Popular fallacies, as well as induction and deduction, are treated in Chapter 8; because fallacies represent errors of reasoning, a knowledge of induction and deduction can make clear how and why fallacies occur. Each chapter ends with an advertisement illustrating the element of argument treated in that chapter.

I have provided examples, readings, discussion questions, and writing suggestions that are, I hope, both practical and stimulating. With the exception of several student dialogues, the examples are real, not invented; they have been taken from speeches, editorial opinions, letters to the editor, advertisements, interviews, and news reports. They reflect the liveliness and complexity that invented examples often suppress.

The forty selections and nine advertisements in Part One support the discussions in several important ways. First, they illustrate the elements of argument; in each chapter, one or more essays have been analyzed to emphasize the chapter's principles of argument. Second, they are drawn from current publications and cover as many different subjects as possible to convince students that argument is a pervasive force in the world they read about and live in. Third, some of the essays are obviously flawed and thus enable students to identify the kinds of weaknesses they should avoid in their own essays.

Part Two takes up the process of writing, researching, and presenting arguments. Chapter 9 explains how to find a topic, define the issues that it embraces, organize the information, and draft and revise an argument. Chapter 10 introduces students to the business of finding sources and using these sources effectively in research papers. The chapter concludes with two annotated student research papers, one of which employs the materials of literature and the Modern Language Association (MLA) documentation system, the other of which represents research in the social and natural sciences and uses a modified American Psychological Association (APA) documentation style. Chapter 11 provides guidelines for presenting an argument orally.

Part Three, Opposing Viewpoints, exhibits arguers in action, using informal and formal language, debating head-on. The subjects of its fifty-seven selections and eight cartoons capture headlines every day, and despite their immediacy, they are likely to arouse passions and remain controversial for a long time. Whether as matters of national policy or personal choice, they call for decisions based on familiarity with competing views.

Part Four, Classic Arguments, reprints eight selections that have stood the tests of both time and the classroom. They are among the arguments that teachers find invaluable in any composition course.

The instructor's manual, *Resources for Teaching* Elements of Argument, provides additional suggestions for using the book, as well as for finding and using the enormous variety of materials available in a course on argument.

A new companion website at <www.bedfordstmartins.com/ rottenberg> includes annotated links for students and instructors looking for further information on controversial topics, online debates, and rhetorical theory.

A briefer edition, *The Structure of Argument*, Third Edition, is available for instructors who prefer a shorter text with fewer readings. It presents only Parts One and Two, an appendix of Classic Arguments, and the appendix, Arguing about Literature, from the longer edition.

NEW TO THIS EDITION

This edition is substantially larger and richer than the previous edition. Revising a successful textbook — the publisher says that *Elements of Argument* is the best-selling book of its kind — presents both a challenge and an opportunity. The challenge is to avoid undoing features that have been well received in the earlier editions. The opportunity is to tap into the experiences of instructors and students who have used the earlier editions and to make use of their insights to improve what needs improvement. In Chapters 3 and 4, for example, five writer's guides respond to instructors' suggestions by offering students step-by-step plans for writing the most commonly assigned essays in the course: a causal paper, an evaluation paper, a proposal paper, a definition paper, and a comparison paper.

The principles and concerns of the book have not changed. Rather, I have included a greater breadth of material to increase the book's usefulness as a teaching tool. Several important new features have been added. Part One includes annotations for twelve sample analysis arguments, a section on responding to visual argument (in Chapter 2), and annotated Web links to accompany each short debate. Part Two now includes a revised and expanded research chapter with detailed instructions for using online and computer sources and a new chapter on presenting an argument orally. And in Part Three, annotated Web links accompany each controversial topic.

To help students sharpen their visual reading skills and make better use of the advertisements and cartoons included in the book, a new section in Chapter 2 includes an advertisement accompanied by a sample analysis that shows students how to analyze and respond to a visual argument. For the short debates, we have retained two popular topics from the fifth edition — treatment for drug addictions and animal rights — and added four familiar and timely subjects: reforming the jury system, cloning, ebonics, and women in the military. Annotated Web links now accompany each of these debates, encouraging students to conduct further research online.

In addition to providing detailed information on evaluating, using, and documenting online and computer sources, Chapter 10, Researching an Argumentative Paper, includes instructions for compiling an annotated bibliography. The new Chapter 11, Presenting an Argument Orally, discusses the important differences between the spoken and the written word and provides guidelines for presenting an argument orally using multimedia and other presentation aids. A persuasive speech by a student is included as a model.

Part Three, Opposing Viewpoints, retains five popular topics from the fifth edition — Affirmative Action, Euthanasia, Freedom of Speech, Punishment, and Sex and Violence in Popular Culture — with selections that reflect the changes in law and public opinion. The three new topics — corporate responsibility, privacy in the information age, and sexual harassment — are not only among the most controversial and newsworthy subjects engaging American society today, but they are also subjects that interest and affect college students at school, at work, and at home. Part Four, Classic Arguments, now includes a provocative essay by Margaret Mead on warfare as a cultural invention.

Finally, the appendix, Arguing about Literature, which provides information on the principal elements of fiction, drama, and poetry, now includes a selection from each of the three genres in addition to a student essay analyzing a short story.

Sixty-three of the 129 selections in the sixth edition are new. Taken as a whole, the changes in the sixth edition should enhance the versatility of the book, deepen students' awareness of how pervasive argument is, and increase their ability to think critically and communicate persuasively.

This book has profited by the critiques and suggestions of reviewers and instructors who responded to a questionnaire. I appreciate the thoughtful consideration given to previous editions by Nancy E. Adams, Timothy C. Alderman, Yvonne Alexander, John V. Andersen, Lucile G. Appert, William Arfin, Alison K. Armstrong, Karen Arnold, Angel M. Arzán, Mark Edward Askren, Michael Austin, David B. Axelrod, Jacquelyn A. Babush, Peter Banland, Carol A. Barnes, Tim Barnett, Marilyn Barry, Marci Bartolotta, Dr. Bonnie C. Bedford, Frank Beesley, Don Beggs, Martine Bellen, Bruce Bennett, Maureen Dehler Bennett, Chester Benson, Robert H. Bentley, Scott Bentley, Arthur E.

Bervin, Patricia Bizzell, Don Black, Kathleen Black, Stanley S. Blair, Laurel Boyd, Mary Virginia Brackett, Robert J. Branda, Dianne Brehmer, Alan Brown, Paul L. Brown, Bill Buck, W. K. Buckley, Alison A. Bulsterbaum, Clarence Bussinger, Deborah N. Byrd, Gary T. Cage, Ruth A. Cameron, Dr. Rita Carey, Barbara R. Carlson, Eric W. Cash, Donna R. Chaney, Gail Chapman, Linda D. Chinn, Roland Christian, Gina Claywell, Dr. John O. Clemonts, Tammy S. Cole, Dr. Thomas S. Costello, Martha J. Craig, David J. Cranmer, Edward Crothers, Sara Cutting, Jo Ann Dadisman, Sandra Dahlberg, Mimi Dane, Judy Davidson, Dr. Cynthia C. Davis, Philip E. Davis, Stephanie Demma, Loretta Denner, Cecile de Rocher, Julia Dietrich, Marcia B. Dinnech, Felicia A. Dixon, Jane T. Dodge, Ellen Donovan, L. Leon Duke, P. Dunsmore, Bernard Earley, Carolyn Embree, Carolyn L. Engdahl, Gwyn Enright, David Estes, Kristina Faber, Lester Faigley, Faridoun Farroth, B. R. Fein, Delia Fisher, Catherine Fitzgerald, Evelyn Flores, David D. Fong, Donald Forand, Mary A. Fortner, Alice R. France, Leslye Friedberg, Sondra Frisch, Richard Fulkerson, Maureen Furniss, Diane Gabbard, Donald J. Gadow, Eric Gardner, Frieda Gardner, Gail Garloch, Darcey Garretson, Victoria Gaydosik, E. R. Gelber-Beechler, Scott Giantralley, Michael Patrick Gillespie, Paula Gillespie, Wallace Gober, Sara Gogol, Stuart Goodman, Joseph Gredler, Lucie Greenberg, Mildred Buza Gronek, Marilyn Hagans, Linda L. Hagge, Lee T. Hamilton, Carolyn Han, Phillip J. Hanse, Pat Hardré, Susan Harland, A. Leslie Harris, Carolyn G. Hartz, Theresia A. Hartz, Fredrik Hausmann, Michael Havens, William Hayes, Ursula K. Heise, Anne Helms, Tena Lea Helton, Peter C. Herman, Diane Price Herndl, Heidi Hobbs, William S. Hochman, Sharon E. Hockensmith, Andrew J. Hoffman, Joyce Hooker, Richard S. Hootman, Clarence Hundley, Patrick Hunter, Richard Ice, Mary Griffith Jackson, Ann S. Jagoe, Katherine James, Ruth Jeffries, Owen Jenkins, Ruth Y. Jenkins, Iris Jennings, Linda Johnson, Janet Jubnke, E. C. Juckett, Catherine Kaikowska, George T. Karnezis, Richard Katula, Mary Jane Kearny, Joanne Keel, Patricia Kellogg-Dennis, N. Kesinger, Susan Kincaid, Joanne Kirkland, Judith Kirscht, Nancy Klug, John H. Knight, Paul D. Knoke, Frances Kritzer, George W. Kuntzman, Barbara Ladd, M. Beardsley Land, Marlene J. Lang, Lisa Lebduska, Sara R. Lee, William Levine, Mary Levitt, Diana M. Liddle, Jack Longmale, Cynthia Lowenthal, Marjorie Lynn, Marcia MacLennan, Nancy McGee, Patrick McGuire, Ray McKerrow, Michael McKoski, Pamela J. McLagen, Suzanne McLaughlin, Dennis McMillan, Donald McQuade, Christina M. McVay, D'Ann Madewell, Beth Madison, Susan Maloney, Dan M. Manolescu, Barbara A. Manrigue, Joyce Marks, Quentin E. Martin, Michael Matzinger, Charles May, Jean-Pierre Meterean, Ekra Miezan, Carolyn R. Miller, Lisa K. Miller, Logan D. Moon, Dennis D. Moore, Dan Morgan, Karen L. Morris, Curt Mortenson, Philip A. Mottola, Thomas Mullen, Charlotte A. Myers, Joan Naake, Michael B. Naas, Joseph Nassar, Byron Nelson, Elizabeth A. Nist, Jody Noerdlinger, Paralee F. Norman, Dr. Mary Jean Northcutt, Thomas O'Brien, James F. O'Neil, Mary O'Riordan, Arlene Okerland, Renee Olander, Amy Olsen, Richard D. Olson, Steven Olson, Lori Jo Oswald, Sushil K. Oswald, Gary Pak, Linda J. Palumbo, Jo Patterson, Laurine Paule, Leland S. Person, Betty Peters, Nancy L. Peterson, Susan T. Peterson, Steve Phelan, Gail W. Pieper, Gloria Platzner, Mildred Postar, Ralph David Powell, Jr., Teresa Marie Purvis, Barbara E. Rees, Karen L. Regal, Pat Regel, Charles Reinhart, Thomas C. Renzi, Janice M. Reynolds, Douglas F. Rice, G. A. Richardson, Beverly A. Ricks, Katherine M. Rogers, Marilyn Mathias Root, Judith Klinger Rose, Cathy Rosenfeld, Robert A. Rubin, Norma L. Rudinsky, Lori Ruediger, Cheryl W. Ruggiero, Richard Ruppel, Victoria Anne Sager, Joseph L. Sanders, Suzette Schlapkohl, Sybil Schlesinger, Richard Schneider, Eileen Schwartz, Esther L. Schwartz, Eugene Senff, Jeffrey Seyall, Ron Severson, Lucy Sheehey, William E. Sheidley, Sallye J. Sheppeard, Sally Bishop Shigley, John Shout, Dr. Barbara L. Siek, Thomas Simmons, Michael Simms, Jacqueline Simon, Richard Singletary, Roger L. Slakey, Thomas S. Sloane, Beth Slusser, Denzell Smith, Rebecca Smith, Margaret Smolik, Katherine Sotol, Donald L. Soucy, Minoo Southgate, Linda Spain, Richard Spilman, Sarah J. Stafford, Jim Stegman, Martha L. Stephens, Arlo Stoltenberg, Elissa L. Stuchlik, Judy Szaho, Andrew Tadie, Fernanda G. Tate-Owens, R. Terhorst, Marguerite B. Thompson, Arline R. Thorn, Mary Ann Trevathan, Sandia Tuttle, Whitney G. Vanderwerff, Jennie VerSteeg, David L. Wagner, Jeanne Walker, James Wallace, Linda D. Warwick, Carol Adams Watson, Roger D. Watson, Karen Webb, Raymond E. Whelan, Betty E. White, Julia Whitsitt, Toby Widdicombe, Mary Louise Willey, Heywood Williams, Matthew C. Wolfe, Alfred Wong, Bonnie B. Zitz, and Laura Zlogar. The instructor's manual is the better for the contribution of Gail Stygall of the University of Washington. Fred Kemp of Texas Tech University drafted the section on responding online in Chapter 2, and Barbara Fister of Gustavus Adolphus College revised Chapter 10's discussion of information technologies; my thanks to them both.

I am grateful to freelancer Jessica Fox and to the people at Bedford/St. Martin's whose efforts have made the progress of the sixth edition a pleasure as well as a business: Charles Christensen, Joan Feinberg, Elizabeth Schaaf, Steve Scipione, Sandy Schechter, Eva Pettersson, Nicole Simonsen, and Jennifer Rush. I especially thank Maura Shea, who skillfully managed the progress of a sixth edition as if she had been doing it all her life and was a joy to work with as well, and Deborah Baker, the production editor, who earned my gratitude for indulging my crankiness and dealing so successfully with problems large and small.

Brief Contents

PART THREE

Opposing Viewpoints   433

PART FOUR

Classic Arguments   661

Contents

A report from the National Bioethics Advisory Commission warns of the health risks involved in somatic cell nuclear transfer cloning in humans and concludes that cloning is unethical — appealing to human vanity, narcissism, and avarice.

The president of the American Federation of Teachers maintains that if the United States were to adopt a childswap system, in which children were periodically and randomly redistributed to new parents, we and our lawmakers would quickly work to ensure that all children were provided with equal medical and educational opportunities.

An author makes a satirical attempt to rewrite segments of our nation's historic documents in the "plain" language of contemporary speech.

A scholar's caustic commentary on student-faculty relations indicts college as a ludicrously inappropriate preparation for the unforgiving world outside.

A journalist interviews an African American linguistics professor at Stanford University who asserts that "teaching approaches that take into account the vernacular dialect of kids work more effectively than those that don't."

A professor at Yale law school favors an affirmative action pyramid for schools, which narrows as it moves upward. Underprivileged students

exposure to sleaze, blood, and violence has made him, like other members of society, less sensitive. "And what happens to an unblushing society?"

PART FOUR

Classic Arguments   661

Imprisoned for sedition in ancient Athens, the philosopher Socrates explains to an old friend why an individual is never justified in breaking the laws of a government, no matter how convinced he is that a law is wrong.

An eighteenth-century satirist concocts a chilling, ironic solution to the problems of Irish poverty and overpopulation.

The author of *Walden* explains why it is reasonable, and often imperative, to disobey laws that one believes to be unjust.

This manifesto by the women of the 1848 Seneca Falls Convention adapts the language and structure of the Declaration of Independence to emphasize that half of America still waited to be freed from the chains of tyranny.

A famous anthropologist challenges the notion that warfare is a biological or sociological inevitability and proposes instead that war is a cultural invention.

In this 1946 essay, the author of *Nineteen Eighty-Four* suggests why the hand that pens a stale metaphor should not be trusted with the reins of government.

ELEMENTS OF
ARGUMENT

The Structure of Argument

CHAPTER ONE

Understanding Argument

THE NATURE OF ARGUMENT

A conversation overheard in the school cafeteria:

"Hey, how come you didn't order the meat loaf special? It's pretty good today."

"Well, I read this book about vegetarianism, and I've decided to give up meat. The book says meat's unhealthy and vegetarians live longer."

"Don't be silly. Americans eat lots of meat, and we're living longer and longer."

"Listen, this book tells how much healthier the Danes were during World War II because they couldn't get meat."

"I don't believe it. A lot of these health books are written by quacks. It's pretty dumb to change your diet after reading one book."

These people are having what most of us would call an argument, one that sounds dangerously close to a quarrel. There are, however, significant differences between the colloquial meaning of argument as a quarrel and its definition as a process of reasoning and advancing proof, although even the exchange reported above exhibits some of the characteristics of formal argument. The kinds of arguments we deal with in this text are not quarrels. They often resemble ordinary discourse about controversial issues. You may, for example, overhear a conversation like this one:

"This morning while I was trying to eat breakfast I heard an announcer describing the execution of that guy in Texas who raped

and murdered a teenaged couple. They gave him an injection, and it took him ten minutes to die. I almost lost my breakfast listening to it."

"Well, he deserved it. He didn't show much pity for his victims, did he?"

"Okay, but no matter what he did, capital punishment is really awful, barbaric. It's murder, even if the state does it."

"No, I'd call it justice. I don't know what else we can do to show how we feel about a cruel, pointless murder of innocent people. The punishment ought to be as terrible as we can make it."

Each speaker is defending a value judgment about an issue that tests ideas of good and evil, right and wrong, and that cannot be decided by facts.

In another kind of argument the speaker or writer proposes a solution for a specific problem. Two men, both under twenty, are engaged in a conversation.

"I'm going to be broke this week after I pay my car insurance. I don't think it's fair for males under twenty to pay such high rates. I'm a good driver, much better than my older sister. Why not consider driving experience instead of age or sex?"

"But I always thought that guys our age had the most accidents. How do you know that driving experience is the right standard to apply?"

"Well, I read a report by the Highway Commission that said it's really driving experience that counts. So I think it's unfair for us to be discriminated against. The law's behind the times. They ought to change the insurance laws."

In this case someone advocates a policy that appears to fulfill a desirable goal — making it impossible to discriminate against drivers just because they are young and male. Objections arise that the arguer must attempt to answer.

In these three dialogues, as well as in all the other arguments you will read in this book, human beings are engaged in explaining and defending their own actions and beliefs and opposing those of others. They do this for at least two reasons: to justify what they do and think both to themselves and to their opponents and, in the process, to solve problems and make decisions, especially those dependent on a consensus between conflicting views.

Unlike the examples cited so far, the arguments you will read and write will not usually take the form of dialogues, but arguments are implicit dialogues. Even when our audience is unknown, we write to persuade the unconvinced, to acquaint them with good reasons for changing their minds. As one definition has it, "Argumentation is the art of influencing others, through the medium of reasoned discourse, to believe or act as we wish them to believe or act."[1] This process is inherently dramatic; a good argument can create the kinds of tensions generated at sporting events. Who will win? What are the factors that enable a winner to emerge? One of the most popular and enduring situations on television is the courtroom debate, in which two lawyers (one, the defense attorney, the hero, unusually knowledgeable and persuasive; the other, the prosecuting attorney, bumbling and corrupt) confront each other before an audience of judge and jury that must render a heart-stopping verdict. Tensions are high because a life is in the balance. In the classroom the stakes are neither so intimidating nor so melodramatic, but even here a well-conducted argument can throw off sparks.

Of course, not all arguments end in clear victories for one side or another. Nor should they. The French philosopher Joseph Joubert said, "It is better to debate a question without settling it than to settle a question without debating it." In a democratic society of competing interests and values, a compromise between two or more extreme points of view may be the only viable solution to a vexing problem. Although formal debates under the auspices of a debating society, such as take place on many college campuses, usually end in winners and losers, real-life problems, both public and private, are often resolved through negotiation. Courtroom battles may result in compromise, and the law itself allows for exemptions and extenuating circumstances. Elsewhere in this book we speak of the importance of tradeoffs in social and political transactions, giving up one thing in return for another.

Keep in mind, however, that some compromises will not be morally defensible. In searching for a middle ground, the thoughtful arguer must determine that the consequences of a negotiated solution will contribute to "the common good," not, in the words of one essayist, merely the good of "the sovereign self." (In Chapter 9 you will find a detailed guide for writing arguments in which you look for common ground.)

Most of the arguments in this book will deal with matters of public controversy, an area traditionally associated with the study of argument. As the word *public* suggests, these matters concern us as members of a community. "They are," according to one rhetorician, "the problems of war and peace, race and creed, poverty, wealth, and population, of democracy and communism. . . . Specific issues arise on which we must take decision from time to time. One day it is Suez, another Cuba. One week it is the Congo, another it is the plight of the American farmer or the railroads. . . . On these subjects

---

[1] J. M. O'Neill, C. Laycock, and R. L. Scale, *Argumentation and Debate* (New York: Macmillan, 1925), p. 1.

the experts as well as the many take sides."[2] Today the issues are different from the issues that writers confronted more than twenty years ago. Today we are concerned about illegal immigration, bilingual education, gun control, gay rights, drug abuse, prayer in school, to name only a few.

Clearly, if all of us agreed about everything, if harmony prevailed everywhere, the need for argument would disappear. But given what we know about the restless, seeking, contentious nature of human beings and their conflicting interests, we should not be surprised that many controversial questions, some of them as old as human civilization itself, will not be settled nor will they vanish despite the energy we devote to settling them. Unresolved, they are submerged for a while and then reappear, sometimes in another form, sometimes virtually unchanged. Capital punishment is one such stubborn problem; abortion is another. Nevertheless, we value the argumentative process because it is indispensable to the preservation of a free society. In *Areopagitica,* his great defense of free speech, John Milton, the seventeenth-century poet, wrote, "I cannot praise a fugitive and cloistered virtue, unexercised and unbreathed, that never sallies out and sees her adversary." How can we know the truth, he asked, unless there is a "free and open encounter" between all ideas? "Give me liberty to know, to utter, and to argue freely according to conscience, above all liberties."

WHY STUDY ARGUMENT?

Perhaps the question has already occurred to you: Why *study* argument? Since you've engaged in some form of the argumentative process all your life, is there anything to be learned that experience hasn't taught you? We think there is. If you've ever felt frustration in trying to decide what is wrong with an argument, either your own or someone else's, you might have wondered if there were rules to help in the analysis. If you've ever been dissatisfied with your attempt to prove a case, you might have wondered how good arguers, the ones who succeed in persuading people, construct their cases. Good arguers do, in fact, know and follow rules. Studying and practicing these rules can provide you with some of the same skills.

You will find yourself using these skills in a variety of situations, not only in arguing important public issues. You will use them, for example, in your academic career. Whatever your major field of study — the humanities, the social sciences, the physical sciences,

---

[2]Karl R. Wallace, "Toward a Rationale for Teachers of Writing and Speaking," *English Journal,* September 1961, p. 386.

business — you will be required to defend views about materials you have read and studied.

Humanities. Why have some of the greatest novels resisted translation into great films?

Social Science. What is the evidence that upward social mobility continues to be a positive force in American life?

Physical Science. What will happen to the world climate as the amount of carbon dioxide in the atmosphere increases?

Business. Are the new tax laws beneficial or disadvantageous to the real estate investor?

For all these assignments, different as they may be, you would use the same kinds of analysis, research techniques, and evaluation. The conventions or rules for reporting results might differ from one field of study to another, but for the most part the rules for defining terms, evaluating evidence, and arriving at conclusions cross disciplinary lines. Many employers, not surprisingly, are aware of this. One sheriff in Arizona advertised for an assistant with a degree in philosophy. He had discovered, he said, that the methods used by philosophers to solve problems were remarkably similar to the methods used in law enforcement.

Whether or not you are interested in serving as sheriff's assistant, you will encounter situations in the workplace that call for the same analytical and argumentative skills employed by philosophers and law enforcement personnel. Almost everywhere — in the smallest businesses as well as the largest corporations — a worker who can articulate his or her views clearly and forcefully has an important advantage in gaining access to positions of greater interest and challenge. Even when they are primarily informative, the memorandums, reports, instructions, questions, and explanations that issue from offices and factories obey the rules of argumentative discourse.

You may not anticipate doing the kind of writing or speaking at your job that you will practice in your academic work. It is probably true that in some careers, writing constitutes a negligible part of a person's duties. But outside the office, the studio, and the salesroom, you will be called on to exhibit argumentative skills as a citizen, as a member of a community, and as a consumer of leisure. In these capacities you can contribute to decision making if you are knowledgeable and prepared. By writing or speaking to the appropriate authorities, you can argue for a change in the meal ticket plan at your school or the release of pornographic films at the neighborhood theater or against a change in automobile insurance rates. Most of us are painfully aware of opportunities we lost because we were uncertain of how to proceed, even in matters that affected us deeply.

A course in argumentation offers another invaluable dividend: It can help you to cope with the bewildering confusion of voices in the world around you. It can give you tools for distinguishing between what is true and what is false, what is valid and what is invalid, in the claims of politicians, promoters of causes, newscasters, advertisers, salespeople, teachers, parents and siblings, employers and employees, neighbors, friends, and lovers, any of whom may be engaged at some time in attempting to persuade you to accept a belief or adopt a course of action. It can even offer strategies for arguing with yourself about a personal dilemma.

So far we have treated argument as an essentially pragmatic activity that benefits the individual. But choosing argument over force or evasion has clear moral benefits for society as well. We can, in fact, defend the study of argumentation for the same reasons that we defend universal education despite its high cost and sometimes controversial results. In a democracy, widespread literacy ultimately benefits all members of society, not only those who are the immediate beneficiaries of education, because only an informed citizenry can make responsible choices. One distinguished writer explains that "democracy depends on a citizenry that can reason for themselves, on men who know whether a case has been proved, or at least made probable."[3]

It is not too much to say that argument is a civilizing influence, the very basis of democratic order. In repressive regimes, coercion, which may express itself in a number of reprehensible forms — censorship, imprisonment, exile, torture, or execution — is a favored means of removing opposition to establishment "truth." In free societies, argument and debate remain the preeminent means of arriving at consensus.

Of course, rational discourse in a democracy can and does break down. Confrontations with police at abortion clinics, shouting and heckling at a meeting to prevent a speaker from being heard, student protests against university policies — such actions have become common in recent years. The demands of the demonstrators are often passionately and sincerely held, and the protesters sometimes succeed through force or intimidation in influencing policy changes. When this happens, however, we cannot be sure that the changes are justified. History and experience teach us that reason, to a far greater degree than other methods of persuasion, ultimately determines the rightness or wrongness of our actions.

A piece of folk wisdom sums up the superiority of reasoned argument as a vehicle of persuasion: "A man convinced against his will

---

[3]Wayne C. Booth, "Boring from Within: The Art of the Freshman Essay," adapted from a speech delivered to the Illinois Council of College Teachers of English in May 1963.

is of the same opinion still." Those who accept a position after engaging in a dialogue offering good reasons on both sides will think and act with greater willingness and conviction than those who have been coerced or denied the privilege of participating in the decision.

WHY WRITE?

If we agree that studying argumentation provides important critical tools, one last question remains: Why *write*? Isn't it possible to learn the rules by reading and talking about the qualities of good and bad arguments? Not quite. All writers, both experienced and inexperienced, will probably confess that looking at what they have written, even after long thought, can produce a startled disclaimer: But that isn't what I meant to say! They know that more analysis and more hard thinking are in order. Writers are also aware that words on paper have an authority and a permanency that invite more than casual deliberation. It is one thing to make an assertion, to express an idea or a strong feeling in conversation, and perhaps even to deny it later; it is quite another to write out an extended defense of your own position or an attack on someone else's that will be read and perhaps criticized by people unsympathetic to your views.

Students are often told that they must become better thinkers if they are to become better writers. It works the other way, too. In the effort to produce a clear and convincing argument, a writer matures as a thinker and a critic. The very process of writing calls for skills that make us better thinkers. Writing argumentative essays tests and enlarges important mental skills — developing and organizing ideas, evaluating evidence, observing logical consistency, expressing ourselves clearly and economically — that we need to exercise all our lives in our various social roles, whether or not we continue to write after college.

THE TERMS OF ARGUMENT

One definition of argument, emphasizing audience, has been given earlier: "Argumentation is the art of influencing others, through the medium of reasoned discourse, to believe or act as we wish them to believe or act." A distinction is sometimes made between argument and persuasion. Argument, according to most authorities, gives primary importance to logical appeals. Persuasion introduces the element of ethical and emotional appeals. The difference is one of emphasis. In real-life arguments about social policy, the distinction is hard to measure. In this book we use the term *argument* to represent forms of discourse that attempt to persuade readers or listeners to accept a claim, whether acceptance is based on logical or on emotional appeals or, as is usually the case, on both. The following brief definition includes other elements: *An argument is a statement or statements offering support for a claim.*

An argument is composed of at least three parts: the claim, the support, and the warrant.[4]

The Claim

The claim (also called a *proposition*) answers the question "What are you trying to prove?" It may appear as the thesis statement of your essay, although in some arguments it may not be stated directly. There are three principal kinds of claim (discussed more fully in Chapter 3): claims of fact, of value, and of policy. (The three dialogues at the beginning of this chapter represent these three kinds of claim respectively.) *Claims of fact* assert that a condition has existed, exists, or will exist and are based on facts or data that the audience will accept as being objectively verifiable:

> The present cocaine epidemic is not unique. From 1885 to the 1920s, cocaine was as widely used as it is today.

> Horse racing is the most dangerous sport.

> California will experience colder, stormier weather for the next ten years.

All these claims must be supported by data. Although the last example is an inference or an educated guess about the future, a reader will probably find the prediction credible if the data seem authoritative.

Claims of value attempt to prove that some things are more or less desirable than others. They express approval or disapproval of standards of taste and morality. Advertisements and reviews of cultural events are one common source of value claims, but such claims emerge whenever people argue about what is good or bad, beautiful or ugly.

> The opera *Tannhäuser* provides a splendid viewing as well as listening experience.

> Football is one of the most dehumanizing experiences a person can face. — Dave Meggyesy

> Ending a patient's life intentionally is absolutely forbidden on moral grounds. — Presidential Commission on Medical Ethics, 1983

---

[4]Some of the terms and analyses used in this text are adapted from Stephen Toulmin's *The Uses of Argument* (Cambridge: Cambridge University Press, 1958).

Claims of policy assert that specific policies should be instituted as solutions to problems. The expression *should, must,* or *ought to* usually appears in the statement.

> Prisons should be abolished because they are crime-manufacturing concerns.

> Our first step must be to immediately establish and advertise drastic policies designed to bring our own population under control. — Paul Ehrlich, biologist

> The New York City Board of Education should make sure that qualified women appear on any new list of candidates for Chancellor of Education.

Policy claims call for analysis of both fact and value. (A full discussion of claims follows in Chapter 3.)

The Support

Support consists of the materials used by the arguer to convince an audience that his or her claim is sound. These materials include *evidence* and *motivational appeals.* The evidence or data consist of facts, statistics, and testimony from experts. The motivational appeals are the ones that the arguer makes to the values and attitudes of the audience to win support for the claim. The word *motivational* points out that these appeals are the reasons that move an audience to accept a belief or adopt a course of action. For example, in his argument advocating population control, Ehrlich first offered statistical evidence to prove the magnitude of the population explosion. But he also made a strong appeal to the generosity of his audience to persuade them to sacrifice their own immediate interests to those of future generations. (See Chapter 5 for detailed discussion of support.)

The Warrant

The warrant is an inference or an assumption, a belief or principle that is taken for granted. A warrant is a guarantee of reliability; in argument it guarantees the soundness of the relationship between the support and the claim. It allows the reader to make the connection between the support and the claim.

Warrants or assumptions underlie all the claims we make. They may be stated or unstated. If the arguer believes that the audience shares his assumption, he may feel it unnecessary to express it. But if he thinks that the audience is doubtful or hostile, he may decide to state the assumption to emphasize its importance or argue for its validity.

This is how the warrant works. In the dialogue beginning this chapter, one speaker made the claim that vegetarianism was more healthful than a diet containing meat. As support he offered the evidence that the authors of a book he had read recommended vegetarianism for greater health and longer life. He did not state his warrant — that the authors of the book were trustworthy guides to theories of healthful diet. In outline form the argument looks like this:

CLAIM: Adoption of a vegetarian diet leads to healthier and longer life.

SUPPORT: The authors of *Becoming a Vegetarian Family* say so.

WARRANT: The authors of *Becoming a Vegetarian Family* are reliable sources of information on diet.

A writer or speaker may also need to offer support for the warrant. In the case cited above, the second speaker is reluctant to accept the unstated warrant, suggesting that the authors may be quacks. The first speaker will need to provide support for the assumption that the authors are trustworthy, perhaps by introducing proof of their credentials in science and medicine. Notice that although the second speaker accepts the evidence, he cannot agree that the claim has been proved unless he also accepts the warrant. If he fails to accept the warrant — that is, if he refuses to believe that the authors are credible sources of information about diet — then the evidence cannot support the claim.

The following example demonstrates how a different kind of warrant, based on values, can also lead an audience to accept a claim.

CLAIM: Laws making marijuana illegal should be repealed.

SUPPORT: People should have the right to use any substance they wish.

WARRANT: No laws should prevent citizens from exercising their rights.

Support for repeal of the marijuana laws often consists of medical evidence that marijuana is harmless. Here, however, the arguer contends that an important ethical principle is at work: Nothing should prevent people from exercising their rights, including the right to use any substance, no matter how harmful. Let us suppose that the reader agrees with the supporting statement, that individuals should have the right to use any substance. But to accept the claim, the reader must also agree with the principle expressed in the warrant — that government should not interfere with the individual's right. He or she can then agree that laws making marijuana illegal should be repealed. Notice that this warrant, like all warrants, certifies that the relationship between the support and the claim is sound.

One more important characteristic of the warrant deserves mention. In many cases, the warrant is a more general statement of belief than the claim. It can, therefore, support many claims, not only the one in a particular argument. For example, the warrant you have just read — "No laws should prevent citizens from exercising their rights" — is a broad assumption or belief that we take for granted and that can underlie claims about many other practices in American society. (For more on warrants, see Chapter 6.)

Definition, Language, Logic

In addition to the claim, the support, and the warrant, several other elements of clear, persuasive prose are crucial to good argument. For this reason we have devoted separate chapters to each of them.

One of the most important is definition. In fact, many of the controversial questions you will read or write about are primarily arguments of definition. Such terms as *abortion, pornography, racism, poverty, addiction,* and *mental illness* must be defined before useful solutions to the problems they represent can be formulated. (Chapter 4 deals with definition.)

Another important resource is the careful use of language, not only to define terms and express personal style but also to reflect clarity of thought and avoid the clichés and outworn slogans that frequently substitute for fresh ideas. (See Chapter 7 for more on language.)

Last, we have included an examination of induction and deduction, the classic elements of logic. Understanding the way in which these reasoning processes work can help you to determine the truth and validity of your own and other arguments and to identify faulty reasoning. (Induction and deduction are covered in Chapter 8.)

THE AUDIENCE

All arguments are composed with an audience in mind. We have already pointed out that an argument is an implicit dialogue or exchange. Often the writer of an argument about a public issue is responding to another writer or speaker who has made a claim that needs to be supported or opposed. In writing your own arguments, you should assume that there is a reader who may not agree with you. Throughout this book, we will continue to refer to ways of reaching such a reader.

Speechmakers are usually better informed than writers about their audience. Some writers, however, are familiar with the specific persons or groups who will read their arguments; advertising copywriters are a conspicuous example. They discover their audiences through sophisticated polling and marketing techniques and direct their messages to a well-targeted group of prospective buyers. Other professionals may be required to submit reports to persuade a specific and clearly defined audience of certain beliefs or courses of action: An engineer may be asked by an environmental interest group to defend his plans for the building of a sewage treatment plant; or a town planner may be called on to tell the town council why she believes that rent control may not work; or a sales manager may find it necessary to explain to his superior why a new product should be launched in the Midwest rather than the South.

In such cases the writer asks some or all of the following questions about the audience:

> Why has this audience requested this report? What do they want to get out of it?
>
> How much do they already know about the subject?
>
> Are they divided or agreed on the subject?
>
> What is their emotional involvement with the issues?

Assessing Credibility

Providing abundant evidence and making logical connections between the parts of an argument may not be enough to win agreement from an audience. In fact, success in convincing an audience is almost always inseparable from the writer's credibility, or the audience's belief in the writer's trustworthiness. Aristotle, the Greek philosopher who wrote a treatise on argument that has influenced its study and practice for more than two thousand years, considered credibility — what he called *ethos* — the most important element in the arguer's ability to persuade the audience to accept his or her claim.

Aristotle named "intelligence, character, and goodwill" as the attributes that produce credibility. Today we might describe these qualities somewhat differently, but the criteria for judging a writer's credibility remain essentially the same. First, the writer must convince the audience that he is knowledgeable, that he is as well informed as possible about the subject. Second, he must persuade his audience that he is not only truthful in the presentation of his evidence but also morally upright and dependable. Third, he must show that, as an arguer with good intentions, he has considered the interests and needs of others as well as his own.

As an example in which the credibility of the arguer is at stake, consider a wealthy Sierra Club member who lives on ten acres of a magnificent oceanside estate and who appears before a community planning board to argue against future development of the area. His claim is that more building will destroy the delicate ecological balance of the area. The board, acting in the interests of all the citizens of the community, will ask themselves: Has the arguer proved that his information about environmental impact is complete and accurate? Has he demonstrated that he sincerely desires to preserve the wilderness, not merely his own privacy and space? And has he also made clear that he has considered the needs and desires of those who might want to live in a housing development by the ocean? If the answers to all these questions are yes, then the board will hear the arguer with respect, and the arguer will have begun to establish his credibility.

A reputation for intelligence, character, and goodwill is not often won overnight. And it can be lost more quickly than it is won. Once a writer or speaker has betrayed an audience's belief in her character or judgment, she may find it difficult to persuade an audience to accept subsequent claims, no matter how sound her data and reasoning are. "We give no credit to a liar," said Cicero, "even when he speaks the truth."

Political life is full of examples of lost and squandered credibility. After it was discovered that President Lyndon Johnson had deceived the American public about U.S. conduct in the Vietnam War, he could not regain his popularity. After President Gerald Ford pardoned former President Richard Nixon for his complicity in the Watergate scandal, Ford was no longer a serious candidate for reelection. After proof that President Clinton had lied to a grand jury and the public about his sexual behavior, public approval of his political record remained high, but approval of his moral character declined and threatened to diminish his influence.

We can see the practical consequences when an audience realizes that an arguer has been guilty of a deception — misusing facts and authority, suppressing evidence, distorting statistics, violating the rules of logic. But suppose the arguer is successful in concealing his or her manipulation of the data and can persuade an uninformed audience to take the action or adopt the idea that he or she recommends. Even supposing that the argument promotes a "good" cause, is the arguer justified in using evasive or misleading tactics?

The answer is no. To encourage another person to make a decision on the basis of incomplete or dishonestly used data is profoundly unethical. It indicates lack of respect for the rights of others — their right to know at least as much as you do about the subject, to be allowed to judge and compare, to disagree with you if they challenge your own interests. If the moral implications are still not clear, try to imagine yourself not as the perpetrator of the lie but as the victim.

There is also a danger in measuring success wholly by the degree to which audiences accept our arguments. Both as writers and readers, we must be able to respect the claim, or proposition, and what it tries to demonstrate. Toulmin has said: "To conclude that a proposition is true, it is not enough to know that this [person] or that finds it 'credible': the proposition itself must be *worthy* of credence."[5]

---

[5] *An Examination of the Place of Reason in Ethics* (Cambridge: Cambridge University Press, 1964), p. 71.

Acquiring Credibility

You may wonder how you can acquire credibility. You are not yet an expert in many of the subjects you will deal with in assignments, although you are knowledgeable about many other things, including your cultural and social activities. But there are several ways in which you can create confidence by your treatment of topics derived from academic disciplines, such as political science, psychology, economics, sociology, and art, on which most assignments will be based.

First, you can submit evidence of careful research, demonstrating that you have been conscientious in finding the best authorities, giving credit, and attempting to arrive at the truth. Second, you can adopt a thoughtful and judicious tone that reflects a desire to be fair in your conclusion. Tone expresses the attitude of the writer toward his or her subject. When the writer feels strongly about the subject and adopts a belligerent or complaining tone, for example, he or she forgets that readers who feel differently may find the tone disagreeable and unconvincing. In the following excerpt a student expresses his feelings about standard grading — that is, grading by letter or number on a scale that applies to a whole group.

> You go to school to learn, not to earn grades. To be educated, that's what they tell you. "He's educated, he graduated magna cum laude." What makes a magna cum laude man so much better than a man that graduates with a C? They are both still educated, aren't they? No one has a right to call someone less educated because they got a C instead of an A. Let's take both men and put them in front of a car. Each car has something wrong with it. Each man must fix his broken car. Our C man goes right to work while our magna cum laude man hasn't got the slightest idea where to begin. Who's more educated now?

Probably a reader who disagreed with the claim — that standard grading should not be used — would find the tone, if not the evidence itself, unpersuasive. The writer sounds as if he is defending his own ability to do something that an honors graduate can't do, while ignoring the acknowledged purposes of standard grading in academic subjects. He sounds, moreover, as if he's angry because someone has done him an injury. Compare the preceding passage to the following one, written by a student on the same subject.

> Grades are the play money in a university Monopoly game. As long as the tokens are offered, the temptation will be largely irresistible to play for them. Students are so busy taking notes, doing tests, and getting tokens that they have forgotten to ask: Of what worth is all this? Or perhaps they ask and the grade is their answer.
>
> One certainly learns something in the passive lecture-note-read-note-test process: how to do it all more efficiently next time (in the

hope of eventually owning Boardwalk and Park Place). As Marshall McLuhan has said, we learn what we do. In this process most students come to view learning as studying and remembering what other people have learned. They assume that knowledge is logically and for practical reasons divided up into discrete pieces called "disciplines" and that the highest knowledge is achieved by specializing in a discipline. By getting good grades in a lot of disciplines they conclude they have learned a lot. They have indeed, and it is too bad.[6]

Most readers would consider this writer more credible than the first, in part because he has adopted a tone that seems moderate and impersonal. That is, he does not convey the impression that he is interested only in defending his own grades. Notice also that the language of this passage suggests a higher level of learning and research.

Sometimes, of course, an expression of anger or even outrage is appropriate and morally justified. But if readers do not share your sense of outrage, you must try to reach them through a more moderate approach. In his autobiography, Benjamin Franklin recounted his attempts to acquire the habit of temperate language in argument:

> Retaining . . . the habit of expressing myself in terms of modest diffidence, never using when I advance anything that may possibly be disputed, the words *certainly, undoubtedly,* or any others that give the air of positiveness to an opinion; but rather say, *I conceive,* or *I apprehend* a thing to be so or so; *it appears to me,* or *I should think it so or so for such and such reasons,* or *I imagine* it to be so, or *it is so* if *I am not mistaken.* — This habit I believe has been of great advantage to me, when I have had occasion to inculcate my opinions and persuade men into measures that I have been from time to time engaged in promoting.[7]

This is not to say that the writer must hedge his or her opinions or confess uncertainty at every point. Franklin suggests that the writer must recognize that other opinions may also have validity and that, although the writer may disagree, he or she respects the other opinions. Such an attitude will also dispose the reader to be more generous in evaluating the writer's argument.

A final method of establishing credibility is to produce a clean, literate, well-organized paper, with evidence of care in writing and proofreading. Such a paper will help persuade the reader to take your efforts seriously.

Now let us turn to one of the most famous arguments in American history and examine its elements.

---

[6]Roy E. Terry in "Does Standard Grading Encourage Excessive Competitiveness?" *Change,* September 1974, p. 45.

[7]*The Autobiography of Benjamin Franklin,* ed. Louis P. Masur (Boston: Bedford Books, 1993), pp. 39–40. Italics are Franklin's.

The Declaration of Independence

THOMAS JEFFERSON

When in the course of human events, it becomes necessary for one people to dissolve the political bands which have connected them with another, and to assume among the Powers of the earth, the separate and equal station to which the Laws of Nature and Nature's God entitle them, a decent respect to the opinions of mankind requires that they should declare the causes which impel them to the separation.

We hold these truths to be self-evident, that all men are created equal, that they are endowed by their Creator with certain unalienable Rights, that among these are Life, Liberty and the pursuit of Happiness.

That to secure these rights, Governments are instituted among Men, deriving their just powers from the consent of the governed.

That whenever any Form of Government becomes destructive of these ends, it is the Right of the People to alter or to abolish it, and to institute a new Government laying its foundation on such principles and organizing its powers in such form, as to them shall seem most likely to effect their Safety and Happiness. Prudence, indeed, will dictate that Governments long established should not be changed for light and transient causes; and accordingly all experience hath shown that mankind are more disposed to suffer, while evils are sufferable, than to right themselves by abolishing the forms to which they are accustomed. But when a long train of abuses and usurpations pursuing invariably the same Object evinces a design to reduce them under absolute Despotism, it is their right, it is their duty, to throw off such government, and to provide new Guards for their future security.

Such has been the patient sufferance of these Colonies; and such 5 is now the necessity which constrains them to alter their former Systems of Government. The history of the present King of Great Britain is a history of repeated injuries and usurpations, all having in direct object the establishment of an absolute Tyranny over these States. To prove this, let Facts be submitted to a candid world.

He has refused his Assent to Laws, the most wholesome and necessary for the public good.

He has forbidden his Governors to pass Laws of immediate and pressing importance, unless suspended in their operation till his Assent should be obtained; and when so suspended, he has utterly neglected to attend to them.

He has refused to pass other Laws for the accommodation of large districts of people, unless those people would relinquish the right of Representation in the Legislature, a right inestimable to them and formidable to tyrants only.

He has called together legislative bodies at places unusual, uncomfortable, and distant from the depository of their Public Records, for the sole purpose of fatiguing them into compliance with his measures.

He has dissolved Representative Houses repeatedly, for oppos- 10 ing with manly firmness his invasions on the rights of the people.

He has refused for a long time, after such dissolutions, to cause others to be elected; whereby the Legislative Powers, incapable of Annihilation, have returned to the People at large for their exercise; the State remaining in the mean time exposed to all the danger of invasion from without, and convulsions within.

He has endeavored to prevent the population of these States; for that purpose obstructing the Laws of Naturalization of Foreigners; refusing to pass others to encourage their migration hither, and raising the conditions of new Appropriations of Lands.

He has obstructed the Administration of Justice, by refusing his Assent to Laws for establishing Judiciary Powers.

He has made Judges dependent on his Will alone, for the tenure of their offices, and the amount and payment of their salaries.

He has erected a multitude of New Offices, and sent hither 15 swarms of Officers to harass our People, and eat out their substance.

He has kept among us, in time of peace, Standing Armies without the consent of our Legislature.

He has affected to render the Military independent of and superior to the Civil Power.

He has combined with others to subject us to jurisdictions foreign to our constitution, and unacknowledged by our laws; giving his Assent to their acts of pretended Legislation:

For quartering large bodies of armed troops among us:

For protecting them, by a mock Trial, from Punishment for any 20 Murders which they should commit on the Inhabitants of these States:

For cutting off our Trade with all parts of the world:

For imposing Taxes on us without our Consent:

For depriving us in many cases, of the benefits of Trial by Jury:

For transporting us beyond Seas to be tried for pretended offenses:

For abolishing the free System of English Laws in a Neighbouring 25 Province, establishing therein an Arbitrary government, and enlarging its boundaries so as to render it at once an example and fit instrument for introducing the same absolute rule into these Colonies:

For taking away our Charters, abolishing our most valuable Laws, and altering fundamentally the Forms of our Governments:

For suspending our own legislatures, and declaring themselves invested with Power to legislate for us in all cases whatsoever.

He has abdicated Government here, by declaring us out of his Protection and waging War against us.

He has plundered our seas, ravaged our Coasts, burnt our towns and destroyed the Lives of our people.

He is at this time transporting large Armies of foreign Mercenar- 30 ies to compleat the works of death, desolation and tyranny, already begun with circumstances of Cruelty & perfidy scarcely paralleled in the most barbarous ages, and totally unworthy the Head of a civilized nation.

He has constrained our fellow Citizens taken Captive on the high Seas to bear Arms against their Country, to become the executioners of their friends and Brethren, or to fall themselves by their Hands.

He has excited domestic insurrections amongst us, and has endeavored to bring on the inhabitants of our frontiers, the merciless Indian Savages, whose known rule of warfare is an undistinguished destruction of all ages, sexes, and conditions.

In every stage of these Oppressions We Have Petitioned for Redress in the most humble terms. Our repeated petitions have been answered only by repeated injury. A Prince, whose character is thus marked by every act which may define a Tyrant, is unfit to be the ruler of a free People.

Not have We been wanting in attention to our British brethren. We have warned them from time to time of attempts by their legislature to extend an unwarrantable jurisdiction over us. We have reminded them of the circumstances of our emigration and settlement here. We have appealed to their native justice and magnanimity and we have conjured them by the ties of our common kindred to disavow these usurpations, which would inevitably interrupt our connections and correspondence. They too have been deaf to the voice of justice and of consanguinity. We must, therefore, acquiesce in the necessity, which denounces our Separation, and hold them, as we hold the rest of mankind, Enemies in War, in Peace Friends.

We, therefore, the Representatives of the United States of Amer- 35 ica, in General Congress, Assembled, appealing to the Supreme Judge of the world for the rectitude of our intentions, do, in the Name, and by Authority of the good People of these Colonies, solemnly publish and declare, That these United Colonies are, and of Right ought to be, Free and Independent States; that they are Absolved from all Allegiance to the British Crown, and that all political connection between them and the State of Great Britain, is and ought to be totally dissolved; and that as Free and Independent States, they have full power to levy War, conclude Peace, contract

Alliances, establish Commerce, and to do all other Acts and Things which Independent States may of right do. And for the support of this Declaration, with a firm reliance on the protection of Divine Providence, we mutually pledge to each other our lives, our Fortunes and our sacred Honor.

Analysis

Claim: What is Jefferson trying to prove? *The American colonies are justified in declaring their independence from British rule.* Jefferson and his fellow signers might have issued a simple statement such as appears in the last paragraph, announcing the freedom and independence of these United Colonies. Instead, however, they chose to justify their right to do so.

Support: What does Jefferson have to go on? The Declaration of Independence bases its claim on two kinds of support: *factual evidence* and *motivational appeals* or appeals to the values of the audience.

Factual Evidence: Jefferson presents a long list of specific acts of tyranny by George III, beginning with "He has refused his Assent to Laws, the most wholesome and necessary for the public good." This list constitutes more than half the text. Notice how Jefferson introduces these grievances: "The history of the present King of Great Britain is a history of repeated injuries and usurpations, all having in direct object the establishment of an absolute Tyranny over these States. *To prove this, let Facts be submitted to a candid world*" (italics for emphasis added). Jefferson hopes that a recital of these specific acts will convince an honest audience that the United Colonies have indeed been the victims of an intolerable tyranny.

Appeal to Values: Jefferson also invokes the moral values underlying the formation of a democratic state. These values are referred to throughout. In the second and third paragraphs he speaks of equality, "Life, Liberty and the pursuit of Happiness," "just powers," "consent of the governed," and in the fourth paragraph, safety. In the last paragraph he refers to freedom and independence. Jefferson believes that the people who read his appeal will, or should, share these fundamental values. Audience acceptance of these values constitutes the most important part of the support. Some historians have called the specific acts of oppression cited by Jefferson trivial, inconsequential, or distorted. Clearly, however, Jefferson felt that the list of specific grievances was vital to definition of the abstract terms in which values are always expressed.

Warrant: How does Jefferson get from support to claim? *People have a right to revolution to free themselves from oppression.* This warrant is explicit: "But when a long train of abuses and usurpations pursuing invariably the same Object evinces a design to reduce them under absolute Despotism, it is their right, it is their duty, to throw off such government, and to provide new Guards for their future security." Some members of Jefferson's audience, especially those whom he accuses of oppressive acts, will reject the principle that any subject people have earned the right to revolt. But Jefferson believes that the decent opinion of mankind will accept this assumption. Many of his readers will also be aware that the warrant is supported by seventeenth-century political philosophy, which defines government as a social compact between the government and the governed.

If Jefferson's readers do, in fact, accept the warrant and if they also believe in the accuracy of the factual evidence and share his moral values, then they will conclude that his claim has been proved — that Jefferson has justified the right of the colonies to separate themselves from Great Britain.

Audience: The Declaration of Independence is addressed to several audiences: to the American colonists; to the British people; to the British Parliament; to the British king, George III; and to humanity or a universal audience.

Not all the American colonists were convinced by Jefferson's argument. Large numbers remained loyal to the king and for various reasons opposed an independent nation. In the next-to-the-last paragraph, Jefferson refers to previous addresses to the British people. Not surprisingly, most of the British citizenry as well as the king also rejected the claims of the Declaration. But the universal audience, the decent opinion of humanity, found Jefferson's argument overwhelmingly persuasive. Many of the liberal reform movements of the eighteenth and nineteenth centuries were inspired by the Declaration. In basing his claim on universal principles of justice and equality, Jefferson was certainly aware that he was addressing future generations.

Definition: Several significant terms are not defined. Modern readers will ask for further definition of "all men are created equal," "Life, Liberty and the pursuit of Happiness," "Laws of Nature and Nature's God," among others. We must assume that the failure to explain these terms more strictly was deliberate, in part because Jefferson thought that his readers would understand the references — for example, to the eighteenth-century belief in freedom as the birthright of all human beings — and in part because he wished the terms to be understood as universal principles of justice, applicable in all struggles, not merely those of the colonies against the king of England. But a failure to narrow the terms of argument can have unpredictable consequences. In later years the Declaration of Independence would be used to justify other rebellions, including the secession of the South from the Union in 1861.

Language: Although some stylistic conventions of eighteenth-century writing would not be observed today, Jefferson's clear, elegant, formal prose — "a surprising mixture of simplicity and majesty," in the words of one writer — remains a masterpiece of English prose and persuades us that we are reading an important document. Several devices are worth noting:

1. *Parallelism,* or balance of sentence construction, gives both emphasis and rhythm to the statements in the introduction (first four paragraphs) and the list of grievances.
2. *Diction* (choice of words) supports and underlines the meaning: nouns that have positive connotations — *safety, happiness, prudence, right, duty, Supreme Judge, justice;* verbs and verbals that suggest negative actions (taken by the king) — *refused, forbidden, dissolved, obstructed, plundered, depriving, abolishing.*
3. The *tone* suggests reason and patience on the part of the author or authors (especially paragraphs 5, 33, 34).

Logic: As a logical pattern of argument, the Declaration of Independence is largely *deductive.* Deduction usually consists of certain broad general statements which we know or believe to be true and which lead us to other statements that follow from the ones already laid down. The Declaration begins with such general statements, summarizing a philosophy of government based on the equality of men, the inalienable rights derived from the Creator, and the powers of the governed. These statements are held to be "self-evident" — that is, not needing proof — and if we accept them, then it follows that a revolution is necessary to remove the oppressors and secure the safety and happiness to which the governed are entitled. The particular grievances against the king are proof that the king has oppressed the colonies, but they are not the basis for revolution.

The fact that Jefferson emphasized the universal principles underlying the right of revolution meant that the Declaration of Independence could appeal to all people everywhere, whether or not they had suffered the particular grievances in Jefferson's list.

EXERCISES

1. From the following list of claims, select the ones you consider most controversial. Tell why they are difficult to resolve. Are the underlying assumptions controversial? Is support hard to find or disputed? Can

you think of circumstances under which some of these claims might be resolved?

a. Congress should endorse the right-to-life amendment.

b. Solar power can supply 20 percent of the energy needs now satisfied by fossil and nuclear power.

c. Homosexuals should have the same job rights as heterosexuals.

d. Rapists should be treated as mentally ill rather than depraved.

e. Whale hunting should be banned by international law.

f. Violence on television produces violent behavior in children who watch more than four hours a day.

g. Both creationism and evolutionary theory should be taught in the public schools.

h. Mentally defective men and women should be sterilized or otherwise prevented from producing children.

i. History will pronounce Reggie Jackson a greater all-around baseball player than Joe DiMaggio.

j. Bilingual instruction should not be permitted in the public schools.

k. Some forms of cancer are caused by a virus.

l. Dogs are smarter than horses.

m. Curfews for teenagers will reduce the abuse of alcohol and drugs.

n. The federal government should impose a drinking age of twenty-one.

o. The United States should proceed with unilateral disarmament.

p. Security precautions at airports are out of proportion to the dangers of terrorism.

q. Bodybuilding cannot be defined as a sport; it is a form of exhibitionism.

2. Report on an argument you have heard recently. Identify the parts of that argument — claim, support, warrant — as they are defined in this chapter. What were the strengths and weaknesses in the argument you heard?

3. Choose one of the more controversial claims in the previous list and explain the reasons it is controversial. Is support lacking or in doubt? Are the warrants unacceptable to many people? Try to go as deeply as you can, exploring, if possible, systems of belief, traditions, societal customs. You may confine your discussion to personal experience with the problem in your community or group. If there has been a change over the years in the public attitude toward the claim, offer what you think may be an explanation for the change.

4. Write your own argument for or against the value of standard grading in college.

5. Discuss an occasion when a controversy arose that the opponents could not settle. Describe the problem, and tell why you think the disagreement was not settled.

CHAPTER TWO

Responding to Argument

Most of us learn how to read, to listen, and to write arguments by attending critically to the arguments of those who have already mastered the important elements as well as those who have not. As we acquire skill in reading, we learn to uncover the clues that reveal meaning and to become sensitive to the kinds of organization, support, and language that experienced writers use in persuading their audiences. Listening, too, is a skill often underrated but increasingly important in an era when the spoken voice can be transmitted worldwide with astonishing speed. In becoming more expert listeners, we can engage in discussions with a wide and varied audience and gain proficiency in distinguishing between responsible and irresponsible speech.

A full response to any argument means more than understanding the message. It also means evaluating, deciding whether the message is successful and then determining *how* it succeeds or fails in persuading us. In making these judgments about the written and spoken arguments of others, we learn how to deliver our own. We try to avoid what we perceive to be flaws in another's arguments, and we adapt the strategies that produce clear, honest, forceful arguments.

RESPONDING AS A CRITICAL READER

You already know how essential critical reading can be to mastery of most college subjects, but its importance for reading and writing about argument, where meaning is often complex and multi-layered, can hardly be overestimated. Critical, or close, reading of arguments leads to greater comprehension and more thorough evaluation. The first step is comprehension — understanding what the author is trying to prove. Then comes evaluation — careful judgment of the extent to which the author has succeeded.

Good readers are never merely passive recipients of the material. They engage in active dialogue with the author, as if he or she were present, asking questions, offering objections, expressing approval. They often write comments in the margins of the book as they read or in a notebook they reserve for this purpose. Clearly, the more information they have about the author and the subject as well as the circumstances surrounding it — an event in the news, for example — the easier and more productive their reading of any material will be. But whatever their level of preparation, they have learned to extract meaning by attending to clues both in the material itself and in their knowledge of the world around them.

Here are a few strategies for close reading of an argument.

1. Pay attention to the title — and the subtitle. They can provide a good deal of information.
   a. The title can tell you what the essay is about. It may even state the purpose of the argument in specific terms, as in "Cocaine Is Even Deadlier Than We Thought" (p. 56), the title of one of the essays in this book.
   b. It can make reference to other writing that you will recognize. The title of the article that follows, "The Pursuit of Whining" (p. 28), brings to mind the phrase in the Declaration of Independence, "the pursuit of Happiness." The subtitle clinches the connection: "Affirmative Action circa 1776."
   c. It can express the author's attitude toward the subject. In the title quoted above, we realize that "whining," because it has negative connotations, will probably be attacked as a means of achieving happiness. The subtitle adds the rather surprising suggestion that the author is unfriendly to some aspects of the American Revolution.
2. As you read the essay for the first time, look for the main idea and the structure of the whole essay. Make a skeleton outline in your mind or on paper. Remember that your purpose in reading an argument is to learn what the author wants to prove and how he or she proves it, and to frame a response to it as you read. At this stage, avoid concentrating on details. Reading is a complex mental operation, and you cannot do everything at once.

   In a well-written essay, even a long one, the main idea and the organization should emerge clearly from a careful reading. Every argument, however long and complicated, has a beginning, a middle, and an end. It will offer a claim and several parts devoted to support. (Development of an important point may take two or more paragraphs.)

3. You will probably find the main idea — also known as the *thesis statement* or *claim* — in one of the first two or three paragraphs. Remember, however, that the beginning of an argument often has other purposes; it may lay out not the author's position but the position that the author will oppose or background for the whole argument.

4. Pay attention to topic sentences. The topic sentence is usually but not always the first sentence of a paragraph. It is the general statement that controls the details and examples in the paragraph.

5. Don't overlook the language signposts, especially the transitional words and phrases that tell you whether the writer will change direction or offer support for a previous point — words and phrases like *but, however, nevertheless, yet, moreover, for example, at first glance, more important, the first reason,* and so on.

6. Select the method for vocabulary search that suits you best: either guessing the meaning of an unfamiliar word from the context and going on or else looking it up immediately. It's true that the first method makes for more rapid reading and is sometimes recommended by teachers of reading, but guessing can be risky. Keep a good dictionary handy. If you are at all in doubt about a word that seems crucial to meaning, check your guess before you go too far in what may be the wrong direction.

7. If you use a colored marker to highlight main points, use it sparingly. Marking passages in color is meant to direct you to the major ideas and reduce the necessity for rereading the whole passage when you review.

8. Don't be timid about asking questions of the text. No author is infallible. Some authors are not always clear. Ask any questions whose answers are necessary to improve your comprehension. Disagree with the author if you feel confident of the support for your view. After you have read the whole argument, you may discover that most of your early questions have been answered. If not, this may be a signal to read the article again. Be cautious about concluding that the author hasn't proved his point.

9. Reading an assigned work is usually a solitary activity, but what follows a reading should be shared. Talk about the material with classmates or others who have read it. You probably know that discussion of a book or a movie strengthens both your memory of details and your understanding of the whole. And defending or modifying your evaluation will mean going back to the text and finding clues that you may have overlooked. Not least, it can be fun to discuss even something you didn't enjoy.

The following essay is annotated by a student as he reads. He is already familiar, as you are, with the Declaration of Independence. After reading and commenting on the essay, he adds a brief summary for his own review.

The Pursuit of Whining: Affirmative Action circa 1776

JOHN PATRICK DIGGINS

Anything to do with "the pursuit of happiness"? Who's doing the whining in 1776?

Is this about affirmative action or the Revolution? Or both?

Usually means that a second glance will show the opposite

Means it's not what it seems

So he's against aff. action because it violates the D of I?

Seems to be his thesis; is group opportunity bad?

All politics, we are now told, will not be local but universal, a struggle over values. In these "culture wars," a candidate who can touch the core nerve of American values will be sure to be elected. How will affirmative action stand up to such a contest?

At first glance, affirmative action appears to be consistent with America's commitment to egalitarianism, which derives from the Declaration of Independence and its ringing pronouncement that "all men are created equal" and are "endowed by their creator with certain unalienable rights." Actually affirmative action, as carried out, has little to do with equality and is so dependent on biology, ancestry, and history that it subverts the individualist spirit of the Declaration.

But the second part of the Declaration, which no one remembers, may affirm affirmative action as the politics of group opportunity.

The Declaration held rights to be equal and unalienable because in the state of nature, before social conventions had been formed, "Nature and Nature's God" (Jefferson's phrase) gave no person or class the authority to dominate over others. Aristocracy became such a class, and the idea of equality was not so much

---

John Patrick Diggins teaches history at the Graduate Center of the City University of New York. This column appeared in the *New York Times* on September 25, 1995.

Reason for the Revolution

Interesting point—today's affirmative action is like yesterday's aristocracy (both claim privileges of birth).

The founding fathers were against inherited privileges.

So far, he's proved that first part of D of I argues against affirmative action.

But the second part, listing grievances, is consistent with it.

Thinks the colonists are crybabies!

an accurate description of the human species as it was a protest against artificial privilege and hereditary right.

Today we have a new identity politics 5 of entitlement, and who one is depends on ethnic categories and descriptions based on either ancestry or sex. This return to a pseudo-aristocratic politics of privilege based on inherited rights by reason of birth means that equality has been replaced by diversity as the criteri[on] of governmental decisions.

Jefferson loved diversity, but he and Thomas Paine trusted the many and suspected the few who saw themselves entitled to preferential treatment as an accident of birth. Paine was unsparing in his critique of aristocracy as a parasitic "no-ability." Speaking for the colonists, many of whom had worked their way out of conditions of indentured servitude, he insisted that hereditary privilege was "as absurd as an hereditary mathematician, or an hereditary wise man; and as ridiculous as an hereditary poet-laureate."

But if America's egalitarian critique of aristocratic privilege could be in conflict with affirmative action, the second part of the Declaration may be perfectly consistent with it. Here begins the art of protest as the Declaration turns to the colonists' grievances, and we are asked to listen to a long tale of woe. Instead of admitting that they simply had no desire to cough up taxes, even to pay for a war that drove the French out of North America and thus made possible a situation where settlers were now secure enough to demand self-government, the colonists blamed King George for every outrage conceivable.

"He has erected . . . swarms of offices to harass our people and eat out their substance." Because the King, in response to the colonists' refusal to pay for the cost of protection, withdrew such protection, he is charged with abdicating "his allegiance and protection: he has plundered our seas, ravaged our coasts, burnt our towns, destroyed the lives of our people." Even Edmund Burke, the British parliamentarian and orator who supported the colonists, saw them as almost paranoid, "protestants" who protest so much that they would "snuff the approach of tyranny in every tainted breeze."

The ultimate <u>hypocrisy</u> comes when Jefferson accuses the King of once tolerating the slave trade, only "he is now exciting those very people to rise up in arms among us, and to purchase their liberty of which he has deprived them, by murdering the people upon whom he has obtruded them." The notion that slavery was forced upon the innocent colonists, who in turn only sought to be free of "tyranny," suggests the extent to which <u>the sentiment of the Revolution grumbles with spurious charges.</u>

The Declaration voiced America's first 10 proclamation of victimology. Whatever the theoretical complexities embedded in the doctrine of equality, the Declaration demonstrated that any politics that has <u>its own interests uppermost</u> is best put forward in the language of victimization and <u>paranoia.</u>

The very vocabulary of the document ("harass," "oppress," and so on) is consistent with affirmative action, where <u>white racists and male chauvinists</u> have replaced King George as the specter of complaint.

Seeing themselves as sufferers to whom awful things happen, the colonists blamed their alleged oppressors and never acknowledged that they had any responsibility for the situation in which they found themselves.

What then is America's core value? Is it equality and civic virtue? Or is it the struggle for power that legitimizes itself in

An ending that's all questions. the more successful, and least demand-
I like it. But they're fake ques- ing, shameless politics of whining?
tions. He knows the answers
and wants us to agree with
him.

Summary: Is affirmative action consistent with the Declaration of Independence? On that subject the two parts of the Declaration contradict each
other. The first part says that equality and individual rights are the principles of the American Revolution. Because the founding fathers opposed
privileges awarded on account of ancestry and history, they would be
against affirmative action. But in the second part of the Declaration, the
grievances of the colonists sound like the complaints of groups today that
claim they are victims of oppression and want special privileges because of
their ancestry and history. Today America must choose between equality
and privileges for special groups. Note: From The Declaration of Independence, a book by Carl Becker, I found out that the excerpts in paragraph 9
come from an earlier draft of the Declaration. This argument about slavery
was omitted from the final draft because Jefferson thought that it was
weaker than the others. So was it fair to include it here?

RESPONDING AS A WRITER

The following essay is a claim of value in which an author argues
that a belief or a form of behavior is either desirable or undesirable.
Here, as the title suggests, the author claims that competitive sports
are destructive. In arguments about values, the author may or may
not suggest a solution to the problem caused by the belief or behavior. If so, the solution will be implicit — that is, unexpressed, or
undeveloped — as is the case here, and the emphasis will remain on
support for the claim.

Keep in mind that an essay of this length can never do justice to
a complicated and highly debatable subject. It will probably lack sufficient evidence, as this one does, to answer all the questions and
objections of readers who enjoy and approve of competitive games.
What it can do is provoke thought and initiate an intelligent discussion.

No-Win Situations
ALFIE KOHN

Intro: personal experience

I learned my first game at a birthday party. You remember it: X players scramble for X-minus-one chairs each time the music stops. In every round a child is eliminated until at the end only one is left triumphantly seated while everyone else is standing on the sidelines, excluded from play, unhappy . . . losers.

This is how we learn to have a good time in America.

Competition

Several years ago I wrote a book called *No Contest,* which, based on the findings of several hundred studies, argued that *Warrant* competition undermines self-esteem, poisons relationships, and holds us back from doing our best. I was mostly interested in the win/lose arrangement that defines our workplaces and classrooms, but I found myself nagged by the following question: If competition is so destructive and counterproductive during the week, why do we take for granted that it suddenly becomes benign and even desirable on the weekend?

This is a particularly unsettling line of inquiry for athletes or parents. Most of us, after all, assume that competitive sports teach all sorts of useful lessons and, indeed, that games by definition must produce a winner and a loser. But I've come *Claim or thesis statement* to believe that recreation at its best does not require people to try to triumph over others. Quite to the contrary.

This article by Alfie Kohn, author of *No Contest: The Case against Competition* (1986) and a contributing editor to *Psychology Today,* appeared in *Women's Sports and Fitness Magazine* (July–August 1990).

Terry Orlick, a sports psychologist at   5
the University of Ottawa, took a look at
musical chairs and proposed that we keep
the basic format of removing chairs but
change the goal; the point becomes to fit
everyone on a diminishing number of
seats. At the end, a group of giggling children tries to figure out how to squish
onto a single chair. Everybody plays to
the end; everybody has a good time.

Support: expert opinion,
alternatives to competitive
games

Orlick and others have devised or
collected hundreds of such games for
children and adults alike. The underlying theory is simple: All games involve
achieving a goal despite the presence of
an obstacle, but nowhere is it written that
the obstacle has to be someone else. The
idea can be for each person on the field to
make a specified contribution to the goal,
or for all the players to reach a certain
score, or for everyone to work with her
partners against a time limit.

Refuting the opposing view

Note the significance of an "opponent" becoming a "partner." The entire
dynamic of the game shifts, and one's attitude toward the other players changes
with it. Even the friendliest game of tennis
can't help but be affected by the game's
inherent structure, which demands that
each person try to hit the ball where the
other can't get to it. You may not be a ma-
licious person, but to play tennis means
that you try to make the other person fail.

No advantages
in competition

I've become convinced that not a
single one of the advantages attributed to
sports actually requires competition. Running, climbing, biking, swimming, aerobics — all offer a fine workout without
any need to try to outdo someone else.

1) Some people point to the camaraderie
that results from teamwork, but that's
precisely the benefit of cooperative activity, whose very essence is that *everyone*
on the field is working together for a common goal. By contrast, the distinguishing
feature of team competition is that a given

player works with and is encouraged to feel warmly toward only half of those present. Worse, a we-versus-they dynamic is set up, which George Orwell once called "war minus the shooting."

2) The dependence on sports to provide a sense of accomplishment or to test one's wits is similarly misplaced. One can aim instead at an objective standard (How far did I throw? How many miles did we cover?) or attempt to do better than last week. Such individual and group striving — like cooperative games — provides satisfaction and challenge without competition.

If large numbers of people insist that we can't do without win/lose activities, the first question to ask is whether they've ever tasted the alternative. When Orlick taught a group of children noncompetitive games, two-thirds of the boys and all of the girls preferred them to the kind that require opponents. If our culture's idea of fun requires beating someone else, it may just be because we don't know any other way. 10

3) It may also be because we overlook the psychological costs of competition. Most people lose in most competitive encounters, and it's obvious why that causes self-doubt. But even winning doesn't build character. It just lets us gloat temporarily. Studies have shown that feelings of self-worth become dependent on external sources of evaluation as a result of competition. Your value is defined by what you've done and who you've beaten. The whole affair soon becomes a vicious circle: The more you compete, the more you *need* to compete to feel good about yourself. It's like drinking salt water when you're thirsty. This process is bad enough for us; it's a disaster for our children.

4) While this is going on, competition is having an equally toxic effect on our relationships. By definition, not everyone

can win a contest. That means that each child inevitably comes to regard others as obstacles to his or her own success. Competition leads children to envy winners, to dismiss losers (there's no nastier epithet in our language than "loser!"), and to be suspicious of just about everyone. Competition makes it difficult to regard others as potential friends or collaborators; even if you're not my rival today, you could be tomorrow.

This is not to say that competitors will always detest one another. But trying to outdo someone is not conducive to trust — indeed it would be irrational to trust a person who gains from your failure. At best, competition leads one to look at others through narrowed eyes; at worst, it invites outright aggression.

Changing the Structure of Sports

Conclusion

But no matter how many bad feelings erupt during competition, we have a marvelous talent for <u>blaming the individuals rather than focusing on the structure of the game itself, a structure that makes my success depend on your failure.</u> Cheating may just represent the logical conclusion of this arrangement rather than an aberration. And sportsmanship is nothing more than an artificial way to try to limit the damage of competition. If we weren't set against each other on the court or the track, we wouldn't need to keep urging people to be good sports; they might well be working *with* each other in the first place.

New idea that confirms his claim

As radical or surprising as it may 15 sound, the problem isn't just that we compete the wrong way or that we push winning on our children too early. <u>The problem is competition itself.</u> What we need to be teaching our daughters and sons is that it's possible to have a good time — a better time — without turning the playing field into a battlefield.

Organization

While there are numerous conventional patterns of organization (see Chapter 9), it is worth pointing out that most essays of more than 750 words are rarely perfect examples of such patterns. Authors mix structures wherever it seems necessary to make a stronger case. The pattern of organization in this essay is primarily a *defense of the main idea* — that competitive sports are psychologically unhealthy. But because the claim is highly controversial, the author must also try to *refute the opposing view* — that competition is rewarding and enjoyable.

The *claim,* expressed as the *thesis statement* of the essay, appears at the end of paragraph 4: "recreation at its best does not require people to try to triumph over others. Quite the contrary." The three-paragraph introduction recounts a relevant personal experience as well as the reasons that prompted Kohn to write his essay. Because we are all interested in stories, the recital of a personal experience is a popular device for introducing almost any subject (see "The Childswap Society," p. 260).

The rest of the essay, until the last two paragraphs, is devoted to summarizing the benefits of cooperative play and the disadvantages of competitive sport. The emphasis is overwhelmingly on the disadvantages as stated in the third paragraph: "competition undermines self-esteem, poisons relationships and holds us back from doing our best." This is the *warrant,* the assumption that underlies the claim. In fact, Kohn is here referring to a larger study that he wrote about competition in workplaces and classrooms. We must accept this broad generalization, which applies to many human activities, before we can agree that the claim about competition in sports is valid.

The last two paragraphs sum up his argument that "The problem is competition itself" (para. 15) — the structure of the game, rather than the people who play. Notice that this summary does not merely repeat the main idea. Like many thoughtful summaries, it also offers *a new idea* about good sportsmanship that confirms his conclusion.

Support

Because the author knows that competitive sports are hugely popular not only in the United States but in many other parts of the world, he must give most of his argument to refuting the specific claims of those who value the spirit of competition. Kohn relies for support on examples from common experience and on the work of Terry Orlick, a sports psychologist. The examples from experience are ones that most of us will recognize. Here we are in a position to judge for ourselves, without the mediation of an expert, whether the influence of competition in sports is as hurtful as Kohn insists. Orlick's research suggests a solution — adaptations of familiar games that will provide enjoyment but avoid competition.

On the other hand, the results from studies by one psychologist whose work we aren't able to verify and the mention of "studies" in paragraph 3 without further attribution are probably not enough to answer all the arguments in favor of competition. Critics may also ask if Kohn has offered support for one of his contentions — that competition "holds us back from doing our best" (para. 3). (Support for this may appear in one of Kohn's books.)

In addition, Kohn fails to make clear distinctions between competitive sports for children, who may find it difficult to accept defeat, and for adults, who understand the consequences of any competitive game and are psychologically equipped to deal with them. Readers may therefore share Kohn's misgivings about competition for children but doubt that his criteria apply equally to adults.

Style

The language is clear and direct. Kohn's article, which appeared in a women's sports magazine, is meant for the educated general reader, not the expert. This is also the audience for whom most student papers are written. But the written essay need not be unduly formal. Kohn uses contractions and the personal pronouns "I" and "you" to establish a conversational context. One of the particular strengths of his style is the skillful use of transitional expressions, words like "this" and "also" and clauses like "This is not to say that" and "Note the significance of" to make connections between paragraphs and new ideas.

The tone is temperate despite the author's strong feelings about the subject. Other authors, supporting the same argument, have used language that borders on the abusive about coaches and trainers of children's games. But a less inflammatory voice is far more effective with an audience that may be neutral or antagonistic.

You will find it helpful to look back over the essay to see how the examples we've cited and others work to fulfill the writer's purpose.

RESPONDING AS A CRITICAL LISTENER

Of course, not all public arguments are written. Oral arguments on radio and television now enjoy widespread popularity and influence. In fact, their proliferation means that we listen far more than we talk, read, or write. Today the art of listening has become an indispensable tool for learning about the world we live in. One informed critic predicts that the dissemination of information and opinions through the electronic media will "enable more and more Americans to participate directly in making the laws and policies by which they are governed."[1]

Because we are interested primarily in arguments about public issues — those that involve democratic decision making — we will not be concerned with the afternoon television talk shows that are largely devoted to personal problems. (Occasionally, however, *Oprah* and *Sally Jessy Raphael* introduce topics of broad social significance.) More relevant to the kinds of written arguments you will read and write about in this course are the television and radio shows that also examine social and political problems. The most intelligent and responsible programs usually consist of a panel of experts — politicians, journalists, scholars — led by a neutral moderator (or one who, at least, allows guests to express their views). Some of these programs are decades old; others are more recent — *Meet the Press, Face the Nation, Firing Line, The McLaughlin Group, The NewsHour with Jim Lehrer.* An outstanding radio show, *Talk of the Nation* on National Public Radio, invites listeners, who are generally informed and articulate, to call in and ask questions of, or comment on remarks by, experts on the topic of the day.

Several enormously popular radio talk shows are hosted by people with strong, sometimes extreme ideological positions. They may use offensive language and insult their listeners in a crude form of theater. Among the most influential shows are those of Don Imus and Howard Stern. In addition, elections and political crises bring speeches and debates on radio and television by representatives of a variety of views. Some are long and formal, written texts that are simply read aloud, but others are short and impromptu.

Whatever the merits or shortcomings of individual programs, significant general differences exist between arguments on radio and television and arguments in the print media. These differences include the degree of organization and development and the risk of personal attacks.

First (excluding for the moment the long, prepared speeches), contributions to a panel discussion must be delivered in fragments, usually no longer than a single paragraph, weakened by time constraints, interruptions, overlapping speech, memory gaps, and real or feigned displays of derision, impatience, and disbelief by critical panelists. Even on the best programs, the result is a lack of both coherence — or connections between ideas — and solid evidence that requires development. Too often we are treated to conclusions with little indication of how they were arrived at.

---

[1] Lawrence K. Grossman, *The Electronic Republic: Reshaping Democracy in the Information Age* (New York: Viking, 1995).

The following brief passage appeared in a newspaper review of "Resolved: The flat tax is better than the income tax," a debate on *Firing Line* by an impressive array of experts. It illustrates some of the difficulties that accompany programs attempting to capture the truth of a complicated issue on television or radio.

> "It is absolutely true," says a proponent. "It is factually untrue," counters an opponent. "It's factually correct," responds a proponent. "I did my math right," says a proponent. "You didn't do your math right," says an opponent. At one point in a discussion of interest income, one of the experts says, "Oh, excuse me, I think I got it backward."

No wonder the television critic called the exchange "disjointed and at times perplexing."[2]

In the sensational talk shows the participants rely on personal experience and vivid anecdotes, which may not be sufficiently typical to prove anything.

Second, listeners and viewers of all spoken arguments are in danger of evaluating them according to criteria that are largely absent from evaluation of written texts. It is true that writers may adopt a *persona* or a literary disguise, which the tone of the essay will reflect. But many readers will not be able to identify it or recognize their own response to it. Listeners and viewers, however, can hardly avoid being affected by characteristics that are clearly definable: a speaker's voice, delivery, bodily mannerisms, dress, and physical appearance. In addition, listeners may be adversely influenced by clumsy speech containing more slang, colloquialisms, and grammar and usage errors than written texts that have had the benefit of revision.

But if listeners allow consideration of physical attributes to influence their judgment of what the speaker is trying to prove, they are guilty of an ad hominem fallacy — that is, an evaluation of the speaker rather than the argument. This is true whether the evaluation is favorable or unfavorable. (See pp. 305–06 for a discussion of this fallacy.)

Talk shows may indeed be disjointed and perplexing, but millions of us find them both instructive and entertaining. Over time we are exposed to an astonishing variety of opinions from every corner of American life, and we also acquire information from experts who might not otherwise be available to us. Then there is the appeal of hearing the voices, seeing the faces of people engaged in earnest, sometimes passionate, discourse — a short, unrehearsed drama in which we also play a part as active listeners in a far-flung audience.

---

[2] Walter Goodman, "The Joys of the Flat Tax, Excluding the Equations," *New York Times*, December 21, 1995, sec. C, p. 14.

Guidelines to Critical Listening

Listening is hearing with attention, a natural and immensely important human activity, which, unfortunately, many people don't do very well. The good news is that listening is a skill that can be learned and, unlike some other skills, practiced every day without big investments of money and effort.

Here are some of the characteristics of critical listening most appropriate to understanding arguments.

1. Above all, listening to arguments requires concentration. If you are distracted, you cannot go back as you do with the written word to clarify a point or recover a connection. Devices such as flow sheets and outlines can be useful aids to concentration. In following a debate, for example, judges and other listeners often use flow sheets — distant cousins of baseball scorecards — to record the major points on each side and their rebuttals. For roundtable discussions or debates you can make your own simple flow chart to fill out as you listen, with columns for claims, different kinds of support, and warrants. Leave spaces in the margin for your questions and comments about the soundness of the proof. An outline is more useful for longer presentations, such as lectures. As you listen, try to avoid being distracted by facts alone. Look for the overall pattern of the speech.

2. Listeners often concentrate on the wrong things in the spoken argument. We have already noted the distractions of appearance and delivery. Research shows that listeners are likely to give greater attention to the dramatic elements of speeches than to the logical ones. But you can enjoy the sound, the appearance, and the drama of a spoken argument without allowing these elements to overwhelm what is essential to the development of a claim.

3. Good listeners try not to allow their prejudices to prevent careful evaluation of the argument. This doesn't mean accepting everything or even most of what you hear. It means trying to avoid premature judgments about what is actually said. This precaution is especially relevant when the speakers and their views are well known and the listener has already formed an opinion about them, favorable or unfavorable.

RESPONDING TO A VISUAL ARGUMENT

Man has been communicating by pictures longer than he has been using words. With the development of photography in this century we are using pictures as a means of communication to such an extent that in some areas they overshadow verbal language.[3]

---

[3] Paul Wendt, "The Language of Pictures," in S. I. Hayakawa, ed. *The Use and Misuse of Language* (Greenwich, Conn.: Fawcett, 1962), p. 175.

You've probably seen some of the powerful images in photographic journalism to which the author refers: soldiers in battle, destruction by weather disasters, beautiful natural landscapes, inhuman living conditions, the great mushroom cloud of early atomic explosions. These photographs and thousands of others encapsulate arguments of fact, value, and policy. We don't need to read their captions to understand what they tell us: *The tornado devastated the town. The Grand Canyon is our most stupendous national monument. We must not allow human beings to live like this.* The pictures stay with us long after we have forgotten the words that accompanied them.

Photographs, of course, function everywhere as instruments of persuasion. Animal rights groups show pictures of brutally mistreated dogs and cats; children's rights advocates publish pictures of sick and starving children in desolate refugee camps. On a very different scale, alluring photographs from advertisers — travel agencies, restaurants, sporting goods manufacturers, clothiers, jewelers, movie studios — promise to fulfill our dreams of pleasure.

But photographs are not the only visual images we respond to. We are also susceptible to other kinds of illustrations and to signs and symbols which over the years have acquired connotations, or suggestive significance. The flag or bald eagle, the shamrock, the crown, the cross, the hammer and sickle, and the swastika can all rouse strong feelings for or against the ideas they represent. These symbols may be defined as abbreviated claims of value. They summarize the moral, religious, and political principles by which groups of people live and often die. In commercial advertisements we recognize symbols that aren't likely to enlist our deepest loyalties but, nevertheless, have impact on our daily lives: the apple with a bite in it, the golden arches, the Prudential rock, Joe Camel, and a thousand others.

In fact, a closer look at commercial and political advertising, which is heavily dependent on visual argument and is something we are all familiar with, provides a useful introduction to this complex subject. We know that advertisements, with or without pictures, are short arguments, often lacking fully developed support, whose claims of policy urge us to take an action: Buy this product or service; vote for this candidate or issue. The claim may not be directly expressed, but it will be clearly implicit. In print, on television, or on the Internet, the visual representation of objects, carefully chosen to appeal to a particular audience, can be as important as, if not more important than, any verbal text.

In a political advertisement, for example, we often see a picture of the candidate surrounded by a smiling family. The visual image is by now a cliché, suggesting traditional values — love and security, the importance of home and children. Even if we know little or nothing about his or her platform, we are expected to make a sympathetic connection with the candidate.

In a commercial advertisement the image may be a picture of a real or fictitious person to whom we will react favorably. Consider the picture on a jar of spaghetti sauce. As a famous designer remarked, "When you think about it, sauce is mostly sauce. It's the label that makes the difference."[4] And what, according to the designer, does the cheerful face of Paul Newman on jars of his spaghetti sauce suggest to the prospective buyer? "Paul Newman. Paul Newman. Paul Newman. Blue eyes. All the money goes to charity. It's humanitarian, funny, and sexy. Selling this is like falling off a log." Not a word about the quality of the sauce.

Even colleges, which are also selling a product, must think of appropriate images to attract their prospective customers — students. Today the fact that more women than men are enrolled in college has caused some schools to rethink their images. One college official explained:

> We're having our recruiting literature redesigned, and we've been thinking about what's a feminine look and what's a masculine look. We have a picture of a library with a lot of stained glass, and people said that was kind of a feminine cover. Now we're using a picture of the quadrangle.[5]

In addition to the emblem itself, the designer pays careful attention to a number of other elements in the ad: colors, light and shadow, foreground and background, relative sizes of pictures and text, and placement of objects on the page or screen. Each of these contributes to the total effect, although we may be unaware of how the effect has been achieved. (In the ad that follows, you will be able to examine some of the psychological and aesthetic devices at work.)

When there is no verbal text, visual images are less subject to analysis and interpretation. For one thing, if we are familiar with the objects in the picture, we see the whole image at once, and it registers immediately. The verbal message is linear and takes far longer to be absorbed. Pictures, therefore, appear to need less translation. Advertisers and other arguers depend on this characteristic to provide quick and friendly acceptance of their claims, although the image may, in fact, be deceptive.

This expectation of easy understanding poses a danger with another visual ally of the arguer — the graph or chart. Graphics give us factual information at a glance. In addition to the relative ease with which they can be read, they are "at their best . . . instruments for reasoning about quantitative information. . . . Of all methods for

---

[4] Tibor Kalman, "Message: Sweet-Talking Spaghetti Sauce," *New York Times Magazine,* December 13, 1998, p. 81.

[5] *New York Times,* December 6, 1998, p. 38.

analyzing and communicating statistical information, well-designed data graphics are usually the simplest and at the same time the most powerful."[6]

Nevertheless, they may mislead the quick reader. Graphics can lie. "The lies are told about the major issues of public policy — the government budget, medical care, prices, and fuel economy standards, for example. The lies are systematic and quite predictable, nearly always exaggerating the rate of recent change."[7]

Visual images, then, for all their apparent immediacy and directness, need to be read with at least the same attention we give to the verbal message if we are to understand the arguments they represent.

Questions for Analysis

1. What does the arguer want me to do or believe? How important is the visual image in persuading me to comply?
2. Has the visual image been accompanied by sufficient text to answer questions I may have about the claim?
3. Are the visual elements more prominent than the text? If so, why?
4. Is the visual image representative of a large group, or is it an exception that cannot support the claim?
5. Does the arrangement of elements in the message tell me what the arguer considers most important? If so, what is the significance of this choice?
6. Can the validity of this chart or graph be verified?
7. Does the visual image lead me to entertain unrealistic expectations? (Can using this shampoo make hair look like that shining cascade on the television screen? Does the picture of the candidate for governor, shown answering questions in a classroom of eager, smiling youngsters, mean that he has a viable plan for educational reform?)

SAMPLE ANALYSIS OF AN ADVERTISEMENT

We have pointed out that a commercial advertisement is a short argument that makes an obvious policy claim, which may or may not be explicit: *You should buy this product.* Depending on the medium — television, print, radio, or Internet — an ad may convey its message through language, picture, or sound.

Here is how one analyst of advertising sums up the goals of the advertiser: (1) attract attention, (2) arouse interest, (3) stimulate

---

[6] Edward R. Tufte, *The Visual Display of Quantitative Information* (Cheshire, Conn.: Graphics Press, 1983), introduction.

[7] Tufte, *The Visual Display,* p. 76.

desire, (4) create conviction, and (5) get action.[8] Needless to say, not every ad successfully fulfills all these objectives. If you examine the ad reproduced here, you can see how the advertiser brings language and visual image together in an attempt to support the claim.

First of all, you must imagine the principal objects of the ad in color — white bread on one side, red ravioli on the other. Of course, the advertiser, Chef Boyardee, expects the reader to find the ravioli more attractive. Like most pictures of food, these are designed to attract attention and arouse interest. Whether they stimulate desire depends on a number of things that the advertiser cannot control — who the reader is, how much the reader likes such food, how hungry he or she is at the time of the reading, and so on.

Notice the word *simple,* which is printed in bright red in the headline. This word emphasizes both the visual image (the clear, uncluttered arrangement of the pictures, lots of white space, the neat lineup of the comparative data) and the content message as well (that is, that the claim is unambiguous and uncontroversial). Simplicity is not always a positive attribute, but to advertisers the word *simple* is a magic wand that dispels the buyer's fear of whatever might be complicated or obscure.

You may not be immediately aware that the word *simple* makes a connection with the word *goodness,* also in bright red, in the lower right corner. One analyst points to this arrangement as "an extremely important dimension" because "when we read, the eye moves from the upper left corner of the page to the lower right corner."[9] The ravioli, too, appear on the preferred side, the right, where the eye will pause or encounter the end of the message. It is the emphatic position.

Support for the claim that Chef Boyardee Beef Ravioli should be your choice appears in the data under the pictures. The data here are limited to numbers, as the headline predicts: "An after-school lesson in simple mathematics." Again, even the visual arrangement of the numbers suggests openness and clarity. The numbers themselves are meant to create conviction. The advertiser, however, omits any authority for them, and critics have noted that such numbers on containers are sometimes inaccurate. Not surprisingly, the advertiser concentrates on fat content because in this respect, perhaps *only* in this respect, is the ravioli superior. (Arguers about social issues also engage in this strategy of calculated omission.)

Additional support appears in the paragraph below. Here, too, the spacing is open, generous, and easy to read, and we learn about

---

[8] J. V. Lund, *Newspaper Advertising* (New York: Prentice-Hall, 1947), p. 83.

[9] Torben Vestergaard and Kim Schroder, *The Language of Advertising* (Oxford: Oxford University Press, 1986), p. 44.

An after-school lesson
in simple mathematics.

Peanut Butter & Jelly Sandwich
(2 Tbsp PB, 1Tbsp Jelly, 2 Slices Bread)

Calories 360
Calories from Fat 150
Fat 18g

Chef Boyardee® Beef Ravioli
(1 cup serving)

Calories 230
Calories from Fat 45
Fat 5g

An after-school meal doesn't have to be a fat fest. Consider a hot

bowl of Chef Boyardee® Beef Ravioli. One serving has fewer calories and

less than 1/3 the fat of a PB&J. Chef Boyardee Beef Ravioli is made with

enriched pasta, sun-ripened tomatoes and 100% USDA-

inspected beef. With no preservatives.

So when your kids come home starving

after school, give them something you both like.

Thank goodness

for Chef Boyardee

See product label for information on sodium and other nutrients.

International Home Foods, Inc.

other healthful qualities of the beef ravioli. The advertiser *seems* to allege that its product is distinctive in regard to these good things. But, in fact, they are true for almost all pasta and meat sold in the United States, and all preservatives, contrary to the advertiser's implication, are not harmful. Other producers have made equally ambiguous claims. Schlitz Beer boasted in its ads that its bottles were steam-sterilized, without revealing that bottles of all other beer companies were also steam-sterilized.[10]

The warrant that underlies the claim becomes clear in the last one-sentence paragraph. We've been aware all along that the appeal is not to children, the chief consumers of peanut-butter and jelly sandwiches. The phrase "your kids" tells us that the appeal is directed to parents. We now understand the unexpressed warrant: Parents can be counted on to provide what is most healthful for their children.

It's worth noting, too, that the paragraph of text probably doesn't play a significant role in the argument. The emphasis rests on the picture and the chart, and the advertiser counts on them to make an impression that will persuade the reader to buy its product even if he or she doesn't read the text. Their place in the upper half of the ad is like a headline and the first paragraph of a news story, which is all that many people read.

Is the ad successful in getting action? The advertiser has tried to establish itself, in both the visual and the verbal content of its message, as a friend of the reader, open, truthful, committed to the health of children. It has assumed that the fat content of food is of high importance to the parents who read the ad. And perhaps it is, but despite the apparent validity of the warrant, the success of the ad is unpredictable. The plump red ravioli may appeal to the parent, but many children will prefer the sandwich, and for reasons that advertisers can't control, the parent may choose what the children *want.* Advertisers who show pictures of expensive toys on children's television programs have already learned this lesson.

RESPONDING ONLINE

You have learned that writers need the responses of readers and other writers to improve their writing. As the influence of computers permeates our society and more people rely on the Internet to send electronic mail (*e-mail*), it has become ever easier for writers to distribute their writing and for readers to respond to it. Only a decade ago, if you wanted feedback for your writing, you had to either read it aloud to others or copy and distribute it by hand or postal mail. Both methods were cumbersome and time-consuming, even expensive. Electronic networks now allow your writing to be distributed almost instantaneously to dozens or even thousands of readers with virtually no copying or mailing costs. Readers can respond to you

---

[10] Daniel J. Boorstin, *The Image; or, What Happened to the American Dream?* (New York: Atheneum, 1962), p. 214.

just as quickly and cheaply. Even though there can be pitfalls and problems with communicating online, the overall ease of use encourages writers to seek, and readers to provide, editorial feedback.

Guidelines for Responding Online

You know that in face-to-face conversation the words themselves constitute only a part of your message. Much of what you say is communicated through your body language and tone of voice. Written words provide a much narrower channel of communication, which is why you must be more careful when you write to someone than when you speak directly to them. Electronic writing, however, especially through e-mail, fosters a casualness and immediacy that often fools writers into assuming they are talking privately rather than writing publicly. Online you may find yourself writing quickly, carelessly, and intimately; without the help of your tone and body language, you may end up being seriously misunderstood. Words written hastily are often read much differently than intended; this is especially true when the writer attempts an ironic or sarcastic tone. For example, if a classmate walks up to you with a critical comment about one of your sentences and you respond by saying "I didn't realize you were so smart," the words, if unaccompanied by a placating smile and a pleasant, jocular tone, may come across as sarcastic or hostile. In e-writing, the same words appear without the mitigating body language and may be perceived as harsh, possibly insulting. You must keep this danger in mind as you respond online or risk alienating your reader.

Keep in mind, too, that e-mail may be read not only by your addressee but also by anyone with whom the addressee chooses to share your message. An intemperate or indiscreet message may be forwarded to other classmates or your instructor, or, depending on the limits of the system, to many other readers whom you do not know.

Experienced online communicators advocate a set of network etiquette guidelines called *netiquette*. Here are some generally accepted netiquette rules:

- Keep your sentences short and uncomplicated.

- Separate blocks of text — which should be no more than four or five lines long — by blank lines. For those rare occasions when a comment requires more than ten or fifteen consecutive lines of text, use subheadings on separate lines to guide your reader.

- Refer specifically to the text to which you are responding. You may want to quote directly from it, cutting and pasting phrases or sentences from the document to help show exactly what you are responding to.

- Greet the person(s) to whom you are writing politely and by name.

- Be wary about attempting to be funny. Humor, as just explained, often requires a context, tone of voice, and body language to emphasize that it is not to be taken seriously. Writing witty comments that are sure to be taken humorously calls for skill and care, and e-mail messages usually are written too quickly for either.

- Avoid profanity or invective, and be wary of brusque or abrupt statements. Consider how you would feel if someone wrote to you that way.

- Avoid discussion of politics or religion unless that is the specific topic of your message.

- Do not ridicule public figures. Your reader may not share your opinions of, say, Senator Edward Kennedy or radio talk show host Rush Limbaugh.

- Frame all comments in a helpful, not critical, tone. For instance, rather than beginning a critique with "I found a number of problems in your text," you may want to start out more like this: "You have some good ideas in this paper, and with a few changes I think it will do well."

EXERCISES

Prereading

1. If you haven't read "Kids in the Mall: Growing Up Controlled" (p. 64), do the following. Take note of the title of the book in which this excerpt appears. Now, write down briefly what you guess the attitude of the author will be toward his subject. Tell which words in the titles of the excerpt and the book suggest his approach. Next, read the quotation that heads the essay and the first paragraph. If you think there are further clues here, explain briefly how you interpreted them. (For example, did your own experience with malls enter into your thinking as you read?)

   Keep your notes. Refer to them after you have read the whole article (and perhaps discussed it in class). How well did your preparation help you to find the main point and understand the examples that supported it? Are there other things you might do to improve your prereading?

Annotating

2. Choose an editorial of at least two paragraphs in a newspaper or your school paper on a controversial subject that interests you. The title will probably reveal the subject. Annotate the editorial as you read, ques-

tioning, agreeing, objecting, offering additional ideas. (The annotation of the "The Pursuit of Whining," p. 28, will suggest ways of doing this, although your personal responses are what make the annotation useful.) Then read the editorial again. You should discover that annotating the article caused you to read more carefully, more critically, with greater comprehension and a more focused response.

Evaluating

3. Summarize the claim of the editorial in one sentence. Omit the supporting data and concentrate on the thesis. Then explain briefly your reaction to it. Has the author proved his or her point? Your annotation will show you where you expressed doubt or approval. If you already know a good deal about the subject, perhaps you will be reasonably confident of your judgment. If not, you may find that your response is tentative and that you need to read further for more information about the subject and to consult guidelines for making evaluations about the elements of argument.

Listening

4. People sometimes object to lectures as an educational tool. Think about some of the specific lectures you have listened to recently, and analyze the reasons that you liked or disliked them (or liked some aspects and disliked others). Do you think that you learned everything that the lecturer intended you to learn? If the results were doubtful, how much did your listening skills, good or bad, contribute to the result? Should the lecturer have done something differently to improve your response?

5. Watch (and *listen* to) one of the afternoon talk shows like *Oprah Winfrey* in which audiences discuss a controversial social problem. (The *TV Guide* and daily newspapers often list the subject. Past topics on *Oprah* include when parents abduct their children and when children kill children.) Write a critical review of the discussion, mentioning as completely as you can the major claims, the most important evidence, and the declared or hidden warrants. (Unspoken warrants or assumptions may be easier to identify in arguments on talk shows where visual and auditory clues can reveal what participants try to hide.) How much did the oral format contribute to success or failure of the argument(s)?

6. Listen to one of the television talk shows that feature invited experts. Write a review, telling how much you learned about the subject(s) of discussion. Be specific about the elements of the show that were either helpful or unhelpful to your understanding.

7. Listen with a friend or friends to a talk show discussion. Take notes as you listen. Then compare notes to discover if you agree on the outstanding points, the degree to which claims have been supported, and the part that seeing or hearing the discussion played in your evaluation. If there is disagreement about any of the elements, how do you account for it?

Online

8. With three or four of your classmates select an argumentative essay in this book that all of you agree to read. Each of you should draft a response to the essay, either agreeing or disagreeing with the author's position, citing evidence to support your position. Then each of you prepare a letter soliciting a response to your draft from the members of your group. For example, you may want to state what your objective was, suggest what you think are the strengths and weaknesses of the draft, and ask what sort of revisions seem appropriate. E-mail the letter and the draft to each of your peer responders. Based on their comments, which should either be e-mailed to you or handwritten on a printed copy of your draft, revise your draft.

CHAPTER THREE

Claims

Claims, or propositions, represent answers to the question: "What are you trying to prove?" Although they are the conclusions of your arguments, they often appear as thesis statements. Claims can be classified as *claims of fact, claims of value,* and *claims of policy.*

CLAIMS OF FACT

Claims of fact assert that a condition has existed, exists, or will exist and that their support consists of factual information — information such as statistics, examples, and testimony that most responsible observers assume can be verified.

Many facts are not matters for argument: Our own senses can confirm them, and other observers will agree about them. We can agree that a certain number of students were in the classroom at a particular time, that lions make a louder sound than kittens, and that apples are sweeter than potatoes.

We can also agree about information that most of us can rarely confirm for ourselves — information in reference books, such as atlases, almanacs, and telephone directories; data from scientific resources about the physical world; and happenings reported in the media. We can agree on the reliability of such information because we trust the observers who report it.

However, the factual map is constantly being redrawn by new data in such fields as history and science that cause us to reevaluate our conclusions. For example, the discovery of the Dead Sea Scrolls in 1947 revealed that some books of the Bible — Isaiah, for one — were

51

far older than we had thought. Researchers at New York Hospital–Cornell Medical Center say that many symptoms previously thought inevitable in the aging process are now believed to be treatable and reversible symptoms of depression.[1]

In your conversations with other students you probably generate claims of fact every day, some of which can be verified without much effort, others of which are more difficult to substantiate.

> CLAIM: Most of the students in this class come from towns within fifty miles of Boston.

To prove this the arguer would need only to ask the students in the class where they come from.

> CLAIM: Students who take their courses pass/fail make lower grades than those who take them for specific grades.

In this case the arguer would need to have access to student records showing the specific grades given by instructors. (In most schools the instructor awards a letter grade, which is then recorded as a pass or a fail if the student has elected this option.)

> CLAIM: The Red Sox will win the pennant this year.

This claim is different from the others because it is an opinion about what will happen in the future. But it can be verified (in the future) and is therefore classified as a claim of fact.

More complex factual claims about political and scientific matters remain controversial because proof on which all or most observers will agree is difficult or impossible to obtain.

> CLAIM: Bilingual programs are less effective than English-only programs in preparing students for higher education.

> CLAIM: The only life in the universe exists on this planet.

Not all claims are so neatly stated or make such unambiguous assertions. Because we recognize that there are exceptions to most generalizations, we often qualify our claims with words such as *generally, usually, probably,* and *as a rule.* It would not be true to state flatly, for example, "College graduates earn more than high school graduates." This statement is generally true, but we know that some high school graduates who are electricians or city bus drivers or sanitation workers earn more than college graduates who are schoolteachers or nurses or social workers. In making such a claim, therefore, the writer should qualify it with a word that limits the claim.

To support a claim of fact, the writer needs to produce sufficient and appropriate data — that is, examples, statistics, and testimony

---

[1] *New York Times,* February 20, 1983, sec. 22, p. 4.

from reliable sources. Provided this requirement is met, the task of establishing a factual claim would seem to be relatively straightforward. But as you have probably already discovered in ordinary conversation, finding convincing support for factual claims can pose a number of problems. Whenever you try to establish a claim of fact, you will need to ask at least three questions about the material you plan to use: *What are sufficient and appropriate data? Who are the reliable authorities?* and *Have I made clear whether my statements are facts or inferences?*

Sufficient and Appropriate Data

The amount and kind of data for a particular argument depend on the importance and complexity of the subject. The more controversial the subject, the more facts and testimony you will need to supply. Consider the claim "The murder rate in New York City is lower this year than last year." If you want to prove the truth of this claim, obviously you will have to provide a larger quantity of data than for a claim that says, "By following three steps, you can train your dog to sit and heel in fifteen minutes." In examining your facts and opinions, an alert reader will want to know if they are accurate, current, and typical of other facts and opinions that you have not mentioned.

The reader will also look for testimony from more than one authority, although there may be cases where only one or two experts who have achieved a unique breakthrough in their field will be sufficient. These cases would probably occur most frequently in the physical sciences. The Nobel Prize winners James Watson and Francis Crick, who first discovered the structure of the DNA molecule, are an example of such experts. However, in the case of the so-called Hitler diaries that surfaced in 1983, at least a dozen experts — journalists, historians, bibliographers who could verify the age of the paper and the ink — were needed to establish that they were forgeries.

Reliable Authorities

Not all those who pronounce themselves experts are trustworthy. Your own experience has probably taught you that you cannot always believe the reports of an event by a single witness. The witness may be poorly trained to make accurate observations — about the size of a crowd, the speed of a vehicle, his distance from an object. Or his own physical conditions — illness, intoxication, disability — may prevent him from seeing or hearing or smelling accurately. The circumstances under which he observes the event — darkness, confusion, noise — may also impair his observation.

In addition, the witness may be biased for or against the outcome of the event, as in a hotly contested baseball game, where the observer sees the play that he wants to see. You will find the problems associated with the biases of witnesses to be relevant to your work as a reader and writer of argumentative essays.

You will undoubtedly want to quote authors in some of your arguments. In most cases you will not be familiar with the authors. But there are guidelines for determining their reliability: the rank or title of the experts, the acceptance of their publications by other experts, their association with reputable universities, research centers, or think tanks. For example, for a paper on euthanasia you might decide to quote from an article by Paul Ramsey, identified as the Harrington Spear Paine Professor of Religion at Princeton University. For a paper on prison reform you might want to use material supplied by Tom Murton, a professional penologist, formerly superintendent in the Arkansas prison system, now professor of criminology at the University of Minnesota. Most readers of your arguments would agree that these authors have impressive credentials in their fields.

What if several respectable sources are in conflict? What if the experts disagree? After a preliminary investigation of a controversial subject, you may decide that you have sufficient material to support your claim. But if you read further, you may discover that other material presented by equally qualified experts contradicts your original claim. In such circumstances you will find it impossible to make a definitive claim. (On pp. 166–68, in the treatment of support of a claim by evidence, you will find a more elaborate discussion of this vexing problem.)

Facts or Inferences

We have defined a fact as a statement that can be verified. An inference is "a statement about the unknown on the basis of the known."[2] The difference between facts and inferences is important to you as the writer of an argument because an inference is an *interpretation,* or an opinion reached after informed evaluation of evidence. As you and your classmates wait in your classroom on the first day of the semester, a middle-aged woman wearing a tweed jacket and a corduroy skirt appears and stands in the front of the room. You don't know who this woman is. However, based on what you do know about the appearance of many college teachers and the fact that teachers usually stand in front of the classroom, you may

---

[2]S. I. Hayakawa, *Language in Thought and Action* (New York: Harcourt, Brace, Jovanovich, 1978), p. 35.

infer that this woman is your teacher. You will probably be right. But you cannot be certain until you have more information. Perhaps you will find out that this woman has come from the department office to tell you that your teacher is sick and cannot meet the class today.

You have probably come across a statement such as the following in a newspaper or magazine: "Excessive television viewing has caused the steady decline in the reading ability of children and teenagers." Presented this way, the statement is clearly intended to be read as a factual claim that has been or can be proved. But it is an inference. The facts, which can be, and have been, verified, are (1) the reading ability of children and teenagers has declined and (2) the average child views television for six or more hours a day. (Whether this amount of time is "excessive" is also an opinion.) The cause-and-effect relation between the two facts is an interpretation of the investigator, who has examined both the reading scores and the amount of time spent in front of the television set and *inferred* that one is the cause of the other. The causes of the decline in reading scores are probably more complex than the original statement indicates. Since we can seldom or never create laboratory conditions for testing the influence of television separate from other influences in the family and the community, any statement about the connection between reading scores and television viewing can only be a guess.

By definition, no inference can ever do more than suggest probabilities. Of course, some inferences are much more reliable than others and afford a high degree of probability. Almost all claims in science are based on inferences, interpretations of data on which most scientists agree. Paleontologists find a few ancient bones from which they make inferences about an animal that might have been alive millions of years ago. We can never be absolutely certain that the reconstruction of the dinosaur in the museum is an exact copy of the animal it is supposed to represent, but the probability is fairly high because no other interpretation works so well to explain all the observable data — the existence of the bones in a particular place, their age, their relation to other fossils, and their resemblance to the bones of existing animals with which the paleontologist is familiar.

Inferences are profoundly important, and most arguments could not proceed very far without them. But an inference is not a fact. The writer of an argument must make it clear when he or she offers an inference, an interpretation, or an opinion that it is not a fact.

Defending a Claim of Fact

Here are some guidelines that should help you to defend a factual claim. (We'll say more about support of factual claims in Chapter 5.)

1. Be sure that the claim — what you are trying to prove — is clearly stated, preferably at the beginning of your paper.
2. Define terms that may be controversial or ambiguous. For example, in trying to prove that "radicals" had captured the student government, you would have to define "radicals," distinguishing them from "liberals" or members of other ideological groups, so that your readers would understand exactly what you meant.
3. As far as possible, make sure that your evidence — facts and opinions, or interpretations of the facts — fulfills the appropriate criteria. The data should be sufficient, accurate, recent, typical; the authorities should be reliable.
4. Make clear when conclusions about the data are inferences or interpretations, not facts. For example, you might write, "The series of lectures titled Modern Architecture, sponsored by our fraternity, was poorly attended because the students at this college aren't interested in discussions of art." What proof could you offer that this *was* the reason and that your statement was a *fact*? Perhaps there were other reasons that you hadn't considered.
5. Emphasize your most important evidence by placing it at the beginning or the end of your paper (the most emphatic positions in an essay) and devoting more space to it.

SAMPLE ANNOTATED ANALYSIS: CLAIM OF FACT

Cocaine Is Even Deadlier Than We Thought
LOUIS L. CREGLER AND HERBERT MARK

To the Editor:

In his July 3 letter about recreational cocaine use, Dr. Carl C. Pfeiffer notes that some of the toxic effects of cocaine on the heart have long been known to those versed in pharmacology. We wish to point out that cardiologists and neurologists

Introduction: reason for the letter — to provide new data

Louis L. Cregler, M.D., was the assistant chief of medicine, and Herbert Mark, M.D., was the chief of medicine at the Bronx Veterans Administration Medical Centre when this article appeared in the *New York Times* on July 30, 1986.

are seeing additional complications not previously known. Indeed, little information on the cardiovascular effects of cocaine appeared until recently.

As Dr. Pfeiffer says, cocaine sensitizes the heart to the normal stimulant effects of the body's adrenaline. This ordinarily makes the heart beat much faster and increases blood pressure significantly. Cocaine abuse has also been associated with *Support: effects on the heart* strokes, heart attacks (acute myocardial infarctions), and sudden deaths. Individuals with weak blood vessels (aneurysms or arteriovenous malformations) in the head are at greatest risk of having a stroke. With the sudden surge in blood pressure, a blood vessel can burst. Cocaine can also cause blood vessels supplying the heart muscle itself to undergo vasoconstriction (coronary spasm), and this can produce a heart attack.

Support: deaths from cocaine Deaths have been reported after ad-
use ministration of cocaine by all routes. Most such deaths are attributed to cocaine intoxication, leading to generalized convulsions, respiratory failure, and cardiac arrhythmias, minutes to hours after administration. Much of this information is so new that it has not found its way into the medical literature or standard textbooks.

Conclusion: claim of fact — Cocaine abuse continues to escalate in
dangers of increasing use American society. It is estimated that 30 million Americans have used it and some 5 million use it regularly. As cocaine has become less expensive, its availability and purity are increasing. It has evolved from a minor problem into a major threat to public health. And as use has increased, greater numbers of emergency-room visits, cocaine-related heart problems, and sudden deaths have been reported. With so many people using cocaine, it is not unexpected that more strokes, heart attacks, and sudden cardiac deaths will be taking place.

Louis L. Cregler, M.D.
Herbert Mark, M.D.

Analysis

The authors of this letter supply data to prove that the deadly effects of cocaine exceed those that are already well known in medicine and pharmacology. Four aspects of this factual claim are noteworthy. First, it is a response to a letter that, according to the authors, ignored significant new evidence. Many factual claims originate in just this way — as answers to previous claims. Second, the authors, both physicians at a large medical center, apparently have expert knowledge of the scientific data they report. Third, the effects of cocaine use are precisely and vividly described. It is, in fact, these specific references to the damage done to heart and blood vessels that make the claim particularly convincing. Finally, the authors make this claim in order to promote a change in our attitudes toward the use of cocaine; they do not call on their readers to abstain from cocaine. This use of a factual claim as a first step in calling for changes in attitude and behavior is a familiar and often effective argumentative strategy.

A NOTE ON CAUSAL ARGUMENT

Causal argument attempts to establish a relationship between two events or conditions by speculating about cause and effect. Suppose you read a report that states that more women than men are enrolled in colleges and universities. You may wonder what has caused this development or what are and will be the consequences for society of a population in which women are better educated than men. Your essay could answer one of these questions by examining one event or condition for either its causes or its effects. In a long paper you could answer both questions.

Several of the essays in this book use cause-and-effect development to support their claims. "Cocaine Is Even Deadlier Than We Thought" (p. 56) briefly summarizes the dangerous effects of an illegal drug. "Happiness Is a Warm Planet" (p. 77) suggests that a cause, global warming, will produce beneficial effects for human beings. "Abductions and Abductionists" (p. 184) begins with an effect — the belief in abduction of humans by aliens — and provides probable causes for this belief.

Such arguments — although we engage in them every day, both formally and informally — are more complicated than they seem and often highly controversial. For one thing, the cause of even the most ordinary event involving human behavior is not always easy to identify. Events usually have more than one cause and often have a chain of causes that began well before the immediate cause. We can often find evidence of this complexity when we ask the question "Why?" about events in our own lives. In literature, too, we see the search for meaning in a chain of events. Macbeth does not murder King Duncan only because Lady Macbeth urges him to do so. He has already heard a prophecy that he will be king; in addition, he has tasted power in his recent elevation to Thane of Cawdor. Even after we have learned about these provocations, we look for other causes in his character and his history.

Second, we cannot perform the kinds of controlled experiments in human behavior that verify causes in the physical sciences. We are told, for example, that married men live longer than unmarried men. It would be interesting and useful to know why, but the answer will probably not be found in the laboratory. For the present the causes, certainly more than one and rooted in psychology, can only be guessed.

Lastly, when two things occur in close proximity, we may leap to the conclusion that one thing is the cause of the other. Superstitions are the most familiar examples of such thinking. One book sums up the difficulty this way:

> Scientists are keenly aware of how easy it is to uncover associations and how hard it is to determine whether these links are actually cause-and-effect relationships. If you select a group of people and compile data about their health, lifestyle, and environment, you could uncover hundreds of associations. You may find direct associations between shirt size and blood pressure, or body weight and ownership of Ford pickup trucks. . . . But few of these links would be causal. . . . The physical height of children increases as their lifetime total of hours spent watching television increases. Does television watching promote physical growth?[3]

Yet, despite the problems associated with isolating the causes of things both ordinary and mysterious, the importance of sound cause-and-effect reasoning can hardly be overestimated. Think how few advances medical science could make before researchers had proved that certain organisms cause disease. In the social sciences causes are much harder to find, but solutions for crime, poverty, poor education, bigotry, and dozens of other problems depend in large part on uncovering them.

Elsewhere in this book you will find other references to cause-and-effect argument: causal connection (p. 157), doubtful-cause fallacy (p. 303), and cause credibility (p. 354).

Writer's Guide to the Causal Paper
Writing an Essay of Cause and Effect

1. You can begin your argument by describing the situation and by stating both your claim and your reasons for addressing this question. We

---

[3]Theodore Schick Jr. and Lewis Vaughan, *How to Think about Weird Things* (Mountain View, Calif.: Mayfield, 1995), p. 179.

often undertake the examination of causes and effects to explain or solve a problem.

2. Make an outline or notes of the main ideas that will support your claim. In a paper of fewer than 700 words, you probably cannot follow a long chain of causes. In fact, you may discover that only one important cause or effect deserves development in a short paper. In "Divorce and Our National Values" (p. 295), the author provides extended proof for one significant cause of divorce — our commitment to self-fulfillment.

3. Since causes are often hard to identify, you should use as many examples, studies by experts, graphs, etc. as you can accommodate to prove that there is a pattern, that the cause of some condition is not an anomaly or irregularity. In "Abductions and Abductionists" (p. 184), Curtis Peebles provides at least five causes for belief in alien abduction.

4. If your evidence shows that some causes in your outline seem stronger than others, emphasize the strong causes, and omit those for which the evidence is weak.

5. Be cautious in predicting that certain effects follow or will follow a particular cause or causes, and qualify your predictions. This means avoiding words like *always* and *never*. The past may not be a reliable guide to the future, and experts make predictions that sometimes are proved wrong.

6. When no solid evidence can be found, an educated guess can sometimes serve as a modest substitute. Educated guesses are reasonable inferences that are based on experience and common sense and are capable of proof. Analogies and comparisons to similar situations can be helpful, but remember that analogies are not proof.

7. Anticipate objections to your own explanations and predictions. If the objections are widely held, acknowledge them and try to point out their weaknesses.

8. Your essay may also rebut statements about cause and effect with which you disagree. Ideas that you oppose — for good reasons, of course — will inspire some of your most stimulating and insightful essays. In other college courses you may have acquired data that contradict conclusions about situations you are familiar with.

CLAIMS OF VALUE

Unlike claims of fact, which attempt to prove that something is true and which can be validated by reference to the data, claims of value make a judgment. They express approval or disapproval. They attempt to prove that some action, belief, or condition is right or wrong, good or bad, beautiful or ugly, worthwhile or undesirable.

CLAIM: Democracy is superior to any other form of government.

CLAIM: Killing animals for sport is wrong.

CLAIM: The Sam Rayburn Building in Washington is an aesthetic failure.

Some claims of value are simply expressions of tastes, likes and dislikes, or preferences and prejudices. The Latin proverb "De gustibus non est disputandum" states that we cannot dispute about tastes. Suppose you express a preference for chocolate over vanilla. If your listener should ask why you prefer this flavor, you cannot refer to an outside authority or produce data or appeal to her moral sense to convince her that your preference is justified.

Many claims of value, however, can be defended or attacked on the basis of standards that measure the worth of an action, a belief, or an object. As far as possible, our personal likes and dislikes should be supported by reference to these standards. Value judgments occur in any area of human experience, but whatever the area, the analysis will be the same. We ask the arguer who is defending a claim of value: *What are the standards or criteria for deciding that this action, this belief, or this object is good or bad, beautiful or ugly, desirable or undesirable? Does the thing you are defending fulfill these criteria?*

There are two general areas in which people often disagree about matters of value: aesthetics and morality. They are also the areas that offer the greatest challenge to the writer. What follows is a discussion of some of the elements of analysis that you should consider in defending a claim of value in these areas.

Aesthetics is the study of beauty and the fine arts. Controversies over works of art — the aesthetic value of books, paintings, sculpture, architecture, dance, drama, and movies — rage fiercely among experts and laypeople alike. They may disagree on the standards for judging or, even if they agree about standards, may disagree about how successfully the art object under discussion has met these standards.

Consider a discussion about popular music. Hearing someone praise the singing of a well-known vocalist, Sheila Jordan, you might ask why she is so highly regarded. You expect Jordan's fan to say more than "I like her" or "Man, she's great." You expect the fan to give reasons to support his claim. "She's unique," he says. He shows you a short review from a widely read newspaper that says, "Her singing is filled with fascinating phrasings, twists, and turns, and she's been compared with Billie Holiday for her emotional intensity. . . . She can be so heart-wrenching that conversations stop cold." Her fan agrees with the criteria for judging a singer given by the author of the review: uniqueness, fascinating phrasings, emotional intensity.

You may not agree that these are the only standards or even the significant ones for judging a singer. But the establishment of standards itself offers material for a discussion or an argument. You may argue about the relevance of the criteria, or, agreeing on the criteria, you may argue about the success of the singer in meeting them. Perhaps you prefer cool singers to intense ones. Or, even if you choose intensity over coolness, you may not think Sheila Jordan can be described as "expressive." Moreover, in any arguments about criteria, differences in experience and preparation acquire importance. You would probably take for granted that a writer with formal musical training who has listened carefully to dozens of singers over a period of years, who has read a good deal of musical criticism and discussed musical matters with other knowledgeable people would be a more reliable critic than someone who lacked these qualifications.

It is probably not surprising then, that, despite wide differences in taste, professional critics more often than not agree on criteria and whether an art object has met the criteria. For example, almost all movie critics agree that *Citizen Kane* and *Gone with the Wind* are superior films. They also agree that *Plan 9 from Outer Space,* a horror film, is terrible.

Value claims about morality express judgments about the rightness or wrongness of conduct or belief. Here disagreements are as wide and deep as in the arts. The first two examples on page 60 reveal how controversial such claims can be. Although you and your reader may share many values — among them a belief in democracy, a respect for learning, and a desire for peace — you may also disagree, even profoundly, about other values. The subject of divorce, for example, despite its prevalence in our society, can produce a conflict between people who have differing moral standards. Some people may insist on adherence to absolute standards, arguing that the values they hold are based on immutable religious precepts derived from God and biblical scripture. Since marriage is sacred, divorce is always wrong, they say, whether or not the conditions of society change. Other people may argue that values are relative, based on the changing needs of societies in different places and at different times. Since marriage is an institution created by human beings at a particular time in history to serve particular social needs, they may say, it can also be dissolved when other social needs arise. The same conflicts between moral values might occur in discussions of abortion or suicide.

As a writer you cannot always know what system of values your reader holds. Yet it might be possible to find a rule on which almost all readers agree. One such rule was expressed by the eighteenth-century German philosopher Immanuel Kant: "Man and, in general, every rational being exists as an end in itself and not merely as a means to be arbitrarily used by this or that will." Kant's prescription urges us not to subject any creature to a condition that it has not freely chosen. In other words, we cannot use other creatures, as in slavery, for our own purposes. (Some philosophers would extend this rule to the treatment of animals by human beings.) This standard of judgment has, in fact, been invoked in recent years against medical experimentation on human beings in prisons and hospitals without their consent and against the sterilization of poor or mentally defective women without their knowledge of the decision.

Nevertheless, even where people agree about standards for measuring behavior, a majority preference is not enough to confer moral value. If in a certain neighborhood a majority of heterosexual men decide to harass a few gay men and lesbians, that consensus does not make their action right. In formulating value claims, you should be prepared to ask and answer questions about the way in which your value claims and those of others have been arrived at. Lionel Ruby, an American philosopher, sums it up in these words: "The law of rationality tells us that we ought to justify our beliefs by evidence and reasons, instead of asserting them dogmatically."[4]

Of course, you will not always be able to persuade those with whom you argue that your values are superior to theirs and that they should therefore change their attitudes. Nor, on the other hand, would you want to compromise your values or pretend that they were different to win an argument. What you can and should do, however, as Lionel Ruby advises, is give *good reasons* that you think one thing is better than another. If as a child you asked why it was wrong to take your brother's toys, you might have been told by an exasperated parent, "Because I say so." Some adults still give such answers in defending their judgments, but such answers are not arguments and do nothing to win the agreement of others.

Writer's Guide to the Evaluation Paper
Defending a Claim of Value

The following suggestions are a preliminary guide to the defense of a value claim. (We discuss value claims further in Chapter 5.)

1. Try to make clear that the values or principles you are defending are important and relatively more significant than other values. Keep in mind that you and your readers may differ about their relative importance. For example, although your readers may agree with you that brilliant photography is important in a film, they may think that a well-written script is even more crucial to its success. And although they may agree that freedom of the press is a mainstay of democracy, they may regard the right to privacy as even more fundamental.
2. Suggest that adherence to the values you are defending will bring about good results in some specific situation or bad results if respect for the values is ignored. You might argue, for example, that a belief in freedom

---

[4]*The Art of Making Sense* (New York: Lippincott, 1968), p. 271.

of the press will make citizens better informed and the country stronger while a failure to protect this freedom will strengthen the forces of authoritarianism.

3. Since value terms are abstract, use examples and illustrations to clarify meanings and make distinctions. Comparisons and contrasts are especially helpful. If you use the term *heroism,* can you provide examples to differentiate between *heroism* and *foolhardiness* or *exhibitionism*?

4. Use testimony of others to prove that knowledgeable or highly regarded people share your values.

SAMPLE ANNOTATED ANALYSIS: CLAIM OF VALUE

Kids in the Mall: Growing Up Controlled
WILLIAM SEVERINI KOWINSKI

Butch heaved himself up and loomed over the group. "Like it was different for me," he piped. "My folks used to drop me off at the shopping mall every morning and leave me all day. It was like a big free baby-sitter, you know? One night they never came back for me. Maybe they moved away. Maybe there's some kind of a Bureau of Missing Parents I could check with."

— Richard Peck
Secrets of the Shopping Mall,
a novel for teenagers

Introduction: interesting personal anecdote

From his sister at Swarthmore, I'd heard about a kid in Florida whose mother picked him up after school every day, drove him straight to the mall, and left him there until it closed — all at his insistence. I'd heard about a boy in Washington who, when his family moved from one suburb to another, pedaled his bi-

---

William Severini Kowinski is a freelance writer who has been the book review editor and managing arts editor of the *Boston Phoenix.* This excerpt is from his book *The Malling of America: An Inside Look at the Great Consumer Paradise* (1985).

cycle five miles every day to get back to his old mall, where he once belonged.

These stories aren't unusual. The mall is a common experience for the majority of American youth; they have probably been going there all their lives. Some ran within their first large open space, saw their first fountain, bought their first toy, and read their first book in a mall. They may have smoked their first cigarette or first joint, or turned them down, had their first kiss or lost their virginity in the mall parking lot. Teenagers in America now spend more time in the mall than anywhere else but home and school. Mostly it is their choice, but some of that mall time is put in as the result of two-paycheck and single-parent households, and the lack of other viable alternatives. But are these kids being harmed by the mall?

Additional examples of mall experience

I wondered first of all what difference it makes for adolescents to experience so many important moments in the mall. They are, after all, at play in the fields of its little world and they learn its ways; they adapt to it and make it adapt to them. It's here that these kids get their street sense, only it's mall sense. They are learning the ways of a large-scale, artificial environment; its subtleties and flexibilities, its particular pleasures and resonances, and the attitudes it fosters.

Reasons for the author's interest

The presence of so many teenagers for so much time was not something mall developers planned on. In fact, it came as a big surprise. But kids became a fact of mall life very easily, and the International Council of Shopping Centers found it necessary to commission a study, which they published along with a guide to mall managers on how to handle the teenage incursion.

Expert opinion

The study found that "teenagers in 5 suburban centers are bored and come to the shopping centers mainly as a place to go. Teenagers in suburban centers spent more time fighting, drinking, littering and walking than did their urban counterparts, but presented fewer overall problems." The report observed that "adolescents congregated in groups of two to four and predominantly at locations selected by them rather than management." This probably had something to do with the decision to install game arcades, which allow management to channel these restless adolescents into naturally contained areas away from major traffic points of adult shoppers.

Why the malls encourage adolescent presence

The guide concluded that mall management should tolerate and even encourage the teenage presence because, in the words of the report, "The vast majority support the same set of values as does shopping center management." *The same set of values* means simply that mall kids are already preprogrammed to be consumers and that the mall can put the finishing touches to them as hard-core, lifelong shoppers just like everybody else. That, after all, is what the mall is about. So it shouldn't be surprising that in spending a lot of time there, adolescents find little that challenges the assumption that the goal of life is to make money and buy products, or that just about everything else in life is to be used to serve those ends.

Disadvantages: a) Exposure to high-consumption society

Growing up in a high-consumption society already adds inestimable pressure to kids' lives. Clothes consciousness has invaded the grade schools, and popularity is linked with having the best, newest clothes in the currently acceptable styles. Even what they read has been affected. "Miss [Nancy] Drew wasn't obsessed with her wardrobe," noted the *Wall Street Journal.* "But today the mystery in teen fiction for girls is what outfit the heroine will wear next." Shopping has become a survival skill and there is certainly no better place to learn it than the mall, where its importance is powerfully reinforced and certainly never questioned.

The mall as a university of suburban materialism, where Valley Girls and Boys from coast to coast are educated in consumption, has its other lessons in this era of change in family life and sexual mores and their economic and social ramifications. The plethora of products in the mall, plus the pressure on teens to buy them, may contribute to the phenomenon that psychologist David Elkind calls "the hurried child": kids who are exposed to too much of the adult world too quickly and must respond with a sophistication that belies their still-tender emotional development. Certainly the adult products marketed for children — form-fitting designer jeans, sexy tops for preteen girls — add to the social pressure to look like an adult, along with the home-grown need to understand adult finances (why mothers must work) and adult emotions (when parents divorce).

Kids spend so much time at the mall partly because their parents allow it and even encourage it. The mall is safe, doesn't seem to harbor any unsavory activities, and there is adult supervision; it is, after all, a controlled environment. So the temptation, especially for working parents, is to let the mall be their baby-sitter. At least the kids aren't watching TV. But the mall's role as a surrogate mother may be more extensive and more profound.

Karen Lansky, a writer living in Los 10 Angeles, has looked into the subject, and she told me some of her conclusions about the effects on its teenaged denizens of the mall's controlled and controlling environment. "Structure is the dominant idea, since true 'mall rats' lack just that in their home lives," she said, "and adolescents about to make the big leap into growing up crave more structure than our modern society cares to acknowledge."

b) Social pressures to buy

c) Mall as babysitter

d) Mall as substitute for home

Karen pointed out some of the elements malls supply that kids used to get from their families, like warmth (Strawberry Shortcake dolls and similar cute and cuddly merchandise), old-fashioned mothering ("We do it all for you," the fast-food slogan), and even home cooking (the "homemade" treats at the food court).

e) Encouragement of passivity

The problem in all this, as Karen Lansky sees it, is that while families nurture children by encouraging growth through the assumption of responsibility and then by letting them rest in the bosom of the family from the rigors of growing up, the mall as a structural mother encourages passivity and consumption, as long as the kid doesn't make trouble. Therefore all they learn about becoming adults is how to act and how to consume.

f) Undemanding jobs

Kids are in the mall not only in the passive role of shoppers — they also work there, especially as fast-food outlets infiltrate the mall's enclosure. There they learn how to hold a job and take responsibility, but still within the same value context. When *CBS Reports* went to Oak Park Mall in suburban Kansas City, Kansas, to tape part of their hour-long consideration of malls, "After the Dream Comes True," they interviewed a teenaged girl who worked in a fast-food outlet there. In a sequence that didn't make the final program, she described the major goal of her present life, which was to perfect the curl on top of the ice-cream cones that were her store's specialty. If she could do that, she would be moved from the lowly soft-drink dispenser to the more prestigious ice-cream division, the curl on top of the status ladder at her restaurant. These are the achievements that are important at the mall.

Example

Other benefits of such jobs may also be overrated, according to Laurence D. Steinberg of the University of California at Irvine's social ecology department, who did a study on teenage employment. Their jobs, he found, are generally simple, mindlessly repetitive and boring. They don't really learn anything, and the jobs don't lead anywhere. Teenagers also work primarily with other teenagers; even their supervisors are often just a little older than they are. "Kids need to spend time with adults," Steinberg told me. "Although they get benefits from peer relationships, without parents and other adults it's one-side socialization. They hang out with each other, have age-segregated jobs, and watch TV."

Perhaps much of this is not so terrible or even so terribly different. Now that they have so much more to contend with in their lives, adolescents probably need more time to spend with other adolescents without adult impositions, just to sort things out. Though it is more concentrated in the mall (and therefore perhaps a clearer target), the value system there is really the dominant one of the whole society. Attitudes about curiosity, initiative, self-expression, empathy, and disinterested learning aren't necessarily made in the mall; they are mirrored there, perhaps a bit more intensely — as through a glass brightly.

Besides, the mall is not without its educational opportunities. There are bookstores, where there is at least a short shelf of classics at great prices, and other books from which it is possible to learn more than how to do sit-ups. There are tools, from hammers to VCRs, and products, from clothes to records, that can help the young find and express themselves. There are older people with stories, and places to be alone or to talk one-on-one with a kindred spirit. And there is always the passing show.

The mall itself may very well be an education about the future. I was struck with the realization, as early as my first

Details

Advantages: a) Time with other adolescents

b) Educational opportunities

15

*Conclusion; claim of value
mall as a controlled environment that teaches a few
valuable lessons*

forays into Greengate, that the mall is only one of a number of enclosed and controlled environments that are part of the lives of today's young. The mall is just an extension, say, of those large suburban schools — only there's Karmelkorn instead of chem lab, the ice rink instead of the gym: It's high school without the impertinence of classes.

Growing up, moving from home to school to the mall — from enclosure to enclosure, transported in cars — is a curiously continuous process, without much in the way of contrast or contact with unenclosed reality. Places must tend to blur into one another. But whatever differences and dangers there are in this, the skills these adolescents are learning may turn out to be useful in their later lives. For we seem to be moving inexorably into an age of preplanned and regulated environments, and this is the world they will inherit.

Still, it might be better if they had more of a choice. One teenaged girl confessed to *CBS Reports* that she sometimes felt she was missing something by hanging out at the mall so much. "But I'm here," she said, "and this is what I have."

Analysis

Kowinski has chosen to evaluate one aspect of an extraordinarily successful economic and cultural phenomenon — the commercial mall. He asks whether the influence of the mall on adolescents is good or bad. The answer seems to be a little of both. The good values may be described as exposure to a variety of experiences, a protective structure for adolescents who often live in unstable environments, and immersion in a world that may well serve as an introduction to adulthood. But the bad values, which Kowinski thinks are more influential (as the title suggests) are those of the shoppers' paradise, a society that believes in acquisition and consumption of goods as ultimate goals, and too much control over the choices available to adolescents. The tone of the judgment, however, is moderate and reflects a balanced, even scholarly, attitude. More than other arguments, the treatment of values requires such a voice, one which respects differences of opinion among readers. But serious doesn't mean heavy. His style is formal but highly readable, brightened by interesting examples and precise details. The opening paragraph is a strikingly effective lead.

Some of his observations are personal, but others are derived from studies by professional researchers, from *CBS Reports* to a well-known writer on childhood. These studies give weight and authority to his conclusions. Here and there we detect an appealing sympathy for adolescents who spend time in their controlled mall environments.

Like any thoughtful social commentator, Kowinski casts a wide net. He sees the mall not only as a hangout for teens but as a good deal more, an institution that offers insights into family life and work, the changing urban culture, the nature of contemporary entertainment, even glimpses of a somewhat forbidding future.

CLAIMS OF POLICY

Claims of policy argue that certain conditions should exist. As the name suggests, they advocate adoption of policies or courses of action because problems have arisen that call for solution. Almost always *should* or *ought to* or *must* is expressed or implied in the claim.

CLAIM: Voluntary prayer should be permitted in public schools.

CLAIM: A dress code should be introduced for all public high schools.

CLAIM: A law should permit sixteen-year-olds and parents to "divorce" each other in cases of extreme incompatibility.

CLAIM: Mandatory jail terms should be imposed for drunk driving violations.

In defending such claims of policy you may find that you must first convince your audience that a problem exists. This will require that, as part of your longer argument, you make a factual claim, offering data to prove that present conditions are unsatisfactory. You may also find it necessary to refer to the values that support your claim. Then you will be ready to introduce your policy, to persuade your audience that the solution you propose will solve the problem.

We will examine a policy claim in which all these parts are at work. The claim can be stated as follows: "The time required for an undergraduate degree should be extended to five years." Immediate agreement with this policy among student readers would certainly not be universal. Some students would not recognize a problem. They would say, "The college curriculum we have now is fine. There's no need for a change. Besides, we don't want to spend more time in school." First, then, the arguer would have to persuade a skeptical audience that there is a problem — that four years of college are no longer enough because the stock of knowledge in almost all fields of study continues to increase. The arguer would provide data to show that students today have many more choices in history, literature, and science than students had in those fields a generation ago. She would also emphasize the value of greater knowledge and more schooling compared to the value of other goods the audience cherishes, such as earlier independence. Finally, the arguer would offer a plan for implementing her policy. Her plan would have to consider initial psychological resistance, revision of the curriculum, costs of more instruction, and costs of lost production in the workforce. Most important, she would point out the benefits for both individuals and society if this policy were adopted.

In this example, we assumed that the reader would disagree that a problem existed. In many cases, however, the reader may agree that there is a problem but disagree with the arguer about the way to solve it. Most of us, no doubt, agree that we want to reduce or eliminate the following problems: misbehavior and vandalism in schools, drunk driving, crime on the streets, child abuse, pornography, pollution. But how should we go about solving those problems? What public policy will give us well-behaved, diligent students who never destroy school property? Safe streets where no one is ever robbed or assaulted? Loving homes where no child is ever mistreated? Some members of society would choose to introduce rules or laws that punish infractions so severely that wrongdoers would be unwilling or unable to repeat their offenses. Other members of society would prefer policies that attempt to rehabilitate or re-educate offenders through training, therapy, counseling, and new opportunities.

Writer's Guide to the Proposal Paper
Defending a Claim of Policy

The following steps will help you organize arguments for a claim of policy.

1. Make your proposal clear. The terms in the proposal should be precisely defined.
2. If necessary, establish that there is a need for a change. When changes have been resisted, present reasons that explain this resistance. (It is

often wrongly assumed that people cling to cultural practices long after their significance and necessity have eroded. But rational human beings observe practices that serve a purpose. The fact that you and I may see no value or purpose in the activities of another is irrelevant.)

3. Consider the opposing arguments. You may want to state the opposing arguments in a brief paragraph before answering them in the body of your argument.

4. Devote the major part of your essay to proving that your proposal is an answer to the opposing arguments and enumerating its distinct benefits for your readers.

5. Support your proposal with solid data, but don't neglect the moral considerations and the commonsense reasons, which may be even more persuasive.

SAMPLE ANNOTATED ANALYSIS: CLAIM OF POLICY

The Real Victims
ALBERT SHANKER

Introduction: statement of the problem — violence and disorder in schools

It's increasingly clear that the biggest roadblock to improving the achievement of U.S. students is violence and disorder in our schools. Education reformers say we must set high standards for student achievement and create curriculums and assessments embodying these standards — and I agree with them. But high standards and excellent curriculums and assessments are not enough. Indeed, they will be worthless if students cannot learn because they are constantly afraid of being hit by a stray bullet or because their classes are dominated by disruptive students. This is just common sense.

Albert Shanker was the president of the American Federation of Teachers until his death in 1997. His weekly column, "Where We Stand," appeared in the *New York Times* Week in Review section for over twenty-five years. This column is from February 19, 1995.

Support: examples of school violence

A couple of weeks ago, *Washington Post* columnist Courtland Milloy told the story of a girl who had seen some classmates stab another student and was so terrified by the possibility of reprisals that she quit school ("An Education in Self-Help," January 29, 1995). This story has a relatively happy ending: The girl went on to earn a GED and is now attending college. But for every one who is motivated to continue her education the way this girl did, there are thousands and tens of thousands who are intimidated and distracted and are lost to school and learning.

Classroom disruption is more pervasive than school violence and just as fatal to learning. If there is one student in a class who constantly yells, curses out the teacher, and picks on other students who are trying to listen or participate in class, you can be sure that most of the teacher's time will not be devoted to helping the other youngsters learn math or science or English; it will be spent figuring out how to contain this student. And it does not take many such students to ruin the learning of the great majority of youngsters in a school.

Support: examples of disruption

Reason the problem is not solved

School officials seem generally to be at a loss. In Washington, D.C., and elsewhere, students who have been caught bringing guns or drugs to school or who have hurt other students may simply be transferred to another school or suspended for a little while. There seems to be a high level of tolerance for this kind of behavior where there should be none. And when it comes to chronically disruptive students, we are even more tolerant. Little happens to kids who merely keep others from learning.

Consequences of failure to solve:

Parents are painfully aware of these problems. That's why both African American and white parents put safe and orderly schools at the top of their list of

a) Private schools
b) Vouchers

things that would improve student achievement. And that is undoubtedly why vouchers and tuition tax credits are so popular — especially among many parents of kids in inner-city schools. These parents are saying, "If your schools are so violent and disorderly that our children can't learn — and are not even safe — let us put them in schools that won't tolerate kids who behave that way."

Rebuttal of expert view

Many education experts insist that our first responsibility is to the few violent and disruptive kids. They say these kids have the "right" to an education and we need to keep them in class and in school so we can help them overcome their problems. But what about the "rights" of the twenty-five or thirty kids in every class who come to school ready to work? Why are we willing to threaten their safety and learning? I'm not advocating putting violent or disruptive kids out on the streets. We need alternative programs for these youngsters, but we also need to change a system that sacrifices the overwhelming majority of children for a handful — without even doing the handful any good.

Claim of policy: alternative programs

Consequences of failure to solve: learning the wrong lessons

Most children come to school believing that doing right matters, but they soon learn to question that belief. Say a youngster in kindergarten does something that is way out of line — he knocks another kid down and kicks him. The other five-year-olds are sure something terrible is going to happen to this child, and they are very glad they're not in his place. Well, what happens? Probably the teacher gets in trouble for reporting the child. So the children's sense of justice — their belief that acting naughty has consequences — begins to be eroded. The youngster who defied the teacher becomes the de facto leader of the class, and peer pressure now encourages the other children to ignore what the teacher tells them to do. At a very early age, kids are taught a bad lesson — nothing will happen if they break the rules — and whatever else they learn in English or math or science, this lesson remains consistent throughout school.

Conclusion: summary

We have an irrational system, and it's no wonder that angry parents are calling for vouchers, tuition tax credits — anything that would allow them to get their kids out of schools where a few violent and disruptive kids call the shots. What this means, though, is that 98 percent of students would be leaving public schools to get away from the 2 percent. Wouldn't it make a lot more sense just to move the 2 percent?

Analysis

Shanker argues that disruptive students should be removed from their classes, but in only two places does he make the policy explicit, referring to "alternative programs" and moving "the 2 percent." Instead, he devotes almost the whole of his essay to proving that a policy to remove disruptive students is absolutely necessary. Even the title reveals the emphasis of the essay. The real victims are children who are prevented from learning by violence in the classroom, and it is their needs that must be addressed.

A reader can guess why Shanker adopts such a rhetorical strategy. Many policy claims require the arguer to first prove that a problem exists — in effect, establishing a claim of fact — and often this is the most important task. Since a policy that expels or removes students from a regular classroom, while not new, is still hotly debated, the advocate of such a policy must make a strong case for it. Shanker acknowledges the objections to his policy in paragraph 6 and answers them.

Shanker emphasizes two unfortunate consequences of a failure to adopt his policy recommendation. One is the cost imposed on children who want to learn and are prevented from doing so. Development of this idea begins in the second paragraph and occupies most of the essay. Its strength lies in its appeal to our sense of fairness. There is also an implicit appeal to fear. The withdrawal of children to safer, often private schools weakens the public school system. Shanker obviously believes that his readers will agree that public schools are worth saving.

The second consequence is more difficult to measure. It is the wrong moral lesson absorbed by children when they see that hurtful behavior goes unpunished. Although a psychological effect cannot easily be proved by numbers, unlike the exodus of children to private schools, most readers will recognize it as one common to their experience.

Despite the fact that we know little or nothing about the details of a removal policy, Shanker's argument suggests that, if the necessity for a change of policy is made sufficiently strong, the way for its adoption has been prepared.

READINGS FOR ANALYSIS

Happiness Is a Warm Planet
THOMAS GALE MOORE

President Clinton convened a conference on global warming yesterday, as the White House agonizes over its posture at the forthcoming talks in Kyoto, Japan, on a worldwide global warming treaty. Mr. Clinton is eager to please his environmentalist supporters, but industry, labor and members of the Senate have told the administration that this treaty would wreck the economy, cost millions of jobs and provoke a flight of investment to more hospitable climes.

A crucial point gets lost in the debate: Global warming, if it were to occur, would probably *benefit* most Americans.

If mankind had to choose between a warmer or a cooler climate, we would certainly choose the former: Humans, nearly all other animals and most plants would be better off with higher temperatures. The climate models suggest, and so far the record confirms, that under global warming nighttime winter temperatures would rise the most, and daytime summer temperatures the least. Most Americans prefer a warmer climate to a colder one — and that preference is justified. More people die of the cold than of the heat; more die in the winter than the summer. Statistical evidence suggests that the climate predicted for the end of the next century might reduce U.S. deaths by about 40,000 annually.

Thomas Gale Moore is a senior fellow at the Hoover Institution. His book *A Politically Incorrect View of Global Warming: Foreign Aid Masquerading as Climate Policy* was published in 1998 by the Cato Institute. This article appeared in the *Wall Street Journal* on October 7, 1997.

In addition, less snow and ice would reduce transportation delays and accidents. A warmer winter would cut heating costs, more than offsetting any increase in air conditioning expenses in the summer. Manufacturing, mining and most services would be unaffected. Longer growing seasons, more rainfall and higher concentrations of carbon dioxide would benefit plant growth. Already there is evidence that trees and other plants are growing more vigorously. Although some locales may become too dry, too wet or too warm, on the whole mankind should benefit from an upward tick in the thermometer.

What about the economic effects? In the pessimistic view of the   5
Intergovernmental Panel on Climate Change, the costs of global warming might be as high as 1.5 percent of the U.S. gross domestic product by the end of the next century. The cost of reducing carbon dioxide emissions, however, would be much higher. William Cline of the Institute for International Economics has calculated that the cost of cutting emissions by one-third from current levels by 2040 would be 3.5 percent of worldwide GDP. The IPCC also reviewed various estimates of losses from stabilizing emissions at 1990 levels, a more modest objective, and concluded that the cost to the U.S. economy would be at least 1.5 percent of GDP by 2050, with the burden continuing to increase thereafter.

The forecast cost of warming is for the end of the next century, not the middle. Adjusting for the time difference, the cost to the U.S. from a warmer climate at midcentury, according to the IPCC, would be at most 0.75 percent of GDP, meaning that the costs of holding carbon dioxide to 1990 levels would be twice the gain from preventing any climate change. But the benefit-cost calculus is even worse. The administration is planning to exempt Third World nations, such as China, India and Brazil, from the requirements of the treaty. Under such a scheme, Americans would pay a huge price for virtually no benefit.

And even if the developing countries agreed to return emissions to 1990 levels, greenhouse gas concentrations would not be stabilized. Since for many decades more carbon dioxide would be added to the atmosphere than removed through natural processes, the buildup would only slow; consequently temperatures would continue to go up. Instead of saving the full 0.75 percent of GDP by keeping emissions at 1990 levels, we would be saving much less.

It is true that whatever dangers global warming may pose, they will be most pronounced in the developing world. It is much easier for rich countries to adapt to any long-term shift in weather than it is for poor countries, which tend to be much more dependent on agriculture. Poor countries lack the resources to aid their flora and fauna in adapting, and many of their farmers earn too little to survive a shift to new conditions. But the best insurance for these poor countries is an increase in their wealth, which would diminish their dependence on agriculture and make it easier for them to adjust to changes in weather, including increases in precipitation and possible flooding or higher sea level. Subjecting Americans to high taxes and onerous regulations will help neither them — we could buy less from them — nor us.

The optimal way to deal with potential climate change is not to embark on a futile attempt to prevent it, but to promote growth and prosperity so that people will have the resources to deal with the normal set of natural disasters. Based on the evidence, including historical records, global warming is likely to be good for most of mankind. The additional carbon, rain and warmth should promote the plant growth necessary to sustain an expanding world population. Global change is inevitable; warmer is better; richer is healthier.

Reading and Discussion Questions

1. This article is a claim of value in which the author tries to prove that something is good or bad — in this case, that a warmer climate would be better than a cold one. How many different reasons does he give to support his claim?
2. Moore offers a solution for the problems of a warm planet. Does this solution have shortcomings? If so, what are they?
3. Moore, an economist, spends the greater part of his argument on the economic consequences of global warming. Do you think he should have tried to develop other effects? Give examples of data that seem insufficient.
4. How much of the author's evidence comes from experts? If more testimony is needed, what kind should it be?

Writing Suggestions

5. To ascertain whether Moore is right about the consequences of global warming, you will have to consult experts who disagree with him. They will not be hard to find. Most of those who have studied climatic changes think we are in trouble. Based on the testimony of other experts, write a paper that refutes some of Moore's claims.
6. Moore says that most of mankind would choose to live in a warm climate (para. 3). If you could choose, would you live in a tropical climate? A subtropical climate? In your answer, try to go beyond the most superficial reasons, like being tan all year long. Provide sufficient detail and personal background to bring to life the various reasons that would govern your choice.

A White Woman of Color

JULIA ÁLVAREZ

Growing up in the Dominican Republic, I experienced racism within my own family — though I didn't think of it as racism. But there was definitely a hierarchy of beauty, which was the main currency in our daughters-only family. It was not until years later, from the vantage point of this country and this education, that I realized that this hierarchy of beauty was dictated by our coloring. We were a progression of whitening, as if my mother were slowly bleaching the color out of her children.

The oldest sister had the darkest coloring, with very curly hair and "coarse" features. She looked the most like Papi's side of the family and was considered the least pretty. I came next, with "good hair," and skin that back then was a deep olive, for I was a tomboy — another dark mark against me — who would not stay out of the sun. The sister right after me had my skin color, but she was a good girl who stayed indoors, so she was much paler, her hair a golden brown. But the pride and joy of the family was the baby. She was the one who made heads turn and strangers approach asking to feel her silken hair. She was white white, an adjective that was repeated in describing her color as if to deepen the shade of white. Her eyes were brown, but her hair was an unaccountable towheaded blond. Because of her coloring, my father was teased that there must have been a German milkman in our neighborhood. How could *she* be *his* daughter? It was clear that this youngest child resembled Mami's side of the family.

It was Mami's family who were *really* white. They were white in terms of race, and white also in terms of class. From them came the fine features, the pale skin, the lank hair. Her brothers and uncles went to schools abroad and had important businesses in the country. They also emulated the manners and habits of North Americans. Growing up, I remember arguments at the supper table on whether or not it was proper to tie one's napkin around one's neck, on how much of one's arm one could properly lay on the table, on whether

Novelist and poet Julia Álvarez is originally from the Dominican Republic but emigrated to the United States with her parents at age ten. Her work includes the novels *How the García Girls Lost Their Accents* (1991), *In the Time of the Butterflies* (1994), and *¡Yo!* (1997); two books of poems, *Homecoming: New and Collected Poems* (1996) and *The Other Side* (1995); and a collection of nonfiction essays, *Something to Declare* (1998). She teaches literature and creative writing at Middlebury College. This essay appeared in *Half and Half: Writers on Growing Up Biracial and Bicultural,* edited by Claudine C. O'Hearn (1998).

spaghetti could be eaten with the help of a spoon. My mother, of course, insisted on all the protocol of knives and forks and on eating a little portion of everything served; my father, on the other hand, defended our eating whatever we wanted, with our hands if need be, so we could "have fun" with our food. My mother would snap back that we looked like *jibaritas* who should be living out in the country. Of course, that was precisely where my father's family came from.

Not that Papi's family weren't smart and enterprising, all twenty-five brothers and sisters. (The size of the family in and of itself was considered very country by some members of Mami's family.) Many of Papi's brothers had gone to the university and become professionals. But their education was totally island — no fancy degrees from Andover and Cornell and Yale, no summer camps or school songs in another language. Papi's family still lived in the interior versus the capital, in old-fashioned houses without air conditioning, decorated in ways my mother's family would have considered, well, tasteless. I remember antimacassars on the backs of rocking chairs (which were the living-room set), garish paintings of flamboyant trees, ceramic planters with plastic flowers in bloom. They were *criollos* — creoles — rather than cosmopolitans, expansive, proud, colorful. (Some members had a sixth finger on their right — or was it their left hand?) Their features were less aquiline than Mother's family's, the skin darker, the hair coarse and curly. Their money still had the smell of the earth on it and was kept in a wad in their back pockets, whereas my mother's family had money in the Chase Manhattan Bank, most of it with George Washington's picture on it, not Juan Pablo Duarte's.

It was clear to us growing up then that lighter was better, but there was no question of discriminating against someone because he or she was dark-skinned. Everyone's family, even an elite one like Mami's, had darker-skinned members. All Dominicans, as the saying goes, have a little black behind the ears. So, to separate oneself from those who were darker would have been to divide *una familia,* a sacrosanct entity in our culture. Neither was white blood necessarily a sign of moral or intellectual or political superiority. All one has to do is page through a Dominican history book and look at the number of dark-skinned presidents, dictators, generals, and entrepreneurs to see that power has not resided exclusively or even primarily among the whites on the island. The leadership of our country has been historically "colored."

But being black was something else. A black Dominican was referred to as a "dark Indian" (*indio oscuro*) — unless you wanted to come to blows with him, that is. The real blacks were the Haitians who lived next door and who occupied the Dominican Republic for twenty years, from 1822 to 1844, a fact that can still so inflame the Dominican populace you'd think it had happened last year. The denial of the Afro-Dominican part of our culture reached its climax during the dictatorship of Trujillo, whose own maternal grandmother was Haitian. In 1937, to protect Dominican race purity, Trujillo ordered the overnight genocide of thousands (figures range from 4,000 to 20,000) of Haitians by his military, who committed this atrocity using only machetes and knives in order to make this planned extermination look like a "spontaneous" border skirmish. He also had the Dominican Republic declared a white nation despite the evidence of the mulatto senators who were forced to pass this ridiculous measure.

So, black was not so good, kinky hair was not so good, thick lips not so good. But even if you were *indio oscuro con pelo malo y una bemba de aquí a Baní,* you could still sit in the front of the bus and order at the lunch counter — or the equivalent thereof. There was no segregation of races in the halls of power. But in the aesthetic arena — the one to which we girls were relegated as females — lighter was better. Lank hair and pale skin and small, fine features were better. All I had to do was stay out of the sun and behave myself and I could pass as a pretty white girl.

Another aspect of my growing up also greatly influenced my thinking on race. Although I was raised in the heart of a large family, my day-to-day caretakers were the maids. Most of these women were dark-skinned, some of Haitian background. One of them, Misiá, had been spared the machetes of the 1937 massacre when she was taken in and hidden from the prowling *guardias* by the family. We children spent most of the day with these women. They tended to us, nursed us when we were sick, cradled us when we fell down and scraped an elbow or knee (as a tomboy, there was a lot of this scraping for me), and most important, they told us stories of *los santos* and *el barón del cementerio,* of *el cuco* and *las ciguapas,* beautiful dark-skinned creatures who escaped capture because their feet were turned backwards so they left behind a false set of footprints. These women spread the wings of our imaginations and connected us deeply to the land we came from. They were the ones with the stories that had power over us.

We arrived in Nueva York in 1960, before the large waves of Caribbean immigrants created little Habanas, little Santo Domingos, and little San Juans in the boroughs of the city. Here we encountered a whole new kettle of wax — as my malapropping Mami might have said. People of color were treated as if they were inferior, prone to violence, uneducated, untrustworthy, lazy — all the "bad" adjectives we were learning in our new language. Our dark-skinned aunt, Tía Ana, who had lived in New York for several decades and so was the authority in these matters, recounted stories of discrimination on buses and subways. These Americans were so blind! One drop of black and you were black. Everyone back home would have known that Tía Ana was not black: she had "good hair" and her skin color was a light *indio*. All week, she worked in a *factoría* in the Bronx, and when she came to visit us on Saturdays to sew our school clothes, she had to take three trains to our nice neighborhood where the darkest face on the street was usually her own.

We were lucky we were white Dominicans or we would have had   10 a much harder time of it in this country. We would have encountered a lot more prejudice than we already did, for white as we were, we found that our Latino-ness, our accents, our habits and smells, added "color" to our complexion. Had we been darker, we certainly could not have bought our mock Tudor house in Jamaica Estates. In fact, the African American family who moved in across the street several years later needed police protection because of threats. Even so, at the local school, we endured the bullying of classmates. "Go back to where you came from!" they yelled at my sisters and me in the playground. When some of them started throwing stones, my mother made up her mind that we were not safe and began applying to boarding schools where privilege transformed prejudice into patronage.

"So where are you from?" my classmates would ask.

"Jamaica Estates," I'd say, an edge of belligerence to my voice. It was obvious from my accent, if not my looks, that I was not *from* there in the way they meant being from somewhere.

"I mean *originally.*"

And then it would come out, the color, the accent, the cousins with six fingers, the smell of garlic.

By the time I went off to college, a great explosion of American   15 culture was taking place on campuses across the country. The civil rights movement, the Vietnam War and subsequent peace movement, the women's movement, were transforming traditional definitions of American identity. Ethnicity was in: my classmates wore long braids like Native Americans and peasant blouses from Mexico and long, diaphanous skirts and dangly earrings from India. Suddenly, my foreignness was being celebrated. This reversal felt affirming but also disturbing. As huipils, serapes, and embroidered dresses proliferated about me, I had the feeling that my ethnicity had become a commodity. I resented it.

When I began looking for a job after college, I discovered that being a white Latina made me a nonthreatening minority in the eyes of these employers. My color was a question *only* of culture, and if I kept my cultural color to myself, I was "no problem." Each time I was hired for one of my countless "visiting appointments" — they were never permanent "invitations," mind you — the inevitable questionnaire would accompany my contract in which I was to check off my RACE: CAUCASIAN, BLACK, NATIVE AMERICAN, ASIAN, HISPANIC, OTHER. How could a Dominican divide herself in this way? Or was I really a

Dominican anymore? And what was a Hispanic? A census creation — there is no such culture — how could it define who I was at all? Given this set of options, the truest answer might have been to check off OTHER.

For that was the way I had begun to think of myself. Adrift from any Latino community in this country, my culture had become an internal homeland, periodically replenished by trips "back home." But as a professional woman on my own, I felt less and less at home on the island. My values, the loss of my Catholic faith, my lifestyle, my wardrobe, my hippy ways, and my feminist ideas separated me from my native culture. I did not subscribe to many of the mores and constraints that seemed to be an intrinsic part of that culture. And since my culture had always been my "color," by rejecting these mores I had become not only Americanized but whiter.

If I could have been a part of a Latino community in the United States, the struggle might have been, if not easier, less private and therefore less isolating. These issues of acculturation and ethnicity would have been struggles to share with others like me. But all my North American life I had lived in shifting academic communities — going to boarding schools, then college, and later teaching wherever I could get those yearly appointments — and these communities reflected the dearth of Latinos in the profession. Except for friends in Spanish departments, who tended to have come from their countries of origin to teach rather than being raised in this country as I was, I had very little daily contact with Latinos.

Where I looked for company was where I had always looked for company since coming to this country: in books. At first the texts that I read and taught were the ones prescribed to me, the canonical works which formed the content of the bread-and-butter courses that as a "visiting instructor" I was hired to teach. These texts were mostly written by white male writers from Britain and the United States, with a few women thrown in and no Latinos. Thank goodness for the occasional creative writing workshop where I could bring in the multicultural authors I wanted. But since I had been formed in this very academy, I was clueless where to start. I began to educate myself by reading, and that is when I discovered that there were others out there like me, hybrids who came in a variety of colors and whose ethnicity and race were an evolving process, not a rigid paradigm or a list of boxes, one of which you checked off.

This discovery of my ethnicity on paper was like a rebirth. I had 20 been going through a pretty bad writer's block: the white page seemed impossible to fill with whatever it was I had in me to say. But listening to authors like Maxine Hong Kingston, Toni Morrison, Gwendolyn Brooks, Langston Hughes, Maya Angelou, June Jordan, and to Lorna Dee Cervantes, Piri Thomas, Rudolfo Anaya, Edward Rivera, Ernesto Galarza (that first wave of Latino writers), I began to hear the language "in color." I began to see that literature could reflect the otherness I was feeling, that the choices in fiction and poetry did not have to be bleached out of their color or simplified into either/or. A story could allow for the competing claims of different parts of ourselves and where we came from.

Ironically, it was through my own stories and poems that I finally made contact with Latino communities in this country. As I published more, I was invited to read at community centers and bilingual programs. Latino students, who began attending colleges in larger numbers in the late seventies and eighties, sought me out as a writer and teacher "of color." After the publication of *How the García Girls Lost Their Accents,* I found that I had become a sort of spokesperson for Dominicans in this country, a role I had neither sought nor accepted. Of course, some Dominicans refused to grant me any status as a "real" Dominican because I was "white." With the color word there was also a suggestion of class. My family had not been among the waves of economic immigrants that left the island in the seventies, a generally darker-skinned, working-class group, who might have been the maids and workers in my mother's family house. We had come in 1960, political refugees, with no money but with "prospects": Papi had a friend who was the doctor at the Waldorf Astoria and who helped him get a job; Mami's family had money in the Chase Manhattan Bank they could lend us. We had changed class in America — from Mami's elite family to middle-class spics — but our background and education and most especially our pale skin had made mobility easier for us here. We had not undergone the same kind of race struggles as other Dominicans; therefore, we could not be "real" Dominicans.

What I came to understand and accept and ultimately fight for with my writing is the reality that ethnicity and race are not fixed constructs or measurable quantities. What constitutes our ethnicity and our race — once there is literally no common ground beneath us to define it — evolves as we seek to define and redefine ourselves in new contexts. My Latino-ness is not something someone can take away from me or leave me out of with a definition. It is in my blood: it comes from that mixture of biology, culture, native language, and experience that makes me a different American from one whose family comes from Ireland or Poland or Italy. My Latino-ness is also a political choice. I am choosing to hold on to my ethnicity and native language even if I can "pass." I am choosing to color my Americanness with my Dominicanness even if it came in a light shade of skin color.

I hope that as Latinos, coming from so many different countries and continents, we can achieve solidarity in this country as the mix that we are. I hope we won't shoot ourselves in the foot in order to maintain some sort of false "purity" as the glue that holds us

together. Such an enterprise is bound to fail. We need each other.
We can't afford to reject the darker or lighter varieties, and to do so
is to have absorbed a definition of ourselves as exclusively one thing
or the other. And haven't we learned to fear that word "exclusive"?
This reductiveness is absurd when we are talking about a group
whose very definition is that of a mestizo race, a mixture of European, indigenous, African, and much more. Within this vast circle,
shades will lighten and darken into overlapping categories. If we cut
them off, we diminish our richness and we plant a seed of ethnic
cleansing that is the root of the bloodshed we have seen in Bosnia
and the West Bank and Rwanda and even our own Los Angeles and
Dominican Republic.

As we Latinos redefine ourselves in America, making ourselves
up and making ourselves over, we have to be careful, in taking up
the promises of America, not to adopt its limiting racial paradigms.
Many of us have shed customs and prejudices that oppressed our
gender, race, or class on our native islands and in our native countries. We should not replace these with modes of thinking that are
divisive and oppressive of our rich diversity. Maybe as a group that
embraces many races and differences, we Latinos can provide a positive multicultural, multiracial model to a divided America.

Reading and Discussion Questions

1. What is the meaning of the title of this essay? Is it an oxymoron?
2. Explain Álvarez's "hierarchy of beauty" (para. 1) in the Dominican Republic. What does she mean by "white in terms of race, and white also
   in terms of class" (para. 3)?
3. Does such a hierarchy of beauty have parallels in the United States? If it
   is not skin color, are other physical attributes rated as good or bad?
   How do you think such preferences arose?
4. Why did Álvarez think of herself as "adrift" (para. 17)? How does
   Álvarez explain the "discovery of my ethnicity" (para. 20)?
5. Álvarez ends her essay by summarizing what she has learned from her
   experience as "a white woman of color." How do the last three paragraphs differ in tone and content from the narrative that precedes it?
   Do you think they are effective? Would the essay have been stronger or
   weaker if she had ended it before the last three paragraphs?

Writing Suggestions

6. Álvarez mentions a number of authors who inspired her with their
   views of otherness (para. 20). Perhaps you are familiar with their works
   or the works of other writers who explore ethnicity in America, such as
   The Joy Luck Club, I Know Why the Caged Bird Sings, Native Son, and
   Reservation Blues. Write a review of a book in which the author describes the experience of being different in the United States.

7. If you know any immigrants — in your own family or perhaps on campus — describe their attempts at acculturation. What aspects of American life have been most challenging for them? What aspects have been easiest to understand and accept?

Taking the Saps

RUSSELL BAKER

There are many explanations for why America is highballing down the low road to Doomsday. One of my favorites is government-sponsored gambling. Any people who let their own government sucker them into throwing their money away on games with prohibitively high odds haven't the wit needed to save great nations from doom.

Here is this human mass that thinks of itself as "the great American people," and what does it amount to? A bunch of saps who sat meekly by while their own once-honorable and respectable government — a government whose flag we saluted every morning before tackling arithmetic — while this once decent government took over the gambling racket from the mob.

The states are chiefly to blame for this, of course, but the Feds quietly acquiesce. When gangsters ran things, muscling in on their rackets could leave you bullet-riddled. Unfortunately the gangsters couldn't do that when government started muscling in. All the gangsters had for enforcing discipline was the machine gun; government had the atom bomb.

It debases a nation to let its governors take over the rackets. It is a no-class thing for a government to do.

You hear the argument that, if millions are determined to 5 gamble anyhow, it's better for government to take their money than for mobsters to do it. Government, the argument goes, will put the money to good use; the mob will use it to set up love nests and indulge depraved tastes.

Everything about this argument is specious, starting with the idea that government will use the money to improve the public condition. Any government that exploits the weakness of its citizens to enrich itself cheapens its own character and thus damages the public interest.

As for the perverse uses to which the mob might put the money, let us not be too quick with denunciations. The mob's record is not so bad.

Russell Baker is the Pulitzer Prize–winning journalist and author of *Growing Up* (1983). His Observer columns of wit and insight have appeared in the *New York Times* since 1962. The column reprinted here is from June 15, 1996.

It has pumped a great deal of its gambling profits into creating Las Vegas, an American entertainment landmark in a class with Disney World, Camden Yards, and Cape Cod. Without Las Vegas, Hollywood would have no place to set half of its movies, and motion picture box-office receipts might suffer gravely, with who knows what consequences for one of the nation's few industries not yet transported to Asia or Latin America.

Let no one suppose that despising government sponsoring of vice marks me as either unduly moral or foolishly sentimental about human nature. I am certain that millions will always enjoy gambling and will continue enjoying it without government assistance.

This appetite should be satisfied, however, by criminals, not by 10 government. Human character is improved when each citizen must settle for himself the moral question of whether the pleasure of vice justifies breaking the law to enjoy it.

As everybody has probably known since pre-biblical times, pleasure's delights are intensified when the pleasure cannot be realized without taking risks. The truth of this antique wisdom was illustrated during the recent "sexual revolution" when the birth-control pill eliminated virtually all the risks of casual sex. As a result sex often declined into just another humdrum social ritual, which might require a delightfully forbidden drug to give it a little zest.

America was a healthier land when its gamblers had to break the law to get rid of their money. As a police reporter long ago in Baltimore, a great horse-player's town, I was struck by the high spirits of American betting men hauled in by the vice squad after a raid on some gambling den.

Being arrested seemed to make their day. They clumped together in the police station waving like celebrities and exchanging jokes while waiting to be bailed out, bantering with the uniformed cops who respected bettors and despised vice squads, and otherwise basking in the rare experience of being under arrest.

It was usually professional gamblers who got caught. What a contrast that robust gambler's America was to the dreary bureaucracies we now find in state-run betting offices and in the sadness of candy-store lines where incurable dreamers queue to buy lottery tickets.

Let us return to an America that worked: Re-criminalize 15 gambling.

Reading and Discussion Questions

1. Find Baker's claim. The warrant appears in the tenth paragraph. Explain how it is related to the claim.
2. Summarize Baker's reasons for opposing government-sponsored gambling. Which issue seems most important to him?

3. What defense of the mob's record does Baker offer? What does he mean when he says: "America was a healthier land when its gamblers had to break the law to get rid of their money" (para. 12)? Did you find this part of the argument convincing?
4. What is the author trying to prove in making an analogy between gambling and sexual activity?
5. What refutation of opposing views do you find? Do you think Baker's rebuttal is persuasive?

Writing Suggestions

6. Because gambling is widespread among all classes in the United States — and in many other societies — its appeal must be strong and nearly universal. Some observers think it is an addiction. What is its appeal? Use your own experience as a gambler, your acquaintance with gamblers, as well as the opinions of psychologists and other experts to explain it.
7. Find evidence from advocates of gambling to justify government sponsorship, especially in state lotteries.
8. Gambling is said to be common on college campuses. What kinds of gambling do college students engage in? Does gambling serve a useful purpose? Is it harmful in any way?

College Life vs. My Moral Code

ELISHA DOV HACK

Many people envy my status as a freshman at Yale College. My classmates and I made it through some fierce competition, and we are excited to have been accepted to one of the best academic and extracurricular programs in American higher education. I have an older brother who attended Yale, and I've heard from him what life at Yale is like.

He spent all his college years living at home because our parents are New Haven residents, and Yale's rules then did not require him to live in the dorms. But Yale's new regulations demand that I spend my freshman and sophomore years living in the college dormitories.

I, two other freshmen and two sophomores have refused to do this because life in the dorms, even on the floors Yale calls "single sex," is contrary to the fundamental principles we have been taught as long as we can remember — the principles of Judaism lived

---

Elisha Dov Hack is a member of the Yale College class of 2001. This article appeared on September 9, 1997, in the *New York Times*.

according to the Torah and 3,000-year-old rabbinic teachings. Unless Yale waives its residence requirement, we may have no choice but to sue the university to protect our religious way of life.

Bingham Hall, on the Yale quadrangle known as the Old Campus, is one of the dorms for incoming students. When I entered it two weeks ago during an orientation tour, I literally saw the handwriting on the wall. A sign titled "Safe Sex" told me where to pick up condoms on campus. Another sign touted 100 ways to make love without having sex, like "take a nap together" and "take a steamy shower together."

That, I am told, is real life in the dorms. The "freshperson" issue 5 of the *Yale Daily News* sent to entering students contained a "Yale lexicon" defining *sexile* as "banishment from your dorm room because your roommate is having more fun than you." If you live in the dorms, you're expected to be part of the crowd, to accept these standards as the framework for your life.

Can we stand up to classmates whose sexual morality differs from ours? We've had years of rigorous religious teaching, and we've watched and learned from our parents. We can hold our own in the intellectual debate that flows naturally from exchanges during and after class. But I'm upset and hurt by this requirement that I live in the dorms. Why is Yale — an institution that professes to be so tolerant and open-minded — making it particularly hard for students like us to maintain our moral standards through difficult college years?

We are not trying to impose our moral standards on our classmates or on Yale. Our parents tell us that things were very different in college dormitories in their day and that in most colleges in the 1950s students who allowed guests of the opposite sex into their dorm rooms were subject to expulsion. We acknowledge that today's morality is not that of the 50s. We are asking only that Yale give us the same permission to live off campus that it gives any lower classman who is married or at least 21 years old.

Yale is proud of the fact that it has no "parietal rules" and that sexual morality is a student's own business. Maybe this is what Dean Richard H. Brodhead meant when he said that "Yale's residential colleges carry . . . a moral meaning." That moral meaning is, basically, "Anything goes." This morality is Yale's own residential religion, which it is proselytizing by force of its regulations.

We cannot, in good conscience, live in a place where women are permitted to stay overnight in men's rooms, and where visiting men can traipse through the common halls on the women's floors — in various stages of undress — in the middle of the night. The dormitories on Yale's Old Campus have floors designated by gender, but there is easy access through open stairwells from one floor to the next.

The moral message Yale's residences convey today is not one that 10 our religion accepts. Nor is it a moral environment in which the five of us can spend our nights, or a moral surrounding that we can call home.

Yale sent me a glossy brochure when it welcomed me as an entering student. It said, "Yale retains a deep respect for its early history and for the continuity that its history provides — a continuity based on constant reflection and reappraisal." Yale ought to reflect on and reappraise a policy that compels us to compromise our religious principles.

Reading and Discussion Questions

1. Summarize Hack's "moral code" in a sentence or two. What examples of conduct does he give to make his definition clear?
2. What solution to his problem does the author propose? Why does Yale refuse to accept the solution? Are Yale's rules justified?
3. Hack says that religious students "may have no choice but to sue the university to protect our religious way of life" (para. 3). What support could he offer in a court of law for his claim that these students should be allowed to live off campus? If you can, ask a legal expert for ideas.
4. Many arguments, like this one between religious students and a university, arise out of a conflict not between good and evil but between two goods. Can you propose a compromise that would satisfy both sides in this case?

Writing Suggestions

5. How do you think Yale could defend the sexual freedom that prevails on its campus? Write an argument setting out the philosophical principles and cultural values that justify tolerance for the practices Hack rejects.
6. Members of some minority groups on college campuses often insist on living together in separate dorms, taking their meals together, engaging in separate activities, etc. In light of today's emphasis on the multicultural experience, should the university allow such segregation?

The Right to Bear Arms

WARREN E. BURGER

Our metropolitan centers, and some suburban communities of America, are setting new records for homicides by handguns. Many of our large centers have up to ten times the murder rate of all of Western Europe. In 1988, there were 9,000 handgun murders in America. Last year, Washington, D.C., alone had more than 400 homicides — setting a new record for our capital.

The Constitution of the United States, in its Second Amendment, guarantees a "right of the people to keep and bear arms." However, the meaning of this clause cannot be understood except by looking to the purpose, the setting, and the objectives of the draftsmen. The first ten amendments — the Bill of Rights — were not drafted at Philadelphia in 1787; that document came two years later than the Constitution. Most of the states already had bills of rights, but the Constitution might not have been ratified in 1788 if the states had not had assurances that a national Bill of Rights would soon be added.

People of that day were apprehensive about the new "monster" national government presented to them, and this helps explain the language and purpose of the Second Amendment. A few lines after the First Amendment's guarantees — against "establishment of religion," "free exercise" of religion, free speech and free press — came a guarantee that grew out of the deep-seated fear of a "national" or "standing" army. The same First Congress that approved the right to keep and bear arms also limited the national army to 840 men; Congress in the Second Amendment then provided:

> A well regulated Militia, being necessary to the security of a free State, the right of the people to keep and bear Arms, shall not be infringed.

In the 1789 debate in Congress on James Madison's proposed Bill of Rights, Elbridge Gerry argued that a state militia was necessary:

> to prevent the establishment of a standing army, the bane of liberty. . . . Whenever governments mean to invade the rights and liberties of the people, they always attempt to destroy the militia in order to raise an army upon their ruins.

We see that the need for a state militia was the predicate of the 5 "right" guaranteed; in short, it was declared "necessary" in order to

---

Warren E. Burger (1907–1995) was chief justice of the United States from 1969 to 1986. This article is from the January 14, 1990, issue of *Parade* magazine.

have a state military force to protect the security of the state. That Second Amendment clause must be read as though the word "because" was the opening word of the guarantee. Today, of course, the "state militia" serves a very different purpose. A huge national defense establishment has taken over the role of the militia of 200 years ago.

Some have exploited these ancient concerns, blurring sporting guns — rifles, shotguns, and even machine pistols — with all firearms, including what are now called "Saturday night specials." There is, of course, a great difference between sporting guns and handguns. Some regulation of handguns has long been accepted as imperative; laws relating to "concealed weapons" are common. That we may be "overregulated" in some areas of life has never held us back from more regulation of automobiles, airplanes, motorboats, and "concealed weapons."

Let's look at the history.

First, many of the 3.5 million people living in the thirteen original Colonies depended on wild game for food, and a good many of them required firearms for their defense from marauding Indians — and later from the French and English. Underlying all these needs was an important concept that each able-bodied man in each of the thirteen independent states had to help or defend his state.

The early opposition to the idea of national or standing armies was maintained under the Articles of Confederation; that confederation had no standing army and wanted none. The state militia — essentially a part-time citizen army, as in Switzerland today — was the only kind of "army" they wanted. From the time of the Declaration of Independence through the victory at Yorktown in 1781, George Washington, as the commander in chief of these volunteer-militia armies, had to depend upon the states to send those volunteers.

When a company of New Jersey militia volunteers reported for 10 duty to Washington at Valley Forge, the men initially declined to take an oath to "the United States," maintaining, "Our country is New Jersey." Massachusetts Bay men, Virginians, and others felt the same way. To the American of the eighteenth century, his state was his country, and his freedom was defended by his militia.

The victory at Yorktown — and the ratification of the Bill of Rights a decade later — did not change people's attitudes about a national army. They had lived for years under the notion that each state would maintain its own military establishment, and the seaboard states had their own navies as well. These people, and their fathers and grandfathers before them, remembered how monarchs had used standing armies to oppress their ancestors in Europe. Americans wanted no part of this. A state militia, like a rifle and powder horn, was as much a part of life as the automobile is today; pistols were largely for officers, aristocrats — and dueling.

Against this background, it was not surprising that the provision concerning firearms emerged in very simple terms with the significant predicate — basing the right on the *necessity* for a "well regulated militia," a state army.

In the two centuries since then — with two world wars and some lesser ones — it has become clear, sadly, that we have no choice but to maintain a standing national army while still maintaining a "militia" by way of the National Guard, which can be swiftly integrated into the national defense forces.

Americans also have a right to defend their homes, and we need not challenge that. Nor does anyone seriously question that the Constitution protects the right of hunters to own and keep sporting guns for hunting game any more than anyone would challenge the right to own and keep fishing rods and other equipment for fishing — or to own automobiles. To "keep and bear arms" for hunting today is essentially a recreational activity and not an imperative of survival, as it was 200 years ago; "Saturday night specials" and machine guns are not recreational weapons and surely are as much in need of regulation as motor vehicles.

Americans should ask themselves a few questions. The Constitution does not mention automobiles or motorboats, but the right to keep and own an automobile is beyond question; equally beyond question is the power of the state to regulate the purchase or the transfer of such vehicle and the right to license the vehicle and the driver with reasonable standards. In some places, even a bicycle must be registered, as must some household dogs.

If we are to stop this mindless homicidal carnage, is it unreasonable:

1. to provide that, to acquire a firearm, an application be made reciting age, residence, employment, and any prior criminal convictions?
2. to require that this application lie on the table for ten days (absent a showing for urgent need) before the license would be issued?
3. that the transfer of a firearm be made essentially as that of a motor vehicle?
4. to have a "ballistic fingerprint" of the firearm made by the manufacturer and filed with the license record so that, if a bullet is found in a victim's body, law enforcement might be helped in finding the culprit?

These are the kinds of questions the American people must answer if we are to preserve the "domestic tranquility" promised in the Constitution.

Reading and Discussion Questions

1. This essay can be divided into three or four parts. Provide headings for these parts.
2. Which part of the essay is most fully developed? What explains the author's emphasis?
3. Why does Burger recount the history of the Second Amendment so fully? Explain his reason for arguing that the Second Amendment does not guarantee the right of individuals to "bear arms."
4. Burger also uses history to argue that there is a difference between legislation against sporting guns and legislation against handguns. Summarize his argument.
5. How effective is his analogy between licensing vehicles and licensing handguns?

Writing Suggestions

6. Other people interpret "the right to bear arms" differently. Look at some of their arguments, and write an essay summarizing their interpretations and defending them.
7. Burger outlines a policy for registration of handguns that would prevent criminal use. But at least one sociologist has pointed out that most guns used by criminals are obtained illegally. Examine and evaluate some of the arguments claiming that registration is generally ineffective.
8. Analyze arguments of the National Rifle Association, the nation's largest gun lobby. Do they answer Burger's claims?

Numbers don't lie.

Take goats, for example.

How many Mongolian goats do you think it takes to get enough fleece to make a single Lands' End Cashmere Sweater? The answer: from *2½ to 4* goats.

And guess how many feet of cotton yarn go into our men's Pinpoint Oxford shirts? 64,306 feet. That's a little over *12 miles* of cotton – in each shirt.

Fact is, we use lots and lots of cotton. Our Stonewashed Jeans are a tough 14¾ oz. cotton denim: a fine, honest fabric. Know how much denim we used in our jeans last year? Enough to fill *23* railroad boxcars.

Now, we're not just playing with numbers here. Numbers tell a lot about Lands' End.

Like the more than *500* crofters – cottage weavers in Scotland–who hand weave the fabric for our Harris Tweed jackets.

Or the *75* inspectors whose job is trying to make sure that everything that wears a Lands' End label deserves it.

In fact, when you consider what all the numbers say about us – and our *passion* to get things right for our customers – doesn't it make you want to see a copy of our catalog? We'd be happy to send you the latest number.

© 1996 Lands' End, Inc.

LANDS' END
Guaranteed. Period.

For a free catalog, call any time, 24 hours a day–

1·800·356·4444 Please mention ad SJ

Name _____

Address _____ Apt. _____

City _____ State _____ Zip _____

Phone ( ) _____ Day/Night (circle one)

Mail to: 1 Lands' End Lane, Dodgeville, WI 53595. **E-Mail: catalogs-sj@landsend.com**

Discussion Questions

1. Notice the headline. The advertiser has supplied lots of numbers. What claim are these numbers meant to support?

2. Did you find the ad interesting to read? Do you think the advertiser was correct in thinking that people would read seven paragraphs about numbers? Explain your answer.

3. What specific aspects of the language might induce people to continue reading even if they find numbers tedious?

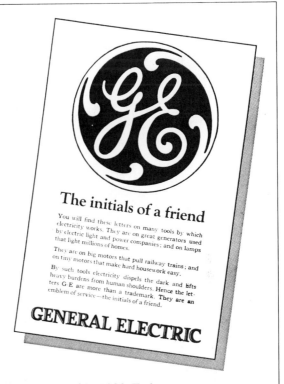

The initials of a friend

You will find these letters on many tools by which electricity works. They are on great generators used by electric light and power companies; and on lamps that light millions of homes.

They are on big motors that pull railway trains; and on tiny motors that make hard housework easy.

By such tools electricity dispels the dark and lifts heavy burdens from human shoulders. Hence the letters G-E are more than a trademark. They are an emblem of service—the initials of a friend.

GENERAL ELECTRIC

This advertisement first appeared in 1923. Today, you'll find our initials on many more things — from appliances, plastics, motors and lighting to financial services and medical equipment. Wherever you see our initials, we want them to mean the same thing to you — the initials of a friend.

We bring good things to life.

Discussion Questions

1. To what need does the ad make an appeal?
2. What devices in the ad — both objects and the choice of objects to discuss — contribute to the effectiveness of the message?
3. How does the company's present-day slogan compare?

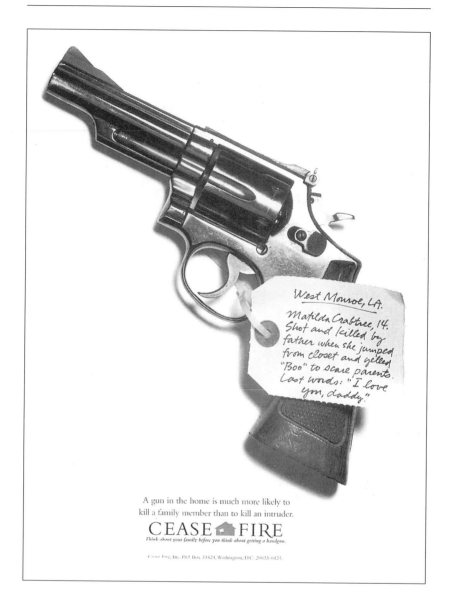

A gun in the home is much more likely to kill a family member than to kill an intruder.

CEASE FIRE

Think about your family before you think about getting a handgun.

Cease Fire, Inc. P.O. Box 33424, Washington, D.C. 20033-0424.

Discussion Questions

1. Would this claim of policy be just as successful if the note were excluded? Would additional facts about guns contribute to its effectiveness?
2. Why is the gun so much larger than the printed message?
3. What is the basis of the emotional appeal? Is there more than one? Does the note go too far in exploiting our emotions?

The Case for Medicalizing Heroin

ALAN DERSHOWITZ

When *Time* magazine has a cover story on the legalization of drugs, and when Oprah Winfrey devotes an entire show to that "unthinkable" proposition, you can be sure that this is an issue whose time has come — at least for serious discussion.

But it is difficult to get politicians to *have* a serious discussion about alternatives to our currently bankrupt approach to drug abuse. Even thinking out loud about the possibility of decriminalization is seen as being soft on drugs. And no elected official can afford to be viewed as less than ferocious and uncompromising on this issue.

Any doubts about that truism were surely allayed when Vice President Bush openly broke with his president and most important supporter over whether to try to make a deal with Panamanian strongman Manuel Noriega, whom the United States has charged with drug-trafficking.

I was one of the guests on the recent Oprah Winfrey show that debated drug decriminalization. The rhetoric and emotions ran high, as politicians and audience members competed over who could be tougher in the war against drugs.

"Call out the marines," "Bomb the poppy fields," "Execute the 5
drug dealers" — these are among the "constructive" suggestions being offered to supplement the administration's simpleminded "just say no" slogan.

Proposals to medicalize, regulate, or in another way decriminalize any currently illegal drug — whether it be marijuana, cocaine, or heroin — were greeted by derision and cries of "surrender." Even politicians who *in private* recognize the virtues of decriminalization must continue to oppose it when the cameras are rolling.

That is why it is so important to outline here the politically unpopular case for an alternative approach.

Ironically, the case is easiest for the hardest drug — heroin. There can be no doubt that heroin is a horrible drug: It is highly

Alan Dershowitz is a professor at Harvard Law School. This essay, originally published in 1988, is reprinted in his book *Contrary to Popular Opinion* (1992).

addictive and debilitating; taken in high, or unregulated, doses, it can kill; when administered by means of shared needles, it spreads AIDS; because of its high price and addictive quality, it makes acquisitive criminals out of desperate addicts. Few would disagree that if we could rid it from the planet through the passage of a law or the invention of a plant-specific herbicide, we should do so.

But since we can neither eliminate heroin nor the demand for it, there is a powerful case for medicalizing as much of the problem as is feasible. Under this proposal, or one of its many variants, the hard-core addict would receive the option of getting his fix in a medical setting, administered by medical personnel.

The setting could be a mobile hospital van or some other facility 10 close to where the addicts live. A doctor would determine the dosage for each addict — a maintenance dosage designed to prevent withdrawal without risking overdose. And the fix would be injected in the medical facility so the addict could not sell or barter the drug or prescription.

This will by no means solve all the problems associated with heroin addiction, but it would ameliorate some of the most serious ones. The maintained heroin addict will not immediately become a model citizen. But much of the desperation that today accounts for the victimization of innocent home-dwellers, store employees, and pedestrians — primarily in urban centers — would be eliminated, and drug-related crime would be significantly reduced.

Today's addict is simply not deterred by the law. He will get his fix by hook or by crook, or by knife or by gun, regardless of the risk. That is what heroin addiction means. Giving the desperate addict a twenty-four-hour medical alternative will save the lives of countless innocent victims of both crime and AIDS.

It will also save the lives of thousands of addicts who now kill themselves in drug shooting galleries by injecting impure street mixtures through AIDS-infected needles.

There will, of course, always be a black market for heroin, even if it were medicalized. Not every addict will accept a medically administered injection, and even some of those who do will supplement their maintenance doses with street drugs. But much of the desperate quality of the constant quest for the fix will be reduced for at least some heroin addicts. And this will have a profound impact on both the quantity and violence of inner-city crime.

Nor would new addicts be created by this medical approach. 15 Only long-term adult addicts would be eligible for the program. And the expenses would be more than offset by the extraordinary savings to our society in reduced crime.

If this program proved successful in the context of heroin addiction, variants could be considered for other illegal drugs such as cocaine and marijuana. There is no assurance that an approach which is successful for one drug will necessarily work for others. Many of the problems are different.

We have already decriminalized two of the most dangerous drugs known to humankind — nicotine and alcohol. Decriminalization of these killers, which destroy more lives than all other drugs combined, has not totally eliminated the problems associated with them.

But we have come to realize that criminalization of nicotine and alcohol causes even more problems than it solves. The time has come to consider whether that is also true of heroin and perhaps of other drugs as well.

For Addicts, Force Is the Best Medicine
SALLY SATEL

Autopsy reports confirmed last week that actor and comedian Chris Farley died December 18 of an overdose of cocaine and morphine. Farley was 33, the same age at which his idol, John Belushi, fatally overdosed on cocaine and heroin in 1982.

Two weeks before Farley's death, another actor, Robert Downey Jr., came before a Los Angeles County municipal judge in a Malibu courtroom on a drug-related charge. The judge, Lawrence Mira, jailed him for six months, having gone easy on him after several earlier convictions. "I'm going to incarcerate you in a way you won't like," Judge Mira told Downey, "but it may save your life."

Indeed it may. And if Farley had had the good fortune to be arrested and come before a tough judge, he might well be alive today. As a psychiatrist who treats drug addicts, I have learned that legal sanctions — either imposed or threatened — may provide the leverage needed to keep them alive by keeping them in treatment. Voluntary help is often not enough. After all, Downey and Farley had already been to some of the nation's finest rehabilitation centers, but their stays were far too brief. "Chris kept trying, and he would go into rehab and he would come out, and sometimes he'd be really healthy," Al Franken, who worked with Farley on *Saturday Night Live,* told a reporter after his death.

It's an all-too-typical story: Addicts avoid treatment for years or take it in small doses, enough to refresh themselves before starting out on another binge. According to the federally funded Drug Abuse

Dr. Sally Satel is a psychiatrist specializing in addiction. This article appeared in the *Wall Street Journal* on January 6, 1998.

Treatment Outcome Study, patients report being addicted for 10 to 15 years on average before first entering treatment. When they do enroll, only one in seven completes a program. Downey, for example, once bailed out after a few days.

At the root of the problem are the misguided though well-meaning attitudes of many drug-treatment professionals. They believe in waiting until a drug user is "motivated" to get help, allowing him to reject help until he is no longer "in denial," and telling addicts that treatment won't work until they "want to do it for themselves." 5

At the same time, the prevailing view holds that an addict is someone suffering from a chronic illness rather than someone whose behavior can be influenced by meaningful consequences. The National Institute on Drug Abuse, part of the National Institutes of Health, even goes so far as to call addiction a "brain disease."

In truth, drugs do affect the brain, but even many of my patients know that stopping is a matter of personal responsibility. In encouraging users to take that responsibility, coercion can be the clinician's best friend. Without it, our work is often in vain.

In the methadone clinic where I work, many patients continue to use cocaine and heroin while receiving counseling and group therapy. Short of ejecting them from the clinic, there is little we doctors can do about this. But sometimes a patient will get a lucky break: He'll get arrested and put on probation with the requirement that he take frequent urine tests and the stipulation that he goes to jail if he fails. With this threat hanging over their heads, patients often test clean — no great surprise to anyone not steeped in therapeutic ideology.

Some addicts themselves recognize the benefits of coercion. One patient told me he planned to get a job as a truck driver. "At least they'll test my urine, and I'll know someone's watching," he said. This patient put his finger on the crying need for built-in controls and individual accountability. When they're there, imposed by a judge or an employer, I can do my job better. The patient and I don't waste time bargaining over how many drug tests he can fail — "C'mon, doc, next week I'll be clean." I don't have to risk straining the treatment relationship by threatening the patient with discharge from the clinic.

Instead, with externally imposed limits and expectations, I am 10 clearly the patient's ally. We are working together toward his recovery, developing strategies to resist temptation and ultimately discovering larger reasons to stay clean, because we both know that there are serious consequences for failing. And it's a myth that addicts have to want treatment. Ample evidence from large-scale studies shows that when they are compelled to treatment by judges or mandated by their employers, these coerced addicts do at least as well as their counterparts who voluntarily enter and complete the program.

It is also well documented that the longer a patient stays in treatment, the more likely he is to avoid future criminal activity and drug use. For example, any patient — whether treated voluntarily or under court order — staying 18 to 24 months in Phoenix House, a residential community program, has a 90 percent chance of being employed and out of legal trouble and a 70 percent chance of being completely drug-free five to seven years after discharge. The Brooklyn, New York, district attorney, who routinely sends nonviolent drug felons to mandatory residential treatment programs instead of prison, finds they remain in treatment two to four times longer than their noncoerced counterparts. They also fare better than their imprisoned counterparts, whose rearrest rate one year after release is more than twice the rate of those who have completed treatment. Treatment is one-third cheaper than incarceration, to boot.

The idea of "harm reduction" — decriminalization, along with medically supervised heroin distribution, needle exchanges, and other such measures — has been gaining currency in the drug debate of late. But addicts would be better off if more of them were arrested and forced to enroll in treatment programs. "I wish the cops could bust an addict for jaywalking or littering," a colleague of mine says, only half-jokingly. "At least then he would get placed in a treatment program where the court would make sure he'd stay." Civil judges can, without arrest, commit some addicts to treatment for their own protection if they are clearly out of control — as Farley appears to have been. More than half the states have statutes, seldom used, that allow civil commitment for alcoholics and drug addicts on the basis of grave disability or a threat to oneself or others.

To be sure, being forced into a program and losing autonomy — either in a residential, a jail-based, or a probationary treatment program — can seem harsh. But the payoff is immense: an opportunity to develop the social competence, trust in others and optimism about the future that are the prerequisites for a life without drugs.

The payoffs for society are substantial, too. Numerous large-scale cost-benefit analyses reveal that every dollar spent on drug treatment saves between $2 and $7 on law enforcement, corrections, health care, lost productivity, and welfare.

To my dismay, some of my treatment colleagues oppose coercion as "punitive." I suppose it may seem that way if one thinks addicts are helpless victims of a brain disease. But addiction is a moral condition as well as a medical one. If we view it in this light, then predictable consequences for failure and rewards for success are the essence of humane therapy.

Discussion Questions

1. What are the bases for Dershowitz's claim that drugs should be legalized?
2. His support consists in part of hypothetical examples of the way that legalized heroin would work. What are the strengths and weaknesses of such evidence?

3. What evidence does Satel supply to support her argument for arrest and forced treatment? Which evidence is most convincing?
4. Does Satel's argument constitute a response to Dershowitz? Why or why not?

TAKING THE DEBATE ONLINE

- **A Wiser Course: Ending Drug Prohibition** <http://www.legalize-usa .org/documents/html/nylawyer.htm> This lengthy essay by the Association of the Bar of the City of New York recommends legalizing drugs and implementing various treatment programs.

- **The Stanton Peele Addiction Web Site: Assumptions about Drugs and the Marketing of Drug Policies** <http://www.peele.net/lib/models .html> This site by Stanton Peele, a consultant for the International Center for Alcohol Policies in Washington, D.C., addresses legalization and treatment programs (including coerced treatment) in relation to the drug policies of the United States.

- **Cascade Policy Institute** <http://www.cascadepolicy.org/addicts .htm> The Cascade Policy Institute presents two letters to the editor published in the January 21, 1998, issue of the *Wall Street Journal:* the first from the Cascade Policy Institute's president and the second from a psychiatrist. Both letters find fault with forcing addicts into treatment because force does not teach addicts about personal and public responsibility.

- **Drug Watch International** <http://www.drugwatch.org> This site, maintained by Drug Watch International — a volunteer, nonprofit information network — promotes a drug-free society and opposes the legalization of drugs.

- **Office of National Drug Control Policy** <http://www.whitehouse-drugpolicy.gov/policy/98ndcs/iii-b.html> This site presents the drug policy of the United States. It does not promote legalization but does call for treatment protocols for prevention.

- **The Harvard Mental Health Letter: Treatment of Drug Abuse and Addiction** <http://www.mentalhealth.com/mag1/p5h-sb04.html> This site defends forced treatment of drug addiction, saying, in part, that many drug addicts are already forced into rehabilitation programs by the current U.S. court system.

- For further information, try entering the terms *drug addiction, rehabilitation programs,* and *drug treatment* into the following search engines: <metafind.com>, <dogpile.com>, <yahoo.com>.

EXERCISES

1. Look for personal advertisements (in which men and women advertise for various kinds of companionship) in a local or national paper or magazine. (The *Village Voice,* a New York paper, is an outstanding source.)

What inferences can you draw about the people who place these ads? About the facts they choose to provide? How did you come to these conclusions? You might also try to infer the reasons that more women than men place ads and why this change has occurred.

2. "I Like Colonel Sanders" is the title of an article that praises ugly architecture, shopping malls, laundromats, and other symbols of "plastic" America. The author claims that these aspects of the American scene have unique and positive values. Defend or refute his claim by pointing out some of the values of these things and giving reasons for your own assessments.

3. A psychiatrist says that in pro football personality traits determine the positions of the players. Write an essay developing this idea and providing adequate evidence for your claim. Or make inferences about the relationship between the personalities of the players and another sport that you know well.

4. At least one city in the world — Reykjavik, the capital of Iceland — bans dogs from the city. Defend or attack this policy by using both facts and values to support your claim.

5. Write a review of a movie, play, television program, concert, restaurant, or book. Make clear your criteria for judgment and their order of importance.

6. The controversy concerning seat belts and air bags in automobiles has generated a variety of proposals, one of which is mandatory use of seat belts in all the states. Make your own policy claim regarding laws about safety devices (the wearing of motorcycle helmets is another thorny subject), and defend it by using both facts and values — facts about safety, values concerning individual freedom and responsibility.

7. Select a familiar ritual, and argue for or against the value it represents. *Examples:* the high school prom, Christmas gift-giving, a fraternity initiation, a wedding, a confirmation or bar mitzvah, a funeral ceremony, a Fourth of July celebration.

8. Choose a recommended policy — from the school newspaper or elsewhere — and argue that it will or will not work to produce beneficial changes. *Examples:* expansion of core curriculum requirements, comprehensive tests as a graduation requirement, reinstitution of a physical education requirement, removal of junk food from vending machines.

Critical Listening

9. Have you ever been a member of a group which tried but failed to solve a problem through discussion? Communication theorists talk about *interference,* defined by one writer as "anything that hinders or lessens the efficiency of communication."[5] Some of the elements of interference in the delivery of oral messages are fatigue, anger, inattention, vague language, personality conflict, and political bias. You will probably be able to think of others. Did any of these elements prevent the group from arriving at an agreement? Describe the situation and the kinds of interference that you noticed.

---

[5]Richard E. Crable, *One to Another* (New York: Harper and Row, 1981), p. 18.

CHAPTER FOUR

Definition

THE PURPOSES OF DEFINITION

Before we examine the other elements of argument, we need to consider definition, a component you may have to deal with early in writing an essay. Definition may be used in two ways: to clarify the meanings of vague or ambiguous terms or as a method of development for the whole essay. In some arguments your claims will contain words that need explanation before you can proceed with any discussion. But you may also want to devote an entire essay to the elaboration of a broad concept or experience that cannot be adequately defined in a shorter space.

The Roman statesman Cicero said, "Every rational discussion of anything whatsoever should begin with a definition in order to make clear what is the subject of dispute." You have probably already discovered the importance of definition in argument. If you have ever had a disagreement with your parents about using the car or drinking or dyeing your hair or going away for a weekend or staying out till three in the morning, you know that you were really arguing about the meaning of the term *adolescent freedom*.

Arguments often revolve around definitions of crucial terms. For example, how does one define *democracy*? Does a democracy guarantee freedom of the press, freedom of worship, freedom of assembly, and freedom of movement? In the United States, we would argue that such freedoms are essential to any definition of *democracy*. But countries in which these freedoms are nonexistent also represent themselves as democracies or governments of the people. In the words of Senator Daniel P. Moynihan, "For years now the most brutal totalitarian regimes have called themselves 'people's' or 'democratic' republics." Rulers in such governments are aware that defining their regimes as democratic may win the approval of people who would otherwise condemn them. In his formidable attack on totalitarianism, *Nineteen Eighty-Four,* George Orwell coined the slogans "War Is Peace" and "Slavery Is Freedom," phrases that represent the corrupt use of definition to distort reality.

But even where there is no intention to deceive, the snares of definition are difficult to avoid. How do you define *abortion*? Is it "termination of pregnancy"? Or is it "murder of an unborn child"? During a celebrated trial in 1975 of a physician who performed an abortion and was accused of manslaughter, the prosecution often used the word *baby* to refer to the fetus, but the defense referred to "the products of conception." These definitions of *fetus* reflected the differing judgments of those on opposite sides. Not only do judgments create definitions; definitions influence judgments. In the abortion trial, the definitions of *fetus* used by both sides were meant to promote either approval or disapproval of the doctor's action.

Definitions can indeed change the nature of an event or a "fact." How many farms are there in the state of New York? The answer to the question depends on the definition of *farm.* In 1979 the *New York Times* reported:

> Because of a change in the official definition of the word "farm," New York lost 20 percent of its farms on January 1, with numbers dropping from 56,000 to 45,000. . . .
> Before the change, a farm was defined as "any place from which $250 or more of agricultural products is sold" yearly or "any place of 10 acres or more from which $50 or more of agricultural products is sold" yearly. Now a farm is "any place from which $1,000 or more of agricultural products is sold" in a year.[1]

A change in the definition of *poverty* can have similar results. An article in the *New York Times,* whose headline reads, "A Revised Definition of Poverty May Raise Number of U.S. Poor," makes this clear.

> The official definition of *poverty* used by the Federal Government for three decades is based simply on cash income before taxes. But in a report to be issued on Wednesday, a panel of experts convened by the [National] Academy of Sciences three years ago at the behest of Congress says the Government should move toward a concept of poverty based on disposable income, the amount left after a family pays taxes and essential expenses.[2]

The differences are wholly a matter of definition. But such differences can have serious consequences for those being defined, most of all in the disposition of billions of federal dollars in aid of various

---

[1]*New York Times,* March 4, 1979, sec. 1, p. 40.
[2]*New York Times,* April 10, 1995, sec. A, p. 1.

kinds. In 1992 the Census Bureau classified 14.5 percent of Americans as poor. Under the new guidelines, at least 15 or 16 percent would be poor, and, under some measures recommended by a government panel, 18 percent would be so defined.

In fact, local and federal courts almost every day redefine traditional concepts that can have a direct impact on our everyday lives. The definition of *family,* for example, has undergone significant changes that acknowledge the existence of new relationships. In January 1990 the New Jersey Supreme Court ruled that a family may be defined as "one or more persons occupying a dwelling unit as a single nonprofit housekeeping unit, who are living together as a stable and permanent living unit, being a traditional family unit or the *functional equivalent* thereof" (italics for emphasis added). This meant that ten Glassboro State College students, unrelated by blood, could continue to occupy a single-family house despite the objection of the borough of Glassboro.[3] Even the legal definition of maternity has shifted. Who is the mother — the woman who contributes the egg or the woman (the surrogate) who bears the child? Several states, acknowledging the changes brought by medical technology, now recognize a difference between the birth mother and the legal mother.

DEFINING THE TERMS IN YOUR ARGUMENT

In some of your arguments you will introduce terms that require definition. We've pointed out that a definition of *poverty* is crucial to any debate on the existence of poverty in the United States. The same may be true in a debate about the legality of euthanasia, or mercy killing. Are the arguers referring to passive euthanasia (the withdrawal of life-support systems) or to active euthanasia (the direct administration of drugs to hasten death)?

It is not uncommon, in fact, for arguments about controversial questions to turn into arguments about the definition of terms. If, for example, you wanted to argue in favor of the regulation of religious cults, you would first have to define *cult.* In so doing, you might discover that it is not easy to distinguish clearly between conventional religions and cults. Then you would have to define *regulation,* spelling out the legal restrictions you favored so as to make them apply only to cults, not to established religions. An argument on the subject might end almost before it began if writer and reader could not agree on definitions of these terms. While clear definitions do not guarantee agreement, they do ensure that all parties understand the nature of the argument.

---

[3]*New York Times,* February 1, 1990, sec. B, p. 5.

Defining Vague and Ambiguous Terms

You will need to define other terms in addition to those in your claim. If you use words and phrases that have two or more meanings, they may appear vague and ambiguous to your reader. In arguments of value and policy abstract terms such as *freedom, justice, patriotism,* and *equality* require clarification. Despite their vagueness, however, they are among the most important in the language because they represent the ideals that shape our laws. When conflicts arise, the courts must define these terms to establish the legality of certain practices. Is the Ku Klux Klan permitted to make disparaging public statements about ethnic and racial groups? That depends on the court's definition of *free speech.* Can execution for some crimes be considered cruel and unusual punishment? That, too, depends on the court's definition of *cruel and unusual punishment.* In addition, such terms as *happiness, mental health, success,* and *creativity* often defy precise definition because they reflect the differing values within a society or a culture.

The definition of *success,* for example, varies not only among social groups but also among individuals within the group. One scientist has postulated five signs by which to measure success: wealth (including health), security (confidence in retaining the wealth), reputation, performance, and contentment.[4] Consider whether all of these are necessary to your own definition of *success.* If not, which may be omitted? Do you think others should be added? Notice that one of the signs — reputation — is defined by the community; another — contentment — can be measured only by the individual. The assessment of performance probably owes something to both the group and the individual.

Christopher Atkins, an actor, gave an interviewer an example of an externalized definition of success — that is, a definition based on the standards imposed by other people:

> Success to me is judged through the eyes of others. I mean, if you're walking around saying, "I own a green Porsche," you might meet somebody who says, "Hey, that's no big deal I own a green Porsche and a house." So all of a sudden, you don't feel so successful. Really, it's in the eyes of others.[5]

So difficult is the formulation of a universally accepted measure for success that some scholars regard the concept as meaningless. Nevertheless, we continue to use the word as if it represented a definable concept because the idea of success, however defined, is

---

[4]Gwynn Nettler, *Social Concerns* (New York: McGraw-Hill, 1976), pp. 196–197.
[5]*New York Times,* August 6, 1982, sec. 3, p. 8.

important for the identity and development of the individual and the group. It is clear, however, that when crossing subcultural boundaries, even within a small group, we need to be aware of differences in the use of the word. If contentment — that is, the satisfaction of achieving a small personal goal — is enough, then a person lying under a palm tree subsisting on handouts from picnickers may be a success. But you should not expect all your readers to agree that these criteria are enough to define *success*.

In arguing about aesthetic matters, whose vocabulary is almost always abstract, the criteria for judgment must be revealed, either directly or indirectly, and then the abstract terms that represent the criteria must be defined. If you want to say that a film is distinguished by great acting, have you made clear what you mean by *great*? That we do not always understand or agree on the definition of *great* is apparent, say, on the morning after the Oscar winners have been announced.

Even subjects that you feel sure you can identify may offer surprising insights when you rethink them for an extended definition. One critic, defining *rock music,* argued that the distinguishing characteristic of rock music was noise — not beat, not harmonies, not lyrics, not vocal style, but noise, "nasty, discordant, irritating noise — or, to its practitioners, unfettered, liberating, expressive noise."[6] In producing this definition, the author had to give a number of examples to prove that he was justified in rejecting the most familiar criteria.

Consider the definition of *race,* around which so much of American history has revolved, often with tragic consequences. Until recently, the only categories listed in the census were white, black, Asian-Pacific, and Native American, "with the Hispanic population straddling them all." But rapidly increasing intermarriage and ethnic identity caused a number of political and ethnic groups to demand changes in the classifications of the Census Bureau. Some Arab Americans, for example, prefer to be counted as "Middle Eastern" rather than white. Children of black-white unions are defined as black 60 percent of the time, while children of Asian-white unions are described as Asian 42 percent of the time. Research is now being conducted to discover how people feel about the terms being used to define them. As one anthropologist pointed out, "Socially and politically assigned attributes have a lot to do with access to economic resources."[7]

---

[6]Jon Pareles, "Noise Evokes Modern Chaos for a Band," *New York Times,* March 9, 1986, sec. H, p. 26.

[7]*Wall Street Journal,* September 9, 1995, sec. B, p. 1.

METHODS FOR DEFINING TERMS

The following strategies for defining terms in an argument are by no means mutually exclusive. You may use all of them in a single argumentative essay.

Dictionary Definition

Giving a dictionary definition is the simplest and most obvious way to define a term. An unabridged dictionary is the best source because it usually gives examples of the way a word can be used in a sentence; that is, it furnishes the proper context.

In many cases, the dictionary definition alone is not sufficient. It may be too broad or too narrow for your purpose. Suppose, in an argument about pornography, you wanted to define the word *obscene.* *Webster's New International Dictionary* (third edition, unabridged) gives the definition of *obscene* as "offensive to taste; foul; loathsome; disgusting." But these synonyms do not tell you what qualities make an object or an event or an action "foul," "loathsome," and "disgusting." In 1973 the Supreme Court, attempting to narrow the definition of *obscenity,* ruled that obscenity was to be determined by the community in accordance with local standards. One person's obscenity, as numerous cases have demonstrated, may be another person's art. The celebrated trials in the early twentieth century about the distribution of novels regarded as pornographic — D. H. Lawrence's *Lady Chatterley's Lover* and James Joyce's *Ulysses* — emphasized the problems of defining obscenity.

Another dictionary definition may strike you as too narrow. *Patriotism,* for example, is defined in one dictionary as "love and loyal or zealous support of one's country, especially in all matters involving other countries." Some readers may want to include an unwillingness to support government policies they consider wrong.

Stipulation

In stipulating the meaning of a term, the writer asks the reader to accept a definition that may be different from the conventional one. He or she does this to limit or control the argument. Someone has said, "Part of the task of keeping definitions in our civilization clear and pure is to keep a firm democratic rein on those with the power, or craving the power, to stipulate meaning." Perhaps this writer was thinking of a term like *national security,* which can be defined by a nation's leaders in such a way as to sanction persecution of citizens and reckless military adventures. Likewise, a term such as *liberation* can be appropriated by terrorist groups whose activities often lead to oppression rather than liberation.

Religion is usually defined as a belief in a supernatural power to be obeyed and worshiped. But in an article entitled "Civil Religion in America," a sociologist offers a different meaning.

> While some have argued that Christianity is the national faith, and others that church and synagogue celebrate only the generalized religion of "the American way of life," few have realized that there actually exists alongside of and rather clearly differentiated from the churches an elaborate and well-institutionalized civil religion in America. This article argues not only that there is such a thing, but also that this religion . . . has its own seriousness and integrity and requires the same care in understanding that any other religion does.[8]

When the author adds, "This religion — there seems no other word for it — was neither sectarian nor in any specific sense Christian," he emphasizes that he is distinguishing his definition of religion from definitions that associate religion and church.

Even the word *violence,* which the dictionary defines as "physical force used so as to injure or damage" and whose meaning seems so clear and uncompromising, can be manipulated to produce a definition different from the one normally understood by most people. Some pacifists refer to conditions in which "people are deprived of choices in a systematic way" as "institutionalized quiet violence." Even where no physical force is employed, this lack of choice in schools, in the workplace, in the black ghettos is defined as violence.[9]

In *Through the Looking-Glass* Alice asked Humpty Dumpty "whether you can make words mean so many different things."

"When I use a word," Humpty Dumpty said scornfully, "it means just what I choose it to mean, neither more nor less."[10]

A writer, however, is not free to invent definitions that no one will recognize or that create rather than solve problems between writer and reader.

Negation

To avoid confusion it is sometimes helpful to tell the reader what a term is *not.* In discussing euthanasia, a writer might say, "By euthanasia I do not mean active intervention to hasten the death of the patient."

---

[8]Robert N. Bellah, "Civil Religion in America," *Daedalus,* Winter 1967, p. 1.

[9]Newton Garver, "What Violence Is," in James Rachels, ed., *Moral Choices* (New York: Harper and Row, 1971), pp. 248–249.

[10]Lewis Carroll, *Alice in Wonderland and Through the Looking-Glass* (New York: Grosset and Dunlap, 1948), p. 238.

A negative definition may be more extensive, depending on the complexity of the term and the writer's ingenuity. The critic of rock music quoted earlier in this chapter arrived at his definition of *noise* by rejecting attributes that seemed misleading. The ex-Communist Whittaker Chambers, in a foreword to a book on the spy trial of Alger Hiss, defined *communism* this way:

> First, let me try to say what Communism is not. It is not simply a vicious plot hatched by wicked men in a subcellar. It is not just the writings of Marx and Lenin, dialectical materialism, the Politburo, the labor theory of value, the theory of the general strike, the Red Army secret police, labor camps, underground conspiracy, the dictatorship of the proletariat, the technique of the coup d'état. It is not even those chanting, bannered millions that stream periodically, like disorganized armies, through the heart of the world's capitals: Moscow, New York, Tokyo, Paris, Rome. These are expressions, but they are not what Communism is about.[11]

This, of course, is only part of the definition. Any writer beginning a definition in the negative must go on to define what the term *is*.

Examples

One of the most effective ways of defining terms in an argument is to use examples. Both real and hypothetical examples can bring life to abstract and ambiguous terms. The writer in the following passage defines *preferred categories* (classes of people who are meant to benefit from affirmative action policies) by invoking specific cases:

> The absence of definitions points up one of the problems with preferred categories. . . . These preferred categories take no account of family wealth or educational advantages. A black whose father is a judge or physician deserves preferential treatment over any nonminority applicant. The latter might have fought his way out of the grinding poverty of Appalachia, or might be the first member of an Italian American or a Polish American family to complete high school. But no matter.[12]

Insanity is a word that has been used and misused to describe a variety of conditions. Even psychiatrists are in dispute about its meaning. In the following anecdote, examples narrow and refine the definition.

> Dr. Zilboorg says that present-day psychiatry does not possess any satisfactory definition of mental illness or neurosis. To illustrate, he

---

[11]*Witness* (New York: Random House, 1952), p. 8.

[12]Anthony Lombardo, "Quotas Work Both Ways," *U.S. Catholic*, February 1974, p. 39.

told a story: A psychiatrist was recently asked for a definition of a "well-adjusted person" (not even slightly peculiar). The definition: "A person who feels in harmony with himself and who is not in conflict with his environment." It sounded fine, but up popped a heckler. "Would you then consider an anti-Nazi working in the underground against Hitler a maladjusted person?" "Well," the psychiatrist hemmed, "I withdraw the latter part of my definition." Dr. Zilboorg withdrew the first half for him. Many persons in perfect harmony with themselves, he pointed out, are in "distinctly pathological states."[13]

Extended Definition

When we speak of an extended definition, we usually refer not only to length but also to the variety of methods for developing the definition. Let's take the word *materialism*. A dictionary entry offers the following sentence fragments as definitions: "1. the doctrine that comfort, pleasure, and wealth are the only or highest goals or values. 2. the tendency to be more concerned with material than the spiritual goals or values." But the term *materialism* has acquired so many additional meanings, especially emotional ones, that an extended definition serves a useful purpose in clarifying the many different ideas surrounding our understanding of the term.

Below is a much longer definition of *materialism,* which appears at the beginning of an essay entitled "People and Things: Reflections on Materialism."[14]

There are two contemporary usages of the term *materialism,* and it is important to distinguish between them. On the one hand we can talk about *instrumental materialism,* or the use of material objects to make life longer, safer, more enjoyable. By instrumental, we mean that objects act as essential means for discovering and furthering personal values and goals of life, so that the objects are instruments used to realize and further those goals. There is little negative connotation attached to this meaning of the word, since one would think that it is perfectly sensible to use things for such purposes. While it is true that the United States is the epitome of materialism in this sense, it is also true that most people in every society aspire to reach our level of instrumental materialism.

On the other hand the term has a more negative connotation, which might be conveyed by the phrase *terminal materialism.* This is the sense critics use when they apply the term to Americans. What they mean is that we not only use our material resources as instruments to make life more manageable, but that we reduce our ultimate goals to the possession of things. They believe that we don't just use our cars to

---

[13]Quoted in *The Art of Making Sense,* p. 48.

[14]Mihaly Csikszentmihalyi and Eugene Rochberg-Halton, "People and Things: Reflections on Materialism," *University of Chicago Magazine,* Spring 1978, pp. 7–8.

get from place to place, but that we consider the ownership of expensive cars one of the central values in life. Terminal materialism means that the object is valued only because it indicates an end in itself, a possession. In instrumental materialism there is a sense of directionality, in which a person's goals may be furthered through the interactions with the object. A book, for example, can reveal new possibilities or widen a person's view of the world, or an old photograph can be cherished because it embodies a relationship. But in terminal materialism, there is no sense of reciprocal interaction in the relation between the object and the end. The end is valued as final, not as itself a means to further ends. And quite often it is only the status label or image associated with the object that is valued, rather than the actual object.

In the essay from which this passage is taken, the authors distinguish between two kinds of materialism and provide an extended explanation, using contrast and examples as methods of development. They are aware that the common perception of materialism — the love of things for their own sake — is a negative one. But this view, according to the authors, doesn't fully account for the attitudes of many Americans toward the things they own. There is, in fact, another more positive meaning that the authors call *instrumental materialism.* You will recognize that the authors are *stipulating* a meaning with which their readers might not be familiar. In their essay they distinguish between *terminal materialism,* in which "the object is valued only because it indicates an end in itself," and *instrumental materialism,* "the use of material objects to make life longer, safer, more enjoyable." Since *instrumental materialism* is the less familiar definition, the essay provides a great number of examples that show how people of three different generations value photographs, furniture, musical instruments, plants, and other objects for their memories and personal associations rather than as proof of the owners' ability to acquire the objects or win the approval of others.

THE DEFINITION ESSAY

The argumentative essay can take the form of an extended definition. An example of such an essay is the one from which we've just quoted, as well as the five essays at the end of this chapter. The definition essay is appropriate when the idea under consideration is so controversial or so heavy with historical connotations that even a paragraph or two cannot make clear exactly what the arguer wants his or her readers to understand. For example, if you were preparing a definition of *patriotism,* you would want to answer some or all of the following questions. You would probably use a number of methods to develop your definition: personal narrative, examples, stipulation, comparison and contrast, and cause-and-effect analysis.

1. *Dictionary definition.* Is the dictionary definition the one I will elaborate on? Do I need to stipulate other meanings?
2. *Personal history.* Where did I first acquire my notions of patriotism? What was taught? How and by whom was it taught?
3. *Cultural context.* Has my patriotic feeling changed in the last few years? Why or why not? Does my own patriotism reflect the mood of the country or the group to which I belong?
4. *Values.* What is the value of patriotism? Does it make me more humane, more civilized? Is patriotism consistent with tolerance of other systems and cultures? Is patriotism the highest duty of a citizen? Do any other values take precedence? What was the meaning of President Kennedy's injunction: "Ask not what your country can do for you; ask rather what you can do for your country"?
5. *Behavior.* How do I express my patriotism (or lack of it)? Can it be expressed through dissent? What sacrifice, if any, would I make for my country?

Writer's Guide to the Definition Paper

The following important steps should be taken when you write an essay of definition.

1. Choose a term that needs definition because it is controversial or ambiguous, or because you want to offer a personal definition that differs from the accepted interpretation. Explain why an extended definition is necessary. Or choose an experience that lends itself to treatment in an extended definition. One student defined *culture shock* as she had experienced it while studying abroad in Hawaii among students of a different ethnic background.
2. Decide on the thesis — the point of view you wish to develop about the term you are defining. If you want to define *heroism,* for example, you may choose to develop the idea that this quality depends on motivation and awareness of danger rather than on the specific act performed by the hero.
3. Begin by consulting the dictionary for the conventional definition, the one with which most readers will be familiar. Make clear whether you want to elaborate on the dictionary definition or take issue with it because you think it is misleading or inadequate.
4. Distinguish wherever possible between the term you are defining and other terms with which it might be confused. If you are defining *love,* can you make a clear distinction between the different kinds of emotional attachments contained in the word?
5. Try to think of several methods of developing the definition — using examples, comparison and contrast, analogy, cause-and-effect analysis. However, you may discover that one method alone — say, use of ex-

amples — will suffice to narrow and refine your definition. See the sample essay "The Nature of Prejudice" on page 135 for an example of such a development.

6. Arrange your supporting material in an order that gives emphasis to the most important ideas.

A NOTE ON COMPARISON AND CONTRAST

One writing assignment in this chapter calls for using comparison or contrast to clarify a term (page 122). But defining terms is not the only use for this argumentative strategy. We can use it to defend or refute all kinds of claims. Comparison is an obvious device for claims of value, in which we argue that one thing is better or worse than another. Advertisers, in their claims of policy, routinely contrast their own products with those of others.

Although we use two words — *compare* and *contrast* — to describe this form of development, the two processes are not really different. In fact, dictionaries list *contrast* as a synonym for *compare* because both words share this meaning: "to set side by side in order to show differences and likenesses." When we make a distinction, a comparison emphasizes likenesses, and a contrast emphasizes differences. But we would not undertake to compare things unless we suspected some contrasts. That is, you might compare headache remedies, but only if you thought there were differences among them.

A comparison-and-contrast essay observes two basic rules. First, it compares two things belonging to the same general class, as in the following questions: How does the 1998 movie *Psycho* compare with the 1960 version directed by Alfred Hitchcock? How do computer games compare with board games such as chess and checkers? How does bilingual education compare with English-only instruction? A popular admonition says, "You can't compare apples and oranges." But you *can* compare them because, like the subjects mentioned above, they share several significant characteristics. You can't compare apples and monkeys because they do not.

Notice that in the article "Addiction Is Not a Disease" (p. 119) the author finds a common element in the condition of disease; this allows him to stress the differences between "real" and "addictive" diseases. In "Gay Marriage, an Oxymoron" (p. 138), the shared element is marriage, which the author defines as possible only for heterosexuals. (An oxymoron is a contradiction.)

Second, the things you compare or contrast must be roughly of the same magnitude. Although Michael Jordan and the kid who shoots baskets in the driveway both play basketball, contrasting them would serve little purpose. Similarly, to compare crime in the

United States with crime in a small tribal society in the rain forest would not be effective.

All successful essays of comparison and contrast do more than simply list the distinguishing characteristics of the subjects. Good essays provide evidence to support their claim that the similarities or differences are meaningful. (No writer wants the reader to say, "So what?") The comparison or contrast should give readers new and useful information, answer a challenging question, lead them to a consideration of some larger issue or even guide them to a solution of a problem.

For example, a recent television newsmagazine report contrasted the upbringing of girls and boys in the United States. We learned that girls are allowed, even encouraged, to express and share their emotions. Boys, on the other hand, are discouraged from expressing them, especially if the emotions are fear or sadness. This was interesting information, but the reporter wanted to establish a reason for emphasizing the contrast. He went on to evaluate the consequences of these patterns for the well-being of boys. In other words, the contrast supported the conclusion that the upbringing of boys was creating serious problems for them that persisted into adulthood.

Another example of the use of comparison to support a controversial claim appears in the short debate at the end of Chapter 8. In arguing that American women soldiers are fit for combat service, Timothy C. Brown (p. 326) compares American with Nicaraguan women soldiers, who were active fighters in their country's civil wars. In response, several letter writers who do not share Brown's view challenge the validity of his comparison.

Writer's Guide to the Comparison Paper
Writing an Essay of Comparison or Contrast

1. Choose subjects worth reading about. Ask yourself: Is there some controversy or misunderstanding about the subject that needs to be clarified? Or some new information that might prove useful? It ought to be clear that you are comparing or contrasting to make an important point.
2. Make sure that the two or more subjects you choose are close enough in essential characteristics to lend themselves to this treatment.
3. Organize your essay in one of two ways. For relatively simple arguments, use the *block method,* in which you first assemble all the support material for one side and then assemble all the material for the other. For example, in a long essay arguing for gun control, one writer has chosen to contrast Seattle in the United States with Vancouver in Canada.[15]

---

[15]Claire Safran, "A Tale of Two Cities — and the Differences Guns Make," *Good Housekeeping,* November 1993.

In a short essay she might begin with this thesis statement: "The twin cities of Seattle and Vancouver resemble each other in many ways, but there is a life and death difference because guns are reasonably restricted in Vancouver but out of control in Seattle." This would be followed by several paragraphs about crime and gun control in Seattle, then several paragraphs about the same conditions in Vancouver. Her conclusion would offer an interpretation of her data. In a comparison-and-contrast essay with many points, your argument will probably be easier to follow if you use another kind of organization — the *alternating* or *point-by-point method*. With this form of development, relevant points of interest are presented, and each city's relationship to these topics is discussed. They might include crime rates, acquisitions of guns, gun injuries and deaths, and penalties for infractions. Which approach you choose depends on the subject and the length of your paper.

4. Use transitional expressions where necessary for coherence. For comparison, use words and phrases like *moreover, in addition, likewise,* and *also*. For contrast, use *but, unlike, however,* and *on the other hand*.

<u>SAMPLE ANNOTATED ANALYSIS</u>

Addiction Is Not a Disease
STANTON PEELE

Why Addiction Is Not a Disease

Medical schools are finally teaching about alcoholism; Johns Hopkins will require basic training for all students and clinicians. . . . Alcoholism, as a chronic disease, offers "a fantastic vehicle to teach other concepts," says Jean Kinney [of Dartmouth's Cork Institute]. . . . William Osler, Kinney remarks, coined the aphorism that "to know syphilis is

---

Stanton Peele, who received his Ph.D. in social psychology from the University of Michigan, is a fellow at the Lindsmith Center, a drug policy think tank in New York City. He is also the coauthor of the best-selling *Love and Addiction* (1975). This excerpt is from *Diseasing of America* (Boston: Houghton Mifflin, 1989).

to know medicine." . . . Now, she says, the same can be said of alcoholism.
— "The Neglected Disease in Medical Education," *Science*[1]

OCD (obsessive-compulsive disorder) is apparently rare in the general population.
— American Psychiatric Association, 1980[2]

The evidence is strong OCD is a common mental disorder that, like other stigmatized and hidden disorders in the past, may be ready for discovery and demands for treatment on a large scale.
— National Institute of Mental Health, 1988[3]

Statement of the problem: definition of addiction as a disease

Exaggeration of the problem

In America today, we are bombarded with news about drug and alcohol problems. We may ask ourselves, "How did we get here?" Alternatively, we may wonder if these problems are really worse now than they were five or ten years ago, or fifty or one hundred. Actually, in many cases the answer is no. Estimates of the number of alcoholics requiring treatment are wildly overblown, and reputable epidemiological researchers find that as little as 1 percent of the population fits the clinical definition of alcoholism — as opposed to the 10 percent figure regularly used by the alcoholism industry. Meanwhile, cocaine use is down. All indicators are that very few young people who try drugs ever become regular users, and fewer still get "hooked."

Real problems of drug users in the ghetto

Of course, we have real problems. The nightly news carries story after story of inner-city violence between crack gangs and of totally desolate urban envi-

---

[1]C. Holden, "The Neglected Disease in Medical Education," *Science* 229 (1985), pp. 741–742.

[2]*Diagnostic and Statistical Manual of Mental Disorders,* 3rd ed. (Washington, D.C.: American Psychiatric Association, 1980).

[3]M. Karno et al., "The Epidemiology of Obsessive-Compulsive Disorder in Five U.S. Communities," *Archives of General Psychiatry* 45 (1988), pp. 1094–1099.

ronments where drugs reign supreme. The cocaine problem has resolved itself — not exclusively, but very largely — into a ghetto problem, like many that face America. A *New York Times* front-page story based on an eight-year study of young drug users showed that those who abuse drugs have a number of serious background problems, and *that these problems don't disappear from their lives when they stop using drugs.*[4] In other words, the sources — and solutions — for what is going on in our ghettos are only very secondarily a matter of drug availability and use.

America is a society broken into two worlds. The reality of the crack epidemic and of inner cities and poor environments sometimes explodes and impinges un-

Broadening of the definition of addiction

pleasantly on our consciousness. For the most part, however, our reality is that of the middle class, which fills our magazines with health stories and warnings about family problems and the strivings of young professionals to find satisfaction. And for some time now, this other world has also focused on addiction. But this new addiction marketplace is only sometimes linked to alcohol and drugs. Even when it is, we have to redefine alcoholism as the new Betty Ford kind, which is marked by a general dull malaise, a sense that one is drinking too much, and — for many, like Betty Ford and Kitty Dukakis — relying on prescribed drugs to make life bearable.

However we define loss-of-control drinking, Betty Ford didn't experience it. But treating problems like hers and those of so many media stars is far more rewarding and profitable than trying to deal with street derelicts or ghetto addicts. At

---

[4]S. Blakeslee, "Eight-Year Study Finds Two Sides to Teen-Age Drug Use," *New York Times,* July 21, 1988, p. 1.

the same time, *everything can be an addiction.* This remarkable truth — which I first described in *Love and Addiction* in 1975 — has so overwhelmed us as a society that we have gone haywire. We want to pass laws to excuse compulsive gamblers when they embezzle money to gamble and to force insurance companies to pay to treat them. We want to treat people who can't find love and who instead (when they are women) go after dopey, superficial men or (when they are men) pursue endless sexual liaisons without finding true happiness. And we want to call all these things — and many, many more — addictions.

Since I was part of the movement to 5
label non-drug-related behaviors as addictions, what am I complaining about? My entire purpose in writing *Love and Addiction* was to explain addictions as part of a larger description of people's lives. Addiction is an experience that people can get caught up in but that still expresses their values, skills at living, and personal resolve — or lack of it. The label *addiction* does not obviate either the meaning of the addictive involvement within people's lives, or their responsibility for their misbehavior or for their choices in continuing the addiction. Forty million Americans have quit smoking. What, then, are we to think about the people who do not quit but who sue a tobacco company for addicting them to cigarettes after they learn they are going to die from a smoking-related ailment?

This discrepancy between understanding addiction within the larger context of a person's life and regarding it as an *explanation* of that life underlies my opposition to the "disease theory" of addiction, which I contest throughout this book. My view of addiction explicitly refutes this theory's contentions that (1) the addiction exists *independently* of the rest of a per-

Examples of the extremes

Claim: addiction as an expression of values

The opposing view that addiction is a disease

son's life and *drives* all of his or her choices; (2) it is progressive and irreversible, so that the addiction *inevitably worsens* unless the person seeks medical treatment or joins an AA-type support group; (3) addiction means the person is incapable of controlling his or her behavior, either in relation to the addictive object itself or — when the person is intoxicated or in pursuit of the addiction — in relation to the person's dealings with the rest of the world. Everything I oppose in the disease view is represented in the passive, *1984*-ish phrase, *alcohol abuse victim,* to replace *alcohol abuser.* On the contrary, this book maintains that people are *active agents* in — not passive victims of — their addictions.

Harmfulness of this view

While I do believe that a host of human habits and compulsions can be understood as addictions, I think the disease version of addiction does *at least* as much harm as good. An addiction does not mean that God in heaven decided which people are alcoholics and addicts. There is no biological urge to form addictions, one that we will someday find under a microscope and that will finally make sense of all these different cravings and idiocies (such as exercising to the point of injury or having sex with people who are bad for you). No medical treatment will ever be created to excise addictions from people's lives, and support groups that convince people that they are helpless and will forever be incapable of controlling an activity are better examples of self-fulfilling prophecies than of therapy.

Growth of an addiction industry

What is this new addiction industry meant to accomplish? More and more addictions are being discovered, and new addicts are being identified, until all of us will be locked into our own little addictive worlds with other addicts like ourselves, defined by the special interests of our neuroses. What a repugnant world to imagine, as well as a hopeless one. Meanwhile, *all of the addictions we define are increasing.* In the first place, we tell people they can never get better from their "diseases." In the second, we constantly find new addicts, looking for them in all sorts of new areas of behavior and labeling them at earlier ages on the basis of more casual or typical behaviors, such as getting drunk at holiday celebrations ("chemical-dependency disease") or checking to see whether they locked their car door ("obsessive-compulsive disorder").

Refutation of the opposing view: dangers in absolving people of responsibility

We must oppose this nonsense by understanding its sources and contradicting disease ideology. . . . Our society is going wrong in excusing crime, compelling people to undergo treatment, and wildly mixing up moral responsibility with disease diagnoses. Indeed, understanding the confusion and self-defeating behavior we display in this regard is perhaps the best way to analyze the failure of many of our contemporary social policies. . . . [We must] confront the actual social, psychological, and moral issues that we face as individuals and as a society — the ones we are constantly repressing and mislabeling through widening our disease nets. It is as though we were creating distorted microscopes that actually muddy our vision and that make our problems harder to resolve into components we can reasonably hope to deal with.

Definition of real disease

What are real diseases? If we are to distinguish between addiction and other diseases, then we first need to understand what have been called diseases historically and how these differ from what are being called diseases today. To do so, let us review three generations of diseases — physical ailments, mental disorders, and addictions.

a) Bodily symptoms

The *first* generation of diseases consists of disorders known through their physical manifestations, like malaria, tuberculosis, cancer, and AIDS. The era of medical understanding that these diseases ushered in began with the discovery of specific microbes that cause particular diseases and for which preventive inoculations — and eventually antibodies — were developed. These maladies are the ones we can unreservedly call diseases without clouding the issue. This first generation of diseases differs fundamentally from what were later called diseases in that the former are *defined by their measurable physical effects.* They are clearly connected to the functioning of the body, and our concern is with the damage the disease does to the body.

b) Behavioral symptoms

The *second* generation of diseases are the so-called mental illnesses (now referred to as emotional disorders). They are not defined in the same way as the first generation. Emotional disorders are apparent to us not because of what we measure in people's bodies but because of the feelings, thoughts, and behaviors that they produce in people, which we can only know from what the sufferers say and do. We do not diagnose emotional disorders from a brain scan; if a person cannot tell reality from fantasy, we call the person mentally ill, no matter what the person's EEG says.

Addiction as a different kind of disease — goal-directed

The *third* generation of diseases — addictions — strays still farther from the model of physical disorder to which the name *disease* was first applied by modern medicine. That is, unlike a mental illness such as schizophrenia, which is indicated by disordered thinking, addictive disorders *are known by the goal-directed behaviors they describe.* We call a person a drug addict who consumes drugs compulsively or excessively and whose life is devoted to seeking out these substances. If an addicted smoker gives up smoking or if a habituated coffee drinker decides to drink coffee only after Sunday dinner, then each ceases to be addicted. We cannot tell whether a person is addicted or will be addicted in the absence of the ongoing behavior — the person with a hypothetical alcoholic predisposition (say, one who has an alcoholic parent or whose face flushes when drinking) but who drinks occasionally and moderately is not an alcoholic.

Clarification of differences between real diseases and addiction

In order to clarify the differences between third-generation and first-generation diseases, we often have to overcome shifting definitions that have been changed solely for the purpose of obscuring crucial differences between problems like cancer and addiction. After a time, we seem not to recognize how our views have been manipulated by such gerrymandered disease criteria. For example, by claiming that alcoholics are alcoholics even if they haven't drunk for fifteen years, alcoholism is made to seem less tied to drinking behavior and more like cancer. Sometimes it seems necessary to remind ourselves of the obvious: that a person does not get over cancer by stopping a single behavior or even by changing a whole life-style, but the sole and essential indicator for successful remission of alcoholism is that the person ceases to drink.

Addictions involve appetites and behaviors. While a connection can be traced between individual and cultural beliefs and first- and second-generation diseases, this connection is most pronounced for addictions. Behaviors and appetites are addictions only in particular cultural contexts — obviously, obesity matters only where people have enough to eat and think it is important to be thin. Symptoms like loss-of-control drinking depend *completely* on cultural and personal meanings, and cultural groups that don't understand how people can lose control of their

Influence of culture on addiction

15

drinking are almost immune to alcoholism. What is most important, however, is not how cultural beliefs affect addictions but how our defining of addictions as diseases affects our views of ourselves as individuals and as a society. . . .

What Is Addiction, and How Do People Get It?

Definition of addiction: distinction between real diseases and addiction

While individual practitioners and recovering addicts — and the whole addiction movement — may believe they are helping people, they succeed principally at expanding their industry by finding more addicts and new types of addictions to treat. I too have argued — in books from *Love and Addiction* to *The Meaning of Addiction* — that addiction *can* take place with any human activity. Addiction is *not,* however, something people are born with. Nor is it a biological imperative, one that means the addicted individual is not able to consider or choose alternatives. The disease view of addiction is equally untrue when applied to gambling, compulsive sex, and everything else that it has been used to explain. Indeed, the fact that people become addicted to all these things *proves* that addiction is not *caused* by chemical or biological forces and that it is not a special disease state.

The nature of addiction: fulfillment of a need

The nature of addiction. People seek specific, essential human experiences from their addictive involvement, no matter whether it is drinking, eating, smoking, loving, shopping, or gambling. People can come to depend on such an involvement for these experiences until — in the extreme — the involvement is totally consuming and potentially destructive. Addiction can occasionally veer into total abandonment, as well as periodic excesses and loss of control. Nonetheless, even in cases where addicts die from their excesses, an addiction must be understood as a human response that is motivated by the addict's desires and principles. All addictions *accomplish something for the addict.* They are ways of coping with feelings and situations with which addicts cannot otherwise cope. What is wrong with disease theories as science is that they are *tautologies;* they avoid the work of understanding *why* people drink or smoke in favor of simply declaring these activities to be addictions, as in the statement "He drinks so much because he's an alcoholic."

Addicts seek experiences that satisfy needs they cannot otherwise fulfill. Any addiction involves three components — the person, the situation or environment, and the addictive involvement or experience (see Table 1). In addition to the individual, the situation, and the experience, we also need to consider the overall cultural and social factors that affect addiction in our society.

Social and cultural differences among addicts: comparison/contrast

The social and cultural milieu. We must also consider the enormous social-class differences in addiction rates. That is, the farther down the social and economic scale a person is, the more likely the person is to become addicted to alcohol, drugs, or cigarettes, to be obese, or to be a victim or perpetrator of family or sexual abuse. How does it come to be that addiction is a "disease" rooted in certain social experiences, and why in particular are drug addiction and alcoholism associated primarily with certain groups? A smaller range of addiction and behavioral problems are associated with the middle and upper social classes. These associations must also be explained. Some addictions, like shopping, are obviously connected with the middle class. Bulimia and exercise addiction are also primarily middle-class addictions.

TABLE 1

The Person	The Situation	The Addictive Experience
Unable to fulfill essential needs	Barren and deprived: disadvantaged social groups, war zones	Creates powerful and immediate sensations; focuses and absorbs attention
Values that support or do not counteract addiction: e.g., lack of achievement motivation	Antisocial peer groups	Provides artificial or temporary sense of self-worth, power, control, security, intimacy, accomplishment
Lack of restraint and inhibition	Absence of supportive social groups; disturbed family structure	
Lack of self-efficacy; sense of powerlessness vis-à-vis the addiction	Life situations: adolescence, temporary isolation, deprivation, or stress	Eliminates pain, uncertainty, and other negative sensations

Examples

Finally, we must explore why addictions of one kind or another appear on our social landscape all of sudden, almost as though floodgates were released. For example, alcoholism was unknown to most colonial Americans and to most Americans earlier in this century; now it dominates public attention. This is not due to greater consumption, since we are actually drinking *less* alcohol than the colonists did. Bulimia, PMS, shopping addiction, and exercise addiction are wholly new inventions. Not that it isn't possible to go back in time to find examples of things that appear to conform to these new diseases. Yet their widespread — almost commonplace — presence in today's society must be explained, especially when the disease — like alcoholism — is supposedly biologically inbred. . . . [20]

Addiction as an active expression of life choices

Are addicts disease victims? The development of an addictive life-style is an accumulation of patterns in people's lives of which drug use is neither a result nor a cause but another example. Sid Vicious was the consummate drug addict, an exception even among heroin users.

Support: examples

Nonetheless, we need to understand the extremes to gain a sense of the shape of the entire phenomenon of addiction. Vicious, rather than being a passive victim of drugs, seemed intent on being and remaining addicted. He avoided opportunities to escape and turned every aspect of his life toward his addictions — booze, Nancy, drugs — while sacrificing anything that might have rescued him — music, business interests, family, friendships, survival instincts. Vicious was pathetic; in a sense, he was a victim of his own life. But his addiction, like his life, was more an active expression of his pathos than a passive victimization.

Addiction theories have been created because it stuns us that people would hurt — perhaps destroy — themselves through drugs, drinking, sex, gambling, and so on. While people get caught up in an addictive dynamic over which they do not have full control, it is at least as accurate to say that people consciously select an addiction as it is to say an addiction has a person under its control. And this is why addiction is so hard to ferret out of the person's life — because it fits the person. The

More examples

bulimic woman who has found that self-induced vomiting helps her to control her weight and who feels more attractive after throwing up is a hard person to persuade to give up her habit voluntarily. Consider the homeless man who refused to go to one of Mayor Koch's New York City shelters because he couldn't easily drink there and who said, "I don't want to give up drinking; it's the only thing I've got."

Support: expert opinion

The researcher who has done the most to explore the personalities of alcoholics and drug addicts is psychologist Craig MacAndrew. MacAndrew developed the MAC scale, selected from items on the MMPI (a personality scale) that distinguish clinical alcoholics and drug abusers from normal subjects and from other psychiatric patients. This scale identifies antisocial impulsiveness and acting out: "an assertive, aggressive, pleasure-seeking character," in terms of which alcoholics and drug abusers closely "resemble criminals and delinquents."[5] These characteristics are not the *results* of substance abuse. Several studies have measured these traits in young men *prior* to [their] becoming alcoholics and in young drug and alcohol abusers.[6] This same kind of antisocial thrill-seeking characterizes most women who become alcoholic. Such women more often have disciplinary problems at school, react to boredom by "stirring up some kind of excitement," engage in more disapproved sexual practices, and have more trouble with the law.[7]

The typical alcoholic, then, fulfills antisocial drives and pursues immediate, sensual, and aggressive rewards while having underdeveloped inhibitions. *Support: results of a survey* MacAndrew also found that another, smaller group comprising both men and women alcoholics — but more often women — drank to alleviate internal conflicts and feelings like depression. This

[5]C. MacAndrew, "What the MAC Scale Tells Us about Men Alcoholics," *Journal of Studies on Alcohol* 42 (1981), p. 617.

[6]H. Hoffman, R. G. Loper, and M. L. Kammeier, "Identifying Future Alcoholics with MMPI Alcoholism Scores," *Quarterly Journal of Studies on Alcohol* 35 (1974), pp. 490–498; M. C. Jones, "Personality Correlates and Antecedents of Drinking Patterns in Adult Males," *Journal of Consulting and Clinical Psychology* 32 (1968), pp. 2–12; R. G. Loper, M. L. Kammeier, and H. Hoffman, "MMPI Characteristics of College Freshman Males Who Later Become Alcoholics," *Journal of Abnormal Psychology* 82 (1973), pp. 159–162; C. MacAndrew, "Toward the Psychometric Detection of Substance Misuse in Young Men," *Journal of Studies on Alcohol* 47 (1986), pp. 161–166.

[7]C. MacAndrew, "Similarities in the Self-Depictions of Female Alcoholics and Psychiatric Outpatients," *Journal of Studies on Alcohol* 47 (1986), pp. 478–484.

group of alcoholics viewed the world, in MacAndrew's words, "primarily in terms of its potentially punishing character." For them, "alcohol functions as a palliation for a chronically fearful, distressful internal state of affairs." While these drinkers also sought specific rewards in drinking, these rewards were defined more by internal states than by external behaviors. Nonetheless, we can see that this group too did not consider normal social strictures in pursuing feelings they desperately desired.

MacAndrew's approach in this research was to identify particular personality types identified by the experiences they looked to alcohol to provide. But even for alcoholics or addicts without *Examples of purposeful* such distinct personalities, the purposeful dynamic is at play. For example, in *The Lives of John Lennon,* Albert Goldman describes how Lennon — who was addicted over his career to a host of drugs — would get drunk when he went out to dinner with Yoko Ono so that he could spill out his resentments of her. In many families, drinking allows alcoholics to express emotions that they are otherwise unable to express. The entire panoply of feelings and behaviors that alcohol may bring about for individual drinkers thus can be motivations for chronic intoxication. While some desire power from drinking, others seek to escape in alcohol; for some drinking is the route to excitement, while others welcome its calming effects. 25

Emotional needs that are Alcoholics or addicts may have more *satisfied by addiction* emotional problems or more deprived backgrounds than others, but probably they are best characterized as feeling powerless to bring about the feelings they want or to accomplish their goals without drugs, alcohol, or some other involvement. Their sense of powerlessness then translates into the belief that the drug or alcohol is extremely powerful. They see in the substance the ability to accomplish what they need or want but can't do on their own. The double edge to this sword is that the person is easily convinced that he or she cannot function without the substance or addiction, that he or she requires it to survive. This sense of personal powerlessness, on the one hand, and of the extreme power of an involvement or substance, on the other, readily translates into addiction.[8]

Conclusion: addiction, unlike a real disease, as a means of coping with problems

People don't manage to become alcoholics over years of drinking simply because their bodies are playing tricks on them — say, by allowing them to imbibe more than is good for them without realizing it until they become dependent on booze. Alcoholics' long drinking careers are motivated by their search for essential experiences they cannot gain in other ways. The odd thing is that — despite a constant parade of newspaper and magazine articles and TV programs trying to convince us otherwise — most people recognize that alcoholics drink for specific purposes. Even alcoholics, however much they spout the party line, know this about themselves. Consider, for example, . . . Monica Wright, the head of a New York City treatment center, [who] describes how she drank over the twenty years of her alcoholic marriage to cope with her insecurity and with her inability to deal with her husband and children. It is impossible to find an alcoholic who does not express similar reasons for his or her drinking, once the disease dogma is peeled away. . . .

---

[8]G. A. Marlatt, "Alcohol, the Magic Elixir," in *Stress and Addiction,* ed. E. Gottheil et al. (New York: Brunner/Mazel, 1987); D. J. Rohsenow, "Alcoholics' Perceptions of Control," in *Identifying and Measuring Alcoholic Personality Characteristics,* ed. W. M. Cox (San Francisco: Jossey-Bass, 1983).

Analysis

Peele is not the only writer to take issue with the popular practice of defining all kinds of mental and social problems as addictions. (A recent satirical newspaper article is entitled, "It's Not Me That's Guilty. My Addiction Just Took Over.") Peele's definition probably can be disputed by many doctors, psychologists, and a powerful industry of self-appointed healers. But definitions that attack popular opinions are often the liveliest and most interesting both to read and to write. In addition, they may serve a useful purpose, even if they are misguided, in encouraging new thinking about apparently intractable problems.

In defense of a controversial definition, an author must do at least two things: (1) make clear why a new definition is needed — that is, why the old definition does not work to explain certain conditions — and (2) argue that the new definition offers a better explanation and may even lead to more effective solutions of a problem.

The first part of Peele's argument is definition by negation. (Notice the title of this section.) Peele insists that the number of drug and alcohol addicts among both the poor and the well-to-do is not nearly so large as practitioners would have it. Next, he points out that addiction is not an explanation of a person's life, as some have insisted, and does not mean that the addict is a victim to be absolved of responsibility for the consequences of his actions. Last, he provides the reasons that addiction is not a disease, basing his argument on the historic definition of disease as a bodily ailment whose physical effects are measurable. Defining mental illness and addiction as diseases is, Peele thinks, an evasion of the truth.

Some readers will question the narrowness of Peele's stipulation. Since the term *disease* has come to signify almost everywhere (including the dictionary) a disorder that need not be biological in origin, these readers may feel that Peele is attacking a nonexistent problem. But in the next section — "What Is Addiction?" — he elaborates on his major point: Addicts are not passive victims. Addiction is a choice, derived from the addict's desires and principles. Because this is the heart of the controversy, Peele devotes the rest of his essay to its development. In "The Nature of Addiction" he gives an overview of the motives that lead addicts to alcohol or drugs. Later, in "Are Addicts Disease Victims?" he enlarges on the descriptions of their behavior and identifies specific reasons for their actions. One of the strengths of his argument is the breadth of the analysis. In a few pages he touches on all the relevant causes of the addict's choices: the individual, the situation, the addictive experience, the social and cultural milieu.

The support for his claim is not exhaustive, but it offers a variety of evidence: examples of familiar individuals and types (Sid Vicious, John Lennon, the bulimic, the homeless man, the head of a treatment center), clear explanations of different kinds of addictive behavior, and a detailed summary of expert opinion.

All this evidence, if it is to work, must make an appeal to the common sense and experience of the reader. As Peele says, "The odd thing is that — despite a constant parade of newspaper and magazine articles and TV programs trying to convince us otherwise — most people recognize that alcoholics drink for specific purposes" (para. 27). Most readers, of course, will not be experts, but if they find the evidence consistent with their knowledge of and experience with addiction, they will find Peele's definition deserving of additional study.

READINGS FOR ANALYSIS

The Nature of Prejudice
GORDON ALLPORT

Before I attempt to define *prejudice,* let us have in mind four instances that I think we all would agree are prejudice.

The first is the case of the Cambridge University student who said, "I despise all Americans. But," he added, a bit puzzled, "I've never met one that I didn't like."

The second is the case of another Englishman, who said to an American, "I think you're awfully unfair in your treatment to Negroes. How *do* Americans feel about Negroes?" The American replied, "Well, I suppose some Americans feel about Negroes just the way you feel about the Irish." The Englishman said, "Oh, come now. The Negroes are human beings."

Then there's the incident that occasionally takes place in various parts of the world (in the West Indies, for example, I'm told). When an American walks down the street the natives conspicuously hold their noses till the American goes by. The case of odor is always interesting. Odor gets mixed up with prejudice because odor has great associative power. We know that some Chinese deplore the odor of Americans. Some white people think Negroes have a distinctive smell and vice versa. An intrepid psychologist recently did

---

Gordon Allport (1897–1967) was a psychologist who taught at Harvard University from 1924 until his death. He was the author of numerous books, among them *Personality: A Psychological Interpretation* (1937). Allport delivered "The Nature of Prejudice" at the Seventeenth Claremont Reading Conference in 1952. The speech was published as a paper in 1952 in the Seventeenth Claremont Reading Conference Yearbook.

an experiment; it went as follows. He brought to a gymnasium an equal number of white and colored students and had them take shower baths. When they were nice and clean he had them exercise vigorously for fifteen minutes. Then he brought his judges in, and each went to the sheeted figures and sniffed. They were to say "white" or "black," guessing at the identity of the subject. The experiment seemed to prove that when we are sweaty we all smell the same way. It's good to have experimental demonstration of the fact.

The fourth example I'd like to bring before you is a piece of writ- 5 ing that I quote. Please ask yourselves who, in your judgment, wrote it. It's a passage about the Jews.

> The synagogue is worse than a brothel. It's a den of scoundrels. It's a criminal assembly of Jews, a place of meeting for the assassins of Christ, a den of thieves, a house of ill fame, a dwelling of iniquity. Whatever name more horrible to be found, it could never be worse than the synagogue deserves.
>
> I would say the same things about their souls. Debauchery and drunkenness have brought them to the level of lusty goat and pig. They know only one thing: to satisfy their stomachs and get drunk, kill, and beat each other up. Why should we salute them? We should not even have the slightest converse with them. They are lustful, rapacious, greedy, perfidious robbers.

Now who wrote that? Perhaps you say Hitler, or Goebbels, or one of our local anti-Semites? No, it was written by Saint John Chrysostom, in the fourth century A.D. Saint John Chrysostom, as you know, gave us the first liturgy in the Christian church, still used in the Orthodox churches today. From it all services of the Holy Communion derive. Episcopalians will recognize him also as the author of that exalted prayer that closes the offices of both matins and evensong in the *Book of Common Prayer.* I include this incident to show how complex the problem is. Religious people are by no means necessarily free from prejudice. In this regard be patient even with our saints.

What do these four instances have in common? You notice that all of them indicate that somebody is "down" on somebody else — a feeling of rejection, or hostility. But also, in all these four instances, there is indication that the person is not "up" on his subject — not really informed about Americans, Irish, Jews, or bodily odors.

So I would offer, first a slang definition of prejudice: *Prejudice is being down on somebody you're not up on.* If you dislike slang, let me offer the same thought in the style of St. Thomas Aquinas. Thomists have defined prejudice as *thinking ill of others without sufficient warrant.*

You notice that both definitions, as well as the examples I gave, specify two ingredients of prejudice. First there is some sort of faulty generalization in thinking about a group. I'll call this the process of *categorization*. Then there is the negative, rejective, or hostile ingredient, a *feeling* tone. "Being down on something" is the hostile ingredient; "that you're not up on" is the categorization ingredient; "thinking ill of others" is the hostile ingredient; "without sufficient warrant" is the faulty categorization.

Parenthetically I should say that of course there is such a thing   10 as *positive* prejudice. We can be just as prejudiced *in favor of* as we are *against*. We can be biased in favor of our children, our neighborhood, or our college. Spinoza makes the distinction neatly. He says that *love prejudice* is "thinking well of others, through love, more than is right." *Hate prejudice,* he says, is "thinking ill of others, through hate, more than is right."

Reading and Discussion Questions

1. This was a speech, obviously not delivered extemporaneously but read to the audience. What characteristics suggest an oral presentation? If you were to revise this essay into a paper, what changes would you make? Why?
2. Allport has arranged his anecdotes carefully. What principle of organization has he used?
3. Allport says that "'thinking ill of others' is the hostile ingredient; 'without sufficient warrant' is the faulty categorization" (para. 9). How would you define the word "warrant" in this part of Allport's definition? How is it related to the definition given on page 11?
4. This essay was written in 1952. Are there any references or examples that seem dated? Why or why not?

Writing Suggestions

5. Some media critics claim that negative prejudice exists in the treatment of certain groups in movies and television. If you agree, select a group that seems to you to be the object of prejudice in these media, and offer evidence of the prejudice and the probable reasons for it. Or disagree with the media critics, and provide evidence that certain groups are *not* the object of prejudice.
6. Can you think of examples of what Allport calls *positive prejudice*? Perhaps you can find instances that are less obvious than the ones Allport mentions. Explain in what way these prejudices represent a love that is "more than is right" (para. 10).

Gay Marriage, an Oxymoron

LISA SCHIFFREN

As study after study and victim after victim testify to the social devastation of the sexual revolution, easy divorce, and out-of-wedlock motherhood, marriage is fashionable again. And parenthood has transformed many baby boomers into advocates of bourgeois norms.

Indeed, we have come so far that the surprise issue of the political season is whether homosexual "marriage" should be legalized. The Hawaii courts will likely rule that gay marriage is legal, and other states will be required to accept those marriages as valid.

Considering what a momentous change this would be — a radical redefinition of society's most fundamental institution — there has been almost no real debate. This is because the premise is unimaginable to many, and the forces of political correctness have descended on the discussion, raising the cost of opposition. But one may feel the same affection for one's homosexual friends and relatives as for any other, and be genuinely pleased for the happiness they derive from relationships, while opposing gay marriage for principled reasons.

"Same-sex marriage" is inherently incompatible with our culture's understanding of the institution. Marriage is essentially a lifelong compact between a man and woman committed to sexual exclusivity and the creation and nurture of offspring. For most Americans, the marital union — as distinguished from other sexual relationships and legal and economic partnerships — is imbued with an aspect of holiness. Though many of us are uncomfortable using religious language to discuss social and political issues, Judeo-Christian morality informs our view of family life.

Though it is not polite to mention it, what the Judeo-Christian 5 tradition has to say about homosexual unions could not be clearer. In a diverse, open society such as ours, tolerance of homosexuality is a necessity. But for many, its practice depends on a trick of cognitive dissonance that allows people to believe in the Judeo-Christian moral order while accepting, often with genuine regard, the different lives of homosexual acquaintances. That is why, though homosexuals may believe that they are merely seeking a small expansion of the definition of marriage, the majority of Americans perceive this change as a radical deconstruction of the institution.

Lisa Schiffren was a speechwriter for former vice president Dan Quayle. This essay appeared in the *New York Times* on March 23, 1996.

Some make the conservative argument that making marriage a civil right will bring stability, an end to promiscuity and a sense of fairness to gay men and women. But they miss the point. Society cares about stability in heterosexual unions because it is critical for raising healthy children and transmitting the values that are the basis of our culture.

Whether homosexual relationships endure is of little concern to society. That is also true of most childless marriages, harsh as it is to say. Society has wisely chosen not to differentiate between marriages, because it would require meddling into the motives and desires of everyone who applies for a license.

In traditional marriage, the tie that really binds for life is shared responsibility for the children. (A small fraction of gay couples may choose to raise children together, but such children are offspring of one partner and an outside contributor.) What will keep gay marriages together when individuals tire of each other?

Similarly, the argument that legal marriage will check promiscuity by gay males raises the question of how a "piece of paper" will do what the threat of AIDS has not. Lesbians seem to have little problem with monogamy, or the rest of what constitutes "domestication," despite the absence of official status.

Finally, there is the so-called fairness argument. The Government gives tax benefits, inheritance rights, and employee benefits only to the married. Again, these financial benefits exist to help couples raise children. Tax reform is an effective way to remove distinctions among earners. 10

If the American people are interested in a radical experiment with same-sex marriages, then subjecting it to the political process is the right route. For a court in Hawaii to assume that it has the power to radically redefine marriage is a stunning abuse of power. To present homosexual marriage as a fait accompli, without national debate, is a serious political error. A society struggling to recover from thirty years of weakened norms and broken families is not likely to respond gently to having an institution central to most people's lives altered.

Reading and Discussion Questions

1. Define the following terms: *oxymoron* (title), *political correctness* (para. 3), *cognitive dissonance* (para. 5). To better understand these terms, try to find other examples of them. Do you agree that political correctness and cognitive dissonance are issues in the debate over gay marriage?
2. Why does Schiffren think that the Hawaiian courts should not be allowed to legalize gay marriage? How does she think the question should be decided?
3. What, according to Schiffren, is the principal reason for marriage? Find the sentence that summarizes her definition. Is her defense of this view

convincing? (This definition will, in fact, constitute the warrant underlying her claim that gay marriages are inadmissible in our society.)

4. Schiffren emphasizes the religious or Judeo-Christian values symbolized in the marital union. Do you think that for most Americans marriage is "imbued with an aspect of holiness" (para. 4)? What evidence can you offer for or against this claim?

5. Schiffren provides at least three reasons against gay marriage. Which do you think is the strongest? The weakest? Can you tell from her discussion which reason the author believes is the most persuasive?

Writing Suggestions

6. Schiffren seems to suggest that the institution of heterosexual marriage has changed little in recent years. Based on what you know and have read about the marriages of previous generations, describe any changes that you observe in marriages today, and explain the reasons for these changes. Has marriage been redefined?

7. In many places in the world, certain kinds of marriages — such as marriages with multiple partners and marriages between close relatives — are prohibited. (You may want to research the arguments that were used against Mormon polygamy when Utah applied for statehood in 1890.) One writer contends that the same kinds of prohibitions should be extended to same-sex marriages, which he characterizes as "equally unnatural" or "harmful." Present your own definition of the institution, and then argue that the state does or does not have an interest in prohibiting some kinds of marriages.

I acquired the painting of my dreams.
Only to discover it was a brilliant forgery.

I bought stocks like they were going out of style.
And they were.

I married for love.
Then found I was being married for money.

I bought myself a Waterman.

There are some decisions one never lives to regret.

Pens write. A Waterman pen expresses. For more than a century, this distinction has remained constant. The creation shown here, for example, has been crafted from sterling silver, painstakingly tooled and balanced to absolute precision. Those who desire such an instrument of expression **()** *will find Waterman pens in a breadth of styles, prices and lacquers.*

*W*ATERMAN
PARIS

© 1989 Waterman Pen Company

Discussion Questions

1. This ad is divided into two parts. The part in small print extols the distinctive attributes of the Waterman pen. Why does the advertiser relegate the description of his pen to the small print?

2. How does the advertiser define a superior "instrument of expression"? Does calling a pen an "instrument of expression" add something to the definition?

3. What contrast is the reader invited to examine in the humorous first part of the ad?

Protect the Jury System, Judge Was the Problem

BARBARA ALLEN BABCOCK

"I personally would have a reasonable doubt, but it's true there is overwhelming evidence that he is possibly guilty."

This statement by an African American man, interviewed on TV shortly before the verdict [was announced] in the O. J. Simpson double-murder trial in October 1995, reveals the tension inherent in our jury system. "Overwhelming evidence" may lead only to the "possibility" of guilt, and in its face, the jury may still entertain sufficient reservations to acquit.

Juries may also make mistakes; may be swayed by passion, prejudice, and sympathy to acquit a guilty person; may misread the evidence, or misconstrue their duty. The first Simpson jurors to speak out seem to be saying that they took quite literally the judge's instruction that they might discount totally the evidence of police officers who lied in some respects. In a sense, they may have become the enforcers of exclusionary rules that many judges no longer follow. Even as individual jurors come forward, however, we are not likely to fully understand the dynamics that led to Simpson's acquittal.

But all who think, as I do, that this verdict is wrong, should not turn their frustration and anger on the criminal jury system itself. Far worse than letting a guilty man go free would be losing faith in, or working fundamental changes on, this most American of institutions.

Even before the Simpson verdicts were in . . . there were legisla- 5 tive moves afoot in California: to do away with the unanimity requirement; to reduce the number of jurors; to abolish peremptory challenges. There are two basic problems with these proposals: First, they rest on a faulty premise that the jury system is broken, and, second, they have the potential to change its operation profoundly in unpredictable ways.

Barbara Allen Babcock is a law professor at Stanford University and a former assistant attorney general under the Carter administration. This article was published in the *Los Angeles Times* on October 8, 1995.

The Price of Liberty

That the jury may make mistakes — or may express through its verdict community sentiment that is, at best, extra-legal — is part of the system, part of the price we pay to have a judgment of the people before we deprive anyone of all liberty. We have always, from the founding of the republic, been willing to sustain the risk that a jury will be wrong. Nothing in the Simpson verdicts changes that.

For every jury that goes awry, there are a hundred that do the right thing. Lawyers on both sides of the criminal system, former jurors, and most academics who have studied juries attest to this. I believe in juries based on my experience as a young lawyer, when I tried many cases — losing some and winning others, representing mostly African American men before mostly African American juries in Washington.

Though losing a verdict is one of life's crushing blows, in virtually all cases I saw close up, the jury made a correct, and wise, decision. More than occasionally, I found that jurors who started with one predisposition — sometimes ones I had chosen because I discerned it — changed their minds through the deliberations.

But no jury in my experience was so mistreated and abused as the Simpson jury. Indeed, it might well be that the mismanagement of the jury helped produce the acquittal. This is the second reason why this case should not be an occasion for sweeping changes: the law of unintended consequences.

We do not know what makes juries work well most of the time — 10 which feature is necessary to proper functioning. The jury comes with certain historical attributes: the mystical number 12; the absolute power, without accountability, to acquit; the judicial filtering of the evidence they will hear; the absence of merit-type qualifications of education or training for service; the requirement that they engage each other to the point of total agreement. No one knows which, if any, of these is essential to the integrity of the institution.

We do know, however, that a jury should be a group put together once in time for a single purpose, that it should be composed of strangers, who know each other only through their deliberations.

This fundamental feature was violated in the Simpson case by a star-struck judge who lost control of the situation. Judge Lance A. Ito caused the jury to spend many hours waiting while he heard and reheard lawyers' arguments, took time off to engage celebrities and, through it all, patronized the jurors — conveying by his tone and manner that their time was not important. He should have taken drastic measures to move the trial along — for example, he might have heard motions in the evenings and held court on Saturdays. Instead, by his leisurely approach, he violated the very premises of the jury and permitted the possibility that they would become a little band with their own agenda.

Legal Statutes and Their Consequences

But Ito, like the judges in most states, was largely on his own in deciding how to deal with this jury. The statutes, and common law, on the selection, care, and instruction of juries are a hodgepodge of piecemeal rules — some adopted in reaction to unpopular verdicts — without concern for how the system, as a whole, will be affected. The most recent addition, for instance, imposed by initiative, removed the right of lawyers to question potential jurors. By the report of both prosecutors and defenders, the unintended consequence of this law has been a dramatic increase in hung juries — because lawyers on both sides are unable to uncover through follow-up questions and direct contact those who may prove to be unreasonable outliers in jury deliberation.

Rather than such reactive legislation, a comprehensive statute that preserved the jury's basic attributes would be a good outcome of the Simpson verdicts. Such a statute should include, for example, provisions regularizing selection practices, including juror questionnaires tailored to the facts of the individual cases; provision for expedited procedures in cases of sequestration, and for more reasonable compensation and treatment of jurors.

Meanwhile, whether or not we agree with the Simpson verdict, 15 all should accept and respect it. The criminal jury system, right or wrong, is still one of our greatest and most characteristically American institutions. Like universal suffrage — a vote for every citizen regardless of class, race, or gender — the jury drawn from the community with absolute power to protect the accused from the state is fundamental to our democracy.

Why Our Jury System Is in Trouble

STEPHEN J. ADLER

As First Lady of the Philippines, Imelda Marcos was famous for throwing the most extraordinary parties. But the one she threw in New York City on July 14, 1990, may have been her most astonishing.

The guests of honor were none other than ten of the twelve jurors who had just cleared Marcos of charges that she had stolen hundreds of millions of dollars belonging to her own people.

"It was so beautiful," marveled juror Yvonne Granberry, 48, a teacher's aide from Harlem. Said another juror, 54-year-old postal worker Anna Sneed: "I can't get over what a simply lovely person Mrs. Marcos is."

Why had the jurors found the defendant so appealing, despite what many observers considered overwhelming evidence to the contrary? Answering that question may uncover one of our legal system's greatest inadequacies: jury stacking. Some jurors succumb too easily to emotional appeals. Some are stymied by complexity. Some filter facts through prejudice. And this isn't always by accident. Through the deceptive, frequently cynical process of jury selection, lawyers can and often do steer some of the least capable and least fair-minded people onto important cases. This helps explain why so many jury verdicts seem to defy logic, reality, and the law.

Lawyers eliminate prospective jurors they believe will be unfavorable by using so-called peremptory challenges, which allow them to reject a limited number of candidates without giving any reason. In the Marcos case the prosecution had six such challenges, while the defense team had ten for Imelda Marcos and her co-defendant, Saudi Arabian arms merchant Adnan Khashoggi, charged with obstruction of justice and mail fraud.

The challenges would all be exercised after the judge's and lawyers' interviews with each prospective juror, the so-called voir dire, translated variously as "to speak the truth" or "true talk." These interviews began Tuesday, March 20, 1990. There were quite a few alert and well-informed juror candidates that morning; the voir dire would eliminate many of them.

Stephen J. Adler was legal editor for the *Wall Street Journal* for six years. This article, which appeared in *Reader's Digest* in December 1994, is condensed from his book *The Jury: Trial and Error in the American Courtroom* (1994).

Chemist David Gong, like other prospects, had filled out a 32-page background questionnaire. It revealed that he liked to read *Science* magazine and didn't watch much TV. He knew that Ferdinand Marcos was the former president of the Philippines and that Imelda Marcos owned an abundance of shoes. But he said that he wouldn't hold this against her because the whole subject was trivial. He was intelligent, respectful, and articulate.

He didn't make it. Khashoggi lawyer James P. Linn wanted to avoid people who tended to be too exacting, not seeing the gray areas of life. Gong came across as too analytical.

Another mark against Gong was that he was Asian. Defense attorneys felt that he would believe in hierarchies and respect authority.

Prospective juror Zachary Berman, 49, had a graduate degree in 10 urban planning and a job with a child-protection agency, investigating abuse. He knew that Khashoggi was wealthy, but he said he had no preconceived ideas about guilt or innocence and had no ill feelings toward Arabs.

Khashoggi lawyers insisted that Berman be struck because he is Jewish. Explained one defense lawyer: "When an American Jew thinks of an Arabian arms trader, he doesn't think of a friend."

Most experienced lawyers pride themselves on spotting favorable jurors, often by relying on ethnic, class, and racial stereotypes, and Khashoggi lawyer Linn was no exception.

A common characteristic of many of the jurors chosen was that they were ill-informed about public affairs, just as the defense had hoped. Pretrial publicity had been consistently negative toward Imelda Marcos. Cartoons made fun of her fondness for shoes. Anyone aware of the media's version, Marcos's attorney, Gerry Spence, would explain later, "had a preconceived prejudice against my client. Even I did."

One of the jurors chosen was Ted Kutzy, a 25-year-old electrical engineer who liked to watch *The Simpsons.* Kutzy said he'd never bought a newspaper, never watched TV news, never heard of Imelda Marcos. The defense lawyers were delighted.

Another chosen was Llewellyn White, a 49-year-old native of 15 Montserrat in the Caribbean and a subway motorman with the New York City Transit Authority. His brother had been shot less than three months earlier, and the killer had not been caught. Asked by Judge John F. Keenan whether that would affect his objectivity, White said, "No, Your Honor, not at all."

But the defense team was nearly certain that White would view the case as a misuse of the criminal-justice system that diverted resources away from street crime. In fact, they planned to attack the prosecution's case partly on the ground that it was a waste of taxpayers' money and courtroom time. "We all agreed he had to stay," a defense lawyer said.

In addition, the lawyers figured that since White had lived for twenty years in a Third World country, he would know that U.S. standards of political corruption aren't necessarily those of other countries. He might prefer not to impose American laws on foreign defendants.

Juror Alan Belofsky described his parents' background as "Jewish/European," an obvious red flag to the Khashoggi lawyers. In addition, his tone of voice and body language were all wrong in a case in which the defense needed sympathy. He was constantly frowning.

But Belofsky was a union man, and Spence was pro-union. Moreover, Spence had his own collection of stereotypes. He favored having Jews on juries because he viewed them as sensitive to persecution. He preferred men to women because he believed men are more forgiving of others' mistakes.

In addition, Belofsky seemed stubborn and argumentative. That 20
made him a potential "hanger" — someone who might hold out and force a hung jury and a mistrial. Despite everyone else's misgivings, Spence insisted that Belofsky must serve.

The trial began on April 3, 1990. The charges came down to this: Imelda Marcos had joined her late husband, the longtime president of the Philippines, in looting the Philippine economy and stashing the money in secret bank accounts. Then she had spent millions on jewelry, real estate, including a $30 million office tower and a $6 million art collection.

After the dictatorship was overthrown, the Marcoses had fled to Hawaii, transferring buildings and artwork they had accumulated in the United States to Khashoggi. Documents had been backdated in an effort to evade a U.S. court freeze on those assets.

The case against Imelda seemed strong. The jurors, however, weren't buying. Sometimes the evidence got lost in the muddle of monetary transactions. But it wasn't just the complexity of the case. Some jurors simply liked Imelda Marcos and felt sorry for her.

Her lawyer, Spence, had sketched her as a decent, generous, and persecuted woman. There she sat each day, dressed somberly in black, fingering her rosary beads, sometimes dabbing away tears with a black, lace-trimmed handkerchief. At one point she sobbed on Spence's shoulder, and the trial was delayed because her blood pressure had risen perilously high.

A few days later Marcos fainted, and the trial was postponed for 25
a week. By that time juror Yvonne Granberry, the teacher's aide, didn't believe Imelda was wicked or cruel. "She always seemed

warm to me," Granberry said. Added postal clerk Anna Sneed, "She didn't seem like a person who would scheme and cheat people. I thought, 'Why are they harassing this sick woman?'"

When the jurors met on Thursday, June 28, 1990, Alan Belofsky was the first to speak. "Imelda was spending money like there's no tomorrow, and she went to a lot of trouble to disguise that. Why would she do that if she thought it was all legitimate?"

Belofsky added that it was clear Ferdinand Marcos had skimmed money off the top of government contracts for years. Meanwhile, Imelda Marcos had been mayor of Manila and had been deeply involved in governmental affairs. "Spence is asking me to believe she's spending all this money and she's not asking where it is coming from." How could she not have known the source of her nearly inexhaustible wealth?

Expecting support for what seemed to him an obvious conclusion, Belofsky was met instead with disagreement, even derision. Just as the defense surmised, White scoffed at the notion that it was illegal for potentates such as Ferdinand Marcos to demand a percentage of businesses' profits. "If you're head of a Third World country, you're it."

Jury forewoman Catherine Balton, a 62-year-old retired office manager, called for a show of hands. The initial vote: 10–2 for acquittal. Only Balton had joined Belofsky.

The next day deliberations grew testier. Belofsky was reduced to 30 asserting, again and again, that Marcos simply must have known what was going on. "Can't you see that Spence was lying?" he'd ask, his voice rising.

Some jurors just laughed. Responded Sandra Alberts, a 39-year-old paralegal, "Don't even listen to the lawyers. They sit around and plot all day with smirks on their faces when they come up with a good idea. Spence can tell us anything. He's not on trial."

Balton also had trouble believing that Imelda Marcos knew nothing about her husband's life of crime. Yet despite the factual evidence of Imelda's extraordinary involvement in her nation's government, other jurors whispered among themselves that because Balton wasn't married, she simply didn't understand how many secrets spouses keep from each other.

Alberts spoke to Balton about her own husband, who would sometimes go off to meetings, and she wouldn't know for sure what he was doing.

"Sandy talked to her real nice," recalls Anna Sneed. "She said it wasn't all cut-and-dried in a marriage. Catherine just loved Sandy and listened to her."

This friendly persuasion seemed to be taking hold. Balton finally 35 changed her vote, not wanting the trial to end in a hung jury.

Belofsky repeated his refrain that on the basis of the evidence, Imelda must have known about her husband's activities. But by Monday, July 2, he was thoroughly disillusioned and frustrated that the other jurors were no longer bothering to listen to his arguments. "It was a holiday weekend," he said afterward. "I wanted to get out. I just rolled with the punches."

When the jury took its final vote that day, the tally was 12–0.

Imelda Marcos was ready to party.

How to Build a Better Jury System

The law says that jury pools must represent a fair cross-section of the population, but voter-registration records, still the sole source of jury lists in 16 states and most federal courts, include only about 70 percent of the adult population. In the future, more state court systems should cull potential jurors from driving and tax records as well.

Many individuals today ignore jury notices; the no-show rate 40 reaches 55 percent in some cities. Court officials should make jury duty more convenient — for example, by allowing people to call each day to see if they're needed and letting them go about their business if they're not. But convenience must be accompanied by firmness; for the most part, jury service should be nonnegotiable.

Most important, peremptory challenges must be eliminated so that lawyers can't manipulate the composition of juries. It's already been done in Great Britain, and now jury selection there takes a matter of minutes or hours, instead of the days or even weeks in America.

With peremptory challenges eliminated, black and white, young and old, transit worker and physicist would all be treated alike. Rather than wonder why they were excluded and doubt the fairness of the system, millions among the formerly spurned would finally get their chance to exercise direct power in a democracy.

Discussion Questions

1. What reasons does Babcock give for defending the jury system even though she disagrees with the jury's verdict in the O. J. Simpson trial?
2. What kinds of changes does she advocate to preserve the basic attributes of the jury system?
3. Babcock and Adler each use a single trial as an example of a jury in operation. Is this an effective argumentative strategy? Why or why not?
4. What elements of the jury selection system does Adler criticize? According to Adler, how do these deficiencies prevent the delivery of justice?

Taking the Debate Online

- **Fully Informed Jury Association: The Independent Jury's Secret Power** <http://www.saf.org/pub/rkba/mirror/whitehouse/political-science/fully-informed-juries/doigart.txt> Don Doig, national coordinator of the Fully Informed Jury Association, investigates the history of the role of the jury, claiming that the jury has the right to judge the law itself and to refuse to condemn the accused if the law can be proven flawed.

- **National Association of Criminal Defense Lawyers: Legislative Priorities** <http://www.criminaljustice.org/LEGIS/priority.htm> This site discusses a number of issues in U.S. crime policy, including grand jury reform, with a goal of achieving a humane and compassionate criminal justice policy for the United States.

- **National Center for Policy Analysis — Idea House: How to Improve American Justice?** <http://www.ncpa.org/~ncpa/oped/dupont/nov2697.html> This opinion editorial of November 26, 1997, from Pete du Pont admits that our legal system is flawed and suggests some improvements to our judicial procedures — especially the jury.

- **Koch Crime Institute Review** <http://www.kci.org/newsletter/1998/nov/criminal_law.htm> This site gathers the comments of criminal court judges from fifteen states who have joined together to analyze the state of criminal law today and to help shape what it should be in the future.

- **First Worldwide Common Law Judicial Conference** <http://www.primenet.com/~jldc/1stWorldwide/doc22.html> This lengthy essay by Sandra Day O'Connor, associate justice of the U.S. Supreme Court, is entitled "Juries: They May Be Broke, But We Can Fix Them."

- **Santa Barbara News-Press: In Defense of the American Jury System** <http://www.west.net/~insight/london/jury.htm> This article written by Scott London for the October 24, 1995, issue of the News-Press, stresses the need to "strengthen the tradition of ordinary people brokering the disputes of their neighbors."

Exercises

1. Choose one of the following statements, and define the italicized term. Make the context as specific as possible (for example, by referring to the Declaration of Independence or your own experience).
   a. All men are created *equal.*
   b. I believe in *God.*
   c. This school doesn't offer a *liberal education.*
   d. The marine corps needs *good men.*
   e. *Friends* is a *better* television show than *Just Shoot Me.*
2. Many recent controversial movements and causes are identified by terms that have come to mean different things to different people.

Choose one of the following and define it, explaining both the favorable and unfavorable connotations of the term. Use examples to clarify the meaning.

a. comparative worth
b. Palestinian homeland
c. affirmative action
d. codependency
e. nationalism

3. Choose two words that are sometimes confused, and define them to make their differences clear. *Examples:* authoritarianism and totalitarianism, envy and jealousy, sympathy and pity, cult and established church, justice and equality, liberal and radical, agnostic and atheist.

4. Define *good parent, good teacher,* or *good husband* or *wife.* Try to uncover the assumptions on which your definition is based. (For example, in defining a good teacher, students sometimes mention the ability of the teacher to maintain order. Does this mean that the teacher alone is responsible for classroom order?)

5. Define any popular form of entertainment, such as *soap opera, western, detective story,* or *science fiction story* or *film.* Support your definition with references to specific shows or books. *Or* define an idealized type from fiction, film, the stage, advertising, or television, describing the chief attributes of that type and the principal reasons for its popularity.

6. From your own experience write an essay describing a serious misunderstanding that arose because two people had different meanings for a term they were using.

7. Write about an important or widely used term whose meaning has changed since you first learned it. Such terms often come from the slang of particular groups: drug users, rock music fans, musicians, athletes, computer programmers, or software developers.

8. Define the differences between *necessities, comforts,* and *luxuries.* Consider how they have changed over time.

Critical Listening

9. Listen for several nights to the local or national news on television or radio. Keep a record of the *kinds* of news items that are repeated. How do you think *news* is defined by the broadcasters? Is it relevant that radio, television, and film have been characterized as the "dramatic media"? Is the definition of *broadcast news* different from *print news*? If so, how do you account for it?

10. You and your friends have probably often argued about subjects that required definition — for example, a good teacher, a good parent, a good popular singer or band, a good movie or television show. Think of a specific discussion. Were you able to reach agreement? How did the acts of listening and talking affect the outcome?

CHAPTER FIVE

Support

TYPES OF SUPPORT: EVIDENCE AND APPEALS TO NEEDS AND VALUES

All the claims you make — whether of fact, of value, or of policy — must be supported. Support for a claim represents the answer to the question, "What have you got to go on?"[1] There are two basic kinds of support in an argument: evidence and appeals to needs and values.

Evidence, as one dictionary defines it, is "something that tends to prove; ground for belief." When you provide evidence, you use facts, including statistics, and opinions, or interpretations of facts — both your own and those of experts. In the following conversation, the first speaker offers facts and the opinion of an expert to convince the second speaker that robots are exceptional machines.

> *"You know, robots do a lot more than work on assembly lines in factories."*
>
> *"Like what?"*
>
> *"They shear sheep, pick citrus fruit, and even assist in neurosurgery. And by the end of the century, every house will have a robot slave."*
>
> *"No kidding. Who says so?"*
>
> *"An engineer who's the head of the world's largest manufacturer of industrial robots."*

---

[1]Stephen Toulmin, *The Uses of Argument* (Cambridge: Cambridge University Press, 1958), p. 98.

A writer often appeals to readers' needs (that is, requirements for physical and psychological survival and well-being) and values (or standards for right and wrong, good and bad). In the following conversation, the first speaker makes an appeal to the universal need for self-esteem and to the principle of helping others, a value the second speaker probably shares.

"I think you ought to come help us at the nursing home. We need an extra hand."

"I'd like to, but I really don't have the time."

"You could give us an hour a week, couldn't you? Think how good you'd feel about helping out, and the old people would be so grateful. Some of them are very lonely."

Although they use the same kinds of support, conversations are less rigorous than arguments addressed to larger audiences in academic or public situations. In the debates on public policy that appear in the media and in the courts, the quality of support can be crucial in settling urgent matters. The following summary of a well-known court case demonstrates the critical use of both evidence and value appeals in the support of opposing claims.

On March 30, 1981, President Ronald Reagan and three other men were shot by John W. Hinckley, Jr., a young drifter from a wealthy Colorado family. Hinckley was arrested at the scene of the shooting. In his trial the factual evidence was presented first: Dozens of reliable witnesses had seen the shooting at close range. Hinckley's diaries, letters, and poems revealed that he had planned the shooting to impress actress Jodie Foster. Opinions, consisting of testimony by experts, were introduced by both the defense and the prosecution. This evidence was contradictory. Defense attorneys produced several psychiatrists who defined Hinckley as insane. If this interpretation of his conduct convinced the jury, then Hinckley would be confined to a mental hospital rather than a prison. The prosecution introduced psychiatrists who interpreted Hinckley's motives and actions as those of a man who knew what he was doing and knew it was wrong. They claimed he was *not* insane by legal definition. The fact that experts can make differing conclusions about the meaning of the same information indicates that interpretations are less reliable than other kinds of support.

Finally, the defense made an appeal to the moral values of the jury. Under the law, criminals judged to be insane are not to be punished as harshly as criminals judged to be sane. The laws assume that criminals who cannot be held responsible for their actions are entitled to more compassionate treatment, confinement to a mental hospital rather than prison. The jury accepted the interpretive

evidence supporting the claim of the defense, and Hinckley was pronounced not guilty by reason of insanity. Clearly the moral concern
for the rights of the insane proved to be decisive.

In your arguments you will advance your claims, not unlike a
lawyer, with these same kinds of support. But before you begin, you
should ask two questions: Which kind of support should I use in convincing an audience to accept my claim? and How do I decide that
each item of support is valid and worthy of acceptance? This chapter presents the different types of evidence and appeals you can use
to support your claim and examines the criteria by which you can
evaluate the soundness of that support.

EVIDENCE

Factual Evidence

In Chapter 3, we defined facts as statements possessing a high
degree of public acceptance. In theory, facts can be verified by experience alone. Eating too much will make us sick; we can get from
Hopkinton to Boston in a half hour by car; in the Northern Hemisphere it is colder in December than in July. The experience of any
individual is limited in both time and space, so we must accept as
fact thousands of assertions about the world that we ourselves can
never verify. Thus we accept the report that human beings landed
on the moon in 1969 because we trust those who can verify it.
(Country people in Morocco, however, received the news with disbelief because they had no reason to trust the reporters of the
event. They insisted on trusting their senses instead. One man said,
"I can see the moon very clearly. If a man were walking around up
there, wouldn't I be able to see him?")

Factual evidence appears most frequently as examples and statistics, which are a numerical form of examples.

Examples

Examples are the most familiar kind of factual evidence. In addition to providing support for the truth of a generalization, examples
can enliven otherwise dense or monotonous prose.

In the following paragraph the writer supports the claim in the
topic sentence by offering a series of specific examples. (The article
claims that most airport security is useless.)

> Meanwhile, seven hijacking incidents occurred last year (twenty-
> one in 1980 and eleven the year before), despite the security system.
> Two involved the use of flammable liquids. . . . In four other cases, hi-
> jackers claimed to have flammables or explosives but turned out to be

bluffing. In the only incident involving a gun, a man brushed past the security system and brandished the weapon on the plane before being wrestled to the ground. One other hijacking was aborted on the ground, and the remaining five were concluded after some expense, fright, and delay — but no injuries or deaths.[2]

Hypothetical examples, which create imaginary situations for the audience and encourage them to visualize what might happen under certain circumstances, can also be effective. The following paragraph, taken from the same article as the preceding paragraph, illustrates the use of hypothetical examples.

But weapons can get through nonetheless. Some are simply overlooked; imagine being one of those 10,000 "screeners" staring at X-rayed baggage, day in and day out. Besides, a gun can be broken down into unrecognizable parts and reassembled past the checkpoint. A hand grenade can be hidden in an aerosol shaving-cream can or a photographer's lens case. The ingredients of a Molotov cocktail can be carried on quite openly; any bottle of, say, duty-free liquor or perfume can be emptied and refilled with gasoline. And the possibilities for bluffing should not be forgotten; once on board, anyone could claim that a bottle of water was really a Molotov cocktail, or that a paper bag contained a bomb.[3]

All claims about vague or abstract terms would be boring or unintelligible without examples to illuminate them. For example, if you claim that a movie contains "unusual sound effects," you will certainly have to describe some of the effects to convince the reader that your generalization can be trusted.

Statistics

Statistics express information in numbers. In the following example statistics have been used to express raw data in numerical form.

Surveys have shown that almost half of all male high school seniors — and nearly 20 percent of all ninth grade boys — can be called "problem drinkers." . . . Over 5,000 teenagers are killed yearly in auto accidents due to drunken driving.[4]

These grim numbers probably have meaning for you, partly because you already know that alcoholism exists even among young teenagers and partly because your own experience enables you to evaluate the numbers. But if you are unfamiliar with the subject, such numbers

---

[2]Patrick Brogan, "The $310 Million Paranoia Subsidy," *Harper's,* September 1982, p. 18.

[3]Ibid.

[4]"The Kinds of Drugs Kids Are Getting Into" (Spring House, Pa.: McNeil Pharmaceutical, n.d.).

may be difficult or impossible to understand. Statistics, therefore, are more effective in comparisons that indicate whether a quantity is relatively large or small and sometimes even whether a reader should interpret the result as gratifying or disappointing. For example, if a novice gambler were told that for every dollar wagered in a state lottery, 50 percent goes back to the players as prizes, would the gambler be able to conclude that the percentage is high or low? Would he be able to choose between playing the state lottery and playing a casino game? Unless he had more information, probably not. But if he were informed that in casino games, the return to the players is over 90 percent and in slot machines and racetracks the return is around 80 percent, the comparison would enable him to evaluate the meaning of the 50 percent return in the state lottery and even to make a decision about where to gamble his money.[5]

Comparative statistics are also useful for measurements over time. A national survey by The Institute for Social Research of the University of Michigan, in which 17,000 of the nation's 2.7 million high school seniors were questioned about their use of drugs, revealed a continuing downward trend.

> 50.9 percent of those questioned in 1989 reported that they had at least tried an illicit drug like marijuana or cocaine, as against 53.9 percent in 1988 and 56.6 percent in 1987.[6]

Diagrams, tables, charts, and graphs can make clear the relations among many sets of numbers. Such charts and diagrams allow readers to grasp the information more easily than if it were presented in paragraph form. The bar graph[7] that is shown on page 157 summarizes the information produced by a poll on gambling habits. A pie chart[8] such as the one on page 158 can also clarify lists of data.

Opinions: Interpretations of the Facts

We have seen how opinions of experts influenced the verdict in the trial of John Hinckley. Facts alone were not enough to substantiate the claim that Hinckley was guilty of attempted assassination. Both the defense and the prosecution relied on experts — psychiatrists — to interpret the facts. Opinions or interpretations about the facts are the inferences discussed in Chapter 3. They are an indispensable source of support for your claims.

Suppose a nightclub for teenagers has opened in your town. That is a fact. What is the significance of it? Is the club's existence

---

[5]Curt Suphee, "Lotto Baloney," *Harper's,* July 1983, p. 201.
[6]*New York Times,* February 14, 1990, sec. A, p. 16.
[7]*New York Times,* May 28, 1989, p. 24.
[8]*Wall Street Journal,* February 2, 1990, sec. B, p. 1.

Want to Bet?

Please tell me whether or not you have done any of the following in the past 12 months:

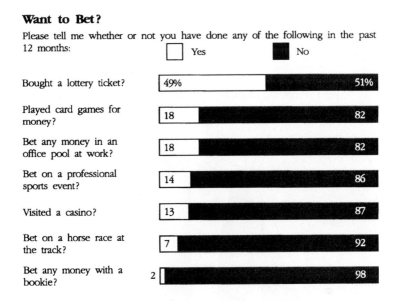

| | Yes | | No |

Bought a lottery ticket?	49%	51%
Played card games for money?	18	82
Bet any money in an office pool at work?	18	82
Bet on a professional sports event?	14	86
Visited a casino?	13	87
Bet on a horse race at the track?	7	92
Bet any money with a bookie?	2	98

Based on a phone survey of 1,412 people nationwide conducted April 13–16, 1989.

Bar graph

good or bad? What consequences will it have for the community? Some parents oppose the idea of a nightclub, fearing that it may allow teenagers to escape from parental control and engage in dangerous activities. Other parents approve of a club, hoping that it will serve as a substitute for unsupervised congregation in the streets. The importance of these interpretations is that they, not the fact itself, help people decide what actions they should take. If the community accepts the interpretation that the club is a source of delinquency, they may decide to revoke the owner's license and close it. As one writer puts it, "The interpretation of data becomes a struggle over power."

Opinions or interpretations of facts generally take three forms: (1) They may suggest the cause for a condition or a causal connection between two sets of data; (2) they may offer predictions about the future; (3) they may suggest solutions to a problem.

1. Causal Connection

Anorexia is a serious, sometimes fatal, disease characterized by self-starvation. It is found largely among young women. Physicians, psychologists, and social scientists have speculated about the causes, which remain unclear. A leading researcher in the field, Hilde Bruch, believes that food refusal expresses a desire to postpone sexual development. Another authority, Joan Blumberg,

Plastic that Goes to Waste

Components of municipal solid waste, by volume

Types of plastic in municipal solid waste, by weight

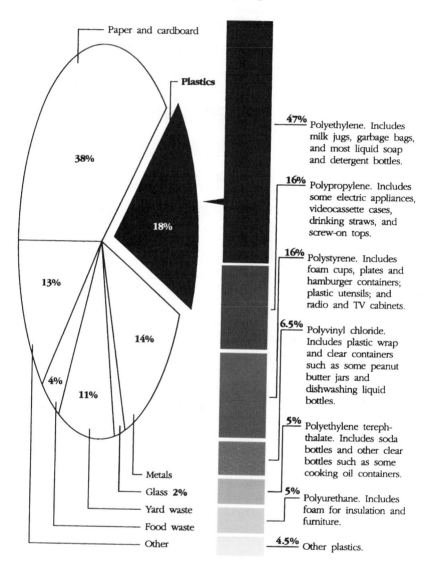

Paper and cardboard

Plastics

38%

18%

13%

14%

4%

11%

Metals

Glass 2%

Yard waste

Food waste

Other

47% Polyethylene. Includes milk jugs, garbage bags, and most liquid soap and detergent bottles.

16% Polypropylene. Includes some electric appliances, videocassette cases, drinking straws, and screw-on tops.

16% Polystyrene. Includes foam cups, plates and hamburger containers; plastic utensils; and radio and TV cabinets.

6.5% Polyvinyl chloride. Includes plastic wrap and clear containers such as some peanut butter jars and dishwashing liquid bottles.

5% Polyethylene terephthalate. Includes soda bottles and other clear bottles such as some cooking oil containers.

5% Polyurethane. Includes foam for insulation and furniture.

4.5% Other plastics.

Source: Franklin Associates Ltd.

Pie chart

believes that one cause may be biological, a nervous dysfunction of the hypothalamus. Still others infer that the causes are cultural, a response to the admiration of the thin female body.[9]

2. Predictions about the Future

In the fall and winter of 1989–90 extraordinary events shook Eastern Europe, toppling Communist regimes and raising more popular forms of government. Politicians and scholars offered predictions about future changes in the region. One expert, Zbigniew Brzezinski, former national security adviser under President Carter, concluded that the changes for the Soviet Union might be destructive.

> It would be a mistake to see the recent decisions as marking a breakthrough for democracy. Much more likely is a prolonged period of democratizing chaos. One will see the rise in the Soviet Union of increasingly irreconcilable conflicts between varying national political and social aspirations, all united by a shared hatred for the existing Communist nomenklatura. One is also likely to see a flashback of a nationalist type among the Great Russians, fearful of the prospective breakup of the existing Great Russian Empire.[10]

3. Solutions to Problems

How shall we solve the problems caused by young people in our cities "who commit crimes and create the staggering statistics in teenage pregnancies and the high abortion rate"? The minister emeritus of the Abyssinian Baptist Church in New York City proposes establishment of a national youth academy with fifty campuses on inactive military bases. "It is a 'parenting' institution. . . . It is not a penal institution, not a prep school, not a Job Corps Center, not a Civilian Conservation Camp, but it borrows from them." Although such an institution has not been tried before, the author of the proposal thinks that it would represent an effort "to provide for the academic, moral, and social development of young people, to cause them to become responsible and productive citizens."[11]

Expert Opinion

For many of the subjects you discuss and write about, you will find it necessary to accept and use the opinions of experts. Based on their reading of the facts, experts express opinions on a variety of

---

[9]Phyllis Rose, "Hunger Artists," *Harper's,* July 1988, p. 82.

[10]*New York Times,* February 9, 1990, sec. A, p. 13.

[11]Samuel D. Proctor, "To the Rescue: A National Youth Academy," *New York Times,* September 16, 1989, sec. A, p. 27.

controversial subjects: whether capital punishment is a deterrent to crime; whether legalization of marijuana will lead to an increase in its use; whether children, if left untaught, will grow up honest and cooperative; whether sex education courses will result in less sexual activity and fewer illegitimate births. The interpretations of the data are often profoundly important because they influence social policy and affect our lives directly and indirectly.

For the problems mentioned above, the opinions of people recognized as authorities are more reliable than those of people who have neither thought about nor done research on the subject. But opinions may also be offered by student writers in areas in which they are knowledgeable. If you were asked, for example, to defend or refute the statement that work has advantages for teenagers, you could call on your own experience and that of your friends to support your claim. You can also draw on your experience to write convincingly about your special interests.

One opinion, however, is not as good as another. The value of any opinion depends on the quality of the evidence and the trustworthiness of the person offering it.

EVALUATION OF EVIDENCE

Before you begin to write, you must determine whether the facts and opinions you have chosen to support your claim are sound. Can they convince your readers? A distinction between the evaluation of facts and the evaluation of opinions is somewhat artificial because many facts are verified by expert opinion, but for our analysis we discuss them separately.

Evaluation of Factual Evidence

As you evaluate factual evidence, you should keep in mind the following questions:

1. Is the evidence up to date? The importance of up-to-date information depends on the subject. If you are defending the claim that suicide is immoral, you will not need to examine new data. For many of the subjects you write about, recent research and scholarship will be important, even decisive, in proving the soundness of your data. "New" does not always mean "best," but in fields where research is ongoing — education, psychology, technology, medicine, and all the natural and physical sciences — you should be sensitive to the dates of the research.

In writing a paper a few years ago warning about the health hazards of air pollution, you would have used data referring only to outdoor pollution produced by automobile and factory emissions. But writing about air pollution today, you would have to take into account new data about indoor pollution, which has become a serious problem as a result of attempts to conserve energy. Because research studies in indoor pollution are continually being updated, recent evidence will probably be more accurate than past research.

2. *Is the evidence sufficient?* The amount of evidence you need depends on the complexity of the subject and the length of your paper. Given the relative brevity of most of your assignments, you will need to be selective. For the claim that indoor pollution is a serious problem, one example would obviously not be enough. For a 750- to 1,000-word paper, three or four examples would probably be sufficient. The choice of examples should reflect different aspects of the problem: in this case, different sources of indoor pollution — gas stoves, fireplaces, kerosene heaters, insulation — and the consequences for health.

Indoor pollution is a fairly limited subject for which the evidence is clear. But more complex problems require more evidence. A common fault in argument is generalization based on insufficient evidence. In a 1,000-word paper you could not adequately treat the causes of conflict in the Middle East; you could not develop workable proposals for health-care reform; you could not predict the development of education in the next century. In choosing a subject for a brief paper, determine whether you can produce sufficient evidence to convince a reader who may not agree with you. If not, the subject may be too large for a brief paper.

3. *Is the evidence relevant?* All the evidence should, of course, contribute to the development of your argument. Sometimes the arguer loses sight of the subject and introduces examples that are wide of the claim. In defending a national health-care plan, one student offered examples of the success of health maintenance organizations, but such organizations, although subsidized by the federal government, were not the structure favored by sponsors of a national health-care plan. The examples were interesting but irrelevant.

Also keep in mind that not all readers will agree on what is relevant. Is the unsavory private life of a politician relevant to his or her performance in office? If you want to prove that a politician is unfit to serve because of his or her private activities, you may first have to convince some members of the audience that private activities are relevant to public service.

4. *Are the examples representative?* This question emphasizes your responsibility to choose examples that are typical of all the examples you do not use. Suppose you offered Vermont's experience to support your claim that passage of a bottle bill would reduce

litter. Is the experience of Vermont typical of what is happening or may happen in other states? Or is Vermont, a small, mostly rural New England state, different enough from other states to make the example unrepresentative?

5. Are the examples consistent with the experience of the audience? The members of your audience use their own experiences to judge the soundness of your evidence. If your examples are unfamiliar or extreme, they will probably reject your conclusion. Consider the following hypothetical description, which is meant to represent the thinking of your generation.

> Imagine coming to a beach at the end of a long summer of wild goings-on. The beach crowd is exhausted, the sand shopworn, hot, and full of debris — no place for walking barefoot. You step on a bottle, and some cop yells at you for littering. The sun is directly overhead and leaves no patch of shade that hasn't already been taken. You feel the glare beating down on a barren landscape devoid of secrets or innocence. You look around at the disapproving faces and can't help but sense, somehow, that the entire universe is gearing up to punish you.
>
> This is how today's young people feel, as members of the 13th generation (born 1961–1981).[12]

If most members of the audience find that such a description doesn't reflect their own expectations or those of their friends, they will probably question the validity of the claim.

Evaluation of Statistics

The questions you must ask about examples also apply to statistics. Are they recent? Are they sufficient? Are they relevant? Are they typical? Are they consistent with the experience of the audience? But there are additional questions directed specifically to evaluation of statistics.

1. Do the statistics come from trustworthy sources? Perhaps you have read newspaper accounts of very old people, some reported to be as old as 135, living in the Caucasus or the Andes, nourished by yogurt and hard work. But these statistics are hearsay; no birth records or other official documents exist to verify them. Now two anthropologists have concluded that the numbers were part of a rural mythology and that the ages of the people were actually within the normal range for human populations elsewhere.[13]

---

[12]Neil Howe and Bill Strauss, *Thirteenth GEN: Abort, Retry, Ignore, Fail?* (New York: Vintage Books, 1993), p. 13.

[13]Richard B. Mazess and Sylvia H. Forman, "Longevity and Age Exaggeration in Vilcabamba, Ecuador," *Journal of Gerontology* (1979), pp. 94–98.

Hearsay statistics should be treated with the same skepticism accorded to gossip or rumor. Sampling a population to gather statistical information is a sophisticated science; you should ask whether the reporter of the statistics is qualified and likely to be free of bias. Among the generally reliable sources are polling organizations such as Gallup, Roper, and Louis Harris and agencies of the U.S. government such as the Census Bureau and the Bureau of Labor Statistics. Other qualified sources are well-known research foundations, university centers, and insurance companies that prepare actuarial tables. Statistics from underdeveloped countries are less reliable for obvious reasons: lack of funds, lack of trained statisticians, lack of communication and transportation facilities to carry out accurate censuses.

2. Are the terms clearly defined?   In an example in Chapter 4, the reference to poverty (p. 107) made clear that any statistics would be meaningless unless we knew exactly how *poverty* was defined by the user. *Unemployment* is another term for which statistics will be difficult to read if the definition varies from one user to another. For example, are seasonal workers employed or unemployed during the off-season? Are part-time workers employed? (In Russia they are unemployed.) Are workers on government projects employed? (During the 1930s they were considered employed by the Germans and unemployed by the Americans.) The more abstract or controversial the term, the greater the necessity for clear definition.

3. Are the comparisons between comparable things?   Folk wisdom warns us that we cannot compare apples and oranges. Population statistics for the world's largest city, for example, should indicate the units being compared. Greater London is defined in one way, greater New York in another, and greater Tokyo in still another. The population numbers will mean little unless you can be sure that the same geographical units are being compared.

4. Has any significant information been omitted?   *The Plain Truth,* a magazine published by the World-Wide Church of God, advertises itself as follows:

> *The Plain Truth* has now topped 5,000,000 copies per issue. It is now the fastest-growing magazine in the world and one of the widest circulated mass-circulation magazines on earth. Our circulation is now greater than *Newsweek.* New subscribers are coming in at the rate of around 40,000 per week.

What the magazine neglects to mention is that it is *free.* There is no subscription fee, and the magazine is widely distributed in drugstores, supermarkets, and airports. *Newsweek* is sold on newsstands and by subscription. The comparison therefore omits significant information.

Evaluation of Opinions

When you evaluate the reliability of opinions in subjects with which you are not familiar, you will be dealing almost exclusively with opinions of experts. Most of the following questions are directed to an evaluation of authoritative sources. But you can also ask these questions of students or of others with opinions based on their own experience and research.

1. Is the source of the opinion qualified to give an opinion on the subject? The discussion on credibility in Chapter 1 (pp. 14–17) pointed out that certain achievements by the interpreter of the data — publications, acceptance by colleagues — can tell us something about his or her competence. Although these standards are by no means foolproof (people of outstanding reputations have been known to falsify their data), nevertheless they offer assurance that the source is generally trustworthy. The answers to questions you must ask are not hard to find: Is the source qualified by education? Is the source associated with a reputable institution — a university or a research organization? Is the source credited with having made contributions to the field — books, articles, research studies? Suppose that in writing a paper on organ transplants you came across an article by Peter Medawar. He is identified as follows:

> Sir Peter Medawar, British zoologist, winner of the 1960 Nobel Prize in Physiology or Medicine, for proving that the rejection by the body of foreign organs can be overcome; president of the Royal Society; head of the National Institute for Medical Research in London; a world leader in immunology.

These credentials would suggest to almost any reader that Medawar was a reliable source for information about organ transplants.

If the source is not so clearly identified, you should treat the data with caution. Such advice is especially relevant when you are dealing with popular works about such subjects as miracle diets, formulas for instant wealth, and sightings of monsters and UFOs. Do not use such data until you can verify them from other, more authoritative sources.

In addition, you should question the identity of any source listed as "spokesperson" or "reliable source" or "an unidentified authority." The mass media are especially fond of this type of attribution. Sometimes the sources are people in public life who plant stories anonymously or off the record for purposes they prefer to keep hidden.

Even when the identification is clear and genuine, you should ask if the credentials are relevant to the field in which the authority claims expertise. So specialized are areas of scientific study today that scientists in one field may not be competent to make judgments in another. William Shockley is a distinguished engineer, a Nobel Prize winner for his contribution to the invention of the electronic transistor. But when he made the claim, based on his own research, that blacks are genetically inferior to whites, geneticists accused Shockley of venturing into a field where he was unqualified to make judgments. Similarly, advertisers invite stars from the entertainment world to express opinions about products with which they are probably less familiar than members of their audience. All citizens have the right to express their views, but this does not mean that all views are equally credible or worthy of attention.

2. Is the source biased for or against his or her interpretation? Even authorities who satisfy the criteria for expertise may be guilty of bias. Bias arises as a result of economic reward, religious affiliation, political loyalty, and other interests. The expert may not be aware of the bias; even an expert can fall into the trap of ignoring evidence that contradicts his or her own intellectual preferences. A British psychologist has said:

> The search for meaning in data is bound to involve all of us in distortion to greater or lesser degree. . . . Transgression consists not so much in a clear break with professional ethics, as in an unusually high-handed, extreme or self-deceptive attempt to promote one particular view of reality at the expense of all others.[14]

Before accepting the interpretation of an expert, you should ask: Is there some reason why I should suspect the motives of this particular source?

Consider, for example, an advertisement claiming that sweetened breakfast cereals are nutritious. The advertisement, placed by the manufacturer of the cereal, provides impeccable references from scientific sources to support its claims. But since you are aware of the economic interest of the company in promoting sales, you may wonder if they have reproduced only facts that favor their claims. Are there other facts that might prove the opposite? As a careful researcher you would certainly want to look further for data about the advantages and disadvantages of sugar in our diets.

It is harder to determine bias in the research done by scientists and university members even when the research is funded by companies interested in a favorable review of their products. If you

---

[14]Liam Hudson, *The Cult of the Fact* (New York: Harper and Row, 1972), p. 125.

discover that a respected biologist who advocates the use of sugar in baby food receives a consultant's fee from a sugar company, should you conclude that the research is slanted and that the scientist has ignored contrary evidence? Not necessarily. The truth may be that the scientist arrived at conclusions about the use of sugar legitimately through experiments that no other scientist would question. But it would probably occur to you that a critical reader might ask about the connection between the results of the research and the payment by a company that profits from the research. In this case you would be wise to read further to find confirmation or rejection of the claim by other scientists.

The most difficult evaluations concern ideological bias. Early in our lives we learn to discount the special interest that makes a small child brag, "My mother (or father) is the greatest!" Later we become aware that the claims of people who are avowed Democrats or Republicans or supply-side economists or Yankee fans or zealous San Franciscans or joggers must be examined somewhat more carefully than those of people who have no special commitment to a cause or a place or an activity. This is not to say that all partisan claims lack support. They may, in fact, be based on the best available support. But whenever special interest is apparent, there is always the danger that an argument will reflect this bias.

3. Has the source bolstered the claim with sufficient and appropriate evidence? In an article attacking pornography, one author wrote, "Statistics prove that the recent proliferation of porno is directly related to the increasing number of rapes and assaults on women."[15] But the author gave no further information — neither statistics nor proof that a cause-effect relation exists between pornography and violence against women. The critical reader will ask, "What are the numbers? Who compiled them?"

Even those who are reputed to be experts in the subjects they discuss must do more than simply allege that a claim is valid or that the data exist. They must provide facts to support their interpretations.

When Experts Disagree

Authoritative sources can disagree. Such disagreement is probably most common in the social sciences. They are called the "soft" sciences precisely because a consensus about conclusions in these areas is more difficult to arrive at than in the natural and physical sciences. Consider the controversy over what determines the best

---

[15]Charlotte Allen, "Exploitation for Profit," *Daily Collegian* [University of Massachusetts], October 5, 1976, p. 2.

interests of the child where both biological and foster parents are engaged in trying to secure custody. Experts are deeply divided on this issue. Dr. Daniel J. Cohen, a child psychologist and director of the Yale Child Study Center, argues that the psychological needs of the child should take precedence. If the child has a stable and loving relationship with foster parents, that is where he should stay. But Bruce Bozer and Bernadine Dohrn of the Children and Family Justice Center at Northwestern University Law School insist that "such a solution may be overly simplistic." The child may suffer in later life when he learns that he has been prevented from returning to biological parents "who fought to get him back."[16]

But even in the natural and physical sciences, where the results of observation and experiment are more conclusive, we encounter heated differences of opinion. A popular argument concerns the extinction of the dinosaurs. Was it the effect of a comet striking the earth? Or widespread volcanic activity? Or a cooling of the planet? All these theories have their champions among the experts.

Environmental concerns also produce lively disagreements. Scientists have lined up on both sides of a debate about the importance of protecting the tropical rain forest as a source of biological, especially mammalian, diversity. Dr. Edward O. Wilson, a Harvard biologist, whose books have made us familiar with the term *biodiversity,* says, "The great majority of organisms appears to reach maximum diversity in the rain forest. There is no question that the rain forests are the world's headquarters of diversity." But in the journal *Science* another biologist, Dr. Michael Mares, a professor of zoology at the University of Oklahoma, argues that "if one could choose only a single South American habitat in which to preserve the greatest mammalian diversity, it would be the dry lands. . . . The dry lands are very likely far more highly threatened than the largely inaccessible rain forests."[17] A debate of more immediate relevance concerns possible dangers in cross-species transplants. One such transplant occurred in December 1995 when a man suffering from AIDS received bone marrow from a baboon in an experiment designed to boost the patient's immune system. Dr. Jonathan S. Allan, of the Southwest Foundation for Biomedical Research in San Antonio, is one of several doctors critical of the guidelines for these procedures, which in his opinion do not protect against possible introduction of new viruses into the general population. In an article for a medical journal, he writes:

> Once the door is opened and a new virus is unleashed, it will be a monumental task to identify a new pathogen, develop adequate screening tests and prevent the spread of that new infection.[18]

---

[16]*New York Times,* September 4, 1994, sec. E, p. 3.
[17]*New York Times,* April 7, 1992, sec. C, p. 4.
[18]*New York Times,* January 9, 1996, sec. C, p. 11.

But other doctors feel that this alarm is unjustified. Dr. Frederick R. Murphy, the dean of the veterinary school at the University of California at Davis, says that "over the years unsterilized biological products derived from animals, products that differ little in risk from xenografts, have often been injected into patients" without major problems.[19]

How can you choose between authorities who disagree? If you have applied the tests discussed so far and discovered that one source is less qualified by training and experience or makes claims with little support or appears to be biased in favor of one interpretation, you will have no difficulty in rejecting that person's opinion. If conflicting sources prove to be equally reliable in all respects, then continue reading other authorities to determine whether a greater number of experts support one opinion rather than another. Although numbers alone, even of experts, don't guarantee the truth, nonexperts have little choice but to accept the authority of the greater number until evidence to the contrary is forthcoming. Finally, if you are unable to decide between competing sources of evidence, you may conclude that the argument must remain unsettled. Such an admission is not a failure; after all, such questions are considered controversial because even the experts cannot agree, and such questions are often the most interesting to consider and argue about.

APPEALS TO NEEDS AND VALUES

Good factual evidence is usually enough to convince an audience that your factual claim is sound. Using examples, statistics, and expert opinion, you can prove, for example, that women do not earn as much as men for the same work. But even good evidence may not be enough to convince your audience that unequal pay is wrong or that something should be done about it. In making value and policy claims, an appeal to the needs and values of your audience is absolutely essential to the success of your argument. If you want to persuade the audience to change their minds or adopt a course of action — in this case, to demand legalization of equal pay for equal work — you will have to show that assent to your claim will bring about what they want and care deeply about.

As a writer, you cannot always know who your audience is; it's impossible, for example, to predict exactly who will read a letter you write to a newspaper. Even in the classroom, you have only partial knowledge of your readers. You may not always know or be able to

---

[19]*New York Times,* January 9, 1996, sec. C, p. 11.

infer what the goals and principles of your audience are. You may not know how they feel about big government, the draft, private school education, feminism, environmental protection, homosexuality, religion, or any of the other subjects you might write about. If the audience concludes that the things you care about are very different from what they care about, if they cannot identify with your goals and principles, they may treat your argument with indifference, even hostility, and finally reject it. But you can hope that decent and reasonable people will share many of the needs and values that underlie your claims.

Appeals to Needs

Suppose that you are trying to persuade Joan Doakes, a friend who is still undecided, to attend college. In your reading you have come across a report about the benefits of a college education written by Howard Bowen, a former professor of economics at Claremont (California) Graduate School, former president of Grinnell College, and a specialist in the economics of higher education. Armed with his testimony, you write to Joan. As support for your claim that she should attend college, you offer evidence that (1) college graduates earn more throughout their lifetime than high school graduates; (2) college graduates are more active and exert greater influence in their communities than high school graduates; and (3) college graduates achieve greater success as partners in marriage and as thoughtful and caring parents.[20]

Joan writes back that she is impressed with the evidence you've provided — the statistics, the testimony of economists and psychologists — and announces that she will probably enroll in college instead of accepting a job offer.

How did you succeed with Joan Doakes? If you know your friend pretty well, the answer is not difficult. Joan has needs that can be satisfied by material success; more money will enable her to enjoy the comforts and luxuries that are important to her. She also needs the esteem of her peers and the sense of achievement that political activity and service to others will give her. Finally, she needs the rootedness to be found in close and lasting family connections.

Encouraged by your success with Joan Doakes, you write the same letter to another friend, Fred Fox, who has also declined to apply for admission to college. This time, however, your argument fails. Fred, too, is impressed with your research and evidence. But college is not for him, and he repeats that he has decided not to become a student.

---

[20]"The Residue of Academic Learning," *Chronicle of Higher Education,* November 14, 1977, p. 13.

Why such a different response? The reason, it turns out, is that you don't know what Fred really wants. Fred Fox dreams of going to Alaska to live alone in the wilderness. Money means little to him, influence in the community is irrelevant to his goals, and at present he feels no desire to become a member of a loving family.

Perhaps if you had known Fred better, you would have offered different evidence to show that you recognized what he needed and wanted. You could have told him that Bowen's study also points out that "college-educated persons are healthier than are others," that "they also have better ability to adjust to changing times and vocations," that "going to college enhances self-discovery" and enlarges mental resources, which encourage college graduates to go on learning for the rest of their lives. This information might have persuaded Fred that college would also satisfy some of his needs.

As this example demonstrates, you have a better chance of persuading your reader to accept your claim if you know what he or she wants and what importance he or she assigns to the needs that we all share. Your reader must, in other words, see some connection between your evidence and his or her needs.

The needs to which you appealed in your letters to Joan and Fred are the requirements for physiological or psychological well-being. The most familiar classification of needs was developed by the psychologist Abraham H. Maslow in 1954.[21] These needs, said Maslow, motivate human thought and action. In satisfying our needs, we attain both long- and short-term goals. Because Maslow believed that some needs are more important than others, he arranged them in hierarchical order from the most urgent biological needs to the psychological needs that are related to our roles as members of a society.

> *Physiological needs.* Basic bodily requirements: food and drink; health; sex
>
> *Safety needs.* Security; freedom from harm; order and stability
>
> *Belongingness and love needs.* Love within a family and among friends; roots within a group or a community
>
> *Esteem needs.* Material success; achievement; power, status, and recognition by others
>
> *Self-actualization needs.* Fulfillment in realizing one's potential

For most of your arguments you won't have to address the audience's basic physiological needs for nourishment or shelter. The desire for health, however, now receives extraordinary attention.

---

[21]*Motivation and Personality* (New York: Harper and Row, 1954), pp. 80–92.

Appeals to buy health foods, vitamin supplements, drugs, exercise and diet courses, and health books are all around us. Many of the claims are supported by little or no evidence, but readers are so eager to satisfy the need for good health that they often overlook the lack of facts or authoritative opinion. The desire for physical well-being, however, is not so simple as it seems; it is strongly related to our need for self-esteem and love.

Appeals to our needs to feel safe from harm, to be assured of order and stability in our lives are also common. Insurance companies, politicians who promise to rid our streets of crime, and companies that offer security services all appeal to this profound and nearly universal need. (We say "nearly" because some people are apparently attracted to risk and danger.) At this writing those who monitor global warming are attempting both to arouse fear for our safety and to suggest ways of reducing the dangers that make us fearful.

The last three needs in Maslow's hierarchy are the ones you will find most challenging to appeal to in your arguments. It is clear that these needs arise out of human relationships and participation in society. Advertisers make much use of appeals to these needs.

Belongingness and love needs

"Whether you are young or old, the need for companionship is universal." (ad for dating service)

"Share the Fun of High School with Your Little Girl!" (ad for a Barbie Doll)

Esteem needs

"Enrich your home with the distinction of an Oxford library."

"Apply your expertise to more challenges and more opportunities. Here are outstanding opportunities for challenge, achievement, and growth." (Perkin-Elmer Co.)

Self-actualization needs

"Be all that you can be." (U.S. Army)

"Are you demanding enough? Somewhere beyond the cortex is a small voice whose mere whisper can silence an army of arguments. It goes by many names: integrity, excellence, standards. And it stands alone in final judgment as to whether we have demanded enough of ourselves and, by that example, have inspired the best in those around us." (*New York Times*)

Of course, it is not only advertisers who use these appeals. We hear them from family and friends, from teachers, from employers, from editorials and letters to the editor, from people in public life.

Appeals to Values

Needs give rise to values. If we feel the need to belong to a group, we learn to value commitment, sacrifice, and sharing. And we then respond to arguments that promise to protect our values. It is hardly surprising that values, the principles by which we judge what is good or bad, beautiful or ugly, worthwhile or undesirable, should exercise a profound influence on our behavior. Virtually all claims, even those that seem to be purely factual, contain expressed or unexpressed judgments. The two scientists quoted in Chapter 3 (pp. 56–57) who presented evidence that cocaine was "deadlier than we thought" did so not for academic reasons but because they hoped to persuade people that using the drug was bad.

For our study of argument, we will speak of groups or systems of values because any single value is usually related to others. People and institutions are often defined by such systems of values. We can distinguish, for example, between those who think of themselves as traditional and those who think of themselves as modern by listing their differing values. One writer contrasts such values in this way:

> Among the values of traditionalism are: merit, accomplishment, competition, and success; self-restraint, self-discipline, and the postponement of gratification; the stability of the family; and a belief in certain moral universals. The modernist ethos scorns the pursuit of success; is egalitarian and redistributionist in emphasis; tolerates or encourages sensual gratification; values self-expression as against self-restraint; accepts alternative or deviant forms of the family; and emphasizes ethical relativism.[22]

Systems of values are neither so rigid nor so distinct from one another as this list suggests. Some people who are traditional in their advocacy of competition and success may also accept the modernist values of self-expression and alternative family structures. Values, like needs, are arranged in a hierarchy; that is, some are clearly more important than others to the people who hold them. Moreover, the arrangement may shift over time or as a result of new experiences. In 1962, for example, two speech teachers prepared a list of what they called "Relatively Unchanging Values Shared by Most Americans."[23] Included were "puritan and pioneer standards of morality" and "perennial optimism about the future." More than thirty years later, an appeal to these values might fall on a number of deaf ears.

You should also be aware of not only changes over time but also different or competing value systems that reflect a multitude of sub-

---

[22]Joseph Adelson, "What Happened to the Schools," *Commentary,* March 1981, p. 37.

[23]Edward Steele and W. Charles Redding, "The American Value System: Premises for Persuasion," *Western Speech,* 26 (Spring 1962), pp. 83–91.

cultures in our country. Differences in age, sex, race, ethnic background, social environment, religion, even in the personalities and
characters of its members define the groups we belong to. Such
terms as *honor, loyalty, justice, patriotism, duty, responsibility, equality, freedom,* and *courage* will be interpreted very differently by different groups.

All of us belong to more than one group, and the values of the
several groups may be in conflict. If one group to which you belong — say, peers of your own age and class — is generally uninter-
ested in and even scornful of religion, you may nevertheless hold to
the values of your family and continue to place a high value on religious belief.

How can a knowledge of your readers' values enable you to
make a more effective appeal? Suppose you want to argue in favor of
a sex education program in the junior high school you attended. The
program you support would not only give students information
about contraception and venereal disease but also teach them about
the pleasures of sex, the importance of small families, and alternatives to heterosexuality. If the readers of your argument are your
classmates or your peers, you can be fairly sure that their agreement will be easier to obtain than that of their parents, especially if
their parents think of themselves as conservative. Your peers are
more likely to value experimentation, tolerance of alternative sexual
practices, freedom, and novelty. Their parents are more likely to
value restraint, conformity to conventional sexual practices, obedience to family rules, and foresight in planning for the future.

Knowing that your peers share your values and your goals will
mean that you need not spell out the values supporting your claim;
they are understood by your readers. Convincing their parents,
however, who think that freedom, tolerance, and experimentation
have been abused by their children, will be a far more challenging
task. In one written piece you have little chance of changing their
values, a result that might be achieved only over a longer period of
time. So you might first attempt to reduce their hostility by suggesting that, even if a community-wide program were adopted, students
would need parental permission to enroll. This might convince some
parents that you share their values regarding parental authority and
primacy of the family. Second, you might look for other values to
which the parents subscribe and to which you can make an appeal.
Do they prize maturity, self-reliance, responsibility in their children?
If so, you could attempt to prove, with authoritative evidence, that
the sex education program would promote these qualities in students who took the course.

But familiarity with the value systems of prospective readers
may also lead you to conclude that winning assent to your argument
will be impossible. It would probably be fruitless to attempt to

persuade a group of lifelong pacifists to endorse the use of nuclear weapons. The beliefs, attitudes, and habits that support their value systems are too fundamental to yield to one or two attempts at persuasion.

EVALUATION OF APPEALS TO NEEDS AND VALUES

If your argument is based on an appeal to the needs and values of your audience, the following questions will help you evaluate the soundness of your appeal.

1. Have the values been clearly defined? If you are appealing to the patriotism of your readers, can you be sure that they agree with your definition? Does patriotism mean "Our country, right or wrong!" or does it mean dissent, even violent dissent, if you think your country is wrong? Because value terms are abstractions, you must make their meaning explicit by placing them in context and providing examples.

2. Are the needs and values to which you appeal prominent in the reader's hierarchy at the time you are writing? An affluent community, fearful of further erosion of quiet and open countryside, might resist an appeal to allow establishment of a high-technology firm, even though the firm would bring increased prosperity to the area.

3. Is the evidence in your argument clearly related to the needs and values to which you appeal? Remember that the reader must see some connection between your evidence and his or her goals. Suppose you were writing an argument to persuade a group of people to vote in an upcoming election. You could provide evidence to prove that only 20 percent of the town voted in the last election. But this evidence would not motivate your audience to vote unless you could provide other evidence to show that their needs were not being served by such a low turnout.

Single-Sex Education Benefits Men Too

CLAUDIUS E. WATTS III

Introduction: background of the problem

The values that the author will defend

Claim of policy: to preserve single-sex education for men

Last week Virginia Military Institute, an all-male state college, got the good news from a federal judge that it can continue its single-sex program if it opens a leadership program at Mary Baldwin College, a nearby private women's school. But it is likely that the government will appeal the decision. Meanwhile, the Citadel, another such institution in Charleston, S.C., remains under attack. Unwittingly, so are some fundamental beliefs prevalent in our society: namely, the value of single-sex education, the need for diversity in education, and the freedom of choice in associating with, and not associating with, whomever one chooses.

When Shannon Faulkner received a preliminary injunction to attend day classes with the Citadel's Corps of Cadets, she was depicted as a nineteen-year-old woman fighting for her constitutional rights, while the Citadel was painted as an outdated and chauvinistic Southern school that had to be dragged into the twentieth century.

But the Citadel is not fighting to keep women out of the Corps of Cadets because there is a grandiose level of nineteenth-century machismo to protect. Rather, we at the Citadel are trying to preserve an educational environment that

---

Lieutenant General Claudius E. Watts III, retired from the U.S. Air Force, is a future faculty member, and former president, of the Citadel in South Carolina. This selection is from the May 3, 1995, edition of the *Wall Street Journal*.

molds young men into grown men of good character, honor, and integrity. It is part of a single-sex educational system that has proven itself successful throughout history.

Support: benefits of single-sex education for men

The benefits of single-sex education for men are clear: Says Harvard sociologist David Riesman, not only is single-sex education an optimal means of character development, but it also removes the distractions of the "mating-dating" game so prevalent in society and enables institutions to focus students on values and academics.

In short, the value of separate education is, simply, the fact it is separate. 5

In October 1992, a federal appeals court ruled that "single-sex education is pedagogically justifiable." Indeed, a cursory glance at some notable statistics bears that out. For instance, the Citadel

a) Retention

has the highest retention rate for minority students of any public college in South Carolina: 67 percent of black students graduate in four years, which is more than 2½ times the national average. Additionally, the Citadel's four-year graduation rate for all students is 70 percent, which compares with 48 percent nationally for all other public institutions and 67 percent

b) Opportunity

nationally for private institutions. Moreover, many of the students come from modest backgrounds. Clearly, the Citadel is not the bastion of male privilege that the U.S. Justice Department, in briefs filed by that agency, would have us all believe.

While the Justice Department continues to reject the court's ruling affirming the values of single-sex education, others continue to argue that because the federal military academies are coeducational, so should the Citadel be. However, it is not the Citadel's primary mission to train officers for the U.S. armed forces. We currently commission approximately 30 percent of our graduates, but only 18 percent actually pursue military careers. At the Citadel, the military model is a means to an end, not the end itself.

Today there are eighty-four women's colleges scattered throughout the United States, including two that are public. *Support: benefits of single-sex education for women* These colleges defend their programs as necessary to help women overcome intangible barriers in male-dominated professions. This argument has merit; women's colleges produce only 4.5 percent of all female college graduates, but have produced one-fourth of all women board members of Fortune 500 companies and one-half of the women in Congress. However, the educational benefits of men's colleges are equally clear; and to allow women alone to benefit from single-sex education seems to perpetuate the very stereotypes that women — including Ms. Faulkner — are trying to correct.

Warrant: men should enjoy the same freedom of choice If young women want and need to study and learn in single-sex schools, why is it automatically wrong for young men to want and need the same? Where is the fairness in this assumption?

"At what point does the insistence 10 that one individual not be deprived of choice spill over into depriving countless individuals of choice?" asks Emory University's Elizabeth Fox Genovese in an article by Jeffrey Rosen published in the February 14 *New Republic.*

Yet, so it is at the Citadel. While one student maintains that she is protecting her freedom to associate, we mustn't forget that the Citadel's cadets also have a freedom — the freedom not to associate. While we have read about one female student's rights, what hasn't been addressed are the rights of the 1,900 cadets who chose the Citadel — and the accompanying discipline and drill — because it offered them the single-sex educational experience they wanted. Why do one student's rights supersede all theirs?

One might be easily tempted to argue on the grounds that Ms. Faulkner is a taxpayer and the Citadel is a tax-supported institution. But if the taxpayer argument holds, the next step is to forbid all public support for institutions that enroll students of only one sex. A draconian measure such as this would surely mean the end of private — as well as public — single-gender colleges.

Backing for warrant: tax-supported education should be equal for men and women

Most private colleges — Columbia and Converse, the two all-female schools in South Carolina, included — could not survive without federal financial aid, tax exemptions, and state tax support in the form of tuition grants. In fact, nearly 900 of Columbia and Converse's female students receive state-funded tuition grants, a student population that is almost half the size of the Corps of Cadets. In essence, South Carolina's two private women's colleges may stand or fall with the Citadel.

Carried to its logical conclusion, then, the effort to coeducate the Citadel might mean the end of all single-sex education — for women as well as men, in private as well as public schools.

Analysis: Support

In 1993 Shannon Faulkner, a woman, was rejected for admission to the Citadel, an all-male state-supported military academy in South Carolina. In 1995, after a long court battle, she was admitted but resigned after a week of physical and emotional stress. The Court was asked to decide if an education equal to that of the Citadel could be provided for women at a nearby school.

Claudius Watts III tackles a subject that is no longer controversial in regard to women's colleges: the virtues of single-sex education. But in this essay he argues that colleges for men only deserve the same right as women's colleges to exclude the opposite sex.

The author has taken care in the limited space available to cover all the arguments that have emerged in the case of Shannon Faulkner. At the end of the opening paragraph he lays out the three ideas he will develop — the value of single-sex education, the need for diversity in education, and freedom of choice. In paragraphs 3 through 6 he supports his case for the benefits of separate education by first quoting a prominent sociologist and then offering statistics to prove that the Citadel population is both diverse and successful. In paragraph 7 he refutes a popular analogy — that since the service academies, like West Point and the Naval Academy, admit women, so should the Citadel. The goals of the Citadel, he says, are broader than those of the service academies. But he does more. In paragraph 8 he provides data that women's colleges produce successful graduates. This reinforces his claim that separate education has advantages over coed schooling. Perhaps it also helps to make friends of opponents who might otherwise be hostile to arguments favoring male privileges.

Notice the transition in paragraph 10. This leads the author to the defense of his last point, the far more elusive concept of freedom of choice and the rights of individuals, ideas whose validity cannot be measured in numbers. He introduces this part of his argument by quoting the words of a supporter of single-sex education, a woman professor at Emory University. He makes a strong appeal to the reader's sense of fairness and belief in the rights of the majority, represented here by the male students at the Citadel. There is also an obvious appeal to fear, an implied threat of the danger to women's colleges, in the next-to-last sentence of the essay. Finally, he invokes logic. If single-sex education cannot be defended for males, neither can it be defended for females. He assumes that against logic there can be no real defense.

Some leading advocates for women's rights have, in fact, agreed with General Watts's arguments for that reason. But those who support both Shannon Faulkner's admission to the Citadel and the sanctity of women's colleges will claim that women, as a disadvantaged group, deserve special consideration, while men do not. (One writer even insisted that the Citadel *needed* women as a civilizing influence.) General Watts's argument, however, should go some distance toward reopening the dialogue.

Not Just Read and Write, but Right and Wrong

KATHLEEN KENNEDY TOWNSEND

In a suburban high school's crowded classroom, a group of juniors explained to me why drugs are difficult to control. "You see, Mrs. Townsend, what if you want a new pair of Reeboks? You could sell drugs and make $250 in an afternoon. It's a lot easier and quicker than working at McDonald's. You'd have to work there a whole week."

In my work helping teachers, I've walked into countless high schools where I could have filled a garbage bag with the trash in the halls. Yet I rarely hear teachers asking students to pick up the garbage — or telling them not to litter in the first place.

Of course, many students obey the law, stay away from drugs, and perform selfless acts: They tutor, work with the elderly, or run antidrug campaigns. But too many lack a sense of duty to a larger community.

A survey conducted for People for the American Way asked just over 1,000 Americans between fifteen and twenty-four what goals they considered important. Three times as many selected career success as chose community service — which finished dead last. Only one-third said they could countenance joining the military or working on a political campaign. During one focus group interview for the study, some young people were asked to name qualities that make this country special. There was a long silence until one young man came up with an answer: "Cable TV."

The study concluded, "Young people have learned only half of 5 America's story.... [They] reveal notions of America's unique character that emphasize freedom and license almost to the complete exclusion of service or participation . . . they fail to perceive a need to reciprocate by exercising the duties and responsibilities of good citizenship."

Failure of Schools

While it is easy enough to blame this problem on the "me-ism" of the Reagan years, it's time to recognize that *it's also the result of deliberate educational policy.* One principal I know speaks for too many

Kathleen Kennedy Townsend is the lieutenant-governor of Maryland. This article first appeared in *The Washington Monthly,* January 1990.

others. "Schools," she says, "cannot impose duties on the students. Students come from different backgrounds. They have different standards."

Twice since 1982 the Maryland Department of Education has sent out questionnaires to local education departments soliciting opinions about values education. The answers are typical of those found across the United States. Many respondents were indifferent, simply stating that values education is "inherent" in teaching. Other answers were more hostile: "Specific training in values is a new development which we do not consider essential," and "A special effort would cause trouble."

The consensus of the high school teachers and administrators participating in a curriculum workshop I ran last summer said it all: "Values — we can't get into that."

Schools across America have simply refused to take responsibility for the character of their students. They wash their hands of the teaching of virtue, doing little to create an environment that teaches children the importance of self-discipline, obligation, and civic participation. As one teacher training text says, "There is no right or wrong answer to any question of value."

Is it any surprise that students tend to agree? These days it   10 seems they're all relativists. A collection of high school interviews quotes one eleventh-grader as saying, "What one person thinks is bad or wrong, another person might think that it is good or right. I don't think morals should be taught because it would cause more conflicts and mess up the student's mind." One of her classmates adds, "Moral values cannot be taught and people must learn what works for them. In other words, 'Whatever gets you through the night, it's alright.'"

Sensitivity Needed

Now it's obvious that the public schools are a ticklish arena for instilling values. Our pluralistic society is justly worried about party lines of any kind. That means that teaching values in the schools — whether as an integral part of the traditional classes or as a separate course — requires subtle skills and real sensitivity to student and community needs. Of course, families and churches should play a part, but neither are as strong or effective as they were a generation ago. Only the schools are guaranteed to get a shot at kids. That's why their current fumbling of anything smacking of right and wrong is so disastrous.

The importance of teaching values in the schools was barely mentioned at the education summit presided over by George Bush at the University of Virginia. The meeting was dominated by talk of federal funding and drug education. The underlying valuelessness of

American education — an obstacle to the intelligent use of scarce resources and a root cause of drug problems — really didn't come up.

Such a curious oversight at Thomas Jefferson's school! Jefferson fought for public education because he believed that the citizen's virtue is the foundation of democracy. Only virtuous citizens, he knew, would resist private gain for the public good. And to know the public good, you have to study literature, philosophy, history, and religion.

For many years, Jefferson's wisdom about education prevailed. James Q. Wilson attributes America's low level of crime during the nineteenth century to the efforts of educators to instill self-discipline. "In the 1830s," he explains, "crime began to rise rapidly. New York had more murders than London, even though New York was only a tiny fraction of the size of London. However, rather than relying on police forces or other government programs, the citizens concentrated on education.

"Sunday schools were started. It was an all-day effort to provide   15
education in morality, education in punctuality, in decency, in following rules, and accepting responsibility, in being generous, in being kind.

"The process was so successful that in the second half of the nineteenth century, despite urbanization, despite the enormous influx into this country of immigrants from foreign countries all over Europe, despite the widening class cleavages, despite the beginning of an industrial proletariat, despite all those things which textbooks today teach us cause crime to go up, crime went down. And it went down insofar as I, or any historian, can tell because this effort to substitute the ethic of self-control for what appeared to be the emerging ethic of self-expression succeeded." In 1830 the average American drank ten gallons of distilled liquor a year. By 1850, it was down to two.

Basic Values

The flavor of this nineteenth-century approach to education is preserved today in many state constitutions. North Dakota's is typical in declaring that public schools should "emphasize all branches of knowledge that tend to impress upon the mind the importance of truthfulness, temperance, purity, public spirit, and respect for honest labor of every kind." In current educational jargon, this approach is called "values inculcation." . . .

In 1981 the California State Assembly considered a bill that spelled out values that should be included in public school instructional materials. Among those values were: honesty, acceptance of responsibility, respect for the individuality of others, respect for the responsibility inherent in being a parent or in a position of authority, the role of the work ethic in achieving personal goals, universal values of right and wrong, respect for property, the importance of the family unit, and the importance of respect for the law.

The bill was defeated.

How have we reached the point where a list of basic values like   20 that is considered unsuitable for schools? . . .

The major criticism of not teaching values is very simple: There are some values that teachers should affirm. Not all values are the same. My daughter is the only girl on her soccer team, and recently some of the boys on the team spit at her. The coach shouldn't have the boys *justify* their actions. He should have them *stop*. He should make sure they know they were wrong. That's what he should do. What he actually did tells you a lot about the schools today. He did nothing.

Reading and Discussion Questions

1. An editorial writer has supplied three subheadings for parts of the essay. The first part lacks a heading. What do you think it should be? Is "Sensitivity Needed" an appropriate headline for the third part?
2. Mention some of the devices Townsend uses to make her essay easy to read and understand.
3. What different kinds of support does Townsend provide to establish her claim? Is the evidence sufficient to prove that instruction in values is necessary?
4. What values above all others would the author seek to promote? Why do you think she has chosen these particular values?
5. Would the nineteenth-century Sunday school effort described by James Q. Wilson work today to reduce crime? Why or why not?
6. Do you think any of the values listed in the 1981 California bill are controversial? Explain.

Writing Suggestions

7. If you have been a student in a public, private, or Sunday school where specific values were taught, directly or through literature and history, describe and evaluate the experience. Was it successful — that is, did the values taught have a meaningful influence on your life?
8. Are there some actions that are always right or wrong, regardless of the circumstances? If you think there are, choose one or two and defend your choice. (You would probably agree with Ted Koppel, who reminds us that they are the Ten Commandments, not the Ten Suggestions.) If, on the other hand, you believe that all values are relative or situational — dependent, that is, on particular circumstances — argue the proposition that any view on the rightness or wrongness of a specific action is contingent on the situation.

Abductions and Abductionists

CURTIS PEEBLES

This book is a chronicle of the flying saucer myth — the system of beliefs that have developed around the idea that alien spacecraft are being seen in Earth's skies. These beliefs did not suddenly spring into existence fully formed. Rather, a set of conflicting ideas originated, the myth was defined, then the beliefs evolved over nearly half a century. Moreover, the flying saucer myth is not a single, monolithic set of doctrines. As soon as the flying saucer myth was defined, schisms began to develop among "believers" — those people who accepted the idea that flying saucers were extraordinary objects. Not all believers held the same beliefs, and these schisms soon led to open warfare. This interaction between believers has been a major influence on the myth's history.

The flying saucer myth not only concerns disk-shaped spaceships and the aliens who supposedly pilot them. Because it also involves how the believers view the role and nature of government, and how the government relates to the people, the U.S. government has had to deal with the flying saucer myth. Presidents have denied their existence; they were a twenty-two-year headache for the Air Force, and were investigated by Congress and the CIA. This interaction both fed the flying saucer myth and brought about the very things the government sought to avoid.

A similar interaction has taken place between the flying saucer myth and the larger society. The flying saucer myth is a mirror to the events of postwar America — the paranoia of the 1950s, the social turmoil of the 1960s, the "me generation" of the 1970s, and the nihilism of the 1980s and the early 1990s. As the flying saucer myth entered popular culture, images and ideas were created which, in turn, shaped the flying saucer myth itself. . . .

Close Encounters of the Third Kind

Although many films had used flying saucer themes, *Close Encounters of the Third Kind* was the only one to fully understand the flying saucer myth. The story is one of ordinary people trying to cope with mythic experiences. Roy Neary (Richard Dreyfuss) is a power company lineman who sees a UFO. He finds himself the victim of subliminal messages which cause him to undertake obsessive,

---

Curtis Peebles is an aerospace historian whose books include *Watch the Skies! A Chronicle of the Flying Saucer Myth* (1994), from which this selection is taken. Bibliographic citations have been cut.

bizarre actions which cause his family to leave. Neary finally realizes he is to go to Devil's Tower, Wyoming. He embarks on an arduous cross-country journey. Overcoming obstacles, he is rewarded with a meeting with the aliens. As the multicolored mothership lifts off with Neary aboard, he rises above his own mundane, earthly existence.

In earlier films, the flying saucers were sources of danger. In *Close* 5 *Encounters of the Third Kind,* the meeting with the aliens was not to be feared, but to be anticipated. It was this "sense of wonder" that was so lacking in such films as *The Thing* or *Earth vs. the Flying Saucer.*

Close Encounters of the Third Kind defined the shape of the aliens. In the film, "they" were short, with large heads, slanted dark eyes, and light gray skins. Their noses were small and their ears were only small holes. The aliens' bodies were elongated and very thin. The fingers were also long. Their overall appearance was that of a fetus. By the early 1980s, this "shape" would come to dominate abduction descriptions.

The Growth of Abduction Reports

Certain UFOlogists began to specialize in abduction cases. The first such "abductionist" was Dr. R. Leo Sprinkle, a psychologist at the University of Wyoming. Sprinkle was frequently quoted by the tabloids and was on the *National Enquirer's* Blue Ribbon Panel. Sprinkle's role was critical in shaping both the development of the abduction myth and its acceptance. His "hypnotic sessions with UFO abductees" began in 1967 and 1968 with three cases. It was not until 1974 that Sprinkle had another abduction case (reflecting the post-Condon Report decline in interest). In 1975 there were two cases. There were three cases each in 1976 and 1977 (after *The UFO Incident*). In 1978 (after *Close Encounters of the Third Kind*), Sprinkle worked with ten subjects, while in 1979 there were eighteen abductees. In 1980 he held the first of his annual conferences for UFO abductees and investigators.

This increase in abduction reports was not limited to Sprinkle. UFOlogist David Webb noted that a 1976 search of UFO literature (covering nearly thirty years) showed only 50 abduction-type cases. Yet, over the next two years, about 100 *more* cases were reported, bringing the total to some 150. By the end of the 1970s, the total number of cases exceeded 200. . . .

Budd Hopkins

With the 1980s, a new abductionist appeared — an artist named Budd Hopkins. Long interested in UFOs, the rise in abduction reports attracted Hopkins's attention in 1976. He met "Steven Kilburn."

Kilburn had a vague memory of being afraid of a stretch of road, but no UFO sighting. To this point, people claiming to have been abducted said they had seen a UFO and/or occupant. This was followed by a period of "missing time." The "abduction" itself was "remembered" under hypnosis. Kilburn had no such memory. When he was hypnotized, however, Kilburn said he was grabbed by a "big wrench" and was taken aboard a UFO.

To Hopkins, this implied a person could be an "abductee" *without* any overt memory. Hopkins began asking people if they had "uneasiness," recurring dreams, or "any event" which might indicate an abduction. It was no longer necessary for a person to have "missing time." *Anyone* could now be an abductee and not realize it. Hopkins believed there might be tens of thousands of abductees — what he called "an invisible multitude." 10

Hopkins published his conclusions in his 1981 book *Missing Time*. He believed "a very long-term, in-depth study is being made of a relatively large sample of humans." The "human specimens" were first abducted as young children. "Monitoring devices" would be implanted in the abductee's nose. This was described as a tiny ball on a long rod. The ball was left in the nasal cavity. The young abductees were then released with no memories of the (alleged) events. Years later, Hopkins believed, once the abductees reached puberty, they would be abducted a second time.

The aliens in Hopkins's abduction cases all followed the shape of those in *The UFO Incident* and *Close Encounters of the Third Kind* — large heads, thin bodies, slanted eyes, and gray skin. The book had several drawings of what became known as "the Grays." *Missing Time* completed the process of defining the shape of the aliens.

Hopkins also speculated on the aliens' motivation. He noted several abductees had scars from childhood. He believed tissue samples were being taken. Hopkins suggested the aliens needed a specific genetic structure. Hopkins also suggested the aliens were taking sperm and ova samples. These, he continued, might be for experiments in producing human/alien hybrids.

This expanded the abduction myth; it was now much more "intrusive." In the Pascagoula case, Hickson claimed he was passively "scanned." Now, tissue samples were being taken which left scars. The alleged abductees also showed emotional scars from their supposed experiences — long-lasting anxiety and fear. The "monitoring devices" were a further intrusion. The taking of sperm and ova was, symbolically, the most intrusive of all. Humans were depicted as helpless before the aliens' overwhelming power, reduced to a lab rat.

Hopkins further developed these themes in his 1987 book *Intruders*. In September 1983, he received a letter from "Kathie Davis." She had read *Missing Time* and wrote him to describe a dream she had had in early 1978 of two small beings in her bedroom. From Davis's 15 accounts and twelve other abductees, Hopkins came to believe the aliens had an unmistakable interest "in the process of human reproduction" going back to the Villas-Boas case.

Hopkins described the process as follows — female abductees were identified as donors during their childhood abductions. The implants allowed the aliens to "track" them. When they reached puberty, they would be reabducted. Ova would be removed, its genetic structure altered with alien characteristics, then replanted back in the human. The female abductees would carry the "baby" several months, then again be abducted. The human/alien child would be removed and brought to term.

Males were not immune to such breeding abductions, according to Hopkins. "Ed Duvall" recalled under hypnosis a sexual encounter with a hybrid alien. In this and other cases, a "suction device" was placed over the penis to remove the sperm. None of these breeding abductions could, according to Hopkins, be described as an erotic experience. "It was very perfunctory," Duvall said, "a detached, clinical procedure."

Once the hybrid children were born, the humans who had "donated" sperm or ova were (yet again) abducted and "shown" their "offspring." The aliens even encouraged the humans to hold the "babies" in a kind of bonding exercise, according to Hopkins. Four women either dreamed or remembered under hypnosis being shown a tiny baby — gray in color and oddly shaped. Kathie Davis claimed to have seen two of her *nine* hybrid children and been allowed to name them. Nor did this cycle of abductions end here. Hopkins claimed the children of abductees were themselves targets for abductions.

Some of Hopkins's abductees gave their impressions of why the aliens were doing these things. "Lucille Forman" had the impression of an alien society "millions of years old, of outstanding technology and intellect but not much individuality or warmth . . . the society was dying . . . children were being born and living to a certain age, perhaps preadolescence, and then dying." The aliens were desperately trying to survive, through both taking new genetic material and exploiting human emotions.

Hopkins painted a progressively darker picture of the "relation- 20 ship" between humans and aliens. "The UFO phenomenon," Hopkins wrote, "seems able to exert nearly complete control over the behavior of the abductees." He continued that the "implants" had "a controlling function as receivers" and that the abductees can "be made to act as surrogates for their abductors." It is a basic tenet of the abduction myth that these alleged events were truly *alien* experiences — that they are not based on science fiction nor psychological aberrations. Hopkins said, "None of these recollections in any way suggests traditional sci-fi gods and devils . . . the aliens are described neither as all-powerful, lordly presences, nor as satanic monsters, but instead as complex, controlling, physically frail beings."

Dr. David Jacobs (a pro-UFO historian) said in a 1986 MUFON[1] paper, "Contactee stories were deeply rooted in a science fiction model of alien behavior [while] abductee stories have a profoundly alien quality to them that are strikingly devoid of cultural programmatic content."

Thomas E. Bullard said that Betty and Barney Hill had no cultural sources from which they could have derived their story, that they were "entirely unpredisposed."

Entirely Unpredisposed?

Consider the following story — a group of men are in a rural area, at night, when they are abducted. They are rendered unconscious, loaded aboard strange flying machines, and taken to a distant place. They are then programmed with false memories to hide the time they were missing. One of them is converted into a puppet of his abductors. They are then released with no overt memories of what happened. But, years later, two of the group begin having strange, surreal dreams about what was done to them.

This story has many elements of abduction stories — loss of control, loss of memory (i.e., one's soul), and loss of humanity. It is not an abduction story. It has nothing to do with UFOs. It is the plot of the 1962 film *The Manchurian Candidate.*

Despite Hopkins's and Jacobs's claims, the abductee myth has numerous similarities with science fiction. Martin Kottmeyer has noted a number of these. In the film *Killers from Space* an abductee has a strange scar and missing memory. In *Invaders from Mars,* the Martians use implants to control humans. This includes not only adults, but their children as well. In the "Cold Hands, Warm Heart" episode of *The Outer Limits,* an astronaut (William Shatner) orbiting Venus loses contact with Earth for eight minutes. After returning to Earth, he has dreams that he landed on Venus and saw a Venusian approaching the ship. His body also starts changing into a Venusian.

"Dying planets" such as "Lucille Forman" described are a standard feature of science fiction — in H. G. Wells's masterpiece *War of the Worlds,* the Martians attacked because Mars was dying and Earth seemed their only hope for survival. Similar "dying planet" themes appeared in the films *This Island Earth, The 27th Day, Killers from Space,* and *Earth vs. the Flying Saucers. The Invaders* were "alien beings from a dying planet."

Crossbreeding between humans and aliens was a common science fiction film plot. They include *Devil Girl from Mars, I Married a*

---

[1]MUFON (Mutual UFO Network) is an international organization dedicated to a scientific study of the UFO phenomenon. — ED.

Monster from Outer Space, The Mysterians, Village of the Damned, Mars Needs Women, and the *Alien* film series.

The shape of aliens in abduction stories is well within the traditions of science fiction. The "bug-eyed monsters" of 1930s and 1940s pulp magazines often had large, bald heads. This was the shape of the projected image of the Wizard in the *Wizard of Oz.* The aliens in the film *Invasion of the Saucer Men* were "bald, bulgy-brained, googly-eyed, no-nosed," fitting the stereotyped image of UFO aliens. Kottmeyer noted that this "prompts worries that abductees are not only plagiarists, but have bad taste as well." In the 1960s, television series such as *The Twilight Zone* and *The Outer Limits* often featured dome-headed aliens. The original pilot for *Star Trek,* "The Cage" (telecast as the two-part episode "The Menagerie"), had short, large-headed, gray-skinned, bald, physically weak aliens with the power to control human minds.

The reasoning behind this particular shape was best expressed by an *Outer Limits* episode called "The Sixth Finger." The story involves the forced forward evolution of a human (David McCallum). As he evolves, his brain grows, his hair recedes, he becomes telepathic, and can control humans. The idea is that apes have small brains, are hairy, and strong. Modern man, in contrast, has a larger brain, has limited body hair, and is weaker. It therefore seems "right" that a future man would have a huge brain, no hair, and be physically frail.

All these similarities between science fiction concepts and the   30
abduction myth caused Kottmeyer to write, "It seems more sensible to flip Hopkins' allegation around. He says nothing about the aliens of UFO abductions resembling 'sci-fi.' I ask, is there anything about UFO aliens that does not resemble science fiction?"

A final note — Hopkins describes a half human/half alien being lacking the ability to feel emotions. It is just such a being which is the most famous character in all of science fiction — Mr. Spock of *Star Trek.* How "logical."

Questions about Hypnosis

Hopkins's abductees had no overt memories until they were hypnotized. The question becomes whether the abduction story is only a product of being hypnotized. A controlled test of hypnotic abduction accounts was conducted in 1977 by Dr. Alvin H. Lawson, a UFOlogist and English professor at California State University, Long Beach. He and others were dissatisfied with the hypnotic regression of abductees. They decided to ask a group of people with no significant UFO knowledge to imagine an abduction under hypnosis. The hypnotic sessions were conducted by Dr. William C. McCall, an M.D. with decades of clinical hypnosis experience. Lawson and the others had expected the imaginary abductees would need prompting. The result was quite different — Lawson wrote later:

What startled us at first was the [subject's] ease and eagerness of narrative invention. Quite often, after introducing the situation — such as, "describe the interior" — Dr. McCall would sit back and the [subject] would talk freely with no more prompting than an occasional, "what's happening, now?"

Lawson compared four imaginary abduction accounts with features of four "real" abduction stories. The chart was an exact match. He concluded:

It is clear from the imaginary narratives that a great many apparent patterns may originate in the mind and so be available to a witness — whether imaginary or "real." If a person who is totally uninformed about UFOs suddenly finds himself in the abduction sequence, it seems safe to assume that the individual's own sensibility will be able to provide under hypnotic regression, pattern details of his encounter which he may or may not have actually experienced in a "real" sense.

The implication of the Lawson study was not that there was a massive number of covert abductions. Rather, it shows that nearly anyone can, under hypnosis, provide an abduction story. Not surprisingly, abductionists and UFO groups have criticized and ignored the Lawson test.

The typical questioning during an abduction hypnotic session goes far beyond "what's happening, now." While researching the book *Mute Evidence,* Daniel Kagan was hypnotized by Dr. Sprinkle. During the session, Dr. Sprinkle said, "Imagine yourself in a spacecraft." There were no UFO images in the recurring dream Kagan was describing. Kagan was so shocked by the attempt to insert a UFO that he came out of the trance. Kagan concluded:

Sprinkle had just demonstrated how much he had probably been responsible for the UFO imagery reported by so many of his hypnotic subjects. It meant that none of Sprinkle's case histories could be taken seriously, because his role as hypnotist could have been the single most powerful factor in introducing UFO images into the subjects' memories.

Another factor is that many of the stories originate with dreams. The dreams are real, but are they dreams of real events? One indication that they are, in fact, only dreams is the wildly irrational and contradictory nature of the stories. This includes one case in which an "abductee" reported hearing a voice from inside a UFO cry out, "I am Jimmy Hoffa!" Other psychological factors include the abductee's own mental state (even "normal" people can have hallucinations) and such organic brain disorders as temporal lobe epilepsy. Finally, there are the effects of personal experiences: under hypnosis, one abductee gave an extremely outlandish description of the aliens; when the hypnotist asked, "Are you sure?" the abductee responded, "No . . . that was something I saw in the

Sunday comic section." Clearly, hypnosis is not the foolproof truth-finding technique the abductionists make it out to be.

In retrospect, it seems clear that the flying saucer myth was always an attempt to find a relationship with the aliens. Earlier myths were about contacts/interactions/struggles between humans and humanlike supernatural beings. Even the conservative Keyhoe had "Operation Lure." The contactees had their own "relationship," rooted in the worldview of the 1950s. When this faded, it was replaced, in the 1960s and 1970s, by the abduction myth, yet another attempt to find a relationship with mythological beings.

This human/alien relationship exactly mirrors society's changing attitudes toward authority, science, and sex. During the contactee era of the 1950s, the grandfatherly "Ike" was president. By the mid-1980s, authority was seen as absolutely evil. Science in the 1950s was seen as utopian. By the 1980s, this had changed into the belief science was antihuman. In 1978, Jose Inacio Alvaro described his alien sexual encounter as being pleasurable. By the 1980s, with the specter of AIDS haunting the bedroom, Hopkins was depicting it as a joyless, technological rape.

The function of mythology is to allow a society to relate to the larger world. This has not changed.

Reading and Discussion Questions

1. The first three paragraphs are an introduction to the chapter. Point out language and particular facts that are designed to prepare you to accept Peebles's claim.
2. How does Peebles explain the similarity in abduction descriptions? Is his explanation plausible? Does anything in your own experience support his explanation?
3. What is the importance of Budd Hopkins in the abduction story? Do you find Hopkins's theories credible? Explain your answer.
4. What does the heading "Entirely Unpredisposed?" mean? How does Peebles develop the idea contained in the title?
5. Summarize Peebles's argument against hypnosis as a means of verifying alien abduction.

Writing Suggestions

6. If you have seen a movie or read a book about alien beings or abductions, describe how the work succeeded or did not succeed in creating credibility.
7. Many books, among them several by Whitney Steiber and *Abduction: Human Experiences with Aliens* (1994) by John Mack, a professor of psychiatry at Harvard University, treat abduction by aliens as a verifiable fact. Look up one of these works, and compare the evidence presented there to the evidence in Peebles's article or his book, mentioned in the biographical note. Confine your discussion to examination of one or two cases.

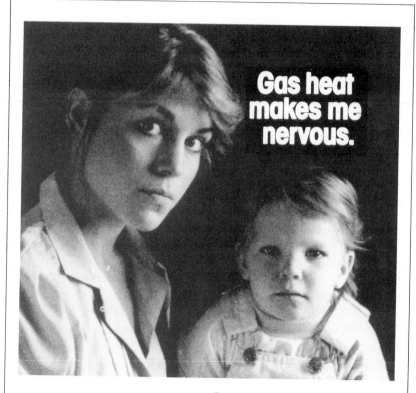

Gas heat makes me nervous.

Gas comes from the big utility.
They don't know my name.
They don't know my family.

If you need prompt service from them,
you have to say, "I smell gas."

That's what scares me most. I think gas heat
is dangerous . . . too dangerous
for my home, my kids.

I heat with oil.

Oil heat...The Intelligent Choice

Metropolitan Energy Council, Inc.

66 Morris Ave., P.O. Box 359, Springfield, NJ 07081 • (201) 379-1100

Discussion Questions

1. What strong emotional appeal does the ad make? Is it justified?
2. How would you verify the validity of the appeal?

Animal Research
Saves Human Lives

HELOISA SABIN

That scene in *Forrest Gump* in which young Forrest runs from his schoolmate tormentors so fast that his leg braces fly apart and his strong legs carry him to safety may be the only image of the polio epidemic of the 1950s etched in the minds of those too young to remember the actual devastation the disease caused. Hollywood created a scene of triumph far removed from the reality of the disease.

Some who have benefited directly from polio research, including that of my late husband, Albert, think winning the real war against polio was just as simple. They have embraced a movement that denounces the very process that enables them to look forward to continued good health and promising futures. This "animal rights" ideology — espoused by groups such as People for the Ethical Treatment of Animals, the Humane Society of the United States and the Fund for Animals — rejects the use of laboratory animals in medical research and denies the role such research played in the victory over polio.

The leaders of this movement seem to have forgotten that year after year in the early fifties, the very words *infantile paralysis* and *poliomyelitis* struck great fear in young parents that the disease would snatch their children as they slept. Each summer public beaches, playgrounds, and movie theaters were places to be avoided. Polio epidemics condemned millions of children and young adults to lives in which debilitated lungs could no longer breathe on their own and young limbs were left forever wilted and frail. The disease drafted tiny armies of children on crutches and in wheelchairs who were unable to walk, run, or jump. In the United States, polio struck down nearly 58,000 children in 1952 alone.

Unlike the braces on Forrest Gump's legs, real ones would be replaced only as the children's misshapen legs grew. Other children and young adults were entombed in iron lungs. The only view of the world these patients had was through mirrors over their heads.

Heloisa Sabin is honorary director of Americans for Medical Progress in Alexandria, Virginia. This essay appeared in the *Wall Street Journal* on October 18, 1995.

These memories, however, are no longer part of our collective cultural memory.

Albert was on the front line of polio research. In 1961, thirty 5 years after he began studying polio, his oral vaccine was introduced in the United States and distributed widely. In the nearly forty years since, polio has been eradicated in the Western Hemisphere, the World Health Organization reports, adding that, with a full-scale effort, polio could be eliminated from the rest of the world by the year 2000.

Without animal research, polio would still be claiming thousands of lives each year. "There could have been no oral polio vaccine without the use of innumerable animals, a very large number of animals," Albert told a reporter shortly before his death in 1993. Animals are still needed to test every new batch of vaccine that is produced for today's children.

Animal activists claim that vaccines really didn't end the epidemic — that, with improvements in social hygiene, polio was dying out anyway, before the vaccines were developed. This is untrue. In fact, advanced sanitation was responsible in part for the dramatic *rise* in the number of paralytic polio cases in the fifties. Improvements in sanitation practices reduced the rate of infection, and the average age of those infected by the polio virus went up. Older children and young adults were more likely than infants to develop paralysis from their exposure to the polio virus.

Every child who has tasted the sweet sugar cube or received the drops containing the Sabin vaccine over the past four decades knows polio only as a word, or an obscure reference in a popular film. Thank heavens it's not part of their reality.

These polio-free generations have grown up to be doctors, teachers, business leaders, government officials, and parents. They have their own concerns and struggles. Cancer, heart disease, strokes, and AIDS are far more lethal realities to them now than polio. Yet, those who support an "animal rights" agenda that would cripple research and halt medical science in its tracks are slamming the door on the possibilities of new treatments and cures.

My husband was a kind man, but he was impatient with those 10 who refused to acknowledge reality or to seek reasoned answers to the questions of life.

The pioneers of polio research included not only the scientists but also the laboratory animals that played a critical role in bringing about the end of polio and a host of other diseases for which we now have vaccines and cures. Animals will continue to be as vital as the scientists who study them in the battle to eliminate pain, suffering, and disease from our lives.

That is the reality of medical progress.

Why We Don't Need Animal Experimentation

PEGGY CARLSON

The issue of animal experimentation has become so polarized that rational thinking seems to have taken a back seat. Heloisa Sabin's October 18 editorial-page article "Animal Research Saves Lives" serves only to further misinform and polarize. She does a great disservice to science to incorrectly portray the debate about animal experimentation as occurring between "animal rights activists" and scientists. The truth is, the value of animal experimentation is being questioned by many scientists.

Mrs. Sabin uses the example of the polio vaccine developed by her husband to justify animal experimentation. However, in the case of the polio vaccine, misleading animal experiments detoured scientists away from reliable clinical studies thereby, according to Dr. Sabin himself, delaying the initial work on polio prevention. It was also unfortunate that the original polio vaccine was produced using monkey cells instead of available human cells as can be done today. The use of monkey cells resulted in viruses with the potential to cause serious disease being transferred to humans when the polio vaccine was administered.

The polio vaccine example cannot logically be used to justify the current level of animal experimentation — several billion dollars and about 30 million animals yearly. Although most people would prefer to believe that the death and suffering of all these animals is justified, the facts do not support that conclusion.

Nearly everything that medicine has learned about what substances cause human cancer and birth defects has come from human clinical and epidemiological studies because animal experiments do not accurately predict what occurs in humans. Dr. Bross, the former Director of Biostatistics at the Roswell Institute for Cancer Research states, "While conflicting animal results have often delayed and hampered advances in the war on cancer, they have never produced a single substantial advance either in the prevention or treatment of cancer." A 1990 editorial in *Stroke* notes that none of the twenty-five compounds "proven" efficacious for treating stroke in animal experiments over the preceding ten years had been effective for use in humans. From human studies alone we have learned how to lessen the risk of heart attacks. Warnings to the public that

Peggy Carlson, M.D., was the research director of the Physicians Committee for Responsible Medicine in Washington, D.C. at the time her letter appeared in the *Wall Street Journal* on November 7, 1995.

195

smoking cigarettes leads to an increased risk of cancer were delayed as researchers sought, unsuccessfully, to confirm the risk by using animals.

Animal tests for drug safety, cancer-causing potential, and toxicity are unreliable, and science is leading us to more accurate methods that will offer greater protection. But if we refuse to acknowledge the inadequacies of animal tests we put a stranglehold on the very progress that will help us. Billions of precious health-care dollars have been spent to fund animal experiments that are repetitious or that have no human relevance.

An uncritical acceptance of the value of animal experiments leads to its overfunding, which, in turn, leads to the underfunding of other more beneficial areas.

Discussion Questions

1. Sabin uses the vaccine against polio as the principal example in her support of animal research. Does this limit her argument? Should she have been more specific in her references to other diseases?
2. What is the significance of Sabin's repeated references to "reality"?
3. Mention all the kinds of support that Carlson provides. Which of the supporting materials is most persuasive?
4. Does Carlson refute all the arguments in Sabin's article? Be specific.
5. Sabin makes strong emotional appeals. Describe them, and decide how large a part such appeals play in her argument. Does Carlson appeal to the emotions of her readers?

TAKING THE DEBATE ONLINE

- **University of Colorado at Boulder: Frequently Asked Questions** <http://www.colorado.edu/Research/animal_resources/faqs.html> This multilayered site examines animal resources at the university and explores many ethical questions on animal research.

- **University of Delaware: Animal Testing — Pro or Con?** <http:// www.ash.udel.edu/incoming/rcap/index.html> This reference tool contains numerous links addressing the pros and cons of animal testing, as well as statistical evidence to back up or condemn the validity of animal research.

- **National Institutes of Health** <http://www.nih.gov/> Investigates America's premier medical research facilities for their treatment of animals.

- **People for the Ethical Treatment of Animals Online** <http://www .peta-online.org> This association unequivocally condemns animal research.

- **Scientific American** **<http://www.sciam.com/>** This site contains links to featured stories about animal experimentation in the February 1997 issue of the magazine.
- **Fund for the Replacement of Animals in Medical Experiments** **<http://www.frame-uk.demon.co.uk/>** This association promotes the researching of alternatives to animal testing.

EXERCISES

1. What kind of evidence would you offer to prove to a skeptic that the moon landings — or any other space ventures — have actually occurred? What objections would you anticipate?
2. A group of heterosexual people in a middle-class community who define themselves as devout Christians have organized to keep a group of homosexuals from joining their church. What kind of support would you offer for your claim that the homosexuals should be welcomed into the church? Address your argument to the heterosexuals unwilling to admit the group of homosexuals.
3. In the summer of 1983, after an alarming rise in the juvenile crime rate, the mayor of Detroit instituted a curfew for young people under the age of eighteen. What kind of support can you provide for or against such a curfew?
4. "Racism [or sexism] is [not] a major problem on this campus [or home town or neighborhood]." Produce evidence to support your claim.
5. Write a full-page advertisement to solicit support for a project or cause that you believe in.
6. How do you account for the large and growing interest in science fiction films and books? In addition to their entertainment value, are there other less obvious reasons for their popularity?
7. According to some researchers soap operas are influential in transmitting values, life-styles, and sexual information to youthful viewers. Do you agree? If so, what values and information are being transmitted? Be specific.
8. Choose one of the following stereotypical ideas and argue that it is true or false or partly both. Discuss the reasons for the existence of the stereotype.
   a. Jocks are stupid.
   b. The country is better than the city for bringing up children.
   c. Television is justly called "the boob tube."
   d. A dog is man's best friend.
   e. Beauty contests are degrading to women.
9. Defend or refute the view that organized sports build character.
10. The philosopher Bertrand Russell said, "Most of the work that most people have to do is not in itself interesting, but even such work has certain advantages." Defend or refute this assertion. Use your own experience as support.

Critical Listening

11. Choose a product advertised on television by many different makers. (Cars, pain relievers, fast food, cereals, and soft drinks are some of the most popular products.) What kinds of support do the advertisers offer? Why do they choose these particular appeals? Would the support be significantly different in print?

12. From time to time advocates of causes speak on campus. The causes may be broadly based — minority rights, welfare cuts, abortion, foreign aid — or they may be local issues, having to do with harassment policy, course requirements, or tuition increases. Attend a meeting or a rally at which a speaker argues his or her cause. Write an evaluation of the speech, paying particular attention to the kinds of support. Did the speaker provide sufficient and relevant evidence? Did he or she make emotional appeals? What signs, if any, reflected the speaker's awareness of the kinds of audience he or she was addressing?

CHAPTER SIX

Warrants

We now come to the third element in the structure of the argument — the warrant. In the first chapter we defined the warrant as an *assumption,* a belief we take for granted, or a general principle. Claim and support, the other major elements we have discussed, are more familiar in ordinary discourse, but there is nothing mysterious or unusual about the warrant. All our claims, both formal and informal, are grounded in warrants or assumptions that the audience must share with us if our claims are to prove acceptable.

These warrants reflect our observations, our personal experience, and our participation in a culture. But because these observations, experiences, and cultural associations will vary, the audience may not always agree with the warrants or assumptions of the writer. The British philosopher Stephen Toulmin, who developed the concept of warrants, dismissed more traditional forms of logical reasoning in favor of a more audience-based, courtroom-derived approach to argumentation. He refers to warrants as "general, hypothetical statements, which can act as bridges" and "entitle one to draw conclusions or make claims."[1] The word *bridges* to denote the action of the warrant is crucial. One dictionary defines warrant as a "guarantee or justification." We use the word *warrant* to emphasize that in an argument it guarantees a connecting link — a bridge — between the claim and the support. This means that even if a reader agrees that the support is sound, the support cannot prove the validity of the claim unless the reader also agrees with the underlying warrant. Recall the sample argument outlined in Chapter 1 (p. 12):

---

[1]Stephen Toulmin, *The Uses of Argument* (Cambridge: Cambridge University Press, 1958), p. 98.

> CLAIM: Adoption of a vegetarian diet leads to healthier and longer life.
>
> SUPPORT: The authors of *Becoming a Vegetarian Family* say so.
>
> WARRANT: The authors of *Becoming a Vegetarian Family* are reliable sources of information on diet.

Notice that the reader must agree with the assumption that the testimony of experts is trustworthy before he or she arrives at the conclusion that a vegetarian diet is healthy. Simply providing evidence that the authors say so is not enough to prove the claim.

The following dialogue offers another example of the relationship between the warrant and the other elements of the argument.

"I don't think that Larry can do the job. He's pretty dumb."

"Really? I thought he was smart. What makes you say he's dumb?"

"Did you know that he's illiterate — can't read above third-grade level? In my book that makes him dumb."

If we put this into outline form, the warrant or assumption in the argument becomes clear.

> CLAIM: Larry is pretty dumb.
>
> EVIDENCE: He can't read above third-grade level.
>
> WARRANT: Anybody who can't read above third-grade level must be dumb.

We can also represent the argument in diagram form, which shows the warrant as a bridge between the claim and the support.

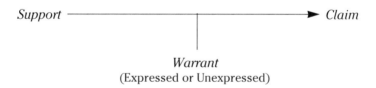

Support ————————————————▶ *Claim*

Warrant
(Expressed or Unexpressed)

The argument above can then be written like this:

Support ————————————————▶ *Claim*
Larry can't read above   He's pretty dumb.
  third-grade level.

Warrant
Anybody who can't read above third-grade
level must be pretty dumb.

Is this warrant valid? We cannot answer this question until we consider the *backing*. Every warrant or assumption rests on something else that gives it authority; this is what we call backing. Backing or authority for the warrant in this example would consist of research data that prove a relationship between stupidity and low reading ability. This particular warrant, we would discover, lacks backing because we know that the failure to learn to read well may be due to a number of things unrelated to intelligence. So if the warrant is unprovable, the claim — that Larry is dumb — is also unprovable, even if the evidence is true. In this case, then, the evidence does not guarantee the soundness of the claim.

Now consider this example of a somewhat more complicated warrant: The beautiful and unspoiled Eastern Shore of Maryland is being discovered by thousands of tourists, vacationers, and developers who will, according to the residents, change the landscape and the way of life, which is now based largely on fishing and farming. In a few years the Eastern Shore may become a noisy, crowded string of resorts. Mrs. Walkup, the Kent County commissioner, says,

> Catering to the wealthy puts property back on the tax rolls, but it's going to make the Eastern Shore look like the rest of the country. Everything that made our way of life so special is being eroded. We are a fragile area. The Eastern Shore is still special, but it is feeling pressure from all directions. Lots of people don't seem to appreciate the fact that God made us to need a little peace and quiet now and then.[2]

In simplified form the argument of those opposed to development would be outlined this way:

CLAIM: Development will bring undesirable changes to the present way of life on the Eastern Shore, a life of farming and fishing, peace and quiet.

SUPPORT: Developers will build express highways, condominiums, casinos, and nightclubs.

WARRANT: A pastoral life of fishing and farming is superior to the way of life brought by expensive, fast-paced modern development.

Notice that the warrant is a broad generalization that can apply to a number of different situations, while the claim is about a specific place and time. It should be added that in other arguments the warrant may not be stated in such general terms. However, even in arguments in which the warrant makes a more specific reference to the claim, the reader can infer an extension of the warrant to other similar arguments. In the vegetarian diet example (p. 3, outlined on p. 12) the warrant mentions a specific book. But it is clear that such

---

[2]Michael Wright, "The Changing Chesapeake," *New York Times Magazine,* July 10, 1983, p. 27.

warrants can be generalized to apply to other arguments in which we accept a claim based on the credibility of the sources.

To be convinced of the validity of Mrs. Walkup's claim, you must first find that the support is true, that the developers plan to introduce drastic changes that will destroy the pastoral life of the Eastern Shore. You may, however, believe that the support is not entirely sound, that the development will be much more modest than residents fear, and that the Eastern Shore will not be seriously altered. Next, you may want to see more justification for the warrant. Is pastoral life superior to the life that will result from large-scale development? Perhaps you have always thought that a life of fishing and farming means poverty and limited opportunities for the majority of the residents. Although the superiority of a way of life is largely a matter of taste and therefore difficult to prove, Mrs. Walkup may need to produce backing for her belief that the present way of life is more desirable than one based on developing the area for new residents and summer visitors. If you find either the support or the warrant unconvincing, you cannot accept the claim.

Remember that a claim is often modified by one or more qualifiers, which limit the claim. Mrs. Walkup might have said, "Development will *probably* destroy *some aspects of* the present way of life on the Eastern Shore." Warrants can also be modified or limited by *reservations,* which remind the reader that there are conditions under which the warrants will not be relevant. Mrs. Walkup might have added, "unless increased prosperity and exposure to the outside world brought by development improve some aspects of our lives."

A diagram of Mrs. Walkup's argument shows the additional elements:

Support ————————————————▶ *Claim*

The developers will build highways, condos, casinos, nightclubs.	Development will bring undesirable changes to life on the Eastern Shore.

Warrant *Qualifier*

A way of life devoted to farming and fishing is superior to a way of life brought by development.	Development will *most likely* bring undesirable changes.

Backing

We have experienced crowds, traffic, noise, rich strangers, and high-rises, and they destroy peace and quiet.

Reservation

But increased development might improve some aspects of our lives.

Claim and support (or lack of support) are relatively easy to uncover in most arguments. One thing that makes the warrant different is that it is often unexpressed and therefore unexamined by both writer and reader because they take it for granted. In the argument about Larry's intelligence, the warrant was stated. But in the argument about development on the Eastern Shore, Mrs. Walkup did not state her warrant directly, although her meaning is perfectly clear. She probably felt that it was not necessary to be more explicit because her readers would understand and supply the warrant.

We can make the discovery of warrants even clearer by examining another argument, in this case a policy claim. We've looked at a factual claim — that Larry is dumb — and a value claim — that Eastern Shore development is undesirable. Now we examine a policy claim that rests on one expressed and one unexpressed warrant. Policy claims are usually more complicated than other claims because the statement of policy is preceded by an array of facts and values. In addition, such claims may represent chains of reasoning in which one argument is dependent on another. These complicated arguments may be difficult or impossible to summarize in a simple diagram, but careful reading, asking the same kinds of questions that the author may have asked about his claim, can help you to find the warrant or chain of warrants that must be accepted before evidence and claim can be linked.

In the article we examine,[3] the author argues for a radical reform in college sports — the elimination of subprofessional intermural team sports, as practiced above all in football and basketball. The claim is clear, and evidence for the professional character of college sports not hard to find: the large salaries paid to coaches, the generous perquisites offered to players, the recruitment policies that ignore academic standing, the virtually full-time commitment of the players, the lucrative television contracts. But can this evidence support the author's claim that such sports do not belong on college campuses? Advocates of these sports may ask, Why not? In the conclusion of the article the author states one warrant or assumption underlying his claim.

> Even if the money to pay college athletes could be found, though, a larger question must be answered — namely, why should a system of professional athletics be affiliated with universities at all? For the truth is that the requirements of athletics and academics operate at cross purposes, and the attempt to play both games at once serves only to reduce the level of performance of each.

In other words, the author assumes that the goals of an academic education on the one hand and the goals of big-time college sports

---

[3]D. G. Myers, "Why College Sports?" *Commentary,* December 1990, pp. 49–51.

on the other hand are incompatible. In the article he develops the ways in which each enterprise harms the other.

But the argument clearly rests on another warrant that is not expressed because the author takes for granted that his readers will supply it: The academic goals of the university are primary and should take precedence over all other collegiate activities. This is an argument based on an authority warrant, the authority of those who define the goals of the university — scholars, public officials, university administrators, and others. (Types of warrants are discussed in the following section.)

This warrant makes clear that the evidence of the professional nature of college sports cited above supports the claim that they should be eliminated. If quasiprofessional college sports are harmful to the primary educational function of the college or university, then they must go. In the author's words, "The two are separate enterprises, to be judged by separate criteria. . . . For college sports, the university is not an educational institution at all; it is merely a locus, a means of coordinating the different aspects of the sporting enterprise."

Arguers will often neglect to state their warrants for one of two reasons: First, like Mrs. Walkup, they may believe that the warrant is obvious and need not be expressed; second, they may want to conceal the warrant in the hope that the reader will overlook its weakness.

What kinds of warrants are so obvious that they need not be expressed? Here are a few that will probably sound familiar.

Mothers love their children.

The more expensive the product, the more satisfactory it will be.

A good harvest will result in lower prices for produce.

First come, first served.

These statements seem to embody beliefs that most of us would share and that might be unnecessary to make explicit in an argument. The last statement, for example, is taken as axiomatic, an article of faith that we seldom question in ordinary circumstances. Suppose you hear someone make the claim, "I deserve to get the last ticket to the concert." If you ask why he is entitled to a ticket that you also would like to have, he may answer in support of his claim, "Because I was here first." No doubt you accept his claim without further argument because you understand and agree with the warrant that is not expressed: "If you arrive first, you deserve to be served before those who come later." Your acceptance of the warrant probably also takes into account the unexpressed backing that is based on a belief in justice: "It is only fair that those who sacrifice time and comfort to be first in line should be rewarded for their trouble."

In this case it may not be necessary to expose the warrant and examine it. Indeed, as Stephen Toulmin tells us, "If we demanded the credentials of all warrants at sight and never let one pass unchallenged, argument could scarcely begin."[4]

But even those warrants that seem to express universal truths invite analysis if we can think of claims for which these warrants might not, after all, be relevant. "First in line," for example, may justify the claim of a person who wants a concert ticket, but it cannot in itself justify the claim of someone who wants a vital medication that is in short supply. Moreover, offering a rebuttal to a long-held but unexamined warrant can often produce an interesting and original argument. If someone exclaims, "All this buying of gifts! I think people have forgotten that Christmas celebrates the birth of Christ," she need not express the assumption — that the buying of gifts violates what ought to be a religious celebration. It goes unstated by the speaker because it has been uttered so often that she knows the hearer will supply it. But one writer, in an essay titled "God's Gift: A Commercial Christmas," argued that, contrary to popular belief, the purchase of gifts, which means the expenditure of time, money, and thought on others rather than oneself, is not a violation but an affirmation of the Christmas spirit.[5]

The second reason for refusal to state the warrant lies in the arguer's intention to disarm or deceive the reader, although the arguer may not be aware of this. For instance, failure to state the warrant is common in advertising and politics, where the desire to sell a product or an idea may outweigh the responsibility to argue explicitly. The following advertisement is famous not only for what it says but for what it does not say:

> In 1918 Leona Currie scandalized a New Jersey beach with a bathing suit cut above her knees. And to irk the establishment even more, she smoked a cigarette. Leona Currie was promptly arrested.
>
> Oh, how Leona would smile if she could see you today.
>
> You've come a long way, baby. *Virginia Slims*. The taste for today's woman.

What is the unstated warrant? The manufacturer of Virginia Slims hopes we will agree that being permitted to smoke cigarettes is a significant sign of female liberation. But many readers would insist that proving "You've come a long way, baby" requires more evidence than women's freedom to smoke (or wear short bathing suits). The shaky warrant weakens the claim.

Politicians, too, conceal warrants that may not survive close scrutiny. In the 1983 mayoral election in Chicago, one candidate

---

[4]*The Uses of Argument* (Cambridge: Cambridge University Press, 1958), p. 106.
[5]Robert A. Sirico, *Wall Street Journal,* December 21, 1993, sec. A, p. 12.

revealed that his opponent had undergone psychiatric treatment. He did not have to state the warrant supporting his claim. He knew that many in his audience would assume that anyone who had undergone psychiatric treatment was unfit to hold public office. This same assumption contributed to the withdrawal of a vice-presidential candidate from the 1972 campaign.

TYPES OF WARRANTS

Arguments may be classified according to the types of warrants offered as proof. Because warrants represent the reasoning process by which we establish the relationship between support and claim, analysis of the major types of warrants enables us to see the whole argument as a sum of its parts.

Warrants may be organized into three categories: "*authoritative, substantive,* and *motivational.*"[6] We have already given examples of these types of warrants in this chapter and in Chapter 1. The *authoritative warrant* (see p. 12) is based on the credibility or trustworthiness of the source. If we assume that the source of the data is authoritative, then we find that the support justifies the claim. A *substantive warrant* is based on beliefs about reliability of factual evidence. In the example on page 200 the speaker assumes, although mistakenly, that the relationship between low reading level and stupidity is a verifiable datum, one that can be proved by objective research. A *motivational warrant,* on the other hand, is based on the needs and values of the audience. For example, the warrant on page 12 reflects a preference for individual freedom, a value that would cause a reader who held it to agree that laws against marijuana should be repealed.

Each type of warrant requires a different set of questions for testing its soundness. The following list of questions will help you to decide whether a particular warrant is valid and can justify a particular claim.

1. *Authoritative* (based on the credibility of the sources)
   Is the authority sufficiently respected to make a credible claim?
   Do other equally reputable authorities agree with the authority cited?
   Are there equally reputable authorities who disagree?

2. *Substantive* (based on beliefs about the reliability of factual evidence)
   Are sufficient examples given to convince us that a general statement is justified? That is, are the examples given representative of the whole community?

---

[6]D. Ehninger and W. Brockriede, *Decision by Debate* (New York: Dodd, Mead, 1953).

If you have argued that one event or condition can bring about another (a cause-and-effect argument), does the cause given seem to account entirely for the effect? Are other possible causes equally important as explanations for the effect?

If you have used comparisons, are the similarities between the two situations greater than the differences?

If you have used analogies, does the analogy explain or merely describe? Are there sufficient similarities between the two elements to make the analogy appropriate?

3. *Motivational* (based on the values of the arguer and the audience)

Are the values ones that the audience will regard as important? Are the values relevant to the claim?

SAMPLE ANNOTATED ANALYSIS

The Case for Torture

MICHAEL LEVIN

Introduction: statement of opposing view

It is generally assumed that torture is impermissible, a throwback to a more brutal age. Enlightened societies reject it outright, and regimes suspected of using it risk the wrath of the United States.

Claim of policy: rebuttal of opposing view

I believe this attitude is unwise. There are situations in which torture is not merely permissible but morally mandatory. Moreover, these situations are moving from the realm of imagination to fact.

Support: hypothetical example to test the reader's belief

Suppose a terrorist has hidden an atomic bomb on Manhattan Island which will detonate at noon on July 4 unless . . . (here follow the usual demands for money and release of his friends from jail). Suppose, further, that he is caught at 10 A.M. of the fateful day, but — preferring death to failure — won't disclose where the bomb is. What do we do? If we follow due

---

Michael Levin is a professor of philosophy at the City College of New York. This essay is reprinted from the June 7, 1982, issue of *Newsweek.*

process — wait for his lawyer, arraign him — millions of people will die. If the only way to save those lives is to subject the terrorist to the most excruciating possible pain, what grounds can there be for not doing so? I suggest there are none. In any case, I ask you to face the question with an open mind.

Torturing the terrorist is unconstitutional? Probably. But millions of lives surely outweigh constitutionality. Torture is barbaric? Mass murder is far more barbaric. Indeed, letting millions of innocents die in deference to one who flaunts his guilt is moral cowardice, an unwillingness to dirty one's hands. If *you* caught the terrorist, could you sleep nights knowing that millions died because you couldn't bring yourself to apply the electrodes?

Once you concede that torture is justi- 5 fied in extreme cases, you have admitted that the decision to use torture is a matter of balancing innocent lives against the means needed to save them. You must now face more realistic cases involving more modest numbers. Someone plants a bomb on a jumbo jet. He alone can disarm it, and his demands cannot be met (or if they can, we refuse to set a precedent by yielding to his threats). Surely we can, we must, do anything to the extortionist to save the passengers. How can we tell 300, or 100, or 10 people who never asked to be put in danger, "I'm sorry, you'll have to die in agony, we just couldn't bring ourselves to . . ."

Here are the results of an informal poll about a third, hypothetical, case. Suppose a terrorist group kidnapped a newborn baby from a hospital. I asked four mothers if they would approve of torturing kidnappers if that were necessary to get their own newborns back. All said yes, the most "liberal" adding that she would administer it herself.

I am not advocating torture as punishment. Punishment is addressed to deeds

Support: hypothetical example

Support: informal poll

Defense of the claim

a) Not punishment but protection of the innocent

irrevocably past. Rather, I am advocating torture as an acceptable measure for preventing future evils. So understood, it is far less objectionable than many extant punishments. Opponents of the death penalty, for example, are forever insisting that executing a murderer will not bring back his victim (as if the purpose of capital punishment were supposed to be resurrection, not deterrence or retribution). But torture, in the cases described, is intended not to bring anyone back but to keep innocents from being dispatched. The most powerful argument against using torture as a punishment or to secure confessions is that such practices disregard the rights of the individual. Well, if the individual is all that important — and he is — it is correspondingly important to protect the rights of individuals threatened by terrorists. If life is so valuable that it must never be taken, the lives of the innocents must be saved even at the price of hurting the one who endangers them.

Hypothetical examples:

b) Analogies with World War II

Better precedents for torture are assassination and preemptive attack. No Allied leader would have flinched at assassinating Hitler, had that been possible. (The Allies did assassinate Heydrich.) Americans would be angered to learn that Roosevelt could have had Hitler killed in 1943 — thereby shortening the war and saving millions of lives — but refused on moral grounds. Similarly, if nation A learns that nation B is about to launch an unprovoked attack, A has a right to save itself by destroying B's military capability first. In the same way, if the police can by torture save those who would otherwise die at the hands of kidnappers or terrorists, they must.

c) Denial that terrorists have rights

There is an important difference between terrorists and their victims that should mute talk of the terrorists' "rights." The terrorist's victims are at risk unintentionally, not having asked to be endangered. But the terrorist knowingly initiated his actions. Unlike his victims, he volunteered for the risks of his deed. By threatening to kill for profit or idealism, he renounces civilized standards, and he can have no complaint if civilization tries to thwart him by whatever means necessary.

Just as torture is justified only to save 10 lives (not extort confessions or recantations), it is justifiably administered only to those *known* to hold innocent lives in their hands. Ah, but how can the authorities ever be sure they have the right malefactor? Isn't there a danger of error and abuse? Won't We turn into Them?

Questions like these are disingenuous in a world in which terrorists proclaim themselves and perform for television. The name of their game is public recognition. After all, you can't very well intimidate a government into releasing your freedom fighters unless you announce that it is your group that has seized its embassy. "Clear guilt" is difficult to define, but when 40 million people see a group of masked gunmen seize an airplane on the evening news, there is not much question about who the perpetrators are. There will be hard cases where the situation is murkier. Nonetheless, a line demarcating the legitimate use of torture can be drawn. Torture only the obviously guilty, and only for the sake of saving innocents, and the line between Us and Them will remain clear.

There is little danger that the Western democracies will lose their way if they choose to inflict pain as one way of preserving order. Paralysis in the face of evil is the greater danger. Some day soon a terrorist will threaten tens of thousands of lives, and torture will be the only way to save them. We had better start thinking about this.

d) Easy identification of terrorists

Conclusion warrant —
"Paralysis in the face of evil is the greater danger."

Analysis

Levin's controversial essay attacks a popular assumption that most people have never thought to question — that torture is impermissible under any circumstances. Levin argues that in extreme cases torture is morally justified to bring about a greater good than the rights of the individual who is tortured.

Against the initial resistance that most readers may feel, Levin makes a strong case. Its strength lies in the backing he provides for the warrant that torture is sometimes necessary. This backing consists in the use of two effective argumentative strategies. One is the anticipation of objections. Unprecedented? No. Unconstitutional? No. Barbaric? No. Second, and more important, are the hypothetical examples that compel readers to rethink their positions and possibly arrive at agreement with the author. Levin chooses extreme examples — kidnapping of a newborn child, planting a bomb on a jumbo jet, detonating an atomic bomb in Manhattan — that draw a line between clear and murky cases and make agreement easier. And he bolsters his moral position by insisting that torture is not to be used as punishment or revenge but only to save innocent lives.

To support such an unpopular assumption the writer must convey the impression that he is a reasonable man, and this Levin attempts to do by a searching definition of terms, the careful organization and development of his argument, including references to the opinions of other people, and the expression of compassion for innocent lives.

Another strength of the article is its readability — the use of contractions, informal questions, conversational locutions. This easy, familiar style is disarming; the reader doesn't feel threatened by heavy admonitions from a writer who affects a superior, moral attitude.

A Proposal to Abolish Grading

PAUL GOODMAN

Let half a dozen of the prestigious Universities — Chicago, Stanford, the Ivy League — abolish grading, and use testing only and entirely for pedagogic purposes as teachers see fit.

Anyone who knows the frantic temper of the present schools will understand the transvaluation of values that would be effected by this modest innovation. For most of the students, the competitive grade has come to be the essence. The naive teacher points to the beauty of the subject and the ingenuity of the research; the shrewd student asks if he is responsible for that on the final exam.

Let me at once dispose of an objection whose unanimity is quite fascinating. I think that the great majority of professors agree that grading hinders teaching and creates a bad spirit, going as far as cheating and plagiarizing. I have before me the collection of essays, *Examining in Harvard College,* and this is the consensus. It is uniformly asserted, however, that the grading is inevitable; for how else will the graduate schools, the foundations, the corporations *know* whom to accept, reward, hire? How will the talent scouts know whom to tap?

By testing the applicants, of course, according to the specific task-requirements of the inducting institution, just as applicants for the Civil Service or for licenses in medicine, law, and architecture are tested. Why should Harvard professors do the testing *for* corporations and graduate schools?

The objection is ludicrous. Dean Whitla, of the Harvard Office of 5 Tests, points out that the scholastic-aptitude and achievement tests used for *admission* to Harvard are a superexcellent index for all-around Harvard performance, better than high-school grades or particular Harvard course-grades. Presumably, these college-entrance tests are tailored for what Harvard and similar institutions want. By the same logic, would not an employer do far better to apply his own job-aptitude test rather than to rely on the vagaries of Harvard section-men? Indeed, I doubt that many employers bother to look at such grades; they are more likely to be interested merely in the fact of a Harvard diploma, whatever that connotes to them.

Paul Goodman (1911–1972) was a college professor and writer whose outspoken views were popular with students during the 1960s. This essay is from *Compulsory Miseducation* (1964).

The grades have most of their weight with the graduate schools —
here, as elsewhere, the system runs mainly for its own sake.

It is really necessary to remind our academics of the ancient history of Examination. In the medieval university, the whole point of
the grueling trial of the candidate was whether or not to accept him
as a peer. His disputation and lecture for the Master's was just that,
a masterpiece to enter the guild. It was not to make comparative
evaluations. It was not to weed out and select for an extramural li-
censor or employer. It was certainly not to pit one young fellow
against another in an ugly competition. My philosophic impression
is that the medievals thought they knew what a good job of work
was and that we are competitive because we do not know. But the
more status is achieved by largely irrelevant competitive evaluation,
the less will we ever know.

(Of course, our American examinations never did have this
purely guild orientation, just as our faculties have rarely had absolute autonomy; the examining was to satisfy Overseers, Elders,
distant Regents — and they as paternal superiors have always
doted on giving grades, rather than accepting peers. But I submit
that this set-up itself makes it impossible for the student to *become* a
master, to *have* grown up, and to commence on his own. He will always be making A or B for some overseer. And in the present atmosphere, he will always be climbing on his friend's neck.)

Perhaps the chief objectors to abolishing grading would be the
students and their parents. The parents should be simply disre-
garded; their anxiety has done enough damage already. For the students, it seems to me that a primary duty of the university is to
deprive them of their props, their dependence on extrinsic valuation
and motivation, and to force them to confront the difficult enterprise
itself and finally lose themselves in it.

A miserable effect of grading is to nullify the various uses of testing. Testing, for both student and teacher, is a means of structuring,
and also of finding out what is blank or wrong and what has been
assimilated and can be taken for granted. Review — including
high-pressure review — is a means of bringing together the fragments, so that there are flashes of synoptic insight.

There are several good reasons for testing, and kinds of test. But 10
if the aim is to discover weakness, what is the point of down-grading
and punishing it, and thereby inviting the student to conceal his
weakness, by faking and bulling, if not cheating? The natural conclusion of synthesis is the insight itself, not a grade for having had it.
For the important purpose of placement, if one can establish in the
student the belief that one is testing *not* to grade and make invidious
comparisons but for his own advantage, the student should normally seek his own level, where he is challenged and yet capable,
rather than trying to get by. If the student dares to accept himself as

he is, a teacher's grade is a crude instrument compared with a student's self-awareness. But it is rare in our universities that students are encouraged to notice objectively their vast confusion. Unlike Socrates, our teachers rely on power-drives rather than shame and ingenuous idealism.

Many students are lazy, so teachers try to goad or threaten them by grading. In the long run this must do more harm than good. Laziness is a character-defense. It may be a way of avoiding learning, in order to protect the conceit that one is already perfect (deeper, the despair that one *never* can be). It may be a way of avoiding just the risk of failing and being down-graded. Sometimes it is a way of politely saying, "I won't." But since it is the authoritarian grown-up demands that have created such attitudes in the first place, why repeat the trauma? There comes a time when we must treat people as adult, laziness and all. It is one thing courageously to fire a do-nothing out of your class; it is quite another thing to evaluate him with a lordly F.

Most important of all, it is often obvious that balking in doing the work, especially among bright young people who get to great universities, means exactly what it says: The work does not suit me, not this subject, or not at this time, or not in this school, or not in school altogether. The student might not be bookish; he might be school-tired; perhaps his development ought now to take another direction. Yet unfortunately, if such a student is intelligent and is not sure of himself, he *can* be bullied into passing, and this obscures everything. My hunch is that I am describing a common situation. What a grim waste of young life and teacherly effort! Such a student will retain nothing of what he has "passed" in. Sometimes he must get mononucleosis to tell his story and be believed.

And ironically, the converse is also probably commonly true. A student flunks and is mechanically weeded out, who is really ready and eager to learn in a scholastic setting, but he has not quite caught on. A good teacher can recognize the situation, but the computer wreaks its will.

Reading and Discussion Questions

1. Goodman divides his argument into several parts, each of which develops a different idea. How would you subtitle these parts?
2. Are some parts of the argument stronger than others? Does Goodman indicate what points he wants to emphasize?
3. Why do you think Goodman calls on "half a dozen of the prestigious Universities" (para. 1) instead of all universities to abolish grading?
4. Where does the author reveal the purposes of his proposal?
5. Most professors, Goodman argues, think that grading hinders teaching. Why, then, do they continue to give grades? How does Goodman reply to their objections?

6. What does Goodman think the real purpose of testing should be? How does grading "nullify the various uses of testing" (para. 9)?

Writing Suggestions

7. Do you agree that grading prevents you from learning? If so, write an essay in which you support Goodman's thesis by reporting what your own experience has been.
8. If you disagree with Goodman, write an essay that outlines the benefits of grading.
9. Is there a better way than grading to evaluate the work of students — a way that would achieve the goals of education Goodman values? Suggest a method, and explain why it would be superior to grading.

Samaritan's Dilemma

ROBERT A. SIRICO

Part of my training as a priest included an assignment at a soup kitchen in Anacostia, a poor section of Washington, D.C. Each Friday a classmate and I would spend the afternoon helping set up, serve, and clean up after a free meal that was offered in the basement of a local Protestant church.

On the first day of our assignment, we met the Catholic nun who ran the operation, which fed between 200 and 500 persons each day. She explained that the numbers would fluctuate, and the pattern seemed to be that the group was the smallest on the days right after the arrival of welfare checks. The nun also said that the soup kitchen had a whosoever-will-may-come policy, meaning there was no means testing.

Sure enough. Whole families would arrive for their meal. I witnessed one person arriving in a taxi. Another couple told me they needed to eat quickly because they were planning to go shopping after dinner.

One Friday during Lent, my classmate and I worked in the kitchen as usual. After serving the meal and cleaning up, we did not eat in the kitchen, as was our custom, since it had served meat and Catholics abstain from eating meat on Fridays during Lent. Instead we went to a seafood pub just down the street.

Robert A. Sirico, a Roman Catholic priest, is president of the Acton Institute for the Study of Religion and Liberty in Grand Rapids, Michigan. This essay appeared in *Forbes* magazine on April 25, 1994.

As we enjoyed a simple fish dinner, something struck me about 5 the nature of our charitable work. We knew that the pub's proprietor lived in the neighborhood and he and his family worked hard to keep the business afloat. It dawned on me that my classmate and I, and the numerous well-intentioned people who contributed food, money, and service to the soup kitchen, were his competitors. Just a block away, we provided a product and a service that made this man's efforts to provide for his own family more difficult.

This story illuminates the moral dilemma that charity to the needy poses. On the face of it a soup kitchen sounds like an unequivocal good. But this requires deeper examination. The first thing we must do, if we are serious in our desire to help the poor better their lot, is to consider the full effect of the programs we organize in their name.

When I worked in the soup kitchen, it pleased me to think of a person coming to us hungry and leaving with a full stomach. Yet for many — perhaps even most — of our clients, the meal was a convenience, not a dire necessity. Perhaps we should have asked diners to help clean or prepare meals in exchange for their food. This would soon have separated those who really needed the meal from those for whom it was a mere convenience.

We must also examine the extent to which such programs help or hinder structural progress in poor areas. Supposing we had served plainer meals — with an emphasis on nutrition over taste and variety. Would we have offered less competition to the fish house proprietor? Would another inexpensive restaurant have opened up — and hired local residents who were then unemployed?

The danger of private charity is that it does not make the recipient part of the division of labor. Therein lies the Samaritan's dilemma: The expectation of charity can lead people to behave in ways that keep them in poverty; their breaking free sometimes requires our withholding help.

Among religious leaders, when we talk of charity, we often speak 10 of the sanctity of the human person. But in our efforts to help the children of God, we ought not overlook the virtue of work. We ought not overlook the dignity that is earned when a person puts his labor to good use. In the Judeo-Christian tradition, sloth is a sin. God gave Adam and Eve the Earth and its wonders as a gift, but He expected them to mix their labor with the resources He provided.

When charity creates a disincentive for an able-bodied person to work, it leads this person down the wrong path. It encourages indolence. Real work provides the individual with the vehicle for a productive and virtuous life. It gives a person self-esteem and a role to play in society.

When government welfare is scaled back, as it surely will be, private charity will be required to an even greater extent. But we will need to be careful about which charities we support. How to know the difference? Bad charity is characterized by the failure to look deeply enough to discover the structural and moral causes of poverty. Men and women of faith will be called to concern themselves not just with the material needs of poor individuals but with their spiritual needs as well.

Reading and Discussion Questions

1. Sirico claims that charity is not always truly helpful. Where does he express the warrant or assumption on which he bases his claim?
2. What particular details of the author's personal experience offer support for his claim? How important are they to his argument?
3. Point out places in the essay that make clear the religious influence on Sirico's analysis. Does the fact that he is a priest lend greater credibility to his claim?
4. What solution does Sirico propose for problems created by some kinds of charity?

Writing Suggestions

5. Have you or someone you know ever offered the kind of charity that Father Sirico describes, i.e., helping people who seemed in need of help? What were your motives? Did your work satisfy you? Did you learn anything new about yourself or the nature of charitable giving that surprised you?
6. Private charity donations in the United States are said to be the most generous in the world, but some prominent people are criticized for their relatively small contributions — for example, Vice President Al Gore was reported to have given only $353 in 1997. If you were a financial advisor to a very rich person, what charities would you choose for his or her gifts? Consider the need of and the impact on (both specific and general) the recipients and society. (Compare Sirico's concern for the "spiritual needs," para. 12, of the poor.)

Get Students Past "Absolutophobia"

ROBERT L. SIMON

A student of mine made this comment: "Of course, I dislike the Nazis, but who is to say they are morally wrong?" Other students in my classes on moral and political philosophy have made similar remarks about apartheid, slavery, and ethnic cleansing. They say it as though it were self-evident; no one, they say, has the right even to criticize the moral views of another group or culture.

In an increasingly multicultural society, it is not surprising that many students believe that criticizing the codes of conduct of other groups and cultures is either unwise or prohibited. They equate such criticism with intolerance and the coercive imposition of a powerful culture's norms on the less powerful.

Does a decent respect for other cultures and practices really require us to refrain from condemning even the worst crimes in human history? Does it make moral judgment impossible?

I maintain that it does not. The growing moral paralysis of some of our best students arises because they have become entangled in abstract premises that, however fashionable they may be, are grounded in confusion and misunderstanding.

To begin with, note that students — and others — who feel that 5 a respect for other cultures requires them not to criticize practices different from their own already are making moral judgments, even if they do not recognize their own presuppositions. They believe, for example, that we ought to respect other cultures, that we ought to be tolerant of practices different from our own, and that we ought to welcome diversity rather than fear it. In fact, not only are they making moral judgments, they are making precisely the ones that should lead to condemnation of the Nazis.

How, then, can we explain this unwillingness to condemn great evils? Although there probably is no simple explanation, several assumptions by students play a role.

The first is that making a moral judgment is, in effect, drawing a line in the sand. Those who make moral judgments are felt to be "absolutists," and, of course, we all know there are no absolutes. The idea seems to be that those who assert absolutes are dogmatic and

Robert L. Simon is professor of philosophy at Hamilton College. He is also author of *Neutrality and the Academic Ethic* (1994). This article, which appeared in the *Education Digest* in October 1997, is condensed from the *Chronicle of Higher Education, 43* (June 27, 1997).

intolerant, and that they advance simple, inflexible general principles that allow no exceptions.

Students, therefore, believe that making moral judgments means that they are closed to further discussion — that they would be taking an inflexible stand that they must maintain, come what may. Perhaps the inflexibility and closed-mindedness of much of what passes for political debate in our society reinforces this image.

But, although there may be some absolutists among us, and perhaps even some "absolutes," there is nothing about moral judgment that requires inflexibility, intolerance, fanaticism, unwillingness to argue and debate, or an inability to recognize that many issues exist on which reasonable people of good will may disagree. In fact, as I've noted, the claim that we ought to be tolerant and willing to consider the viewpoints and arguments of others is itself a moral judgment, one that many of our skeptical students make, however unwilling they may be to acknowledge it.

An antidote to this reluctance to make moral judgments is to re- 10 place "absolutophobia" with an appreciation of the richness, diversity, and openness that make up moral discourse and moral judgment. Discussion of moral issues need not consist of two fanatics asserting conflicting principles they regard as self-evident; it can involve dialogue, the consideration of the points raised by others, and an admission of fallibility on all sides.

The second assumption that students should examine is that we are so inextricably embedded in our own individual perspectives — or those of our social or ethnic group, race, or gender — that the kind of impartiality or detachment from our own viewpoint that moral judgment requires is impossible. One of my students summed up this view on a recent exam paper, arguing that the social constructions of race, gender, and class make impartial assessment of a moral issue impossible.

What this student failed to consider is that if our race, gender, or class memberships really make impartial assessment of evidence impossible, how can we ever be confident that the evidence shows that race, gender, and class actually distort our thinking? Similarly, if we are all so biased, how can we claim that we ought to be tolerant, argue that we ought to respect diversity, or, indeed, defend any social or political goal at all?

Accordingly, although we certainly do need to be aware of biases that may taint our evaluations, asserting that such biases are so pervasive and inescapable that they make objectivity impossible undercuts the very possibility of having reasons for our opinions at all — including reasons for thinking that we are all biased.

Perhaps more important, the students who dismiss the possibility of moral inquiry ignore the role of critical dialogue in detecting and correcting personal or social prejudices. Surely one benefit of moral dialogue with others is that it can expose our own biases and open them to critical examination.

Crude forms of relativism, then, are open to strong logical objec- 15 tion. What, then, makes these views, which are so vulnerable to reasoned criticism, so pervasive? What gives them so strong a hold on so many students?

Part of the answer probably lies in students' interpretations (or misinterpretations) of multiculturalism and postmodernism. As understood by the relativist student, these views suggest that any criticism of another culture's practices is a kind of cultural imperialism. Second, the postmodern rejection of many of the ideals of the Enlightenment is taken to imply that, because we all speak from some particular perspective, truly objective moral knowledge is impossible to attain.

Sophisticated multiculturalists surely do not want to assert that all views are equally justified, for on many issues they claim that multicultural approaches are more justified than traditional ones. Similarly, sophisticated postmodernists surely want to claim that their own critique of many ideals of the Enlightenment is itself well-founded. So if multicultural and postmodernist approaches are to avoid intellectual incoherence, they cannot support the crude relativism that we are hearing from our students.

A more cynical explanation for such relativism rests less on current intellectual trends than on old-fashioned intellectual laziness. Crude relativism is an easy and undemanding position to hold. Rather than think through a problem to a reasoned conclusion, students can throw up their hands and ask, "Well, who's to say, anyway?" This conveniently allows them to ignore the moral issues that arise on their own campuses, such as excessive consumption of alcohol or improper conduct in personal relationships.

What can faculty members do to combat such views, without appearing dogmatic or authoritarian? We can begin by pointing out the hidden contradictions in the relativism espoused by students. That is, students simply cannot have it both ways, claiming that justifiable moral judgments cannot be made and yet that colleges should encourage the values of tolerance and respect for diversity.

Second, faculty members can point out that students them- 20 selves not only expect moral standards to be applied to them, but can offer explicit and coherent arguments for why they should be. Few students will be satisfied by "Who's to say one grade is more deserved than any other?" when that is a professor's explanation for giving them a failing grade on an important examination.

Third, we can demand that students not avoid difficult issues by asking "Who's to say?" but instead require them to state what constitutes a justifiable response to the issue at hand. The "Who's to say?" response should be clearly exposed for what it is — an excuse for refusing to engage in sustained inquiry.

Most important, we can require students to engage in the kinds of reasoning that can appropriately be applied to moral issues. Students can be asked if specific social practices can be defended for all those affected by them, and, if not, whether they can be regarded as fair to anyone. For example, can the support provided for men's and women's athletics on their own campuses be regarded as reasonable from the perspective of both male and female athletes?

Or we might ask students if their own views on different issues are totally consistent. Surely a student who believes both that the affluent have no moral obligations to the disadvantaged and that a 16-year-old girl who is pregnant as the result of rape has an obligation to carry her fetus to term needs to explain how these two views can be compatible.

Although different forms of ethical argument may or may not yield one final moral truth, it is unlikely that people who actually engage in moral reasoning and discussion will be able to conclude that all moral claims are equally reasonable, let alone that the views of the Nazis are as defensible as those of their opponents.

It is possible to reach relativist students, I believe, precisely because, deep down, they are not true moral relativists or skeptics. Rather, they actually hold to a disguised morality that emphasizes tolerance and respect for diversity. 25

However, by denying themselves the moral authority to condemn such great evils of human history as the Holocaust, slavery, and racial oppression, these students lose the basis for morally condemning wrongdoing anywhere, and so must ultimately abandon the very values that led them to advocate tolerance and respect for diversity in the first place.

Isn't it our responsibility as teachers to show, by directly confronting the confusions underlying absolutophobia, that students need not be inflexible dogmatists to have a moral ground on which to stand? If we allow the legitimate desire to avoid moral fanaticism to drive us to the point where even condemnation of the Holocaust is seen as a kind of unwarranted intellectual arrogance, then the truly arrogant and the truly fanatical need not fear moral censure no matter what evil they choose to inflict on us all.

Reading and Discussion Questions

1. Find the three main parts of this essay that are clearly indicated by the author's transitions. Create a summary sentence for each part. (Note that this essay, like many others [see Chapter 2], begins with a personal anecdote.)

2. How does Simon explain the refusal of students to pass judgment? Do the reasons he gives resemble what you have encountered in your own educational experience?
3. The author mentions three types of evil human behavior — the Holocaust, slavery, and racial oppression — as examples of conditions that students ought to condemn. What moral principles would he use to justify his condemnation of these practices?
4. Should Simon have included more examples? If so, where?
5. What, according to the author, is the danger in refusing to condemn wrongdoing?

Writing Suggestions

6. Can you think of activities of other cultures, present or past, that most Americans regard as wrong? For example, do you approve of dog or cock fights, which are illegal in the United States but practiced widely in some countries? Write a defense or a condemnation of some cultural practice you have heard or read about, making clear the moral standards you are using as warrant for your claim.
7. Many people tolerate questionable behavior — adultery, shoplifting, cheating on exams — when others are the victims, but change their minds when they themselves are victimized. If you have had or know about such an experience, describe it, and tell what it taught you about making judgments. (Since this is not an exercise in biography, you may also invent a scenario that lets you come to a conclusion about the limits of tolerance.)

PERHAPS THE MOST BEAUTIFUL THING ABOUT USING ENERGY
MORE EFFICIENTLY ISN'T THE FUEL IT CAN SAVE.

Use natural gas and you'll help protect the environment two ways. First, natural gas is much
cleaner than other fossil fuels. You can also take advantage of our programs to reduce natural gas use up to
30% in your home or business. And that's something that's good for the environment, too.
To find out more, call 1-800-427-3089. You'll be surprised how much you can save.

BostonGas
FOR THESE TIMES, IT'S A NATURAL.

BOS/5

Discussion Questions

1. What advantages of natural gas does this ad stress? Are butterflies superior to plants or other animals as persuasive elements?
2. What warrants or assumptions about the user underlie the advertiser's approach?
3. Contrast this ad with the ad on page 192. Which argument is stronger? Notice that one is negative, the other positive. Does that influence your choice?

Cloning Misperceptions

LEE M. SILVER

Why do four out of five Americans think that human cloning is "against God's will" or "morally wrong"? Why are people so frightened by this technology? One important reason is that many people have a muddled sense of what cloning is. They confuse the popular meaning of the word *clone* and the specific meaning it takes on in the context of biology.

In its popular usage, *clone* refers to something that is a duplicate, or cheaper imitation, of a brand-name person, place, or thing. The British politician Tony Blair has been called a clone of Bill Clinton, and an IBM PC clone is not only built like an IBM PC, it *behaves* like an IBM PC. It is this popular meaning of the word that caused many people to believe that human cloning would copy not just a person's body but a person's consciousness as well. This concept of cloning was at the center of the movie *Multiplicity,* which was released just months before the Dolly announcement. In it, a geneticist makes a clone of the star character played by Michael Keaton and explains that the clone will have "all of his feelings, all of his quirks, all of his memories, right up to the moment of cloning." The clone himself says to the original character, "You are me, I am you." It is this image that Jeremy Rifkin probably had in mind when he criticized the possible application of the sheep cloning technology to humans by saying, "It's a horrendous crime to make a Xerox (copy) of someone."

But this popular image bears absolutely no resemblance to actual cloning technology, in either process or outcome. Scientists cannot make full-grown adult copies of any animal, let alone humans. All they can do is start the process of development over again, using genetic material obtained from an adult. Real biological cloning can only take place at the level of the cell — life *in the general sense.* It is only long after the cloning event is completed that a unique — and independent — life *in the special sense* could emerge in the developing fetus. Once again, it is the inability of many people to appreciate the difference between the two meanings of "life" that is the cause of confusion.

A second reason people fear cloning is based on the notion that a clone is an imperfect imitation of the real thing. This causes some

Lee M. Silver is a professor of molecular biology at Princeton University. This essay is from *Remaking Eden: Cloning and Beyond in a Brave New World* (1997).

people to think that — far from having the same soul as someone else — a clone would have no soul at all. Among the earliest popular movies to explore this idea was *Blade Runner*, in which synthetic people were produced that were just like humans in all respects but one — they had no empathy. (Coincidentally, *Blade Runner* was based on a 1968 book by Philip K. Dick entitled *Do Androids Dream of Electric Sheep?*) And the same general idea of imperfection is explored in *Multiplicity* when a clone of the Michael Keaton character has himself cloned. The clone of the clone is a dimwitted clown because, as the original clone says, "Sometimes you make a copy of a copy and it's not as sharp as the original."

The Irvine, California, rabbi Bernard King was seriously fright- 5 ened by this idea when he asked, "Can the cloning create a soul? Can scientists create the soul that would make a being ethical, moral, caring, loving, all the things we attribute humanity to?" The Catholic priest Father Saunders suggested that "cloning would only produce humanoids or androids — soulless replicas of human beings that could be used as slaves." And Brent Staples, a member of the *New York Times* editorial board, warned that "synthetic humans would be easy prey for humanity's worst instincts."

Yet there is nothing synthetic about the cells used in cloning. They are alive before the cloning process, and they are alive after fusion has taken place. The newly created embryo can only develop inside the womb of a woman in the same way that all embryos and fetuses develop. Cloned children will be full-fledged human beings, indistinguishable in biological terms from all other members of the species. Thus, the notion of a soulless clone has no basis in reality.

When the misperceptions are tossed aside, it becomes clear what a cloned child will be. She, or he, will simply be a later-born identical twin — nothing more and nothing less. And while she may go through life looking similar to the way her progenitor-parent looked at a past point in time, she will be a unique human being, with a completely unique consciousness and a unique set of memories that she will build from scratch.

To many people, the mere word *clone* seems ominous, conjuring up images from movies like *The Boys from Brazil* with evil Nazis intent on ruling the world. How likely is it that governments or organized groups will use cloning as a tool to build future societies with citizens bred to fulfill a particular need?

The Brave New World *Scenario*

"Bokanovsky's Process," repeated the Director. . . . One egg, one embryo, one adult — normality. But a bokanovskified egg will bud, will proliferate, will divide. From eight to ninety-six buds, and every bud will grow into a perfectly formed embryo, and every embryo into a full-sized

adult. Making ninety-six human beings grow where only one grew before. Progress. . . . Identical twins — but not in piddling twos and threes
as in the old viviparous days, when an egg would sometimes accidentally divide; actually by dozens, by scores at a time. . . . "But, alas," the
Director shook his head, "we can't bokanovskify indefinitely." Ninety-six
seemed to be the limit; seventy-two a good average.

Thus did Aldous Huxley present one of the technological underpinnings of his brave new world where cloning would be used "as one
of the major instruments of social stability." With cloning, it was possible to obtain "standard men and women; in uniform batches. The
whole of a factor staffed with the products of a single bokanovskified
egg."

Brave New World evoked powerful feelings within people not   10
only because they could see inklings of the rigid conformity of the
brave new world society within their own, but because the science
was presented in a hyperrealistic manner. Even the most minor
technical details were carefully described.

Huxley, for one, was convinced that political forces would
evolve in the direction he described. In the foreword to the 1946 edition, he wrote: "It is probable that all the world's governments will
be more or less completely totalitarian even before the harnessing
of atomic energy; that they will be totalitarian during and after the
harnessing seems almost certain." It was the *science* that he was less
certain of.

Yet, like so many other twentieth-century intellectuals, Huxley
underestimated the power of technology to turn yesterday's fantasy
into today's reality. Only sixty-four years after he speculated on the
possibility of human cloning, it is on the verge of happening. But
now that one aspect of science has caught up to *Brave New World,*
what can we say about the politics? Will there be governments that
choose to clone?

Definitely not in a democratic society for a very simple reason.
Cloned children cannot appear out of the air. Each one will have to
develop within the womb of a woman (for the time being). And in a
free society, the state cannot control women's bodies and minds in a
way that would be necessary to build an army of clones.

But what about a totalitarian government that wanted to produce clones to serve its own social needs: "Standard men and
women; in uniform batches. The whole of a factory staffed with the
products of a single bokanovskified egg."

This scenario is highly improbable. First, only an extremely con-   15
trolling totalitarian state would have the ability to enslave women *en
masse* to act as surrogate mothers for babies that would be forcibly
removed and raised by the state. Ruling governments this extreme
are rare at the end of the twentieth century. But even if one did
emerge, it is hard to imagine why it would want to clone people.

Would it be to produce an army of powerful soldiers? Any government that could clone would certainly get more fighting power out of high-tech weapons of destruction than even the most muscular and obedient soldier clones.

Would it be to produce docile factory workers? Cloning is not necessary for this objective, which has already been reached throughout many societies. And mind control could be achieved much more effectively with New Age drugs targeted at particular behaviors and emotions (another prediction made by Huxley).

Would it be to produce people with great minds? It is not clear how a government would choose a progenitor for such clones, or what it would do during the twenty years or so that it took for clones to mature into adults. After all that time, a new set of leaders might decide that the wrong characteristics had been chosen for cloning. A better approach would be to simply build a superior system of public education that allowed the brightest children to rise to the top, no matter where on society's ladder they began their lives.

In the end, one is hard-pressed to come up with a single strategic advantage that any government might get from breeding clones rather than allowing a population to regenerate itself naturally. Thus, the Huxleyan use of cloning as a means for building a stable society seems very unlikely. But there is an obvious exception — one that could occur in a state or society controlled by a single egomaniacal dictator with substantial financial and scientific resources.

The example that comes to mind is that of the Japanese cult 20 leader Shoko Asahara. Asahara's group, Aum Shinrikyo, included well-educated chemists who produced nerve gas for the purpose of holding the Japanese government hostage. The group was exposed, and their leader was arrested and put on trial after a lethal gas attack on the Tokyo subway system in March 1995. Based on what we have learned about the group, it is possible that it might have had both the financial and technical resources required to put together the facility and equipment needed for cloning, as well as the power of persuasion required to convince skilled personnel to carry it out. And the aura that Asahara projected was such that he might well have succeeded in convincing women to become pregnant with his clones. Finally, Asahara himself seems to have been exactly the kind of egomaniac who would have preferred child clones over naturally conceived sons.

I doubt that we could stop people like Shoko Asahara from cloning themselves. But would it make any difference? Let us imagine that Asahara had cloned himself into a dozen children. It seems extremely unlikely that these children would have any greater effect on society, twenty years down the road, than sons conceived the old-fashioned way. It's not only that they wouldn't grow up in the same adverse environment that played an important role in turning

Asahara into the cult leader that he became. It's also that they would grow up among different people who would be unlikely to respond to them in exactly the same way that people responded to Asahara. The same could be said for modern-day clones of Adolf Hitler. In both cases, the original men were catapulted into positions of leadership through chance personal or historical events that will never repeat themselves. An adult alive today with Adolf Hitler's mind, personality, and behavior would be more likely to find himself barricaded in a militia outpost or in jail than in the White House or the German Bundesrat.

While Hitler's Third Reich and Asahara's Aum Shinrikyo were both short-lived phenomena, there are still examples of royal families — albeit with little real power today — that have handed down the crown from parent to child over hundreds of years. If after ascending to the throne, Prince Charles of Great Britain decided to place his clone — rather than his eldest son — next in line, would that upset the world order? On the contrary, I doubt if anyone would care.

The Risks of Human Cloning Outweigh the Benefits

*NATIONAL BIOETHICS
ADVISORY COMMISSION*

There is one basis of opposition to somatic cell nuclear transfer cloning on which almost everyone can agree. (A somatic cell is any cell of the embryo, fetus, child, or adult which contains a full complement of two sets of chromosomes; in contrast with a germ cell — that is, an egg or a sperm, which contains only one set of chromosomes. During somatic cell nuclear transfer cloning, the nucleus — which contains a full set of chromosomes — is removed from the somatic cell and transferred to an egg cell which has had its nucleus removed.) There is virtually universal concern regarding the current safety of attempting to use this technique in human beings. Even if there were a compelling case in favor of creating a child in this manner, it would have to yield to one fundamental principle of both medical ethics and political philosophy — the injunction, as it is stated in the Hippocratic canon, to "first, do no harm." In addition, the avoidance of physical and psychological harm was established as a standard for research in the Nuremberg Code, 1946–49.

This article is from *Cloning Human Beings: Reports and Recommendations of the National Bioethics Advisory Commission* (June 1997).

At this time, the significant risks to the fetus and physical well-being of a child created by somatic cell nuclear tranplantation cloning outweigh arguably beneficial uses of the technique.

It is important to recognize that the technique that produced Dolly the sheep was successful in only 1 of 277 attempts. If attempted in humans, it would pose the risk of hormonal manipulation in the egg donor; multiple miscarriages in the birth mother; and possibly severe developmental abnormalities in any resulting child. Clearly the burden of proof to justify such an experimental and potentially dangerous technique falls on those who would carry out the experiment. Standard practice in biomedical science and clinical care would never allow the use of a medical drug or device on a human being on the basis of such a preliminary study and without much additional animal research. Moreover, when risks are taken with an innovative therapy, the justification lies in the prospect of treating an illness in a patient, whereas, here no patient is at risk until the innovation is employed. Thus, no conscientious physician or Institutional Review Board should approve attempts to use somatic cell nuclear transfer to create a child at this time. For these reasons, prohibitions are warranted on all attempts to produce children through nuclear transfer from a somatic cell at this time.

A Difference of Opinion

Even on this point, however, NBAC (National Bioethics Advisory Committee) has noted some difference of opinion. Some argue, for example, that prospective parents are already allowed to conceive, or to carry a conception to term, when there is a significant risk — or even certainty — that the child will suffer from a serious genetic disease. Even when others think such conduct is morally wrong, the parents' right to reproductive freedom takes precedence. Since many of the risks believed to be associated with somatic cell nuclear transfer may be no greater than those associated with genetic disorders, some contend that such cloning should be subject to no more restriction than other forms of reproduction.

And, as in any new and experimental clinical procedure, harms cannot be accurately determined until trials are conducted in humans. Law professor John Robertson noted before NBAC on March 13, 1997 that:

> [The] first transfer [into a uterus] of a human [embryo] clone [will occur] before we know whether it will succeed. . . . [Some have argued therefore] that the first transfers are somehow unethical . . . experimentation on the resulting child, because one does not know what is going to happen, and one is . . . possibly leading to a child who could be disabled and have developmental difficulties. . . . [But the] child who would result would not have existed but for the procedure at issue, and

[if] the intent there is actually to benefit that child by bringing it into being . . . [this] should be classified as experimentation for [the child's] benefit and thus it would fall within recognized exceptions. . . . We have a very different set of rules for experimentation intended to benefit [the experimental subject].

But the argument that somatic cell nuclear transfer cloning experiments are "beneficial" to the resulting child rest on the notion that it is a "benefit" to be brought into the world as compared to being left unconceived and unborn. This metaphysical argument, in which one is forced to compare existence with non-existence, is problematic. Not only does it require us to compare something unknowable — non-existence — to something else, it also can lead to absurd conclusions if taken to its logical extreme. For example, it would support the argument that there is no degree of pain and suffering that cannot be inflicted on a child, provided that the alternative is never to have been conceived. Even the originator of this line of analysis rejects this conclusion.

In addition, it is true that the actual risks of physical harm to the child born through somatic cell nuclear transfer cannot be known with certainty unless and until research is conducted on human beings. It is likewise true that if we insisted on absolute guarantees of no risk before we permitted any new medical intervention to be attempted in humans, this would severely hamper if not halt completely the introduction of new therapeutic interventions, including new methods of responding to infertility. The assertion that we should regard attempts at human cloning as "experimentation for [the child's] benefit" is not persuasive. . . .

Cloning and Individuality

The concept of creating a genetic twin, although separated in time, is one aspect of somatic cell nuclear transfer cloning that most find both troubling and fascinating. The phenomenon of identical twins has intrigued human cultures across the globe, and throughout history. It is easy to understand why identical twins hold such fascination. Common experience demonstrates how distinctly different twins are, both in personality and in personhood. At the same time, observers cannot help but imbue identical bodies with some expectation that identical persons occupy those bodies, since body and personality remain intertwined in human intuition. With the prospect of somatic cell nuclear transfer cloning comes a scientifically inaccurate but nonetheless instinctive fear of multitudes of identical bodies, each housing personalities that are somehow less than distinct, less unique, and less autonomous than usual.

Is there a moral or human right to a unique identity, and if so would it be violated by this manner of human cloning? For such somatic cell nuclear transfer cloning to violate a right to a unique identity, the relevant sense of identity would have to be genetic identity, that is a right to a unique unrepeated genome. Even with the same genes, two individuals — for example homozygous twins — are distinct and not identical, so what is intended must be the various properties and characteristics that make each individual qualitatively unique and different than others. Does having the same genome as another person undermine that unique qualitative identity?

Ignorance and Knowledge

Along these lines of inquiry some question whether reproduction using somatic cell nuclear transfer would violate what philosopher Hans Jonas called a right to ignorance, or what philosopher Joel Feinberg called a right to an open future, or what Martha Nussbaum called the quality of "separateness." Jonas argued that human cloning, in which there is a substantial time gap between the beginning of the lives of the earlier and later twin, is fundamentally different from the simultaneous beginning of the lives of homozygous twins that occur in nature. Although contemporaneous twins begin their lives with the same genetic inheritance, they also begin their lives or biographies at the same time, in ignorance of what the twin who shares the same genome will by his or her choices make of his or her life. To whatever extent one's genome determines one's future, each life begins ignorant of what that determination will be, and so remains as free to choose a future as are individuals who do not have a twin. In this line of reasoning, ignorance of the effect of one's genome on one's future is necessary for the spontaneous, free, and authentic construction of a life and self.

A later twin created by cloning, Jonas argues, knows, or at least 10
believes he or she knows, too much about him or herself. For there is already in the world another person, one's earlier twin, who from the same genetic starting point has made the life choices that are still in the later twin's future. It will seem that one's life has already been lived and played out by another, that one's fate is already determined, and so the later twin will lose the spontaneity of authentically creating and becoming his or her own self. One will lose the sense of human possibility in freely creating one's own future. It is tyrannical, Jonas claims, for the earlier twin to try to determine another's fate in this way.

And even if it is a mistake to believe such crude genetic determinism according to which one's genes determine one's fate, what is important for one's experience of freedom and ability to create a life for oneself is whether one thinks one's future is open and undetermined, and so still to be largely determined by one's own choices. One might try to interpret Jonas' objection so as not to assume either genetic determinism, or a belief in it. A later twin might grant that he or she is not destined to follow in his or her earlier twin's footsteps, but that nevertheless the earlier twin's life would always haunt the later twin, standing as an undue influence on the latter's life, and shaping it in ways to which others' lives are not vulnerable. . . .

Potential Harms to Important Social Values

Those with grave reservations about somatic cell nuclear transfer cloning ask us to imagine a world in which cloning human beings via somatic cell nuclear transfer were permitted and widely practiced. What kind of people, parents, and children would we become in such a world? Opponents fear that such cloning to create children may disrupt the interconnected web of social values, practices, and institutions that support the healthy growth of children. The use of such cloning techniques might encourage the undesirable attitude that children are to be valued according to how closely they meet parental expectations, rather than loved for their own sake. In this way of looking at families and parenting, certain values are at the heart of those relationships, values such as love, nurturing, loyalty, and steadfastness. In contrast, a world in which such cloning were widely practiced would give, the critics claim, implicit approval to vanity, narcissism, and avarice. To these critics, changes that undermine those deeply prized values should be avoided if possible. At a minimum, such undesirable changes should not be fostered by public policies. . . .

Treating People as Objects

Some opponents of somatic cell nuclear cloning fear that the resulting children will be treated as objects rather than as persons. This concern often underlies discussions of whether such cloning amounts to "making" rather than "begetting" children, or whether the child who is created in this manner will be viewed as less than a fully independent moral agent. In sum, will being cloned from the somatic cell of an existing person result in the child being regarded as less of a person whose humanity and dignity would not be fully respected?

One reason this discussion can be hard to capture and to articulate is that certain terms, such as "person," are used differently by different people. What is common to these various views, however, is a shared understanding that being a "person" is different from being the manipulated "object" of other people's desires and expectations. Writes legal scholar Margaret Radin,

> The person is a subject, a moral agent, autonomous and self-governing. An object is a non-person, not treated as a self-governing moral agent. . . . [By] "objectification of persons," we mean, roughly, "what Kant would not want us to do."

That is, to objectify a person is to act towards the person without regard for his or her own desires or well-being, as a thing to be valued according to externally imposed standards, and to control the person rather than to engage her or him in a mutually respectful relationship. Objectification, quite simply, is treating the child as an object — a creature less deserving of respect for his or her moral agency. Commodification is sometimes distinguished from objectification and concerns treating persons as commodities, including treating them as a thing that can be exchanged, bought or sold in the marketplace. To those who view the intentional choice by another of one's genetic makeup as a form of manipulation by others, somatic cell nuclear transfer cloning represents a form of objectification or commodification of the child.

Some may deny that objectification is any more a danger in somatic cell nuclear transfer cloning than in current practices such as genetic screening or, in the future perhaps, gene therapy. These procedures aim either to avoid having a child with a particular condition, or to compensate for a genetic abnormality. But to the extent that the technology is used to benefit the child by, for example, allowing early preventive measures with phenylketonuria, no objectification of the child takes place.

When such cloning is undertaken not for any purported benefit of the child himself or herself, but rather to satisfy the vanity of the nucleus donor, or even to serve the need of someone else, such as a dying child in need of a bone marrow donor, then some would argue that it goes yet another step toward diminishing the personhood of the child created in this fashion. The final insult, opponents argue, would come if the child created through somatic cell nuclear transfer is regarded as somehow less than fully equal to the other human beings, due to his or her diminished physical uniqueness and the diminished mystery surrounding some aspects of his or her future physical development.

Eugenic Concerns

The desire to improve on nature is as old as humankind. It has been played out in agriculture through the breeding of special strains of domesticated animals and plants. With the development of the field of genetics over the past 100 years came the hope that the selection of advantageous inherited characteristics — called eugenics, from the Greek *eugenes* meaning wellborn or noble in heredity — could be as beneficial to humankind as selective breeding in agriculture.

The transfer of directed breeding practices from plants and animals to human beings is inherently problematic, however. To begin, eugenic proposals require that several dubious and offensive assumptions be made. First, that most, if not all people would mold their reproductive behavior to the eugenic plan; in a country that values reproductive freedom, this outcome would be unlikely absent compulsion. Second, that means exist for deciding which human traits and characteristics would be favored, an enterprise that rests on notions of selective human superiority that have long been linked with racist ideology.

Equally important, the whole enterprise of "improving" humankind by eugenic programs oversimplifies the role of genes in determining human traits and characteristics. Little is known about the correlation between genes and the sorts of complex, behavioral characteristics that are associated with successful and rewarding human lives; moreover, what little is known indicates that most such characteristics result from complicated interactions among a number of genes and the environment. While cows can be bred to produce more milk and sheep to have softer fleece, the idea of breeding humans to be superior would belong in the realm of science fiction even if one could conceive how to establish the metric of superiority, something that turns not only on the values and prejudices of those who construct the metric but also on the sort of a world they predict these specially bred persons would face. 20

Nonetheless, at the beginning of this century eugenic ideas were championed by scientific and political leaders and were very popular with the American public. It was not until they were practiced in such a grotesque fashion in Nazi Germany that their danger became apparent. Despite this sordid history and the very real limitations in what genetic selection could be expected to yield, the lure of "improvement" remains very real in the minds of some people. In some ways, creating people through somatic cell nuclear transfer offers eugenicists a much more powerful tool than any before. In selective breeding programs, such as the "germinal choice" method urged by the geneticist H. J. Muller a generation ago, the outcome depended on the usual "genetic lottery" that occurs each time a sperm fertilizes an egg, fusing their individual genetic heritages into a new individual. Cloning, by contrast, would allow the selection of a desired genetic prototype which would be replicated in each of the "offspring," at least on the level of the genetic material in the cell nucleus.

Objections to a Eugenics Program

It might be enough to object to the institution of a program of human eugenic clothing — even a voluntary program — that it would rest on false scientific premises and hence be wasteful and misguided. But that argument might not be sufficient to deter those people who want to push the genetic traits of a population in a particular direction. While acknowledging that a particular set of genes can be expressed in a variety of ways and therefore that cloning (or any other form of eugenic selection) does not guarantee a particular phenotypic manifestation of the genes, they might still argue that certain genes provide a better starting point for the next generation than other genes.

The answer to any who would propose to exploit the science of cloning in this way is that the moral problems with a program of human eugenics go far beyond practical objections of infeasibility. Some objections are those that have already been discussed in connection with the possible desire of individuals to use somatic cell nuclear transfer that the creation of a child under such circumstances could result in the child being objectified, could seriously undermine the value that ought to attach to each individual as an end in themselves, and could foster inappropriate efforts to control the course of the child's life according to expectations based on the life of the person who was cloned.

In addition to such objections are those that arise specifically because what is at issue in eugenics is more than just an individual act, it is a collective program. Individual acts may be undertaken for singular and often unknown or even unknowable reasons, whereas a eugenics program would propagate dogma about the sorts of people who are desirable and those who are dispensable. That is a path that humanity has tread before, to its everlasting shame. And it is a path to whose return the science of cloning should never be allowed to give even the slightest support. . . .

Cloning Is Unethical

In summary, the Commission reached several conclusions in considering the appropriateness of public policies regarding the creation of children through somatic cell nuclear transfer. First and foremost, creating children in this manner is unethical at this time because available scientific evidence indicates that such techniques are not safe at this time. Even if concerns about safety are resolved, however, significant concerns remain about the negative impact of the use of such a technology on both individuals and society. Public opinion on this issue may remain divided. Some people believe that cloning through 25 somatic cell nuclear transfer will always be unethical because it . . . will always risk causing psychological or other harms to the resulting child. In addition, although the Commission acknowledged that there are cases for which the use of such cloning might be considered desirable by some people, overall these cases were insufficiently compelling to justify proceeding with the use of such techniques. . . .

Finally, many scenarios of creating children through somatic cell nuclear transfer are based on the serious misconception that selecting a child's genetic makeup is equivalent to selecting the child's traits or accomplishments. A benefit of more widespread discussion of such cloning would be a clearer recognition that a person's traits and achievements depend heavily on education, training, and the social environment, as well as on genes. Should this type of cloning proceed, however, any children born as a result of this technique should be treated as having the same rights and moral status as any other human being.

Discussion Questions

1. What distinction does Silver make between the popular and the scientific meanings of *clone*? What two definitions of *life* does he emphasize to make his meaning clear?
2. One form of support in Silver's argument depends on references to movies and literature, as well as direct quotations from critics. Look back over the article, and decide if these references make the development stronger. How effective are they if the reader is unfamiliar with the movies or the novel?
3. How does Silver refute the view that totalitarian governments will "produce clones to serve its own social needs" (para. 14)? Is his argument persuasive? Explain your answer.
4. According to the National Bioethics Advisory Commission, why would a conscientious physician decline to perform the cloning procedure?
5. How does the Commission respond to Robertson's defense of cloning? Which argument seems more convincing?
6. Summarize the objections of the Commission to human cloning. The headings as well as the last paragraph are a guide to the issues.
7. Both articles use definitions to defend their arguments. Point out the issues in which definition is important. Do these definitions make it harder or easier to reach a conclusion about this debate? Explain why.

TAKING THE DEBATE ONLINE

- **Philadelphia Inquirer, March 4, 1997: Bah Cloning <http://www
  .med.upenn.edu/bioethics/Cloning/caplan-clone.html>** This short
  essay, written by Arthur Caplan of the Center for Bioethics at the University of Pennsylvania for the Philadelphia Inquirer, asks the layperson not to believe the media hype of human cloning by the unscrupulous

entrepreneur. He insists that we have more control over our technological advances than the media would lead us to believe.

- **The Ethics and Religious Liberty Commission <http://www.erlc .com/Biomed/1997/65Comsn.htm>** This site reflects the unfavorable views on human cloning held by the Ethics and Religious Liberty Commission. It also provides links to other articles relating to cloning and biomedical ethics.

- **Intellectual Capital: There Is More to Cloning than Human Beings — An Interview with Dr. Harry Griffin, January 19, 1998 <http:// www.intellectualcapital.com/issues/98/0219/icinterview.asp>** This is an interview with Dr. Harry Griffin, the assistant director of science at the Roslin Institute in Roslin, Scotland, where the sheep Dolly was cloned. He balks at the ease with which some scientists claim they can clone humans, a difficult and unethical experiment at this time.

- **Science and Technology in Congress: President's Commission Issues Cloning Recommendations <http://www.aaas.org/spp/dspp/ cstc/bulletin/articles/7-97/CLONING.HTM>** This site of the American Association for the Advancement of Science presents an overview of cloning from the perspective of the U.S. Congress.

- **New Scientist: Cloning — A Special Report <http://www.nsplus.com/>** This multilayered site explores issues relating to Dolly and cloning and addresses the implications such scientific advancement has for humans.

- **The Human Cloning Foundation <http://www.humancloning.org/>** This association is wholly in support of human cloning.

EXERCISES

1. What are some of the assumptions underlying the preference for *natural* foods and medicines? Can *natural* be clearly defined? Is this preference part of a broader philosophy? Try to evaluate the validity of the assumption.
2. Is plagiarism wrong? What assumptions about education are relevant to the issue of plagiarism? (Some students defend it. What kinds of arguments do they provide?)
3. Choose an advertisement, and examine the warrants on which the advertiser's claim is based.
4. "Religious beliefs are (or are not) necessary to a satisfactory life." Explain the warrants underlying your claim. Define any ambiguous terms.
5. Should students be given a direct voice in the hiring of faculty members? On what warrants about education do you base your answer?
6. Discuss the validity of the warrant in this statement from *The Watch Tower* (a publication of the Jehovah's Witnesses) about genital herpes: "The sexually loose are indeed 'receiving in themselves the full recompense, which was due for their error' (Romans 1:27)."

7. Read the following passage about suicide by the Greek philosopher Aristotle (adapted from his *Ethics*). Then defend or attack his argument, being careful to make clear both Aristotle's and your own warrants.

> Just as a murderer does not have the right to take a mother from her family or a child from her parents and simultaneously to deny society the use of a productive citizen, so the suicide, even though he or she freely chooses to be his or her own victim, does not possess the right to thus diminish the welfare of so many others.

8. In view of increasing interest in health in general, and nutrition and exercise in particular, do you think that universities and colleges should impose physical education requirements? If so, what form should they take? If not, why not? Defend your reasons.

9. Both state and federal governments have been embroiled in controversies concerning the rights of citizens to engage in harmful practices. In Massachusetts, for example, a mandatory seat-belt law was repealed by rebellious voters who considered the law an infringement of their freedom. What principles do you think ought to guide government regulation of dangerous practices?

10. The author of the following passage, Katherine Butler Hathaway, became a hunchback as a result of a childhood illness. Here she writes about the relationship between love and beauty from the point of view of someone who is deformed. Discuss the warrants on which the author bases her conclusion.

> I could secretly pretend that I had a lover . . . but I could never risk showing that I thought such a thing was possible for me . . . with any man. Because of my repeated encounters with the mirror and my irrepressible tendency to forget what I had seen, I had begun to force myself to believe and to remember, and especially to remember, that I would never be chosen for what I imagined to be the supreme and most intimate of all experience. I thought of sexual love as an honor that was too great and too beautiful for the body in which I was doomed to live.

Critical Listening

11. People often complain that they aren't listened to. Children complain about parents, patients about doctors, wives about husbands, citizens about government. Are the complaints to be taken literally? Or are they based on unexpressed warrants or assumptions about communication? Choose a specific familiar situation, and explain the meaning of the complaint.

12. Barbara Ehrenreich, in a *Time* essay, defends "talk shows of the *Sally Jessy Raphael* variety" as highly moralistic. Listen to a few of these shows — *Ricki Lake, Jerry Springer, Hard Copy* — and determine what moral assumptions about personal relationships and behavior underlie the advice given to the participants by the host and the audience. Do you think Ehrenreich is correct?

CHAPTER SEVEN

Language
and Thought

THE POWER OF WORDS

Words play such a critical role in argument that they deserve special treatment. Elsewhere we have referred directly and indirectly to language: Chapter 4 discusses definitions, and Part Two discusses style — the choice and arrangement of words and sentences — and shows how successful writers express arguments in language that is clear, vivid, and thoughtful. An important part of these writers' equipment is a large and active vocabulary, but no single chapter in a book can give this to you; only reading and study can widen your range of word choices. Even in a brief chapter, however, we can point out how words influence the feelings and attitudes of an audience, both favorably and unfavorably.

One kind of language responsible for shaping attitudes and feelings is *emotive language,* language that expresses and arouses emotions. Understanding it and using it effectively is indispensable to the arguer who wants to move an audience to accept a point of view or undertake an action.

Long before you thought about writing your first argument, you learned that words had the power to affect you. Endearments and affectionate and flattering nicknames evoked good feelings about the speaker and yourself. Insulting nicknames and slurs produced dislike for the speaker and bad feelings about yourself. Perhaps you were told, "Sticks and stones may break your bones, but words will never hurt you." But even to a small child it is clear that ugly words are as painful as sticks and stones and that the injuries are sometimes more lasting.

Nowhere is the power of words more obvious and more familiar than in advertising, where the success of a product may depend on the feelings that certain words produce in the prospective buyer. Even the names of products may have emotive significance. In recent years a new industry, composed of consultants who supply names for products, has emerged. Although most manufacturers agree that a good name won't save a poor product, they also recognize that the right name can catch the attention of the public and persuade people to buy a product at least once. According to an article in the *Wall Street Journal,* a product name not only should be memorable but also should "remind people of emotional or physical experiences." One consultant created the name Magnum for a malt liquor from Miller Brewing Company: "The product is aimed at students, minorities, and lower-income customers." The president of the consulting firm says that Magnum "implies strength, masculinity, and more bang for your buck."[1] This naming of products has been called the "Rumpelstiltskin effect," a phrase coined by a linguist. "The whole point," he said, "is that when you have the right name for a thing, you have control over it."[2]

Even scientists recognize the power of words to attract the attention of other scientists and the public to discoveries and theories that might otherwise remain obscure. A good name can even enable the scientist to visualize a new concept. One scientist says that "a good name," such as "quark," "black hole," "big bang," "chaos," or "great attractor," "helps in communicating a theory and can have substantial impact on financing."

It is not hard to see the connection between the use of words in conversation and advertising and the use of emotive language in the more formal arguments you will be writing. Emotive language reveals your approval or disapproval, assigns praise or blame — in other words, makes a judgment about the subject. Keep in mind that unless you are writing purely factual statements, such as scientists write, you will find it hard to avoid expressing judgments. Neutrality does not come easily, even where it may be desirable, as in news stories or reports of historical events. For this reason you need to attend carefully to the statements in your argument, making sure that you have not disguised judgments as statements of fact. Of course, in attempting to prove a claim, you will not be neutral. You will be revealing your judgment about the subject, first in the selection of facts and opinions and the emphasis you give to them and second in the selection of words.

Like the choice of facts and opinions, the choice of words can be effective or ineffective in advancing your argument, moral or im-

---

[1] *Wall Street Journal,* August 5, 1982, p. 19.
[2] *Harvard Magazine,* July–August 1995, p. 18.

moral in the honesty with which you exercise it. The following discussions offer some insights into recognizing and evaluating the use of emotive language in the arguments you read, as well as into using such language in your own arguments where it is appropriate and avoiding it where it is not.

CONNOTATION

The connotations of a word are the meanings we attach to it apart from its explicit definition. Because these added meanings derive from our feelings, connotations are one form of emotive language. For example, the word *rat* denotes or points to a kind of rodent, but the attached meanings of "selfish person," "evil-doer," "betrayer," and "traitor" reflect the feelings that have accumulated around the word.

In Chapter 4 we observed that definitions of controversial terms, such as *poverty* and *unemployment,* may vary so widely that writer and reader cannot always be sure that they are thinking of the same thing. A similar problem arises when a writer assumes that the reader shares his or her emotional response to a word. Emotive meanings originate partly in personal experience. The word *home,* defined merely as "a family's place of residence," may suggest love, warmth, and security to one person; it may suggest friction, violence, and alienation to another. The values of the groups to which we belong also influence meaning. Writers and speakers count on cultural associations when they refer to our country, our flag, and heroes and enemies we have never seen. The arguer must also be aware that some apparently neutral words trigger different responses from different groups — words such as *cult, revolution, police, beauty contest,* and *corporation.*

Various reform movements have recognized that words with unfavorable connotations have the power not only to reflect but also to shape our perceptions of things. The words *Negro* and *colored* were rejected by the civil rights movement in the 1960s because they bore painful associations with slavery and discrimination. Instead, the word *black,* which was free from such associations, became the accepted designation; more recently, the Reverend Jesse Jackson suggested another term, *African American,* to reflect ethnic origins. People of "Spanish-Hispanic" origin (as they are designated on the 1990 census) are now engaged in a debate about the appropriate term for a diverse population of more than 22 million American residents from Mexico, Puerto Rico, Cuba, and more than a dozen Central and South American countries. To some, the word *Hispanic* is unacceptable because it is an Anglicization and recalls the colonization of America by Spain and Portugal.

The women's liberation movement also insisted on changes that would bring about improved attitudes toward women. The movement condemned the use of *girl* for a female over the age of eighteen and the use in news stories of descriptive adjectives that emphasized the physical appearance of women. And the homosexual community succeeded in reintroducing the word *gay,* a word current centuries ago, as a substitute for words they considered offensive. Now *queer,* a word long regarded as offensive, has been adopted as a substitute for *gay* by a new generation of gays and lesbians, although it is still considered unacceptable by many members of the homosexual community.

Members of certain occupations have invented terms to confer greater respectability on their work. The work does not change, but the workers hope that public perceptions will change if janitors are called custodians, if garbage collectors are called sanitation engineers, if undertakers are called morticians, if people who sell makeup are called cosmetologists. Events considered unpleasant or unmentionable are sometimes disguised by polite terms, called *euphemisms.* During the 1992 to 1993 recession new terms emerged that disguised, or tried to, the grim fact that thousands of people were being dismissed from their jobs: *skill-mix adjustment, workforce-imbalance correction, redundancy elimination, downsizing, indefinite idling,* even a daring *career-change opportunity.* Many people refuse to use the word *died* and choose *passed away* instead. Some psychologists and physicians use the phrase *negative patient care outcome* for what most of us would call *death.* Even when referring to their pets, some people cannot bring themselves to say *put to death* but substitute *put to sleep* or *put down.* In place of a term to describe an act of sexual intercourse, some people use *slept together* or *went to bed together* or *had an affair.*

Polite words are not always so harmless. If a euphemism disguises a shameful event or condition, it is morally irresponsible to use it to mislead the reader into believing that the shameful condition does not exist. In his powerful essay "Politics and the English Language" George Orwell pointed out that politicians and reporters have sometimes used terms like "pacification" or "rectification of frontiers" to conceal acts that result in torture and death for millions of people. An example of such usage was cited by a member of Amnesty International, a group monitoring human rights violations throughout the world. He objected to a news report describing camps in which the Chinese were promoting "reeducation through labor." This term, he wrote, "makes these institutions seem like a cross between Police Athletic League and Civilian Conservation Corps camps." On the contrary, he went on, the reality of "reeducation through labor" was that the victims were confined to "rather unpleasant prison camps." The details he offered about the conditions under which people lived and worked gave substance to his claim.[3] More recently, when news organizations referred to the expulsion of Romanian gypsies from Germany as part of a "deportation treaty," an official of Germany's press agency objected to the use of the word *deportation.* "You must know that by using words such as *deportation* you are causing great sadness. . . . We prefer that you use the term *readmission* or *retransfer.*"[4]

Some of the most interesting changes in language usage occur in modern Bible translations. The vocabulary and syntax of earlier versions have been greatly simplified to make the Bible more accessible to that half of the American public who cannot read above eighth-grade level. Another change responds to arguments by feminists, environmentalists, and multiculturalists for more "inclusive language." God is no longer the *Father,* human beings no longer have *dominion* over creation, and even the word *blindness* as a metaphor for sin or evil has been replaced by other metaphors.

Perhaps the most striking examples of the way that connotations influence our perceptions of reality occur when people are asked to respond to questions of poll-takers. Sociologists and students of poll-taking know that the phrasing of a question, or the choice of words, can affect the answers and even undermine the validity of the poll. In one case poll-takers first asked a selected group of people if they favored continuing the welfare system. The majority answered no. But when the poll-takers asked if they favored government aid to the poor, the majority answered yes. Although the terms *welfare* and *government aid to the poor* refer to essentially the same forms of government assistance, *welfare* has acquired for many people negative connotations of corruption and shiftless recipients.

A *New York Times*/CBS News poll conducted in January 1989 asked, "If a woman wants to have an abortion and her doctor agrees to it, should she be allowed to have an abortion or not?" Sixty-one percent said yes, 25 percent said no, and 25 percent said it depended on the circumstances. But when the pollsters asked, "Should abortion be legal as it is now, or legal only in such cases as rape, incest, or to save the life of the mother, or should it not be permitted at all?" a much higher percentage said that abortion depended on the circumstances. Only 46 percent said it should be legal as it is now, and 41 percent said it should be legal only in such cases as rape, incest, or to save the life of the mother. According to polling experts, people are far more likely to say that they support abortion when the question is asked in terms of the "woman's right to

---

[3]Letter to the *New York Times,* August 30, 1982, p. 25.
[4]*International Herald Tribune,* November 5, 1992.

choose" than when the question asks about "protecting the unborn child." "How the question is framed," say the experts, "can affect the answers."[5]

This is also true in polls concerning rape, another highly charged subject. Dr. Neil Malamuth, a psychologist at the University of California at Los Angeles, says, "When men are asked if there is any likelihood they would force a woman to have sex against her will if they could get away with it, about half say they would. But if you ask them if they would rape a woman if they knew they could get away with it, only about 15 percent say they would." The men who change their answers aren't aware that "the only difference is in the words used to describe the same act."[6]

The wording of an argument is crucial. Because readers may interpret the words you use on the basis of feelings different from your own, you must support your word choices with definitions and with evidence that allows readers to determine how and why you made them.

SLANTING

Slanting, says one dictionary, is "interpreting or presenting in line with a special interest." The term is almost always used in a negative sense. It means that the arguer has selected facts and words with favorable or unfavorable connotations to create the impression that no alternative view exists or can be defended. For some questions it is true that no alternative view is worthy of presentation, and emotionally charged language to defend or attack a position that is clearly right or wrong would be entirely appropriate. We aren't neutral, nor should we be, about the tragic abuse of human rights anywhere in the world or even about less serious infractions of the law, such as drunk driving or vandalism, and we should use strong language to express our disapproval of these practices.

Most of your arguments, however, will concern controversial questions about which people of goodwill can argue on both sides. In such cases, your own judgments should be restrained. Slanting will suggest a prejudice — that is, a judgment made without regard to all the facts. Unfortunately, you may not always be aware of your bias or special interest; you may believe that your position is the only correct one. You may also feel the need to communicate a passionate belief about a serious problem. But if you are interested in persuading a reader to accept your belief and to act on it, you must also ask: If the reader is not sympathetic, how will he or she re-

---

[5]*New York Times,* January 1, 1989, p. 21.
[6]*New York Times,* August 29, 1989, sec. C, p. 1.

spond? Will he or she perceive my words as "loaded" — one-sided and prejudicial — and my view as slanted?

R. D. Laing, a Scottish psychiatrist, defined *prayer* in this way: "Someone is gibbering away on his knees, talking to someone who is not there."[7] This description probably reflects a sincerely held belief. Laing also clearly intended it for an audience that already agreed with him. But the phrases "gibbering away" and "someone who is not there" would be offensive to people for whom prayer is sacred.

The following remark by an editor of *Penthouse* appeared in a debate on women's liberation.

> I haven't noticed that there is such a thing as a rise in the women's liberation movement. It seems to me that it's a lot of minor sound and a tiny fury. There are some bitty bitty groups of some disappointed ladies who have some objective or other.[8]

An unfriendly audience would resent the use of language intended to diminish the importance of the movement: "minor sound," "tiny fury," "bitty bitty groups of some disappointed ladies," "some objective or other." But even audiences sympathetic to the claim may be repelled or embarrassed by intense, colorful, obviously loaded words. In the mid-1980s an English environmental group, London Greenpeace, began to distribute leaflets accusing the McDonald's restaurants of a wide assortment of crimes. The leaflets said in part:

> McDollars, McGreedy, McCancer, McMurder, McDisease, McProfits, McDeadly, McHunger, McRipoff, McTorture, McWasteful, McGarbage.
>
> This leaflet is asking you to think for a moment about what lies behind McDonald's clean, bright image. It's got a lot to hide. . . .
>
> McDonald's and Burger King are two of the many U.S. corporations using lethal poisons to destroy vast areas of Central American rain forest to create grazing pastures for cattle to be sent back to the States as burgers and pet food. . . .
>
> What they don't make clear is that a diet high in fat, sugar, animal products and salt . . . and low in fiber, vitamins and minerals — which describes an average McDonald's meal — is linked with cancers of the breast and bowel, and heart disease. . . .[9]

Even readers who share the belief that McDonald's is not a reliable source of good nutrition might feel that London Greenpeace has gone too far, and that the name-calling, loaded words, and exaggera-

---

[7]"The Obvious," in David Cooper, ed. *The Dialectics of Liberation* (Penguin Books, 1968), p. 17.

[8]"Women's Liberation: A Debate" (Penthouse International Ltd., 1970).

[9]*New York Times*, August 6, 1995, sec. E, p. 7. In 1990 McDonald's sued the group for libel. In June 1997, after the longest libel trial in British history, the judge ruled in favor of the plaintiff, awarding McDonald's $60,000. In March 1999 an appeal partially overturned the verdict, and reduced the damages awarded to McDonald's by approximately one-third.

tion have damaged the credibility of the attackers more than the reputation of McDonald's.

We find slanting everywhere, not only in advertising and propaganda, where we expect to find it, but in news stories, which should be strictly neutral in their recounting of events, and in textbooks. In the field of history, for example, it is often difficult for scholars to remain impartial about significant events. Like the rest of us, they may approve or disapprove, and their choice of words will reflect their judgments.

The following passage by a distinguished Catholic historian describes the events surrounding the momentous decision by Henry VIII, king of England, to break with the Roman Catholic Church in 1534, in part because of the Pope's refusal to grant him a divorce from the Catholic princess Catherine of Aragon so that he could marry Anne Boleyn.

> The *protracted* delay in receiving an annulment was very *irritating* to the *impulsive* English king. . . . Gradually Henry's former *effusive* loyalty to Rome gave way to a settled conviction of the tyranny of the papal power, and there *rushed* to his mind the recollections of efforts of earlier English rulers to restrict that power. A few *salutary* enactments against the Church might *compel* a favorable decision from the Pope.
>
> Henry seriously opened his campaign against the Roman Church in 1531, when he *frightened* the clergy into paying a fine of over half a million dollars for violating an *obsolete* statute . . . and in the same year he *forced* the clergy to recognize himself as supreme head of the Church. . . .
>
> His *subservient* Parliament then empowered him to stop the payments of annates to the Pope and to appoint bishops in England without recourse to the papacy. *Without waiting longer* for the decision from Rome, he had Cranmer, *one of his own creatures*, whom he had just named Archbishop of Canterbury, declare his marriage null and void. . . .
>
> Yet Henry VIII encountered considerable *opposition* from the *higher clergy*, from the monks, and from many *intellectual leaders*. . . . A *popular uprising* — the Pilgrimage of Grace — was *sternly* suppressed, and such men as the *brilliant* Sir Thomas More and John Fisher, the *aged* and *saintly* bishop of Rochester, were beheaded because they retained their former belief in papal supremacy.[10] [Italics added]

In the first paragraph the italicized words help make the following points: that Henry was rash, impulsive, and insincere and that he was intent on punishing the church (the word *salutary* means healthful or beneficial and is used sarcastically). In the second paragraph the choice of words stresses Henry's use of force and the cowardly submission of his followers. In the third paragraph the adjectives describing the opposition to Henry's campaign and those who were ex-

---

[10]Carlton J. H. Hayes, *A Political and Cultural History of Modern Europe,* vol. 1 (New York: Macmillan, 1933), pp. 172–173.

ecuted emphasize Henry's cruelty and despotism. Within the limits of this brief passage the author has offered support for his strong indictment of Henry VIII's actions, both in defining the statute as obsolete and in describing the popular opposition. In a longer exposition you would expect to find a more elaborate justification with facts and authoritative opinion from other sources.

The advocate of a position in an argument, unlike the reporter or the historian, must express a judgment, but the preceding examples demonstrate how the arguer should use language to avoid or minimize slanting and to persuade readers that he or she has come to a conclusion after careful analysis. The careful arguer must not conceal his or her judgments by presenting them as if they were statements of fact, but must offer convincing support for his or her choice of words and respect the audience's feelings and attitudes by using temperate language.

Depending on the circumstances, *exaggeration* can be defined, in the words of one writer, as "a form of lying." An essay in *Time* magazine, "Watching Out for Loaded Words," points to the danger for the arguer in relying on exaggerated language as an essential part of the argument.

> The trouble with loaded words is they tend to short-circuit thought. While they may describe something, they simultaneously try to seduce the mind into accepting a prefabricated opinion about the something described.[11]

PICTURESQUE LANGUAGE

Picturesque language consists of words that produce images in the mind of the reader. Students sometimes assume that vivid picture-making language is the exclusive instrument of novelists and poets, but writers of arguments can also avail themselves of such devices to heighten the impact of their messages.

Picturesque language can do more than render a scene. It shares with other kinds of emotive language the power to express and arouse deep feelings. Like a fine painting or photograph, it can draw readers into the picture where they partake of the writer's experience as if they were also present. Such power may be used to delight, to instruct, or to horrify. In 1741 the Puritan preacher Jonathan Edwards delivered his sermon "Sinners in the Hands of an Angry God," in which people were likened to repulsive spiders hanging over the flames of Hell to be dropped into the fire whenever a wrathful God was pleased to release them. The congregation's reaction to

---

[11]*Time,* May 24, 1982, p. 86.

Edwards's picture of the everlasting horrors to be suffered in the netherworld included panic, fainting, hysteria, and convulsions. Subsequently Edwards lost his pulpit in Massachusetts, in part as a consequence of his success at provoking such uncontrollable terror among his congregation.

Language as intense and vivid as Edwards's emerges from very strong emotion about a deeply felt cause. In an argument against abortion, a surgeon recounts a horrifying experience as if it were a scene in a movie.

> You walk toward the bus stop. . . . It is all so familiar. All at once you step on something soft. You feel it with your foot. Even through your shoe you may have the sense of something unusual, something marked by a special "give." It is a foreignness upon the pavement. Instinct pulls your foot away in an awkward little movement. You look down, and you see . . . a tiny naked body, its arms and legs flung apart, its head thrown back, its mouth agape, its face serious. A bird, you think, fallen from the nest. But there is no nest here on 73rd Street, no bird so big. It is rubber, then. A model, a . . . a joke. And you bend to see. Because you must. And it is no joke. Such a gray softness can be but one thing. It is a baby, and dead. You cover your mouth, your eyes. You are fixed. Horror has found its chink and crawled in, and you will never be the same as you were. Years later you will step from a sidewalk to a lawn, and you will start at its softness and think of that upon which you have just trod.[12]

Here the use of the pronoun *you* serves to draw readers into the scene and intensify their experience.

The rules governing the use of picturesque language are the same as those governing other kinds of emotive language. Is the language appropriate? Is it too strong, too colorful for the purpose of the message? Does it result in slanting or distortion? What will its impact be on a hostile or indifferent audience? Will they be angered, repelled? Will they cease to read or listen if the imagery is too disturbing?

We expect strong language in arguments about life and death. For subjects about which your feelings are not so passionate, your choice of words will be more moderate. The excerpt below, from an article arguing against repeal of Sunday closing laws, creates a sympathetic picture of a market-free Sunday. Most readers, even those who oppose Sunday closing laws, would enjoy the picture and perhaps react more favorably to the argument.

> Think of waking in the city on Sunday. Although most people no longer worship in the morning, the city itself has a reverential air. It comes to life slowly, even reluctantly, as traffic lights blink their orders to empty streets. Next, joggers venture forth, people out to get the

---

[12]Richard Selzer, *Mortal Lessons: Notes on the Art of Surgery* (New York: Simon and Schuster, 1974), pp. 153–154.

paper, families going to church or grandma's. Soon the city is its Sunday self: People cavort with their children, discuss, make repairs, go to museums, gambol. Few people go to work, and any shopping is incidental. The city on Sunday is a place outside the market. Play dominates, not the economy.[13]

CONCRETE AND ABSTRACT LANGUAGE

Writers of argument need to be aware of another use of language — the distinction between concrete and abstract. Concrete words point to real objects and real experiences. Abstract words express qualities apart from particular things and events. *Beautiful roses* is concrete; we can see, touch, and smell them. *Beauty* in the eye of the beholder is abstract; we can speak of the quality of beauty without reference to a particular object or event. *Returning money found in the street to the owner, although no one has seen the discovery* is concrete. *Honesty* is abstract. In abstracting we separate a quality shared by a number of objects or events, however different from each other the individual objects or events may be.

Writing that describes or tells a story leans heavily on concrete language. Although arguments also rely on the vividness of concrete language, they use abstract terms far more extensively than other kinds of writing. Using abstractions effectively, especially in arguments of value and policy, is important for two reasons: (1) Abstractions represent the qualities, characteristics, and values that the writer is explaining, defending, or attacking; and (2) they enable the writer to make generalizations about his or her data. Equally important is knowing when to avoid abstractions that obscure the message.

In some textbook discussions of language, abstractions are treated as inferior to concrete and specific words, but such a distinction is misleading. Abstractions allow us to make sense of our experience, to come to conclusions about the meaning of the bewildering variety of emotions and events we confront throughout a lifetime. One writer summarized his early history as follows: "My elementary school had the effect of *destroying any intellectual motivation,* of *stifling* all *creativity,* of *inhibiting personal relationships* with either my teachers or my peers" (emphasis added). Writing in the humanities and in some social and physical sciences would be impossible without recourse to abstractions that express qualities, values, and conditions.

---

[13]Robert K. Manoff, "New York City, It Is Argued, Faces 'Sunday Imperialism,'" *New York Times,* January 2, 1977, sec. 4, p. 13.

You should not, however, expect abstract terms alone to carry the emotional content of your message. The effect of even the most suggestive words can be enhanced by details, examples, and anecdotes. One mode of expression is not superior to the other; both abstractions and concrete detail work together to produce clear, persuasive argument. This is especially true when the meanings assigned to abstract terms vary from reader to reader.

In establishing claims based on the support of values, for example, you may use such abstract terms as *religion, duty, freedom, peace, progress, justice, equality, democracy,* and *pursuit of happiness.* You can assume that some of these words are associated with the same ideas and emotions for almost all readers; others require further explanation. Suppose you write, "We have made great progress in the last fifty years." One dictionary defines *progress* as "a gradual betterment," another abstraction. How will you define "gradual betterment" for your readers? Can you be sure that they have in mind the same references for progress that you do? If not, misunderstandings are inevitable. You may offer examples: supersonic planes, computers, shopping malls, nuclear energy. Many of your readers will react favorably to the mention of these innovations, which to them represent progress; others, for whom these inventions represent change but not progress, will react unfavorably. You may not be able to convince all of your readers that "we have made great progress," but all of them will now understand what you mean by "progress." And intelligent disagreement is preferable to misunderstanding.

Abstractions tell us what conclusions we have arrived at; details tell us how we got there. But there are dangers in either too many details or too many abstractions. For example, a writer may present only concrete data without telling readers what conclusions are to be drawn from them. Suppose you read the following:

> To Chinese road-users, traffic police are part of the grass . . . and neither they nor the rules they're supposed to enforce are paid the least attention. . . . Ignoring traffic-lights is only one peculiarity of Chinese traffic. It's normal for a pedestrian to walk straight out into a stream of cars without so much as lifting his head; and goodness knows how many Chinese cyclists I've almost killed as they have shot blindly in front of me across busy main roads.[14]

These details would constitute no more than interesting gossip until we read, "It's not so much a sign of ignorance or recklessness . . . but of fatalism." The details of specific behavior have now acquired a significance expressed in the abstraction *fatalism.*

---

[14]Philip Short, "The Chinese and the Russians," *The Listener,* April 8, 1982, p. 6.

A more common problem, however, in using abstractions is omission of details. Either the writer is not a skilled observer and cannot provide the details, or he or she feels that such details are too small and quiet compared to the grand sounds made by abstract terms. These grand sounds, unfortunately, cannot compensate for the lack of clarity and liveliness. Lacking detailed support, abstract words may be misinterpreted. They may also represent ideas that are so vague as to be meaningless. Sometimes they function illegitimately as short cuts (discussed on pp. 253–60), arousing emotions but unaccompanied by good reasons for their use. The following paragraph exhibits some of these common faults. How would you translate it into clear English?

> We respectively petition, request, and entreat that due and adequate provision be made, this day and the date hereinafter subscribed, for the satisfying of these petitioners' nutritional requirements and for the organizing of such methods of allocation and distribution as may be deemed necessary and proper to assure the reception by and for said petitioners of such quantities of baked cereal products as shall, in the judgment of the aforesaid petitioners, constitute a sufficient supply thereof.[15]

If you had trouble decoding this, it was because there were almost no concrete references — the homely words *baked* and *cereal* leap out of the paragraph like English signposts in a foreign country — and too many long words or words of Latin origin when simple words would do: *requirements* instead of *needs, petition* instead of *ask.* An absence of concrete references and an excess of long Latinate words can have a depressing effect on both writer and reader. The writer may be in danger of losing the thread of the argument, the reader at a loss to discover the message.

The paragraph above, according to James B. Minor, a lawyer who teaches courses in legal drafting, is "how a federal regulation writer would probably write, 'Give us this day our daily bread.'" This brief sentence with its short, familiar words and its origin in the Lord's Prayer has a deep emotional effect. The paragraph composed by Minor deadens any emotional impact because of its preponderance of abstract terms and its lack of connection with the world of our senses.

That passage was invented to educate writers in the government bureaucracy to avoid inflated prose. But writing of this kind is not uncommon among professional writers, including academics. If the subject matter is unfamiliar and the writer an acknowledged expert, you may have to expend a special effort in penetrating the language. But you may also rightly wonder if the writer is making unreasonable demands on you.

---

[15]*New York Times,* May 10, 1977, p. 35.

The human race is now entering upon a new phase of evolutionary consciousness and progress, a phase in which, impelled by the forces of evolution itself, it must converge upon itself and convert itself into one single human organism infused by a reconciliation of knowing and being in their inner unity and destined to make a qualitative leap into a higher form of consciousness as we know it, or otherwise destroy itself. For the entire universe is one vast field, potential for incarnation, and achieving incandescence here and there of reason and spirit. And in the whole world of *quality* with which by the nature of our minds we necessarily make contact, we here and there apprehend preeminent value. This can be achieved only if we recognize that we are unable to focus our attention on the particulars of the whole, without diminishing our comprehension of the whole, and of course, conversely, we can focus on the whole only by diminishing our comprehension of the particulars which constitute the whole.[16]

You probably found this paragraph even more baffling than the previous example. Although there is some glimmer of meaning here — that mankind must attain a higher level of consciousness, or perish — you should ask whether the extraordinary overload of abstract terms is justified. In fact, most readers would be disinclined to sit still for an argument with so little reference to the real world. One critic of social science prose maintains that if preeminent thinkers like Bertrand Russell can make themselves clear but social scientists continue to be obscure, "then you can justifiably suspect that it might all be nonsense."[17]

Finally, there are the moral implications of using abstractions that conceal a disagreeable reality. George Orwell pointed them out more than forty years ago in "Politics and the English Language." Another essayist, Joseph Wood Krutch, in criticizing the attitude that cheating "doesn't really hurt anybody," observed, "'It really doesn't hurt anybody' means it doesn't do that abstraction called society any harm." The following news story reports a proposal with which Orwell and Krutch might have agreed. His intention, says the author, is to "slow the hand of any President who might be tempted to unleash a nuclear attack."

> It has long been feared that a President could be making his fateful decision while at a "psychological distance" from the victims of a nuclear barrage; that he would be in a clean, air-conditioned room, surrounded by well-scrubbed aides, all talking in abstract terms about appropriate military responses in an international crisis, and that he might well push to the back of his mind the realization that hundreds of millions of people would be exterminated.

---

[16]Ruth Nanda Anshen, "Credo Perspectives," introduction to James Bryant Conant, *Two Modes of Thought* (New York: Simon and Schuster, 1964), p. x.

[17]Stanislav Andreski, *Social Sciences as Sorcery* (New York: St. Martin's Press, 1972), p. 86.

So Roger Fisher, professor of law at Harvard University, offers a simple suggestion to make the stakes more real. He would put the codes needed to fire nuclear weapons in a little capsule, and implant the capsule next to the heart of a volunteer, who would carry a big butcher knife as he accompanied the President everywhere. If the President ever wanted to fire nuclear weapons, he would first have to kill, with his own hands, that human being.

He has to look at someone and realize what death is — what an innocent death is. "It's reality brought home," says Professor Fisher.[18]

The moral lesson is clear: It is much easier to do harm if we convince ourselves that the object of the injury is only an abstraction.

SHORT CUTS

Short cuts are arguments that depend on readers' responses to words. Short cuts, like other devices we have discussed so far, are a common use of emotive language but are often mistaken for valid argument.

Although they have power to move us, these abbreviated substitutes for argument avoid the hard work necessary to provide facts, expert opinion, and analysis of warrants. Even experts, however, can be guilty of using short cuts, and the writer who consults an authority should be alert to that authority's use of language. Two of the most common uses of short cuts are clichés and slogans.

Clichés

"I'm against sloppy, emotional thinking. I'm against fashionable thinking. I'm against the whole cliché of the moment."[19] This statement by the late Herman Kahn, the founder of the Hudson Institute, a famous think tank, serves as the text for this section. A cliché is an expression or idea grown stale through overuse. Clichés in language are tired expressions that have faded like old photographs; readers no longer see anything when clichés are placed before them. Clichés include phrases like "cradle of civilization," "few and far between," "rude awakening," "follow in the footsteps of," "fly in the ointment."

But more important to recognize and avoid are clichés of thought. A cliché of thought may be likened to a formula, which one dictionary defines as "any conventional rule or method for doing something, especially when used, applied, or repeated without thought." Clichés of thought represent ready-made answers to questions, stereotyped solutions to problems, "knee-jerk" reactions. Two writers who call these

---

[18]*New York Times,* September 7, 1982, sec. C, p. 1.
[19]*New York Times,* July 8, 1983, sec. B, p. 1.

forms of expression "mass language" describe it this way: "Mass language is language which presents the reader with a response he is expected to make without giving him adequate reason for having this response."[20] These "clichés of the moment" are often expressed in single words or phrases. For example, the phrase "Gen X" has been repeated so often that it has come to represent an indisputable truth for many people, one they no longer question. The acceptance of this cliché, however, conceals the fact that millions of very different kinds of people from ages eighteen to thirty-five are being thoughtlessly lumped together as apathetic and lazy.

Certain cultural attitudes encourage the use of clichés. The liberal American tradition has been governed by hopeful assumptions about our ability to solve problems. A professor of communications says that "we tell our students that for every problem there must be a solution."[21] But real solutions are hard to come by. In our haste to provide them, to prove that we can be decisive, we may be tempted to produce familiar responses that resemble solutions.

History teaches us that a solution to an old and serious problem is almost always accompanied by unexpected drawbacks. As the writer quoted in the previous paragraph warns us, "Life is not that simple. There is no one answer to a given problem. There are multiple solutions, all with advantages and disadvantages." By solving one problem, we often create another. Automobiles, advanced medical techniques, industrialization, and liberal divorce laws have all contributed to the solution of age-old problems: lack of mobility, disease, poverty, domestic unhappiness. We now see that these solutions bring with them new problems that we nevertheless elect to live with because the advantages seem greater than the disadvantages. A well-known economist puts it this way: "I don't look for solutions; I look for trade-offs. I think the person who asks, 'What is the solution to this problem?' has a fundamental misconception of the way the world works. We have trade-offs, and that's all we have."[22]

This means that we should be skeptical of solutions promising everything and ignoring limitations and criticism. Such solutions have probably gone around many times. Having heard them so often, we are inclined to believe that they have been tried and proven. Thus they escape serious analysis.

Some of these problems and their solutions represent the fashionable thinking to which Kahn objected. They confront us every-

---

[20]Richard E. Hughes and P. Albert Duhamel, *Rhetoric: Principles and Usage* (Englewood Cliffs, N.J.: Prentice-Hall, 1962), p. 161.

[21]Malcolm O. Sillars, "The New Conservatism and the Teacher of Speech," *Southern Speech Journal* 21 (1956), p. 240.

[22]Thomas Sowell, "Manhattan Report" (edited transcript of *Meet the Press*) (New York: International Center for Economic Policy Studies, 1981), p. 10.

where, like the public personalities who gaze at us week after week from the covers of magazines and tabloid newspapers at the checkout counter in the supermarket. Alarms about the failures of public education, about drug addiction or danger to the environment or teenage pregnancy are sounded throughout the media continuously. The same solutions are advocated again and again: "Back to basics"; "Impose harsher sentences"; "Offer sex education." Their popularity, however, should not prevent us from asking: Are the problems as urgent as their prominence in the media suggests? Are the solutions workable? Does sufficient evidence exist to justify their adoption?

Your arguments will not always propose solutions. They will sometimes provide interpretations of or reasons for social phenomena, especially for recurrent problems. Some explanations have acquired the status of folk wisdom, like proverbs, and careless arguers will offer them as if they needed no further support. One object of stereotyped responses is the problem of juvenile delinquency, which liberals attribute to poverty, lack of community services, meaningless education, and violence on television. Conservatives blame parental permissiveness, decline in religious influence, lack of individual responsibility, lenient courts. Notice that the interpretations of the causes of juvenile delinquency are related to an ideology, to a particular view of the world that may prevent the arguer from recognizing any other way of examining the problem. Other stereotyped explanations for a range of social problems include inequality, competition, self-indulgence, alienation, discrimination, technology, lack of patriotism, excessive governmental regulation, and lack of sufficient governmental regulation. All of these explanations are worthy of consideration, but they must be defined and supported if they are to be used in a thoughtful, well-constructed argument.

Although formulas change with the times, some are unexpectedly hardy and survive long after critics have revealed their weaknesses. Overpopulation is often cited as the cause of poverty, disease, and war. It can be found in the writing of the ancient Greeks 2,500 years ago. "That perspective," says the editor of *Food Monitor,* a journal published by World Hunger Year, Inc., "is so pervasive that most Americans have simply stopped thinking about population and resort to inane clucking of tongues."[23] If the writer offering overpopulation as an explanation for poverty were to look further, he or she would discover that the explanation rested on shaky data. Singapore, the most densely populated country in the world (11,574 persons per square mile) is also one of the richest ($16,500 per capita income per year). Chad, one of the most sparsely populated (11 persons per square mile) is also one of the poorest ($190 per capita

---

[23]Letter to the *New York Times,* October 4, 1982, sec. A, p. 18.

income per year).[24] Strictly defined, overpopulation may serve to explain some instances of poverty; obviously it cannot serve as a blanket to cover all or even most instances. "By repeating stock phrases," one columnist reminds us, "we lose the ability, finally, to hear what we are saying."

Slogans

> I have always been rather impressed by those people who wear badges stating where they stand on certain issues. The badges have to be small, and therefore the message has to be small, concise, and without elaboration. So it comes out as "I hate something" or "I love something," or ban this or ban that. There isn't space for argument, and I therefore envy the badge-wearer who is so clear-cut about his or her opinions.[25]

The word *slogan* has a picturesque origin. A slogan was the war cry or rallying cry of a Scottish or Irish clan. From that early use it has come to mean a "catchword or rallying motto distinctly associated with a political party or other group" as well as a "catch phrase used to advertise a product."

Slogans, like clichés, are short, undeveloped arguments. They represent abbreviated responses to often complex questions. As a reader you need to be aware that slogans merely call attention to a problem; they cannot offer persuasive proof for a claim in a dozen words or less. As a writer you should avoid the use of slogans that evoke an emotional response "without giving [the reader] adequate reason for having this response."

Advertising slogans are the most familiar. Some of them are probably better known than nursery rhymes: "Got milk?" "L'Oréal, because I'm worth it," "Nike, just do it." Advertisements may, of course, rely for their effectiveness on more than slogans. They may also give us interesting and valuable information about products, but most advertisements give us slogans that ignore proof — short cuts substituting for argument.

The persuasive appeal of advertising slogans heavily depends on the connotations associated with products. In Chapter 5 (see p. 171, under "Appeals to Needs and Values"), we discussed the way in which advertisements promise to satisfy our needs and protect our values. Wherever evidence is scarce or nonexistent, the advertiser must persuade us through skillful choice of words and phrases (as well as pictures), especially those that produce pleasurable feel-

---

[24]*World Almanac and Book of Facts,* 1995 (New York: World Almanac, 1995), pp. 754, 818.

[25]Anthony Smith, "Nuclear Power — Why Not?" *The Listener,* October 22, 1981, p. 463.

ings. "Let it inspire you" is the slogan of a popular liqueur. It suggests a desirable state of being but remains suitably vague about the nature of the inspiration. Another familiar slogan — "Noxzema, clean makeup" — also emphasizes a quality that we approve of, but what is "clean" makeup? Since the advertisers are silent, we are left with warm feelings about the word and not much more.

Advertising slogans are persuasive because their witty phrasing and punchy rhythms produce an automatic yes response. We react to them as we might react to the lyrics of popular songs, and we treat them far less critically than we treat more straightforward and elaborate arguments. Still, the consequences of failing to analyze the slogans of advertisers are usually not serious. You may be tempted to buy a product because you were fascinated by a brilliant slogan, but if the product doesn't satisfy, you can abandon it without much loss. However, ignoring ideological slogans coined by political parties or special-interest groups may carry an enormous price, and the results are not so easily undone.

Ideological slogans, like advertising slogans, depend on the power of connotation, the emotional associations aroused by a word or phrase. In the 1960s and 1970s, a period of well-advertised social change, slogans flourished; they appeared by the hundreds of thousands on buttons, T-shirts, and bumper stickers. One of them read, "Student Power!" To some readers of the slogan, distrustful of young people and worried about student unrest on campuses and in the streets, the suggestion was frightening. To others, mostly students, the idea of power, however undefined, was intoxicating. Notice that "Student Power!" is not an argument; it is only a claim. (It might also represent a warrant.) As a claim, for example, it might take this form: Students at this school should have the power to select the faculty. Of course, the arguer would need to provide the kinds of proof that support his or her claim, something the slogan by itself cannot do. Many people, whether they accepted or rejected the claim, supplied the rest of the argument without knowing exactly what the issues were and how a developed argument would proceed. They were accepting or rejecting the slogan largely on the basis of emotional reaction to words.

American political history is, in fact, a repository of slogans. Leaf through a history of the United States and you will come across "Tippecanoe and Tyler, too," "manifest destiny," "fifty-four forty or fight," "make the world safe for democracy," "the silent majority," "the domino theory," "the missile gap," "the window of vulnerability." Each administration tries to capture the attention and allegiance of the public by coining catchy phrases. Roosevelt's New Deal in 1932 was followed by the Square Deal and the New Frontier. Today, slogans must be carefully selected to avoid offending groups that are sensitive to the ways in which words affect their interests.

In 1983 Senator John Glenn, announcing his candidacy for president, talked about bringing "old values and new horizons" to the White House. "New horizons" apparently carried positive connotations. His staff, however, worried that "old values" might suggest racism and sexism to minorities and women.

A professor of politics and international affairs at Princeton University explains why public officials use slogans, despite their obvious shortcomings:

> Officials long have tried to capture complicated events and to dominate public discussion of foreign policy by using simple phrases and slogans. They engage in phrase-making in order to reach wide audiences. . . .
>
> Slogans and metaphors often express the tendencies of officials and academics who have a common wish to be at once sweeping, unequivocal, easily understood, and persuasive. The desire to capture complicated phenomena through slogans stems also from impatience with the particular and unwillingness or inability to master interrelationships.[26]

Over a period of time slogans, like clichés, can acquire a life of their own and, if they are repeated often enough, come to represent an unchanging truth we no longer need to examine. "Dangerously," says the writer quoted above, "policy makers become prisoners of the slogans they popularize."

The arguments you write will not, of course, be one-sentence slogans. Unfortunately, many longer arguments amount to little more than sloganeering or series of suggestive phrases strung together to imitate the process of argumentation. Following are two examples. The first is taken from a full-page magazine advertisement in 1983, urging the formation of a new political party. The second is part of the second inaugural address of George C. Wallace, governor of Alabama, in 1971. These extracts are typical of the full advertisement and the full speech.

> We can't dislodge big money from its domination over the two old parties, but we can offer the country something better: a new party that represents the people and responds to their needs. . . . How can we solve any problem without correcting the cause — the structure of the Dem/Rep machine and the power of the military-industrial establishment? . . . The power of the people could be a commanding force if only we could get together — Labor, public-interest organizations, blacks, women, antinuclear groups, and all the others.[27]

> The people of the South and those who think like the South, represent the majority viewpoint within our constitutional democracy, but they are not organized and do not speak with a loud voice. Until the day arrives when the voice of the people of the South and those who think

---

[26]Henry Bienen, "Slogans Aren't the World," *New York Times,* January 16, 1983, sec. 4, p. 19.

[27]*The Progressive,* September 1983, p. 38.

like us is, within the law, thrust into the face of the bureaucrats, only then can the "people's power" express itself legally and ethically and get results. . . . Too long, oh, too long, has the voice of the people been silenced by their own disruptive government — by governmental bribery in quasi-governmental handouts such as H.E.W. and others that exist in America today! An aroused people can save this nation from those evil forces who seek our destruction. The choice is yours. The hour is growing late![28]

Whatever power these recommendations might have if their proposals were more clearly formulated, as they stand they are collections of slogans and loaded words. (Even the language falters: Can the voice of the people be thrust into the face of the bureaucrats?) We can visualize some of the slogans as brightly colored banners: "Dislodge Big Money!" "Power to the People!" "Save This Nation from Evil Forces!" "The Choice Is Yours!" Do all the groups mentioned share identical interests? If so, what are they? Given the vagueness of the terms, it is not surprising that arguers on opposite sides of the political spectrum — loosely characterized as liberal and conservative — sometimes resort to the same clichés and slogans: the language of populism, or a belief in the virtues of the "common people" in these examples.

Slogans have numerous shortcomings as substitutes for the development of an argument. First, their brevity presents serious disadvantages. Slogans necessarily ignore exceptions or negative instances that might qualify a claim. They usually speak in absolute terms without describing the circumstances in which a principle or idea might not work. Their claims therefore seem shrill and exaggerated. In addition, brevity prevents the sloganeer from revealing how he or she arrived at conclusions.

Second, slogans may conceal unexamined warrants. When Japanese cars were beginning to compete with American cars, the slogan "Made in America by Americans" appeared on the bumpers of thousands of American-made cars. A thoughtful reader would have discovered in this slogan several implied warrants: American cars are better than Japanese cars; the American economy will improve if we buy American; patriotism can be expressed by buying American goods. If the reader were to ask a few probing questions, he or she might find these warrants unconvincing.

Silent warrants that express values hide in other popular and influential slogans. "Pro-life," the slogan of those who oppose abortion, assumes that the fetus is a living being entitled to the same rights as individuals already born. "Pro-choice," the slogan of those who favor abortion, suggests that the freedom of the pregnant

[28]Second Inaugural Address as governor of Alabama, January 18, 1971.

woman to choose is the foremost or only consideration. The words *life* and *choice* have been carefully selected to reflect desirable qualities, but the words are only the beginning of the argument.

Third, although slogans may express admirable sentiments, they often fail to tell us how to achieve their objectives. They address us in the imperative mode, ordering us to take an action or refrain from it. But the means of achieving the objectives may be nonexistent or very costly. If the sloganeer cannot offer workable means for implementing his or her goals, he or she risks alienating the audience.

Sloganeering is one of the recognizable attributes of propaganda. Propaganda for both good and bad purposes is a form of slanting, of selecting language and facts to persuade an audience to take a certain action. Even a good cause may be weakened by an unsatisfactory slogan. The slogans of some organizations devoted to fundraising for people with physical handicaps have come under attack for depicting those with handicaps as helpless. According to one critic, the popular slogan "Jerry's kids" promotes the idea that Jerry Lewis is the sole support of children with muscular dystrophy. Perhaps increased sensitivity to the needs of people with disabilities will produce new words and new slogans. If you assume that your audience is sophisticated and alert, you will probably write your strongest arguments, devoid of clichés and slogans.

SAMPLE ANNOTATED ANALYSIS

The Childswap Society
SANDRA FELDMAN

Introduction: reference to a sci-fi story that suggests her subject

Many years ago, when I was a teenager, I read a science fiction story that I've never been able to forget. It came back to me with special force this holiday season because I was thinking about this country's national shame — a child poverty rate of 25 percent — and about our lack of urgency in dealing with the

The subject: the problem of child neglect

Sandra Feldman is president of the American Federation of Teachers. This essay appeared in the *New York Times* on January 4, 1998, as part of an ongoing "Where We Stand" advertising campaign for the American Federation of Teachers.

problems this poverty creates.

The story described a society with a national child lottery which was held every four years. Every child's name was put into it — there were no exceptions — and children were randomly redistributed to new parents, who raised them for the next four years.

Babies were not part of this lottery. Parents got to keep their newborn children until the next lottery, but then they became part of the national childswap. The cycle was broken every third swap and kids were sent back to their original parents until the next lottery. So by the time you were considered an adult, at age 26, the most time you could have spent with your birth parents was 10 years. The other 16 were simply a matter of chance.

The Luck of the Draw

Maybe one of your new parents would be the head of a gigantic multinational company and the most powerful person in the country or the president of a famous university. Or you might find yourself the child of a family living in a public housing project or migrant labor camp.

The whole idea sounded horrible to me, but people in the childswap society took the lottery for granted. They didn't try to hide their children or send them away to other countries; childswapping was simply part of their culture. And one thing the lottery did was to make the whole society very conscientious about how things were arranged for kids. After all, you never knew where your own child would end up after the next lottery, so in a very real sense everyone's child was — *virtues of the childswap society* or could be — yours. As a result, children growing up under this system got everything they needed to thrive, both physically and intellectually, and the society itself was harmonious.

Further development and support: contrast of the childswap society with American society

What if someone wrote a story about what American society in the late twentieth century takes for granted in the arrangements for its children? We might not want to admit it, but don't we take for granted that some kids are going to have much better lives than others? Of course. We take for granted that some will get the best medical treatment and others will be

(implicit warrant: All children are entitled to decent lives.)

able to get little or none. We take for granted that some kids will go to beautiful, well-cared-for schools with top-notch curriculums, excellent libraries, and computers for every child and others will go to schools where there are not enough desks and textbooks to go around — wretched places where even the toilets don't work.

We take for granted that teachers in wealthy suburban schools will be better paid and better trained than those in poor inner-city or rural schools. We take for granted, in so many ways, that the children whom the lottery of birth has made the most needy will get the least. "After all," we say to ourselves, "it's up to each family to look after its own. If some parents can't give their children what they need to thrive, that's *their* problem."

What Would Happen?

transition to conclusion

Obviously I'm not suggesting that the United States adopt a childswap system. The idea makes me cringe, and, anyway, it's just a fable. But I like to imagine what would happen if we did.

Conclusion: Claim of Policy

We'd start with political figures and their children and grandchildren, with governors and mayors and other leaders. What do you suppose would happen when they saw that their children would

We should treat all children as if they were our own. have the same chance as the sons and daughters of poor people — no more and no less? What would happen to our schools and health-care system — and our shameful national indifference to children who are not ours?

    I bet we'd quickly find a way to set things straight and make sure *all* children had an equal chance to thrive. 10

Analysis

    This essay concerns a serious educational challenge — equalizing opportunities for all children in this country, whatever their social or economic status. This subject might appear in a State of the Union address or another formal public-policy pronouncement before a large audience. In this essay the author has chosen to treat the subject as if she were engaged in a dialogue with the reader, speaking in familiar language that is neither technical, scholarly, nor literary. But despite its informality, it retains the patterns and grammar of written, not spoken, discourse.

    Feldman begins with a kind of introduction that you've already encountered in other essays, an anecdote recounting a personal experience. Because this anecdote consumes a third of the essay, we know that the author considers it a crucial element in her appeal. Although no single personal experience unaccompanied by other evidence provides enough support to change public policy, it can gain our attention and arouse suspense. It can be effective in arguments about policies where personal feelings are relevant and where scientific research has little or no influence on the conclusion. And the use of the personal pronoun throughout ("I," "you," and "we") — even if the subject of the essay is not the author, as in this case — can often make a broad generalization seem more immediate.

    Other stylistic devices contribute to the informality of the language. Feldman uses contractions such as "didn't," "can't," and "I've" to maintain the closeness to ordinary speech. In addition, she introduces expressions like "I bet" and the word "kids" for children and homely examples, like "even the toilets don't work." She also inserts rhetorical questions — to which she knows the answers — as a way of provoking thought about the issues. Even using "and" and "but" to begin sentences, a practice frowned on in technical and scientific papers, emphasizes the conversational style of the argument.

In a technical or scientific paper expression of the author's personality and feelings might divert attention from the objective research on which a sound conclusion rests. Feldman's language is appropriate for an article on the op-ed page of a newspaper or a column like "My Turn" in *Newsweek*. In an essay on the future of children or, for that matter, on any subject about human welfare that stirs compassion, the language of personal concern can go far in persuading the reader to sympathize with the arguer and her claim.

READINGS FOR ANALYSIS

Life, Liberty, Whatever
MARK LEYNER

On June 1, 1998, President Clinton issued an executive memorandum directing Federal departments and agencies to rewrite all official documents that are sent to the public in "plain language" by the year 2002. In light of the President's call for clarity, it seems appropriate, even patriotic, to rework some of our nation's historic documents — not only to rid them of mandarin obfuscation, but also to update their language, making them accessible to a new generation of Americans.

The Unanimous Declaration of the
Thirteen United States of America

When in the course of human events it becomes necessary for one people to dissolve the political bands which have connected them with another, and to assume among the powers of the earth, the separate and equal station to which the laws of nature and of nature's God entitle them, a decent respect to the opinions of mankind requires that they should declare the causes which impel them to the separation. . . .

Look, sometimes you gotta do what you gotta do. We're Americans. We're not English. O.K.? We're not into the whole foggy, yes mum, no mum, cross-dressing, spanking, seedy seaside resort thing. And just because we might occasionally "overindulge" and binge on

---

Mark Leyner is a novelist and author of *The Tetherballs of Bougainville* (1997). This article appeared in the *New York Times* on July 19, 1998.

johnnycakes and salt cod because we're (admittedly) so totally obsessed with establishing diplomatic and military relations with, like, rich, handsome allies (I think France really, really likes us) doesn't mean we don't deserve a corner office in the great firm of nations. Without going into all the gory details, here's basically why we want the separation. Bottom line: You can be treated like dirt for just so long. (Also, F.Y.I.: George III is a certifiable nutjob). Anyway. . . . England, thanks for the language and everything. Oh, and thanks especially for the system of jurisprudence (without which none of us would be employed). But, as George Michael said: "All we have to see/Is that I don't belong to you/And you don't belong to me/Freedom/I won't let you down/Freedom/I will not give you up/Freedom/Gotta have some faith in the sound."

The Bill of Rights

Amendment I
Congress shall make no law respecting an establishment of religion, or prohibiting the free exercise thereof; or abridging the freedom of speech or of the press; or the right of the people peaceably to assemble, and to petition the government for a redress of grievances.

You have the right to be as totally obnoxious as you want. 5 Really! (There are exceptions. I mean, you can't yell "Sarin attack!" in the middle of *The Horse Whisperer,* for instance. But, like, who'd want to anyway?)

Amendment II
A well-regulated militia being necessary to the security of a free State, the right of the people to keep and bear arms shall not be infringed.

Want to attend your child's T-ball game brandishing an AK-47, with cartridge bandoliers slung across your bare, sweating, obscenity-strewn chest? You can.

Amendment III
No soldier shall, in time of peace, be quartered in any house without the consent of the owner, nor in time of war, but in a manner to be prescribed by law.

You cannot be forced, in peacetime, to entertain a buxom Navy Seal in your home, nor can you be compelled to watch her do one-armed pushups.

Amendment IV
The right of the people to be secure in their persons, houses, papers, and effects, against unreasonable searches and seizures, shall not be violated, and no warrants shall issue but upon probable cause, 10

*supported by oath or affirmation, and particularly describing the place
to be searched, and the persons or things to be seized.*

Basically, cops can't burst into your house in the middle of the
night, beat you, and trash your possessions, unless: (1) They have
the wrong address. (2) They feel like it.

Amendment V

*No person shall be held to answer for a capital, or otherwise infa-
mous crime, unless on a presentment or indictment of a grand jury, except in cases arising in the land or naval forces, or in the militia, when
in actual service in time of war or public danger; nor shall any person
be subject for the same offense to be twice put in jeopardy of life or
limb; nor shall be compelled in any criminal case to be a witness
against himself, nor be deprived of life, liberty, or property, without due
process of law; nor shall private property be taken for public use without just compensation.*

This is another amendment for criminals. Nice people with jobs
don't need to worry about this one.

Amendment VI

*In all criminal prosecutions, the accused shall enjoy the right to a
speedy and public trial, by an impartial jury of the State and district
wherein the crime shall have been committed, which district shall have
been previously ascertained by law, and to be informed of the nature
and cause of the accusation; to be confronted with the witnesses
against him; to have compulsory process for obtaining witnesses in his
favor, and to have the assistance of counsel for his defense.*

You have the right to glower at the venal, lying scum who testify 15
against you.

Amendment VII

*In suits at common law, where the value in controversy shall ex-
ceed twenty dollars, the right of trial by jury shall be preserved, and no
fact tried by a jury shall be otherwise re-examined in any court of the
United States, than according to the rules of the common law.*

Medical malpractice? Defective product? Slip-and-fall accident?
Think liability. . . . Pain and suffering. . . . Loss of consortium. . . .

Sue! Nobody redistributes wealth like a righteous jury. Free con-
sultation. No fee unless you collect. Call 1-800-7TH-AMEN.

Amendment VIII

*Excessive bail shall not be required, nor excessive fines imposed,
nor cruel and unusual punishments inflicted.*

Condemned inmates cannot be macheted to death, burned alive, 20
frozen alive, dunked in piranha tanks, defenestrated, crushed in in-

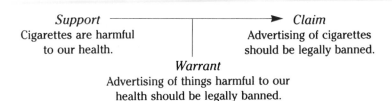

loopholes galore — expresses precisely the degree of loss of autonomy that we are able to tolerate.

Analysis

A deductive argument proceeds from a general statement that the writer assumes to be true to a conclusion that is more specific. Deductive reasoning is commonplace, although seldom so pure as the definition suggests. In Kramer's article the conclusion appears at the end of paragraph 3: "divorce expresses our overriding respect for autonomy, for the unique and separate self." The major premise or general statement may be summed up as "Self-actualization is an important American value," and the minor premise as "Divorce is an expression of self-actualization."

Kramer's defense of the major premise is admirable. Despite its brevity, the article brims with significant quotations and instructive examples from literature, psychiatry, and social and economic history that began, as he reminds us, with a "bill of divorcement" (para. 7) from England in 1776.

Finding support for the minor premise is a more difficult exercise because the reader here confronts a *specific* consequence of self-fulfillment — divorce. In all arguments, details and examples test the strength of our generalizations, and while self-actualization is suitably vague, divorce is not. We know that it does not always represent liberation for both partners. Kramer is aware of the problem. In the same paragraph he has insisted both that divorce "signals social progress" and that it is "destructive" (para. 12). He knows that his critics will call on him to reconcile this contradiction.

So far Kramer's argument has been largely factual, proof of the existence of the American ideal. Now he advances onto shakier ground in an examination of values: "the question is whether any other compelling value counterbalances the siren song of self-improvement" (para. 12).

Kramer then responds to those therapists who value a different ideal — that of mutuality, cooperation, and compromise rather than self-assertion. He admires such virtues but finds them unlikely to prevail against the ideal of self-fulfillment that pervades all areas of American life. Divorce, he believes, is simply one expression of that ideal, and he rejects the proposition that we should "ask the institution of marriage to play by different rules" (para. 17).

In deductive argument the conclusion must be true. Questions of social behavior, however, are not so easily proved. We accept the conclusions in such cases if they are plausible — well supported and consistent with experience. Within the limits of this brief essay, Kramer's findings are convincing.

One other element is worth noting: Kramer's objectivity, his role as observer rather than advocate. For the most part, he has excluded himself from the argument. We suspect that, as a psychiatrist, he supports values of self-expression, but in this article he is describing not his own views but those of most Americans. He does not explicitly defend divorce; he explains it. On the whole, this is an effective strategy. We do not need to agree on the morality of self-fulfillment to accept his conclusion.

A NOTE ON THE SYLLOGISM AND THE TOULMIN MODEL

In examining the classical deductive syllogism, you may have noticed the resemblance of its three-part outline to the three-part structure of claim, support, and warrant that we have used throughout the text to illustrate the elements of argument. We mentioned that the syllogism was articulated over two thousand years ago by the Greek philosopher Aristotle. By contrast, the claim-support-warrant structure is based on the model of argument proposed by the modern British philosopher Stephen Toulmin.

Now, there is every reason to think that all models of argument will share some similarities. Nevertheless, the differences between the formal syllogism and the informal Toulmin model suggest that the latter is a more effective instrument for writers who want to know which questions to ask, both before they begin and during the process of developing their arguments.

The syllogism is useful for laying out the basic elements of an argument, as we have seen in several examples. It lends itself more readily to simple arguments. The following syllogism summarizes a familiar argument.

MAJOR PREMISE: Advertising of things harmful to our health should be legally banned.

MINOR PREMISE: Cigarettes are harmful to our health.

CONCLUSION: Therefore, advertising of cigarettes should be legally banned.

Cast in the form of a Toulmin outline, the argument looks like this:

CLAIM: Advertising of cigarettes should be legally banned.

SUPPORT (EVIDENCE): Cigarettes are harmful to our health.

WARRANT: Advertising of things harmful to our health should be legally banned.

or in diagram form:

Support ──────────────┬──────────▶ *Claim*
Cigarettes are harmful   │   Advertising of cigarettes
to our health.   │   should be legally banned.

Warrant
Advertising of things harmful to our
health should be legally banned.

In both the syllogism and the Toulmin model the principal elements of the argument are expressed in three statements. You can see that the claim in the Toulmin model is the conclusion in the syllogism — that is, the proposition that you are trying to prove. The evidence (support) in the Toulmin model corresponds to the minor premise in the syllogism. And the warrant in the Toulmin model resembles the major premise of the syllogism.

But the differences are significant. One difference is the use of language. The syllogism represents an argument "in which the validity of the assumption underlying the inference 'leap' is uncontested."[3] That is, the words "major premise" seem to suggest that the assumption has been proved. They do not emphasize that an analysis of the premise — "Advertising of things harmful to our health should be legally banned" — is necessary before we can decide that the conclusion is acceptable. Of course, a careful arguer will try to establish the truth and validity of all parts of the syllogism, but the terms in which the syllogism is framed do not encourage him or her to examine the real relationship among the three elements. Sometimes the enthymeme (see p. 293), which uses only two elements in the argument and suppresses the third, makes analyzing the relationship even more difficult.

In the Toulmin model, the use of the term *warrant* indicates that the validity of the proposition must be established to *guarantee* the claim or make the crossing from support to claim. It makes clear that the arguer must ask *why* such advertising must be banned.

Nor is the term *minor premise* as useful to the arguer as "support." The word *support* instructs the arguer that he or she must take steps to provide the claim with factual evidence or an appeal to values.

A second difference is that while the syllogism is essentially static, with all three parts logically locked into place, the Toulmin model suggests that an argument is a *movement* from support to claim by way of the warrant, which acts as a bridge. Toulmin introduced the concept of warrant by asking "How do you get there?"

---

[3]Wayne E. Brockenreide and Douglas Ehninger, "Toulmin on Argument: An Interpretation and Application," *Contemporary Theories of Rhetoric: Selected Readings,* ed. Richard L. Johannesen (New York: Harper and Row, 1971), p. 245. This comparative analysis is indebted to Brockenreide and Ehninger's influential article.

(His first two questions, introducing the claim and support, were, "What are you trying to prove?" and "What have you got to go on?")

Lastly, recall that in addition to the three basic elements, the Toulmin model offers supplementary elements of argument. The *qualifier,* in the form of words like "probably" or "more likely," shows that the claim is not absolute. The *backing* offers support for the validity of the warrant. The *reservation* suggests that the validity of the warrant may be limited. These additional elements, which refine and expand the argument itself, reflect the real flexibility and complexity of the argumentative process.

COMMON FALLACIES

In this necessarily brief review it would be impossible to discuss all the fallacies listed by logicians, but we can examine the ones most likely to be found in the arguments you will read and write. Fallacies are difficult to classify, first, because there are literally dozens of systems for classifying, and second, because under any system there is always a good deal of overlap. Our discussion of the reasoning process, however, tells us where faulty reasoning occurs.

Inductive fallacies, as we know, result from the wrong use of evidence: That is, the arguer leaps to a conclusion on the basis of an insufficient sample, ignoring evidence that might have altered his or her conclusion. Deductive fallacies, on the other hand, result from a failure to follow the logic of a series of statements. Here the arguer neglects to make a clear connection between the parts of his or her argument. One of the commonest strategies is the introduction of an irrelevant issue, one that has little or no direct bearing on the development of the claim and serves only to distract the reader.

It's helpful to remember that, even if you cannot name the particular fallacy, you can learn to recognize it and not only refute it in the arguments of others but avoid it in your own as well.

1. Hasty Generalization

In Chapter 5 (see pp. 160–62) we discussed the dangers in drawing conclusions on the basis of insufficient evidence. Many of our prejudices are a result of hasty generalization. A prejudice is literally a judgment made before the facts are in. On the basis of experience with two or three members of an ethnic group, for example, we may form the prejudice that all members of the group share the characteristics that we have attributed to the two or three in our experience. (See Gordon Allport, "The Nature of Prejudice," on p. 135.)

Superstitions are also based in part on hasty generalization. As a result of a very small number of experiences with black cats, broken mirrors, Friday the thirteenth, or spilled salt, some people will assume a cause-and-effect relation between these signs and misfortunes. *Superstition* has been defined as "a notion maintained despite evidence to the contrary." The evidence would certainly show that, contrary to the superstitious belief, in a lifetime hundreds of such "unlucky" signs are not followed by unfortunate events. To generalize about a connection is therefore unjustified.

2. Faulty Use of Authority

Faulty use of authority — the attempt to bolster claims by citing the opinions of experts — was discussed in Chapter 5. Both writers and readers need to be especially aware of the testimony of authorities who may disagree with those cited. In circumstances where experts disagree, you are encouraged to undertake a careful evaluation and comparison of credentials.

3. Post Hoc or Doubtful Cause

The entire Latin term for this fallacy is *post hoc, ergo propter hoc,* meaning, "After this, therefore because of this." The arguer infers that because one event follows another event, the first event must be the cause of the second. But proximity of events or conditions does not guarantee a causal relation. The rooster crows every morning at 5:00 and, seeing the sun rise immediately after, decides that his crowing has caused the sun to rise. A month after A-bomb tests are concluded, tornadoes damage the area where the tests were held, and residents decide that the tests caused the tornadoes. After the school principal suspends daily prayers in the classroom, acts of vandalism increase, and some parents are convinced that failure to conduct prayer is responsible for the rise in vandalism. In each of these cases, the fact that one event follows another does not prove a causal connection. The two events may be coincidental, or the first event may be only one, and an insignificant one, of many causes that have produced the second event. The reader or writer of causal arguments must determine whether another more plausible explanation exists and whether several causes have combined to produce the effect. Perhaps the suspension of prayer was only one of a number of related causes: a decline in disciplinary action, a relaxation of academic standards, a change in school administration, and changes in family structure in the school community.

In the previous section we saw that superstitions are the result not only of hasty generalization but also of the willingness to find a cause-and-effect connection in the juxtaposition of two events. A belief in astrological signs also derives from erroneous inferences about cause and effect. Only a very few of the millions of people who consult the astrology charts every day in newspapers and magazines have submitted the predictions to statistical analysis. A curious reader might try this strategy: Save the columns, usually at the beginning or end of the year, in which astrologers and clairvoyants make predictions for events in the coming year, allegedly based on their reading of the stars and other signs. At the end of the year evaluate the percentage of predictions that were fulfilled. The number will be very small. But even if some of the predictions prove true, there may be other less fanciful explanations for their accuracy.

In defending simple explanations against complex ones, philosophers and scientists often refer to a maxim called *Occam's razor,* a principle of the medieval philosopher and theologian William of Occam. A modern science writer says this principle "urges a preference for the simplest hypothesis that does all we want it to do."[4] Bertrand Russell, the twentieth-century British philosopher, explained it this way:

> It is vain to do with more what can be done with fewer. That is to say, if everything in some science can be interpreted without assuming this or that hypothetical entity, there is no ground for assuming it. I have myself found this a most fruitful principle in logical analysis.[5]

In other words, choose the simpler, more credible explanation wherever possible.

We all share the belief that scientific experimentation and research can answer questions about a wide range of natural and social phenomena: evolutionary development, hurricanes, disease, crime, poverty. It is true that repeated experiments in controlled situations can establish what seem to be solid relations suggesting cause and effect. But even scientists prefer to talk not about cause but about an extremely high probability that under controlled conditions one event will follow another.

In the social sciences cause-and-effect relations are especially susceptible to challenge. Human experiences can seldom be subjected to laboratory conditions. In addition, the complexity of the social environment makes it difficult, even impossible, to extract one cause from among the many that influence human behavior.

4. False Analogy

Many analogies are merely descriptive and offer no proof of the connection between the two things being compared. In recent years a debate has emerged between weight-loss professionals about the wis-

---

[4]Martin Gardner, *The Whys of a Philosophical Scrivener* (New York: Quill, 1983), p. 174.

[5]*Dictionary of Mind, Matter and Morals* (New York: Philosophical Library, 1952), p. 166.

dom of urging overweight people to lose weight for health reasons. Susan Wooley, director of the eating disorders clinic at the University of Cincinnati and a professor of psychiatry, offered the following analogy in defense of her view that dieting is dangerous.

> We know that overweight people have a higher mortality rate than thin people. We also know that black people have a higher mortality rate than white people. Do we subject black people to torturous treatments to bleach their skin? Of course not. We have enough sense to know skin-bleaching will not eliminate sickle-cell anemia. So why do we have blind faith that weight loss will cure the diseases associated with obesity?"[6]

But it is clear that the false analogy between black skin and excessive weight does not work. The color of one's skin does not cause sickle-cell anemia, but there is an abundance of proof that excess weight influences mortality.

Historians are fond of using analogical arguments to demonstrate that particular circumstances prevailing in the past are being reproduced in the present. They therefore feel safe in predicting that the present course of history will follow that of the past. British historian Arnold Toynbee argues by analogy that humans' tenure on earth may be limited.

> On the evidence of the past history of life on this planet, even the extinction of the human race is not entirely unlikely. After all, the reign of man on the Earth, if we are right in thinking that man established his present ascendancy in the middle paleolithic age, is so far only about 100,000 years old, and what is that compared to the 500 million or 900 million years during which life has been in existence on the surface of this planet? In the past, other forms of life have enjoyed reigns which have lasted for almost inconceivably longer periods — and which yet at last have come to an end.[7]

Toynbee finds similarities between the limited reigns of other animal species and the possible disappearance of the human race. For this analogy, however, we need to ask whether the conditions of the past, so far as we know them, at all resemble the conditions under which human existence on earth might be terminated. Is the fact that human beings are also members of the animal kingdom sufficient support for this comparison?

5. Ad Hominem

The Latin term *ad hominem* means "against the man" and refers to an attack on the person rather than on the argument or the issue. The assumption in such a fallacy is that if the speaker proves to be

---

[6]*New York Times,* April 12, 1992, sec. C, p. 43.

[7]*Civilization on Trial* (New York: Oxford University Press, 1948), pp. 162–163.

unacceptable in some way, his or her statements must also be judged unacceptable. Attacking the author of the statement is a strategy of diversion that prevents the reader from giving attention where it is due — to the issue under discussion.

You might hear someone complain, "What can the priest tell us about marriage? He's never been married himself." This ad hominem accusation ignores the validity of the advice the priest might offer. In the same way an overweight patient might reject the advice on diet by an overweight physician. In politics it is not uncommon for antagonists to attack each other for personal characteristics that may not be relevant to the tasks they will be elected to perform. They may be accused of infidelity to their partners, homosexuality, atheism, or a flamboyant social life. Even if certain accusations should be proved true, voters should not ignore the substance of what politicians do and say in their public offices.

This confusion of private life with professional record also exists in literature and the other arts. According to their biographers, the American writers Thomas Wolfe, Robert Frost, and William Saroyan — to name only a few — and numbers of film stars, including Charlie Chaplin, Joan Crawford, and Bing Crosby, made life miserable for those closest to them. Having read about their unpleasant personal characteristics, some people find it hard to separate the artist from his or her creation, although the personality and character of the artist are often irrelevant to the content of the work.

Ad hominem accusations against the person do *not* constitute a fallacy if the characteristics under attack are relevant to the argument. If the politician is irresponsible and dishonest in the conduct of his or her personal life, we may be justified in thinking that the person will also behave irresponsibly and dishonestly in public office.

6. False Dilemma

As the name tells us, the false dilemma, sometimes called the *black-white fallacy,* poses an either-or situation. The arguer suggests that only two alternatives exist, although there may be other explanations of or solutions to the problem under discussion. The false dilemma reflects the simplification of a complex problem. Sometimes it is offered out of ignorance or laziness, sometimes to divert attention from the real explanation or solution that the arguer rejects for doubtful reasons.

You may encounter the either-or situation in dilemmas about personal choices. "At the University of Georgia," says one writer, "the measure of a man was football. You either played it or worshiped those who did, and there was no middle ground."[8] Clearly

---

[8]Phil Gailey, "A Nonsports Fan," *New York Times Magazine,* December 18, 1983, sec. 6, p. 96.

this dilemma — "Love football or you're not a man" — ignores other measures of manhood.

Politics and government offer a wealth of examples. In an interview with the *New York Times* in 1975, the Shah of Iran was asked why he could not introduce into his authoritarian regime greater freedom for his subjects. His reply was, "What's wrong with authority? Is anarchy better?" Apparently he considered that only two paths were open to him — authoritarianism or anarchy. Of course, democracy was also an option, which, perhaps fatally, he declined to consider.

7. Slippery Slope

If an arguer predicts that taking a first step will lead inevitably to a second, usually undesirable step, he or she must provide evidence that this will happen. Otherwise, the arguer is guilty of a slippery-slope fallacy.

Asked by an inquiring photographer on the street how he felt about censorship of a pornographic magazine, a man replied, "I don't think any publication should be banned. It's a slippery slope when you start making decisions on what people should be permitted to read. . . . It's a dangerous precedent." Perhaps. But if questioned further, the man should have offered evidence that a ban on some things leads inevitably to a ban on everything.

Predictions based on the danger inherent in taking the first step are commonplace:

> Legalization of abortion will lead to murder of the old and the physically and mentally handicapped.
>
> The Connecticut law allowing sixteen-year-olds and their parents to divorce each other will mean the death of the family.
>
> If we ban handguns, we will end up banning rifles and other hunting weapons.

Distinguishing between probable and improbable predictions — that is, recognizing the slippery-slope fallacy — poses special problems because only future developments can verify or refute predictions. For example, in 1941 the imposition of military conscription aroused some opponents to predict that the draft was a precursor of fascism in this country. Only after the war, when 10 million draftees were demobilized, did it become clear that the draft had been an insufficient sign for a prediction of fascism. In this case the slippery-slope prediction of fascism might have been avoided if closer attention had been paid to other influences pointing to the strength of democracy.

Slippery-slope predictions are simplistic. They ignore not only the dissimilarities between first and last steps but also the complexity of the developments in any long chain of events.

8. Begging the Question

If the writer makes a statement that assumes that the very question being argued has already been proved, the writer is guilty of begging the question. In a letter to the editor of a college newspaper protesting the failure of the majority of students to meet the writing requirement because they had failed an exemption test, the writer said, "Not exempting all students who honestly qualify for exemption is an insult." But whether the students are honestly qualified is precisely the question that the exemption test was supposed to resolve. The writer has not proved that the students who failed the writing test were qualified for exemption. She has only made an assertion *as if* she had already proved it.

In an effort to raise standards of teaching, some politicians and educators have urged that master teachers be awarded higher salaries. Opponents have argued that such a proposal begs the question because it assumes that the term *master teachers* can be or has already been defined.

Circular reasoning is an extreme example of begging the question: "Women should not be permitted to join men's clubs because the clubs are for men only." The question to be resolved first, of course, is whether clubs for men only should continue to exist.

9. Straw Man

The straw-man fallacy consists of an attack on a view similar to but not the same as the one your opponent holds. It is a familiar diversionary tactic. The name probably derives from an old game in which a straw man was set up to divert attention from the real target that a contestant was supposed to knock down.

One of the outstanding examples of the straw-man fallacy occurred in the famous Checkers speech of Senator Richard Nixon. In 1952 during his vice-presidential campaign, Nixon was accused of having appropriated $18,000 in campaign funds for his personal use. At one point in the radio and television speech in which he defended his reputation, he said:

> One other thing I probably should tell you, because if I don't they will probably be saying this about me, too. We did get something, a gift, after the election.
>
> A man down in Texas heard Pat on the radio mention the fact that our two youngsters would like to have a dog, and, believe it or not, the day before we left on this campaign trip we got a message from Union Station in Baltimore saying they had a package for us. We went down to get it. You know what it was?
>
> It was a little cocker spaniel dog, in a crate that he had sent all the way from Texas, black and white, spotted, and our little girl, Tricia, the six-year-old, named it Checkers.

> And, you know, the kids, like all kids, loved the dog, and I just want to say this, right now, that regardless of what they say about it, we are going to keep it.[9]

Of course, Nixon knew that the issue was the alleged misappropriation of funds, not the ownership of the dog, which no one had asked him to return.

10. Two Wrongs Make a Right

The two-wrongs-make-a-right fallacy is another example of the way in which attention may be diverted from the question at issue.

After President Jimmy Carter in March 1977 attacked the human rights record of the Soviet Union, Russian officials responded:

> As for the present state of human rights in the United States, it is characterized by the following facts: millions of unemployed, racial discrimination, social inequality of women, infringement of citizens' personal freedom, the growth of crime, and so on.[10]

The Russians made no attempt to deny the failure of *their* human rights record; instead they attacked by pointing out that the Americans are not blameless either.

11. Non Sequitur

The Latin term *non sequitur,* which means "it does not follow," is another fallacy of irrelevance. An advertisement for a book, *Worlds in Collision,* whose theories about the origin of the earth and evolutionary development have been challenged by almost all reputable scientists, states:

> Once rejected as "preposterous"! Critics called it an outrage! It aroused incredible antagonism in scientific and literary circles. Yet half a million copies were sold and for twenty-seven years it remained an outstanding bestseller.

We know, of course, that the popularity of a book does not bestow scientific respectability. The number of sales, therefore, is irrelevant to proof of the book's theoretical soundness — a non sequitur.

12. Ad Populum

Arguers guilty of the *ad populum* fallacy make an appeal to the prejudices of the people (*populum* in Latin). They assume that their claim can be adequately defended without further support if they

---

[9]Radio and television address of Senator Nixon from Los Angeles on September 23, 1952.

[10]*New York Times,* March 3, 1977, p. 1.

emphasize a belief or attitude that the audience shares with them. One common form of *ad populum* is an appeal to patriotism, which may allow arguers to omit evidence that the audience needs for proper evaluation of the claim. In the following advertisement the makers of Zippo lighters made such an appeal in urging readers to buy their product.

> It's a grand old lighter. Zippo — the grand old lighter that's made right here in the good old U.S.A.
>
> We truly make an all-American product. The raw materials used in making a Zippo lighter are all right from this great land of ours.
>
> Zippo windproof lighters are proud to be Americans.

13. Appeal to Tradition

In making an appeal to tradition, the arguer assumes that what has existed for a long time and has therefore become a tradition should continue to exist *because* it is a tradition. If the arguer avoids telling his or her reader *why* the tradition should be preserved, he or she may be accused of failing to meet the real issue.

The following statement appeared in a letter defending the membership policy of the Century Club, an all-male club established in New York City in 1847 that was under pressure to admit women. The writer was a Presbyterian minister who opposed the admission of women.

> I am totally opposed to a proposal which would radically change the nature of the Century. . . . A club creates an ethos of its own over the years, and I would deeply deplore a step that would inevitably create an entirely different kind of place.
>
> A club like the Century should surely be unaffected by fashionable whims. . . .[11]

14. Faulty Emotional Appeals

In some discussions of fallacies, appeals to the emotions of the audience are treated as illegitimate or "counterfeit proofs." All such appeals, however, are *not* illegitimate. As we saw in Chapter 5 on support, appeals to the values and emotions of an audience are an appropriate form of persuasion. You can recognize fallacious emotional appeals if (1) they are irrelevant to the argument or draw attention from the issues being argued or (2) they appear to conceal another purpose. Here we treat two of the most popular appeals — to pity and to fear.

Appeals to pity, compassion, and natural willingness to help the unfortunate are particularly hard to resist. The requests for aid by

---

[11]David H. C. Read, letter to the *New York Times,* January 13, 1983, p. 14.

most charitable organizations — for hungry children, victims of disaster, stray animals — offer examples of legitimate appeals. But these appeals to our sympathetic feelings should not divert us from considering other issues in a particular case. It would be wrong, for example, to allow a multiple murderer to escape punishment because he or she had experienced a wretched childhood. Likewise, if you are asked to contribute to a charitable cause, you should try to learn how many unfortunate people or animals are being helped and what percentage of the contribution will be allocated to maintaining the organization and its officers. In some cases the financial records are closed to public review, and only a small share of the contribution will reach the alleged beneficiaries.

Appeals to fear are likely to be even more effective. But they must be based on evidence that fear is an appropriate response to the issues and that it can move an audience toward a solution to the problem. (Fear can also have the adverse effect of preventing people from taking a necessary action.) Insurance companies, for example, make appeals to our fears of destitution for ourselves and our families as a result of injury, unemployment, sickness, and death. These appeals are justified if the possibilities of such destitution are real and if the insurance will provide relief. It would also be legitimate to arouse fear of the consequences of drunk driving, provided, again, that the descriptions were accurate. On the other hand, it would be wrong to induce fear that fluoridation of public water supplies causes cancer without presenting sound evidence of the probability. It would also be wrong to instill a fear of school integration unless convincing proof were offered of undesirable social consequences.

An emotional response by itself is not always the soundest basis for making decisions. Your own experience has probably taught you that in the grip of a strong emotion like love or hate or anger you often overlook good reasons for making different and better choices. Like you, your readers want to be given the opportunity to consider all the available kinds of support for an argument.

On Nation and Race

ADOLF HITLER

There are some truths which are so obvious that for this very reason they are not seen or at least not recognized by ordinary people. They sometimes pass by such truisms as though blind and are most astonished when someone suddenly discovers what everyone really ought to know. Columbus's eggs lie around by the hundreds of thousands, but Columbuses are met with less frequency.

Thus men without exception wander about in the garden of Nature; they imagine that they know practically everything and yet with few exceptions pass blindly by one of the most patent principles of Nature's rule: the inner segregation of the species of all living beings on this earth.

Even the most superficial observation shows that Nature's restricted form of propagation and increase is an almost rigid basic law of all the innumerable forms of expression of her vital urge. Every animal mates only with a member of the same species. The titmouse seeks the titmouse, the finch the finch, the stork the stork, the field mouse the field mouse, the dormouse the dormouse, the wolf the she-wolf, etc.

Only unusual circumstances can change this, primarily the compulsion of captivity or any other cause that makes it impossible to mate within the same species. But then Nature begins to resist this with all possible means, and her most visible protest consists either in refusing further capacity for propagation to bastards or in limiting the fertility of later offspring; in most cases, however, she takes away the power of resistance to disease or hostile attacks.

This is only too natural.   5

Any crossing of two beings not at exactly the same level produces a medium between the level of the two parents. This means: The offspring will probably stand higher than the racially lower parent, but not as high as the higher one. Consequently, it will later succumb in the struggle against the higher level. Such mating is contrary to the will of Nature for a higher breeding of all life. The precondition for this does not lie in associating superior and inferior, but in the total vic-

---

Adolf Hitler (1889–1945) became the Nazi dictator of Germany in the mid-1930s. "On Nation and Race" (editor's title) begins Chapter 11 of *Mein Kampf* (*My Struggle*), vol. 1, published in 1925.

tory of the former. The stronger must dominate and not blend with the weaker, thus sacrificing his own greatness. Only the born weakling can view this as cruel, but he after all is only a weak and limited man; for if this law did not prevail, any conceivable higher development of organic living beings would be unthinkable.

The consequence of this racial purity, universally valid in Nature, is not only the sharp outward delimitation of the various races, but their uniform character in themselves. The fox is always a fox, the goose a goose, the tiger a tiger, etc., and the difference can lie at most in the varying measure of force, strength, intelligence, dexterity, endurance, etc., of the individual specimens. But you will never find a fox who in his inner attitude might, for example, show humanitarian tendencies toward geese, as similarly there is no cat with a friendly inclination toward mice.

Therefore, here, too, the struggle among themselves arises less from inner aversion than from hunger and love. In both cases, Nature looks on calmly, with satisfaction, in fact. In the struggle for daily bread all those who are weak and sickly or less determined succumb, while the struggle of the males for the female grants the right or opportunity to propagate only to the healthiest. And struggle is always a means for improving a species' health and power of resistance and, therefore, a cause of its higher development.

If the process were different, all further and higher development would cease and the opposite would occur. For, since the inferior always predominates numerically over the best, if both had the same possibility of preserving life and propagating, the inferior would multiply so much more rapidly that in the end the best would inevitably be driven into the background, unless a correction of this state of affairs were undertaken. Nature does just this by subjecting the weaker part to such severe living conditions that by them alone the number is limited, and by not permitting the remainder to increase promiscuously, but making a new and ruthless choice according to strength and health.

No more than Nature desires the mating of weaker with stronger 10
individuals, even less does she desire the blending of a higher with a lower race, since, if she did, her whole work of higher breeding, over perhaps hundreds of thousands of years, might be ruined with one blow.

Historical experience offers countless proofs of this. It shows with terrifying clarity that in every mingling of Aryan blood with that of lower peoples the result was the end of the cultured people. North America, whose population consists in by far the largest part of Germanic elements who mixed but little with the lower colored peoples, shows a different humanity and culture from Central and South America, where the predominantly Latin immigrants often mixed with the aborigines on a large scale. By this one example, we can clearly and distinctly recognize the effect of racial mixture. The Germanic inhabitant of the American continent, who has remained racially pure and unmixed, rose to be master of the continent; he will remain the master as long as he does not fall a victim to defilement of the blood.

The result of all racial crossing is therefore in brief always the following:

(a) Lowering of the level of the higher race;

(b) Physical and intellectual regression and hence the beginning of a slowly but surely progressing sickness.

To bring about such a development is, then, nothing else but to 15 sin against the will of the eternal creator.

And as a sin this act is rewarded.

When man attempts to rebel against the iron logic of Nature, he comes into struggle with the principles to which he himself owes his existence as a man. And this attack must lead to his own doom.

Here, of course, we encounter the objection of the modern pacifist, as truly Jewish in its effrontery as it is stupid! "Man's role is to overcome Nature!"

Millions thoughtlessly parrot this Jewish nonsense and end up by really imagining that they themselves represent a kind of conqueror of Nature; though in this they dispose of no other weapon than an idea, and at that such a miserable one, that if it were true no world at all would be conceivable.

But quite aside from the fact that man has never yet conquered 20 Nature in anything, but at most has caught hold of and tried to lift one or another corner of her immense gigantic veil of eternal riddles and secrets, that in reality he invents nothing but only discovers everything, that he does not dominate Nature, but has only risen on the basis of his knowledge of various laws and secrets of Nature to be lord over those other living creatures who lack this knowledge — quite aside from all this, an idea cannot overcome the preconditions for the development and being of humanity, since the idea itself depends only on man. Without human beings there is no human idea in this world; therefore, the idea as such is always conditioned by the presence of human beings and hence of all the laws which created the precondition for their existence.

And not only that! Certain ideas are even tied up with certain men. This applies most of all to those ideas whose content originates, not in an exact scientific truth, but in the world of emotion, or, as it is so beautifully and clearly expressed today, reflects an "inner experience." All these ideas, which have nothing to do with cold logic as such, but represent only pure expressions of feeling, ethical conceptions, etc., are chained to the existence of men, to whose intellectual imagination and creative power they owe their existence. Precisely in this case the preservation of these definite races and men is the precondition for the existence of these ideas. Anyone, for example, who really desired the victory of the pacifistic idea in this world with all his heart would have to fight with all the means at his disposal for the conquest of the world by the Germans; for, if the opposite should occur, the last pacifist would die out with the last German, since the rest of the world has never fallen so deeply as our own people, unfortunately, has for this nonsense so contrary to Nature and reason. Then, if we were serious, whether we liked it or not, we would have to wage wars in order to arrive at pacifism. This and nothing else was what Wilson, the American world savior, intended, or so at least our German visionaries believed — and thereby his purpose was fulfilled.

In actual fact the pacifistic-humane idea is perfectly all right perhaps when the highest type of man has previously conquered and subjected the world to an extent that makes him the sole ruler of this earth. Then this idea lacks the power of producing evil effects in exact proportion as its practical application becomes rare and finally impossible. Therefore, first struggle and then we shall see what can be done. Otherwise mankind has passed the high point of its development and the end is not the domination of any ethical idea but barbarism and consequently chaos. At this point someone or other may laugh, but this planet once moved through the ether for millions of years without human beings and it can do so again some day if men forget that they owe their higher existence, not to the ideas of a few crazy ideologists, but to the knowledge and ruthless application of Nature's stern and rigid laws.

Everything we admire on this earth today — science and art, technology and inventions — is only the creative product of a few peoples and originally perhaps of *one* race. On them depends the existence of this whole culture. If they perish, the beauty of this earth will sink into the grave with them.

However much the soil, for example, can influence men, the result of the influence will always be different depending on the races in question. The low fertility of a living space may spur the one race to the highest achievements; in others it will only be the cause of bitterest poverty and final undernourishment with all its consequences. The inner nature of peoples is always determining for the manner in which outward influences will be effective. What leads the one to starvation trains the other to hard work.

All great cultures of the past perished only because the origi- 25
nally creative race died out from blood poisoning.

The ultimate cause of such a decline was their forgetting that all culture depends on men and conversely; hence that to preserve a certain culture the man who creates it must be preserved. This preservation is bound up with the rigid law of necessity and the right to victory of the best and stronger in this world.

Those who want to live, let them fight, and those who do not want to fight in this world of eternal struggle do not deserve to live.

Even if this were hard — that is how it is! Assuredly, however, by far the harder fate is that which strikes the man who thinks he can overcome Nature, but in the last analysis only mocks her. Distress, misfortune, and diseases are her answer.

The man who misjudges and disregards the racial laws actually forfeits the happiness that seems destined to be his. He thwarts the triumphal march of the best race and hence also the precondition for all human progress, and remains, in consequence, burdened with all the sensibility of man, in the animal realm of helpless misery.

It is idle to argue which race or races were the original represen- 30 tative of human culture and hence the real founders of all that we sum up under the word *humanity*. It is simpler to raise the question with regard to the present, and here an easy, clear answer results. All the human culture, all the results of art, science, and technology that we see before us today, are almost exclusively the creative product of the Aryan. This very fact admits of the not unfounded inference that he alone was the founder of all higher humanity, therefore representing the prototype of all that we understand by the word *man*. He is the Prometheus of mankind from whose bright forehead the divine spark of genius has sprung at all times, forever kindling anew that fire of knowledge which illumined the night of silent mysteries and thus caused man to climb the path to mastery over the other beings of this earth. Exclude him — and perhaps after a few thousand years darkness will again descend on the earth, human culture will pass, and the world turn to a desert.

Reading and Discussion Questions

1. Find places in the essay where Hitler attempts to emphasize the scientific objectivity of his theories.
2. Are some passages difficult to understand? (See, for example, paragraph 13.) How do you explain the difficulty?
3. In explaining his ideology, how does Hitler misinterpret the statement that "Every animal mates only with a member of the same species" (para. 3)? How would you characterize this fallacy?
4. Hitler uses the theory of evolution and his interpretation of the "survival of the fittest" to justify his racial philosophy. Find the places in the text where Hitler reveals that he misunderstands the theory in its application to human beings.
5. What false evidence about race does Hitler use in his assessment of the racial experience in North America? Examine carefully the last sentence of paragraph 11: "The Germanic inhabitant of the American continent, who has remained racially pure and unmixed, rose to be master of the continent; he will remain the master as long as he does not fall a victim to defilement of the blood."

6. What criticism of Jews does Hitler offer? How does this criticism help to explain Hitler's pathological hatred of Jews?
7. Hitler believes that pacifism is a violation of "Nature and reason" (para. 21). Would modern scientists agree that the laws of nature require unremitting struggle and conflict between human beings — until the master race conquers?

Writing Suggestion

8. Do some research in early human history to discover the degree of truth in this statement: "All the human culture, all the results of art, science, and technology that we see before us today, are almost exclusively the creative product of the Aryan" (para. 30). You may want to limit your discussion to one area of human culture.

A Reasonable Life
FERENC MÁTÉ

A recent Department of Education report was released after extensively surveying nine million school kids. Eighth graders were asked how often in the last six months they had talked to a parent about their schoolwork. Half of them responded, "Once or twice, or not at all." And one-third responded, "Never." This is madness. What *do* we talk to them about? Haircuts? Sunglasses? Somebody's latest facial relocation? Do we talk at all? Or have we simply, under the relentless, crushing demand of longer and longer hours of commuting and work, and the grueling task of keeping up premises and appearances, become completely deaf and dumb, save for our prerecorded patter about the weather, baseball scores, and new weeds in the lawn. Have we taken a cue from junk bonds, junk food, junk mail, and junked our minds as well?

It is no mystery where our children learned not to use their minds: from us. According to a 1988 National Geographic survey, fully half of all Americans didn't know that the then Soviet Union was in the Warsaw Pact. In fact, one out of ten actually believed that America was. Six out of ten did not know the population of the United States, and half of them didn't know that Contras and Sandinistas had been fighting in Nicaragua. Now these might not have been life-and-death issues to them, but when the government had been

---

Ferenc Máté was born in Hungary. Escaping at the age of eleven after the suppression of the Revolution of 1956, he has lived in Vancouver, New York, and Paris. Reprinted here are excerpts from his eighth book, *A Reasonable Life: Toward a Simpler, Secure, More Humane Existence* (1997).

spending nearly half of their tax dollars protecting them from the Warsaw Pact and the Sandinista devils, one would think that, if nothing else, simple curiosity about where their money is being flushed would keep them in touch with the outside world. The rest of their ignorance our children picked up on their own. They never had to think. From earliest childhood they have been *told* everything by television, advertising, teachers, and politicians.

I think most of us agree that fundamental social changes have to come. But those will take time. There are changes that we need to make at once before another generation of our children wastes away. Major social and physical menaces have bloomed in our society these last few decades to which our schools have reacted barely at all, while at the same time they have embraced all technical innovation as the newest savior. These threats have to be addressed and countered and the earlier we start the better. Call them Survival Studies, or Social Self-Defense. They should start in kindergarten.

Livestock and Politicians

We should have a quick combined course in animal husbandry and government just so our kids could learn to distinguish good-for-the-garden bullshit from the other kind.

New-History

Given the devastation of our planet triggered by the greed and overconsumption of a relatively small number of ignorant, power-hungry "blobs," would it not make sense to teach our children not about demented kings and queens and princes of industry, and the grotesquely motivated pyramids and edifices they built in their own honor, but about the great gentle masses through the ages, the nameless, harmless humanity? Would it not make sense to teach our children how humble, simple people — the peasants, the craftsmen, the fishermen, the country doctor — managed to live through the centuries? They should be our heroes, for they have withstood endless misery at the hands of the well-remembered, with whose life stories we bore our children now.

Religious Studies

It is most curious that we leave the teachings of the kindest and wisest men of history to mostly ignored courses at universities. Would the wisdom of Buddha, Jesus, and Mohammed and the teachings of myriad native tribes, with their all-encompassing view of man, Nature, life, and the universe, not be an infinitely more sound

foundation for our children than obscure details about which insecure, jingoistic runt defeated which rabid loony where?

It is this lack of an overview of life, this lack of an attempt to give
an overall perspective to the relationship between man and man,
man and the earth, man and history, that leads to a morally and
philosophically hollow citizenry, led by men and women who are
convinced that "A Philosophy of Life" is a long-running soap on the
tube every morning.

The Environment

It is safe to say that there is no greater current threat to our children than the destruction by their elders of the world around them.
To give them a broad understanding of the results of all of our actions is essential. They need to understand that no human action
lives in isolation; it has a result that, in some small way, can affect us
all. And small things add up.

It is time for a Children's Bill of Rights. Every child born on this
Earth has a God-given right to clean air, clean water, clean food,
tranquility, and unspoiled natural beauty. (And, on his birthday, all
the rocky-road ice-cream he can eat.) Children should be taught
that. Should be taught to demand it. Should be taught, if the need
arises, to fight for it.

Along with their rights they should be taught a Bill of Responsi-   10
bilities. As Solzhenitsyn so profoundly observed, "Western civilization has spent three hundred years demanding rights, with almost
no mention of responsibilities." First responsibility: Think through
completely what you plan to do. Second responsibility: Don't do it;
there are too many people doing it already. You'll just end up making a mess and who'll clean up after you? You lived fine without it so
far, so why bother? Have another beer.

Farming

Every child, by the time he leaves elementary school, should
know first hand — *not from bloody video!* — how to grow his own
food, raise chickens, and cook them, so that when this crack-a-joke,
house-of-gadgets of a society crumbles, and the last investment
banker lies dead of starvation in front of an empty deli, he can be
happily whistling in the fields with his little hoe.

Building

And know how to build his own house out of wood, stone, sticks
and mud.

It is not difficult to figure out what constitutes a reasonable life. You can, if you like pain, do it by elimination, by listing your daily activities and asking yourself "How does it feel?"

1. Being shocked awake from a deep sleep in middream by a heartless gadget every morning. Answer: Torture.

2. Breaking Olympic records in the Career-Octathelon: rising, 15 crawling, dumping, showering, shaving, clipping nose hairs, graysuiting (or Nairing, spraying-hair-until-bullet-proof-helmet, clownfacing and dressing), chomping, slurping, cursing, and dashing to car. Answer: Humiliating.

3. Lurching, stopping, bumping, gridlocking while holding back caffeine rush so you don't tear off your car roof and serial-kill the first hundred people you find. Answer: Trying.

4. Being locked in office or factory with the boss hovering over you, smiling when you need to scream, nodding politely when you want to smash his nose flat with your forehead. Answer: Unbearable.

5. Lunching lumpy tepid mush with the combined fragrance of Pine-Scent and puppy chow. Answer: Don't remind me.

6. Repeating all of the above 10,000 times before you die. Answer: No way!

Or you can simply ask yourself what you would like to do if you 20 could retire today. Most people would say, "Get a little house with a garden in the country or in a small town and live happily ever after."

So what are you waiting for? Why not sell the house, pack up the kids, kiss the boss goodbye, and head for the hills?

For economic security, emotional calm, diversity of work, and living in complete harmony with nature, nothing can surpass the classic, mostly self-sufficient, country family. As John Berger said, "It is the only class of people with a built-in resistance to consumerism." And it also has a built-in resistance to unemployment, recessions, inflation, deflation, traffic jams, and crime. In other words, it is the only class with a built-in ability to tell the hectic, frantic world to drop dead! How can *anything* feel better than that?!

And the social strength of the self-sufficient family is even greater. There simply exists no tighter or more stable social unit than a country family and its neighbors, all of whom share the same problems, same hopes, same harvests, and same droughts. After a lifetime of research in both psychology and anthropology, Carl Jung found the hamlet or village to be the ideal human habitation. So did Lewis Mumford, who spent the last decades of his life in upstate New York in his beloved hamlet of Amenia.

Eventually society will change — it will have to. It will realize that neither environmental salvation nor our social happiness lies in monstrous, impersonal cities, but out in the country in close contact with Nature, real neighbors, and our real selves. But if we sit and wait for the sick behemoth of a world to awaken and change direction, we'll all die of old age before it turns its head. If you want to have a reasonable life you will have to go and find it for yourself. You won't have far to look.

Small towns in North America are dying — except for those that 25 have become quaint shopping malls for the rich, and are already dead. Some of the others want to be revitalized so badly, welcome strangers with such open arms, that they even offer free housing for those who venture there. And as for good land, no place offers more than North America. Nor is there a broader choice of vegetation and climate anywhere.

I realize that most of you will recoil in mortal terror at the mere thought of having torn from you the wonders of the city — steady job, museums, operas, Dunkin' Donuts — but I assure you life goes on without them. And is better. Much more satisfying replacements await you in the country. . . .

It can be done.

Your immediate fearful cry will be that you are by profession a computer RAM-byter microfries boot-chipper — and how in God's name can you survive in the country? Easy. Because long before you became any of the above obscenities, you were a perfectly normal human being to whom digging, hoeing, gathering, and hammer-swinging come infinitely more naturally than does byting RAMs. And the best way to learn to do something is by doing it. You don't need a million magazines, books, or videos to teach you; the best book on each subject will do. But you will need some clear thinking, imagination, and good old-fashioned common sense. If you're stuck, look around. Go visit and ask questions. It's a good way to meet the neighbors and people love to help. And the more you can learn from those around you, especially those who have lived and worked on the land and know the soil, know the seasons, the more confident and comfortable you will be.

But no matter how expert you become at self-sufficiency, you will not be able to grow bathroom taps or light bulbs. Hence the need for supplementary cash. The most important step is to ween yourself off the things that cost money. Your TV should stay where it belongs — in the factory in Japan. Not only won't you waste money buying it, but you also won't be tempted by the tons of gaudy rubble it tries to sell. Try to make some of the simple things you need. It's a lot more fun than shelling out money at a store, you'll feel a lot prouder of it, and you will probably never replace it because you're much too vain to throw out your precious handiwork.

There is no need to go to extremes. You need not try to make a 30 watch from old car parts, nor eyeglasses from a pile of sand. But you can easily reinvent things that you now see only in old movies, like sewing on a button instead of throwing out the shirt, patching holes in clothes, or even sewing them from scratch, darning, knitting, toy-making, furniture-making, preserving fruit and vegetables, and, as a last resort, cooking.

The cash that you do need can be found both in small towns and in the country, although admittedly in smaller quantities than in the city, but, as I said, you will need much less. The most important thing to realize, especially for those who think the country has no jobs, is that there are a jillion jobs but not the kind that require eight hours a day until you die. So while there might be no room for an en-tire accountant, there will certainly be work for a tenth of one. And while a full-time notary or lawyer or moritician would starve, a fifth or a tenth of each would thrive. On Fred Smith's island, a desktop publisher drives the ambulance and is the local fax man. In other words, specialists beware, but generalists who can combine, say, brain surgery with a little tree pruning and sausage-making will get on just fine.

The best part of having a wide range of jobs is not only that vari-ety is the spice of life, but also that in variety lies security. If the de-mand for brain surgery diminishes, the demand for sausages might rise, and so on. . . .

Some people would object on a historical basis, saying that country life has been a dead-end in the past. While that may have been true forty years ago, it is no more. We have made great leaps in small equipment such as inexpensive motor-tillers, more hardy vari-eties of plants, good organic pest-control information, excellent soil conservation information, speedy transportation to market (and the tourist market coming to your door), and the ever-growing demand for tasty, healthy, unpesticided food. And even more important are the new portable jobs made possible by fax machines, computers, modems, and general technology that provide today's country life with more potential and variety than was ever dreamed of in the past.

So there you have it — a few things to escape to. Of course there are others; cabins in the woods, fishing boats, sailboats, and desert islands. But if you find the notion of immediately cutting city ties and heading for the hills far-fetched, too drastic, too irreversible, then at least do this: dump the TV set; cut up all credit cards, coupons, green stamps, crossword puzzles; cancel all subscriptions, prescriptions, addictions, memberships, affiliations, commitments and obligations, aerobics classes, kung fu classes, shrink appoint-ments, hair appointments, and the ten-part doggy-dancing lessons you gave Fido for Christmas, and go home after work, just sit there in the dark, and try to figure out what this madness is all about. And what, if anything, it has to do with you. You might just come up with a better, more reasonable life. . . .

In a reasonable world, the need for taxes would be greatly re- 35 duced, as would the need for governments that spend them. With small communities nearly self-reliant, or reliant only on neighbors, and everyone known by and dependent on those around him, our million fatuous laws could be sent to museum shelves. Reasonable, decent human conduct would be taught and enforced by all. We could once again become like the truly democratic corners of 1800s America, where, "Each citizen developed his civic mores informally, through conversations on street corners or in the square; in the day-to-day encounters in the shops; on the walks that took him past public buildings and houses of worship and settings of great natural beauty — that took him, if only for a moment, out of his private self."

What central governments remained would no longer be led by the belligerent, mentally limited, and emotionally callow of recent history, who attained their posts only through zeal for power, political conniving, and vicious public relations. They would be led by the truly wise, who have shown ability and deep concern for humanity through their lives. Candidates would not emerge after years of favor-gaining, kowtowing, and vulgar fund-raising, which gives those who promised Big Money the most, an advantage. They would be nominated by a Nobel-type committee, made up of the nation's most thoughtful citizens, who would base their decisions on a life of merit. The candidates could skip the year of numbing travel, posing, grinning, raving, glad-handing, posturing, and, as Bill Clinton said, "Learning nothing." They would instead, as we all had to do in school, write a simple, clear, easy-to-read essay (without the aid of speechwriters and hucksters) which, before being presented to the nation, would be examined by an esteemed, knowledgeable academy, judged for comprehension of problems and the feasibility of offered remedies. In other words, the academy would edit out the bullshit. This short and lucid essay, in point form if need be, conspicuously free of resonating moronities such as "It's morning in America" and "A thousand points of light," could then be presented to all, before election time. They could be discussed point by point, in family circles, on front porches, hamlet greens, shops, or village squares, without confounding advertising that, along with special interest and lobby groups, would be exiled to Saint Helena. An oral test would make sure the candidates comprehend their duties. We would then no longer have photo-op celebrities as leaders but true public *servants,* whose concentrated efforts go to making our schools and hospitals as sacred as banks and malls, and to keeping our streets swept and the sewers flowing. No less and no more.

Reading and Discussion Questions

1. Find examples on pages 321 to 323 of the following logical fallacies and other weaknesses of argumentation: (1) exaggeration, (2) name-calling, (3) false dilemma, (4) slippery slope, (5) failure to define terms, (6) selective use of examples and quotations.
2. What aspects of American life does Máté criticize? Pick the specific aspects with which you agree and disagree, and provide examples from your own experience.
3. What is your reaction to the author's humor, or attempts at humor? Is it effective as argument? Why or why not?
4. Does the school curriculum described on pages 317 to 319 sound practical? Can you point out strengths and weaknesses?
5. How would you characterize the election process described on page 323? Does it represent an improvement over today's practices? What would you include in a "simple, clear, easy-to-read essay" (para. 36) that would satisfy a knowledgeable academy and help ensure your election? How long would it have to be?
6. At times the author seems indifferent to history, science, and art. Where are "the great gentle masses" (para. 5)? Were food and air in the past always "clean" (para. 9)? If life on the farm or in the village was so satisfying, why have many millions of people deserted that life for the city? How would the author answer the economists who can explain the advantages of division of labor? Why does he lump museums and operas together with Dunkin' Donuts?

Writing Suggestions

7. *A Reasonable Life* describes one man's ideal society. For more than two thousand years people have written about ideal societies or utopias. (*Utopia,* a word coined by Sir Thomas More in 1516 to describe such a community, means "nowhere" in Greek.) What aspects of present-day life would be very different in a utopia of your own creation? Among many other things, writers and filmmakers who design utopias treat education, courtship and marriage, child rearing, religion, form of government, and personal freedom. Describe your ideal version of something you feel strongly about.
8. *Dystopia* is the opposite of the ideal society. You may be familiar with *Nineteen Eighty-Four* by George Orwell, *Brave New World* by Aldous Huxley, and *Walden Two* by B. F. Skinner — books about societies created by behavioral engineering. Many contemporary science fiction novels and films also describe a world gone terribly wrong. If you have read or seen any of these works, choose one (or more), and tell how it reflects our fears of certain trends and changes in modern life.
9. The author of *A Reasonable Life* thinks that life in the country or a village is superior in almost every way to life in the city. Write an argument defending your own preference.

CHERYL SILAS had a highway collision, was hit twice from behind, and then sold three cars for us.

When Cheryl unbuckled her shoulder harness and lap belt, it took her a moment to realize her Saturn coupe was really a mess. And that, remarkably, she wasn't. That's when she decided to get another SC.

Several other people arrived at similar conclusions. A policeman at the accident scene came in soon after and ordered himself a sedan. As did a buddy of his, also on the force. Then Cheryl's brother, glad he still had a sister, bought yet another Saturn in Illinois.

Now, good referrals are important to any product. And we're always glad to have them. But we'd be more than happy if our customers found less dramatic ways to help spread the word.

A DIFFERENT KIND OF COMPANY. A DIFFERENT KIND OF CAR.

© 1991 Saturn Corporation. M.S.R.P. of 1992 Saturn SC shown is $12,415, including retailer prep and optional sunroof. Tax, license, transportation and other options additional. If you'd like to know more about Saturn, and our new sedans and coupe, please call us at 1-800-522-5000.

Discussion Questions

1. What example of inductive reasoning does the advertiser use? How would you evaluate the probability of the conclusion?

2. To what extent does the use of an alleged real person in a narrative contribute to the effectiveness of the advertiser's pitch? Should the ad have contained more factual information?

Women Unfit for Combat?
Au Contraire!

TIMOTHY C. BROWN

From Kelly Flinn to *G.I. Jane,* controversy has raged in recent months over whether women are fit for military service. As a ten-year Marine veteran, I am convinced that women have what it takes to serve with distinction, even in combat roles. The best evidence: the experience of the Nicaraguan contras.

All combat requires exceptional physical stamina, courage, discipline under fire, and technical competence, but these demands are even greater on guerrillas fighting an extended war. Fighting without artillery, air support, or firepower superiority calls for more than the guts and skills of regular infantry troops. It demands a level of endurance and stamina closer to that of special-warfare units like the Navy's Seals. The story of Nicaragua's women commandos, who comprised 7 percent of the entire contra army, serves as an excellent reality check of how American women, if given the opportunity and encouragement, could perform effectively in combat.

A few anecdotes gathered from surviving records and recent in-depth interviews illustrate the point. Angélica Maria (like the other women in this story, referred to by the nom de guerre she used during the war) had been a front-line infantry combatant for six years when, in 1986, she took command of her platoon during a battle in which all its officers had been killed. A legend among her male peers (who still treat her as their equal, if not superior), Angélica Maria then continued as the commander of her almost all-male platoon until, wounded in combat for a seventh time, she was forced to seek medical attention.

La China was a *correo,* or unarmed intelligence runner, before becoming a uniformed commando. In 1980, still in her teens, she traveled alone on foot for more than one hundred fifty miles, from the Honduran border almost to Costa Rica, contacting small peasant resistance groups then forming throughout the central mountain highlands.

Daysi was a paramedic. But she would invariably drop her med- 5 ical kit, grab her AK-47, and join the fray whenever the shooting

---

Timothy C. Brown is a research fellow at Stanford's Hoover Institution. This article appeared in the *Wall Street Journal* on September 30, 1997.

started, resuming her medical duties only when a comrade was wounded. On April 5, 1985, during a battle at El Guapinol, deep in Nicaragua's central mountain highlands, she was killed by an incoming 105mm artillery round. After Daysi's death, fellow commandos, mostly male, renamed their unit the Maritza Zeledon battalion, after their heroine's real name.

Altogether some two thousand women served as volunteer front-line contra fighters, while another two thousand served as correos, and more than one thousand died in combat. Nicaragua's contra women served as equals. They received the same combat training as men — unlike the U.S. Marines, the contra army made no "special adjustments" — and then joined local guerrilla units as front-line combatants. They earned the respect of their male counterparts. In a recent study, a few male former contra commandos admitted to having had initial doubts about female participation in combat. But without exception they came to view their female comrades as a valuable addition to their forces.

The contras did accommodate the special needs of their female contingent. Pregnant commandos were moved to the rear, helped through their confinement, and then assigned support roles if they wished. The contras even provided "day care" for their children when necessary. Asked why, one senior former contra commander seemed surprised by the question. "We had to," he said. "They were too valuable to lose."

Even under these limited circumstances, women contras remained commandos and were not exempt from combat. Poignant photographs taken during the last major battle of the contra war depict women commandos nursing babies in their arms, supporting combat packs on their backs and AK-47s on their shoulders, while advancing to the front under intense bombardment from nearby Sandinista BM-21 rocket launchers.

Is the contra experience really applicable to the American case? I believe the answer clearly is yes. In terms of the demands of infantry warfare, women have proved themselves capable of fighting under even the most arduous of conditions. Whether the women of the Gulf War, those who served with me in the Marines, or women police officers I know who are fighting crime today on America's meanest streets, American women have clearly demonstrated ample dedication, stamina, and just plain guts.

Whether the U.S. should assign women to combat roles may still 10 be debated on the basis of cultural beliefs and values. But whether or not women can do the job is no longer in doubt. If given the opportunity, America's women can and will serve their country with distinction, as did Nicaragua's women contras.

Women Are Not a Warrior Class

JAMES COLLINS, PAUL L. HACKETT,
AND BILL NORTON

Timothy C. Brown's vivid images of heroic Nicaraguan contra women fighting for their freedom against the Sandinistas alongside their approving male counterparts are, indeed, inspiring. They are also totally irrelevant to the debate over the proper role for women in the twenty-first-century American military ("Women Unfit for Combat? Au Contraire!" editorial page, September 30). No objective observer really doubts that on an individual basis there are some women who could endure the rigors of combat or even thrive in such a challenging environment. Certainly, when put in desperate, life-threatening conditions, when one's very survival or the survival of one's country is at stake (for example, envision the likely reaction of Israeli women if faced with a blitzkrieg invasion by a combined Arab force), many women would rise to the challenge.

Unfortunately, this is far removed from the situation facing the American armed forces today, where a combination of feminist activists, lawyers, politicians with their fingers in the equal opportunity wind, and senior military officers more concerned with career enhancement than military readiness have combined to create an environment in which double standards are the rule and no realistic assessment of a woman's ability to perform a combat role can be made because a negative result is, by definition, politically unacceptable. Until and unless this changes, and the question of women in combat is allowed to be considered objectively instead of as an attempt to engage in misguided social engineering, no real progress can be made. Worse, those who ultimately pay the price in blood, suffering, and death, if military readiness and discipline are sacrificed, will, as usual, not be the politicians, professors, and pundits, but our sons and daughters.

James Collins

Can women master the skills and strategies of combat as well as men? Yes. Can women mentally endure the rigors of combat as well as men? Yes. Can women meet the physical rigors of combat at the level required by the U.S. forces and in particular the U.S. Marine Corps? Absolutely not.

These letters appeared in the *Wall Street Journal* on October 9, 1997, in response to Timothy C. Brown's essay.

I make this assessment based on first-hand knowledge having spent six months in a company with an all-female platoon; i.e. TBS "C" Company 3789. A real rifle company it was not, but for those of us who served the big green machine (USMC) we know the physical requirements at least for that six-month period are as close as any non-grunt is going to get to the real thing.

The members of our female platoon literally couldn't come close 5 to carrying their weight. Were there some women who could carry their weight and physically cut it? Absolutely. Unfortunately, they were the exception. If a male Marine officer had physically performed at a comparable level to the average female Marine officer, he would have been kicked out. Marine Corps grunts are the Olympic gold medalists when it comes to combat. If for the sake of diversity and political correctness we want to include women in combat, then consider the cost of that decision: the silver medal in combat is defeat.

Paul L. Hackett

There is an overarching reason why women should never be in combat units. A bond develops among infantrymen which organizational scholars identify as cohesion. It is defined as the willingness to subordinate self-interest to the needs and well-being of the group.

Women destroy cohesion for three reasons. The first arises from differential standards. Suboptimal performance is not an option when in harm's way. Those who cannot contribute equally have no place. Next, there are sexual tensions that cannot be resolved. I do not mean to address the issues of rape or harassment as they are codified but rather the consensual liaisons that occur. Are the unit members focused on mission or love interest? How are these conflicting goals reconciled when the first incoming round impacts? How do the have-nots react — those yearning for companionship but excluded from it? Finally, there is the issue of physical inferiority. Egalitarianism is a bankrupt concept. If not, may I have forty million a year to play for the Bulls like Michael Jordan? The reality is that he is a gifted athlete, I am not. The very essence of "differently gifted" carries the implicit message that we all have limitations. Explicitly, there are some things that we cannot do.

The argument has been framed by feminists in terms of career opportunities for women. Why, they ask, should women be barred from advancement solely because of gender? The central issue is not career advancement for women but the combat readiness of a warrior class. That objective is sufficiently important that it must have primacy over misguided humanism.

My gravest concern is the absence of leadership in the military. High-ranking officers are essentially political appointees, serving at the pleasure of the commander-in-chief. Collectively, they behave as his sycophants. When our sitting president was (by his admission) dodging the draft in England and not inhaling dope, I was leading a reconnaissance platoon in the central highlands of Vietnam. His contempt for the military was revealed long ago and endures unchanged.

Bill Norton

Discussion Questions

1. Brown uses an analogy with Nicaraguan women fighters as the main rhetorical device in support of his claim that American women are also capable of combat. Briefly summarize the main points of the Nicaraguan experience on which he draws.
2. In the next-to-last paragraph Brown argues that the analogy is relevant. Since American women have never served in combat, what proof does he offer of their fitness for this role?
3. The three letters that respond to Brown make different points, but one point emerges more than once. What is it? Does it offer an effective refutation of Brown's claim?
4. Notice that two of the letters refer to personal experience in the armed services. Is this kind of evidence more persuasive than the largely objective argument in the first letter?
5. Some of the objections that Brown tries to refute have also been made concerning female police officers and firefighters. Do you think the history of women in those professions is relevant to a decision about women in combat?

TAKING THE DEBATE ONLINE

- **Gender Gap: Women Warriors** <http://www.gendergap.com/military .warriors.HTM> This vast site illustrates the history of women in military service.

- **NATO Review: Recognizing the role of women in NATO's military forces** <http://www.nato.int/docu/review/articles/9705-08.htm> Major General Harris, chair of the Committee on Women in NATO, argues that recognizing the contributions of women in today's military forces will be beneficial to the military as a whole and to the Alliance.

- **Family Research Council's Perspective: Women Going to Combat?** <http://www.frc.org/perspective/pv94b1wc.html> Robert L. Maginnis, a policy analyst with the Family Research Council and a retired lieutenant colonel in the U.S. Army, critiques the Clinton administration's aim to place women in combat roles. He is disappointed that "liberal notions of affirmative action, quotas, and 'equal opportunity' are now more important than military necessity and two centuries of tradition."

- **Feminist Majority Condemns Push to Resegregate Military Training as Giant Step Backwards for Women, June 5, 1997 <http://www .feminist.org/news/pr/pr060597.html>** The Feminist Majority and other national women's rights organizations have submitted signed testimony to the U.S. Senate Committee on Armed Services opposing gender-segregated basic military training. Issues of sexual harassment, they claim, are now being used to distance women from their goals of equality in the U.S. military.

- **The Heritage Foundation: Congress Should Hold Hearings before Allowing Women in Combat, July 24, 1994 <http://www.heritage.org/ library/categories/natsec/bgu230.html>** John Luddy, a policy analyst for the Heritage Foundation, believes that placing women "in or near combat units will damage military effectiveness." He believes that "Congress can stop the [Clinton] Administration from using the military as a laboratory for social engineering."

- **International Christian Media: Who Killed Kara Hultgreen? <http:// www.usaradio.com/pov/articles/art4795.fcr.html>** This short essay by Christopher Corbett claims that placing women in combat flies in the face of the "biblical distinction between men and women, both physical and emotional."

- **Washington Post Opinions, January 3, 1998: Women in Combat — The Opposing View <http://www.ccnet.com/~suntzu75/news_archives/ 1998/military/mus98005.htm>** This article raises four interesting points in its condemnation of women in combat.

EXERCISES

Decide whether the reasoning in the following examples is faulty. Explain your answers.

1. The presiding judge of a revolutionary tribunal, on being asked why people were being executed without trial: "Why should we put them on trial when we know that they're guilty?"
2. Since good nutrition is essential to the health of its citizens, the government should punish people who eat junk food.
3. Children who watch *Frasier* rather than *Friends* receive higher grades in school. So it must be true that *Frasier* is more educational than *Friends*.
4. The meteorologist predicted the wrong amount of rain for May. Obviously the meteorologist is unreliable.
5. Women ought to be permitted to serve in combat. Why should men be the only ones to face death and danger?
6. If Cher uses Equal, it must taste better than Sweet 'n Low.
7. People will gamble anyway, so why not legalize gambling in this state?
8. Because so much money was spent on public education in the last decade while educational achievement declined, more money to improve education can't be the answer to reversing the decline.

9. He's a columnist for the campus newspaper, so he must be a pretty good writer.

10. We tend to exaggerate the need for standard English. You don't need much standard English for most jobs in this country.

11. It's discriminatory to mandate that police officers must conform to a certain height and weight.

12. A doctor can consult books to make a diagnosis, so a medical student should be able to consult books when being tested.

13. Because this soft drink contains so many chemicals, it must be unsafe.

14. Core requirements should be eliminated. After all, students are paying for their education, so they should be able to earn a diploma by choosing the courses they want.

15. We should encourage a return to arranged marriages in this country since marriages based on romantic love haven't been very successful.

16. I know three redheads who have terrible tempers, and since Annabel has red hair, I'll bet she has a terrible temper, too.

17. Supreme Court Justice Byron White was an All-American football player while at college, so how can you say that athletes are dumb?

18. Benjamin H. Sasway, a student at Humboldt State University in California, was indicted for failure to register for possible conscription. Barry Lynn, president of Draft Action, an antidraft group, said, "It is disgraceful that this administration is embarking on an effort to fill the prisons with men of conscience and moral commitment."

19. You know Jane Fonda's exercise videos must be worth the money. Look at the great shape she's in.

20. James A. Harris, former president of the National Education Association: "Twenty-three percent of schoolchildren are failing to graduate, and another large segment graduate as functional illiterates. If 23 percent of anything else failed — 23 percent of automobiles didn't run, 23 percent of the buildings fell down, 23 percent of stuffed ham spoiled — we'd look at the producer."

21. A professor at Rutgers University: "The arrest rate for women is rising three times as fast as that of men. Women, inflamed by the doctrines of feminism, are pursuing criminal careers with the same zeal as business and the professions."

22. Physical education should be required because physical activity is healthful.

23. George Meany, former president of the AFL-CIO, in 1968: "To these people who constantly say you have got to listen to these younger people, they have got something to say, I just don't buy that at all. They smoke more pot than we do and if the younger generation are the hundred thousand kids that lay around a field up in Woodstock, New York, I am not going to trust the destiny of the country to that group."

24. That candidate was poor as a child, so he will certainly be sympathetic to the poor if he's elected.

25. When the federal government sent troops into Little Rock, Arkansas, to enforce integration of the public school system, the governor of Arkansas attacked the action, saying that it was as brutal an act of intervention as Russia's sending troops into Hungary to squelch the Hun-

garians' rebellion. In both cases, the governor said, the rights of a freedom-loving, independent people were being violated.

26. Governor Jones was elected two years ago. Since that time constant examples of corruption and subversion have been unearthed. It is time to get rid of the man responsible for this kind of corrupt government.

27. Are we going to vote a pay increase for our teachers, or are we going to allow our schools to deteriorate into substandard custodial institutions?

28. You see, the priests were right. After we threw those virgins into the volcano, it quit erupting.

29. The people of Rome lost their vitality and desire for freedom when their emperors decided that the way to keep them happy was to provide them with bread and circuses. What can we expect of our own country now that the government gives people free food and there is a constant round of entertainment provided by television?

30. From Mark Clifton, "The Dread Tomato Affliction" (proving that eating tomatoes is dangerous and even deadly): "Ninety-two point four percent of juvenile delinquents have eaten tomatoes. Fifty-seven point one percent of the adult criminals in penitentiaries throughout the United States have eaten tomatoes. Eighty-four percent of all people killed in automobile accidents during the year have eaten tomatoes."

31. From Galileo, *Dialogues Concerning Two New Sciences*: "But can you doubt that air has weight when you have the clear testimony of Aristotle affirming that all elements have weight, including air, and excepting only fire?"

32. Robert Brustein, artistic director of the American Repertory Theatre, commenting on a threat by Congress in 1989 to withhold funding from an offensive art show: "Once we allow lawmakers to become art critics, we take the first step into the world of Ayatollah Khomeini, whose murderous review of *The Satanic Verses* still chills the heart of everyone committed to free expression." (The Ayatollah Khomeini called for the death of the author, Salman Rushdie, because he had allegedly committed blasphemy against Islam in his novel.)

Critical Listening

33. Listen carefully to a speech by a candidate for public office. Note any fallacies or lapses in logical thinking. Do some kinds of fallacies seem more common than others?

PART TWO

Writing, Researching, and Presenting Arguments

CHAPTER NINE

Writing an Argumentative Paper

The person who understands how arguments are constructed has an important advantage in today's world. Television commercials, political speeches, newspaper editorials, and magazine advertisements, as well as many communications between individuals, all draw on the principles we have examined in the preceding chapters. By now you should be fairly adept at picking out claims, support, and warrants (explicit or unstated) in these presentations. The next step is to apply your skills to writing an argument of your own. The process of using what you have learned will enhance your ability to analyze critically the marketing efforts with which we are all bombarded every day. Mastering the writing of arguments also gives you a valuable tool for communicating with other people in school, on the job, and even at home.

In this chapter we will move through the various stages involved in creating an argumentative paper: choosing a topic, defining the issues, organizing the material, writing the essay, and revising. We will also consider the more general question of how to use the principles already discussed in order to convince a real audience. The more carefully you follow the guidelines set out here and the more thought you give to your work at each point, the better you will be able to utilize the art of argument when this course is over.

FINDING AN APPROPRIATE TOPIC

An old British recipe for jugged hare is said to begin, "First, catch your hare." To write an argumentative paper, you first must choose your topic. This is a relatively easy task for someone writing an argument as part of his or her job — a lawyer defending a client, for example, or an advertising executive presenting a campaign. For a student, however, it can be daunting. Which of the many ideas in the world worth debating would make a good subject?

Several guidelines can help you evaluate the possibilities. Perhaps your assignment limits your choices. If you have been asked to write a research paper, you obviously must find a topic on which research is available. If your assignment is more open-ended, you need a topic that is worth the time and effort you expect to invest in it. In either case, your subject should be one that interests you. Don't feel you have to write about what you know — very often finding out what you don't know will turn out to be more satisfying. You should, however, choose a subject that is familiar enough for you to argue about without fearing you're in over your head.

Invention Strategies

As a starting point, think of conversations you've had in the past few days or weeks that have involved defending a position. Is there some current political issue you're concerned about? Some dispute with friends that would make a valid paper topic? One of the best sources is controversies in the media. Keep your project in mind as you watch TV, read, or listen to the radio. You may even run into a potential subject in your course reading assignments or classroom discussions. Fortunately for the would-be writer, nearly every human activity includes its share of disagreement.

As you consider possible topics, write them down. One that looks unlikely at first glance may suggest others or may have more appeal when you come back to it later. Further, simply putting words on paper has a way of stimulating the thought processes involved in writing. Even if your ideas are tentative, the act of converting them into phrases or sentences can often help in developing them.

Evaluating Possible Topics

Besides interesting you, your topic must interest your audience. Who is the audience? For a lawyer it is usually a judge or jury; for a columnist, anyone who reads the newspaper in which his or her column appears. For the student writer, the audience is to some extent hypothetical. You should assume that your paper is directed at readers who are reasonably intelligent and well informed, but who have no specific knowledge of the subject. It may be useful to imagine you are writing for a local or school publication — this may be the case if your paper turns out well.

Be sure, too, that you choose a topic with two sides. The purpose of an argument is to defend or refute a thesis, which means the thesis must be debatable. In evaluating a subject that looks promising, ask yourself: Can a case be made for the opposing view? If not, you have no workable ground for building your own case.

Finally, check the scope of your thesis. Consider how long your paper will be, and whether you can do justice to your topic in that amount of space. For example, suppose you want to argue in favor of worldwide nuclear disarmament. Is this a thesis you can support persuasively in a short paper? One way to find out is by listing the potential issues or points about which arguers might disagree. Consider the thesis: "The future of the world is in danger as long as nuclear weapons exist." Obviously this statement is too general. You would have to specify what you mean by the future of the world (the continuation of human life? of all life? of the earth itself?) and exactly how nuclear weapons endanger it before the claim would hold up. You could narrow it down: "Human beings are error-prone; therefore as long as nuclear weapons exist there is the chance that a large number of people will be killed accidentally." Though this statement is more specific and includes an important warrant, it still depends on other unstated warrants: that one human being (or a small group) is in the position to discharge a nuclear weapon capable of killing a large number of people; that such a weapon could, in fact, be discharged by mistake, given current safety systems. Can you expect to show sufficient evidence for these assumptions in the space available to you?

By now it should be apparent that arguing in favor of nuclear disarmament is too broad an undertaking. A more workable approach might be to defend or refute one of the disarmament proposals under consideration by the U.S. Congress, or to show that nuclear weapons pose some specific danger (such as long-term water pollution) that is sufficient reason to strive for disarmament.

Can a thesis be too narrow? Certainly. If this is true of the one you have chosen, you probably realized it when you asked yourself whether the topic was debatable. If you can prove your point convincingly in a paragraph, or even a page, you need a broader thesis.

At this preliminary stage, don't worry if you don't know exactly how to word your thesis. It's useful to write down a few possible phrasings to be sure your topic is one you can work with, but you need not be precise. The information you unearth as you do research will help you to formulate your ideas. Also, stating a thesis in final terms is premature until you know the organization and tone of your paper.

To This Point

Let's assume you have surveyed a range of possible topics and chosen one that provides you with a suitable thesis for your paper. Before you go on, check your thesis against the following questions:

1. Is this topic one that will interest both me and my audience?
2. Is the topic debatable?
3. Is my thesis appropriate in scope for a paper of this length?
4. Do I know enough about my thesis to have a rough idea of what ideas to use in supporting it and how to go about finding evidence to back up these ideas?

DEFINING THE ISSUES

Preparing an Initial Outline

An outline, like an accounting system or a computer program, is a practical device for organizing information. Nearly every elementary and high school student learns how to make an outline. What will you gain if you outline your argument? Time and an overview of your subject. The minutes you spend organizing your subject at the outset generally save at least double the time later, when you have few minutes to spare. An outline also enables you to see the whole argument at a glance.

Your preliminary outline establishes an order of priority for your argument. Which supporting points are issues to be defended, which are warrants, and which are evidence? Which supporting points are most persuasive? By constructing a map of your territory, you can identify the research routes that are likely to be most productive. You can also pinpoint any gaps in your reasoning.

List each issue as a main heading in your outline. Next, write below it any relevant support (or sources of support) that you are aware of. Then reexamine the list and consider which issues appear likely to offer the strongest support for your argument. You should number these in order of importance.

Case Study: Coed Bathrooms

To see how we raise and evaluate issues in a specific context, let's look at a controversy that surfaced recently at a large university. Students living in coed dorms elected to retain their coed bathrooms. The university administration, however, withdrew its approval, in part because of growing protests from parents and alumni.

The students raised these issues:

1. The rights of students to choose their living arrangements
2. The absence of coercion on those who did not wish to participate
3. The increase in civility between the sexes as a result of sharing accommodations

4. The practicality of coed bathrooms, which preclude the necessity for members of one sex to travel to a one-sex bathroom on another floor
5. The success of the experiment so far

On the other side, the administration introduced the following issues:

1. The role of the university *in loco parentis*
2. The necessity for the administration to retain the goodwill of parents and alumni
3. The dissatisfaction of some students with the arrangement
4. The inability of immature students to respect the right of others and resist the temptation of sexual activity

Now let's analyze these issues, comparing their strengths and weaknesses.

1. It is clear that not all the issues in this dispute were equally important. The arguers decided, therefore, to give greater emphasis to the issues that were most likely to be ultimately persuasive to their audiences and less attention to those that were difficult to prove or narrower in their appeal. The issue of convenience, for example, seemed a minor point. How much cost is imposed in being required to walk up or down a flight of stairs?

2. It was also clear that, as in several of the other cases we have examined, the support consisted of both factual data and appeals to values. In regard to the factual data, each side reported evidence to prove that

a. The experiment was or was not a success.
b. Civility had or had not increased.
c. The majority of students did or did not favor the plan.
d. Coercion had or had not been applied.

The factual data were important. If the administration could prove that the interests of some students had been injured, then the student case for coed bathrooms would be weakened.

But let us assume that the factual claims either were settled or remained in abeyance. We now turn our attention to a second set of issues, a contest over the values to be served.

3. Both sides claimed adherence to the highest principles of university life. Here the issues, while no easier to resolve, offered greater opportunity for serious and fruitful discussion.

The first question to be resolved was that of democratic control. The students asserted, "We should be permitted to have coed bathrooms because we can prove that the majority of us want them." The students hoped that the university community would agree with the implied analogy: that the university community should resemble a political democracy and that students should have full rights as citizens of that community. (This is an argument also made in regard to other areas of university life.)

The university denied that it was a democracy in which students had equal rights and insisted that it should not be. The administration offered its own analogical proof: Students are not permitted to hire their own teachers or to choose their manner of instruction, their courses of study, their grades, or the rules of admission. The university, they insisted, represented a different kind of community, like a home, in which the experienced are required to lead and instruct the inexperienced.

Students responded by pointing out that coed bathrooms or any other aspect of their living arrangements were areas in which *they* were experts and that freedom to choose living arrangements was not to be confused with a demand for equal participation in academic matters. Moreover, it was also true that in recent years the verdict had increasingly been rendered in favor of rights of special groups as against those of institutions. Students' rights have been among those that have benefited from the movement toward freedom of choice.

4. The second issue was related to the first but introduced a practical consideration, namely, the well-being of the university. The administration argued that more important than the wishes of the students in this essentially minor dispute was the necessity for retaining the support and goodwill of parents and alumni, who are ultimately responsible for the very existence of the university.

The students agreed that this support was necessary but felt that parents and alumni could be persuaded to consider the good reasons in the students' argument. Some students were inclined to carry the argument over goals even further. They insisted that if the university could maintain its existence only at the cost of sacrificing principles of democracy and freedom, then perhaps the university had forfeited its right to exist.

In making our way through this debate, we have summarized a procedure for tackling the issues in any controversial problem.

1. Raise the relevant issues and arrange them in order of importance. Plan to devote more time and space to issues you regard as crucial.
2. Produce the strongest evidence you can to support your factual claims, knowing that the opposing side or critical readers may try to produce conflicting evidence.
3. Defend your value claims by finding support in the fundamental principles with which most people in your audience would agree.
4. Argue with yourself. Try to foresee what kinds of refutation are possible. Try to anticipate and meet the opposing arguments.

ORGANIZING THE MATERIAL

Once you are satisfied that you have identified all the issues that will appear in your paper, you should begin to determine what kind of organization will be most effective for your argument. Now is the time to organize the results of your thinking into a logical and persuasive form. If you have read about your topic, answered questions, and acquired some evidence, you may already have decided on ways to approach your subject. If not, you should look closely at your outline now, recalling your purposes when you began your investigation, and develop a strategy for using the information you have gathered to achieve those purposes.

The first point to establish is what type of thesis you plan to present. Is your intention to make readers aware of some problem? To offer a solution to the problem? To defend a position? To refute a position held by others? The way you organize your material will depend to a great extent on your goal. With that goal in mind, look over your outline and reevaluate the relative importance of your issues. Which ones are most convincing? Which are backed up by the strongest support? Which ones relate to facts, and which concern values?

With these points in mind, let us look at various ways of organizing an argumentative paper. It would be foolish to decide in advance how many paragraphs a paper ought to have; however, you can and should choose a general strategy before you begin writing. If your thesis presents an opinion or recommends some course of action, you may choose simply to state your main idea and then defend it. If your thesis argues against an opposing view, you probably will want to mention that view and then refute it. Both these organizations introduce the thesis in the first or second paragraph (called the *thesis paragraph*). A third possibility is to start establishing that a problem exists and then introduce your thesis as the solution; this method is called *presenting the stock issues*. Although these three approaches sometimes overlap in practice, examining each one individually can help you structure your paper. Let's take a look at each arrangement.

Defending the Main Idea

All forms of organization will require you to defend your main idea, but one way of doing this is simple and direct. Early in the paper state the main idea that you will defend throughout your argument. You can also indicate here the two or three points you intend to develop in support of your claim; or you can raise these later as they come up. Suppose your thesis is that widespread vegetarianism would solve a number of problems. You could phrase it this way: "If the majority of people in this country adopted a vegetarian diet, we would see improvements in the economy, in the health of our people, and in moral sensitivity." You would then develop each of the claims in your list with appropriate data and warrants. Notice that the thesis statement in the first (thesis) paragraph has already outlined your organizational pattern.

Defending the main idea is effective for factual claims as well as policy claims, in which you urge the adoption of a certain policy and give the reasons for its adoption. It is most appropriate when your thesis is straightforward and can be readily supported by direct statements.

Refuting the Opposing View

Refuting an opposing view means to attack it in order to weaken, invalidate, or make it less credible to a reader. Since all arguments are dialogues or debates — even when the opponent is only imaginary — refutation of the other point of view is always implicit in your arguments. As you write, keep in mind the issues that an opponent may raise. You will be looking at your own argument as an unsympathetic reader may look at it, asking yourself the same kinds of critical questions and trying to find its weaknesses in order to correct them. In this way every argument you write becomes a form of refutation.

How do you plan a refutation? Here are some general guidelines.

1. If you want to refute the argument in a specific essay or article, read the argument carefully, noting all the points with which you disagree. This advice may seem obvious, but it cannot be too strongly emphasized. If your refutation does not indicate scrupulous familiarity with your opponent's argument, he or she has the right to say, and often does, "You haven't really read what I wrote. You haven't really answered my argument."

2. If you think that your readers are sympathetic to the opposing view or are not familiar with it, summarize it at the beginning of your paper, providing enough information to give readers an understanding of exactly what you plan to refute. When you summarize, it's important to be respectful of the opposition's views. You don't want to alienate readers who might not agree with you at first.

3. If your argument is long and complex, choose only the most important points to refute. Otherwise the reader who does not have the original argument on hand may find a detailed refutation hard to follow. If the argument is short and relatively simple — a claim supported by only two or three points — you may decide to refute all of them, devoting more space to the most important ones.

4. Attack the principal elements in the argument of your opponent.

   a. Question the evidence. (See pp. 160–66 in the text.) Question whether your opponent has proved that a problem exists.

b. Attack the warrants or assumptions that underlie the claim. (See pp. 206–07 in the text.)

c. Attack the logic or reasoning of the opposing view. (Refer to the discussion of fallacious reasoning on pp. 302–12 in the text.)

d. Attack the proposed solution to a problem, pointing out that it will not work.

5. Be prepared to do more than attack the opposing view. Supply evidence and good reasons in support of your own claim.

Finding the Middle Ground

Although an argument, by definition, assumes a difference of opinion, we know that opposing sides frequently find accommodation somewhere in the middle. As you mount your own argument about a controversial issue, you need not confine yourself to support of any of the differing positions. You may want to acknowledge that there is some justice on all sides and that you understand the difficulty of resolving the issue.

Consider these guidelines for an argument that offers a compromise between competing positions:

1. Early in your essay explain the opposing positions. Make clear the major differences separating the two (or more) sides.

2. Point out, whenever possible, that the opposing sides already agree to some exceptions to their stated positions. Such evidence may prove that the opposing sides are not so extreme as their advocates insist. Several commentators, writing about the budget conflict between Democrats and Republicans in late 1998, adopted this strategy, suggesting that compromise was possible because the differences were narrower than the public believed.

3. Make clear your own moderation and sympathy, your own willingness to negotiate. An example of this attitude appears in an essay on abortion in which the author infers how Abraham Lincoln might have treated the question of abortion rights.

> In this debate I have made my own position clear. It is a pro-life position (though it may not please all pro-lifers), and its model is Lincoln's position on slavery from 1854 until well into the Civil War: tolerate, restrict, discourage. Like Lincoln's, its touchstone is the common good of the nation, not the sovereign self. Like Lincoln's position, it accepts the legality but not the moral legitimacy of the institution that it seeks to contain. It invites argument and negotiation; it is a gambit, not a gauntlet.[1]

---

[1]George McKenna, "On Abortion: A Lincolnian Position," *The Atlantic Monthly*, September 1995, p. 68. (A gauntlet or glove is flung down in order to challenge an opponent to combat; a gambit is the opening move in a chess game, or in the words of one dictionary, "a concession that invites discussion." — ED.)

4. If you favor one side of the controversy, acknowledge that opposing views deserve to be considered. For example, in another essay on abortion, the author, who supports abortion rights, says,

> Those of us who are pro-choice must come to terms with those thoughtful pro-lifers who believe that in elevating the right to privacy above all other values, the most helpless form of humanity is left unprotected and is, in fact, defined away. They deserve to have their views addressed with sympathy and moral clarity.[2]

5. Provide evidence that accepting a middle ground can offer marked advantages for the whole society. Wherever possible, show that continued polarization can result in violence, injustice, and suffering.

6. In offering a solution that finds a common ground, be as specific as possible, emphasizing the part that you are willing to play in reaching a settlement. In an essay titled "Pro-Life and Pro-Choice? Yes!" the author concludes with this:

> Must those of us who abhor abortion, then, reconcile ourselves to seeing it spread unchecked? By no means. We can refuse to practice it ourselves — or, if we are male, beseech the women who carry our children to let them be born, and promise to support them, and mean it and do it. We can counsel and preach to others; those of us who are religious can pray. . . . What we must not do is ask the state to impose our views on those who disagree.[3]

On a different subject, a debate on pornography, the author, who is opposed to free distribution of obscene material, nevertheless refuses to endorse censorship.

> I think that, by enlarging the First Amendment to protect, in effect, freedom of expression, rather than freedom of speech and of the press, the courts made a mistake. The courts have made other mistakes, but I do not know a better way of defining the interests of the community than through legislation and through the courts. So I am willing to put up with things I think are wrong in the hope that they will be corrected. I know of no alternative that would always make the right decisions.[4]

Presenting the Stock Issues

Presenting the stock issues, or stating the problem before the solution, is a type of organization borrowed from traditional debate format. It works for policy claims when an audience must be con-

---

[2]Benjamin C. Schwarz, "Judge Ginsburg's Moral Myopia," *New York Times,* July 30, 1993, sec. A, p. 27.

[3]George Church, *Time,* March 6, 1995, p. 108.

[4]Ernest van den Haag, *Smashing Liberal Icons: A Collection of Debates* (Washington, D.C.: Heritage Foundation, 1981), p. 101.

vinced that a need exists for changing the status quo (present conditions) and for introducing plans to solve the problem. You begin by establishing that a problem exists (need). You then propose a solution (plan), which is your thesis. Finally, you show reasons for adopting the plan (advantages). These three elements — need, plan, and advantages — are called the stock issues.

For example, suppose you wanted to argue that measures for reducing acid rain should be introduced at once. You would first have to establish a need for such measures by defining the problem and providing evidence of damage. Then you would produce your thesis, a means for improving conditions. Finally you would suggest the benefits that would follow from implementation of your plan. Notice that in this organization your thesis paragraph usually appears toward the middle of your paper, although it may also appear at the beginning.

Ordering Material for Emphasis

Whichever way you choose to work, you should revise your outline to reflect the order in which you intend to present your thesis and supporting ideas. Not only the placement of your thesis paragraph but also the wording and arrangement of your ideas will determine what points in your paper receive the most emphasis.

Suppose your purpose is to convince the reader that cigarette smoking is a bad habit. You might decide to concentrate on three unpleasant attributes of cigarette smoking: (1) it is unhealthy; (2) it is dirty; (3) it is expensive. Obviously, these are not equally important as possible deterrents. You would no doubt consider the first reason the most compelling, accompanied by evidence to prove the relationship between cigarette smoking and cancer, heart disease, emphysema, and other diseases. This issue, therefore, should be given greater emphasis than the others.

There are several ways to achieve emphasis. One is to make the explicit statement that you consider a certain issue the most important.

> Finally, and *most importantly,* human culture is often able to neutralize or reverse what might otherwise be genetically advantageous consequences of selfish behavior.[5]

This quotation also reveals a second way — placing the material to be emphasized in an emphatic position, either first or last in the paper. The end position, however, is generally more emphatic.

A third way to achieve emphasis is to elaborate on the material to be emphasized, treating it at greater length, offering more data and reasons for it than you give for the other issues.

---

[5]Peter Singer, *The Expanding Circle* (New York: New American Library, 1982), p. 171.

Considering Scope and Audience

With a working outline in hand that indicates the order of your thesis and claims, you are almost ready to begin turning your notes into prose. First, however, it is useful to review the limits on your paper to be sure your writing time will be used to the best possible advantage.

The first limit involves scope. As mentioned earlier, your thesis should introduce a claim that can be adequately supported in the space available to you. If your research has opened up more aspects than you anticipated, you may want to narrow your thesis to one major subtopic. Or you could emphasize only the most persuasive arguments for your position (assuming these are sufficient to make your case) and omit the others. In a brief paper (three or four pages), three issues are probably all you have room to develop. On the other hand, if you suspect your thesis can be proved in one or two pages, look for ways to expand it. What additional issues might be brought in to bolster your argument? Alternatively, is there a larger issue for which your thesis could become a supporting idea?

Other limits on your paper are imposed by the need to make your points in a way that will be persuasive to an audience. The style and tone you choose depend not only on the nature of the subject but also on how you can best convince readers that you are a credible source. *Style* in this context refers to the elements of your prose — simple versus complex sentences, active versus passive verbs, metaphors, analogies, and other literary devices. *Tone* is the approach you take to your topic — solemn or humorous, detached or sympathetic. Style and tone together compose your voice as a writer.

Many students assume that every writer has only one voice. In fact, a writer typically adapts his or her voice to the material and the audience. Perhaps the easiest way to appreciate this is to think of two or three works by the same author that are written in different voices. Or compare the speeches of two different characters in the same story, novel, or film. Every writer has individual talents and inclinations that appear in most or all of his or her work. A good writer, however, is able to amplify some stylistic elements and diminish others, as well as to change tone, by choice.

It is usually appropriate in a short paper to choose an *expository* style, which emphasizes the elements of your argument rather than your personality. You many want to appeal to your readers' emotions as well as their intellects, but keep in mind that sympathy is most effectively gained when it is supported by believable evidence. If you press your point stridently, your audience is likely to be suspicious rather than receptive. If you sprinkle your prose with jokes or metaphors, you may diminish your credibility by detracting from the substance of your case. Both humor and analogy can be useful tools, but they should be used with discretion.

You can discover some helpful pointers on essay style by reading the editorials in newspapers such as the *New York Times,* the *Washington Post,* or the *Wall Street Journal.* The authors are typically addressing a mixed audience comparable to the hypothetical readers of your own paper. Though their approaches vary, each writer is attempting to portray himself or herself as an objective analyst whose argument deserves careful attention.

Again, remember your goals. You are trying to convince your audience of something; an argument is, by its nature, directed at people who may not initially agree with its thesis. Therefore, your voice as well as the claims you make must be convincing.

To This Point

The organizing steps that come between preparation and writing are often neglected. Careful planning at this stage, however, can save much time and effort later. As you prepare to start writing, you should be able to answer the following questions:

1. Is the purpose of my paper to persuade readers to accept a potentially controversial idea, to refute someone else's position, or to propose a solution to a problem?
2. Can or should my solution also incorporate elements of compromise and negotiation?
3. Have I decided on an organization that is likely to accomplish this purpose?
4. Does my outline arrange my thesis and issues in an appropriate order to emphasize the most important issues?
5. Does my outline show an argument whose scope suits the needs of this paper?
6. What questions of style and tone do I need to keep in mind as I write to ensure that my argument will be persuasive?

WRITING

Beginning the Paper

Having found a claim you can defend and the voice you will adopt toward your audience, you must now think about how to begin. An introduction to your subject should consist of more than just the first paragraph of your paper. It should invite the reader to give attention to what you have to say. It should also point you in the direction you will take in developing your argument. You may want to begin the actual writing of your paper with the thesis paragraph. It is useful to consider the whole paragraph rather than simply the thesis statement for two reasons. First, not all theses are effectively expressed in a single sentence. Second, the rest of the paragraph will be closely related to your statement of the main idea. You may show why you have chosen this topic or why your audience will benefit from reading your paper. You may introduce your warrant, qualify your claim, and in other ways prepare for the body of your argument. Because readers will perceive the whole paragraph as a unit, it makes sense to approach it that way.

Consider first the kind of argument you intend to present. Does your paper make a factual claim? Does it address values? Does it recommend a policy or action? Is it a rebuttal of some current policy or belief? The answers to those questions will influence the way you introduce the subject.

If your thesis makes a factual claim, you may be able to summarize it in one or two opening sentences. "Whether we like it or not, money is obsolete. The currency of today is not paper or coin, but plastic." Refutations are easy to introduce in a brief statement: "Contrary to popular views on the subject, the institution of marriage is as sound today as it was a generation ago."

A thesis that defends a value is usually best preceded by an explanatory introduction. "Some wars are morally defensible" is a thesis that can be stated as a simple declarative opening sentence. However, readers who disagree may not read any further than the first line. Someone defending this claim is likely to be more persuasive if he or she first gives an example of a situation in which war is or was preferable to peace or presents the thesis less directly.

One way to keep such a thesis from alienating the audience is to phrase it as a question. "Are all wars morally indefensible?" Still better would be to prepare for the question:

> Few if any of us favor war as a solution to international problems. We are too vividly aware of the human suffering imposed by armed conflict, as well as the political and financial turmoil that inevitably result. Yet can we honestly agree that no war is ever morally defensible?

Notice that this paragraph gains appeal from use of the first person *we*. The author implies that he or she shares the readers' feelings but has good reasons for believing those feelings are not sufficient grounds for condemning all wars. Even if readers are skeptical, the conciliatory phrasing of the thesis should encourage them to continue reading.

For any subject that is highly controversial or emotionally charged, especially one that strongly condemns an existing situation or belief, you may sometimes want to express your indignation directly. Of course, you must be sure that your indignation can be justified. The author of the following introduction, a physician and writer, openly admits that he is about to make a case that may offend readers.

> Is there any polite way to introduce today's subject? I'm afraid not. It must be said plainly that the media have done about as sorry and dishonest a job of covering health news as is humanly possible, and that when the media do not fail from bias and mendacity, they fail from ignorance and laziness.[6]

If your thesis advocates a policy or makes a recommendation, it may be a good idea, as in a value claim, to provide a short background. The following paragraph introduces an argument favoring relaxation of controls in high schools.

> "Free the New York City 275,000" read a button worn by many young New Yorkers some years ago. The number was roughly the total of students enrolled in the City's high schools.
>   The condition of un-freedom which is described was not, however, unique to the schools of one city. According to the Carnegie Commission's comprehensive study of American public education, *Crisis in the Classroom,* public schools across the country share a common characteristic, namely, "preoccupation with order and control." The result is that students find themselves the victims of "oppressive and petty rules which give their schools a repressive, almost prison-like atmosphere."[7]

There are also other ways to introduce your subject. One is to begin with an appropriate quotation.

> "Reading makes a full man, conversation makes a ready man, and writing makes an exact man." So Francis Bacon told us around 1600. Recently I have been wondering how Bacon's formula might apply to present-day college students.[8]

Or you may begin with an anecdote. In the following introduction to an article about the relation between cancer and mental attitude, the author recounts a personal experience.

> Shortly after I moved to California, a new acquaintance sat in my San Francisco living room drinking rose-hip tea and chainsmoking. Like so many residents of the Golden West, Cecil was "into" all things healthy, from jogging to *shiatsu* massage to kelp. Tobacco didn't seem to fit, but he told me confidently that there was no contradiction. "It all

---

[6]Michael Halberstam, "TV's Unhealthy Approach to Health News," *TV Guide,* September 20–26, 1980, p. 24.

[7]Alan Levine and Eve Carey, *The Rights of Students* (New York: Avon Books, 1977), p. 11.

[8]William Aiken, "The Conversation on Campus Today Is, Uh . . . ," *Wall Street Journal,* May 4, 1982, p. 18.

has to do with energy," he said. "Unless you have a lot of negative energy about smoking cigarettes, there's no way they can hurt you; you won't get cancer."[9]

Finally, you may introduce yourself as the author of the claim.

> I wish to argue an unpopular cause: the cause of the old, free elective system in the academic world, or the untrammeled right of the undergraduate to make his own mistakes.[10]

> My subject is the world of Hamlet. I do not of course mean Denmark, except as Denmark is given a body by the play; and I do not mean Elizabethan England, though this is necessarily close behind the scenes. I mean simply the imaginative environment that the play asks us to enter when we read it or go to see it.[11]

You should, however, use such introductions with care. They suggest an authority about the subject that you shouldn't attempt to assume unless you can demonstrate that you are entitled to it.

Guidelines for Good Writing

In general, the writer of an argument follows the same rules that govern any form of expository writing. Your style should be clear and readable, your organization logical, your ideas connected by transitional phrases and sentences, your paragraphs coherent. The main difference between an argument and other kinds of expository writing, as noted earlier, is the need to persuade an audience to adopt a belief or take an action. You should assume your readers will be critical rather than neutral or sympathetic. Therefore, you must be equally critical of your own work. Any apparent gap in reasoning or ambiguity in presentation is likely to weaken the argument.

As you read the essays in this book and elsewhere, you will discover that good style in argumentative writing shares several characteristics:

- Variety in sentence structure: a mixture of both long and short sentences, different sentence beginnings
- Rich but standard vocabulary: avoidance of specialized terms unless they are fully explained, word choice appropriate to a thoughtful argument
- Use of details and examples to illustrate and clarify abstract terms, principles, and generalizations

---

[9]Joel Guerin, "Cancer and the Mind," *Harvard Magazine,* November–December 1978, p. 11.

[10]Howard Mumford Jones, "Undergraduates on Apron Strings," *Atlantic Monthly,* October 1955, p. 45.

[11]Maynard Mack, "The World of Hamlet," *Yale Review,* June 1952, p. 502.

You should take care to avoid the following:

- Unnecessary repetition: making the same point without new data or interpretation
- Exaggeration or stridency, which can create suspicion of your fairness and powers of observation
- Short paragraphs of one or two sentences, which are common in advertising and newspaper writing to get the reader's attention but are inappropriate in a thoughtful essay

In addition to these stylistic principles, seven general points are worth keeping in mind:

1. Although *you,* like *I,* should be used judiciously, it can be found even in the treatment of weighty subjects. Here is an example from an essay by the distinguished British mathematician and philosopher, Bertrand Russell.

> Suppose you are a scientific pioneer and you make some discovery of great scientific importance and suppose you say to yourself, "I am afraid this discovery will do harm": you know that other people are likely to make the same discovery if they are allowed suitable opportunities for research; you must therefore, if you do not wish the discovery to become public, either discourage your sort of research or control publication by a board of censors.[12]

Don't be afraid to use *you* or *I* when it is useful to emphasize the presence of the person making the argument.

2. Don't pad. This point should be obvious; the word *pad* suggests the addition of unnecessary material. Many writers find it tempting, however, to enlarge a discussion even when they have little more to say. It is never wise to introduce more words into a paper that has already made its point. If the paper turns out to be shorter than you had hoped, it may mean that you have not sufficiently developed the subject or that the subject was less substantial than you thought when you selected it. Padding, which is easy to detect in its repetition and sentences empty of content, weakens the writer's credibility.

3. For any absolute generalization — a statement containing words such as *all* or *every* — consider the possibility that there may be at least one example that will weaken the generalization. Such a precaution means that you won't have to backtrack and admit that your generalization is not, after all, universal. A student who was arguing against capital punishment for the reason that all killing was wrong suddenly paused in her presentation and added, "On the

---

[12]"Science and Human Life," in *What Is Science?* edited by James R. Newman (New York: Simon and Schuster, 1955), p. 12.

other hand, if given the chance, I'd probably have been willing to kill Hitler." This admission meant that she recognized important exceptions to her rule and that she would have to qualify her generalization in some significant way.

4. When offering an explanation, especially one that is complicated or extraordinary, look first for a cause that is easier to accept, one that doesn't strain credibility. (In Chapter 8, we called attention to this principle. See pp. 302–03.) For example, years ago a great many people were bemused by reports about the mysterious Bermuda Triangle, which had apparently swallowed up ships and planes since the mid-nineteenth century. The forces at work were variously described as space-time warps, UFOs that transported earthlings to other planets, and sea monsters seeking revenge. But a careful investigation revealed familiar, natural causes. A reasonable person interested in the truth would have searched for more conventional explanations before accepting the bizarre stories of extraterrestrial creatures. He or she would also exercise caution when confronted by conspiracy theories that try to account for controversial political events, such as the assassination of John F. Kennedy.

5. Check carefully for questionable warrants. Your outline should specify your warrants. When necessary, these should be included in your paper to link claims with support. Many an argument has failed because it depended on an unstated warrant with which the reader did not agree. If you were arguing for a physical education requirement at your school, you might make a good case for all the physical and psychological benefits of such a requirement. But you would certainly need to introduce and develop the warrant on which your claim was based — that it is the proper function of a college or university to provide the benefits of a physical education. Many readers would agree that physical education is valuable, but they might question the assumption that an academic institution should introduce a nonintellectual enterprise into the curriculum. At any point where you draw a controversial or tenuous conclusion, be sure your reasoning is clear and logical.

6. Avoid conclusions that are merely summaries. Summaries may be needed in long technical papers, but in brief arguments they create endings that are without force or interest. In the closing paragraph you should find a new idea that emerges naturally from the development of the whole argument.

7. Strive for a paper that is unified, coherent, and emphatic where appropriate. A *unified* paper stays focused on its goal and directs each claim, warrant, and piece of evidence toward that goal. Extraneous information or unsupported claims impair unity. *Coherence* means that all ideas are fully explained and adequately connected by transitions. To ensure coherence, give especially close

attention to the beginnings and ends of your paragraphs: Is each new concept introduced in a way that shows it following naturally from the one that preceded it? *Emphasis,* as we have mentioned, is a function partly of structure and partly of language. Your most important claims should be placed where they are certain of receiving the reader's attention: key sentences at the beginning or end of a paragraph, key paragraphs at the beginning or end of your paper. Sentence structure can also be used for emphasis. If you have used several long, complex sentences, you can emphasize a significant point by stating it briefly and simply. You can also create emphasis with verbal flags, such as "The primary issue to consider . . ." or "Finally, we cannot ignore. . . ."

All clear expository prose will exhibit the qualities of unity, coherence, and emphasis. But the success of an argumentative paper is especially dependent on these qualities because the reader may have to follow a line of reasoning that is both complicated and unfamiliar. Moreover, a paper that is unified, coherent, and properly emphatic will be more readable, the first requisite of an effective argument.

REVISING

The final stage in writing an argumentative paper is revising. The first step is to read through what you have written for mistakes. Next, check your work against the guidelines listed under "Organizing the Material" and "Writing." Have you omitted any of the issues, warrants, or supporting evidence on your outline? Is each paragraph coherent in itself? Do your paragraphs work together to create a coherent paper? All the elements of the argument — the issues raised, the underlying assumptions, and the supporting material — should contribute to the development of the claim in your thesis statement. Any material that is interesting but irrelevant to that claim should be cut. Finally, does your paper reach a clear conclusion that reinforces your thesis?

Be sure, too, that the style and tone of your paper are appropriate for the topic and the audience. Remember that people choose to read an argument because they want the answer to a troubling question or the solution to a recurrent problem. Besides stating your thesis in a way that invites the reader to join you in your investigation, you must retain your audience's interest through a discussion that may be unfamiliar or contrary to their convictions. The outstanding qualities of argumentative prose style, therefore, are clarity and readability.

Style is obviously harder to evaluate in your own writing than organization. Your outline provides a map against which to check the structure of your paper. Clarity and readability, by comparison, are somewhat abstract qualities. Two procedures may be helpful. The first is to read two or three (or more) essays by authors whose style you admire and then turn back to your own writing. Awkward spots in your prose are sometimes easier to see if you get away from it and respond to someone else's perspective than if you simply keep rereading your own writing.

The second method is to read aloud. If you have never tried it, you are likely to be surprised at how valuable this can be. Again, start with someone else's work that you feel is clearly written, and practice until you achieve a smooth rhythmic delivery that satisfies you. And listen to what you are reading. Your objective is to absorb the patterns of English structure that characterize the clearest, most readable prose. Then read your paper aloud, and listen to the construction of your sentences. Are they also clear and readable? Do they say what you want them to say? How would they sound to a reader? According to one theory, you can learn the rhythm and phrasing of a language as you learn the rhythm and phrasing of a melody. And you will often *hear* a mistake or a clumsy construction in your writing that has escaped your eye in proofreading.

PREPARING THE MANUSCRIPT

Print your typed essay on one side of 8½-by-11-inch white computer paper, double-spacing throughout. Leave margins of 1 to 1½ inches on all sides, and indent each paragraph one-half inch or five spaces. Unless a formal outline is part of the paper, a separate title page is unnecessary. Instead, beginning about one inch from the top of the first page and flush with the left margin, type your name, the instructor's name, the course title, and the date, each on a separate line; then double-space and type the title, capitalizing the first letter of the words of the title except for articles, prepositions, and conjunctions. Double-space and type the body of the paper.

Number all pages at the top right corner, typing your last name before each page number in case pages are mislaid. If an outline is included, number its pages with lowercase roman numerals.

Use the spell-check and grammar-check functions of your word-processing program, and proofread the paper carefully for other mistakes. Correct the errors, and reprint the pages in question. If you have used a typewriter, make corrections with liquid correction fluid, or, if there are only a few mistakes, cross them out and neatly write the correction above the line.

REVIEW CHECKLIST
FOR ARGUMENTATIVE PAPERS

A successful argumentative paper meets the following criteria:

1. It presents a thesis that is of interest to both the writer and the audience, is debatable, and can be defended in the amount of space available.
2. Each statement offered in support of the thesis is backed up with enough evidence to give it credibility. Data cited in the paper come from a variety of sources. All quotations and direct references to primary or secondary sources are fully documented.
3. The warrants linking claims to support are either specified or implicit in the author's data and line of reasoning. No claim should depend on an unstated warrant with which skeptical readers might disagree.
4. The thesis is clearly presented and adequately introduced in a thesis paragraph, which indicates the purpose of the paper.
5. Supporting statements and data are organized in a way that builds the argument, emphasizes the author's main ideas, and justifies the paper's conclusions.
6. All possible opposing arguments are anticipated and refuted.
7. The paper is written in a style and tone appropriate to the topic and the intended audience. The author's prose is clear and readable.
8. The manuscript is clean, carefully proofed, and typed in an acceptable format.

CHAPTER TEN

Researching an Argumentative Paper

The success of any argument, short or long, depends in large part on the quantity and quality of the support behind it. Research, therefore, can be crucial for any argument outside your own experience. Most papers will benefit from research in the library and elsewhere because development of the claim requires facts, examples, statistics, and informed opinions that are available only from primary and secondary research sources. This chapter offers information and advice to help you work through the steps of writing a research paper, from getting started to preparing the finished product.

GETTING STARTED

The following guidelines will help you keep your research on track:

1. Focus your investigation on building your argument, not merely on collecting information about the topic. Do follow any promising leads that turn up from the sources you consult, but don't be diverted into general reading that has no direct bearing on your thesis.

2. Look for at least two pieces of evidence to support each point you make. If you cannot find sufficient evidence, you may need to revise or abandon the point.

3. Use a variety of sources. Seek evidence from different kinds of sources (books, magazines, websites, government reports, even personal interviews with experts) and from different fields.

4. Be sure your sources are authoritative. We have already pointed out elsewhere the necessity for examining the credentials of

sources. Although it may be difficult or impossible for those outside the field to conclude that one authority is more trustworthy than another, some guidelines are available. Articles and essays in scholarly journals are probably more authoritative than articles in college newspapers. Authors whose credentials include many publications and years of study at reputable institutions are probably more reliable than newspaper columnists and the so-called man in the street. However, we can judge reliability much more easily if we are dealing with facts and inferences than with values and emotions.

5. Don't let your sources' opinions outweigh your own. Your paper should demonstrate that the thesis and ideas you present are yours, arrived at after careful reflection and supported by research. The thesis need not be original, but your paper should be more than a collection of quotations or a report of the facts and opinions you have been reading. It should be clear to the reader that the quotations and other materials support *your* claim and that *you* have been responsible for finding and emphasizing the important issues, examining the data, and choosing between strong and weak opinions.

6. Prepare for research by identifying potential resources and learning how they work. Make sure you know how to use the library's catalog and other databases available either in the library or through the campus network. For each database that looks useful, explore how to execute a subject search, how to refine a search, and how to print out or download results. Make sure you know how to find books, relevant reference materials, and journals. Find out whether interlibrary loan is an option and how long it takes. If you plan to use government publications, find out if your library is a depository for federal documents. Identify relevant organizions using the *Encyclopedia of Associations* and visit their websites. Finally, discuss your topic with a librarian at the reference desk to make sure you haven't overlooked anything.

MAPPING RESEARCH: A SAMPLE OUTLINE

To explore a range of research activities, let's suppose that you are preparing a research paper, six to ten pages long. You have chosen to defend the following thesis: *Conventional zoos should be abolished because they are cruel to animals and cannot provide the benefits to the public that they promise.* To keep your material under control and give direction to your reading, you would sketch a preliminary outline, which might look like this:

Why We Don't Need Zoos

I. Moral Objection: Animals have fundamental right to liberty
   A. Must prove animals are negatively affected by captivity
      1. research?

    2. research?

  B. Must refute claims that captivity is not detrimental to animals

    1. Brownlee's description of dolphin: "seeming stupor"; eating "half-heartedly"; not behaving like wild dolphins

    2. Personal experience: watching leopards running in circles in cages for hours

II. Practical Objection: Zoos can't accomplish what they claim to be their goals

  A. "Educational benefits" zoo provides are inaccurate at best: Public is not learning about wild animals at all but about domesticated descendants of same (support with research from [I.A] above)

  B. Conservation programs at zoos are ineffective

    1. It's difficult to breed animals in zoos

    2. Resultant offspring, when there is any, is victim of inbreeding. Leads to inferior stock that will eventually die out (research?)

Now you need to begin the search for the materials that will support your argument. There are two principal ways of gathering the materials — primary research and secondary research. Most writers will not want to limit themselves to one kind of research, but one method may work better than another for a particular project.

USING SOURCES: PRIMARY RESEARCH

Primary research involves looking for firsthand information. By *firsthand* we mean information taken directly from the original source, including field research (interviews, surveys, personal observations, or experiments). If your topic relates to a local issue involving your school or community, or if it focuses on a story that has never been reported by others, field research may be more valuable than anything available in the library. However, the library can be a source of firsthand information. Memoirs and letters written by witnesses to past events, photographs, contemporary news reports of historical events, or expert testimony presented at congressional hearings are all primary sources that may be available in your library. The Internet, too, can be a source of primary data. A discussion list, newsgroup, or chat room focused on your topic may give you a means to converse with activists and contact experts. Websites of certain organizations provide documentation of their views, unfiltered by others' opinions. The text of laws, court opinions, bills, debates in Congress, environmental impact statements, and even selected declassified FBI files can be found through government-sponsored websites. Other sites present statistical data or the text of historical or political documents.

One of the rewards of primary research is that it often generates new information, which in turn produces new interpretations of familiar conditions. It is a favored method for anthropologists and sociologists, and most physical and natural scientists use observation and experiment at some point as essential tools in their research. Notice that both of the student research papers at the end of this chapter used firsthand information gained from personal observation and interviews in addition to their secondary library research.

Consider the sample thesis that *zoos should be abolished.* Remember that you need to prove that *zoos are cruel to animals* and that *they cannot provide the benefits to the public that they promise.* It is possible to go directly to primary sources without consulting books or journals. For example:

- Phone the local area chapter of any animal rights group and ask to interview members on their opinions concerning zoos.

- Talk to the veterinarian on call at your local zoo and ask about animal injuries, illnesses, neuroses, and so forth.

- Search the World Wide Web for sites sponsored and developed by the groups associated with the animal rights movement. Many such informational sites will provide the text of current or proposed laws concerning this issue.

- Locate Internet newsgroups or discussion lists devoted to animal rights and identify experts in the field such as animal scientists who would be willing to provide authoritative opinions for your paper.

The information gleaned from primary research can be used directly to support your claim, or can provide a starting point for secondary research at the library.

USING SOURCES: SECONDARY RESEARCH

Secondary research involves locating commentary and analysis of your topic. In addition to raw evidence found through primary research, secondary sources provide a sense of how others are examining the issues and can provide useful information and analysis. Secondary sources may be written for a popular audience, ranging from news coverage, to popular explanations of research findings, to social analysis, to opinion pieces. Or they may be scholarly publications — experts presenting their research and theories to other researchers. These sources might also come in the form of analytical reports written to untangle possible courses of action, such as a report written by staff members for a congressional committe or an analysis of an issue by a think tank that wants to use the evidence it has gathered to influence public opinion.

Whatever form it may take, be sure when you use a secondary source that you consider the author's purpose and the validity of the material presented to ensure that is useful evidence for your argument. An opinion piece published in a small-town paper, for example, may be a less impressive source for your argument than an analysis written by a former cabinet member. A description of a scientific discovery published in a magazine will carry less weight as evidence than the article written by the scientists making the discovery, presenting their research findings in a scientific journal.

The nature of your topic will determine which route you follow to find good sources. If the topic is current, you may find it more important to use articles than books and might bypass the library catalog altogether. If the topic has to do with social policy or politics, government publications may be particularly useful, though they would be unhelpful for a literary paper. If the topic relates to popular culture, the Internet may provide more information than more traditional publications. Consider what kinds of sources will be most useful as you choose your strategy. If you aren't certain which approaches fit your topic best, consult with a librarian at the reference desk.

Selecting and Searching Databases

You will most likely use one or more *databases* (online catalogs of reference materials) to locate books and articles on your topic. The library catalog is a database of books and other materials owned by the library; other databases may cover articles in popular or specialized journals and may even provide the full text of articles. Some databases may be available only in the library; others may be accessible all over campus. Here are some common features that appear in many databases.

Keyword or subject searching: You might have the option of searching a database by *keyword* — using the words that you think are most relevant to your search — or by subject. Typically, a keyword search will search for any occurrence of your search term in titles, notes, or the descriptive headings provided by database catalogers or indexers. The advantage to keyword searching is that you can use terms that come naturally to you to cast your net as widely as possible. The disadvantage is that there may be more than one way to express your topic and you may not capture all the relevant materials unless you use the right keywords.

With *subject searching,* you use search terms from a list of subject headings (sometimes called *descriptors*) established by the creators of the database. To make searching as efficient as possible, they choose one word or phrase to express a subject. Every time a new source is entered into the database, the indexers describe it using words from the list of subject headings: When you use the list to search the database, you retrieve every relevant source. You might find that a database lists these subject headings through a thesaurus feature. The sophisticated researcher will always pay attention to the subject headings or descriptors generally listed at the bottom of a record for clues to terms that might work best and for related terms that might be worth trying.

Searching for more than one concept: Most database searches allow you to combine terms using the connectors *and, or,* and *not.* These connectors (also known as *Boolean operators*) group search terms in different ways. If you search for zoos *and* animal rights, for example, the resulting list of sources will include only those that deal with both zoos and animal rights, leaving out any that deal with only one subject and not the other. If you connect terms with *or,* your list will contain sources that deal with either concept: A search for dogs *or* cats will create a list of sources that cover either animal. *Not* excludes concepts from a search. A search for animal rights *not* furs will search for the concept animal rights and then cut out any sources that deal with furs.

Limiting a search: Most databases have some options for limiting a search by a number of variables, such as publication date, language, or format. If you find a large number of sources in a database search, you might limit your search to sources published in English in the past three years. If you need a visual aid for a presentation, you might limit a search of the library's catalog to videos, and so on.

Truncating search terms with wild cards: At times you will search for a word that has many possible endings. A wild card is a symbol that, placed at the end of a word root, allows for any possible ending for a word. For example, *animal** will allow a search for *animal* or *animals.*

Options for saving records: You may have the opportunity to print, download to a disk, or e-mail to yourself the citations you find in a database. Many databases have a feature for marking just the records you want so you save only those of interest.

Help screens: Most databases offer some kind of online help that explains how to use the database effectively. If you invest five minutes getting familiar with the basics of a database, it may save you twenty minutes later.

Types of Databases

The library catalog: If you want to search for books, videos, or periodical publications, the library catalog is the database to search. Most libraries now have computerized catalogs, but some still have a card catalog. In either case, the type of information provided is the same. Every book in the library has an entry in the catalog that gives its author, title, publisher, date, length, and subject headings and perhaps some notes about its contents. It also gives the call number or location on the shelf and often some indication as to whether it is currently available. You can search the catalog for an author, title, subject, or keyword. Most online catalogs have ways of combining and limiting searches and for printing results. Remember when searching the catalog, though, that entries are created for whole books and not for specific parts of them. If you use too narrow search terms, you may not find a book that has a chapter that includes exactly what you are looking for. Use broad search terms, and check the subject headings for search terms that will work best. Plan to browse the shelves and examine the tables of contents of the books that you find through the catalog to see which, in fact, are most helpful for your topic.

Sample Online Catalog Record
You searched for the TITLE: animal rights movement

```
CALL #        Z7164.C45 M38 1994.
AUTHOR        Manzo, Bettina, 1943-
TITLE         The animal rights movement in the United States, 1975-
              1990 : an annotated bibliography / by Bettina Manzo.
IMPRINT       Metuchen, N.J. : Scarecrow Press, 1994.
PHYS DESCR    xi, 296 p. ; 23 cm.
NOTE          Includes indexes.
CONTENTS      Animal rights movement -- Activists and organizations --
              Philosophy, ethics, and religion -- Law and legislation
              -- Factory farming and vegetarianism -- Trapping and
              fur industry -- Companion animals -- Wildlife --
              Circuses, zoos, rodeos, dog
SUBJECT       Animal rights movement --United States --Bibliography.
              Animal rights --United States --Bibliography.
              Animal experimentation --United States --Bibliography.
OCLC #        30671149.
ISBN/ISSN     GB95-17241.
```

General periodical databases: If you want to search for articles, you can find a number of options at your library. Most libraries have a generalized database of periodical articles that may include citations, citations with abstracts (brief summaries), or the entire text of articles. *Searchbank, Ebscohost, Infotrac, Readers' Guide Abstracts,* and *ProQuest* are all online indexes of this type. Ask a librarian what is available in your library. These are particularly good for finding current information in fairly nonspecialized sources, though they may include some scholarly journals. If you are looking for articles published before the 1980s — say, for news accounts published when the atomic bomb was dropped on Hiroshima — you would most likely need to use a print index such as the *Readers' Guide to Periodical Literature,* which began publication in 1900.

Specialized databases: In addition to these general databases, you may find you need to delve deeper into a particular subject area. Every academic discipline has some sort of in-depth index to its research, and though the materials they cover tend to be highly specialized, they can provide more substantial support for your claims because they tend to cover sources written by experts in their fields. These resources may be available in electronic or print form:

Art Index

Biological Abstracts (the online version is known as *Biosis*)

Business Periodicals Index

ERIC (focused on education research)

Index Medicus (*Medline* or *PubMed* online)

Modern Languages Association International Bibliography (*MLA Bibliography* online)

Psychological Abstracts (*PsychInfo* or *PsychLit* online)

Sociological Abstracts (*Sociofile* online)

Check with a librarian to find out which specialized databases or indexes that relate to your topic are available in your library.

Database services: In addition to individual databases, many libraries subscribe to database services that provide access to a number of databases from one search screen. *FirstSearch,* for example, provides access to a variety of subject-specific databases as well as *WorldCat,* a massive database of library catalogs. *Lexis/Nexis* is a collection of databases to over a billion texts, most of them available in full text; it is a strong source for news coverage, legal research, and business information. These may be available to you through the

Web anywhere on campus. Again, a visit with a librarian will help you quickly identify what your library has available.

Encyclopedias

General and specialized encyclopedias offer quick overviews of topics and easy access to factual information. They also tend to have excellent selective bibliographies, pointing you toward useful sources. You will find a wide variety of encyclopedias in your library's reference collection; you may also have an online encyclopedia, such as *Britannica Online,* available through the Web anywhere on campus. Some specialized encyclopedias include the following:

Encyclopedia of African American History and Culture

Encyclopedia of American Social History

Encyclopedia of Bioethics

Encyclopedia of Educational Research

Encyclopedia of Hispanic Culture in the United States

Encyclopedia of International Relations

Encyclopedia of Philosophy

Encyclopedia of Sociology

Encyclopedia of the United States in the Twentieth Century

Encyclopedia of World Cultures

International Encyclopedia of Communications

McGraw-Hill Encyclopedia of Science and Technology

Political Handbook of the World

Statistical Resources

Often statistics are used as evidence in an argument. If your argument depends on establishing that one category is bigger than another, that the majority of people hold a certain opinion, or that one group is more affected by something than another group, statistics can provide the evidence you need. Of course, as with any other source, you need to be sure that your statistics are as reliable as possible and that you are reporting them responsibly.

It isn't always easy to find things counted the way you want. If you embark on a search for numbers to support your argument, be prepared to spend some time locating and interpreting data. Always read the fine print that explains how and when the data were gathered. Some sources for statistics include these:

U.S. Bureau of the Census: This government agency produces a wealth of statistical data, much of it available on CD-ROM or through the Web at <http://www.census.gov/>. A handy compilation of their most useful tables is found in the one-volume annual handbook, *Statistical Abstract of the United States,* which also includes statistics from other government sources.

Other federal agencies: Numerous federal agencies gather statistical data. Among these are the National Center for Education Statistics, the National Center for Health Statistics, the National Bureau of Labor Statistics, and the Federal Bureau of Investigation, which annually compiles national crime statistics. One handy place to find a wide variety of federal statistics is a website called *FedStats* at <http://www.fedstats.gov/>.

United Nations: Compilations of international data published by the United Nations include the *Demographic Yearbook* and *Statistical Yearbook.* Some statistics are also published by U.N. agencies such as the Food and Health Organization. Some are available from the U.N. website at <http://www.un.org/>.

Opinion polls: Several companies conduct opinion polls, and some of these are available in libraries. One such compilation is the Gallup Poll series, which summarizes public opinion polling from 1935 to the present. Other poll results are reported by the press. Search a database that covers news publications by using your topic and *polls* as keywords to help you locate some summaries of results.

Government Publications

Beyond statistics, government agencies compile and publish a wealth of information. For topics that concern public welfare, health, education, politics, foreign relations, earth sciences, the environment, or the economy, government documents may provide just the information you need.

The U.S. federal government is the largest publisher in the world. Its publications are distributed free to libraries designated as document depositories across the country. If your library is not a depository, chances are there is a regional depository somewhere nearby. Local, state, and foreign governments are also potential sources of information.

Federal documents distributed to depository libraries are indexed in *The Monthly Catalog of U.S. Government Documents,* available in many libraries as an electronic database. These include congressional documents such as hearings and committee reports, presidential papers, studies conducted by the Education Department or the Centers for Disease Control, and so on. Many government documents are available through the Internet. If you learn about a government publication through the news media, chances are you will be able to obtain a copy at the website of the sponsoring agency or congressional body. In fact, government publications are among the most valuable of resources available on the Web because they are rigorously controlled for content. You know you are looking at a U.S. federal government site when you see *.gov* before the first slash in the URL.

Searching the Web

The World Wide Web is becoming an increasingly important resource for researchers. It is particularly helpful if you are looking for information about organizations, current events, political debates, popular culture, or government-sponsored research and activities. It is not an especially good place to look for literary criticism, historical analysis, or scholarly research articles, which are still more likely to be published in traditional ways. Biologists reporting on an important experiment, for example, are more likely to submit an article about it to a prestigious journal in the field than simply post their results on the Web.

Because anyone can publish whatever they like on the Web, searching for good information can be frustrating. Search engines operate by means of automated programs that gather information about sites and match search terms to whatever is out there, regardless of quality. A search engine may locate thousands of Web documents on a topic, but most are of little relevance and dubious quality. The key is to know in advance what information you need and who might have produced it. For example, if your topic has to do with some aspect of free speech and you know that the American Civil Liberties Union is involved in the issue, a trip to the ACLU home page may provide you with a wealth of information, albeit from a particular perspective. If your state's pollution control agency just issued a report on water quality in the area, you may find the report published at their website or the e-mail address of someone who could send it to you. The more you know about your topic before you sit down to surf, the more likely you will use your time productively.

If you have a fairly broad topic and no specific clues about where it might be covered, you may want to start your search using a selective guide to good sites. For example, the University of Texas maintains an excellent directory to sites relating to Latin America. Subject guides that selectively list valuable sites can be found at the *Argus Clearinghouse* at <http://www.clearinghouse.net>, the University of California's *Infomine* at <http://lib-www.ucr.edu/>, and the *World Wide Web Virtual Library* project at <http://www.vlib.org/Home.html>. Reference librarians will also be able to point you to quality sites that relate to your topic.

If you have a fairly specific topic in mind or are looking for a particular organization or document on the Web, a search engine can help you find it. No matter what search engine you choose, find out how it works, how it ranks results, and how deeply it indexes Web pages. Some search engines will retrieve more results than others simply because of the way the program gathers information from sites. As with databases, there are usually ways to refine a search and improve your results. Many search engines offer an advanced search option that may provide some useful options for refining and limiting a search.

It is important to know what will not be retrieved by a search engine. Because publishing and transmitting texts on the Web is relatively easy, it is becoming more common for libraries to subscribe to databases and electronic journals that are accessed through a Web browser. You may have *Britannica Online* and *Lexis/Nexis* as options on your library's home page. However, the contents of those subscriptions will be available only to your campus community and will not be searched by general Web search engines.

READING WITH A PURPOSE

When you begin studying your sources, read first to acquire general familiarity with your subject. Make sure that you are covering both sides of the question — in this case arguments both for and against the existence of zoos — as well as facts and opinions from a variety of sources. In investigating this subject, you will encounter data from biologists, ecologists, zoo directors, anthropologists, animal-rights activists, and ethical philosophers; their varied points of view will contribute to the strength of your claim.

As you read, look for what seem to be the major issues. They will probably be represented in all or most of your sources. For the claim about zoos the major issues may be summarized as follows: (1) the fundamental right wild animals have to liberty; (2) the harm done to animals who are denied this right and kept in captivity. On the other side, these issues will emerge: (1) the lack of concrete evidence that animals suffer or are harmed by being in zoos; (2) the benefits, in terms of entertainment, education, and conservation efforts that the public derives from zoos. The latter two, of course, are the issues you will have to refute. Your note taking should emphasize these important issues.

Record questions as they occur to you in your reading. Why do zoos exist? What are their major goals, and how well do they meet them? What happens to animals who are removed from the wild and placed in zoos? What happens to animals born and reared in captivity? How do these groups compare with their wild counterparts, who are free to live in their natural habitats? Do animals really have a right to liberty? What are the consequences of denying them this right? Are there consequences to humanity?

Evaluating Sources

The sources you find provide useful information that you need for your paper and help you support your claims. One key to supporting claims effectively is to make sure you have the best evidence available. It is tempting when searching a database or the Web to take the first sources that look good, print them or copy them, and not give them another thought until you are sitting down to compose your argument — only to discover that the sources aren't as valuable as they could be. Sources that looked pretty good at the beginning of your research may turn out to be less useful once you have learned more about the topic. And a source that seems interesting at first glance may turn out to be a rehash or digest of a much more valuable source, something you realize only when you sit down and look at it carefully.

To find the right stuff, be a critical thinker from the start of your research process. Scan and evaluate the references you encounter throughout your search. As you examine options in a database, choose sources that use relevant terms in their titles, seem directed to an appropriate audience, and are published in places that will look good in your Works Cited list. For example, a Senate Foreign Relations Committee report will be more impressive as a source than a comparable article in *Good Housekeeping.* An article from the scholarly journal *Foreign Affairs* will carry more clout than an article from *Reader's Digest,* even if they are on the same subject.

Skim and quickly evaluate each source that looks valuable.

- Is it relevant to your topic?
- Does it provide information you haven't found elsewhere?
- Can you learn anything about the author, and does what you learn inspire confidence?

As you begin to learn more about your topic and develop an outline, you can use sources to help direct your search. If a source mentions an organization, for example, you may use that clue to run a search on the Web for that organization's home page. If a newspaper story refers to a study published in a scientific journal, you may want to seek out that study to see the results of the research first-hand. And if you have a source that includes references to other publications, scan through them, and see which might also prove helpful to you. When you first started your research, chances are you weren't quite sure what you were looking for. Once you are familiar with your topic, you need to concentrate on finding sources that will best support the claims you want to make, and your increasing familiarity with the issue will make it easier to identify the best sources. That may mean a return trip to the library.

Once you have selected some useful sources to support your claims, make a more in-depth evaluation to be sure you have the best evidence available.

- Is it current enough? Have circumstances changed since this text was published?
- Is the author someone I want to call on as an expert witness? Does the author have the experience or credentials to make a solid argument that carries weight with my readers?
- Is it reliable information for my purposes? It may be highly opinionated, but are the basic facts it presents confirmed in other sources? Is the evidence presented in the text convincing?

These questions are not always easy to answer. In some cases, articles will include some information about the author, such as where he or she works. In other cases, no information or even an author's name is given. In that case, it may help to evaluate the publication and its reputation. If you aren't familiar with a publication and don't feel confident making your own judgment, see if it is described in Katz's *Magazines for Libraries,* which evaluates the reputation and quality of periodicals.

Web sites pose particular challenges. Look for some mention of when the site was last updated to help you determine currency. Look for a link to an author's personal home page, often found at the bottom of a Web page, or for information about a sponsoring agency to learn more about who created the page and why. It may be possible, even if there is not a clear link to this information, to erase part of the URL after the first slash to find out where the information is posted. For example, the URL for a site dealing with wiretapping in the digital age is <http://www.aclu.org/issues/cyber/wiretap _brother.html>. If you want to find out more about the sponsoring organization, erase the URL until only <http://www.aclu.org/> remains. There you will find the home page for the American Civil Liberties Union and an About the ACLU link where their mission is discussed.

Some clues are available in the URL of the page: A site that has *.gov* in its domain name is a U.S. federal site of some sort and bears the imprimatur of its sponsoring agency. Government-sponsored

Web sites are carefully edited for content. A site with *.edu* is based at a college or university but may not be of particular academic integrity since most colleges allow their students and staff to post material without restriction. A site with *.k12* is based in a school and is generally oriented to a young audience. If the URL includes *.org,* the site belongs to a nonprofit organization of some sort, and its contents probably reflect the concerns of that organization. A *.com* site is a commercial site, though it may not be dedicated to commercial activity; individuals that access the Internet through a commercial Internet service provider have *.com* in their site addresses. And sites outside the United States have URLs that end with a two-letter country abbreviation, such as *.uk* for United Kingdom.

Above all, read the information provided on a website with care. Judge it as you would any text. Does it make sense? Does it provide authoritative evidence for its claims? Can you confirm the information it presents in other sources? Is this the best source available for my purposes?

Taking Notes

While everyone has his or her own method for taking notes, here are a few suggestions that should be useful to any writer, including those working on a word processor.

Summarize instead of quoting long passages, unless you feel the quotation is more effective than anything you can write and can provide crucial support for your argument. Summarizing as you read can save you a great deal of time.

When you do quote, make sure to quote exactly. Copy the material word for word, leaving all punctuation exactly as it appears and inserting ellipsis points if you delete material. Make sure to enclose all quotations in quotation marks and to copy complete information about your source, including page numbers and publishing information as well as the author's name and the title of the book or article. If you quote an article that appears in an anthology or collection, make sure you record complete information about the book itself.

Record complete bibliographical information for each source *as you use it.* That way you will have all the information necessary to document your paper when you need it. Some people find it useful to keep two sets of note cards: one set for the bibliographical information and one set for the notes themselves. Each source appears on one card by itself, ready to be arranged in alphabetical order for the Works Cited or References page of the paper.

If you use a word processor, you can record information in any number of ways; the best may be to open a file for each source, enter the bibliographic information, and directly type into the file a series of potentially useful quotations, paraphrases, and summaries.

Note
Card
with
Quotation

> Hediger   25
>
> "The wild animal, with its marked tendency to escape, is notorious for the fact that it is never completely released from that all-important activity, avoiding enemies, even during sleep, but is constantly on the alert."

Note
Card
with
Summary

> Hediger   25
>
> Animals who live in the wild have to be on the watch for predators constantly.

For each entry, make sure to note the correct page reference as you go along, and indicate clearly whether you are quoting, paraphrasing, or summarizing. The material you record can then be readily integrated into your research paper by cutting and pasting from the source files, thus eliminating the need to retype and reducing the chance of error. Resist the temptation to record nothing but direct quotations; this will only postpone the inevitable work of summarizing, paraphrasing, and composing involved in thinking critically about your topic.

As you take notes, refer to your outline frequently to ensure that you are acquiring sufficient data to support all the points you intend to use. You will also be revising your outline during the course of your research, as issues are clarified and new ones emerge. Keeping close track of your outline will prevent you from recording material that is interesting but not relevant. If you aren't sure whether you will want to use a certain piece of information later, don't copy the whole passage. Instead, make a note for future reference so that you can find it again if you need it. Taking too many notes is, however, preferable to taking too few, a problem that will force you to go back

*Note
Card
with
Statistics*

> Reiger   32
>
> By end of decade, worldwide extinction rate will
> be one species per hour.
>
> Other statistics, too, in Reiger, "The Wages of
> Growth," <u>Field and Stream</u>, July 1981:32.

*Bibliography
Note
Card*

> Hediger, Heini. <u>The Psychology and Behavior</u>
> <u>of Animals in Zoos and Circuses</u>. Trans.
> Geoffrey Sircom. New York: Dover, 1968.

to the library for missing information. For the ideas and quotations in your notes, you should always take down enough information to enable you to find the references again as quickly as possible.

When researching your topic, you will find words and ideas put together by other people that you will want to use in your paper. Relying on the knowledge of others is an important part of doing research; expert opinions and eloquent arguments will help support your claims when your own expertise is limited. But remember, this is *your* paper. Your ideas and your insights into other people's ideas are just as important as the information you uncover at the library. Try to achieve a balance between solid information and original interpretation.

Quoting

You may want to quote passages or phrases from your sources if they express an idea in words more effective than your own. In this particular project, you might come across a statement that provides succinct, irrefutable evidence for an issue you wish to support. If the author of this statement is a professional in his or her field, someone with a great deal of authority on the subject, it would be appropriate to quote that author. Suppose, during the course of your research for the zoo paper, you find that many sources agree that zoos don't have the money or space necessary to maintain large enough animal populations to ensure successful captive breeding programs. But so far you only have opinions to that effect. You have been unable to find any concrete documentation of this fact until you come across Ulysses S. Seal's address to the National Zoological Park Symposia for the Public, September 1982. Here is how you could use Seal's words in your paper (using reference citation style of the American Psychological Association):

> Bear in mind that "none of these [zoo] budgets is allocated specifically for species preservation. Zoos have been established primarily as recreational institutions and are only secondarily developing programs in conservation, education and research" (Seal, 1982, p. 74).

Notice the use of brackets (not parentheses) in the first sentence, which enclose material that did not appear in the original source but is necessary for clarification. Brackets must be used to indicate any such changes in quoted material.

Quotations should be introduced logically and gracefully in your text. Make sure that the quoted material either supports or illustrates the point you have just made or the point you are about to make and that your writing remains grammatically correct once the quotation is introduced.

Quotations are an important tool for establishing your claims, but it is important not to overuse them. If you cannot say most of what you want to say in your own words, you probably haven't thought hard enough about what it is you want to say.

Paraphrasing

Paraphrasing involves restating the content of an original source in your own words. It is most useful when the material from your source is too long for your paper, can be made clearer to the reader by rephrasing, or is written in a style markedly different from your own.

A paraphrase should be as true to the original source as you can make it: Do not change the tone or the ideas, or even the order in which the ideas are presented. Take care not to allow your own opinions to creep into your paraphrase of someone else's argument.

Your readers should always be aware of which arguments belong to you and which belong to outside sources.

Like a quotation, a paraphrase must *always* include documentation, or you will be guilty of plagiarism. Even though you are using your own words, the ideas in a paraphrase belong to someone else, and that person deserves credit for them. One final caveat: When putting a long passage into your own words, beware of picking up certain expressions and turns of phrase from your source. If you do end up using your source's exact words, make sure to enclose them in quotation marks.

Below is a passage from Shannon Brownlee's "First It Was 'Save the Whales,' Now It's 'Free the Dolphins'" (*Discover*, December 1986, pp. 70–72), along with a good paraphrase of the passage and two unacceptable paraphrases.

ORIGINAL PASSAGE

But are we being good caretakers by holding a dolphin or a sea lion in a tank? Yes, if two conditions are met: that they're given the best treatment possible and, no less important, that they're displayed in a way that educates and informs us. Captive animals must be allowed to serve as ambassadors for their species (Brownlee, 1986, p. 72).

A PARAPHRASE THAT PLAGIARIZES

In "First It Was 'Save the Whales,' Now It's 'Free the Dolphins,'" Shannon Brownlee (1986) argues that it's all right for people to hold animals in captivity as long as (1) the animals are treated as well as possible, and (2) the animals are displayed in a way that educates the public. Brownlee insists that animals be allowed to serve as "ambassadors for their species" (p. 72).

A PARAPHRASE THAT ALTERS THE
MEANING OF THE ORIGINAL PASSAGE

According to Shannon Brownlee (1986), a captive animal is being treated fairly as long as it's kept alive and its captivity gives people pleasure. In her essay, "First It Was 'Save the Whales,' Now It's 'Free the Dolphins,'" she argues that people who keep animals in cages are responsible to the animals in only two ways: (1) they should treat their captives as well as possible (even if a small tank is all that can be provided), and (2) they should make sure that the spectators enjoy watching them (p. 72).

A GOOD PARAPHRASE

Shannon Brownlee (1986) holds that two criteria are necessary in order for the captivity of wild animals to be considered worthwhile.

First, the animals should be treated as well as possible. Second, their captivity should have educational value for the people who come to look at them. "Captive animals," Brownlee claims, "must be allowed to serve as ambassadors for their species" (p. 72).

Summarizing

A summary is like a paraphrase, but it involves shortening the original passage as well as putting it in your own words. It gives the gist of the passage. Summarizing is useful when the material from your source is too long for the purposes of your paper. As with a paraphrase, a summary should not alter the meaning of the original passage.

In the paper at the end of this chapter, for instance, the statement, "It is generally acknowledged that there is a great deal of difficulty involved in breeding zoo animals" is not a direct quotation, but the idea comes from Jon Luoma's article in *Audubon*. The statement in the paper is both a summary and a paraphrase. Returning to the source makes it clear that neither quoting nor paraphrasing would have been suitable choices in this instance, since for the writer's purposes it was possible to reduce the following passage from Luoma's article to one sentence.

> But the successful propagation of entire captive species poses awesome management problems. . . . Sanford Friedman, the Minnesota Zoo's director of biological programs, had explained to me that long-term maintenance of a species in captivity demands solutions to these fundamental problems. "First, we have to learn *how* to breed them. Second, we have to decide *who* to breed. And third, we have to figure out *what* to do with them and their offspring once we've bred them."

This passage is far too long to include in a brief research paper, but it is easily summarized without losing any of its effectiveness.

Avoiding Plagiarism

Plagiarism is the use of someone else's words or ideas without adequate acknowledgment — that is, presenting such words or ideas as your own. Putting something in your own words is not in itself a defense against plagiarism; the source of the ideas must be identified as well. Giving credit to the sources you use serves three important purposes: (1) it reflects your own honesty and seriousness as a researcher; (2) it enables the reader to find the source of the reference and read further, sometimes to verify that the source has been correctly used; and (3) it adds the authority of experts to your argument. Deliberate plagiarism is nothing less than cheating and theft, and it is an offense that deserves serious punishment. Accidental plagiarism can be avoided if you take a little care when researching and writing your papers.

The writer of the zoo paper, for instance, uses and correctly introduces the following direct quotation by James Rachels (para. 4):

> As James Rachels (1976) writes:
>
> Humans have a right to liberty because they have various other interests that will suffer if their freedom is unduly restricted. The right to liberty--the right to be free of external constraints on one's actions--may then be seen as derived from a more basic right not to have one's interests needlessly harmed. (p. 210)

If the writer of the zoo paper had chosen to state this idea more briefly, in her own words, the result might have been something like this: "Human beings believe in their fundamental right to liberty because they all agree that they would suffer without it. The right to liberty, then, stems from the right not to suffer unnecessarily." Although the wording has been significantly altered, if this statement appeared as is, undocumented, the author of the paper would be guilty of plagiarism because the ideas are not original. To avoid plagiarism, the author needs to include a reference to James Rachels at the beginning of the summary and a citation of the page number at the end. Taking care to document sources is an obvious way to avoid plagiarism. You should also be careful in taking notes and, when writing your paper, indicating where your ideas end and someone else's ideas begin.

When taking notes, make sure either to quote word-for-word *or* to paraphrase: one or the other, not a little bit of both. If you quote, enclose any language that you borrow from other sources in quotation marks. That way, when you look back at your note cards weeks later, you won't mistakenly assume that the language is your own. If you know that you aren't going to use a particular writer's exact words in your paper, then take the time to summarize that person's ideas right away. That will save you time and trouble later.

When using someone else's ideas in your paper, always let the reader know where that person's ideas begin and end. Here is an example from the zoo paper (para. 10):

> When zoo animals do mate successfully, the offspring is often weakened by inbreeding. According to geneticists, this is because a population of 150 breeder animals is necessary in order to "assure the more or less permanent survival of a species in captivity" (Ehrlich & Ehrlich, 1981, p. 211).

The phrase "according to geneticists" indicates that the material to follow comes from another source, cited parenthetically at the end of the borrowed material. If the student had not included the phrase "according to geneticists," it might look as if she only borrowed the passage in quotation marks, and not the information that precedes that passage.

Material that is considered common knowledge — that is, familiar or at least accessible to the general public — does not have to be documented. The author of *Hamlet,* the date the Declaration of Independence was signed, or the definition of *misfeasance,* while open to dispute (some scholars, for example, claim that William Shakespeare did not write *Hamlet*) are indisputably considered to be common knowledge in our culture. Unfortunately, it is not always clear whether a particular fact *is* common knowledge. Although too much documentation can clutter a paper and distract the reader, it's still better to cite too many sources than to cite too few and risk being accused of dishonesty. In general, if you are unsure whether or not to give your source credit, you should document the material.

Keeping Research under Control

Your preliminary outline provides guideposts for your research. You will need to revise it as you go along to make room for new ideas and evidence and for the questions that come up as you read. Rather than try to fit each new piece of information into your outline, you can use the numbering or lettering system in your outline to cross-reference your notebooks or file cards.

As much as possible, keep all materials related to the same point in the same place. You might do this by making a separate pile of file cards for each point and its support and questions or by reserving several pages in your notebook for information bearing on each point.

How do you know when you have done enough research? If you have kept your outline updated, you have a visual record of your progress. Check this against the guidelines on pages 358–59. Is each point backed by at least two pieces of support? Do your sources represent a range of authors and of types of data? If a large proportion of your support comes from one book, or if most of your references are to newspaper articles, you probably need to keep working. On the other hand, if your notes cite five different authorities making essentially the same point, you may have collected more data than you need. It can be useful to point out that more than one authority holds a given view and to make notes of examples that are notably different from one another. But it is not necessary to take down all the passages or examples expressing the same idea.

To This Point

Before you leave the library or your primary sources for your typewriter, check to make sure your research is complete.

1. Does your working outline show any gaps in your argument?
2. Have you found adequate data to support your claim?
3. Have you identified the warrants linking your claim with data and ensured that these warrants too are adequately documented?
4. If you intend to quote or paraphrase sources in your paper, do your notes include exact copies of all statements you may want to use and complete references?
5. Have you answered all the relevant questions that have come up during your research?
6. Do you have enough information about your sources to document your paper?

COMPILING AN ANNOTATED BIBLIOGRAPHY

An annotated bibliography is a list of sources that includes the usual bibliographic information followed by a paragraph describing and evaluating each source. Its purpose is to provide information about each source in a bibliography so that the reader has an overview of the resources related to a given topic.

For each source in an annotated bibliography, the same bibliographic information included in a Works Cited or References list is provided, alphabetized by author. Each reference also has a short paragraph that describes the work, its main focus, and, if appropriate, the methodology used in or the style of the work. An annotation might note special features such as tables or illustrations. Usually an annotation evaluates the source by analyzing its usefulness, reliability, and overall significance for understanding the topic. An annotation might include some information on the credentials of the author or the organization that produced it.

A SAMPLE ANNOTATION USING THE MLA CITATION STYLE

Warner, Marina. "Pity the Stepmother." New York Times. 12 May
    1991, late ed.: D17. Lexis/Nexis Universe 12 Dec. 1998
    <http://web.lexis-nexis.com/universe/form/academic/
    univ_gennews.html>.

The author asserts that many fairy tales feature absent or cruel mothers, transformed by romantic editors such as the Grimm brothers into stepmothers because the idea of a wicked mother desecrated an ideal. She argues that figures in fairy tales should be viewed in their historical context and that social conditions often affected the way that motherhood figured in fairy tales. Warner, a novelist and author of books on the images of Joan of Arc and the Virgin Mary, writes persuasively about the social roots of a fairy-tale archetype.

A SAMPLE ANNOTATION USING THE APA CITATION STYLE

"Don't Zoos Contribute to the Saving of Species from Extinction?" Animal Rights Resource Site. Envirolink Network. 14 Dec. 1998 <http://arrs.envirolink.org/Faqs+Ref/ar-faq/Q68.html>.

This website provides arguments against the idea that zoos save species from extinction. Breeding in captivity doesn't always work, and the limited gene pool creates problems. Habitat restoration is difficult, and until the problems of poaching and pollution are solved, the habitat will be dangerous for reintroduced species. Meanwhile, the individual animals living in zoos lose their freedom because of an abstract and possibly faulty concept. This website, part of the Animal Rights Resource Site sponsored by the Envirolink organization, is brief but outlines the major arguments against zoos' role in preserving species.

MLA SYSTEM FOR CITING PUBLICATIONS

One of the simplest methods of crediting sources is the Modern Language Association (MLA) in-text system, which is used in the research paper on fairy tales in this chapter. In the text of your paper, immediately after any quotation, paraphrase, or anything else you wish to document, simply insert a parenthetical mention of the author's last name and the page number on which the material appeared. You don't need a comma after the author's name or an abbreviation of the word "page" or "p." For example, the following sentence appears in the fairy tale paper (para. 8):

Famines in the seventeenth century often reduced the peasantry to a diet of "bad black bread, acorns, and roots" (Weber 96).

The parenthetical reference tells the reader that the information in this sentence came from page 96 of the book or article by Eugen Weber that appears in the Works Cited, at the end of the paper. The complete reference on the Works Cited page provides all the information readers need to locate the original source in the library:

Weber, Eugen. "Fairies and Hard Facts: The Reality of Folktales."
Journal of the History of Ideas 42 (1981): 93-113.

If the author's name is mentioned in the same sentence, it is also acceptable to place only the page numbers in parentheses; it is not necessary to repeat the author's name. For example (para. 24):

Bettelheim sees symbolic meaning in every motif and element in the story, and assumes that children interpret these symbolically as well (159-66).

Some sources do not name an author. To cite a work with an unknown author, give the title, or a recognizable shortened form, in the text of your paper. If the work does not have numbered pages, often the case in Web pages or nonprint sources, do not include page numbers. For example:

In some cases Sephardic Jews, "converted" under duress, practiced Christianity openly and Judaism in secret until recently ("Search for the Buried Past").

The list of works cited includes all material you have used to write your research paper. This list appears at the end of your paper and always starts on a new page. Center the title Works Cited, double-space between the title and the first entry, and begin your list, which should be arranged alphabetically by author. Each entry should start at the left margin; indent all subsequent lines of the entry five spaces. Number each page, and double-space throughout.

Another method of documenting sources is to use notes, either footnotes (at the foot of the page) or endnotes (on a separate page at the end of the paper). The note method is not as commonly used today as the in-text system because reference notes repeat almost all the information already given on the Works Cited page. If footnotes or endnotes are used, most word processing programs have functions that make the insertion of these notes convenient.

Nevertheless, it is a valid method, so we illustrate it here. Superscript numbers go at the end of the sentence or phrase being referenced:

Roman authors admit to borrowing frequently from earlier Greek writers for their jokes, although no joke books in the original Greek survive today.[1]

The reference note for this citation would be:

[1]Alexander Humez and Nicholas Humez, Alpha to Omega (Boston: Godine, 1981) 79.

On the Works Cited page this reference would be:

Humez, Alexander, and Nicholas Humez. Alpha to Omega. Boston: Godine, 1981.

Notice that the page number for a book citation is given in the note but not the reference and that the punctuation differs. Otherwise the information is the same. Number the notes consecutively throughout your paper.

One more point: *Content notes,* which provide additional information not readily worked into a research paper, are also indicated by superscript numbers. Susan Middleton's paper on fairy tales features four such notes, included on a Notes page before the list of Works Cited.

Following are examples of the citation forms you are most likely to need as you document your research. In general, for both books and magazines, information should appear in the following order: author, title, and publication information. Each item should be followed by a period. When using as a source an essay that appears in this book, follow the citation model for "Material reprinted from another source," unless your instructor indicates otherwise. Consult the *MLA Handbook for Writers of Research Papers,* Fifth Edition, by Joseph Gibaldi (New York: Modern Language Association of America, 1999) for other documentation models and a list of acceptable shortened forms of publishers.

A BOOK BY A SINGLE AUTHOR

Gubar, Susan. Racechanges: White Skin, Black Face in American Culture. New York: Oxford UP, 1997.

AN ANTHOLOGY OR COMPILATION

Dark, Larry, ed. Prize Stories 1997: The O. Henry Awards. New York: Anchor, 1997.

A BOOK BY TWO AUTHORS

Alderman, Ellen, and Caroline Kennedy. The Right to Privacy. New York: Vintage, 1995.

Note: This form is followed even for two authors with the same last name.

Ehrlich, Paul, and Anne Ehrlich. Extinction: The Causes and
Consequences of the Disappearance of Species. New York:
Random, 1981.

A BOOK BY TWO OR MORE AUTHORS

Heffernan, William A., Mark Johnston, and Frank Hodgins. Literature:
Art and Artifact. San Diego: Harcourt, 1987.

If there are more than three authors, name only the first and add:
"et al." (and others).

A BOOK BY A CORPORATE AUTHOR

Poets & Writers, Inc. The Writing Business: A Poets & Writers
Handbook. New York: Poets & Writers, 1985.

A WORK IN AN ANTHOLOGY

Head, Bessie. "Woman from America." Wild Women: Contemporary
Short Stories by Women Celebrating Women. Ed. Sue Thomas.
Woodstock: Overlook, 1994. 45-51.

AN INTRODUCTION, PREFACE, FOREWORD, OR AFTERWORD

Callahan, John F. Introduction. Flying Home and Other Stories. By
Ralph Ellison. Ed. John F. Callahan. New York: Vintage, 1996.

MATERIAL REPRINTED FROM ANOTHER SOURCE

Hutchinson, Earl Ofari. "The Fallacy of Talkin' Black." The Crisis in
Black and Black. Los Angeles: Middle Passage, 1998. Rpt. in
Elements of Argument: A Text and Reader. Annette T. Rottenberg.
6th ed. Boston: Bedford/St. Martin's, 2000. 276.

A MULTIVOLUME WORK

Skotheim, Robert Allen, and Michael McGiffert, eds. Since the Civil
War. Vol. 2 of American Social Thought: Sources and
Interpretations. 2 vols. Reading: Addison, 1972.

AN EDITION OTHER THAN THE FIRST

Charters, Ann, ed. The Story and Its Writer: An Introduction to Short
Fiction, 5th ed. Boston: Bedford/St. Martin's, 1999.

A TRANSLATION

Allende, Isabel. The House of the Spirits. Trans. Magda Bogin. New
York: Knopf, 1985.

A REPUBLISHED BOOK

Weesner, Theodore. The Car Thief. 1972. New York: Vintage-Random,
1987.

Note: The only information about original publication you need to provide is the publication date, which appears immediately after the title.

A BOOK IN A SERIES

Eady, Cornelius. Victims of the Latest Dance Craze. Omnation Press Dialogues on Dance Series 5. Chicago: Omnation, 1985.

AN ARTICLE FROM A DAILY NEWSPAPER

Doctorow, E. L. "Quick Cuts: The Novel Follows Film into a World of
Fewer Words." New York Times 15 Mar. 1999, sec. B: 1+.

AN ARTICLE FROM A PERIODICAL

Schulhofer, Stephen. "Unwanted Sex." Atlantic Monthly Oct. 1998:
55-66.

AN UNSIGNED EDITORIAL

"Medium, Message." Editorial. Nation 28 Mar. 1987: 383-84.

ANONYMOUS WORKS

"The March Almanac." Atlantic Mar. 1995: 20.
Citation World Atlas. Maplewood: Hammond, 1987.

**AN ARTICLE FROM A JOURNAL WITH SEPARATE
PAGINATION FOR EACH ISSUE**

Brewer, Derek. "The Battleground of Home: Versions of Fairy Tales."
Encounter 54.4 (1980): 52-61.

**AN ARTICLE IN A JOURNAL WITH CONTINUOUS
PAGINATION THROUGHOUT THE VOLUME**

McCafferty, Janey. "The Shadders Go Away." New England Review and
Bread Loaf Quarterly 9 (1987): 332-42.

Note that the issue number is not mentioned here; because the volume has continuous pagination throughout the year, only the volume number 9 is needed.

A REVIEW

Walker, David. Rev. of A Wave, by John Ashbery. Field 32 (1985):
63-71.

AN INTERVIEW

Hines, Gregory. Interview. With D. C. Denison. Boston Globe Magazine
29 Mar. 1987: 2.

Note: An interview conducted by the author of the paper would be documented as follows:

Hines, Gregory. Personal interview. 29 Mar. 1987.

AN ARTICLE IN A REFERENCE WORK

"Bylina." The Princeton Encyclopedia of Poetry and Poetics. Ed. Alex
Preminger. Enlarged ed. Princeton: Princeton UP, 1974.

A GOVERNMENT DOCUMENT

United States. National Endowment for the Arts. 1989 Annual Report.
Washington: Office of Public Affairs, 1990.

Frequently the Government Printing Office (GPO) is the publisher of federal government documents.

REPORTS

Gura, Mark. The Gorgeous Mosaic Project: A Work of Art by the Schoolchildren of the World. Teacher's packet. East Brunswick:
Children's Atelier, 1990. ERIC ED 347 257.

Kassebaum, Peter. Cultural Awareness Training Manual and Study
Guide. ERIC, 1992. ED 347 289.

The ERIC number at the end of the entry indicates that this source is available through ERIC (Educational Resource Information Center); some libraries have these available on microfiche. The number indicates which report to look for. Some ERIC documents were published elsewhere, as in the first example. If no other publishing information is given, treat ERIC (with no city given) as the publisher, as shown in the second entry. Reports are also published by NTIS (National Technical Information Service), state geological surveys, organizations, institutes within universities, and so on and may be called "technical reports," or "occasional papers." Be sure to include the source and the unique report number, if given.

COMPUTER SOFTWARE

XyQuest. XyWrite. Vers. III Plus. Computer Software. XyQuest, 1988.
PC-DOS 2.0, 384KB, disk.

Note here that the version is given in roman numerals, since it appears that way in the title; usually software versions are given in decimals (e.g., Vers. 2.1).

MATERIAL ACCESSED THROUGH A COMPUTER SERVICE

Boynton, Robert S. "The New Intellectuals." Atlantic Monthly Mar. 1995. Atlantic Unbound. America Online. 3 Mar. 1995. Keyword: Atlantic.

A CD-ROM

Corcoran, Mary B. "Fairy Tale." Grolier Multimedia Encyclopedia. CD-ROM. Danbury: Grolier, 1995.

AN UNPUBLISHED MANUSCRIPT

Leahy, Ellen. "An Investigation of the Computerization of Information Systems in a Family Planning Program." Unpublished master's degree project. Div. of Public Health, U of Massachusetts, Amherst, 1990.

A LETTER TO THE EDITOR

Flannery, James W. Letter. New York Times Book Review 28 Feb. 1993: 34.

PERSONAL CORRESPONDENCE

Bennett, David. Letter to the author. 3 Mar. 1993.

A LECTURE

Calvino, Italo. "Right and Wrong Political Uses of Literature." Symposium on European Politics. Amherst College, Amherst. 25 Feb. 1976.

A FILM

The Voice of the Khalam. Prod. Loretta Pauker. With Leopold Senghor, Okara, Birago Diop, Rubadiri, and Francis Parkes. Contemporary Films/McGraw-Hill, 1971. 16 mm, 29 min.

Other pertinent information to give in film references, if available, is the writer and director (see model for radio/television program for style).

A TELEVISION OR RADIO PROGRAM

The Shakers: Hands to Work, Hearts to God. Narr. David McCullough. Dir. Ken Burns and Amy Stechler Burns. Writ. Amy Stechler

Burns, Wendy Tilghman, and Tom Lewis. PBS. WGBY, Springfield. 28 Dec. 1992.

A VIDEOTAPE

Style Wars! Videotape. Prod. Tony Silver and Henry Chalfont. New Day Films, 1985. 69 min.

A PERFORMANCE

Quilters: A Musical Celebration. By Molly Newman and Barbara Damashek. Dir. Joyce Devlin. Musical dir. Faith Fung. Mt. Holyoke Laboratory Theatre, South Hadley, MA. 26 Apr. 1991. Based on The Quilters: Women and Domestic Art by Patricia Cooper and Norma Bradley Allen.

A CARTOON

Henley, Marian. "Maxine." Cartoon. Valley Advocate 25 Feb. 1993: 39.

A WEBSITE

Fairy Tales: Origins and Evolution. Ed. Christine Daaé. 12 Dec. 1998 <http://www.darkgoddess.com/fairy/>.

Include the title if available; the author's name if available or, if not, a generic description such as "Home page"; the sponsoring organization or institution except in the case of commercial sponsorship; date of access; and URL in angle brackets.

A PAGE WITHIN A WEBSITE

"Don't Zoos Contribute to the Saving of Species from Extinction?" Animal Rights Resource Site. Envirolink Network. 14 Dec. 1998 <http://arrs.envirolink.org/faqs+Ref/ar-faq/Q68.html>.

A BOOK AVAILABLE ON THE WEB

Kramer, Heinrich, and James Sprenger. The Malleus Maleficarum. Trans. Montague Summers. New York: Dover, 1971. 14 Dec. 1998 <http://www.geocities.com/Athens/2962/witchcraze/malleus_2_ii_html>.

In this case the book had been previously published, and information about its original publication was included at the site.

AN ARTICLE FROM AN ELECTRONIC JOURNAL

Minow, Mary. "Filters and the Public Library: A Legal and Policy Analysis." First Monday 2.12 (1 Dec. 1997). 28 Nov. 1998 <http:www.firstmonday.dk/issues/issue2_12/minow/index.html>.

AN ARTICLE FROM A FULL-TEXT DATABASE AVAILABLE
THROUGH THE WEB

Warner, Marina. "Pity the Stepmother." New York Times. 12 May
    1991, late ed.: D17. Lexis/Nexis Universe 12 Dec. 1998.
    <http://web.lexis-nexis.com/universe/form/academic/
    univ_gennews.html>.

Include the original source information and the name of the database, access date, and URL.

AN ARTICLE FROM A CD-ROM FULL-TEXT DATABASE

"Tribal/DNC Donations." News from Indian Country. (Dec. 1997).
    Ethnic Newswatch. CD-ROM. Softline. 12 Oct. 1998.

Include the original source information and the name of the database, the designation *CD-ROM,* the publisher of the CD-ROM, and the electronic publication data, if available.

AN ARTICLE FROM AN ELECTRONIC REFERENCE WORK

"Folk Arts." Britannica Online. Encyclopaedia Britannica. 14 Dec.
    1998. <http://www.eb.com:180/>.

A PERSONAL E-MAIL COMMUNICATION

Franz, Kenneth. "Re: Species Reintroduction." E-mail to the author.
    12 Oct. 1998.

AN E-MAIL COMMUNICATION POSTED TO A DISCUSSION LIST

Lee, Constance. "Re: Mothers and Stepmothers." Online posting.
    10 Sept. 1998. Folklore Discussion List <mglazer@panam.edu>.

If the address of the discussion list archives is known, include that information in angle brackets; if not, place the moderator's e-mail address in angle brackets.

A POSTING TO A WEB FORUM

DeYoung, Chris. Online posting. 12 Dec. 1998. Issues: Gay Rights. 14
    Dec. 1998 <http://community.cnn.com/cgi-bin/WebX?14@52
    .7bmLaPoSc49^0@.ee7239c/12479>.

Include the author, header (if any) in quotation marks, the designation *Online posting,* the date of the posting, the name of the forum, the date of access, and the URL.

A NEWSGROUP POSTING

Vining, Philip. "Zoos and Infotainment." Online posting. 16 Oct. 1998.
    12 Dec. 1998. <news: alt.animals.ethics.vegetarian>.

Include the author, header in quotation marks, the designation *Online posting,* the date of posting, the date of access, and the name of the newsgroup.

A SYNCHRONOUS COMMUNICATION

Krishnamurthi, Ashok. Online discussion of cyberlaw and the media. "Reinventing Copyright in a Digital Environment." 25 Oct. 1998. MediaMOO. 25 Oct. 1998 <telnet://purple-crayon.media .mit.edu:8888/>.

To cite a synchronous communication from a MUD or a MOO, include the name of the speaker, a description of the event, the date, the forum, the date of access, and the electronic address.

SAMPLE RESEARCH PAPER (MLA STYLE)

The following paper, prepared in the MLA style, was written for an advanced composition course. Told to compose a research paper on a literary topic, Susan Middleton chose to write on fairy tales — a subject literary enough to satisfy her instructor, yet general enough to encompass her own interest in developmental psychology. But as she explored the subject, she found herself reading in a surprising array of disciplines, including folklore, anthropology, and history. Although she initially expected to report on the psychological importance of fairy tales, Middleton at last wrote an argument about the importance of their historical and cultural roots. Her paper, as is typical for literary papers, anchors its argument in the events and details of its chosen text, "Hansel and Gretel." But it also makes effective use of sources to help readers understand that there is more to the tale than a story that sends children happily off to sleep.

When a Fairy Tale Is Not Just a Fairy Tale

By

Susan Middleton

Professor Herrington

English 2A

May 1999

Include a title page if an outline is part of the paper. If no outline is required, include name, instructor's name, course name, and date at the upper left corner of page 1.

Writer's name; page number

Topic outline. Some instructors require a thesis statement under "Outline" heading and before the outline itself.

Outline

I. Introduction:

   A. Dictionary definition of "fairy tale"

   B. Thesis: "Hansel and Gretel" has historical roots

II. Origin and distribution of tale

III. Historical basis of motifs

   A. Physical and economic hardship

      1. Fear of the forest

      2. Poverty and starvation

      3. Child abandonment

      4. Fantasies of finding treasure

   B. Cruel stepmother

   C. Wicked witch

      1. Eating meat associated with cannibalism and upper classes

      2. Elderly caretaker for unwanted children

      3. Witches in community

      4. Witchcraft as remnant of ancient fertility religion

IV. Rebuttals to historical approach

   A. Motivation for telling realistic tales

   B. Psychological interpretations

      1. Fairy tales dreamlike, not literal

      2. Freudian interpretation

V. Conclusion

Middleton 1

When a Fairy Tale Is Not Just a Fairy Tale

"Hansel and Gretel" is a well-known fairy tale, beloved of many children in both Europe and North America.[1] Although it has no fairies in it, it conforms to the definition of "fairy tale" given in Merriam-Webster's Collegiate Dictionary, Tenth Edition: "a story (as for children) involving fantastic forces and beings (as fairies, wizards, and goblins)." As anyone familiar with this tale will remember, Hansel and Gretel are two children on an adventure in the woods, where they encounter a wicked witch in a gingerbread house, who plans to fatten and eat them. Through their ingenuity they outsmart her, burn her up in her own oven, and return home triumphantly with a hoard of riches found in her house.

We think of fairy tales as being lighthearted fantasies that entertain but don't have much relevance to daily life. We often borrow the word to describe a movie with an unlikely plot, or a person not quite grounded in reality: "Oh, he's living in a fairy tale world; he hasn't got his head on his shoulders." In fact, the second definition of "fairy tale" in Webster's is "a made-up story usually designed to mislead."

So what is the meaning of "Hansel and Gretel"? Is it simply a story of make-believe, or something more? Fairy tales are told, read, and heard in the context of a time and place. Today we are exposed to them through illustrated storybooks, cartoons, and film. But in Europe, before technologies in printing made mass publishing possible, folktales were passed on orally. Women were the primary tellers of folktales, though they were later gathered and published by male writers such as Charles Perrault and the Grimm Brothers ("Tales"). They were told by adults mostly for adult audiences, although people often first heard them as children. They served to entertain and to relieve the boredom of repetitive work in the fields during the day and in the home in the evening (Weber 93, 113). In peasant and aboriginal communities, that is often still the case (Taggart 437).

I believe that "Hansel and Gretel" has historical meaning. Embedded in this simple narrative is a record of the

---

Side annotations:

Title centered

Raised, super-script number refers to notes giving information at the end of the paper.

Writer briefly summarizes tale to orient readers.

In-text citation of author and pages; citation appears at the end of the sentence before the period.

Thesis with claim of fact that the writer must support

experiences and events once common in the lives of the people who first told and listened to it.

Where did "Hansel and Gretel" come from? We do not know for certain. In oral form this tale shows wide distribution. Different versions have been recorded all over Europe, India, Japan, Africa, the Caribbean, Pacific Islands, and among native North and South Americans ("Hansel and Gretel"). As with all folktales, there is no agreement among folklorists[2] about whether all these versions migrated from one place to another, sprang up independently, or derive from some combination of the two ("Hansel and Gretel"). Most oral versions of it have been recorded in Europe (Aarne 117). This does not prove that the tale originated there--it may simply reflect the eagerness of people in Europe during the nineteenth and twentieth centuries to record their own folk history--but it is the best guideline for now.

The tale may be very ancient, since folktales can be passed on faithfully from one generation to another without change. (The origins of "Cinderella," for example, can be traced back to China in the ninth century [Thompson, Folktale 126].) But we can't know that for sure. So, even though "Hansel and Gretel" may have originated hundreds or even thousands of years ago, it probably is only safe to compare a tale with the historical period when the tale was first recorded. For "Hansel and Gretel" this means Europe in the seventeenth to nineteenth centuries.[3]

Eugen Weber is one historian who sees direct parallels between the characters and motifs in "Hansel and Gretel" (and other Grimms' fairy tales) and the social and economic conditions in Europe during this period. One of the central themes in the tale is poverty and abandonment. Recall how the tale begins: Hansel and Gretel live with their parents near a huge forest; their father is a woodcutter. The family is facing starvation because there is a famine. Twice their parents abandon them in the woods to save themselves. The first time the children are able to find their way home, but the second time they get lost.

Reference to dictionary article — page number not necessary

Square brackets used to represent parentheses within parentheses

Specific support from the tale cited

Middleton   3

As Weber points out, until the middle of the
nineteenth century, the forest, especially for northern
Europeans, carried the real potential for encountering
danger in the form of robbers, wild animals, and getting
lost (96-97). Moreover, conditions of poverty, starvation,
early death, and danger from unknown adults were
common throughout Europe for peasants and the working
class (96). The majority of Europeans at the beginning of
the eighteenth century were farmers, and the average life
expectancy was about twenty-five years (Treasure 660,
667). Famines in the seventeenth century often reduced
the peasantry to a diet of "bad black bread, acorns, and
roots" (Weber 96). Hansel and Gretel are treated by the
witch to a dinner of pancakes and sugar, milk, nuts, and
apples (101). This may not sound particularly nourishing
to our ears because we assume a healthy dinner must have
vegetables and/or meat. But when you're starving,
anything is likely to taste good; this would have been a
sumptuous meal for Hansel and Gretel.

Childhood was thought of differently then than today.
"Valued as an extra pair of hands or deplored as an extra
mouth to feed, the child belonged to no privileged realm of
play and protection from life's responsibilities" (Treasure
664). Social historian John Boswell estimates that anywhere
from 10 to 40 percent of children in towns and cities were
abandoned during the eighteenth century. Parental
motivation included removing the stigma of illegitimate or
physically deformed children, being unable to support their
children and hoping to give them a better life with strangers,
desiring to promote one child's inheritance over another's,
or simply lacking interest in raising the child (48, 428).

Weber points out that peasants had very little cash
and didn't use banks. Hiding and finding treasure--gold,
silver, and jewelry--was a much more common occurrence
two centuries ago than it is today (101), a kind of lottery
for the poor. In this light, the riches the children find in
the witch's house could reflect the common person's
fantasy of striking it rich.

Consecutive references immediately following an identified source ("Weber") cite only the pages within the source without repeating the source.

Narrative details linked to historical facts

Source cited after direct quotation

Writer's interpretation of one aspect of the story

Middleton   4

A central motif in the story is the stepmother who
wants to abandon the children to keep herself and her
husband from starving. (The father, at first reluctant,
eventually gives in to his wife's plan.) As Weber and others
have noted, stepmothers were not unusual in history. The
death rate among childbearing women was much higher in
past centuries than it is today. When women died in
childbirth, there was strong economic motivation for
fathers to remarry. In the seventeenth and eighteenth
centuries, 20 to 80 percent of widowers remarried within
the year of their wife's death. By the mid-nineteenth
century, after life expectancy rose, only 15 percent of
widowers did so (94, 112).

What accounts for the stereotype of the heartless
stepmother? Warner argues that mothers, not stepmothers,
actually appeared in many of the tales in their original forms,
until romantic editors, like the Grimm brothers, "rebelled
against this desecration of motherhood and changed mothers
into wicked stepmothers" (D17). Weber suggests that
stepmothers were assigned the role of doing evil to children for
economic reasons: The family would risk losing its good name
and perhaps its land if a biological parent killed a child (107).
There is also the issue of inheritance from the stepmother's
point of view: If her husband dies, her husband's children, not
she, would inherit the land and property. Literary and legal
evidence of stepmothers plotting to eliminate stepchildren,
especially stepsons, shows up in European literature as far
back as two millennia ago (Boswell 128).

Another major theme in "Hansel and Gretel" is the
wicked witch, which also shows up in lots of other fairy
tales. One of the common beliefs about witches was that
they ate children. According to the words of a purported
witch in the <u>Malleus Maleficarum</u>, a treatise on witchcraft
published originally around 1486, "[we] cook them in a
cauldron until the whole flesh comes away from the bones
to make a soup that may be easily drunk" (Kramer and
Sprenger, ch. 2, para. 12). The authors of this work were
alarmists, describing in sometimes improbable terms the

Reference to a
newspaper

Transition to new
topic: witches

evil behavior of witches, but the question remains: Were there witches in European history, and if so, where did the reputation for eating children come from?

Weber notes that in fairy tales only evil figures eat meat of any kind, whether animal or human flesh. Before the middle of the nineteenth century the peasantry rarely ate meat, but the aristocracy and bourgeoisie did. This discrepancy may be the origin of the motif in some fairy tales of evil figures of upper-class background wanting to eat children (112, 101). Weber seems to imply that child-eating witches symbolized to the peasantry either resentment of or paranoia about the aristocracy.

Although the witch's cottage in "Hansel and Gretel" is not described as grand or large, there are other allusions to wealth and comfort. The witch puts the two children to bed between clean sheets, a luxury for much of the peasantry, who slept on straw and for whom bed lice were a common reality (Treasure 661-62). And of course there is the hoard of coin money and jewelry the children later discover there. Perhaps more significantly, the witch herself has a lot of power, just as the aristocracy was perceived to have, including the power to deceive and take away life.

David Bakan suggests that the historical basis for the witch is the unmarried elderly woman in the community who took in unwanted, illegitimate children and was often paid to do this (66-67). There is also evidence that witchcraft, ranging from white magic to sorcery (black magic), was practiced by both individual women and men among the peasantry during this time. For example, "the 'cunning folk' were at least as numerous in sixteenth-century England as the parish clergy. Moreover, in their divinatory, medical, and religious functions they were far more important in peasant society than were the official clergy" (Horsley 697). Witches were called on to influence the weather, provide love potions, find lost objects, midwife, identify thieves, and heal illnesses (698). Some services performed by witches were ambiguous: "Apparently some peasants would conjure the storms or weather

Middleton   6

spirits to avoid striking their own fields--but to strike someone else's instead," but for the most part the wisewomen
and sorcerers were different people (698).

The idea that an organized witch cult, as portrayed by
the Catholic Church during the Middle Ages, actually
existed is dismissed today by most social historians. Jesse
Nash thinks we should reconsider the possibility that some
of the behavior witches were accused of, including ritual
cannibalism and sexual orgies in the woods, actually
occurred in some form (12). He sees witchcraft as "a
surviving remnant of a religion which was concerned with
the fertility of crops, animals, humans, and with the
alteration of seasons and with the identification of humans
with animals" (13). These practices date back to a matriar-
chal goddess religion which flourished in Europe 5,000 to
7,000 years ago, before invasion of the patriarchal cultures

Source within a source cited

from India (Marija Gimbutas in Nash 12). This religion
included human sacrifice and was based on the concept of
maintaining balance in the universe: The goddess of life
was at the same time the goddess of death. Wood-wives and
fairies, who lived in the forest, "were mediators of sacred
knowledge to their communities" (16).

Nash suggests that in Europe, although Christianity
became the official way of thinking about the world, it did
not replace the old beliefs entirely, despite strong attempts
by the Church to eliminate them. Religious beliefs and practices can persist hidden for generations if need be.[4] The
peasants were able to live with and practice both Christianity and paganism in combination for centuries (25).

So we have seen there is validity to the claim that many
of the motifs of "Hansel and Gretel" have historical roots.

Having supported her major claim, the writer contin- ues by anticipat- ing and address- ing possible rebuttals.

However, one might well ask why people would want to hear
stories so close to their own experiences. If oral tales during
this time were meant as entertainment mostly for adults,
wouldn't they want something to take their minds off their
troubles? Weber suggests a couple of motivations for telling
fairy tales. One was to experience "the delights of fear" (97).
Fairy tales were told along with ghost stories, gossip, jokes,

and fables. I suspect it was similar to the thrill some people get today watching scary movies with happy endings.

Second, fairy tales helped to explain how the world worked. To most people not able to read, the world of cause and effect was mysterious and could only be explained through symbolism and analogy. Folktales had been used in church sermons since the fourteenth century (Weber 110, Zipes 22). Two sources cited at once

But the industrial age ushered in the scientific revolution, and with it came the concept of explaining the unknown by breaking it down into working parts (Weber 113). Reading became available to large numbers of people. By this time fairy tales were no longer meaningful ways to explain the world for ordinary adults, so they became the province of children's entertainment (113).

Folklorist Alan Dundes thinks it is naive to assume fairy tales have literal meaning. In recent years he and a number of other people have looked to psychology to explain the origin of fairy tales. "Fairy tales are like dreams--can you find the historic origin of dreams?" (Dundes). In their structure and characters fairy tales do have a number of dreamlike aspects: They rarely state the feelings of the hero directly, and all inner experiences of the hero are projected outward into objects in nature and other people (Tatar 91). The other characters seem not to have separate lives of their own; all their actions and intentions relate to the hero (Brewer 55). Also, magical things happen: Elements of nature speak, granting favors to the hero or threatening success or even life. In one version of "Hansel and Gretel," for example, a white duck talks to the children and carries them across a lake on their way home.

Competing theories presented

Telephone interview — no page numbers

The symbolic nature of fairy tales, however, doesn't deny the validity of examining them for historical origins. As anyone who has recorded their own dreams knows, people and objects from mundane, daily life show up regularly in them. Sometimes these elements are disguised as symbols, but other times they are transparently realistic. Similarly, the talking duck and the gingerbread house in "Hansel and Gretel" may be unreal, but other themes have more literal counterparts in history.

Middleton   8

One of the most quoted interpreters of fairy tales is psychologist Bruno Bettelheim, whose The Uses of Enchantment analyzes fairy tales in Freudian terms. In his view, "Hansel and Gretel" represents the task each of us as children must face in coming to terms with anxiety--not the anxiety of facing starvation and being literally abandoned in the woods, but the ordinary fear of separating from our parents (especially mother) in the process of growing up to become independent adults. Bettelheim sees symbolic meaning in every motif and element in the story, and assumes that children interpret these symbolically as well (159-66).

Partial validity of competing theories acknowledged

Undeniably, there are themes in "Hansel and Gretel"-- as in many of our most common fairy tales--that strike deep psychological chords with both children and adults. The wicked stepmother is a good example: Children often fantasize they are really stepchildren or adopted as a way to account for feeling victimized and abused by their parents. "In real life this fantasy occurs among children with a very high frequency" (Bakan 76).

Having qualified her major claim in light of other theories, student goes on to reiterate the support of her major claim in her conclusion.

These themes help to explain the enduring popularity of fairy tales among middle-class children over the last two centuries. But we cannot treat fairy tales as if they spring full-blown from the unconscious and tell us nothing about the past. For the people who told and heard "Hansel and Gretel" in the seventeenth to nineteenth centuries in Europe, the tale was describing events and phenomena that happened, if not to them, then to someone they knew. Everyone in rural communities was likely to have been exposed, whether in person or by hearsay, to some elderly woman claiming powers to alter weather patterns, heal the sick, cast spells, midwife, or take in illegitimate babies. Stepmothers were common, poverty and famine ongoing, and abandonment and child abuse very real. In addition to providing entertainment, tales like "Hansel and Gretel" reassured teller and listener alike that the ordinary physical hardships, which for most of us today are fictions, were possible to overcome.

Middleton   9

Notes

[1] We in the United States know it primarily in printed form, as it has come to us from Germany. Between 1812 and 1857, the Grimm brothers, Jacob and Wilhelm, published several editions of <u>Kinder und Hausmarchen</u> (<u>Children's and Household Tales</u>) (Zipes 6, 41, 79). In addition to "Hansel and Gretel," this book included over 200 other folktales (though not all of them were fairy tales). The anthology increased in popularity until by the turn of the twentieth century it outsold all other books in Germany except the Bible (Zipes 15). To date it has been translated into some seventy languages (Denecke).

[2] Folklorists collect folktales from around the world and analyze them. Tales are categorized according to <u>type</u> (basic plot line) and <u>motifs</u> (elements within the tale). Two widely used references for folklorists are Antti Aarne's <u>Types of the Folklore</u> and Stith Thompson's <u>Motif-index</u>. "Hansel and Gretel" is type 327A in the Aarne classification.

[3] The Grimms were the first to record tale type 327A in 1812 (see note 1). A related tale about Tom Thumb (tale type 327B) was first recorded by Charles Perrault from France in 1697 (Thompson, <u>Folktale</u> 37, 182).

[4] Consider the example of Sephardic Jews who "converted" to Christianity under duress in Spain in the fifteenth century. Some of them moved to North America, and their descendants continued to practice Christianity openly and Judaism in secret until recently ("Search for the Buried Past").

Content notes appear at the end of the paper, before Works Cited.

Space included between superscript number and beginning of note

Indent five spaces to superscript number; rest of note is flush left.

Middleton   10

Sources arranged
alphabetically by
author's last
name or by title

First line flush left
in citation, rest
indented five
spaces

Book

Periodical

Encyclopedia
article

Interview

An online book

Radio broadcast

Works Cited

Aarne, Antti. The Types of the Folklore: Classification and
Bibliography. Trans. and ed. Stith Thompson. 2nd rev.
ed. FF Communications 184. Helsinki: Suomalainen
Tiedeakatemia, 1964.

Bakan, David. Slaughter of the Innocents. Toronto:
Canadian Broadcasting System, 1971.

Bettelheim, Bruno. The Uses of Enchantment: The Meaning
and Importance of Fairy Tales. 1976. New York:
Vintage, 1977.

Boswell, John. The Kindness of Strangers: The
Abandonment of Children in Western Europe from
Late Antiquity to the Renaissance. New York:
Pantheon, 1988.

Brewer, Derek. "The Battleground of Home: Versions of
Fairy Tales." Encounter 54.4 (1980): 52-61.

Denecke, Ludwig. "Grimm, Jacob Ludwig Carl and Wilhelm
Carl." Encyclopaedia Britannica: Micropaedia. 1992 ed.

Dundes, Alan. Telephone interview. 10 Feb. 1993.

"Fairy tale." Merriam-Webster's Collegiate Dictionary. 10th
ed. 1993.

"Hansel and Gretel." Funk & Wagnalls Standard Dictionary
of Folklore, Mythology, and Legend. Ed. Maria Leach.
New York: Funk & Wagnalls, 1949.

Horsley, Richard A. "Who Were the Witches? The Social
Roles of the Accused in the European Witch Trials."
Journal of Interdisciplinary History 9 (1979):
689-715.

Kramer, Heinrich, and James Sprenger. The Malleus
Maleficarum. Trans. Montague Summers. New York:
Dover, 1971. 14 Dec. 1998. <http://www.geocities
.com/Athens/2962/witchcraze/malleus_2_ii
_html>.

Nash, Jesse. "European Witchcraft: The Hidden Tradition."
Human Mosaic 21.1-2 (1987): 10-30.

"Search for the Buried Past." The Hidden Jews of New Mexico. Prod. Nan Rubin. WFCR, Amherst, MA. 13 Sept.
1992.

Middleton   11

Taggart, James M. " 'Hansel and Gretel' in Spain and
    Mexico." Journal of American Folklore 99 (1986):
    435-60.

"The Tales and Their Tellers." Ed. Christine Daaé. Fairy
    Tales: Origins and Evolution. 12 Dec. 1998.
    <http://www.darkgoddess.com/fairy/tellers.htm>.

Tatar, Maria. "Folkloristic Phantasies: Grimm's Fairy Tales
    and Freud's Family Romance." Fairy Tales as Ways of
    Knowing: Essays on Marchen in Psychology, Society
    and Literature. Ed. Michael M. Metzger and Katharina
    Mommsen. Germanic Studies in America 41. Berne:
    Lang, 1981. 75-98.

Thompson, Stith. The Folktale. New York: Holt, 1946.

---. Motif-index of Folk-literature: A Classification of
    Narrative Elements in Folktales, Ballads, Myths,
    Fables, Mediaeval Romances, Exempla, Fabliaux,
    Jest-books, and Local Legends. Rev. ed. 6 vols. plus
    index. Bloomington: Indiana UP, 1957.

Treasure, Geoffrey R. R. "European History and Culture:
    The Emergence of Modern Europe, 1500-1648." Ency-
    clopaedia Britannica: Macropaedia. 1992 ed. 657-83.

Warner, Marina. "Pity the Stepmother." New York Times.
    12 May 1991, late ed.: D17. Lexis/Nexis Universe 12
    Dec. 1998. <http://web.lexis-nexis.com/universe/
    form/academic/univ_gennews.html>.

Weber, Eugen. "Fairies and Hard Facts: The Reality of Folk-
    tales." Journal of the History of Ideas 42 (1981):
    93-113.

Zipes, Jack. The Brothers Grimm: From Enchanted Forests
    to the Modern World. New York: Routledge, 1988.

A page within
a Web site

Article in an
edited anthology

Two consecutive
works by the
same author

Volume in a multi-
volume revised
edition

Newspaper
online from a
computer service

APA SYSTEM FOR CITING PUBLICATIONS

Instructors in the social sciences might prefer the citation system of the American Psychological Association (APA). Like the MLA system, the APA system calls for a parenthetical citation in the text of the paper. Unlike the MLA system, the APA system includes the year of publication in the parenthetical reference. Here is an example:

> Even though many South American countries rely on the drug trade for their economic survival, the majority of South Americans disapprove of drug use (Gorriti, 1989, p. 72).

The complete publication information for Gorriti's article will appear at the end of your paper, on a page titled "References." (Sample citations for the "References" page appear below.)

If your list of references includes more than one work written by the same author in the same year, cite the first work as *a* and the second as *b*. For example, Gorriti's second article of 1989 would be cited in your paper as (Gorriti, 1989b).

Following are examples of the citation forms you are most likely to use. If you need the format for a type of publication not listed here, consult the *Publication Manual of the American Psychological Association,* Fourth Edition (1994).

A BOOK BY A SINGLE AUTHOR

Briggs, J. (1988). Fire in the crucible: The alchemy of creative genius. New York: St. Martin's Press.

MULTIPLE WORKS BY THE SAME AUTHOR IN THE SAME YEAR

Gardner, H. (1982a). Art, mind, and brain: A cognitive approach to creativity. New York: Basic.

Gardner, H. (1982b). Developmental psychology: An introduction (2nd ed.). Boston: Little, Brown.

AN ANTHOLOGY OR COMPILATION

Gioseffi, D. (Ed.). (1988). Women on war. New York: Simon & Schuster.

A BOOK BY TWO OR MORE AUTHORS OR EDITORS

Atwan, R., & Roberts, J. (Eds.). (1996). Left, right, and center: Voices from across the political spectrum. Boston: Bedford Books.

Note: List the names of *all* the authors or editors, no matter how many.

A BOOK BY A CORPORATE AUTHOR

International Advertising Association. (1977). Controversy advertising: How advertisers present points of view on public affairs. New York: Hastings House.

A WORK IN AN ANTHOLOGY

Mukherjee, B. (1988). The colonization of the mind. In Gioseffi, D. (Ed.) Women on war (pp. 140-142). New York: Simon & Schuster.

AN INTRODUCTION, PREFACE, FOREWORD, OR AFTERWORD

Hemenway, R. (1984). Introduction. In Z. N. Hurston, Dust tracks on a road. Urbana: University of Illinois Press, ix-xxxix.

AN EDITION OTHER THAN THE FIRST

Gumpert, G., & Cathcart, R. (Eds.). (1986). Inter/media: Interpersonal communication in a media world (3rd ed.). New York: Oxford University Press.

A TRANSLATION

Sartre, J. P. (1962). Literature and existentialism. (B. Frechtman, Trans.). New York: Citadel Press. (Original work published 1949.)

A REPUBLISHED BOOK

James, W. (1969). The varieties of religious experience: A study in human nature. London: Collier Books. (Original work published 1902.)

A BOOK IN A SERIES

Berthrong, D. J. (1976). The Cheyenne and Arapaho ordeal: Reservation and agency life in the Indian territory, 1875-1907. Vol. 136. The civilization of the American Indian series. Norman: University of Oklahoma Press.

A MULTIVOLUME WORK

Mussen, P. H. (Ed.). (1983). Handbook of child psychology (4th ed., Vols. 1-4). New York: Wiley.

AN ARTICLE FROM A DAILY NEWSPAPER

Hottelet, R. C. (1990, March 15). Germany: Why it can't happen again. Christian Science Monitor, p. 19.

AN ARTICLE FROM A PERIODICAL

Gorriti, G. A. (1989, July). How to fight the drug war. Atlantic
  Monthly, 70-76.

AN ARTICLE IN A JOURNAL WITH CONTINUOUS
PAGINATION THROUGHOUT THE VOLUME

Cockburn, A. (1989). British justice, Irish victims. The Nation, 249,
  554-555.

AN ARTICLE FROM A JOURNAL WITH SEPARATE
PAGINATION FOR EACH ISSUE

Mukerji, C. Visual language in science and the exercise of power: The
  case of cartography in early modern Europe. Studies in Visual
  Communication, 10(3), 30-45.

AN ARTICLE IN A REFERENCE WORK

Frisby, J. P. (1990). Direct perception. In M. W. Eysenck (Ed.),
  Blackwell dictionary of cognitive psychology (pp. 95-100).
  Oxford: Basil Blackwell.

A GOVERNMENT PUBLICATION

United States Dept. of Health, Education, and Welfare. (1973). Current
  ethical issues in mental health. Washington, DC: U.S. Government
  Printing Office.

AN ABSTRACT

Fritz, M. (1990/1991). A comparison of social interactions using a
  friendship awareness activity. Education and Training in Mental
  Retardation, 25, 352-359. (From Psychological Abstracts, 1991,
  78, Abstract No. 11474)

When the dates of the original publication and of the abstract differ,
give both dates separated by a slash.

AN ANONYMOUS WORK

The status of women: Different but the same. (1992-1993). Zontian,
  73(3), 5.

If the primary contributors to developing the program are known,
begin the reference with those as the author(s) instead of the corporate author. If you are citing a documentation manual rather than
the program itself, add the word "manual" before the closing
bracket. If there is additional information needed for retrieving the
program (such as report and/or acquisition numbers), add this at
the end of the entry, in parentheses after the last period.

A DATABASE SOURCE (INFORMATION SERVICE)

LeSourd, S. J. (1992, April). The psychology of perspective
consciousness. Paper presented at the annual meeting of the
American Educational Research Association, San Francisco. (ERIC
Document Reproduction Service No. ED 348 296)

Treat an ERIC document as a database source only if the primary or
sole place to find it is from ERIC; if the source was previously published and is readily available in printed form, treat it as a journal
article or published book.

MATERIAL ACCESSED THROUGH A COMPUTER SERVICE

Boynton, R. S. (1994, March 3). The new intellectuals [3 parts]. The
Atlantic Monthly Online: [On-line serial]. Available America
Online: Directory: The Atlantic Monthly Online: Main Menu: News-
stand: Folder: The Atlantic Monthly 40-99669: File: The New
Intellectuals: Article: The New Intellectuals Parts 1-3.

A REVIEW

Harris, I. M. (1991). [Review of Rediscovering masculinity: Reason,
language, and sexuality]. Gender and Society, 5, 259-261.

Give the author of the review, not the author of the book being reviewed. Use this form for a film review also. If the review has a title,
place it before the bracketed material, and treat it like an article title.

A LETTER TO THE EDITOR

Pritchett, J. T., & Kellner, C. H. (1993). Comment on spontaneous
seizure activity [Letter to the editor]. Journal of Nervous and
Mental Disease, 181, 138-139.

PERSONAL CORRESPONDENCE

B. Ehrenreich (personal communication, August 7, 1992).

(B. Ehrenreich, personal communication, August 7, 1992.)

Cite all personal communications to you (such as letters, memos,
and telephone conversations) in text only, *without* listing them
among the references. The phrasing of your sentences will determine which of the two above forms to use.

AN UNPUBLISHED MANUSCRIPT

McIntosh, P. (1988). White privilege and male privilege: A personal
account of coming to see correspondences through work in

women's studies. Working Paper 189. Unpublished manuscript, Wellesley College, Center for Research on Women, Wellesley, MA.

A LECTURE

Kagan, J. (1968, April 30). A theoretical look at child development. Albert F. Blakeslee Lecture, Smith College, Northampton, MA.

PROCEEDINGS OF A MEETING, PUBLISHED

Guerrero, R. (1972/1973). Possible effects of the periodic abstinence method. In W. A. Uricchio & M. K. Williams (Eds.), Proceedings of a Research Conference on Natural Family Planning (pp. 96-105). Washington, DC: Human Life Foundation.

If the date of the symposium or conference is different from the date of publication, give both, separated by a slash. If the proceedings are published annually, treat the reference like a periodical article.

A FILM

Golden, G. (Producer). (1975). Changing images: Confronting career stereotypes [Film]. Berkeley: University of California.

A VIDEOTAPE

Cambridge Video (Producer). (1987). Setting educational/vocational goals [Video]. Charleston, WV: Cambridge Career Products.

COMPUTER SOFTWARE

UnionSquareware (1987). Squarenote, the ideal librarian [Computer program]. Somerville, MA: Author.

A WEBSITE

Daaé, C. (1996). Fairy Tales: Origins and Evolution [Online]. Available: <http://www.darkgoddess.com/fairy/>[1998, December 12].

A PAGE WITHIN A WEBSITE

Don't Zoos Contribute to the Saving of Species from Extinction? (No date). In Animal Rights Resource Site. 14 Dec. 1998. Available: <http:// arrs.envirolink.org/faqs+Ref/ar-faq/Q68.html> [12 Dec. 1998].

A BOOK AVAILABLE ON THE WEB

Kramer, H., & Sprenger, J. (1971). The Malleus Maleficarum. (M. Summers, Trans.) New York: Dover. Available:

<http://www.geocities.com/Athens/2962/witchcraze/
malleus_2_ii_html> [1998, 14 December].

AN ARTICLE FROM AN ELECTRONIC JOURNAL

Minow, M. (1997). Filters and the Public Library: A Legal and Policy
   Analysis. [Online] First Monday 2 (12), 123 paragraphs.
   Available: <http://www.firstmonday.dk/issues/issue2_12/
   minow/index.html> [1998, 12 November].

AN ARTICLE FROM A FULL-TEXT DATABASE AVAILABLE
THROUGH THE WEB

Warner, M. (1991, May 12). Pity the Stepmother. New York
   Times. P.D17 (1 p.). Available: Lexis/Nexis Universe
   <http://web.lexis-nexis.com/universe/form/academic/
   univ_gennews.html—Newspapers—All Available Dates> [1998, December 12].

AN ARTICLE FROM A CD-ROM FULL-TEXT DATABASE

Tribal/DNC Donations. (1997, December). News from Indian Country
   10 (12), 1–2. [CD-ROM]. Available: Softline/Ethnic Newswatch
   [1998, October 12].

AN ARTICLE FROM AN ELECTRONIC REFERENCE WORK

Folk Arts. (No date). In Britannica Online. [Online] Available:
   <http://www.eb.com:180> [1998, December 14].

A PERSONAL E-MAIL COMMUNICATION

Franz, K. (kfranz@innov.edu). (1998, October 12) Re: Species
   reintroduction. E-mail to Amanda Repp (Amanda_Repp
   @innov.edu).

AN E-MAIL COMMUNICATION POSTED TO A DISCUSSION LIST

Lee, C. (1998, September 10). Re: Mothers and Stepmothers.
   Folklore Discussion List [Online]. Available E-mail:
   folklore@listserv.tamu.edu [1998, September 15].

A POSTING TO A WEB FORUM

DeYoung, C. (1998, December 12). [Online]. Issues: Gay Rights.
   Available: <http://community.cnn.com/cgi-bin/
   WebX?14@52.7bmLaPoSc49^0@.ee7239c/12479> [1988,
   December 14].

A NEWSGROUP POSTING

Vining, P. (1988, October 16). Zoos and Infotainment. [Online]. Available: news:alt.animals.ethics.vegetarian [1998, December 12].

A SYNCHRONOUS COMMUNICATION

Krishnamurthi, A. (1988, October 25). Reinventing Copyright in a Digital Environment. In <u>MediaMOO</u> [Online]. Available telnet://purple -crayon.media.mit.edu:8888/[1998, October 1998].

SAMPLE RESEARCH PAPER (APA STYLE)

The following paper urges a change in our attitude toward zoos. Arguing the value claim that it is morally wrong for humans to exploit animals for entertainment, the student combines expert opinion gathered from research with her own interpretations of evidence. She is always careful to anticipate and represent the claims of the opposition before going on to refute them.

The student uses the APA style, modified to suit the preferences of her writing instructor. APA style requires a title page with a centered title, author, affiliation, and a short title that can be used as a "running head" on each page. An abstract page follows the title page and includes a one-paragraph abstract or summary of the article. Amanda Repp was told she could omit the title page and abstract recommended by the APA. A full description of APA publication conventions can be found in the *Publication Manual of the American Psychological Association,* Fourth Edition (1994).

Amanda Repp   Zoos   1

English 102-G

Mr. Kennedy

Fall 1999

Why Zoos Should Be Eliminated

    Zoos have come a long way from their grim beginnings.
Once full of tiny cement-block steel cages, the larger zoos now
boast simulated jungles, veldts, steppes, and rain forests, all
in an attempt to replicate the natural habitats of the incarcerated animals. The attempt, however admirable, is misguided.
It is morally wrong to keep wild animals in captivity, and no
amount of replication, no matter how realistic, can compensate for the freedom these creatures are denied.

    Peter Batten (1976) argues that a wild animal's life "is
spent in finding food, avoiding enemies, sleeping, and in
mating or other family activities. . . . Deprivation of any of
these fundamentals results in irreparable damage to the
individual" (p. 1). The fact that humans may be stronger or
smarter than beasts does not give them the right to ambush
and exploit animals for the purposes of entertainment.

    We humans take our own liberty quite seriously.
Indeed, we consider liberty to be one of our inalienable
rights. But too many of us apparently feel no obligation to
grant the same right to animals, who, because they cannot
defend themselves against our sophisticated methods of
capture and because they do not speak our language,
cannot claim it for themselves.

    But the right to liberty is not based on the ability to
claim it, or even on the ability to understand what it is. As
James Rachels (1976) writes:

> Humans have a right to liberty because they have
> various other interests that will suffer if their
> freedom is unduly restricted. The right to liberty--the
> right to be free of external constraints on one's
> actions--may then be seen as derived from a more
> basic right not to have one's interests needlessly
> harmed. (p. 210)

Animals, like people, have interests that are harmed if they
are kept in captivity: They are separated from their
families and prevented from behaving according to their

Marginal notes:

Short title and page number, per APA style. Some instructors may prefer the student's name instead of the short title as a running head.

First paragraph ends with thesis

Citation includes author, date of publication, and page number. Ellipses (. . .) indicate omitted passage; period after ellipses indicates that the omission included the end of a sentence.

Long quotations of more than 40 words are set off as block quotations. Start a new line on a five-space indented margin, double space throughout, and put the page number of the quotations in parentheses after the final punctuation.

natural instincts by being removed from the lives they
know, which are the lives they were meant to lead.

Summary of an opposing argument

Some argue that animals' interests are not being
harmed when they are kept in zoos or aquariums--that no
damage is being done to the individual--but their claims are
highly disputable. For example, the Zurich Zoo's Dr. Heini
Hediger (1985) protests that it is absurd to attribute

Writer suggests flaw in comparison.

human qualities to animals at all, but he nevertheless
resorts to a human analogy: "Wild animals in the zoo
rather resemble estate owners. Far from desiring to escape
and regain their freedom, they are only bent on defending
the space they inhabit and keeping it safe from invasion"

Refutation of opposing argument based on evidence from personal experience

(p. 9). How can Dr. Hediger explain the actions of the
leopards and cheetahs I have seen executing figure eights
off the walls and floors of their cages for hours on end? I
have watched, spellbound by their grace but also horrified;
it is impossible to believe that these animals do not want
their freedom. An estate owner would not spend his time
running frantically around the perimeters of his property.
These cats know they are not lords of any estate. The
senseless repetition of their actions suggests that the cats
know that they are caged and that there is nothing to
defend against, no "estate" to protect.

Writer summarizes, then points out a weakness in, a second opposing argument.

Shannon Brownlee (1986) also believes that there is
no concrete evidence that incarcerated animals are
suffering or unhappy, but she weakens her own case in her
description of Jackie, a dolphin in captivity who "spends
the day in a seeming stupor" and "chews on the mackerel
half-heartedly" at feeding time (p. 70). Clearly there is
something wrong with Jackie; this becomes apparent when
Brownlee contrasts Jackie's lethargic behavior with that of
wild dolphins cavorting in the bay. Brownlee points out that
Jackie has never tried to escape through a hole in his
enclosure, although he knows it is there. But this fact does
not necessarily mean that Jackie enjoys captivity. Instead,
it may mean that Jackie's spirit has been broken and that

Writer questions an unstated warrant in the argument.

he no longer remembers or cares what his earlier days
were like. Granted we have no way of knowing what Jackie

Zoos   3

is really feeling, but does that give us the right to assume that he is not feeling anything?

To be fair, Brownlee does not go that far. She does allow Jackie one emotional state, attributing his malaise to boredom. But perhaps if the author were removed from members of her family, as well as all other members of her species, and prevented from engaging in activities that most mattered to her, she would recognize Jackie's problems as something more than boredom. In any case, why should we inflict boredom on Jackie, or any other animal, just because we happen to have the means to do so?

Having registered these basic objections to zoos--that keeping any creature in captivity is a fundamental infringement on that creature's right to liberty and dignity--I want to take a closer look at the zoo as an institution, in order to assess fairly its goals and how it tries to meet them. Most zoo professionals today maintain that zoos exist for two main reasons: to educate humans and to conserve animal species. These are both admirable goals, certainly, but as Seal (1985) notes, "none of these [zoo] budgets is allocated specifically for species preservation. Zoos have been established primarily as recreational institutions and are only secondarily developing programs in conservation, education, and research" (p. 74). The fact is most zoos do not have the money, space, or equipment required to make significant contributions in this area. The bulk of their money goes to the upkeep of the animals and exhibits--that is, to put it crudely, to the displays.

On behalf of the education a zoo provides, a common argument is that there is nothing like seeing the real thing. But what you see in the zoo is not a real thing at all. According to a statement from the Animal Rights Resource Site, "The conditions under which animals are kept in zoos typically distorts their behavior significantly" (How will people see). Many zoo and aquarium animals, like Jackie the dolphin, have been domesticated to the point of lethargy, in part because they are being exhibited alone or with only one other member of their species, when what

Margin annotations:

Writer shifts to the second half of her argument.

Clarifying word in square brackets

Another opposing argument, with refutation

Summarizes two expert opinions that zoos do not help endangered species

they are used to is traveling in groups and finding their own food, instead of being fed. Anyone who wants to see the real thing would be better off watching some of the excellent programming about nature and wildlife that appears on public television.

As for conservation, it is clearly a worthwhile effort, but zoos are not effective agents of species preservation. It is generally acknowledged that it is difficult to breed zoo

Author, date, page cited parenthetically

animals (Luoma, 1982, p. 104). Animals often do not reproduce at all--quite possibly because of the artificial, and consequently unsettling, circumstances in which they live. When zoo animals do mate successfully, the offspring is often weakened by inbreeding. According to geneticists, this is because a population of 150 breeder animals is necessary in order to "assure the more or less permanent survival of

Source with two authors cited parenthetically

a species in captivity" (Ehrlich & Ehrlich, 1981, p. 211). Few zoos have the resources to maintain populations that size. When zoos rely on smaller populations for breeding (as many do), the species' gene pool becomes more and more limited, "vigor and fecundity tend to decline" (Ehrlich & Ehrlich, 1981, p. 212), and this can eventually lead to extinction. In other words, we are not doing these animals any favors by trying to conserve them in zoos. Indeed, Wilson (1995) writes that "all the zoos in the world today can sustain a maximum of only 2,000 species of mammals, birds, reptiles, and amphibians, out of about 24,000 known to exist" (p. 57). Reserves and preservations, which have room for the larger populations necessary for successful conservation efforts and which can concentrate on breeding animals rather than on displaying them, are much more suitable for these purposes.

For what purposes, then, are zoos suitable? Are they even necessary? At present, they must house the many generations of animals that have been bred there, since these animals have no place else to go. Most animals in captivity cannot go back to the wild for one of two reasons. The first is that the creatures would be unable to survive there, since their instincts for finding their own food and protecting themselves from predators, or even the weather,

Zoos   5

have been greatly diminished during their time spent in
captivity (Morton, 1985, p. 155). Perhaps this
is why Jackie the dolphin chooses to remain in his
enclosure.

Paraphrase with
source cited
parenthetically

The other reason animals cannot return to the wild is
an even sadder one: In many cases, their natural habitats
no longer exist. Thanks to deforesting and clearing of land
for homes, highways, factories, and shopping malls--which
are continually being built with no regard for the plant and
animal life around them--ecosystems are destroyed constantly, driving increasing numbers of species from their
homes. Air and water pollution and toxic waste, results of
the ever-increasing urbanization and industrialization
throughout the world, are just some of the agents of this
change. It is a problem I wish to address in closing.

If zoos were to leave breeding programs to more
appropriate organizations and to stop collecting animals,
the zoo as an institution would eventually be phased out.
Animals would cease to be exhibits and could resume being
animals, and the money previously used to run zoos could
be put to much better use. Ideally it could be used to
investigate why endangered species are endangered, and
why so many of the original habitats of these species have
disappeared. Most important, it could be used to explore
how we can change our habits and reorient our behavior,
attitudes, and priorities, so we can begin to address these
issues.

Writer closes by
proposing a solu-
tion of her own.

The problem of endangered species does not exist in a
vacuum; it is a symptom of a much greater predicament.
Humankind is responsible for this predicament, and it is up
to us to recognize this before it is too late. Saving a selected
species here and there will do none of us any good if those
species can exist only in isolated, artificial environments,
where they will eventually breed themselves into extinction. The money that has been concentrated on such efforts
should be devoted instead to educating the public about the
endangered planet--not just its animals--or, like the animals,
none of us will have any place to go.

Zoos 6

References start
a new page

A book with two
authors

A work in an
anthology

An article from a
periodical

For each refer-
ence, flush left on
first line, then in-
dent three spaces
on subsequent
lines

An article
online from a
computer service

References

Batten, P. (1976). Living trophies. New York: Crowell.

Brownlee, S. (1986, December). First it was "save the
whales," now it's "free the dolphins." Discover,
70-72.

Ehrlich, P., & Ehrlich, A. (1981). Extinction: The
causes and consequences of the disappearance of
species. New York: Random House.

Hediger, H. (1985). From cage to territory. In R.
Kirchschofer (Ed.), The world of zoos: A survey
and gazetteer (pp. 9-20). New York: Viking.

How will people see wild animals and learn about
them without zoos? (No date). In Animal
Rights Resource Site. 14 Dec. 1998. Available:
<http://arrs.envirolink.org/faqs+Ref/
ar-faq/Q70.html> [12 Dec. 1998].

Luoma, J. (1982, November). Prison or ark?
Audubon, 102-109.

Morton, E. S. (1985). The realities of reintroducing
species to the wild. In J. R. Hoage (Ed.), Animal
extinctions: What everyone should know (pp. 147-
158). National Zoological Park Symposia for the
Public series. Washington, DC: Smithsonian
Institution.

Rachels, J. (1976). Do animals have a right to
liberty? In T. Regan & P. Singer (Eds.), Animal
rights and human obligations (pp. 205-223).
Englewood Cliffs, NJ: Prentice-Hall.

Seal, U. S. (1985). The realities of preserving species
in captivity. In J. R. Hoage (Ed.), Animal
extinctions: What everyone should know (pp.
147-158). National Zoological Park Symposia for
the Public series. Washington, DC: Smithsonian Institution.

Wilson, E. (1995, October 30). Wildlife: Legions of the
doomed. Time. pp. 57-62. Available: Lexis/Nexis
Universe. <http://web.lexis-nexis.com/universe/
form/academic/univ_gennews.html>. All maga-
zines--All Available Dates [1998, December 12].

Presenting an Argument Orally

Speech is the basic skill overlooked by many who urge a return to the Three R's. The ability to speak clearly and persuasively, and to think on one's feet can be as vital to success as reading and writing. Beginning with the job interview, speech classifies a person.[1]

You already know a good deal about the power of persuasive speech. You've not only listened to it, from parents, teachers, preachers, coaches, friends, and enemies; you've practiced it yourself with varying degrees of success.

A classics scholar points out that the oratorical techniques we use today were "invented in antiquity and have been used to great effect ever since."[2] But history is not our only guide to the principles of public speaking. Much of what we know about the power of persuasive speech is knowledge based on lifelong experience — things we learn in everyday discourse with different kinds of people who respond to different appeals. Early in life you learned that you did not use the same language or the same approach to argue with your mother or your teacher as you used with your sibling or your friend. You learned, or tried to learn, how to convince people to listen to you and to trust you because you were truthful and knew what you were talking about. And perhaps equally important, if you won the argument, you wanted to make it clear that your victory would not mean hardship for the loser. (No obvious gloating). Although speeches to a larger, less familiar audience will require much more preparation,

---

[1] Fred M. Hechinger, "About Education," *New York Times,* May 11, 1988, sec. B, p. 7.

[2] Mary Lefkowitz, "Classic Oratory," *New York Times,* January 24, 1999, sec. W, p. 15.

many of the rules of argument that guided you in your personal encounters can be made to work for you in more public arenas.

You will often be asked to make oral presentations in your college classes. Many jobs, both professional and nonprofessional, will call for speeches to groups of fellow employees or prospective customers, to community groups, and even government officials. Wherever you live, there will be controversies and public meetings about schooling and political candidates, about budgets for libraries and road repairs and pet control. The ability to rise and make your case before an audience is one that you will want to cultivate as a citizen of a democracy. Great oratory is probably no longer the most powerful influence in our society, and computer networks have usurped the role of oral communication in many areas of public life. But whether it's in person or on television there is still a significant role for a live presenter, a real human being to be seen and heard.

Some of your objectives as a writer will also be relevant to you as a speaker: making the appropriate appeal to an audience, establishing your credibility, finding adequate support for your claim. But other elements of argument will be different: language, organization, and the use of visual and other aids.

Before you begin a brief examination of these elements, keep in mind the larger objectives of the speech-maker. A good introduction to the process of influencing an audience is *the motivated sequence.*[3] This outline, created by a professor of speech communication, lists the five steps that must be taken in order to motivate an audience to adopt a policy, an action, or a belief.

1. Getting attention (attention step)
2. Showing the need: describing the problem (need step)
3. Satisfying the need: presenting the solution (satisfaction step)
4. Visualizing the results (visualization step)
5. Requesting action or approval (action step)

Perhaps you noticed that these steps resemble the steps taken by advertisers. (That list appears in the sample analysis of an ad in Chapter 2.) The resemblance is not accidental. According to the author of the motivated sequence, this is a description of the way "people systematically think their way through to a decision."

As you read the following discussions of audience, credibility, language, organization, support, and visual and aural aids, try to think of occasions in your own experience when you were aware of these elements in spoken argument, formal or informal.

---

[3]Alan H. Munroe and Douglas Ehninger, *Principles of Speech Communication* (Glenview, Ill.: Scott, Foresman, 1969), p. 261.

THE AUDIENCE

Most speakers who confront a live audience already know something about the members of that audience. They may know why the audience is assembled to hear the particular speaker, their vocations, their level of education, and their familiarity with the subject. They may know whether the audience is friendly, hostile, or neutral to the views that the speaker will express. Analyzing the audience is an essential part of speech preparation. If speakers neglect it, both audience and speaker will suffer. At some time all of us have been trapped as members of an audience, forced to listen to a lecture, a sermon, an appeal for action when it was clear that the speaker had little or no idea what we were interested in or capable of understanding. In such situations the speaker who seems indifferent to the needs of the audience will also suffer because the audience will either cease to listen or reject his claim outright.

In college classes students who make assigned speeches on controversial topics are often encouraged to first survey the class. Questionnaires and interviews can give the speaker important clues to the things he should emphasize or avoid: They will tell him whether he should give both sides of a debatable question, introduce humor, use simpler language, and bring in visual or other aids.

But even where such specific information is not immediately available, speakers are well advised to find out as much as they can about the beliefs and attitudes of their audience from other sources. They will then be better equipped to make the kinds of appeals — to reason and to emotion — that the audience is most responsive to. For example, two young evangelists for a religious group (not students at the university) were invited to visit a speech class and present an argument for joining their group. The visitors knew that the class was learning the principles of persuasive speaking; they had no other information about the listeners. After the speech, the students in the class asked questions about some practices of the religious group which had received unfavorable media attention, but the speakers turned aside all questions, saying they did not engage in argument but were instructed only to describe the rewards of joining their group. Before some other audience, such a strategy might have been emotionally satisfying and ultimately persuasive. For this class, however, which was prepared to look for hard evidence, logic, and valid assumptions, the refusal to answer questions suggested evasion and indifference to the interests of their audience. Class evaluations of the speech revealed, to no one's surprise, that the visitors had failed to motivate their listeners.

If you know something about your audience, ask yourself what impression your clothing, gestures and bodily movements, voice, and general demeanor might convey. It might be worth pointing out here that the visitors cited above arrived dressed in three-piece suits and sporting crew cuts to confront an audience in tee shirts, torn jeans, and long hair. The fact that both speakers and listeners were the same age was not quite enough to overcome an impression of real differences. Make sure, too, that you understand the nature of the occasion — is it too solemn for humor? too formal for personal anecdotes? — and the purpose of the meeting, which can influence your choice of language and the most effective appeal.

CREDIBILITY

The evaluation of audience and the presentation of your own credibility are closely related. In other words, what can you do to persuade this particular audience that you are a reliable exponent of the views you are expressing? Credibility, as you learned in Chapter 1, is another name for *ethos* (the Greek word from which the English word *ethics* is derived) and refers to the honesty, moral character, and intellectual competence of the speaker.

Public figures, whose speeches and actions are reported in the media, can acquire (or fail to acquire) reputations for being endowed with those characteristics. And there is little doubt that a reputation for competence and honesty can incline an audience to accept an argument that would be rejected if offered by a speaker who lacks such a reputation. One study, among many that report similar results, has shown that the same speech will be rated highly by an audience that thinks the Surgeon General of the United States has delivered it but treated with much less regard if they hear it delivered by a college sophomore.

How, then, does a speaker who is unknown to the audience or who boasts only modest credentials convince his listeners that he is a responsible advocate? From the moment the speaker appears before them, members of the audience begin to make an evaluation, based on external signs, such as clothing and mannerisms. But the most significant impression of the speaker's credibility will be based on what the speaker says and how he says it. Does the speaker give evidence that he knows the subject? Does he seem to be aware of the needs and values of the audience? Especially if he is arguing an unpopular claim, does he seem modest and conciliatory?

An unknown speaker is often advised to establish his credentials in the introduction to his speech, to summarize his background and experience as proof of his right to argue the subject he has chosen. A prize-winning and widely reprinted speech by a student begins with these words:

> When you look at me, it is easy to see several similarities between us. I have two arms, two legs, a brain, and a heart just like you. These are my

hands, and they are just like yours. Like you, I also have wants and de-sires; I am capable of love and hate. I can laugh and I can cry. Yes, I'm just like you, except for one very important fact — I am an ex-con.[4]

This is a possibly risky beginning — not everybody in the audi-ence will be friendly to an ex-con — but it signifies that the speaker brings some authority to his subject, which is prison reform. It also attests to the speaker's honesty and may rouse sympathy among certain listeners. (To some in the audience, the speaker's allusions to his own humanity will recall another moving defense, the famous speech by Shylock, the Jewish money-lender, in Shakespeare's *The Merchant of Venice*.)

The speaker will often use an admission of modesty as proof of an honest and unassuming character. He presents himself not as an expert but as one well aware of his limitations. Such an appeal can generate sympathy in the audience (if they believe him) and a sense of identification with the speaker.

The professor of classics quoted earlier has analyzed the speech of a former senator who defended President Clinton at his impeach-ment trial. She found that the speaker "made sure his audience un-derstood that he was one of them, a friend, on their level, not above them. He denied he was a great speaker and spoke of his friendship with Mr. Clinton." As the writer points out, this confession brings to mind the speech by Mark Antony in *Julius Caesar:*

> I am no orator, as Brutus is,
> But (as you know me all) a plain blunt man
> That loves my friend; (3.2.226–28)

The similarity of these attempts at credibility, separated by al-most four hundred years (to say nothing of the fact that Aristotle wrote about *ethos* 2,500 years ago) tells us a good deal about the en-during influence of *ethos* or character on the speaker's message.

ORGANIZATION

Look at the student speech at the end of this chapter. The orga-nization of this short speech — the usual length of speeches deliv-ered in the classroom — is easily mastered and works for all kinds of claims.

At the end of the first paragraph the speaker states what he will try to prove, that a vegetarian diet contributes to prevention of chronic diseases. In the third paragraph the speaker gives the four

---

[4] Richard M. Duesterbeck, "Man's Other Society," in Wil Linkugel, R. R. Allen, and Richard Johannesen, eds., *Contemporary American Speeches* (Belmont, Calif.: Wadsworth, 1965), p. 264.

points that he will develop in his argument for vegetarianism. Following the development of these four topics, the conclusion urges the audience to take action, in this case, to stop eating meat.

This basic method of organizing a short speech has several virtues. First, the claim or thesis statement that appears early in a short speech, if the subject is well chosen, can engage the interest of the audience at once. Second, the list of topics guides the speaker in planning and developing his speech. Moreover, it tells the audience what to listen for as they follow the argument.

A well-planned speech has a clearly defined beginning, middle, and end. The beginning, which offers the introduction, can take a number of forms, depending on the kind of speech and its subject. Above all, the introduction must win the attention of the audience, especially if they have been required to attend, and encourage them to look forward to the rest of the speech. The authors of the motivated sequence suggest seven basic attention-getters: (1) referring to the subject or occasion, (2) using a personal reference, (3) asking a rhetorical question, (4) making a startling statement of fact or opinion, (5) using a quotation, (6) telling a humorous anecdote, (7) using an illustration.[5]

The speeches by the ex-con and the vegetarian provide examples of two of the attention-getters cited above — using a personal reference and asking a rhetorical question. In another kind of argument, a claim of fact, the student speaker uses a combination of devices to introduce her claim that culturally deprived children are capable of learning:

> In Charles Schulz's popular cartoon depiction of happiness, one of his definitions has special significance for the American school system. The drawing shows Linus, with his eyes closed in a state of supreme bliss, a broad smile across two-thirds of his face and holding a report card upon which is a big bold "A." The caption reads: "Happiness is finding out you're not so dumb after all." For once, happiness is not defined as a function of material possessions, yet even this happiness is practically unattainable for the "unteachables" of the city slums. Are these children intellectually inferior? Are they unable to learn? Are they not worth the time and the effort to teach? Unfortunately, too many people have answered "yes" to these questions and promptly dismissed the issue.[6]

The middle or body of the speech is, of course, the longest part. It will be devoted to development of the claim that appeared at the beginning. The length of the speech and the complexity of the subject will determine how much support you provide. Some points

---

[5] Monroe and Ehninger, p. 206.

[6] Carolyn Kay Geiman, "Are They Really 'Unteachables'?" in Linkugel, Allen, and Johannesen, p. 123.

will be more important than others and should therefore receive more extended treatment. Unless the order is chronological, it makes sense for the speaker to arrange the supporting points in emphatic order, that is, the most important at the end because this may be the one that listeners will remember.

The conclusion should be brief; some rhetoricians suggest that the ending should constitute five percent of the total length of the speech. For speeches that contain several main points with supporting data, you may need to summarize. Or you may return to one of the attention-getters mentioned earlier. One writer recommends this as "the most obvious method" of concluding speeches, "particularly appropriate when the introduction has included a quotation, an interesting anecdote, a reference to an occasion or a place, an appeal to the self-interest of the audience, or a reference to a recent incident."[7]

An example of such an ending appears in a speech given by Bruce Babbitt, Secretary of the Interior, in 1996. Speaking to an audience of scientists and theologians, the Secretary defended laws that protected the environment. This is how the speech began:

> A wolf's green eyes, a sacred blue mountain, the words from Genesis, and the answers of children all reveal the religious values manifest in the 1977 Endangered Species Act.

(The children Babbitt refers to had written answers to a question posed at an "eco-expo" fair, "Why Save the Environment?")

And this is the ending of the speech:

> I conclude here tonight by affirming that those religious values remain at the heart of the Endangered Species Act, that they make themselves manifest through the green eyes of the grey wolf, through the call of the whooping crane, through the splash of the Pacific salmon, through the voices of America's children.
>
> We are living between the flood and the rainbow: between the threats to creation on the one side and God's covenant to protect life on the other.
>
> Why should we save endangered species?
>
> Let us answer this question with one voice, the voice of the child at that expo, who scrawled her answer at the very bottom of the sheet: "Because we can."[8]

The speaker must also ensure the smooth flow of his argument throughout. Coherence, or the orderly connections between ideas,

---

[7] James C. McCroskey, *An Introduction to Rhetorical Communication* (Englewood Cliffs, New Jersey: Prentice-Hall, 1968), p. 204.

[8] Calvin McLeod Logue and Jean DeHart, eds., *Representative American Speeches 1995–1996* (New York: Wilson, 1996), p. 70ff.

is even more important in speech than in writing because the listener cannot go back to uncover these connections. The audience listens for expressions that serve as guideposts — words, phrases, and sentences to indicate which direction the argument will take. The student speech on vegetarianism uses these words among others: *next, then, finally, here, first of all, whereas, in addition, secondly, in fact, now, in conclusion.* Other expressions can also help the listener to follow the development. Each of the following examples from real speeches makes a bridge from a previous idea to a new one: "Valid factual proof, right? No, wrong!" "Consider an illustration of this misinformation." "But there is another way." "Up to this point, I've spoken only of therapy." "And so we face this new challenge." "How do we make this clear?" "Now, why is this so important?"

LANGUAGE

> It should be observed that each kind of rhetoric has its own appropriate style. That of written prose is not the same as that of spoken oratory.
>
> — Aristotle

In the end, your speech depends on the language. No matter how accurate your analysis of the audience, how appealing your presentation of self, how deep your grasp of the material, if the language does not clearly and emphatically convey your argument, the speech will probably fail. Fortunately, the effectiveness of language does not depend on long words or complex sentence structure; quite the contrary. Most speeches, especially those given by beginners to small audiences, are distinguished by an oral style that respects the rhythms of ordinary speech and sounds spontaneous.

The vocabulary you choose, like the other elements of spoken discourse we have discussed, is influenced by the kind of audience you confront. A student audience may be entertained or moved to identification with you and your message if you use the slang of your generation; an assembly of elderly church members at a funeral may not be so generous. Use words that both you and your listeners are familiar with, language that convinces the audience you are sharing your knowledge and opinions, neither speaking down to them nor over their heads. As one writer puts it, "You never want to use language that makes the audience appear ignorant or stupid."

Make sure, too, that the words you use will not be considered offensive by some members of your audience. Today we are all sensitive, sometimes hypersensitive, to terms we once used freely if not wisely. One word, improperly used, can cause some listeners to reject the whole speech.

The short speeches you give will probably not be devoted to elaborating grand abstractions, but it is not only abstract terms that need definition. When you know your subject very well, you forget that others can be ignorant of it. Think whether the subject is one that the particular audience you are addressing is not likely to be familiar with. If this is the case, then explain even the basic terms. In one class a student who had chosen to discuss a subject about which he was extremely knowledgeable, betting on horse races, neglected to define clearly the words *exacta, subfecta, trifecta, parimutuel* and others, leaving his audience fairly befuddled.

Wherever it is appropriate, use concrete language with details and examples that create images and cause the listener to feel as well as think. One student speaker used strong words to good effect in providing some unappetizing facts about hot dogs: "In fact, the hot dog is so adulterated with chemicals, so contaminated with bacteria, so puffy with gristle, fat, water, and lacking in protein, that it is nutritionally worthless."[9]

Another speech on a far more serious subject offered a personal experience with vivid details. The student speaker was a hemophiliac making a plea for blood donations.

> I remember the three long years when I couldn't even walk because repeated hemorrhages had twisted my ankles and knees to pretzel-like forms. I remember being pulled to school in a wagon while other boys rode their bikes and pushed to my table. I remember sitting in the dark empty classroom by myself during recess while the others went out in the sun to run and play. And I remember the first terrible day at the big high school when I came on crutches and built-up shoes carrying my books in a sack around my neck.[10]

As a rule, the oral style demands simpler sentences. That is because the listener must grasp the grammatical construction without the visual clues of punctuation available on the printed page. Simpler means shorter and more direct. Use subject-verb constructions without a string of phrases or clauses preceding the subject or interrupting the natural flow of the sentence. Use the active voice frequently. In addition to assuring clarity for the audience, such sentences are easier for the speaker to remember and to say. (The sentences in the paragraph above are long, but notice that the sentence elements of subject, verb, and subordinate clause are arranged in the order dictated by natural speech.)

---

[9] Donovan Ochs and Anthony Winkler, *A Brief Introduction to Speech* (New York: Harcourt, Brace, Jovanovich, 1979), p. 74.

[10] Ralph Zimmerman, "Mingled Blood," in Linkugel, Allen, and Johannesen, p. 200.

Simpler, however, does not mean less impressive. A speech before any audience may be simply expressed without loss of emotional or intellectual power. "The Nature of Prejudice" in Chapter 4 is a noteworthy example. First delivered as a speech to an audience of experts, it nevertheless reflects the characteristics of conversation. One of the most eloquent short speeches ever delivered in this country is the surrender speech in 1877 by Chief Joseph of the Nez Perce Tribe, which clearly demonstrates the power of simple words and sentences.

> I am tired of fighting. Our chiefs are killed. Looking Glass is dead. Toohulsote is dead. The old men are all dead. It is the young men who say no and yes. He who led the young men is dead. It is cold and we have no blankets. The little children are freezing to death. My people, some of them, have run away to the hills and have no blankets, no food. No one knows where they are — perhaps they are freezing to death. I want to have time to look for my children and see how many of them I can find. Maybe I shall find them among the dead. Hear me, my chiefs. I am tired. My heart is sad and sick. From where the sun now stands I will fight no more forever.[11]

If you are in doubt about the kind of language in which you should express yourself, you might follow Lincoln's advice: "Speak so that the most lowly can understand you, and the rest will have no difficulty."

A popular stylistic device — repetition and balance or parallel structure — can emphasize and enrich parts of your message. Look back to the balanced sentences of the passage from the student speaker on hemophilia, sentences beginning with "I remember." Almost all inspirational speeches, including religious exhortation and political oratory, take advantage of such constructions, whose rhythms evoke an immediate emotional response. It is one of the strengths of Martin Luther King Jr.'s "I Have a Dream." Keep in mind that the ideas in parallel structures must be similar and that, for maximum effectiveness, they should be used sparingly in a short speech. Not least, the subject should be weighty enough to carry this imposing construction.

SUPPORT

The support for a claim is essentially the same for both spoken and written arguments. Factual evidence, including statistics, and expert opinion, as well as appeals to needs and values, are equally

---

[11] M. Gidley, *Kopet: A Documentary Narrative of Chief Joseph's Last Years.* (Chicago: Contemporary Books, 1981), p. 31.

important in oral presentations. But time constraints will make a difference. In a speech the amount of support that you provide will be limited to the capacity of listeners to digest and remember information that they cannot review. This means that you must choose subjects that can be supported adequately in the time allotted. The speech by Secretary Babbitt, for example, on saving the environmental protection laws, developed material on animals, national lands, water, his own history, religious tradition, and the history of environmental legislation, to name only the most important. It would have been impossible to defend his proposition in a half-hour speech. Although his subject was far more limited, the author of the argument for vegetarianism could not do full justice to his claim for lack of time. Meat-eaters would find that some of their questions remain unanswered, and even those listeners friendly to the author's claim might ask for more evidence from authoritative sources.

While both speakers and writers use logical, ethical, and emotional appeals in support of their arguments, the forms of presentation can make a significant difference. The reasoning process demanded of listeners must be relatively brief and straightforward, and the supporting evidence readily assimilated. The ethical appeal or credibility of the speaker is affected not only by what he says but by his appearance, bodily movements, and vocal expressions. And the appeal to the sympathy of the audience can be greatly enhanced by the presence of the speaker. Take the excerpt from the speech of the hemophiliac. The written descriptions of pain and heartbreak are very moving, but place yourself in the audience, looking at the victim and imagining the suffering experienced by the human body standing in front of you. No doubt the effect would be deep and long-lasting, perhaps more memorable even than the written word.

Because the human instrument is so powerful, it must be used with care. You have probably listened to speakers who used gestures and voice inflections that had been dutifully rehearsed but were obviously contrived and worked, unfortunately, to undermine rather than support the speaker's message and credibility. If you are not a gifted actor, avoid gestures, body language, and vocal expressions that are not truly felt.

Some speech theorists treat support or proofs as *nonartistic* and *artistic*. The nonartistic support — factual data, expert opinion, examples — is considered objective and verifiable. Its acceptability should not depend on the character and personality of the speaker. It is plainly different from the artistic proof, which is subjective, based on the values and attitudes of the listener, and therefore more difficult for the speaker to control. This form of support is called artistic because it includes creative strategies within the power of the speaker to manipulate. In earlier parts of this chapter we have discussed the artistic proofs, ways of establishing credibility, and recognizing the values of the audience.

PRESENTATION AIDS

Charts, Graphs, Handouts

Some speeches, though not all, will be enhanced by visual and other aids: charts, graphs, maps, models, objects, handouts, recordings, and computer technology. These aids, however, no matter how visually or aurally exciting, should not overwhelm your own oral presentation. The objects are not the stars of the show. They exist to make your spoken argument more persuasive.

Charts and graphs, large enough and clear enough to be seen and understood, can illuminate speeches that contain numbers of any kind, especially statistical comparisons. You can make a simple chart yourself, on paper for use with an easel or a transparency for use with a slide projector. Enlarged illustrations or a model of a complicated machine — say, the space shuttle — would help a speaker to explain its function. You already know that photographs or videos are powerful instruments of persuasion, above all in support of appeals for humanitarian aid, for both people and animals.

Court cases have been won or lost on the basis of diagrams or charts that purport to prove the innocence or guilt of a defendant. Such aids do not always speak for themselves. No matter how clear they are to the designer, they may be misinterpreted or misunderstood by a viewer. Some critics have argued that the jury in the O. J. Simpson case failed to understand the graphs of DNA relationships that experts for the prosecution displayed during the trial. Before you show any diagrams or charts of any complexity to your audience, ask friends if they find them easy to understand.

The use of a handout also requires planning. It's probably unwise to put your speech on hold while the audience reads or studies a handout that requires time and concentration. Confine the subject matter of handouts to material that can be easily grasped as you discuss or explain it.

Audio

Audio aids may also enliven a speech or even be indispensable to its success. One student played a recording of a scene from *Romeo and Juliet*, spoken by a cast of professional actors, to make a point about the relationship between the two lovers. Another student chose to define several types of popular music, including rap, goth, heavy metal, and techno. But he used only words, and the lack of any musical demonstration meant that the distinctions remained unclear.

Video

With sight, sound, and movement, a video can illustrate or reinforce the main points of a speech. A speech warning people not to drink and drive will have a much greater effect if enhanced by a video showing the tragic and often gruesome outcome of car accidents caused by drunk driving. Schools that teach driver's education frequently rely on these bone-chilling videos to show their students that getting behind the wheel is a serious responsibility, not a game. If you want to use video, check to make sure that a VCR and television are available to you. Most schools have an audio-visual department that manages the delivery, set-up, and return of all equipment.

Multimedia

Multimedia presentation software programs enable you to combine several different media such as text, charts, sound, and still or moving pictures into one unit. In the business world, multimedia presentations are commonly used in situations where you have a limited amount of time to persuade or teach a fairly large audience. For instance, the promotion director of a leading teen magazine is trying to persuade skeptical executives that a magazine website would increase sales and advertising revenue. Since the magazine is sold through newsstand and subscription, some executives question whether the cost of creating and maintaining a website outweighs the benefits. Using multimedia presentation software, the promotion director can Integrate: demographic charts and graphs showing that steadily increasing numbers of teenagers surf the Web, a segment from a television news program reporting that many teens shop online (an attraction for advertisers), and downloaded pages from a competitor's website to demonstrate that others are already reaping the benefits of the Internet. With several studies reporting that people today are increasingly "visual" in their learning styles, multimedia software may be the most effective aid for an important presentation.

Though effective when done well, technically complicated presentations require large amounts of time and careful planning. First you must ensure that your computer is powerful enough to adeptly handle presentation software such as Microsoft Powerpoint, Lotus Freelance, Harvard Graphics, Adobe Persuasion, Cintel Charisma, and Asymetrix Compel. Then you need to familiarize yourself with the program. Most presentation software programs come equipped with helpful tutorials. If the task of creating your own presentation from scratch seems overwhelming, you can use one of the many pre-formatted presentation templates — you will simply need to customize the content. Robert Stephens, the founder of the Geek Squad, a Minneapolis-based business that provides on-site emergency response to computer problems, gives the following tips for multimedia presentations:

1. In case of equipment failure, always bring two of everything.
2. Back up your presentation not only on floppy disk, but on CD-ROM, or a Zip drive.
3. Avoid live visits to the Internet. Because connections can fail or be painfully slow, and sites can move or disappear, if you must visit the Internet in your presentation, download the appropriate pages onto your hard drive ahead of time. It will still look like a live visit.
4. In the end, technology cannot replace creativity. Make sure that you are using multimedia to reinforce not replace your main points.[12]

Make sure that any necessary apparatus will be available at the right time. If you have never used the devices you need for your presentation, practice using them before the speech. Few things are more disconcerting for the speechmaker and the audience than a speaker who is fumbling with his materials, unable to find the right picture or to make a machine work.

SAMPLE PERSUASIVE SPEECH

The following speech was delivered by C. Renzi Stone to his public speaking class at the University of Oklahoma. Told to prepare a persuasive speech, C. Renzi Stone chose to speak about the health benefits of vegetarianism. Note his attention-grabbing introduction.

---

[12] Robert Stephens as paraphrased in "When Your Presentation Crashes . . . Who You Gonna Call?" by Eric Matson, *Fast Company*, February/March 1997, p. 130.

Live Longer and Healthier:
Stop Eating Meat!

C. RENZI STONE

What do Steve Martin, Dustin Hoffman, Albert Einstein, Jerry Garcia, Michael Stipe, Eddie Vedder, Martina Navratilova, Carl Lewis, and 12 million other Americans all have in common? All of these well-known people were or are vegetarians. What do they know that we don't? Consuming a regimen of high-fat, high-protein flesh foods is a sure-fire prescription for disaster, like running diesel fuel through your car's gasoline engine. In the book *Why Do Vegetarians Eat Like That?* David Gabbe asserts that millions of people today are afflicted with chronic diseases that can be directly linked to the consumption of meat. Eating a vegetarian diet can help prevent many of those diseases.

In 1996, 12 million Americans identified themselves as vegetarians. That number is twice as many as in the decade before. According to a recent National Restaurant Association poll found in *Health* magazine, one in five diners say they now go out of their way to choose restaurants that serve at least a few meatless entrees. Obviously, the traditionally American trait of a meat-dominated society has subsided in recent years.

In discussing vegetarianism today, first I will tell how vegetarians are perceived in society. Next, I will introduce several studies validating my claim that a meatless diet is extraordinarily healthy. I will then show how a veggie diet can strengthen the immune system and make the meatless body a shield from unwanted diseases such as cancer and heart disease. Maintaining a strict vegetarian diet can also lead to a longer life. Finally, I will put an image into the audience's mind of a meatless society that relies on vegetables for the main course at breakfast, lunch, and dinner.

Moving to my first point, society generally holds two major misperceptions about vegetarians. First of all, society often perceives vegetarians as a radical group of people with extreme principles. In this view, vegetarians are seen as a monolithic group of people who choose to eat vegetables because they are opposed to the killing of animals for food. The second major misconception is that because vegetarians do not eat meat, they do not get the proper amounts of essential vitamins and minerals often found in meat.

Here is my response to these misconceived notions. First of all, 5 vegetarians are not a homogeneous group of radicals. Whereas many vegetarians in the past did join the movement on the principle that killing animals is wrong, many join the movement today mainly for its health benefits. In addition, there are many different levels of vegetarianism. Some vegetarians eat nothing but vegetables. Others don't eat red meat but do occasionally eat chicken and fish.

Secondly, contrary to popular opinion, vegetarians get more than enough vitamins and minerals in their diet and generally receive healthier nourishment than meat eaters. In fact, in an article for *Health* magazine, Peter Jaret states that vegetarians actually get larger amounts of amino acids due to the elimination of saturated fats which are often found in meat products. Studies show that the health benefits of a veggie lifestyle contribute to increased life expectancy and overall productivity.

Hopefully you now see that society's perceptions of vegetarians are outdated and just plain wrong. You are familiar with many of the problems associated with a meat-based diet, and you have heard many of the benefits of a vegetarian diet. Now try to imagine how you personally can improve your life by becoming a vegetarian.

Can you imagine a world where people retire at age eighty and lead productive lives into their early 100s? Close your eyes and think about celebrating your seventieth wedding anniversary, seeing your great-grandchildren get married, and witnessing 100 years of world events and technological innovations. David Gabbe's book refers to studies that have shown a vegetarian diet can increase your life expectancy up to fifteen years. A longer life is within your reach, and the diet you eat has a direct impact on your health and how you age.

In conclusion, vegetarianism is a healthy life choice, not a radical cult. By eliminating meat from their diet, vegetarians reap the benefits of a vegetable-based diet that helps prevent disease and increase life expectancy. People, take heed of my advice. There are many more sources of information available for those who want to take a few hours to research the benefits of the veggie lifestyle. If you don't believe my comments, discover the whole truth for yourself.

Twelve million Americans know the health benefits that come 10 with being a vegetarian. Changing your eating habits can be just as easy as making your bed in the morning. Sure, it takes a few extra minutes and some thought, but your body will thank you in the long run.

You only live once. Why not make it a long stay?

PART THREE

Opposing Viewpoints

THE FOLLOWING SECTION contains a variety of opposing viewpoints on eight controversial questions. These questions generate conflict among experts and laypeople alike for two principal reasons. First, even when the facts are not in dispute, they may be interpreted differently by opposing sides. Example: Do the statistics prove that capital punishment is or is not a deterrent to crime? Second, and certainly more difficult to resolve, equally worthwhile values may be in conflict. Example: In dealing with hateful or racist speech, should we decide in favor of the freedom of the individual to speak or the responsibility of the government to protect?

Opposing Viewpoints lends itself to classroom debates, both formal and informal. It can also serve as a useful source of informed opinions which can lead to further research. First, read all the articles in one of the Opposing Viewpoints. Then select a topic for your research paper, either one suggested in this book (see Topics for Research at the end of each chapter) or another approved by your teacher. You may wish to begin your research by choosing material to support your claim from two or three articles in the text or by exploring recommended sources on the Web (see Taking the Debate Online at the end of each chapter).

In reading, analyzing, and preparing your own responses to the opposing viewpoints, you should ask the following questions about each controversy:

1. Are there two — or more — different points of view on the subject? Do all sides make clear what they are trying to prove? Summarize their claims.
2. Do all sides share the same goals? If not, how are they different?
3. How important is definition of key terms? Do all sides agree on the definitions? If so, what are they? If not, how do they differ? Does definition become a significant issue in the controversy?
4. How important is factual and opinion evidence in support of the claims? Does the support fulfill the appropriate criteria? If not, what are its weaknesses? Is the support conflicting? Do the authorities — both the arguers and the experts they quote — have convincing credentials?
5. Do the arguers base any part of their arguments on needs and values that their readers are expected to share? What are they? Do the arguers provide examples of the ways these values function? Are these values implicit or explicit in the arguments? Is there a conflict of values? If so, which seem more important?
6. What warrants or assumptions underlie the claims? Are they implicit or explicit? Do the arguers examine them for the reader? Are the warrants acceptable? If not, point out their weaknesses.
7. What are the main issues? Is there a genuine debate — that is, does each side try to respond to arguments on the other side?
8. Do the arguers propose solutions to a problem? Are the advantages of their proposals clear? Are there obvious disadvantages to implementation of their solutions?
9. Does each argument follow a clear and orderly organization, one that lends itself to a good outline? If not, what are the weaknesses?
10. Does language play a part in the argument? Are there any examples of misuse of language — slanted or loaded words, clichés, slogans, euphemisms, or other short cuts?
11. Do the arguers show an awareness of audience? How would you describe the audience(s) for whom the various arguments are presented?
12. Do you think that one side won the argument? Can you find examples of negotiation and compromise, of attempts to establish a common ground? Explain your answer in detail.

CHAPTER TWELVE

Affirmative Action

More than thirty-five years after the enactment of laws and rules to promote affirmative action, it is under attack on several fronts — by government, business, and education. The legal bases for affirmative action are the Civil Rights Act of 1964 and two executive orders signed by President Lyndon Johnson in 1965. (The Equal Employment Opportunities Act of 1972 was charged with enforcing their provisions.) The original objective of these actions was elimination of the barriers to employment and schooling for women and members of minority groups. To that end, government contractors and educational institutions receiving federal funds were required to set up affirmative action programs.

The earliest policies were designed to protect traditionally disadvantaged groups against discrimination. This meant *ignoring* race and gender criteria, which had prevented qualified women and members of racial and ethnic groups, especially African Americans, from participating fully in American life. In the 1970s, however, affirmative action underwent significant changes with the introduction of quotas, which were intended not merely to remove barriers but to compensate for the effects of past discrimination. Employers and school officials were now compelled to hire, or show that they had made efforts to hire, a specific percentage of African Americans, Hispanics, Native Americans, or women. (Asian Americans and Jews are almost never included in these quotas.)

As a result of these changes, Americans express ambivalence about the benefits of affirmative action to the whole society. In one poll 54 percent of the respondents said that "affirmative action has been good for the country." But when affirmative action was defined as "mandatory preferences," 75 percent of respondents opposed it.

That is because most Americans believe that mandatory preferences mean quotas, a violation of the American ideal that people should be judged as individuals, not as members of a group. They are uneasy about judgments made according to criteria, such as race and gender, that may have little to do with effort or ability to perform a job.

Proponents argue that affirmative action has been successful in enlarging opportunities and increasing diversity at work and at school. And until discrimination no longer prevents minorities and women from equal access to jobs, housing, and education, affirmative action laws should remain firmly on the books.

Court actions have reflected the ambivalence of the American public. Judges, in acknowledging the claims of reverse discrimination by white plaintiffs, have struck down some affirmative action programs in employment, but they have allowed others to remain. In education, however, it seems clear that the role of affirmative action is shrinking. A federal court in March 1996 ruled against a race-based admissions policy at the University of Texas Law School. Other schools in the same federal judicial circuit have been affected. More than a dozen states (including California, Arizona, Pennsylvania, Washington, Colorado, and Michigan) have enacted legislation to dismantle affirmative action programs that determine college admissions and employment. As a result, in 1998 attendance by African Americans and Hispanic Americans declined at some of the top law and medical schools but increased at many second-tier schools. A number of colleges and universities now offer financial aid to students on the basis of family income and educational merit rather than race.

Racial Justice on the Cheap
STEPHEN L. CARTER

I often feel that I should oppose all racial preferences in admission to college and professional school. But I don't. When the law school admission season rolls around during the winter, I find myself drawn to the folders of applicants who are not white, as though to something rare and precious. Those folders I give an extra bit of scrutiny, looking, perhaps, for reasons to recommend a *Yes*. I am not trying to get the numbers right and I do not believe that the standards applied by colleges or professional schools are racist; rather, I find myself wanting others to have the same leg up that I had. The

Stephen L. Carter is William Nelson Cromwell Professor of Law at Yale University and a former clerk to Supreme Court Justice Thurgood Marshall. This selection is from his book *Reflections of an Affirmative Action Baby* (1991). His other books include *Civility* (1998), *Integrity* (1996), and *The Culture of Disbelief* (1993). [Bibliographic citations have been cut.]

question is whether I can square this instinct with what I have said about the damage that preferences do. One of the principal mistaken emphases (or perhaps a public relations problem) of the modern diversity movement . . . is that it often seems in its rhetoric to press toward circumventing or eradicating standards, rather than training us and pushing us until we are able to meet them. There is an important distinction between this modern approach and the more traditional understanding of affirmative action as a program that would help a critical mass of us gain the necessary training to meet the standards of our chosen fields rather than seeking to get around them. Not the least of the difficulties is that the more time we spend arguing that various standards for achievement are culturally inappropriate, the more other people are likely to think we are afraid of trying to meet them.

My own view is that, given training, given a chance, we as a people need fear no standards. That is why I want to return the special admission programs to their more innocent roots, as tools for providing that training and that chance for students who might not otherwise have it. A college or university is not fulfilling its educational missions if it fails to take a hard look at the applicant pool to be sure that it is not missing highly motivated students — some of them people of color, some of them not — who might not be "sure things" but who show good evidence of being positioned to take advantage of what the school can offer. This means taking risks, but that is what higher educational institutions ought to be doing — not to fill a quota or to look good on paper or to keep student activists quiet, and certainly not to bring into the student body a group of students who will thereafter be called upon to represent the distinctive voices of oppressed people (imagine the brouhaha were a professor to take this idea seriously in calling on students in class discussion), but because the purveying of knowledge, the reason universities exist, is a serious enterprise, and one professors should undertake joyfully, even when it isn't easy and even when there is a risk of failure.

Of course, the students who are admitted because a school has decided to take a chance on them will not look as good on paper as those who are admitted because they are sure things; and the odds are that those with the better paper records will be the better performers, too, which is why grades and test scores are considered in the first place. The school, then, is admitting more than one group of students. Many students are admitted because of their paper qualifications, and these are the ones on which the school is likely to pin its highest hopes for academic attainment. The rest are admitted because they have benefited from one preference or another: legacy (as children of alumni are sometimes called), athlete, geography, even in some places music. And some receive a preference because of race.

All the beneficiaries of preferences, not just those who have earned a place through racial preferences, would have been excluded had only a paper record been used. But although every college has its stereotypes of the dumb jock and the stupid legacy, there is a qualitative difference between these characterizations and the conscious or unconscious racial nature of similar comments about the beneficiaries of racially conscious affirmative action. For just as a different standard for admission or hiring reinforces a double standard for the measurement of success, it also reinforces a double standard for the consequence of failure. When a person admitted because of membership in a special category does not succeed, that lack of success is often attributed to others in the same category. The stereotype of the dumb jock exists because of the widespread perception (a correct one) that athletes are frequently admitted on paper records for which other students would be rejected. When people of color are admitted in the same fashion, the damage is worse, because the double standard reinforces an already existing stereotype, and because the stereotype, like the program, sorts explicitly according to race. Consequently, if our success rate at elite colleges turns out to be lower than that of white students (as, thus far, it is), we can scarcely avoid having the fact noticed and, in our racially conscious society, remembered as well.

This risk is a predictable consequence of double standards and   5
cannot be avoided. It can, however, be reduced. The best way to reduce the risk would be to eliminate racial preferences, and over time, as the competitive capacity of people of color continues to improve. A more immediate solution is for those students who are admitted as a consequence of affirmative action, while on the college campus and while in professional school and while pursuing their careers — in short, *for the rest of their professional lives* — to bend to their work with an energy that will leave competitors and detractors alike gasping in admiration. The way to turn this potential liability into a powerful asset is to make our cadre of professionals simply too good to ignore.

To accomplish this goal, the first thing that an opportunity-based affirmative action must do is to abandon the pretense that it will in any significant way compensate for present educational disadvantage. Programs of preferential admissions will not wipe away the lingering effects of struggling through the inner-city public schools about which the nation long ago ceased to care. To bring onto college campuses students whose academic abilities have been severely damaged by the conditions in which they have been forced to learn would be a recipe for failure. At best, affirmative action can take those students of color who have already shown the greatest potential and place them in environments where their minds will be tested and trained, the campuses of elite colleges and professional schools.

Besides, the evidence has long suggested, and recent studies have confirmed, that educational disadvantage is but one of a cluster of problems reducing the likelihood that students of color will attend or complete college. In the past decade, despite rising test scores, a higher rate of high school graduation, and affirmative action programs galore, college attendance by black students is down. In particular, the proportion of black youth aged eighteen to twenty-four who have been enrolled in college has plummeted. In 1976, 33.4 percent of that group were or had been enrolled in college, representing nearly half of black high school graduates; this compared very favorably with the 33.0 percent of white youth of the same age with enrollment experience, representing 40 percent of white high school graduates. Ten years later, although the high school graduation rate rose, the percentage of black youth with enrollment experience dropped to 28.6 percent, representing only 37.4 percent of high school graduates, while the equivalent percentages for white youth barely changed at all.

Debate over the causes of this decline continues, and some of the candidates — for example, the rising involvement with the drug culture, the large number of young black men caught up in the criminal justice system, and the appeal of competing career choices, such as the military — are beyond the control of educational institutions. (Besides, the drug culture and criminal justice arguments are plainly insufficient to explain why the rate of high school graduation would be *up* so sharply.) There is common agreement, however, that a principal difficulty is the high cost, especially at the nation's most exclusive universities, which makes alternative career choices more attractive. This is why preferential financial assistance (for all its obvious problems) might actually be a more logical and efficient solution than preferential admission. As this manuscript was being completed, a debate erupted over the decision (subsequently modified) by the United States Department of Education to deny federal funds to schools offering preferential financial aid packages on the basis of race.[1] This decision, defended on the ground that federal aid should be administered in a color-blind manner, created a dilemma for colleges interested in keeping both minority recruitment and academic standards at high levels. If one argues that affirmative action is impermissible, then schools are left with only the market mechanism — money — as a tool for enticing onto their campuses excellent students who are not white. A genuine believer in market solutions should allow participants in the market to bid for scarce resources — and by all accounts, first-rate students of color are such a resource. One might want to

---

[1] The compromise resolution was that schools may not use federal funds for racially preferential scholarships but may fund such scholarships from other sources.

argue that this bidding is not fair, but if colleges can rely on neither preferential admission nor bidding to attract students who are not white, they plainly can do no more than pay lip service to the ideal of "minority recruitment." . . .

With the proper goal in mind, then, a degree of racial conscious-ness *in college and perhaps professional school admission* can plausi-bly be justified — but just a degree, and just barely. The educational sphere is the place for action because the proper goal of all racial preferences is opportunity — a chance at advanced training for highly motivated people of color who, for whatever complex set of reasons, might not otherwise have it. So justified, the benefit of a racial preference carries with it the concomitant responsibility not to waste the opportunity affirmative action confers. What matters most is what happens *after* the preference.

I call this vision of professional achievement and racial prefer- 10 ence the affirmative action pyramid, and it works much as the name implies: The role of preference narrows as one moves upward. And although I do not want to say arbitrarily *This is the spot,* what is clear is that as one climbs toward professional success, at some point the preferences must fall away entirely. Possibly a slight preference is justified in college admission, not as a matter of getting the numbers right, and certainly not as a matter of finding the right set of hitherto excluded points of view, but as a matter of giving lots of people from different backgrounds the chance — only the chance — to have an education at an elite college or university. But when that opportu-nity has been exercised, when the student has shown what he or she can do, the rationale for a preference at the next level is slimmer. So an even slighter affirmative action preference for professional school admission, while possibly justified on similar grounds, is less important, and a little bit harder to defend, than a program at the college level.

And when one's training is done, when the time comes for entry to the job market, I think it is quite clear that among professionals,[2] the case for preference evaporates. The candidate has by this time had six or seven or eight years of training at the highest level; it is a bit silly, as well as demeaning, to continue to insist that one's college and professional school performance is not a very accurate barome-ter of one's professional possibilities. The time has come, finally, to stand or fall on what one has actually achieved. And, of course, as one passes the point of initial entry and moves up the ladder of one's chosen field, all of the arguments run the other way; the time

---

[2] I make no claim here about the propriety of affirmative action in labor markets demanding less in the way of educational credentials.

for preference has gone, and it is time instead to stand proudly on
one's own record. The preferences cannot go on forever. Sooner or
later, talent and preparation, rather than skin color, must tell.

Affirmative Action Must Go
SHELBY STEELE

There are many indications that affirmative action may soon
provoke what it has never provoked before: a national debate on
group preferences that will be so open and contentious that no important politician will be able to avoid a hard yea or nay position.

This has all been started by the threat of another of those California statewide initiatives in which some long-simmering public bitterness explodes onto the ballot and is then argued out in the national
village of talk radio. Next year, Californians are to vote on the appropriateness of preferential treatment by sex, race, and ethnic origin as
a form of social redress. What an odd opportunity: to vote in secret on
the idea that some citizens should be preferred over others in public
employment, contracting, and higher education.

I wish my parents had had such a vote back in the 1950s, when I
was languishing in a segregated elementary school created by white
preferential treatment. My guess is that Californians will vote as my
parents would surely have voted then: against preferences of any kind.

Significantly, most of the new interest in affirmative action
seems to be political rather than social. The buzz is all about how
the issue will wedge the Democrats into white male moderates on
one flank and minorities and women on the other — an ugly reseg-
regation of America's "civil rights" party that will make President
Clinton even more vulnerable than he already is.

There is little talk about affirmative action as public policy. One   5
reason, I think, is that affirmative action has always been what might
be called iconographic public policy — policy that ostensibly exists
to solve a social problem but actually functions as an icon for the
self-image people hope to gain by supporting the policy. From the
beginning, affirmative action could be cited as evidence of white social virtue and of emerging black power — the precise qualities that
America's long history of racism had denied to each side.

Shelby Steele, a research fellow at the Hoover Institute, Stanford University, is
the author of two books, *A Dream Deferred: The Second Betrayal of Black Freedom in
America* (1998) and *The Content of Our Characters: A New Vision of Race in America*
(1990). This column appeared in the *New York Times* on March 1, 1995.

Had America worked from the 1960s on to educate blacks to the same standards as whites, had it truly labored to eradicate discrimination, there would be more virtue and power on both sides of the racial divide today. The disingenuousness of affirmative action — born of the black struggle for freedom — can be seen in two remarkable facts: Middle-class white women have benefited from it far more than any other group, and 46 percent of all black children live in poverty.

The perniciousness of an iconographic social policy is that you cannot be against it without seeming to be against what it purports to represent. The white who argues against affirmative action looks like a racist and the black looks like an Uncle Tom. Iconographic policies perpetuate themselves by hiding behind what they represent. This is why, after twenty-five years, affirmative action is one of the least evaluated social policies in American history. The price for accepting its illusion of virtue and power is ignorance.

Not only do we blind ourselves to the workings of a social policy that becomes an icon, but in search of a flattering self-image we justify the policy by vague ideals like "diversity." And the emptiness of these ideals makes the policy unaccountable for any result it may have, so it remains an icon whether or not it accomplishes anything in the real world.

Diversity policies (today's euphemism for affirmative action) exist in virtually every important institution even though no one really knows what diversity means. Both proportionate and disproportionate representation reflect diversity; integration is one kind of diversity and segregation another. Here is an idealism that destroys accountability in social policy, and a language of willed ignorance in which the words mean only that the speaker has good intentions.

Still, as much as I loathe affirmative action — for the indignity 10 and Faustian bargain it presents to minorities, for the hypocrisy and shameless self-congratulation it brings out in its white supporters — I must admit that it troubles me to see its demise so glibly urged from the political right. The Republican presidential aspirants are stumbling over one another to condemn it. While they are right to do so — and right is right even when it is nothing more than right — there is also the matter of moral authority. And this is something anyone who wants to dismantle affirmative action will have to earn.

I would ask those who oppose preferences to acknowledge and account for the reality of black alienation. As a black, I still fear discrimination, still have the feeling that it is waiting for me in public America. Discrimination does not justify preferential treatment, but I want to know that the person who stands with me against preferences understands the problem that inspired them.

To my mind there is only one way to moral authority for those of us who want affirmative action done away with: to ask that discrimination by race, gender, or ethnicity be a criminal offense, not just civil. If someone can go to jail for stealing my car stereo, he ought to do considerably more time for stifling my livelihood and well-being by discriminating against me.

If this means there will be many trials and lawsuits, so be it. When the pressure is put precisely on the evil you want to eradicate, then individuals and institutions will quickly learn not only what discrimination is but also what fairness is — and fairness is a concept so confused by decades of affirmative action that many now believe it can be reached only through discrimination.

Ending affirmative action must involve more than bringing down an icon. It must also involve an extension of democratic principles to what might be an extreme degree in a racially homogeneous society. But in a society like ours, discrimination is the greatest and most disruptive social evil. In a multiracial democracy of individuals, you have to make it a felony.

Race, Not Class
NATHAN GLAZER

Only a few months ago, affirmative action seemed sacrosanct, having survived under two Republican presidents who opposed it but were incapable of modifying it in any way. Now suddenly the policy is threatened by complete abolition. But even confirmed opponents might quail before the cold-turkey withdrawal now made possible by the massive upthrust of political opinion. Is there any alternative to extinction, and should we try to find it?

One of the most popular alternatives to complete abolition is the replacement of race-based affirmative action with class-based affirmative action. It is preference on the basis of race that arouses anger and a sense of injustice among whites, just as it arouses such feelings among blacks. When whites believe that race alone excludes them from consideration for jobs or limits their opportunities to enter selective colleges, universities, and professional schools, many will feel the same anger blacks do.

Proponents of class-based affirmative action assert it would do much of what race-based affirmative action attempts to do, and

---

Nathan Glazer, a professor of education and sociology at Harvard University, is the author or editor of numerous books, including *We Are All Multiculturalists Now* (1998). This article is reprinted from the April 5, 1995, edition of the *Wall Street Journal.*

would not arouse the same hostility. Nor is there any bar to such preference, apparently, in the Constitution or in civil rights law. Of course, it could not achieve the same results for blacks as race-based affirmative action. But since blacks are to be found disproportionately among the poor (they form 12 percent of the population, but 30 percent or more of the population in poverty), many could move up because of their poverty. Class-based affirmative action would reduce the irritation and anger of those excluded, because of the moral legitimacy of this ground of preference. It would also reduce the cases of inequity, few as they may be, in which blacks of professional and high-income backgrounds get preference on the basis of race over poorer whites.

A Bad Idea

But class-based affirmative action is a bad idea, whose weaknesses become apparent when we review the areas in which affirmative action operates. Consider the preference to government contractors on grounds of race. This was designed to increase the number of black businessmen, and it has been ineffective in doing so, because we do not know the levers that will turn people averse to entrepreneurship into eager small-business men willing to undertake the risks, long hours, and stresses. (Koreans have the highest rate of self-employment of any racial or ethnic group, but not because of any government preference in bidding for contracts, even though they are apparently eligible for preference because they are "Asian.")

How would one qualify for eligibility for preference in bidding 5 for government contracts when the racial criterion is replaced by the economic? Would it be current income, to demonstrate that the bidder is truly poor? Could a poor contractor fulfill the contract? Would it be the income of the bidder's family of origin? What sense would that make? After all, how many children of prosperous parents undertake the hard and risky life of the small-business man? And who would the new businessmen of impoverished backgrounds be replacing, but other small-business men of almost equally impoverished backgrounds?

This area of affirmative action is peculiarly afflicted by dissembling and fraud. Is the contractor truly a "minority" or a "woman"— rather than a white contractor seeking a minority cover or a woman covering for her husband? Matters in this regard would not be improved if we replaced race by class. In the case of race-based preference in government contracts, abolition is clearly preferable to class-based preference.

Class-based preference makes as little sense in another area of affirmative action, admission to colleges, universities, and professional schools. We already have a huge and expensive system of federal loans and grants, supplemented by state programs and individual institutional scholarships, to make it possible for those without parental or their own income to get higher education. These do not cover all costs, but it is the assumption in American higher education that students will work to help pay for their education, and almost all, rich or poor, do. One can imagine covering all costs for higher education for everyone, as European countries attempt to do, but the costs would be enormous, and the beneficiaries for the most part would be white and Asian.

The problem African Americans face in entering institutions of higher education is performance, and performance is affected by poverty. But then the direct answer is programs to raise performance, or to reduce poverty. We know that substantial efforts have been expended on both objectives, and how frustratingly difficult it has been to make progress on either. The only effect of preference on grounds of class could be to increase the number of poor whites and Asians in institutions of higher education, and to reduce the number of blacks.

When it comes to employment, it is also hard to see what class-based affirmative action would achieve. Those aspiring to well-paid skilled work, as electricians, plumbers, and the like; to work as policemen, firemen, sanitation workers; to teaching jobs — in all of which strong affirmative action programs exist — are not typically from well-to-do backgrounds.

In each area of employment, defined means of entry and promo- 10 tion have been developed: apprenticeship and union membership for skilled work, civil-service examinations for city jobs. Endless effort has been devoted to opening apprenticeship programs, union membership, and city work forces to blacks, and there has been some modest success, particularly in police forces, but these successes could not have been achieved by class-based affirmative action. Those struggling to enter such programs do not see themselves as particularly advantaged, and would resent the notion that a preference should be given to those poorer than they are when they themselves struggle against poverty.

Affirmative action is afflicted with irrational and illogical preference categories and with fraud. Much of this can and should be stripped away. But at its heart is a reality that cannot be wished away. This is the distinctive condition of American blacks, scarred by a history of oppression no other group, save American Indians, can match. African Americans are a group still uniquely isolated and segregated.

Whatever the weight of the logic that led to the inclusion of Hispanic Americans and Asian Americans in affirmative action at its beginnings, it no longer applies. Both groups now consist in their majority of immigrants and their children. American society and institutions have no special obligation beyond nondiscrimination for these groups. Asian Americans in general already have more education and as much income as most Americans. Hispanic Americans are more poorly off, but their circumstances are explained far more by lower average education, language difficulties, and recent immigration than by discrimination. Neither group should be included in legal requirements for affirmative action. American Indians raise other issues, but their condition is already addressed by a great deal of special legislation.

A Terrible Rejection

Affirmative action was occasioned by the civil rights revolution, and was designed for blacks. The problems it was intended to address are still with us, and in some respects are more serious than they were thirty years ago. Affirmative action has done precious little to ameliorate these problems, but I am concerned that African Americans will see the abandonment of affirmative action for them as a terrible rejection by an indifferent and hostile society. It would have consequences — for example, a sharp reduction in the number of blacks in selective colleges and professional schools — that we should not accept, whatever the value of the principle that justifies them.

Just what form affirmative action for blacks should take, where it should be applied, and who should benefit require further discussion. At the very least, voluntary affirmative action, which would certainly be maintained in colleges and universities, by major corporations, and by many cities, even in the absence of federal regulations, should be encouraged. There are legal and constitutional problems here, but they should not be allowed to stand in the way of voluntary efforts to deal with our greatest domestic problem.

Affirmative Action: A Tale of Two Women
MANDALIT DEL BARCO

The issue of affirmative action is being debated across the country, having sparked such buzzwords and phrases as "angry white males," "preferential treatment," and "reverse discrimination." The policy's original intent in the late 1960s was to redress past discrimination and provide opportunities for underrepresented groups, including Latinos and women. Supporters of affirmative action say the playing fields in schools, jobs, and contracts are still not level for many minorities, and that affirmative action is still crucial for ensur-

Mandalit del Barco is a Los Angeles–based reporter for National Public Radio and the radio program *Latino USA*. She was a contributing editor to *Sí,* when this article appeared in the Fall–Winter 1995 issue.

ing equal access. Critics, meanwhile, charge that affirmative action has stigmatized the very people it was supposed to have benefited, and created new victims in those who are passed over for jobs, college admissions, and so on. Some advocate abolishing affirmative action altogether, while others call for reforms, suggesting that the best solution could be to simply recast the policy in terms of the economically disadvantaged. All sides seem to agree the problem is one of fairness, though they may disagree about what is fair. *Sí* spoke with two prominent Mexican American women, Linda Chavez and Antonia Hernández, who have opposing views on this issue, which has at times divided those within the same ethnic group, including the Latino community.

Linda Chavez is a Mexican American woman out of the mold: She is fiercely and consistently conservative in the matter of affirmative action. The articulate staff director of the Commission on Civil Rights during the Reagan administration is today the president of the Center for Equal Opportunity, a nonprofit research group in Washington, D.C. Chavez is a columnist, a TV commentator, and author of the book *Out of the Barrio: Toward a New Politics of Hispanic Assimilation.* She will soon publish her second book, *A House Divided: Race and the Politics of Multiculturalism.* Linda Chavez's views are shaped not only by an extensive education, but also by her personal experience of ethnicity in this country. She belongs to the old community of *Mexicános* in the Southwest. "The only immigrant in my family in recent memory was probably my great grandfather, who was from England," says Chavez, a native of New Mexico. "On my father's side, my family goes back to the seventeenth century. On my mother's, there were Irish and English immigrants."

Sí: What is your definition of affirmative action?

Chavez: Affirmative action was originally construed to cast a wider net or provide training opportunities to enable people to compete. Those intentions were transformed in the late sixties and early seventies into programs that emphasize race or ethnicity as qualifications to promote the ideas of diversity. Diversity for its own sake. I find that offensive and I would like to see those programs abolished.

Sí: Why?   5

Chavez: They are more than offensive. Racial preferences granted by the State are unconstitutional. They violate the letter as well as the spirit of the civil rights laws. The Civil Rights Act of 1964 is unequivocal in that respect. 703-J of Title Seven says, "Nothing in this Act shall be interpreted to require preferences on the basis of race, color, or national origin."

Racial preferences are also patronizing, and ultimately, a very racist concept. They imply that, somehow, you cannot apply the same standards to blacks and Hispanics as you do to whites, because minorities will not be able to meet them. This is a misguided notion promoted by many liberals.

Sí: What do you say to those people who feel they never would have made it to where they are had it not been for affirmative action?

Chavez: If they would not have made it because they would not have found the opportunities, that is one thing. But if they have been admitted under a separate set of standards, and then held to a different standard of performance, I find it wrong.

Another thing that concerns me about the affirmative action programs is that they are a perpetual motion machine: Once they start, they go on forever. A student can be admitted by a college under one of those programs. After graduation, he or she can get into law school under another affirmative action program. After law school, he or she might still use affirmative action programs to get a job. If as a professional he or she does not make it to the top, people would say that there is a glass ceiling preventing this person from succeeding. An individual who cannot stand on his or her own in any given position perhaps should not be in it at all.

Sí: Yet people who favor affirmative action say its programs are still needed to level the playing field. Students who come from a school that was economically disadvantaged, and lack opportunities available to others, need that extra help.

Chavez: I do not disagree with that, that is what affirmative action was initially. But kids of middle-class families, whose parents are sometimes college-educated, are given a preference at Berkeley or Stanford based solely on their ethnic background. My children, for example, are often recruited. I have one son who is a senior now. He has been given a book on how to apply for affirmative action and scholarships. We live in one of the most affluent communities in America. He has not faced discrimination in his life, and he is not economically or socially disadvantaged. He should not be held to a lower standard and given a preference simply on the basis of his mother's ethnicity.

That is the core of the problem: Programs do not reach out to the kids who are disadvantaged and who come from inner-city schools.

The effort should not concentrate on admissions for law or medical schools. The emphasis should be a place in education at the elementary and secondary school levels. Here, the process begins. Children are prepared to compete on their own. Four years of math, science, and a foreign language are far more important to the long-term progress of both blacks and Hispanics than anything that can be done at a later time.

Sí: What is your own experience with affirmative action?

Chavez: I have been chosen for jobs on the basis of being a Mexican American woman. Each time, it has been an unmitigated disaster. There was a presumption that I thought in a certain way, and that I was going to serve a certain function. When it turned out I was not interested in being the token Hispanic, things did not work out well. There have been other times when the affirmative action prejudice stigmatized me. I had to constantly demonstrate that I have earned my position.

Once, I actively went after an affirmative action program. This was in 1969. The Ford Foundation had established a series of generous fellowships for blacks, Mexican American, and American Indians. I applied for one of them. The interviewer — who happened to be Anglo — complimented me on my ability to speak English. "My, you speak English so well," he said. Well, English is my only fluent language. English is my first language, as it is for most third-generation Mexican Americans. In addition, I was then pursuing a Ph.D. in English literature. I found the comment demeaning and insulting. The interview went downhill from there.

They also found my G.R.E. scores "too high" and that somehow this meant that I could not be an authentic Mexican American. That very sour experience was caused by people who thought they were doing people like me a favor.

Sí: Do you think your position might polarize people over the issue of race, when the real problem Americans face is, as many say, disappearing jobs?

Chavez: The most vociferous opposition comes from universities, not from working-class people who have seen their income diminish because of economic restructuring. The opposition underestimates the great damage affirmative action has done to race relations in this country. Indeed, there has been an increase in racial hostility. 20

Sí: Do you see a connection between the issues of affirmative action and immigration?

Chavez: Yes. People for Proposition 187 — an anti-immigrant initiative on the 1994 California ballot — were worried not just about a large number of newcomers, but about an increasing number of people eligible for affirmative action. Also, a lot of the anti-immigrant sentiment is a reflection of dissatisfaction with programs such as bilingual education, and the sense that immigrants create a whole new huge clientele for programs that are draining resources. People are angry about welfare. I am convinced that 187 won by such a large margin because welfare was on the ballot.

Sí: What is your view of Latino immigration in the United States?

Chavez: I am all for immigration, and maybe for higher immigration levels than the current ones. Immigrants come with tremendous entrepreneurial spirit. They are risk takers, they invest a lot in succeeding. But historically, American immigration has worked only if immigrants do not stay outside the mainstream, and stop functioning in their own language. The problem with Latino immigration is public policy regarding bilingual education.

What could also be destructive is the apparent rush to change   25
immigration law. A moratorium on immigration, worker registries, a national I.D. card are all bad ideas.

Affirmative action divides more neatly along conservative and liberal lines. The immigration debate is much more divided. Some of the people who are most virulently anti-immigrant are those who consider themselves liberals. We are living in interesting times.

Antonia Hernández finds her story is not unique among Mexican Americans. Her family lived in Texas, but was deported when her father was eight years old. "I also was eight when I came here," remembers Hernández. "My dad brought us to Juárez. We lived here while my father put the documents together. I remember going to the interview with the immigration officers. They told my dad that, technically, we were citizens through derivative birth. It was the month of June. We crossed the border to El Paso, and they gave us our *mica*,[1] but our uncle could not come to pick us up from Los Angeles till September. We lived in Las Cruces and worked in the cotton fields."

Hernández's memories flow with ease. "My uncle came in a beautiful Chevrolet. We all got in the car, all crunched up, and on the way to Los Angeles, they were playing on the radio two songs I will never forget: Sarah Vaughan's 'Tender Lovin'' and Connie Francis's 'Lipstick on Your Collar.' When I hear those songs, I go back to that trip from El Paso to Los Angeles. I did migrant work. My parents were industrial laborers. The usual story."

Her story, though, is not common at all. From her humble origins, Hernández has come to be a well-known leader in the defense of Latino rights. She is president and general counsel of the Mexican American Legal Defense and Education Fund (MALDEF), an organization noted for its triumphs in class actions against discrimination, including widely publicized redistricting cases. She began her advocacy career during the Chicano movement in the early seventies, and continued her passionate service to the community at the Los Angeles Center for Law and Justice, and the Legal Foundation of Los Angeles. She is currently advising on the legal challenge to California's anti-immigrant initiative, Proposition 187.

---

[1] A Mexican term for the government-issued green card allowing immigrants to work in the United States for a limited number of years. — ED.

Sí: In your opinion, what is affirmative action?   30

Hernández: Affirmative action is a court-sanctioned vehicle for diversifying the work force and opening opportunities for people who have been excluded in the past. Affirmative action is not quotas. It does not allow people to get by. In colleges and universities, affirmative action programs diversify the student body by considering a variety of factors for admission. But there is no affirmative action for grades. That is up to the student.

Same thing in the work force. For example: In the past, there were height requirements for police officers. That was devastating for women, since not many of them are six feet tall, particularly Latinas. Since height has little to do with your ability to perform the job, we went to court and challenged the requirement.

After a complete review of police responsibilities and the physical ability needed to fulfill them, the height requirement was changed. The quality standards were not lowered. That is the beauty of affirmative action. It gives the flexibility to find new standards that are more relevant, more current, taking into account our past and present history of discrimination and exclusion.

Sí: In which ways do you feel affirmative action has been successful?

Hernández: All you have to do is look at the statistics. And quite   35
frankly, I would not be here if it were not for affirmative action. I was an immigrant kid out of East Los Angeles. Without affirmative action I would not have been given an opportunity to go to UCLA and explore horizons that were never opened to my parents. "Huppies"— upwardly mobile Hispanics — do not acknowledge sometimes that affirmative action has opened doors for them. They feel uncomfortable with what they perceive as a negative tag. We need to openly say we are examples of the success of affirmative action.

Sí: Can you talk about your own experience with affirmative action?

Hernández: I am a kid out of Garfield High School in East Los Angeles. I am a pretty bright individual, and I had decent grades. I was just dirt poor. My parents lived in the projects and I dreamed of going to Cal State L.A., because it was just across the street, in the neighborhood. That was as far as my dreams would take me. While I was in college, I was exposed to UCLA. I applied and was admitted. I did relatively well at UCLA because my grades were pretty decent, and my LSAT scores were also very good. I do not know whether I got in the door through affirmative action or regular admission. But it does not matter. I was given an opportunity and, I am sure, I was judged by standards other than just grades and test scores. They saw in me the burning determination, the drive, the willingness to work. That is what made me a success. I am not the only one. It happened to thousands of Latinos who went to medical school, to architecture school, you name it.

Sí: One argument people make against affirmative action is that it brings with it the stigma of being seen as undeserving. Do people think that you were given a break, that the standards were lowered when applied to you?

Hernández: I do not know if the standards were lowered. But they did give me a break. But it is no different than the breaks other people have been given. Children of alumni are given a very special break and get admitted automatically to the best universities. The perception that this is a society based on merit is one of our biggest myths. To some degree, I think I was also less qualified than other entering students. I came from Garfield High School. If you compare what it offered in the early sixties to other public schools, I was not getting an equal opportunity education. But I will tell you: I did not get in because I was given the proper grounding. I did not get in because I was given every privilege bestowed on alumni's kids. Am I stigmatized by this? No.

Sí: Linda Chavez and others argue: Why should we continue to 40 base jobs, hiring, promotions, admissions, on a surname or the color of your skin?

Hernández: There is a basic assumption people make, that race is no longer a factor in this country. Race is a more prevalent factor now, but in a much more subtle way than before. Up until the sixties, regardless of how rich you were in Texas, if you were Mexican American, you were not admitted to certain colleges and universities. Look at the census. My kids are by no means poor. Should they get "a break" because their name is Hernández? I would venture to think, probably not. But my little Ben, who looks very Mexican, is not going to be judged by how well he is prepared. Group identity is still based on gender and skin pigmentation.

Sí: You were born in Mexico. Do you see a connection between affirmative action and emerging anti-immigration policies such as Proposition 187?

Hernández: Absolutely. This country is going through a real nervous breakdown. I do not mean it in a negative way. The national complexion is changing. The dynamics of who is an American is changing. In addition to Latinos, there are high concentrations of Armenians, Koreans, Iranians, and Russian Jews in large American cities. The country is feeling uncomfortable. Being American is not about looking a certain way. It is a state of [m]ind, an ideal, an attitude. It is what we believe in: individualism, and participatory democracy.

Is Affirmative Action on the Way Out? Should It Be?

RANDALL KENNEDY

Affirmative action as a "hand up" for "people who have had a hard time" comports with the best justification for efforts that offer special assistance to individuals associated with groups that have been historically oppressed in the United States. In other words, reparative justice is the best rationale for affirmative action — offering a benefit to certain people in order to offset the disadvantages they inherited as a consequence of deep-seated social pathologies such as racism and sexism.

This justification is prominent in the public's understanding of affirmative action. It has sometimes given way, however, to other, more dubious, justifications. In the landmark 1978 case of *Regents of California v. Bakke,* for example, Justice Powell's pivotal opinion rejected generalized claims of reparative justice as a proper basis for affirmative action in higher education. In its stead, he embraced the idea of intellectual diversity. I have never been persuaded that taking race (or gender) into account to assure the presence of varying perspectives in a classroom is a weightier justification than attempting to repair decades, indeed centuries, of racial and gender oppression.

Affirmative action has greatly benefited large numbers of women of all hues and racial minorities of all genders. It has done so by enabling them to attain educational and occupational advancements in numbers and at a pace that would otherwise have been unlikely if not impossible. It has also signaled publicly and vividly a desire to repudiate the policies of the past that relegated women and minorities to an inferior role in the nation's life. These consequences of affirmative action have redounded not only to the benefit of those who have been the direct recipients of special assistance. They have redounded to the benefit of the nation as a whole.

Affirmative action does have significant costs as well. It has often stigmatized its direct beneficiaries, exacerbated racial resentments, and deepened overall an already deeply entrenched habit of racial and gender selectivity in public and private affairs. Thirty years ago, the benefits of affirmative action clearly outweighed the drawbacks (though the drawbacks should have always been evident and troublesome). Now the case is much closer.

Randall Kennedy is a professor at the Harvard law school and the author of *Race, Crime, and the Law* (1997). This essay is from *Commentary,* March 1998.

As for the future, I am ambivalent about affirmative action and 5
think that ambivalence is a good posture to adopt. On the one hand,
I am deeply impressed by the toxic consequences of drawing racial
distinctions among people in this multiracial society, particularly
when the racial line-drawing is done by the government. On the
other hand, I am profoundly worried about the prospect of slowing
the reconstruction of America, slowing the process by which women
and minorities are belatedly becoming integrated into all sectors of
the nation's life.

I am also worried that the destruction of affirmative action will
not lead to a widespread assault against all racial line-drawing but
only against racial line-drawing that adversely affects men and
whites. After all, police officers are authorized to take race into account in deciding whom to question and detain for purposes of fighting crime. This practice is deeply resented in minority communities
and is profoundly counterproductive. Yet it receives little attention
in comparison to affirmative action.

Affirmative action will be cut back in various ways but will not
be wholly removed as a significant force in American life anytime
soon. This is so for both troubling and heartening reasons. I will end
by noting one of the heartening reasons. Many, many Americans,
whatever their ideological vantage point, are decently concerned
when they see an important forum in which women or racial minorities are absent or conspicuously few in number. That is why conservatives who say that they abhor affirmative action *love* the presence
of Clarence Thomas, Thomas Sowell, and Walter Williams. That is
why every presidential administration since the Kennedy administration, including that of Ronald Reagan, has made sure to have at
least one black member of the cabinet.

It is right for Americans to reconsider whether race-selective
and gender-selective affirmative action is the best available way to
continue the process of deepening our democracy. It is also right
for Americans to insist, however, that somehow that process be
continued.

Testimony before a Congressional Committee

CARL COHEN

Mr. Chairman and Members of the Committee:

Good morning. My name is Carl Cohen; I am a professor of philosophy at the University of Michigan, in Ann Arbor. I am grateful for the opportunity to express my vigorous support for the Equal Opportunity Act of 1995, and to present, in the few minutes at my disposal, the essence of the argument against preference by ethnic group. A list of references on this topic — in law reviews and elsewhere — has been submitted to the Committee for your convenience.

The object of the Equal Opportunity Act of 1995 is to prohibit our federal government from giving preference based on race or on sex — and to prohibit the government from requiring or encouraging others to give such preference. Why in the world would any fair-minded person object to that? Surely there is no ground for complaint if our government does *not* discriminate! But many well-intentioned people do complain, struggling to retain group preferences — some because they seek to engineer a *redistribution* of goods to match the proportions of the races and the sexes, and some because they think that such preferences give *compensation* for past injuries. Reasons of both kinds are deeply mistaken. The moral case against group preference — whether in the form of quotas, or goals and timetables, or numerical targets, or whatever — is overwhelming.

The Constitutional case against it, resting upon the Due Process Clause of the Fifth Amendment addressed to the government of the United States, and the Equal Protection Clause of the Fourteenth Amendment addressed to the several states, I leave to the lawyers; you know it well.

But underlying these clauses of our constitution, Mr. Chairman, and underlying also the unambiguous language of the Civil Rights Act of 1964, there lies a *moral* foundation — a universal understanding of right conduct that does not depend upon the words of any clause or statute, but stems directly from our recognition of the moral equality of persons, and the obligation — certainly the obligation of democratic governments — to treat persons equally.

Carl Cohen is a professor of philosophy at the University of Michigan. On December 7, 1995, he testified before the U.S. House of Representatives Committee on the Judiciary Subcommittee on the Constitution, chaired by Representative Charles T. Canady. His comments were published in *Measure*, January–February 1996.

Here is the nub of it: To give favor to males or to females, to 5
whites or to blacks or to persons of any color, *because* of their sex
or color, is morally wrong because doing so is intrinsically *unfair.*
Color, nationality, sex are not attributes that entitle anyone to more
(or less) of the good things of life, or to any special favor (or disfa-
vor). When in the past whites or males did receive such preference
that was deeply wrong; it is no less wrong now when the colors or
sexes are reversed. Justice Thurgood Marshall long ago made it
clear that the plain words of federal law "proscribe racial discrimination . . . against whites on the same terms as racial discrimination
against non-whites." [*McDonald v. Santa Fe Trail Transportation Co.*
(1976) 427 U.S. 273, at 280] Equality applies to all.

But what of those who have been badly hurt by earlier racial discrimination; do they not deserve to be compensated? Yes; persons
may indeed be entitled to remedy for unlawful injury done to them
because they were black or brown or female. We give such remedy,
rightly — but it is the *injury* for which remedy is given, not the skin
color or sex. There is all the difference in the world between compensation for injury and preference by race.

When preference is naked — given flatly by skin color or by
sex — the inevitable result is the award of advantages to some who
deserve no advantage and the imposition of burdens upon some
who deserve no burden. Most often those who benefit did not suffer
the wrong for which "compensation" is supposedly being given;
those who are disadvantaged by the preference most often did not
do any wrong whatever, and certainly not that earlier wrong to a minority group for which the preference is alleged redress.

The oppression of blacks and some other minorities in our country has been grievous, a stain on our history; no honest person will
deny that. But the notion that we can redress that historical grievance by giving preference now to persons in the same racial or sexual *group* as those earlier wronged is a mistake, a blunder. It
supposes that rights are possessed by *groups,* and that therefore
advantages given to some minority group now can be payment for
earlier injuries to other members of that minority. But moral entitle-
ments are not held by groups. Whites as a group do not have rights;
blacks as a group do not have rights. Rights are possessed by *persons,* individual human persons. And when persons are entitled to
be made whole for some injury earlier done to them, the duty owed
is not to members of their race or sex or nationality, not to their
group, but to *them* as individuals. The effort to defend preference as
group compensation fails because it fundamentally misconceives
the relation between wrongs and remedies.

Does this mean that affirmative action must be abandoned? That
depends upon what is meant by affirmative action, of course. In its
original sense affirmative action was intended to insure the *elimina-*

tion of racially discriminatory practices — that is the sense in which the phrase is used in the Civil Rights Act of 1964 — and there is nothing in the bill before us that would hinder that honorable aim. But if by affirmative action one means (as most Americans now do mean) preferential devices designed to bring about *redistribution* of the good things of life to match ethnic proportions in the population, affirmative action in that sense must be rejected — because the preferences it employs are inconsistent with the equal treatment of all persons. No sound principles, constitutional or moral, justify discriminating by race or sex to achieve some predetermined numerical distribution of goods. This defense of preference fails for the same reason all other defenses of preference fail: it contravenes the equal treatment of individual persons that fair process demands.

This principle of equal treatment is the moral foundation upon 10 which the Equal Protection Clause of the Fourteenth Amendment ultimately rests; our Supreme Court has repeatedly emphasized that the rights guaranteed by that clause are *individual* rights, the rights of *persons* ["No state shall . . . deny to any person . . . "] and not the rights of groups. And that is why, Mr. Chairman, every program relying upon naked preference by race or sex, whether in the form of set-asides in the award of contracts, or bonuses for hiring persons of certain colors, or extra credit to bidders in the competition for broadcast licenses, or additional consideration in competitive employment, or promotion, or admission systems — all such preferences — *and whether defended as compensatory or as redistributive* — must be *unjust.*

Some will reply: "It's easy for you, a white male, to say 'No more preference' after you and yours have enjoyed so much preference over the generations. But the tables are turned now and you get a taste of your own medicine. We were oppressed yesterday, so we are entitled to advantage today; it's your turn to pay."

The anger is understandable, but the reasoning is bad. Racial and sexual vindictiveness, like preference itself, is the product of "*groupthink*" — the confused conviction that one group has an entitlement, another group a debt; again supposing that racial or sexual *groups* are the bearer of rights. It is that very blunder that led us, long ago, to the evils flowing from categorization by race, differential treatment by race. It was wrong then and it is wrong now. We cannot bring those evils to an end by rejuvenating that practice with new beneficiaries and new victims. The only way the injustice of racial discrimination will be brought to an end is through a national determination, morally resolute and backed by law where that is appropriate, *never again* to give preference by race or color or sex. We do not, we cannot right the wrongs of times past by engaging now in the same invidious practices that engendered those wrongs. Justice Scalia [in *City of Richmond v. Croson* (1989) 488 U.S. 469, at 524] put it succinctly: "Where injustice is the game, turnabout is not fair play."

The truth of this moral principle has been recognized by virtually every great statesman of recent times. Nelson Mandela has said it forcefully: color of skin is *not relevant* in public affairs. Martin Luther King Jr. said it beautifully: in a decent society what counts is not the color of our skin but "the content of our character." Racial or sexual preference makes it impossible to deal with individuals as the *persons* they truly are, but instead obliges us to treat them first as members of their group. It gives and takes on grounds having no genuine relevance to what is given or taken. It is inescapably unjust.

Let us seek to respond justly to injury, giving appropriate remedy where remedy is due, without regard to sex or color of skin. And let us see to it that our federal government, in its dealings with citizens and groups, is scrupulously impartial. The Equal Opportunity Act of 1995, by forbidding our government to give racial or sexual preference or to require others to do so, cannot insure equal treatment in every sphere of course, but does surely move in the right direction.

The case against racial preference has another dimension, Mr. 15 Chairman, which my limited time permits me to outline only very briefly. Beyond its unfairness, racial preference is *injurious,* counterproductive. And this in three contexts, quickly noted:

1. *Preference corrupts and damages the institutions that practice it.* Where employees are appointed or promoted, or contracts let, on grounds not relevant to the work to be done, it is *inevitable* that the quality of work done will suffer. Minorities are most certainly not less qualified; but *whenever* we select on the basis of race, whether favoring minority or majority, we select stupidly and corrupt the process. Basketball players we would not dream of selecting to reflect racial proportions; we know very well what that would do to the quality of play. And to the retort: "But the players selected would still be qualified to play!" we would respond with laughter. All institutions must suffer similarly when race and sex illegitimately enter the appointment or admission or promotion process.

2. *Preference corrupts the society at large.* Resentment, produced by preference, is unavoidable and is already widespread; the product of resentment is distrust, and before long, hostility. The corrupting spiral leads eventually to ugly racial incidents, which in turn ignite the fires of racial hatred. Racial tension in our country today grows ever more pronounced; since the early 1970s, when racial preferences began in earnest, race relations have been going downhill. Racial antagonism has come to infect almost all of public life; we see it in our public schools and playgrounds, on our streets, in offices and in factories, even in legislatures. I have been teaching at the University of Michigan since 1955; I report to you what my stu-

dents know well, and what all the talk about diversity and multiculturalism cannot hide: preferential affirmative action on our campus (as on many campuses around the nation) has driven race relations among us to a point lower than it has ever been. The story is long and complicated and has many variants, but the short of it is this: give preference by race and you create hostility by race. And for that we Americans are paying, and we will pay, a dreadful price.

3. Finally, *preference is injurious to the very persons it was supposed to assist.* Individual members of minorities may benefit, of course — but the minority group is not helped, it is *subverted* when preference is given. Preference results inevitably in the appointment and admission of persons on grounds irrelevant to their duties or their studies. The manifest disparity in resultant performance is everywhere seen as the product of that preference, so that the nasty stereotypes of racial inferiority — *which are not true!* — are *reinforced* by the preferential devices that were supposed to give support to previously disadvantaged groups. If some demon had sought to concoct a scheme aimed at undermining the credentials of minority businessmen, minority professionals and students, to stigmatize them permanently and to humiliate them publicly, there could have been no more cruel or ingenious plan devised than the preferential affirmative action that is now rampant in our country.

Mr. Chairman, I express my thanks for the opportunity to outline here the moral case against preference. On these argumentative bones I have not had the time to put much flesh. But the case against preference by race and sex is truly compelling. Preference is *wrong,* intrinsically unjust, ethically confused. It is moreover socially *counterproductive:* damaging to those who practice it, injurious to the society in which it breeds, and above all cruelly hurtful to the minorities who were to have been helped by it. The Equal Opportunity Act of 1995 is one valuable step on the road to the elimination of naked racial preference.

THINKING AND WRITING ABOUT AFFIRMATIVE ACTION

Questions for Discussion and Writing

1. Both Chavez and Carter, members of minority groups, agree on what Carter calls "the affirmative action pyramid." Explain how this might change some practices on affirmative action today.

2. Why does Kennedy think that "ambivalence is a good posture to adopt"? Several other writers are also ambivalent. Explain some of the contradictions that trouble them.

3. What does Steele mean by "iconographic public policy"? What does he see as the consequences of such policy? Does the remedy he proposes

to replace affirmative action seem reasonable as a solution to the problems of discrimination?

4. Why does Glazer believe that preferences based on class and income rather than race are "a bad idea"? Which of the reasons that he defends is strongest?

5. Chavez, Hernández, and Carter use personal experience to defend their positions. If you have already formed an opinion about affirmative action, did any of their stories persuade you to change your mind or at least entertain a doubt about your position?

6. Several authors claim that affirmative action has damaged both minorities and whites in different ways. But they do not all therefore conclude that affirmative action must go. How do they reconcile these two apparently contradictory points of view?

7. Cohen claims that the "moral case against group preference . . . is overwhelming." Summarize his argument. Cohen also asserts that racial preference is "*injurious,* counterproductive." Do any of the other writers agree with these conclusions?

8. In the cartoon below, identify *Brown Decision, Voting Rights Bill,* and *Emancipation Proclamation,* and explain their relevance to the point of the cartoon.

Topics for Research

The effect of new college admissions policies on African American and Hispanic American students

The effect of affirmative action on women

The birth of affirmative action in 1965

Affirmative action policies of my campus: goals and results

Changing affirmative action policies in the 1990s

TAKING THE DEBATE ONLINE

- **Americans United for Affirmative Action <www.auaa.org/>** This site is a comprehensive online affirmative action resource and home page for the civil rights organization founded by Martin Luther King III.

- **American Association of Law Libraries Committee on Diversity <http://vls.law.vill.edu/library/diversit/affirmat.htm>** This pro–affirmative action site, maintained by the American Association of Law Libraries Committee on Diversity, is divided into three comprehensive lists:
  - General issues having to do with the Affirmative Action Act,
  - California's Proposition 209 in particular,
  - *Hopwood et al. v. State of Texas et al.* A case where four caucasian students claimed that because of their race they were denied admission to State of Texas Law School, while less qualified African American and Mexican American students were accepted.

- **The Conservative Digest <http://www.conservative-digest.com/affirm/affirm.htm>** This comprehensive site purports that "affirmative action employs state-sponsored discrimination . . . to 'right' . . . past discrimination." Its many links cover a myriad of topics, including political personalities, court cases, university debates, and public policies.

- **Affirmative Action for Immigrants? <http://pw2.netcom.com/~jimrobb/index.html>** This site bemoans the fact that recent immigrants to the United States are reaping more of the benefits of affirmative action than the original recipients — African Americans and Native Americans.

- **Equalists: Replace Affirmative Action with Affirmative Equality to reduce racism, sexism, hate, and hate crimes! <http://members.aol.com/mdpetersen/mw2/aavae.htm>** This site proposes replacing affirmative action with affirmative equality, a policy guaranteeing legal protection for anyone who has been stereotyped and harassed because of their race or gender.

- **The American Association for Affirmative Action <www.affirmativeaction.org/>** This is the homepage for the American Association for Affirmative Action — a great resource.

CHAPTER THIRTEEN

Corporate Responsibility

A corporation is defined in law as "an organization enjoying legal personality for the purposes of carrying on certain activities." The corporations mentioned in the following articles are all businesses for profit. Typically, they raise capital by selling shares of stock to stockholders who are nominally responsible for the decisions made by the corporation.

Corporations are not new. They existed in some form in ancient Rome and in medieval England. Nor is the idea of corporate responsibility new. In 1890 the Sherman Anti-Trust Act was the first of several such laws to prohibit business practices that restricted competition. In the first half of the twentieth century social reformers expressed strong opposition to sweatshops, which employed women, children, and the elderly at long hours and low wages in unsanitary conditions.

Now these concerns have reemerged as companies move operations to developing countries where costs of production are much lower. Some of the most popular American products are now made abroad under what critics cite as "less than ideal labor conditions." But corporate responsibility has come to mean not only increased sensitivity to fair working conditions, including decent wages and a refusal to hire children, but also a commitment to philanthropy and the support of social causes, like education. In addition, corporations are now asked to accept responsibility for any damage their products might inflict. The 1997 tobacco settlement, in which tobacco companies promised to pay billions of dollars in reparations to the states, may be only the beginning of a concerted attack on the manufacturers of guns and automobiles, which also injure people.

On the other side are those who argue that a corporation should not be held responsible for satisfying popular demand for a product. It is the users who should be held accountable for their choices. A number of economists insist that the corporation is obliged only to fulfill its commitment to its stockholders to make a profit. They argue that the private corporation is not bound to make social policy and should not do so — as a matter of democratic principle. Nor should corporations be routinely condemned for paying lower wages abroad to people who would otherwise be even less gainfully employed or not at all.

The dilemma is summed up by a writer in *Newsweek* reporting on the ability of corporations to practice good works: "You can afford the luxury of goodness only if you make a buck or two for shareholders."

Prohibition II . . .

RICHARD KLEIN

America has already had one disastrous experiment in Prohibition. The tobacco settlement announced last week puts us on the verge of another. Like the first Prohibition in this century, this new one promises an explosive increase in black markets, smuggling, criminality, and general cynicism. What's more, every indication is that the measures proposed by the settlement will serve not to diminish but to *increase* smoking. The settlement calls for spending hundreds of millions of dollars on efforts to discourage and deglamorize tobacco use. But emphasizing that tobacco is dangerous and disapproved will enhance the glamour, prestige, and attractiveness of cigarettes — particularly among the young.

The pattern has been clear for some time. At an August 1995 press conference, President Clinton announced that dramatically more young people had been smoking since 1991. He cited statistics indicating that smoking had increased 30 percent among tenth-graders and a shocking 40 percent among ninth-graders. Children are smoking more and starting earlier, a trend that has continued and even accelerated over the past two years. Yet this generation of youngsters has been subjected to the most intense and systematic antismoking propaganda in the history of the world. Every adult

Richard Klein is a professor of French at Cornell University. He is the author of *Cigarettes are Sublime* (1993) and *Eat Fat* (1996). This essay, along with the next one by Elizabeth M. Whelan, appeared in the *Wall Street Journal* on June 26, 1997.

institution of authority has admonished them not to smoke, from the earliest stages of their development. Parental pressure and media stereotypes reinforce the antismoking message. Yet more and more of the young are finding it cool to light up.

The anti-antismoking backlash isn't limited to high schoolers. In movies, where for a while only villains smoked, cigarettes today seem almost as sexy and glamorous as they were in the heyday of Bogie and Bacall. And consider the chic of cigar bars springing up around the country and the success of magazines and products that cater to their aficionados. As smoking has been demonized and tabooed, it has naturally become eroticized and seductive. The Internet is rife with sites where cigarette fetishists exchange otherwise mild pornography that depicts men and women lighting up.

Cigarettes have traditionally served as children's first important introduction to adult pleasures. Adolescents are drawn to cigarettes for all the reasons that our censors are so eager to ban them. They understand them as a way of experimenting with being grown up. They use them as the gateway to the temptations and intensities that adults wish their children would never know.

Throughout their history, cigarettes have appealed to adoles-   5
cents with even a slight taste for rebellion against society's strictures and an inclination to revolt against its hypocrisies. Women have taken a particular pleasure in transgressing the taboo against feminine smoking. That scandalous pleasure may be found today in the spectacle of women smoking fat cigars while lounging on leather chairs. But the tobacco settlement's proposed measures will transform every form of tobacco into an irresistible lure.

Since their invention nearly two centuries ago, cigarettes have always been associated with risk, menace, and the intimation of mortality. Part of the allure of smoking is the subtle pleasure of elegantly defying death. Thus one doesn't know whether to laugh or cry at the requirement that companies show a decline in teenage smoking over ten years or face stiff fines. Nowhere does the settlement envisage the possibility that these measures will cause smoking among teenagers to increase even more alarmingly.

The settlement requires, for example, that strong warnings cover 25 percent of the front of every cigarette pack. Didn't any of the negotiators notice that teen smoking has jumped in recent years just as warnings have gotten larger and harsher? Are none of them aware that Death Head cigarettes are drop-dead chic in London, where they're sold in black-and-white packs with a large, leering skull and crossbones on the cover? When the new warnings fail to achieve their discouraging intention, will our Solons require pictures of cancerous lungs to be placed on packs, thereby prompting even heavier smoking?

Consider, too, the proposals limiting cigarette advertising and banning promotions. Portugal, with one of the highest per capita rates of smoking in Europe, has banned all cigarette advertising for decades. Canada and New Zealand banned cigarette ads within the past decade; smoking rates in both countries are unchanged. And censorship can only heighten the "forbidden fruit" effect. Some Canadians not long ago proposed that cigarettes be packaged in plain brown paper wrappers. It was the packaging on cigarettes, they argued, that enticed young smokers. The idea was abandoned when someone recalled that pornography is sold in plain brown paper wrappers and the mere hint of those undistinguished looking bags has come to acquire its own titillating erotic power.

These proposals come at a time of exorbitant rhetorical inflation, when our public officials feel no constraint whatsoever in attributing to tobacco companies the purest sort of evil. Opponents, like the state attorneys general who sued the tobacco companies, argue publicly that they must be "punished" for their criminal deceit. Other prominent critics believe that any deal negotiated with the tobacco companies must necessarily be suspect and probably compromised. They justify this belief by referring to tobacco companies, which sell a legal product, as "the Devil" — with whom, as everyone knows, one negotiates at one's peril. These avatars of our Puritan ancestors, upholders of public morality, sound depressingly like the crusaders of the old Temperance Leagues who used to denounce "the demon rum."

Make no mistake: prohibition is the logical outcome of the to- 10 bacco settlement. For years Food and Drug Administration officials have denied that their ultimate intent was to outlaw cigarettes. But the settlement would take a huge step in that direction by giving the FDA the power not only to regulate nicotine in cigarettes but to eliminate it by 2009. Cigarettes without nicotine are like Scotch without alcohol — or, more exactly, like what in the 1920s was reviled as "near beer." Antismoking critics of the settlement even want to eviscerate the sensible provision that would delay the elimination of nicotine if it would lead to a black market. There can be little question that black markets would develop. Canada was recently obliged to rescind the harshly punitive taxes it imposed on cigarettes when widespread trafficking across the border resulted in increased violence, intolerable demands on law enforcement, and no decline in smoking.

American culture, descended from Puritans, stands at the apogee of one of its regular cycles of repression. The current demonization of tobacco contrasts with other moments in our history, when cigarettes were not only tolerated but celebrated. Think what a GI could buy with a carton of American cigarettes in Europe at the end of World

War II. As cigarettes have become the instrument of the devil, we forget that they were recently considered to be divine. They offer consolation in the face of loss, release after exertions; they are the friend of soldiers, of journalists and actors in the wings, mitigating anxiety and killing boredom. They cut appetite, which is why a lot of women secretly smoke. But most of all they bring the Promethean beauty of cinder, fire, and smoke into the lives of people on the meanest streets and the plushest benches of the world.

The antismoking crusaders who negotiated the tobacco settlement imagine that it is possible for adolescents to hear only half the truth — that cigarettes are poisonous. Inevitably they will learn the whole truth — that cigarettes are a mixed blessing, as a billion people around the world, lighting up, every day discover to their dismay and satisfaction. America may be the first nation to ban cigarettes. It certainly won't be the first to try. Odds are, however, that as the pendulum swings, the censors once again will learn the absurdity of trying to legislate morality and the futility of aiming to stamp out ancient vices.

. . . Or a Payoff to Purveyors of Poison?
ELIZABETH M. WHELAN

Last week, a group of lawyers purporting to represent both national interests (the public health) and local constituencies (the taxpayers of their respective states) reached an accord with the manufacturers of America's leading cause of preventable death — cigarettes. This was touted by many as victory in the war against smoking.

But there is another way to characterize what happened: we were witnessing the creation of a blueprint for the biggest drug payoff of the century — a $368 billion deal by which the cigarette lords would distribute lots of money to silence and pacify their critics, who, in accepting the payoff, would thereby become behind-the-scenes shareholders in the profits of big tobacco. Martin Broughton, chairman of BAT, parent of Brown & Williamson Tobacco, described last week's deal perfectly: "They want to be paid off and we want a peaceful life."

Elizabeth M. Whelan is the president of the American Council on Science and Health. This essay appeared with Richard Klein's "Prohibition II . . . " in the *Wall Street Journal* on June 26, 1997.

And what does public health get in return? Many of the "concessions" listed as part of the deal are already being implemented by local ordinances (bans on vending machines) or are hollow promises for which the industry has already arranged escape clauses. If, for example, youth smoking rates do not decline, the cigarette companies can avoid the financial penalty described in the settlement if they can show, in effect, that they tried their best. And while at first glance the settlement suggests the industry is yielding to Food and Drug Administration regulation, the fine print suggests otherwise. Former FDA chief David Kessler, for one, says that the accord restricts, not expands, the authority already granted to the FDA by the courts to regulate nicotine.

It's easy enough to see why the deal was endorsed by the attorneys general (they'll derive political benefits) and lawyers (they'll derive financial benefits), but why did many of my colleagues in the public health community go along? My explanation begins with the observation that antismoking advocates — most of whom embrace a liberal political agenda — have railed for years about cigarette companies "profiting from killing people." That wording has always suggested to me that these advocates are bothered as much by the profits as by the killing. Now, perhaps, they have decided that levying financial damages against the industry — which, they hope, will take some of the profits out — will somehow make the ongoing carnage more tolerable.

Whatever the parties' motivation, the deal that resulted gave the 5 tobacco industry a major boost by providing limited immunity against future litigation. While technically allowing smokers (or their survivors) to continue to sue cigarette companies for damages caused by smoking, the settlement would put a yearly cap of $5 billion on damages — an amount that is a trivial cost of doing business for the industry. This cap will serve as a disincentive to future plaintiffs' attorneys, who will incur enormous costs in any challenges they choose to mount against the wealthy tobacco companies.

Under the newly proposed settlement, the industry is afforded even more legal protection than it gained in 1965 when Congress slapped the so-called warning label on cigarette packs, thereby giving cigarette manufacturers a federally backed excuse not to give full disclosure of health risks. Now the industry, having paid tax-deductible damages, will be able to return to business as usual for the next twenty-five years. There will be no threat of future industrywide lawsuits. This is analogous to a scenario in which a corporation admits to polluting the water supply, pays some damages, then returns immediately to dumping toxins down the well — and gets away with it.

Litigation has its downside — the risk of becoming excessive and not grounded in science — but the threat of legal action does pose a strong incentive to corporations (and individuals) to remain honest and to behave responsibly.

I was reminded of this recently on a flight to Japan. One business-class cabin I peeked into was thick with cigarette smoke. Naively, I queried the flight attendants: How could the airline assume the risk of liability by allowing the consistent exposure of their employees to this proven noxious substance? The answer: Under workers' compensation laws, the airline, or any other employer, cannot be held liable for health risks in the workplace. In the absence of a legal threat, there is no incentive for a corporation — in this case an airline — to take remedial action. Thus the tobacco deal, by removing the threat of litigation, will bring to a screeching halt many efforts to discourage smoking and curb the outrageous behavior of an industry that is literally selling death.

It's unclear to me why we needed a tobacco deal at all. No other industry suffering an assault of litigation has been afforded protection, even when the products under attack (breast implants, for example) have caused no documented harm. So why are we offering special status to the one legal product in the U.S. that is harmful when used as intended? Why, instead, don't we demand that our government take a "hands off" approach to the future of cigarettes? Why don't we let the industry — as any other would — have its day in court and face the consequences of jury decisions? We would thereby let the free market — not the government bureaucracy, not the runaway state attorney generals — determine the future of cigarettes.

Social Responsibility of Business and Labor
MILTON FRIEDMAN

The view has been gaining widespread acceptance that corporate officials and labor leaders have a "social responsibility" that goes beyond serving the interest of their stockholders or their members. This view shows a fundamental misconception of the character and nature of a free economy. In such an economy, there is one and only one social responsibility of business — to use its resources and engage in activities designed to increase its profits so long as it stays within the rules of the game, which is to say, engages in open and free competition, without deception or fraud. Similarly,

---

Milton Friedman, winner of the Nobel Prize in economics, is a senior research fellow at the Hoover Institution, Stanford University, and Paul Snowden Russell Distinguished Service Professor Emeritus of Economics at the University of Chicago. This essay is excerpted from *Capitalism and Freedom* (1962).

the "social responsibility" of labor leaders is to serve the interests of the members of their unions. It is the responsibility of the rest of us to establish a framework of law such that an individual in pursuing his own interest is, to quote Adam Smith again, "led by an invisible hand to promote an end which was no part of his intention. Nor is it always the worse for the society that it was no part of it. By pursuing his own interest, he frequently promotes that of the society more effectually than when he really intends to promote it. I have never known much good done by those who affected to trade for the public good."[1]

Few trends could so thoroughly undermine the very foundations of our free society as the acceptance by corporate officials of a social responsibility other than to make as much money for their stockholders as possible. This is a fundamentally subversive doctrine. If businessmen do have a social responsibility other than making maximum profits for stockholders, how are they to know what it is? Can self-selected private individuals decide what the social interest is? Can they decide how great a burden they are justified in placing on themselves or their stockholders to serve that social interest? Is it tolerable that these public functions of taxation, expenditure, and control be exercised by the people who happen at the moment to be in charge of particular enterprises, chosen for those posts by strictly private groups? If businessmen are civil servants rather than the employees of their stockholders, then in a democracy they will, sooner or later, be chosen by the public techniques of election and appointment.

And long before this occurs, their decision-making power will have been taken away from them. A dramatic illustration was the cancellation of a steel price increase by U.S. Steel in April 1962 through the medium of a public display of anger by President Kennedy and threats of reprisals on levels ranging from antitrust suits to examination of the tax reports of steel executives. This was a striking episode because of the public display of the vast powers concentrated in Washington. We were all made aware of how much of the power needed for a police state was already available. It illustrates the present point as well. If the price of steel is a public decision, as the doctrine of social responsibility declares, then it cannot be permitted to be made privately.

The particular aspect of the doctrine which this example illustrates, and which has been most prominent recently, is an alleged social responsibility of business and labor to keep prices and wage rates down in order to avoid price inflation. Suppose that at a time when there was upward pressure on prices — ultimately of course

---

[1] Adam Smith, *The Wealth of Nations* (1776), Bk. IV, chapter ii, p. 421 (Cannan, ed., London, 1930).

reflecting an increase in the stock of money — every businessman and labor leader were to accept this responsibility and suppose all could succeed in keeping any price from rising, so we had voluntary price and wage control without open inflation. What would be the result? Clearly product shortages, labor shortages, gray markets, black markets. If prices are not allowed to ration goods and workers, there must be some other means to do so. Can the alternative rationing schemes be private? Perhaps for a time in a small and unimportant area. But if the goods involved are many and important, there will necessarily be pressure, and probably irresistible pressure, for governmental rationing of goods, a governmental wage policy, and governmental measures for allocating and distributing labor.

Price controls, whether legal or voluntary, if effectively enforced 5 would eventually lead to the destruction of the free-enterprise system and its replacement by a centrally controlled system. And it would not even be effective in preventing inflation. History offers ample evidence that what determines the average level of prices and wages is the amount of money in the economy and not the greediness of businessmen or of workers. Governments ask for the self-restraint of business and labor because of their inability to manage their own affairs — which includes the control of money — and the natural human tendency to pass the buck.

One topic in the area of social responsibility that I feel duty-bound to touch on, because it affects my own personal interests, has been the claim that business should contribute to the support of charitable activities and especially to universities. Such giving by corporations is an inappropriate use of corporate funds in a free-enterprise society.

The corporation is an instrument of the stockholders who own it. If the corporation makes a contribution, it prevents the individual stockholder from himself deciding how he should dispose of his funds. With the corporation tax and the deductibility of contributions, stockholders may of course want the corporation to make a gift on their behalf, since this would enable them to make a larger gift. The best solution would be the abolition of the corporate tax. But so long as there is a corporate tax, there is no justification for permitting deductions for contributions to charitable and educational institutions. Such contributions should be made by the individuals who are the ultimate owners of property in our society.

People who urge extension of the deductibility of this kind of corporate contribution in the name of free enterprise are fundamentally working against their own interest. A major complaint made frequently against modern business is that it involves the separation of ownership and control — that the corporation has become a social institution that is a law unto itself, with irresponsible executives who do not serve the interests of their stockholders. This charge is not true. But the direction in which policy is now moving, of permitting corporations to make contributions for charitable purposes and allowing deductions for income tax, is a step in the direction of creating a true divorce between ownership and control and of undermining the basic nature and character of our society. It is a step away from an individualistic society and toward the corporate state.

God versus GE

JOHN F. WELCH JR. AND SISTER PATRICIA DALY

Sister Patricia Daly: Good morning, Mr. Welch, members of the board, and fellow shareholders. My name is Pat Daly. I am a Dominican sister, and I am here representing the Interfaith Center on Corporate Responsibility. ICCR has been raising very critical issues before U.S. corporations for almost thirty years. We represent about $90 billion of investment money.

Today, I would like to discuss the resolution on the necessity for public education about General Electric's pollution around the Hudson Valley. The Hudson River is the largest PCB spill on the planet. It is also the largest Superfund site in the country. Most of those PCBs are in the river because of the past practices of General Electric. We also have been contacted by GE employees in the beautiful Berkshires and along the Housatonic River watershed who are facing similar situations. This is a serious concern for people who have given their lives to General Electric and have been very grateful to be a part of the GE family.

Mr. Welch, we will probably never agree on the science of PCBs. We did agree last year that certainly PCB-contaminated fish should not be eaten by people along the Hudson Valley. We have asked, and we continue to ask, General Electric to work with us on a public-education program. So many people along the Hudson Valley depend on the river to feed their families. It is not common knowledge that people should not be fishing and feeding their families on a regular basis from the Hudson. So we are asking again that you join us in educating people about the hazards they face.

These comments were published in *Harper's Magazine* in August 1998. The comments are from an exchange between John F. Welch Jr., CEO of General Electric, and Sister Patricia Daly that occurred during the April 22 GE shareholders' meeting. On June 3, the Environmental Protection Agency ordered GE to begin dredging the Housatonic River near GE's Pittsfield, Massachusetts, plant, citing PCB levels "among the highest" ever found in the United States.

John F. Welch Jr.: Thank you. Before we have any more comments on this, I would like to put the company's position on PCBs in perspective for all of you.

PCB use by General Electric has always been lawful. It is critical to   5
know that our use of PCBs, every day we ever used them, was lawful. We did not manufacture PCBs; we bought them. Starting in the 1940s, General Electric and every electrical manufacturer used PCBs in electrical equipment for a very important reason: safety. PCBs were used in capacitors and transformers to prevent fires. Government codes mandated the use of PCBs in electrical equipment. In the mid-1970s, the government changed its position and banned the continued production and use of PCBs. Our company complied immediately.

PCBs do not pose health risks. Based on the scientific evidence developed since the 1970s, we simply do not believe that there are any significant adverse health effects from PCBs. More than twenty studies show absolutely no link between workers and others with elevated PCBs in their blood, and cancer and other adverse health effects.

I want to make it very clear to all of you that we, your company, will base our discussion of PCBs, as we have for twenty years, on science, not on bad politics or shouting voices from a few activists. Science will decide this issue. Advocates can shout loudly. They can say anything. They are accountable to no one.

Daly: Mr. Welch, you are right. We are all accountable, and you know who I am accountable to.

Welch: No, I do not. I would like to —

Daly: I truly think my accountability is ultimately to God, which   10
is why —

Welch: And I think mine is also.

Daly: I am not judging that. What I am saying, Mr. Welch, is that this is an issue of public education.

Welch: Sister, why not take public education right to the government and have them educate the public on the situation. It is not our job to educate.

Daly: It is, however. Let's get this absolutely straight. The EPA continues to list PCBs on its suspected-carcinogen list. For you to be saying that PCBs are perfectly harmless is not true. I really want our company to be a credible mover on this. We all remember the images of the CEOs of the tobacco companies swearing that they were telling the truth. Do they have any credibility in the United States today?

Welch: That is an outrageous comparison.   15

Daly: That is an absolutely valid comparison, Mr. Welch.

Welch: It is outrageous.

Daly: Mr. Welch, I am sorry, but we need to have the independent scientific community decide this, not the GE scientific community.

Welch: Twenty-seven studies, twenty-one of them independent, have concluded that there is no correlation between PCB levels and cancer, Sister. You have to stop this conversation. You owe it to God to be on the side of truth here.

Daly: I am on the side of truth. The other consideration here is 20 that this is not just about carcinogens. We are talking about hormonal disruptions, fertility issues, and developmental problems in children. Those are real issues, and certainly those are the issues that my sisters are seeing in schools all along the Hudson River. That is exactly what is going on here.

Welch: Thank you very much for coming, Sister. Let's move on to the next agenda item.

Victims of Everything

JACOB SULLUM

Like you, I've seen innumerable Calvin Klein ads featuring sallow, sullen, scrawny youths. Not once have I had an overwhelming urge to rush out and buy some heroin, and probably neither have you. Yet the death of Davide Sorrenti, a twenty-year-old fashion photographer who overdosed on heroin in February, is now being held up as proof that such images have the power to turn people into junkies.

On Wednesday President Clinton accused the fashion industry of "increasing the allure of heroin among young people" and urged it not to "glamorize addiction" to sell clothes. "We now see on college campuses and in neighborhoods heroin becoming increasingly the drug of choice," he said. "And we know that part of this has to do with the images that are finding their way to our young people."

In reality, heroin is not "the drug of choice" by any stretch of the imagination. In the Government's 1995 National Household Survey on Drug Abuse, 0.1 percent of respondents reported that they had used the drug in the previous month. A nationwide study done in 1994 for the Department of Health and Human Services found about the same level of heroin use among nineteen- to twenty-eight-year-olds; marijuana use was 140 times as common, and alcohol was far and away the most popular intoxicant.

And there is no reason to expect that people attracted to the look promoted by Calvin Klein and other advertisers — a cynical,

Jacob Sullum, a senior editor at *Reason* magazine, is the author of *For Your Own Good: The Anti-Smoking Crusade and the Tyranny of Public Health* (1998). This essay appeared in the *New York Times* on May 23, 1997.

sanitized vision of drug use that pretends to reflect a gritty reality — will also be attracted to heroin any more than suburban teen-agers who wear baggy pants and backward caps will end up shooting people from moving cars.

Nevertheless, the editors of the cutting-edge fashion magazines that helped popularize the heroin-chic look are professing repentance. "With Davide's death," said Long Nguyen, *Detour's* style director, "we realized how powerful fashion pictures are."

And how powerful is that? Leaving aside the point that Mr. Sorrenti, as a producer of these images, can hardly be seen as an unknowing victim of their influence, it is important to keep in mind what pictures can and cannot do. Clearly, they can provoke outrage. They can also pique curiosity, create awareness, and elicit a range of emotional reactions. But they cannot *make* anyone buy jeans or perfume, let alone take up heroin. Nor can they make kids smoke cigars, despite the claims of critics about the power of photos showing cigar-chomping celebrities. A conscious mind must intervene, deciding how to interpret the message and whether to act on it.

Blurring the distinction between persuasion and coercion is often the first step toward censorship. In the 1950s, John Kenneth Galbraith and Vance Packard argued that corporations used advertising to manipulate consumers and create an artificial desire for their products. The federal court that upheld the 1970 ban on broadcast advertising of cigarettes was clearly influenced by such ideas, citing "the subliminal impact of this pervasive propaganda."

We see the same line of thinking today. In calling for restrictions on Web sites promoting alcohol and tobacco, the Center for Media Education, a research group in Washington, warns that "interactivity has a hypnotic and addictive quality that some analysts believe could be stronger than television."

The aim of such arguments is to portray people not as independent moral agents but as mindless automatons. It's a view of human nature that encourages the flight from responsibility to victimhood that we see all around us: the smoker who blames a cigarette maker for his lung cancer, the heavy drinker who blames the liquor company for her baby's birth defects, the mass murderer who blames dirty magazines for inspiring his crimes.

So far no one has called for a ban on glassy-eyed waifs, and the critics of heroin chic have every right to decry the message they believe it sends. But they should be careful not to send a dangerous message themselves: that the dictates of fashion overwhelm our ability to choose.

Barbie Talks Back

SEAN M. FITZGERALD

We were deeply disturbed by the blatantly inaccurate portrayal of the working conditions at one of our contractor facilities described by Anton Foek in your January-February 1997 issue. Not only was the information a gross misrepresentation of the Dynamic factory's current work environment, but it was simply untrue.

Mattel does not currently, *nor has it ever*, manufactured Barbie® dolls at the Dynamic plant in Bangkok.

The third basic principle of the humanist philosophy states that "we are committed to the position that the only thing that can be called knowledge is that which is firmly grounded in the realm of human understanding and *verification*." Since Mr. Foek never contacted us to verify any of the allegations in the story, never spoke to sources in Thailand who may have provided a different perspective, or ever bothered to verify a fact as mundane as the types of products manufactured at Dynamic, we can only assume that his commitment to verification was temporarily misplaced. On the other hand, there may have been a concern on his part that the truth may have simply derailed a good story.

If Mr. Foek had actually visited the plant as he claims, he would most certainly have discovered the glaring inaccuracy upon which his entire story was based. How could he possibly have seen "hundreds of women and children stuffing, cutting, dressing, and assembling Barbie dolls" in a factory that has *never* been responsible for the manufacture of that product?

The charges raised by Mr. Foek concerning working conditions reflect those made by other individuals six years ago. At that time, Mattel immediately investigated the Dynamic facility and found that, while certain safety procedures were not being followed as closely as we would have liked, all other allegations were found to be completely without basis. (Safety procedures have since been updated.) And without question, the allegations of work-related illness and worker fatalities at the Dynamic facility are at best fictional and at worst slanderous.

The wages paid at the Dynamic factory not only meet, but in many instances exceed, those required by national labor laws in Thailand. While the income levels in Thailand may not equal those of the United States in monetary terms, valid research would have

Sean M. Fitzgerald is vice president of corporate communications for Mattel, Inc. This essay, along with Anton Foek's that follows, was published in *The Humanist* in July-August 1997.

compared the purchasing power of the wages and found the Dynamic incomes comparing favorably with other industries in that country. Mr. Foek's assertion that children are involved in the manufacture of our products at Dynamic is absurd — a fact he could easily have *verified* had he investigated the factory's personnel files (a practice we have recently initiated at all our manufacturing facilities and those of our contractors around the world) to ensure that all local laws are being upheld. Mattel creates toys for children, not jobs.

There are many allusions in the story to the still nascent labor movement in Thailand — a movement that must gain visibility and influence to succeed. Frequently, companies like Mattel are unfairly targeted because of their international recognition. Allegations, no matter how sensationalized or untrue, are unjustly made for the sake of the movement. And some reporters, no matter how well meaning, do not question or *verify* the validity of the allegations.

Finally, while the Thai women suffering from lead poisoning highlighted in Mr. Foek's story deserve everyone's extreme sympathy and support, it is impossible that they contracted this ailment from manufacturing any Mattel product. We'd like to *verify* the fact that Mattel *does not, would not, and cannot* exceed the U.S. federal requirement for lead content in any of our products. This requirement translates into an amount so minimal that it is essentially nonexistent.

Mattel, Inc., is a company that is as concerned with the safety and well-being of the men and women around the world who manufacture our products as we are with the quality and safety of the toys themselves.

As we expand our operations around the world, we will continue [10] to make positive changes in manufacturing environments which do not currently meet commonly accepted Western safety and workers' rights standards. However, what possible incentive do we and other responsible multinational companies have to work toward change if we are unjustly and irresponsibly vilified by reporters who are unwilling or unable to meet the same standards of fairness and humanism to which they hold us?

A Reply to Mattel

ANTON FOEK

Mr. Fitzgerald, I am very glad you responded to my article in the January-February 1997 *Humanist*. This gives me an opportunity to reply with some thoughts I consider important.

The points I make in my article, of course, speak well enough for themselves, given that I was on the scene, took the photos, and tape-recorded the interviews from which I quoted. But I also talked with national and international Mattel representatives at the New York Toy Fair, and I reviewed video and written material sent to me by your company.

By contrast, there is no indication in your letter that you, yourself, have entered the factories I discussed or visited the hospitals and talked privately to workers who are sick and dying there. But you do make it clear that you don't believe my findings, saying that Mattel has been "unjustly and irresponsibly vilified." Is this also your response to other eyewitnesses who — after inspecting toy factories in China, Indonesia, and elsewhere where Mattel products are made — reported similar findings in *U.S. News and World Report,* the *Nation,* and on *Dateline NBC* at about the same time my *Humanist* article appeared?

Since I'm not Michael Moore, I won't confront you on television to offer you a plane ticket to Asia, as he did with Phil Knight, chair of Nike, inviting Knight to accompany him on a personal tour of the sweatshops where his company's shoes are made. I prefer to think that we can now move beyond denial and look at the larger picture. For our differences of opinion touch core issues affecting the future of humanity. The essential question is: What is progress? To some, it is the creation of a more inclusive society; to others, it is the amassing of greater individual wealth.

As a former business and financial editor, I understand quite 5 well what is going on at Mattel. Although I respect the prosperity your company has achieved, I condemn and feel it is my duty to reveal at what human cost such wealth is so often obtained. As long as one out of every three children worldwide dies of starvation and disease, as long as 9 percent of our own nation's people are feeding themselves on dog and cat food, and as long as the discrepancies between the rich and the poor are growing wider not narrower, I will speak out for the powerless and exploited.

Anton Foek is a freelance writer who reported Mattel's unsafe working conditions in the January–February 1997 issue of *The Humanist.* Here Foek responds to Sean M. Fitzgerald's defense of Mattel in "Barbie Talks Back." Both essays appeared in the July–August 1997 issue.

My concern, therefore, extends beyond the practices of your company to the realities of the corporate world and our economic system as a whole. Since the sixteenth century, social institutions — including the church and the military — have, one by one, been drawn into the expanding global marketplace. In looking back, we cannot but wonder at what we have wrought.

Fortunately, the Age of Enlightenment inspired in us the idea that our destiny lies in our own hands. A growing technology has served to increase our confidence in that belief. And in acting on that confidence, we have — here and there — promoted more freedom for individuals, more rights for workers, and the enfranchisement of women, minorities, the disabled, and many others.

But here there is a paradox. The more people we accept as equal participants in the life of society, the less the energetic affluent will be able to achieve and maintain their goals of vastly superior wealth. The expansion of democracy worldwide — and the subsequent demise of gulags, concentration camps, and imperialistic wars — must of necessity mean a reduction in disparities between racial, class, and economic groups. For when more people have a voice, and when those voices become a chorus, there is less opportunity for economic elites to dominate.

Thus, the goal of amassing private fortunes works at cross purposes with the goal of extending participatory democracy. By your letter, you show that you are concerned with justice and the future of our world. But are you willing to take the dramatic economic steps necessary to make justice a reality? What is your first priority: market expansion and rising quarterly profits or the eradication of slavelike conditions in sweatshops? When a direct contradiction between these two aims confronts you, what overriding ethical ideal motivates your choice?

Back in the late 1960s, the Beatles sang, "Nothing's gonna change my world." But if we are resistant to change, the world we keep will be a world where some continue to prosper at the expense of others. That's what we have now. And so, when I phoned Bangkok recently to see how some of the people I had interviewed were doing, I learned that one of the women had died.

10

THINKING AND WRITING ABOUT CORPORATE RESPONSIBILITY

Questions for Discussion and Writing

1. In the tobacco settlement debate, do Klein and Whelan argue the same points? Which issues seem most important to Klein? Which issues to Whelan?

2. Friedman's claim that corporations have only one "social responsibility," to their stockholders, is based on a belief in individual freedom of choice. Point out places where he explains the connection. Does his thesis contradict Foek's, as expressed in question 6?
3. Since both Daly and Welch claim scientific research as an ally, how can a reader determine the truth? What is Welch's principal defense against Daly's accusations? Is it convincing?
4. Summarize Sullum's view of the power of advertising. Do you agree? Can you cite examples from experience, as Sullum does, to support your conclusion?
5. In the debate on working conditions in Mattel plants, Fitzgerald and Foek offer opposing data. They also use different argumentative strategies. What examples do you find of logical, ethical, and emotional appeals? Which are the most effective? Which least effective? Explain why.
6. Foek argues a much larger question: "the goal of amassing private fortunes works at cross purposes with the goal of extending participatory democracy." Has he proved his point? What kind of evidence must be provided in support of this claim?
7. For the cartoon, state both its claim of policy and the warrant that underlies it.

Topics for Research

Fashion industry advertising: socially responsible?

What "socially responsible" businesses do (e.g., Tom's of Maine, Ben and Jerry)

Corporate charity versus philanthropy by nonprofit organizations

Gun manufacturers: the case for or against liability

Sweatshop scandals (e.g., Nike, Reebok, Kathie Lee Gifford)

TAKING THE DEBATE ONLINE

- **FDA <www.fda.gov/default.htm>** This site is maintained by the FDA, the nation's foremost consumer protection agency.

- **The California Trade and Commerce Agency's Hardwood Industry Development Program <http://commerce.ca.gov/business/select/communities/hardwood/edaf1997.html>** This site reflects the efforts of the California Trade and Commerce Agency to devise a Hardwood Industry Development Program that would be economically fruitful and environmentally sound.

- **The Internet's Forest Products Resource IRIS <www.primusweb.com/forest/iris070.htm>** This site provides links to a number of ecological groups and lumber companies.

- **Action on Smoking and Health <http://ash.org/>** This national anti-smoking organization was instrumental in banning cigarette commercials on television and radio and smoking on planes, buses, and public areas.

- **Tobacco Industry Information <www.gate.net/~jcannon/tobacco.html>** Tobacco Industry Information provides a free resource center focusing on tobacco industry documents and other informational sources exposing the tactics and objectives of the tobacco industry and its collaborators.

- **Global Economy Nike Campaign <www.globalexchange.org/corpacct/nike/links.html>** This site provides links related to Nike labor issues.

- **Annual Report: Corporate Responsibility <www.nikebiz.com/invest/respons.html>** A pro-Nike site on the company's corporate responsibility.

CHAPTER FOURTEEN

Euthanasia

Euthanasia means "good death" or "mercy killing," that is, causing the death of one who is so ill or disabled that continued existence will produce intolerable suffering. Euthanasia may be active or passive; in the first case, death is deliberately inflicted, sometimes by a relative; in the second case, life-support systems are withdrawn, and the patient dies naturally.

Controversy surrounding the morality of euthanasia has been heightened enormously in recent years because of advances in medical technology that make it possible for human beings, both newborn and old, to be kept alive almost indefinitely, even when severely impaired. As our life span lengthens, more and more people will reach an age when illness and disability create the possibility for euthanasia.

In those cases in which the patient cannot make a rational choice, decisions to prolong or terminate life must be left to families, doctors, and, not infrequently, the courts. Even the definition of *life* is at issue. A person may be declared "brain dead" while vital functions persist. Other problems of definition have become increasingly important. Where a patient has signed a living will, a physician may nevertheless refuse to remove the feeding tube, arguing that continuing to provide nourishment does not constitute "medication, artificial means, or heroic measures." In June 1990 the Supreme Court ruled that a state may pass laws allowing patients to refuse unwanted life-sustaining treatment, provided that the patient has previously expressed "clear and convincing evidence" of such a desire. Since then, legal initiatives for and against euthanasia have appeared on several state ballots. In 1992, after several doctor-assisted suicides by the inventor of a "self-execution machine," Michigan became the first state to make doctor-assisted suicide illegal.

Dr. Jack Kevorkian, a Michigan pathologist who invented the machine, has repeatedly challenged the Michigan state law by continuing to assist people to die (more than a hundred, according to his lawyer). In each of four trials, juries refused to convict Kevorkian of criminal acts. But in November 1998, *60 Minutes* released a videotape that showed Kevorkian injecting lethal drugs into a man with Lou Gehrig's disease who had expressed a desire to die. His death took place on camera. Because Kevorkian had administered the poison himself, he was charged with first-degree murder. On March 26, 1999, after a trial in which the dead man's family defended Dr. Kevorkian, a jury found him guilty of second-degree murder. On April 13, he was sentenced to ten to twenty-five years in prison. A *New York Times* editorial deplored Kevorkian's "reckless campaign to promote assisted suicide of desperately ill people" but acknowledged that he had "helped bring the need for right-to-die reforms to public attention."[1]

More than thirty states have now enacted laws banning assisted suicide. The state of Oregon is presently the only place in the world where physician-assisted suicide is legal. The law, enacted in 1994, allows doctors "to prescribe suicide pills to a terminally ill patient with less than six months to live, who gets a second opinion, makes three requests, and doesn't appear to be suffering from a mental disorder." Both this law and a similar law in New York state have been upheld by state circuit courts of appeal. In 1998 a survey revealed that fifteen persons ended their lives in Oregon assisted by doctors acting under the law.

On one side are those who regard the problems posed by euthanasia as essentially religious: Life is sacred, no matter how severely disabled the patient may be, and no human being can arrogate to him- or herself a decision reserved for God. On the other side are those who insist that it is the quality of life that should influence the decision and that death may be preferable to a severely impaired life. Euthanasia thus becomes an act of charity. In one widely publicized case which tested the limits of the quality-of-life criterion, parents approved denial of food and water to their severely retarded newborn son rather than allow a stomach operation for him.

One final problem confronts us in all the discussions about euthanasia. Will increasingly widespread acceptance of such deaths lead to a more relaxed attitude toward the taking of life in general and toward taking the lives of those in need of constant and lifelong attention in particular? One writer asks if the same principle of withholding food and water from a woman in a coma should be extended "to the thousands of others who fall into a coma every year, and to the many more mentally retarded or deranged, and sufferers of Alzheimer's disease who are a 'burden' on their families."

---

[1]April 15, 1999, p. A 20.

In Defense of
Voluntary Euthanasia

SIDNEY HOOK

A few short years ago, I lay at the point of death. A congestive heart failure was treated for diagnostic purposes by an angiogram that triggered a stroke. Violent and painful hiccups, uninterrupted for several days and nights, prevented the ingestion of food. My left side and one of my vocal cords became paralyzed. Some form of pleurisy set in, and I felt I was drowning in a sea of slime. At one point, my heart stopped beating; just as I lost consciousness, it was thumped back into action again. In one of my lucid intervals during those days of agony, I asked my physician to discontinue all life-supporting services or show me how to do it. He refused and predicted that someday I would appreciate the unwisdom of my request.

A month later, I was discharged from the hospital. In six months, I regained the use of my limbs, and although my voice still lacks its old resonance and carrying power I no longer croak like a frog. There remain some minor disabilities and I am restricted to a rigorous, low-sodium diet. I have resumed my writing and research.

My experience can be and has been cited as an argument against honoring requests of stricken patients to be gently eased out of their pain and life. I cannot agree. There are two main reasons. As an octogenarian, there is a reasonable likelihood that I may suffer another "cardiovascular accident" or worse. I may not even be in a position to ask for the surcease of pain. It seems to me that I have already paid my dues to death — indeed, although time has softened my memories they are vivid enough to justify my saying that I suffered enough to warrant dying several times over. Why run the risk of more?

Secondly, I dread imposing on my family and friends another grim round of misery similar to the one my first attack occasioned. My wife and children endured enough for one lifetime. I know 5 that for them the long days and nights of waiting, the disruption of their professional duties, and their own familial responsibilities counted for nothing in their anxiety for me. In their joy at my recovery they have been forgotten. Nonetheless, to visit another prolonged spell of helpless suffering on them as my life ebbs away, or even worse, if I linger on into a comatose senility, seems altogether gratuitous.

This essay by Sidney Hook (1902–1989), former professor of philosophy at New York University and senior research fellow at the Hoover Institution on War, Revolution, and Peace, was published in the *New York Times* on March 1, 1987.

483

But what, it may be asked, of the joy and satisfaction of living, of basking in the sunshine, listening to music, watching one's grandchildren growing into adolescence, following the news about the fate of freedom in a troubled world, playing with ideas, writing one's testament of wisdom and folly for posterity? Is not all that one endured, together with the risk of its recurrence, an acceptable price for the multiple satisfactions that are still open even to a person of advanced years?

Apparently those who cling to life no matter what think so. I do not.

The zest and intensity of these experiences are no longer what they used to be. I am not vain enough to delude myself that I can in the few remaining years make an important discovery useful for mankind or can lead a social movement or do anything that will be historically eventful, no less event-making. My autobiography, which describes a record of intellectual and political experiences of some historical value, already much too long, could be posthumously published. I have had my fill of joys and sorrows and am not greedy for more life. I have always thought that a test of whether one had found happiness in one's life is whether one would be willing to relive it — whether, if it were possible, one would accept the opportunity to be born again.

Having lived a full and relatively happy life, I would cheerfully accept the chance to be reborn, but certainly not to be reborn again as an infirm octogenarian. To some extent, my views reflect what I have seen happen to the aged and stricken who have been so unfortunate as to survive crippling paralysis. They suffer, and impose suffering on others, unable even to make a request that their torment be ended.

I am mindful too of the burdens placed upon the community, with its rapidly diminishing resources, to provide the adequate and costly services necessary to sustain the lives of those whose days and nights are spent on mattress graves of pain. A better use could be made of these resources to increase the opportunities and qualities of life for the young. I am not denying the moral obligation the community has to look after its disabled and aged. There are times, however, when an individual may find it pointless to insist on the fulfillment of a legal and moral right.

What is required is no great revolution in morals but an enlargement of imagination and an intelligent evaluation of alternative uses of community resources.

Long ago, Seneca observed that "the wise man will live as long as he ought, not as long as he can." One can envisage hypothetical circumstances in which one has a duty to prolong one's life despite its costs for the sake of others, but such circumstances are far removed from the ordinary prospects we are considering. If wisdom is rooted in knowledge of the alternatives of choice, it must be reliably informed of the state one is in and its likely outcome. Scientific medicine is not infallible, but it is the best we have. Should a rational person be willing to endure acute suffering merely on the chance that a miraculous cure might presently be at hand? Each one should be permitted to make his own choice — especially when no one else is harmed by it.

The responsibility for the decision, whether deemed wise or foolish, must be with the chooser.

Active and Passive Euthanasia
JAMES RACHELS

The distinction between active and passive euthanasia is thought to be crucial for medical ethics. The idea is that it is permissible, at least in some cases, to withhold treatment and allow a patient to die, but it is never permissible to take any direct action designed to kill the patient. This doctrine seems to be accepted by most doctors, and it is endorsed in a statement adopted by the House of Delegates of the American Medical Association on December 4, 1973:

> The intentional termination of the life of one human being by another — mercy killing — is contrary to that for which the medical profession stands and is contrary to the policy of the American Medical Association.
>
> The cessation of the employment of extraordinary means to prolong the life of the body when there is irrefutable evidence that biological death is imminent is the decision of the patient and/or his immediate family. The advice and judgment of the physician should be freely available to the patient and/or his immediate family.

However, a strong case can be made against this doctrine. In what follows I will set out some of the relevant arguments and urge doctors to reconsider their views on this matter.

To begin with a familiar type of situation, a patient who is dying of incurable cancer of the throat is in terrible pain, which can no longer be satisfactorily alleviated. He is certain to die within a few days, even if present treatment is continued, but he does not want

James Rachels is editor of *Moral Problems* (1979), a reader on the ethical aspects of contemporary social issues. "Active and Passive Euthanasia" was published in the *New England Journal of Medicine,* vol. 292, in 1975.

to go on living for those days since the pain is unbearable. So he asks the doctor for an end to it, and his family joins in the request.

Suppose the doctor agrees to withhold treatment, as the conventional doctrine says he may. The justification for his doing so is that the patient is in terrible agony, and since he is going to die anyway, it would be wrong to prolong his suffering needlessly. But now notice this. If one simply withholds treatment, it may take the patient longer to die, and so he may suffer more than he would if more direct action were taken and a lethal injection given. This fact provides strong reason for thinking that, once the initial decision not to prolong his agony has been made, active euthanasia is actually preferable to passive euthanasia, rather than the reverse. To say otherwise is to endorse the option that leads to more suffering rather than less, and is contrary to the humanitarian impulse that prompts the decision not to prolong his life in the first place.

Part of my point is that the process of being "allowed to die" can be relatively slow and painful, whereas being given a lethal injection is relatively quick and painless. Let me give a different sort of example. In the United States about one in 600 babies is born with Down's syndrome. Most of these babies are otherwise healthy — that is, with only the usual pediatric care, they will proceed to an otherwise normal infancy. Some, however, are born with congenital defects such as intestinal obstructions that require operations if they are to live. Sometimes, the parents and the doctor will decide not to operate, and let the infant die. Anthony Shaw describes what happens then:

> . . . When surgery is denied [the doctor] must try to keep the infant from suffering while natural forces sap the baby's life away. As a surgeon whose natural inclination is to use the scalpel to fight off death, standing by and watching a salvageable baby die is the most emotionally exhausting experience I know. It is easy at a conference, in a theoretical discussion, to decide that such infants should be allowed to die. It is altogether different to stand by in the nursery and watch as dehydration and infection wither a tiny being over hours and days. This is a terrible ordeal for me and the hospital staff — much more so than for the parents who never set foot in the nursery.[1]

I can understand why some people are opposed to all euthanasia, and insist that such infants must be allowed to live. I think I can also understand why other people favor destroying these babies quickly and painlessly. But why should anyone favor letting "dehydration and infection wither a tiny being over hours and days"? The doctrine that says that a baby may be allowed to dehydrate and wither, but

---

[1] A. Shaw, "Doctor, Do We Have a Choice?" *New York Times Magazine,* January 30, 1972, p. 54.

may not be given an injection that would end its life without suffering, seems so patently cruel as to require no further refutation. The strong language is not intended to offend, but only to put the point in the clearest possible way.

My second argument is that the conventional doctrine leads to 5 decisions concerning life and death made on irrelevant grounds.

Consider again the case of the infants with Down's syndrome who need operations for congenital defects unrelated to the syndrome to live. Sometimes there is no operation, and the baby dies, but when there is no such defect, the baby lives on. Now, an operation such as that to remove an intestinal obstruction is not prohibitively difficult. The reason why such operations are not performed in these cases is, clearly, that the child has Down's syndrome and the parents and doctor judge that because of that fact it is better for the child to die.

But notice that this situation is absurd, no matter what view one takes of the lives and potential of such babies. If the life of such an infant is worth preserving, what does it matter if it needs a simple operation? Or, if one thinks it better that such a baby should not live on, what difference does it make that it happens to have an unobstructed intestinal tract? In either case, the matter of life and death is being decided on irrelevant grounds. It is the Down's syndrome, and not the intestines, that is the issue. The matter should be decided, if at all, on that basis, and not be allowed to depend on the essentially irrelevant question of whether the intestinal tract is blocked.

What makes this situation possible, of course, is the idea that when there is an intestinal blockage, one can "let the baby die," but when there is no such defect there is nothing that can be done, for one must not "kill" it. The fact that this idea leads to such results as deciding life or death on irrelevant grounds is another good reason why the doctrine should be rejected.

One reason why so many people think that there is an important moral difference between active and passive euthanasia is that they think killing someone is morally worse than letting someone die. But is it? Is killing, in itself, worse than letting die? To investigate this issue, two cases may be considered that are exactly alike except that one involves killing whereas the other involves letting someone die. Then, it can be asked whether this difference makes any difference to the moral assessments. It is important that the cases be exactly alike, except for this one difference, since otherwise one cannot be confident that it is this difference and not some other that accounts for any variation in the assessments of the two cases. So, let us consider this pair of cases:

In the first, Smith stands to gain a large inheritance if anything 10 should happen to his six-year-old cousin. One evening while the child is taking his bath, Smith sneaks into the bathroom and drowns the child, and then arranges things so that it will look like an accident.

In the second, Jones also stands to gain if anything should happen to his six-year-old cousin. Like Smith, Jones sneaks in planning to drown the child in his bath. However, just as he enters the bathroom Jones sees the child slip and hit his head, and fall face down in the water. Jones is delighted; he stands by, ready to push the child's head back under if it is necessary, but it is not necessary. With only a little thrashing about, the child drowns all by himself, "accidentally," as Jones watches and does nothing.

Now Smith killed the child, whereas Jones "merely" let the child die. That is the only difference between them. Did either man behave better, from a moral point of view? If the difference between killing and letting die were in itself a morally important matter, one should say that Jones's behavior was less reprehensible than Smith's. But does one really want to say that? I think not. In the first place, both men acted from the same motive, personal gain, and both had exactly the same end in view when they acted. It may be inferred from Smith's conduct that he is a bad man, although that judgment may be withdrawn or modified if certain further facts are learned about him — for example, that he is mentally deranged. But would not the very same thing be inferred about Jones from his conduct? And would not the same further considerations also be relevant to any modification of this judgment? Moreover, suppose Jones pleaded, in his own defense, "After all, I didn't do anything except just stand there and watch the child drown. I didn't kill him; I only let him die." Again, if letting die were in itself less bad than killing, this defense should have at least some weight. But it does not. Such a "defense" can only be regarded as a grotesque perversion of moral reasoning. Morally speaking, it is no defense at all.

Now, it may be pointed out, quite properly, that the cases of euthanasia with which doctors are concerned are not like this at all. They do not involve personal gain or the destruction of normal, healthy children. Doctors are concerned only with cases in which the patient's life is of no further use to him, or in which the patient's life has become or will soon become a terrible burden. However, the point is the same in these cases: The bare difference between killing and letting die does not, in itself, make a moral difference. If a doctor lets a patient die, for humane reasons, he is in the same moral position as if he had given the patient a lethal injection for humane reasons. If his decision was wrong — if, for example, the patient's illness was in fact curable — the decision would be equally regrettable no matter which method was used to carry it out. And if the doctor's decision was the right one, the method used is not in itself important.

The AMA policy statement isolates the crucial issue very well; the crucial issue is "the intentional termination of the life of one human being by another." But after identifying this issue, and forbidding "mercy killing," the statement goes on to deny that the cessation of treatment is the intentional termination of a life. This is where the mistake comes in, for what is the cessation of treatment, in these circumstances, if it is not "the intentional termination of the life of one human being by another"? Of course it is exactly that, and if it were not, there would be no point to it.

Many people will find this judgment hard to accept. One reason, 15 I think, is that it is very easy to conflate the question of whether killing is, in itself, worse than letting die, with the very different question of whether most actual cases of killing are more reprehensible than most actual cases of letting die. Most actual cases of killing are clearly terrible (think, for example, of all the murders reported in the newspapers), and one hears of such cases every day. On the other hand, one hardly ever hears of a case of letting die, except for the actions of doctors who are motivated by humanitarian reasons. So one learns to think of killing in a much worse light than of letting die, for it is not the bare difference between killing and letting die that makes the difference in these cases. Rather, the other factors — the murderer's motive of personal gain, for example, contrasted with the doctor's humanitarian motivation — account for different reactions to the different cases.

I have argued that killing is not in itself any worse than letting die; if my contention is right, it follows that active euthanasia is not any worse than passive euthanasia. What arguments can be given on the other side? The most common, I believe, is the following:

"The important difference between active and passive euthanasia is that, in passive euthanasia, the doctor does not do anything to bring about the patient's death. The doctor does nothing, and the patient dies of whatever ills already afflict him. In active euthanasia, however, the doctor does something to bring about the patient's death: He kills him. The doctor who gives the patient with cancer a lethal injection has himself caused his patient's death; whereas if he merely ceases treatment, the cancer is the cause of the death."

A number of points need to be made here. The first is that it is not exactly correct to say that in passive euthanasia the doctor does nothing, for he does do one thing that is very important: He lets the patient die. "Letting someone die" is certainly different in some respects, from other types of action — mainly in that it is a kind of action that one may perform by way of not performing certain other actions. For example, one may let a patient die by way of not giving medication, just as one may insult someone by way of not shaking his hand. But for any purpose of moral assessment, it is a type of action nonetheless. The decision to let a patient die is subject to moral appraisal in the same way that a decision to kill him would be subject to moral appraisal: It may be assessed as wise or unwise, compassionate or sadistic, right or wrong. If a doctor deliberately let a patient die who was suffering from a routinely curable illness, the doctor would certainly be to blame for what he had done, just as he would be to blame if he had needlessly killed the patient. Charges against him would then be appropriate. If so, it would be no defense at all for him to insist that he didn't "do anything." He would have done something very serious indeed, for he let his patient die.

Fixing the cause of death may be very important from a legal point of view, for it may determine whether criminal charges are brought against the doctor. But I do not think that this notion can be used to show a moral difference between active and passive euthanasia. The reason why it is considered bad to be the cause of someone's death is that death is regarded as a great evil — and so it is. However, if it had been decided that euthanasia — even passive euthanasia — is desirable in a given case, it has also been decided that in this instance death is no greater an evil than the patient's continued existence. And if this is true, the usual reason for not wanting to be the cause of someone's death simply does not apply.

Finally, doctors may think that all of this is only of academic in- 20 terest — the sort of thing that philosophers may worry about but that has no practical bearing on their own work. After all, doctors must be concerned about the legal consequences of what they do, and active euthanasia is clearly forbidden by the law. But even so, doctors should also be concerned with the fact that the law is forcing upon them a moral doctrine that may well be indefensible and has a considerable effect on their practices. Of course, most doctors are not now in the position of being coerced in this matter, for they do not regard themselves as merely going along with what the law requires. Rather, in statements such as the AMA policy statement that I have quoted, they are endorsing this doctrine as a central point of medical ethics. In that statement, active euthanasia is condemned not merely as illegal but as "contrary to that for which the medical profession stands," whereas passive euthanasia is approved. However, the preceding considerations suggest that there is really no moral difference between the two, considered in themselves (there may be important moral differences in some cases in their *consequences,* but, as I pointed out, these differences may make active euthanasia, and not passive euthanasia, the morally preferable option). So, whereas doctors may have to discriminate between active and passive euthanasia to satisfy the law, they should not do any more than that. In particular, they should not give the distinction any added authority and weight by writing it into official statements of medical ethics.

A Modern Inquisition

JACK KEVORKIAN

This is probably the first time that this august body [the American Humanist Association] has been addressed by someone under indictment on two counts of first-degree murder.

The Inquisition is still alive and well. The only difference is that today it's much more dangerous and subtle. The inquisitors don't burn you at the stake anymore; they slowly sizzle you. They make sure you pay dearly for what you do. In fact, they kill you often in a subtle way. My situation is a perfect example of it.

This is not self-pity, understand. I don't regret the position I'm in. I'm not a hero, either — by my definition, anyway. To me, anyone who does what *should* be done is not a hero. And I still feel that I'm only doing what I, as a physician, should do. A license has nothing to do with it; I am a physician and therefore I will act like a physician whenever I can. That doesn't mean that I'm more compassionate than anyone else, but there is one thing I am that many aren't and that's honest.

The biggest deficiency today and the biggest problem with society is dishonesty. It underlies almost every crisis and every problem you can name. It's almost inevitable; in fact, it's unavoidable as you mature. We feel that a little dishonesty greases the wheels of society, that it makes things easier for everybody if we lie a little to each other. But all this dishonesty becomes cumulative after a while. If everyone were perfectly honest at all times, if human nature could stand that, you would find many fewer problems in the world.

When we (my lawyers, sisters, medical technologist, and myself) first started this work [physician-assisted voluntary euthanasia], we didn't expect the explosion of publicity that followed. The mainstream media tried to make my work look very negative — they tried to make me look negative — so that they could denigrate the concept we're working on. They said I should not be identified with the concept, yet they strived to do just that. They insulted and denigrated me and then hoped that it would spill over onto the concept. It didn't work, however; according to the polls, people may be split 50-50 on what they think of me, but they are three-to-one in favor of the concept, and that's never changed.

Now isn't it strange that on a controversial subject of this magnitude — one that cuts across many disciplines — the entire editorial

This speech by Dr. Jack Kevorkian, a proponent of physician-assisted voluntary euthanasia, first appeared in the November–December 1994 issue of *The Humanist;* this excerpt is from the March–April 1995 issue of *Utne Reader.*

policy of the country is on one side? Even on a contentious issue like abortion, there is editorial support for both sides. And our issue — death with dignity — as far as we're concerned, is simpler than abortion. So why is every mainstream editorial writer and newspaper in the country against us on this? Not one has come out in whole-hearted support of us, even though public opinion is on our side.

As I surmise it, they're in a conspiracy, which is not a revelation to many people. But with whom? Well, let's take a look at who's against this: organized religion, organized medicine, and organized big money. That's a lot of power.

Why is organized medicine against this? For a couple of reasons, I think. First, because the so-called profession — which is no longer a profession; it's really a commercial enterprise and has been for a long time — is permeated with religious overtones. The basis of so-called medical ethics is religious ethics. The Hippocratic oath is a religious manifesto. It is not medical. Hippocrates didn't write it; we don't know who did, but we think it's from the Pythagoreans. So if you meet a physician who says "Life is sacred," be careful. We didn't study sanctity in medical school. You are talking to a theologian first, probably a businessperson second, and a physician third.

The second reason that organized medicine is against physician-assisted voluntary euthanasia is the money involved. If a patient's suffering is curtailed by three weeks, can you imagine how much that adds up to in medical care? And a lot of drugs are used in the last several months and years of life, which add up to billions of dollars for the pharmaceutical industry.

This is what is so dismaying to me, what makes me cynical. You 10 have to be cynical in life when you read about a situation that's so terrible and so incorrigible. There are certain ways to deal with it: You can go along with it, which is hard to do; you can go insane, which is a refuge (and some do that); or you can face it with deep cynicism. I've opted for cynicism.

In responding to the religious issues, I ask this: Why not let all the religious underpinnings of medicine apply only to the ethics of religious hospitals and leave the secular hospitals alone? The doctors who work in religious hospitals can refuse to do abortions, they can refuse assisted suicide or euthanasia, they can do anything they want. But they have no right to impose what *they* call a universal medical ethic on secular institutions.

Besides, what is ethics? Can you define it? My definition is simple: Ethics is saying and doing what is right, at the time. And that changes. Seventy-five years ago, if I told you that for Christmas I was going to have a truck deliver ten tons of coal to your house, you would have been delighted. If I told you that today, you would be insulted. Doing the right thing changes with time.

That's true of human society also. There is a primitive society — I don't know which one exactly — whose members were shocked to learn that we embalm our dead, place them in boxes, and then bury them in the ground. Do you know what they do? They eat them. To them, it's ethical and moral and honorable to devour the corpse of your loved one. We're shocked at that, right? It's all a matter of acculturation, time, where you are, and who you are. If I visited this primitive society and I was a real humanist, I'd say, "Oh, that's interesting." And if the so-called savage in turn said "Gee, that's interesting what you do," then he or she would be a humanist. I used to define maturity as the inability to be shocked. So I guess in some ways we're still immature. But if you're truly mature, and a true humanist, you can never be shocked. If they eat their dead, so be it — that's their culture. But you know what our missionaries did, don't you? That's immoral action.

I think you get the gist of my position.

Kevorkian Has Punctured the Ethical Gray Zone Where Most of Us Live

ELLEN GOODMAN

What does Jack Kevorkian demand now? A *court*-assisted suicide?

After the video had rolled, after 22 million Americans had seen him inject potassium chloride into Tom Youk's arm on *60 Minutes,* Kevorkian turned back to the subject that matters the most to him: his own fate. Would he be prosecuted?

Youk was little more than a prop for Jack's act, a dead body he could use in challenging authority. "Either they go or I go," he told Mike Wallace, finally exhibiting the emotion lacking from his death-side manner.

"If I'm acquitted, they go because they know they'll never convict me," he said. "If I am convicted, I will starve to death in prison. So I will go. One of the two of us is going to go. And that's why I did this. The issue has got to be raised to the level where it's finally decided."

Ellen Goodman is a Pulitzer Prize–winning columnist for the *Boston Globe.* This essay appeared on December 3, 1998.

So" we have another scene in the long-running melodrama 5
scripted by and starring the man from Michigan.

How many roles he has played. Dr. Jack, the pathologist who
never had a live patient until he began escorting them to death. Dr.
Jack, the obitiatrist whose first cause was promoting the harvesting
of organs from death row inmates. Dr. Jack, the artist, whose oil
paintings come replete with severed heads and skulls. Now he's trying out for Dr. Jack, the martyr.

I am not surprised that Kevorkian upped the ante, moving from
passive to active euthanasia. Assisted suicide no longer caught the
spotlight. Nor did it catch the eye of the county prosecutor elected
on the promise that he wouldn't waste more tax money trying Dr.
Jack.

But now the new prosecutor has been dared into his duty. He's
charged Kevorkian with homicide. It appears that Dr. Jack will return to the courtroom that he once mocked with his Thomas Jefferson costume. Is this, finally, the climax?

I would never have cast Kevorkian for the lead role in the movement for a more merciful death. He forced the issue of assisted suicide and euthanasia onto the public stage, but he also polarized that
public audience. Nor would I wish him at my deathbed offering these
last words of comfort: "We're going to inject in your right arm. OK?
Okey-doke." *Okey-doke?*

But this time Dr. Jack is doing more than exposing the thin line 10
between passive and active euthanasia. He is pulling the curtain on
public ambivalence. This is where most Americans stand, awk-
wardly balanced: on one side, unease about legalizing the right to assisted death; on the other side, unease about condemning those
who assist in a merciful death.

Michigan is just one example of this ambivalence. This fall the
state overwhelmingly turned down a ballot initiative to legalize assisted suicide. Yet three times, its courts acquitted Kevorkian of assisted suicide. Indeed, the third time, the jurors asked for his
autograph and invited him out to dinner.

The latest challenge delivered by Kevorkian — "either they go
or I go" — has the staged quality of a temperamental actor. But even
the most ardent opponent of doctor-assisted death ranks the likelihood of a homicide conviction as close to zero. The law may not
make a distinction between delivering death to a healthy man or to
one, like Tom Youk, with Lou Gehrig's disease. But jurors do.

As for the lesser charges of assisting suicide and delivering controlled substances, there is enough wiggle room and enough legal
technicalities to make Kevorkian's threat of suicide by starvation
thin, if not empty. The issue will not be "finally decided."

It's only six months since the Supreme Court ruled that there
was no fundamental right to assisted suicide. The justices encour-

aged the country to continue "an earnest and profound debate about the morality, legality, and practicality of physician-assisted suicide." So far only one state — Oregon — has rationally and carefully legalized aid-in-dying.

For the most part, the country remains both reluctant to change 15 the law and reluctant to enforce it. This is the place we have been driven to by a desire for mercy and a longing for caution.

In Holland, where 2.4 percent of the deaths come at the expressed request of a patient, there is a word to describe this ethical gray zone where many of us live. There, doctor-assisted death is *gedogen,* as they say in Dutch: illegal and yet permitted. It's allowed only under strict guidelines for patients suffering unbearable pain and terminal illness.

But here we are literally at a loss for words. We can arrest and we can acquit. But for the terminally and suffering ill, we have yet to agree on what separates the kind from the Kevorkian. We sit in the audience chilled to the bone by Dr. Jack's latest act. But we have done too little to establish guidelines to distinguish a merciful death from an icy "okey-doke."

Consequences of Imposing the Quality-of-Life Ethic
EILEEN DOYLE

Under the American Constitution, all who belong to the human species *are persons* and are guaranteed the protection of their inalienable right to life (and other inalienable rights).

(The only exceptions are living human beings before birth who have unjustly been denied their right to life by the 1973 Supreme Court abortion decisions, *Roe v. Wade* and *Doe v. Bolton.*)

The Constitution adheres to the sanctity of life ethic and the theory of natural rights which state that human beings by their very nature are of intrinsic value — they do not have to earn their value; it belongs to them simply because they are human.

Therefore they are endowed with inalienable rights to life and other rights. The state cannot bestow or take away these inalienable rights because they do not belong to the state to dispose of, but rather to each individual human being. The state exists to protect these rights.

Eileen Doyle, R.N., was the president of New York State Nurses for Life when this essay was written. This selection is from *A Pro-Life Primer on Euthanasia* (1985).

The problem for euthanasia proponents is that under our Con- 5
stitution, euthanasia (killing human beings who are innocent of unjust aggression on others' lives) cannot be legalized. It is obvious
that the American people would not permit them to tear up the Constitution and write a new one to fit their purposes, so they have devised a clever strategy to make it appear that we would be abiding
by the Constitution even while violating it.

First they attack the sanctity-of-life ethic as a religious doctrine
because it is based on the religious belief that human beings are created by God in His Image. They fail to realize that whatever the religious beliefs upon which it was founded, its principles embodied in
our Constitution are right now held dear by the vast majority of
American people.

They propose to replace this sanctity-of-life ethic with a new one
which we call the quality-of-life ethic. But underlying this new ethic
is another religious belief of secular humanism, which believes that
human life is the result of random evolution and denies or questions
the existence of God or at least God's involvement in human
affairs — a remote God.

The Supreme Court has declared that secular humanism as a
world view is a religion in the First Amendment sense *(Torasco v.
Watkins, United States v. Seeger, Welsh v. United States)*.

Redefining Some People

This quality-of-life ethic proposes that some human beings have
a quality of life so poor that they ought not be classified as legal persons with inalienable rights. To be declared a person with human
rights, a human being must be able to pass certain tests. The tests
vary according to who is proposing them but in general, it requires
that to be declared a person (with inalienable rights) a human being
must be able to: think and reason; give or receive love; be useful in
some way; be capable of meaningful life, i.e., able to enjoy or appreciate life.

Those who fail the test would lose legal personhood and have 10
no inalienable rights. Therefore, these human beings could be killed
without violating anyone's inalienable rights.

This is precisely what the Court did in the abortion decisions in
declaring the unborn as not persons, thus allowing them to be killed.
The whole idea is pure legal fiction, a subterfuge to quiet the consciences of the American people who have a horror of killing innocent people.

Killing a "nonperson" demoted to a less-than-human status by
legal fiat seems then to be more like killing a dog or a cat to put it
out of its misery. Then all can pretend that no evil, unjust deed has
been done.

This quality-of-life ethic also holds that even among those who pass the tests of personhood, there may be many who have a quality of life so poor because of grave illness or birth defects that life itself is no longer a value to be preserved for these people. So to take these lives would not be an injustice but a benefit for them.

And finally . . . , this quality-of-life ethic allows that there is a compelling state interest sufficient to deny the inalienable right to life to a class of citizens: permanently dependent, institutionalized people who put an inordinate burden on the state to provide public funds and medical resources for their care.

The Awesome Result

If the proponents of this quality-of-life ethic succeed in having 15 it replace the sanctity-of-life ethic, what would be the consequences?

1. It would destroy the underlying principles embodied in our Constitution, reducing it to a worthless, ineffective, hypocritical document. A new constitution would have to be written to replace it.

2. It would be an injustice to the vast majority of the Americans who adhere to the principles of the Constitution and who treasure our Constitution to have those principles overridden and the Constitution destroyed by a small elite who wish to impose their own set of principles, not accepted by most people.

3. Large numbers of people whose inalienable right to life is now protected by the law of homicide would be killed without their consent because somebody else had decided they are not persons. These could include newborn infants with birth defects, autistic children, psychotic people, senile aged, comatose people, those with severe drug or alcohol addiction, and so on. All these could easily fail the tests of personhood.

Then there are the huge numbers of people who by somebody's definition other than their own have lives not worth living, who could be disposed of.

And finally there are those millions of dependent, institutional- 20 ized people on the public dole eating up the valuable resources of the powerful, so-called nondependent taxpayers. To dispose of them — the dependents — would become a "patriotic duty."

Equal protection of the law would become a mockery.

4. The psychological and spiritual damage to those who do the killing and to those who permit it would corrupt our entire nation. All would be a party to killing and to the lying to ourselves that we are doing good rather than admitting the crimes.

5. Inordinate power, tyrannical power, would be vested in the Supreme Court. For it would be the Court that would ultimately

decide who is and who is not a legal person; who has and who has not a sufficient quality of life to give it value worth preserving; and at what point there is a compelling state interest sufficient to override the inalienable right to life of dependent citizens.

As with the concept of a constitutional right to die, the concept of a quality-of-life ethic becomes absurd as well, when analyzed to its logical conclusions. For we would literally be handing over our priceless freedom and all inalienable rights to an oligarchy of nine justices on the Supreme Court.

And for what? To give power to an elite few to create their idea   25
of a "brave new world"— for themselves, who in turn might become their own victims should misfortune make them dependent and powerless.

Euthanasia for Kids
ARTHUR CAPLAN

The most momentous change in public policy with respect to health care during the past few years is the legalization of physician-assisted suicide in the state of Oregon. Those who favor this landmark change in the law insist that doctors can perform euthanasia without serious abuses. Oregon's law contains many protections to insure that no one is put to death without their consent. But a case from Holland, the country that has the most experience with physician-assisted suicide, raises the question of exactly how steep the slopes surrounding doctor-assisted suicide actually are.

In Holland, as long as a doctor reports an assisted suicide to the local prosecutor and it is clear that the person who was killed had made repeated requests for help in dying, was suffering, and was terminally ill, then no prosecution occurs. The Dutch Parliament formally adopted these protections into law. Thousands of people in Holland have asked for and received physician assistance in bringing about their deaths.

The Dutch seem to have avoided sliding down a slippery slope to involuntary euthanasia. However, their ability to stay off the slope is now in doubt due to a case involving the killing of a baby.

Arthur Caplan is the director of the Center for Bioethics and Trustee Professor of Bioethics at the University of Pennsylvania. He has published many articles and books on philosophy, medicine, health policy, and the biological sciences. This essay is excerpted from his book *Due Consideration: Controversy in the Age of Medical Miracles* (1998).

In Late December of 1994, the Dutch Minister of Justice, Winnie Sorgdrager, announced that the government was bringing charges against Dr. Henk Prins. Prins, a forty-nine-year-old gynecologist on the staff of the Waterland Hospital in Zandaam just north of Amsterdam, admitted killing a three-day-old baby girl at her parents' request in March of 1993.

The baby was born partially paralyzed with a severely deformed 5 brain. Her parents felt that she was in pain. Prins killed the baby after consulting with a number of doctors who confirmed his prognosis that she probably had only weeks to live. Prins felt that even if the baby lived, she would not be able to walk, stand, control her bowel and bladder, and might have had a life of constant pain.

After killing the baby, Prins reported what he had done to the police and the local prosecutor. He felt that he should not be punished for what he had done since the parents had requested the death and since the child's life would, in his view, have been miserable.

Prins's role in the death of a baby shows how hard it is not to slide down the slope toward involuntary killing where active euthanasia by doctors is concerned. Once killing is allowed for those in the health professions, it is difficult to prevent the right to die from being extended to newborns, children, the retarded, the mentally ill, and the senile. The pressure to include those who are neither terminally ill — or mentally competent in the ranks of those endowed with the right to be helped to die becomes enormous. What is worse, those who are vulnerable, such as babies or the retarded, to having others decide they ought be killed are much more at risk in America than they would be in Holland.

Unlike Americans, the Dutch have generous health insurance. Views about the quality of life in Holland are not as colored by the question of how high the meter has run at the hospital billing department. Nor are there public officials proposing to end all health care programs for babies who are the children of illegal aliens or new immigrants or to throw all children of single parents into orphanages. The Prins case shows that the disabled are put at risk when competent adults are granted the right to physician-assisted suicide. Those who seek to extend the right to assisted suicide in the United States would be well advised to think harder about the much sharper angle of the slopes that exist on this side of the Atlantic.

The Supreme Court and
Physician-Assisted Suicide—
The Ultimate Right

MARCIA ANGELL

The U.S. Supreme Court will decide later this year whether to let stand decisions by two appeals courts permitting doctors to help terminally ill patients commit suicide.[1] The Ninth and Second Circuit Courts of Appeals last spring held that state laws in Washington and New York that ban assistance in suicide were unconstitutional as applied to doctors and their dying patients.[2,3] If the Supreme Court lets the decisions stand, physicians in twelve states, which include about half the population of the United States, would be allowed to provide the means for terminally ill patients to take their own lives, and the remaining states would rapidly follow suit. Not since Roe v. Wade has a Supreme Court decision been so fateful.

The decision will culminate several years of intense national debate, fueled by a number of highly publicized events. Perhaps most important among them is Dr. Jack Kevorkian's defiant assistance in some 44 suicides since 1990, to the dismay of many in the medical and legal establishments, but with substantial public support, as evidenced by the fact that three juries refused to convict him even in the face of a Michigan statute enacted for that purpose. Also since 1990, voters in three states have considered ballot initiatives that would legalize some form of physician-assisted dying, and in 1994 Oregon became the first state to approve such a measure.[4] (The Oregon law was stayed pending a court challenge.) Several surveys indicate that roughly two thirds of the American public now support physician-assisted suicide,[5,6] as do more than half the doctors in the

Marcia Angell is executive editor of *The New England Journal of Medicine,* in which this editorial appeared on January 2, 1997. On June 26th of that year, the U.S. Supreme Court unanimously ruled that the U.S. Constitution does not guarantee Americans a right to commit suicide with the help of a physician, leaving the issue to state legislatures to decide.

[1]L. Greenhouse, "High Court to Say If the Dying Have a Right to Suicide Help," *New York Times,* October 2, 1996, p. A1.

[2]Compassion in Dying v. Washington. 79 F:3d 790. 9th Cir. Ct. 1996.

[3]Quill v. Vacco. 80 F:3d 716. 2nd Cir. Ct. 1996.

[4]G. J. Anas, "Death by Prescription — the Oregon Initiative," *New England Journal of Medicine* 331 (1994): pp. 1240–1243.

[5]R. J. Blendon, U. S. Szalay, and R. A. Knox, "Should Physicians Aid Their Patients in Dying? The Public Perspective," *JAMA* 267 (1992): pp. 2658–2662.

[6]J. G. Bachman, K. H. Alcser, D. J. Doukas, R. L. Lichtenstein, A. D. Corning, and H. Brody, "Attitudes of Michigan Physicians and the Public toward Legalizing

United States,[6,7] despite the fact that influential physicians' organizations are opposed. It seems clear that many Americans are now so concerned about the possibility of a lingering, high-technology death that they are receptive to the idea of doctors being allowed to help them die.

In this editorial I will explain why I believe the appeals courts were right and why I hope the Supreme Court will uphold their decisions. I am aware that this is a highly contentious issue, with good people and strong arguments on both sides. The American Medical Association (AMA) filed an amicus brief opposing the legalization of physician-assisted suicide,[8] and the Massachusetts Medical Society, which owns the *Journal,* was a signatory to it. But here I speak for myself, not the *Journal* or the Massachusetts Medical Society. The legal aspects of the case have been well discussed elsewhere, to me most compellingly in Ronald Dworkin's essay in the *New York Review of Books.*[9] I will focus primarily on the medical and ethical aspects.

I begin with the generally accepted premise that one of the most important ethical principles in medicine is respect for each patient's autonomy, and that when this principle conflicts with others, it should almost always take precedence. This premise is incorporated into our laws governing medical practice and research, including the requirement of informed consent to any treatment. In medicine, patients exercise their self-determination most dramatically when they ask that life-sustaining treatment be withdrawn. Although others may sometimes consider the request ill-founded, we are bound to honor it if the patient is mentally competent — that is, if the patient can understand the nature of the decision and its consequences.

A second starting point is the recognition that death is not fair 5 and is often cruel. Some people die quickly, and others die slowly but peacefully. Some find personal or religious meaning in the process, as well as an opportunity for a final reconciliation with loved ones. But others, especially those with cancer, AIDS, or progressive neurologic disorders, may die by inches and in great anguish, despite every effort of their doctors and nurses. Although nearly all pain can be relieved, some cannot, and other symptoms, such as dyspnea, nausea, and weakness, are even more difficult to

Physician-assisted Suicide and Voluntary Euthanasia," *New England Journal of Medicine* 334 (1996): pp. 303–309.

[7]M. A. Lee, H. D. Nelson, V. P. Tilden, L. Ganzini, T. A. Schmidt, and S. W. Tolle, "Legalizing Assisted Suicide — Views of Physicians in Oregon," *New England Journal of Medicine* 334 (1996): pp. 310–315.

[8]D. M. Gianelli, "AMA to Court: No Suicide Aid," *American Medical News* 1 (November 25, 1996): pp. 1, 27, 28.

[9]R. Dworkin, "Sex, Death, and the Courts," *New York Review of Books,* August 8, 1996.

control. In addition, dying sometimes holds great indignities and existential suffering. Patients who happen to require some treatment to sustain their lives, such as assisted ventilation or dialysis, can hasten death by having the life-sustaining treatment withdrawn, but those who are not receiving life-sustaining treatment may desperately need help they cannot now get.

If the decisions of the appeals courts are upheld, states will not be able to prohibit doctors from helping such patients to die by prescribing a lethal dose of a drug and advising them on its use for suicide. State laws barring euthanasia (the administration of a lethal drug by a doctor) and assisted suicide for patients who are not terminally ill would not be affected. Furthermore, doctors would not be required to assist in suicide; they would simply have that option. Both appeals courts based their decisions on constitutional questions. This is important, because it shifted the focus of the debate from what the majority would approve through the political process, as exemplified by the Oregon initiative, to a matter of fundamental rights, which are largely immune from the political process. Indeed, the Ninth Circuit Court drew an explicit analogy between suicide and abortion, saying that both were personal choices protected by the Constitution and that forbidding doctors to assist would in effect nullify these rights. Although states could regulate assisted suicide, as they do abortion, they would not be permitted to regulate it out of existence.

It is hard to quarrel with the desire of a greatly suffering, dying patient for a quicker, more humane death or to disagree that it may be merciful to help bring that about. In those circumstances, loved ones are often relieved when death finally comes, as are the attending doctors and nurses. As the Second Circuit Court said, the state has no interest in prolonging such a life. Why, then, do so many people oppose legalizing physician-assisted suicide in these cases? There are a number of arguments against it, some stronger than others, but I believe none of them can offset the overriding duties of doctors to relieve suffering and to respect their patients' autonomy. Below I list several of the more important arguments against physician-assisted suicide and discuss why I believe they are in the last analysis unpersuasive.

Assisted suicide is a form of killing, which is always wrong. In contrast, withdrawing life-sustaining treatment simply allows the disease to take its course.

There are three methods of hastening the death of a dying patient: withdrawing life-sustaining treatment, assisting suicide, and euthanasia. The right to stop treatment has been recognized repeatedly since the 1976 case of Karen Ann Quinlan[10] and was affirmed by

---

[10]In re: Quinlan. 70 N.J. 10, 355. A.2d 647. 1976.

the U.S. Supreme Court in the 1990 Cruzan decision[11] and the U.S. Congress in its 1990 Patient Self-Determination Act.[12] Although the legal underpinning is the right to be free of unwanted bodily invasion, the purpose of hastening death was explicitly acknowledged. In contrast, assisted suicide and euthanasia have not been accepted; euthanasia is illegal in all states, and assisted suicide is illegal in most of them.

Why the distinctions? Most would say they turn on the doctor's role: whether it is passive or active. When life-sustaining treatment is withdrawn, the doctor's role is considered passive and the cause of death is the underlying disease, despite the fact that switching off the ventilator of a patient dependent on it looks anything but passive and would be considered homicide if done without the consent of the patient or a proxy. In contrast, euthanasia by the injection of a lethal drug is active and directly causes the patient's death. Assisting suicide by supplying the necessary drugs is considered somewhere in between, more active than switching off a ventilator but less active than injecting drugs, hence morally and legally more ambiguous.

I believe, however, that these distinctions are too doctor-centered and not sufficiently patient-centered. We should ask ourselves not so much whether the doctor's role is passive or active but whether the patient's role is passive or active. From that perspective, the three methods of hastening death line up quite differently. When life-sustaining treatment is withdrawn from an incompetent patient at the request of a proxy or when euthanasia is performed, the patient may be utterly passive. Indeed, either act can be performed even if the patient is unaware of the decision. In sharp contrast, assisted suicide, by definition, cannot occur without the patient's knowledge and participation. Therefore, it must be active — that is to say, voluntary. That is a crucial distinction, because it provides an inherent safeguard against abuse that is not present with the other two methods of hastening death. If the loaded term *kill* is to be used, it is not the doctor who kills, but the patient. Primarily because euthanasia can be performed without the patient's participation, I oppose its legalization in this country.

Assisted suicide is not necessary. All suffering can be relieved if care givers are sufficiently skillful and compassionate, as illustrated by the hospice movement.

---

[11]Cruzan v. Director, Missouri Department of Health. 497 U.S. 261. 110 S. Ct. 2841. 1990.

[12]Omnibus Budget Reconciliation Act of 1990. Pub. L. 101–508, sec. 4206 and 4751. 1994. Stat. 104.1388, 1388–115, and 1388–204 (classified respectively at 42 U.S.C. 1395cc(f) (Medicare) and 1396a(w) (Medicaid).

I have no doubt that if expert palliative care were available to everyone who needed it, there would be few requests for assisted suicide. Even under the best of circumstances, however, there will always be a few patients whose suffering simply cannot be adequately alleviated. And there will be some who would prefer suicide to any other measures available, including the withdrawal of life-sustaining treatment or the use of heavy sedation. Surely, every effort should be made to improve palliative care, as I argued 15 years ago,[13] but when those efforts are unavailing and suffering patients desperately long to end their lives, physician-assisted suicide should be allowed. The argument that permitting it would divert us from redoubling our commitment to comfort care asks these patients to pay the penalty for our failings. It is also illogical. Good comfort care and the availability of physician-assisted suicide are no more mutually exclusive than good cardiologic care and the availability of heart transplantation.

Permitting assisted suicide would put us on a moral "slippery slope." Although in itself assisted suicide might be acceptable, it would lead inexorably to involuntary euthanasia.

It is impossible to avoid slippery slopes in medicine (or in any aspect of life). The issue is how and where to find a purchase. For example, we accept the right of proxies to terminate life-sustaining treatment, despite the obvious potential for abuse, because the reasons for doing so outweigh the risks. We hope our procedures will safeguard patients. In the case of assisted suicide, its voluntary nature is the best protection against sliding down a slippery slope, but we also need to ensure that the request is thoughtful and freely made. Although it is possible that we may someday decide to legalize voluntary euthanasia under certain circumstances or assisted suicide for patients who are not terminally ill, legalizing assisted suicide for the dying does not in itself make these other decisions inevitable. Interestingly, recent reports from the Netherlands, where both euthanasia and physician-assisted suicide are permitted, indicate that fears about a slippery slope there have not been borne out.[14,15,16]

---

[13]M. Angell, "The Quality of Mercy," *New England Journal of Medicine* 306 (1982): pp. 98–99.

[14]P. J. van der Maas, G. van der Wal, I. Haverkate, et al., "Euthanasia, Physician-assisted Suicide, and Other Medical Practices Involving the End of Life in the Netherlands, 1990–1995," *New England Journal of Medicine* 335 (1996): pp. 1699–1705.

[15]G. van der Wal, P. J. van der Maas, J. M. Bosma, et al., "Evaluation of the Notification Procedure for Physician-assisted Suicide in the Netherlands," *New England Journal of Medicine* 335 (1996): pp. 1706–1711.

[16]M. Angell, "Euthanasia in the Netherlands — Good News or Bad?" *New England Journal of Medicine* 335 (1996): pp. 1676–1678.

Assisted suicide would be a threat to the economically and socially vulnerable. The poor, disabled, and elderly might be coerced to request it. Admittedly, overburdened families or cost-conscious doctors might pressure vulnerable patients to request suicide, but similar wrongdoing is at least as likely in the case of withdrawing life-sustaining treatment, since that decision can be made by proxy. Yet, there is no evidence of widespread abuse. The Ninth Circuit Court recalled that it was feared Roe v. Wade would lead to coercion of poor and uneducated women to request abortions, but that did not happen. The concern that coercion is more likely in this era of managed care, although understandable, would hold suffering patients hostage to the deficiencies of our health care system. Unfortunately, no human endeavor is immune to abuses. The question is not whether a perfect system can be devised, but whether abuses are likely to be sufficiently rare to be offset by the benefits to patients who otherwise would be condemned to face the end of their lives in protracted agony.

Depressed patients would seek physician-assisted suicide rather than help for their depression. Even in the terminally ill, a request for assisted suicide might signify treatable depression, not irreversible suffering.

Patients suffering greatly at the end of life may also be depressed, but the depression does not necessarily explain their decision to commit suicide or make it irrational. Nor is it simple to diagnose depression in terminally ill patients. Sadness is to be expected, and some of the vegetative symptoms of depression are similar to the symptoms of terminal illness. The success of antidepressant treatment in these circumstances is also not ensured. Although there are anecdotes about patients who changed their minds about suicide after treatment,[17] we do not have good studies of how often that happens or the relation to antidepressant treatment. Dying patients who request assisted suicide and seem depressed should certainly be strongly encouraged to accept psychiatric treatment, but I do not believe that competent patients should be required to accept it as a condition of receiving assistance with suicide. On the other hand, doctors would not be required to comply with all requests; they would be expected to use their judgment, just as they do in so many other types of life-and-death decisions in medical practice.

Doctors should never participate in taking life. If there is to be assisted suicide, doctors must not be involved.

Although most doctors favor permitting assisted suicide under 15 certain circumstances, many who favor it believe that doctors

---

[17]H. M. Chochinov, K. G. Wilson, M. Enns, et al., "Desire for Death in the Terminally Ill," *American Journal of Psychiatry* 152 (1995): pp. 1185–1191.

should not provide the assistance.[6,7] To them, doctors should be un-ambiguously committed to life (although most doctors who hold this view would readily honor a patient's decision to have life-sustaining treatment withdrawn). The AMA, too, seems to object to physician-assisted suicide primarily because it violates the profession's mission. Like others, I find that position too abstract.[18] The highest ethical imperative of doctors should be to provide care in whatever way best serves patients' interests, in accord with each patient's wishes, not with a theoretical commitment to preserve life no matter what the cost in suffering.[19] If a patient requests help with suicide and the doctor believes the request is appropriate, requiring someone else to provide the assistance would be a form of abandonment. Doctors who are opposed in principle need not assist, but they should make their patients aware of their position early in the relationship so that a patient who chooses to select another doctor can do so. The greatest harm we can do is to consign a desperate patient to unbearable suffering — or force the patient to seek out a stranger like Dr. Kevorkian. Contrary to the frequent assertion that permitting physician-assisted suicide would lead patients to distrust their doctors, I believe distrust is more likely to arise from uncertainty about whether a doctor will honor a patient's wishes.

Physician-assisted suicide may occasionally be warranted, but it should remain illegal. If doctors risk prosecution, they will think twice before assisting with suicide.

This argument wrongly shifts the focus from the patient to the doctor. Instead of reflecting the condition and wishes of patients, assisted suicide would reflect the courage and compassion of their doctors. Thus, patients with doctors like Timothy Quill, who described in a 1991 *Journal* article how he helped a patient take her life,[20] would get the help they need and want, but similar patients with less steadfast doctors would not. That makes no sense.

People do not need assistance to commit suicide. With enough determination, they can do it themselves.

This is perhaps the cruelest of the arguments against physician-assisted suicide. Many patients at the end of life are, in fact, physically unable to commit suicide on their own. Others lack the resources to do so. It has sometimes been suggested that they can simply stop eating and drinking and kill themselves that way. Al-

---

[18]C. K. Cassel and D. E. Meier, "Morals and Moralism in the Debate over Euthanasia and Assisted Suicide," *New England Journal of Medicine* 323 (1990): pp. 750–752.

[19]M. Angell, "Doctors and Assisted Suicide," *Ann R Coll Physicians Surg Can* 24 (1991): pp. 493–494.

[20]T. E. Quill, "Death and Dignity — A Case of Individualized Decision Making," *New England Journal of Medicine* 324 (1991): pp. 691–694.

though this method has been described as peaceful under certain conditions,[21] no one should count on that. The fact is that this argument leaves most patients to their suffering. Some, usually men, manage to commit suicide using violent methods. Percy Bridgman, a Nobel laureate in physics who in 1961 shot himself rather than die of metastatic cancer, said in his suicide note, "It is not decent for society to make a man do this to himself."[22]

My father, who knew nothing of Percy Bridgman, committed suicide under similar circumstances. He was 81 and had metastatic prostate cancer. The night before he was scheduled to be admitted to the hospital, he shot himself. Like Bridgman, he thought it might be his last chance. At the time, he was not in extreme pain, nor was he close to death (his life expectancy was probably longer than six months). But he was suffering nonetheless — from nausea and the side effects of antiemetic agents, weakness, incontinence, and hopelessness. Was he depressed? He would probably have freely admitted that he was, but he would have thought it beside the point. In any case, he was an intensely private man who would have refused psychiatric care. Was he overly concerned with maintaining control of the circumstances of his life and death? Many people would say so, but that was the way he was. It is the job of medicine to deal with patients as they are, not as we would like them to be.

I tell my father's story here because it makes an abstract issue very concrete. If physician-assisted suicide had been available, I have no doubt my father would have chosen it. He was protective of his family, and if he had felt he had the choice, he would have spared my mother the shock of finding his body. He did not tell her what he planned to do, because he knew she would stop him. I also believe my father would have waited if physician-assisted suicide had been available. If patients have access to drugs they can take when they choose, they will not feel they must commit suicide early, while they are still able to do it on their own. They would probably live longer and certainly more peacefully, and they might not even use the drugs.

Long before my father's death, I believed that physician-assisted 20 suicide ought to be permissible under some circumstances, but his death strengthened my conviction that it is simply a part of good medical care — something to be done reluctantly and sadly, as a last resort, but done nonetheless. There should be safeguards to ensure that the decision is well considered and consistent, but they should not be so daunting or violative of privacy that they become

---

[21]J. Lynn and J. F. Childress, "Must Patients Always Be Given Food and Water?" *Hastings Center Report* 13(5) (1983): pp. 17–21.

[22]S. B. Nuland, *How We Die* (New York: Knopf, 1994), p. 152.

obstacles instead of protections. In particular, they should be directed not toward reviewing the reasons for an autonomous decision, but only toward ensuring that the decision is indeed autonomous. If the Supreme Court upholds the decisions of the appeals courts, assisted suicide will not be forced on either patients or doctors, but it will be a choice for those patients who need it and those doctors willing to help. If, on the other hand, the Supreme Court overturns the lower courts' decisions, the issue will continue to be grappled with state by state, through the political process. But sooner or later, given the need and the widespread public support, physician-assisted suicide will be demanded of a compassionate profession.

THINKING AND WRITING ABOUT EUTHANASIA

Questions for Discussion and Writing

1. What is Hook's principal reason for regretting that his request to discontinue the life support was denied? What qualities in the author are reflected in this article? Does the fact that the article is written by the patient himself make the argument more or less powerful? Can Hook's argument for voluntary euthanasia be used to answer Doyle?

2. Does Rachels prove that there is no moral difference between active and passive euthanasia? Is his attempt to meet the arguments of the opposition a convincing tactic? Which of his arguments do you find most persuasive? Why?

3. Kevorkian suggests two reasons for the objections of physicians to euthanasia. Would these reasons explain the objections of Doyle, a nurse? Which parts of Kevorkian's speech, if any, would opponents of euthanasia find persuasive?

4. What opinion of Kevorkian does Goodman express? Can you tell why she feels as she does? Does she indicate in any way what choice she would make about doctor-assisted suicide?

5. Define the "quality of life," as Doyle sees it. According to the author, how does the Constitution of the United States prevent the legalization of euthanasia? What consequences does the author foresee if euthanasia is permitted by law, as abortion is? Do you think her predictions are soundly based?

6. Explain Caplan's reference to "sliding down the slope." Why would physician-assisted suicide be more dangerous in America than in the Netherlands?

7. Does Angell answer all the questions raised by opponents of physician-assisted suicide? On what issues would she and Hook agree?

8. Readers have been familiar with Dracula for over one hundred years, but the cartoon on page 509 might not have been so clearly understood a generation ago. What circumstances have changed?

"This is a surprise—he doesn't want any extraordinary measures taken to resuscitate him."

Drawing by Ed Fisher; © *1992 The New Yorker Magazine.*

Topics for Research

The case of Dr. Jack Kevorkian, the Michigan "suicide doctor"

The hospice solution

The Hemlock Society

Newborns with severe congenital defects: Who should decide?

Noteworthy cases involving the right to die

TAKING THE DEBATE ONLINE

- **Internet Resources: Social Ethical Issues <www.spjc.cc.fl.us/instcomp/ phi1600/resource/res03.html>**   This site links with a number of pro and con euthanasia sites.

- **Respect Life <www.deaconscorner.com/>** A Christian-affiliated site that condemns euthanasia as devaluing of life, God's gift to us.

- **Euthanasia World Directory <www.finalexit.org/>**   This is a huge site filled with resources on euthanasia and right-to-die issues.

- **Information for Research on Euthanasia, Physician-Assisted Suicide, Living Wills, Mercy Killing <www.euthanasia.com>** An enormous anti-euthanasia site addressing legal, medical, and religious issues, among others.

- **Washington Post Top News <www.newsweek.com/nw-srv/topnews/ daily/60min1126.htm>**   *Washington Post* staff writers discuss the *60 Minutes* broadcast.

CHAPTER FIFTEEN

Freedom of Speech

The First Amendment to the Constitution of the United States reads, "Congress shall make no laws respecting an establishment of religion, or prohibiting the free expression thereof; or abridging the freedom of speech, or of the press; or the right of the people peaceably to assemble, and to petition the Government for a redress of grievances." (The first ten amendments were ratified on December 15, 1791, and form what is known as the Bill of Rights.) The arguments in this section will consider primarily the issue of "abridging the freedom of speech, or of the press."

The limits of free speech in the United States are constantly being adjusted as social values change and new cases testing those limits emerge. Several prominent areas of controversy are emphasized in the following selection of essays.

One of the most hotly debated issues has been played out on college campuses. Following federal law, a number of colleges and universities have formulated codes of conduct which define the "correct" ways of naming certain persons, groups, or activities in order to avoid offense to those who have historically been most vulnerable to "hate" speech — African Americans, Jews, women, and gays and lesbians. These policies have frequently provoked opposition from members of the college community on both sides of the political spectrum. Their disagreement is based on a principle enunciated in 1929 by Justice Oliver Wendell Holmes: "the principle of free thought — not free thought for those who agree with us but freedom for the thought that we hate." A few students who have been harshly punished for using "racist, sexist, and homophobic" speech have taken their cases to court. In several cases the courts decided that the policies enforcing strict speech codes were in violation of the First Amendment. College and university officials are now drafting new codes that would define the prohibited language and conduct in narrower and more specific terms.

Probably more controversial and vastly more difficult to control is speech in cyberspace. Congress and the states have begun to enact legislation that would prohibit dissemination of material regarded as offensive. But defenders of free speech argue that cyberspace communication should be private, like posted mail and conversation.

Freedom of speech is also a central issue in arguments over the lyrics of rap songs, which have been accused of advocating violence against police officers and women. Parents have raised concerns about the effects of such lyrics on young listeners and proposed rating labels for some albums. The language in one rap song in the early 1990s, calling for murder of police officers, led to appeals for censorship and boycotts of the record company.

Even nonverbal art forms whose creators express views that offend large groups of people are not immune to issues of free speech. Controversial movies, photography, painting, and sculpture, as well as religious displays on public land and even nude dancing, have all been defended as forms of speech protected by the Constitution.

On Racist Speech

CHARLES R. LAWRENCE III

I have spent the better part of my life as a dissenter. As a high school student, I was threatened with suspension for my refusal to participate in a civil defense drill, and I have been a conspicuous consumer of my First Amendment liberties ever since. There are very strong reasons for protecting even racist speech. Perhaps the most important of these is that such protection reinforces our society's commitment to tolerance as a value, and that by protecting bad speech from government regulation, we will be forced to combat it as a community.

But I also have a deeply felt apprehension about the resurgence of racial violence and the corresponding rise in the incidence of verbal and symbolic assault and harassment to which blacks and other traditionally subjugated and excluded groups are subjected. I am troubled by the way the debate has been framed in response to the

Charles R. Lawrence III is a professor of law at Georgetown University. His article appeared in the October 25, 1989, *Chronicle of Higher Education,* when Lawrence was teaching law at Stanford University. It is adapted from a speech given at a conference of the American Civil Liberties Union.

recent surge of racist incidents on college and university campuses and in response to some universities' attempts to regulate harassing speech. The problem has been framed as one in which the liberty of free speech is in conflict with the elimination of racism. I believe this has placed the bigot on the moral high ground and fanned the rising flames of racism.

Above all, I am troubled that we have not listened to the real victims, that we have shown so little understanding of their injury, and that we have abandoned those whose race, gender, or sexual preference continues to make them second-class citizens. It seems to me a very sad irony that the first instinct of civil libertarians has been to challenge even the smallest, most narrowly framed efforts by universities to provide black and other minority students with the protection the Constitution guarantees them.

The landmark case of *Brown v. Board of Education* is not a case that we normally think of as a case about speech. But *Brown* can be broadly read as articulating the principle of equal citizenship. *Brown* held that segregated schools were inherently unequal because of the *message* that segregation conveyed — that black children were an untouchable caste, unfit to go to school with white children. If we understand the necessity of eliminating the system of signs and symbols that signal the inferiority of blacks, then we should hesitate before proclaiming that all racist speech that stops short of physical violence must be defended.

University officials who have formulated policies to respond to 5 incidents of racial harassment have been characterized in the press as "thought police," but such policies generally do nothing more than impose sanctions against intentional face-to-face insults. When racist speech takes the form of face-to-face insults, catcalls, or other assaultive speech aimed at an individual or small group of persons, it falls directly within the "fighting words" exception to First Amendment protection. The Supreme Court has held that words which "by their very utterance inflict injury or tend to incite an immediate breach of the peace" are not protected by the First Amendment.

If the purpose of the First Amendment is to foster the greatest amount of speech, racial insults disserve that purpose. Assaultive racist speech functions as a preemptive strike. The invective is experienced as a blow, not as a proffered idea, and once the blow is struck, it is unlikely that a dialogue will follow. Racial insults are particularly undeserving of First Amendment protection because the perpetrator's intention is not to discover truth or initiate dialogue but to injure the victim. In most situations, members of minority groups realize that they are likely to lose if they respond to epithets by fighting and are forced to remain silent and submissive.

Courts have held that offensive speech may not be regulated in public forums such as streets where the listener may avoid the speech by moving on, but the regulation of otherwise protected speech has been permitted when the speech invades the privacy of the unwilling listener's home or when the unwilling listener cannot avoid the speech. Racist posters, fliers, and graffiti in dormitories, bathrooms, and other common living spaces would seem to clearly fall within the reasoning of these cases. Minority students should not be required to remain in their rooms in order to avoid racial assault. Minimally, they should find a safe haven in their dorms and in all other common rooms that are a part of their daily routine.

I would also argue that the university's responsibility for ensuring that these students receive an equal educational opportunity provides a compelling justification for regulations that ensure them safe passage in all common areas. A minority student should not have to risk becoming the target of racially assaulting speech every time he or she chooses to walk across campus. Regulating vilifying speech that cannot be anticipated or avoided would not preclude announced speeches and rallies — situations that would give minority-group members and their allies the chance to organize counter-demonstrations or avoid the speech altogether.

The most commonly advanced argument against the regulation of racist speech proceeds something like this: we recognize that minority groups suffer pain and injury as the result of racist speech, but we must allow this hate mongering for the benefit of society as a whole. Freedom of speech is the lifeblood of our democratic system. It is especially important for minorities because often it is their only vehicle for rallying support for the redress of their grievances. It will be impossible to formulate a prohibition so precise that it will prevent the racist speech you want to suppress without catching in the same net all kinds of speech that it would be unconscionable for a democratic society to suppress.

Whenever we make such arguments, we are striking a balance 10 on the one hand between our concern for the continued free flow of ideas and the democratic process dependent on that flow, and, on the other, our desire to further the cause of equality. There can be no meaningful discussion of how we should reconcile our commitment to equality and our commitment to free speech until it is acknowledged that there is real harm inflicted by racist speech and that this harm is far from trivial.

To engage in a debate about the First Amendment and racist speech without a full understanding of the nature and extent of that harm is to risk making the First Amendment an instrument of domination rather than a vehicle of liberation. We have not all known the experience of victimization by racist, misogynist, and homophobic speech, nor do we equally share the burden of the societal harm it inflicts. We are often quick to say that we have heard the cry of the victims when we have not.

The *Brown* case is again instructive because it speaks directly to the psychic injury inflicted by racist speech by noting that the symbolic message of segregation affected "the hearts and minds" of Negro children "in a way unlikely ever to be undone." Racial epithets and harassment often cause deep emotional scarring and feelings of anxiety and fear that pervade every aspect of a victim's life.

Brown also recognized that black children did not have an equal opportunity to learn and participate in the school community if they bore the additional burden of being subjected to the humiliation and psychic assault contained in the message of segregation. University students bear an analogous burden when they are forced to live and work in an environment where at any moment they may be subjected to denigrating verbal harassment and assault. The same injury was addressed by the Supreme Court when it held that sexual harassment that creates a hostile or abusive work environment violates the ban on sex discrimination in employment of Title VII of the Civil Rights Act of 1964.

Carefully drafted university regulations would bar the use of words as assault weapons and leave unregulated even the most heinous of ideas when those ideas are presented at times and places and in manners that provide an opportunity for reasoned rebuttal or escape from immediate injury. The history of the development of the right to free speech has been one of carefully evaluating the importance of free expression and its effects on other important societal interests. We have drawn the line between protected and unprotected speech before without dire results. (Courts have, for example, exempted from the protection of the First Amendment obscene speech and speech that disseminates official secrets, that defames or libels another person, or that is used to form a conspiracy or monopoly.)

Blacks and other people of color are skeptical about the argument that even the most injurious speech must remain unregulated because, in an unregulated marketplace of ideas, the best ones will rise to the top and gain acceptance. Our experience tells us quite the opposite. We have seen too many demagogues elected by appealing to America's racism. We have seen too many good liberal politicians shy away from the issues that might brand them as being too closely allied with us.

Whenever we decide that racist speech must be tolerated because of the importance of maintaining societal tolerance for all unpopular speech, we are asking blacks and other subordinated groups to bear the burden for the good of all. We must be careful that the ease with which we strike the balance against the regulation of racist speech is in no way influenced by the fact that the cost will be borne by others. We must be certain that those who will pay that price are fairly represented in our deliberations and that they are heard.

At the core of the argument that we should resist all government regulation of speech is the ideal that the best cure for bad speech is good, that ideas that affirm equality and the worth of all individuals will ultimately prevail. This is an empty ideal unless those of us who would fight racism are vigilant and unequivocal in that fight. We must look for ways to offer assistance and support to students whose speech and political participation are chilled in a climate of racial harassment.

Civil rights lawyers might consider suing on behalf of blacks whose right to an equal education is denied by a university's failure to ensure a nondiscriminatory educational climate or conditions of employment. We must embark upon the development of a First Amendment jurisprudence grounded in the reality of our history and our contemporary experience. We must think hard about how best to launch legal attacks against the most indefensible forms of hate speech. Good lawyers can create exceptions and narrow interpretations that limit the harm of hate speech without opening the floodgates of censorship.

Everyone concerned with these issues must find ways to engage actively in actions that resist and counter the racist ideas that we would have the First Amendment protect. If we fail in this, the victims of hate speech must rightly assume that we are on the oppressors' side.

Free Speech on the Campus
NAT HENTOFF

A flier distributed at the University of Michigan some months ago proclaimed that blacks "don't belong in classrooms, they belong hanging from trees."

At other campuses around the country, manifestations of racism are becoming commonplace. At Yale, a swastika and the words WHITE POWER! were painted on the building housing the University's Afro-American Cultural Center. At Temple University, a White Students Union has been formed with some 130 members.

Swastikas are not directed only at black students. The Nazi symbol has been spray-painted on the Jewish Student Union at Memphis State University. And on a number of campuses, women have been singled out as targets of wounding and sometimes frightening

Nat Hentoff is the author of *The First Freedom* (1988) and a staff writer for the *Village Voice*. This article appeared in the May 1989 issue of *The Progressive*.

speech. At the law school of the State University of New York at Buffalo, several women students have received anonymous letters characterized by one professor as venomously sexist.

These and many more such signs of the resurgence of bigotry and know-nothingism throughout the society — as well as on campus — have to do solely with speech, including symbolic speech. There have also been physical assaults on black students and on black, white, and Asian women students, but the way to deal with physical attacks is clear: Call the police and file a criminal complaint. What is to be done, however, about speech alone — however disgusting, inflammatory, and rawly divisive that speech may be?

At more and more colleges, administrators — with the enthusi- 5 astic support of black students, women students, and liberal students — have been answering that question by preventing or punishing speech. In public universities, this is a clear violation of the First Amendment. In private colleges and universities, suppression of speech mocks the secular religion of academic freedom and free inquiry.

The Student Press Law Center in Washington, D.C. — a vital source of legal support for student editors around the country — reports, for example, that at the University of Kansas, the student host and producer of a radio news program was forbidden by school officials from interviewing a leader of the Ku Klux Klan. So much for free inquiry on that campus.

In Madison, Wisconsin, the *Capital Times* ran a story in January about Chancellor Sheila Kaplan of the University of Wisconsin branch at Parkside, who ordered her campus to be scoured of "some anonymously placed white-supremacist hate literature." Sounding like the legendary Mayor Frank ("I am the law") Hague of Jersey City, who booted "bad speech" out of town, Chancellor Kaplan said, "This institution is not a lamppost standing on the street corner. It doesn't belong to everyone."

Who decides what speech can be heard or read by everyone? Why, the chancellor, of course. That's what George III used to say, too.

University of Wisconsin political science professor Carol Tebben thinks otherwise. She believes university administrators "are getting confused when they are acting as censors and trying to protect students from bad ideas. I don't think students need to be protected from bad ideas. I think they can determine for themselves what ideas are bad."

After all, if students are to be "protected" from bad ideas, how are 10 they going to learn to identify and cope with them? Sending such ideas underground simply makes them stronger and more dangerous.

Professor Tebben's conviction that free speech means just that has become a decidedly minority view on many campuses. At the

University of Buffalo Law School, the faculty unanimously adopted a "Statement Regarding Intellectual Freedom, Tolerance, and Political Harassment." Its title implies support of intellectual freedom, but the statement warned students that once they enter "this legal community," their right to free speech must become tempered "by the responsibility to promote equality and justice."

Accordingly, swift condemnation will befall anyone who engages in "remarks directed at another's race, sex, religion, national origin, age, or sex preference." Also forbidden are "other remarks based on prejudice and group stereotype."

This ukase is so broad that enforcement has to be alarmingly subjective. Yet the University of Buffalo Law School provides no due-process procedures for a student booked for making any of these prohibited remarks. Conceivably, a student caught playing a Lenny Bruce, Richard Pryor, or Sam Kinison album in his room could be tried for aggravated insensitivity by association.

When I looked into this wholesale cleansing of bad speech at Buffalo, I found it had encountered scant opposition. One protester was David Gerald Jay, a graduate of the law school and a cooperating attorney for the New York Civil Liberties Union. Said the appalled graduate: "Content-based prohibitions constitute prior restraint and should not be tolerated."

You'd think that the law professors and administration at this public university might have known that. But hardly any professors dissented, and among the students only members of the conservative Federalist Society spoke up for free speech. The fifty-strong chapter of the National Lawyers Guild was on the other side. After all, it was more important to go on record as vigorously opposing racism and sexism than to expose oneself to charges of insensitivity to these malignancies.

The pressures to have the "right" attitude — as proved by having the "right" language in and out of class — can be stifling. A student who opposes affirmative action, for instance, can be branded a racist.

At the University of California at Los Angeles, the student newspaper ran an editorial cartoon satirizing affirmative action. (A student stops a rooster on campus and asks how the rooster got into UCLA. "Affirmative action," is the answer.) After outraged complaints from various minority groups, the editor was suspended for violating a publications policy against running "articles that perpetuate derogatory or cultural stereotypes." The art director was also suspended.

When the opinion editor of the student newspaper at California State University at Northridge wrote an article asserting that the sanctions against the editor and art director at UCLA amounted to censorship, he was suspended too.

At New York University Law School, a student was so disturbed by the pall of orthodoxy at that prestigious institution that he wrote to the school newspaper even though, as he said, he expected his letter to make him a pariah among his fellow students.

Barry Endick described the atmosphere at NYU created by "a 20 host of watchdog committees and a generally hostile classroom reception regarding any student comment right of center." This "can be arguably viewed as symptomatic of a prevailing spirit of academic and social intolerance of . . . any idea which is not 'politically correct.'"

He went on to say something that might well be posted on campus bulletin boards around the country, though it would probably be torn down at many of them:

> We ought to examine why students, so anxious to wield the Fourteenth Amendment, give short shrift to the First. Yes, Virginia, there are racist assholes. And you know what, the Constitution protects them, too.

Not when they engage in violence or vandalism. But when they speak or write, racist assholes fall right into this Oliver Wendell Holmes definition — highly unpopular among bigots, liberals, radicals, feminists, sexists, and college administrators:

> If there is any principle of the Constitution that more imperatively calls for attachment than any other, it is the principle of free thought — not free only for those who agree with us, but freedom for the thought we hate.

The language sounds like a pietistic Sunday sermon, but if it ever falls wholly into disuse, neither this publication nor any other journal of opinion — Right or Left — will survive.

Sometimes, college presidents and administrators sound as if they fully understand what Holmes was saying. Last year, for example, when the *Daily Pennsylvanian* — speaking for many at the University of Pennsylvania — urged that a speaking invitation to Louis Farrakhan be withdrawn, University President Sheldon Hackney disagreed.

"Open expression," said Hackney, "is the fundamental principle 25 of a university." Yet consider what the same Sheldon Hackney did to the free-speech rights of a teacher at his own university. If any story distills the essence of the current decline of free speech on college campuses, it is the Ballad of Murray Dolfman.

For twenty-two years, Dolfman, a practicing lawyer in Philadelphia, had been a part-time lecturer in the Legal Studies Department of the University of Pennsylvania's Wharton School. For twenty-two years, no complaint had ever been made against him; indeed, his student course evaluations had been outstanding. Each year students competed to get into his class.

On a November afternoon in 1984, Dolfman was lecturing about personal-service contracts. His style somewhat resembles that of Professor Charles Kingsfield in *The Paper Chase.* Dolfman insists that students he calls on be prepared — or suffer the consequences. He treats all students this way — regardless of race, creed, or sex.

This day, Dolfman was pointing out that no one can be forced to work against his or her will — even if a contract has been signed. A court may prevent the register from working for someone else so long as the contract is in effect but, Dolfman said, there can "be nothing that smacks of involuntary servitude."

Where does this concept come from? Dolfman looked around the room. Finally, a cautious hand was raised: "The Constitution?"

"Where in the Constitution?" No hands. "The Thirteenth Amend- 30 ment," said the teacher. So, what does *it* say? The students were looking everywhere but at Dolfman.

"We will lose our liberties," Dolfman often told his classes, "if we don't know what they are."

On this occasion, he told them that he and other Jews, as ex-slaves, spoke at Passover of the time when they were slaves under the Pharaohs so that they would remember every year what it was like not to be free.

"We have ex-slaves here," Dolfman continued, "who should know about the Thirteenth Amendment." He asked black students in the class if they could tell him what was in that amendment.

"I wanted them to really think about it," Dolfman told me recently, "and know its history. You're better equipped to fight racism if you know all about those post–Civil War amendments and civil-rights laws."

The Thirteenth Amendment provides that "neither slavery nor 35 involuntary servitude . . . shall exist within the United States."

The black students in his class did not know what was in that amendment, and Dolfman had them read it aloud. Later, they complained to university officials that they had been hurt and humiliated by having been referred to as ex-slaves. Moreover, they said, they had no reason to be grateful for a constitutional amendment which gave them rights which should never have been denied them — and gave them precious little else. They had not made these points in class, although Dolfman — unlike Professor Kingsfield — encourages rebuttal.

Informed of the complaint, Dolfman told the black students he had intended no offense, and he apologized if they had been offended.

That would not do — either for the black students or for the administration. Furthermore, there were mounting black-Jewish tensions on campus, and someone had to be sacrificed. Who better than a part-time Jewish teacher with no contract and no union? He was sentenced by — George Orwell would have loved this — the Committee on Academic Freedom and Responsibility.

On his way to the stocks, Dolfman told President Sheldon Hackney that if a part-time instructor "can be punished on this kind of charge, a tenured professor can eventually be booted out, then a dean, and then a president."

Hackney was unmoved. Dolfman was banished from the campus   40 for what came to be a year. But first he was forced to make a public apology to the entire university and then he was compelled to attend a "sensitivity and racial awareness" session. Sort of like a Vietnamese reeducation camp.

A few conservative professors objected to the stigmatization of Murray Dolfman. I know of no student dissent. Indeed, those students most concerned with making the campus more "sensitive" to diversity exulted in Dolfman's humiliation. So did most liberals on the faculty.

If my children were still of college age and wanted to attend the University of Pennsylvania, I would tell them this story. But where else could I encourage them to go?

Ice-T: The Issue Is Creative Freedom

BARBARA EHRENREICH

Ice-T's song "Cop Killer" is as bad as they come. This is black anger — raw, rude, and cruel — and one reason the song's so shocking is that in postliberal America, black anger is virtually taboo. You won't find it on TV, not on the *McLaughlin Group* or *Crossfire,* and certainly not in the placid features of Arsenio Hall or Bernard Shaw. It's been beaten back into the outlaw subcultures of rap and rock, where, precisely because it is taboo, it sells. And the nastier it is, the faster it moves off the shelves. As Ice-T asks in another song on the same album, "Goddamn what a brotha gotta do / To get a message through / To the red, white, and blue?"

But there's a gross overreaction going on, building to a veritable paroxysm of white denial. A national boycott has been called, not just of the song or Ice-T, but of all Time Warner products. The president himself has denounced Time Warner as "wrong" and Ice-T as "sick."

Barbara Ehrenreich, honorary chair of Democratic Socialists of America, is the author of numerous books, including *Blood Rites: Origins and History of the Passions of War* (1997). This article is from the July 20, 1992, issue of *Time.*

Ollie North's Freedom Alliance has started a petition drive aimed at bringing Time Warner executives to trial for "sedition and anarchy." Much of this is posturing and requires no more courage than it takes to stand up in a VFW hall and condemn communism or crack. Yes, "Cop Killer" is irresponsible and vile. But Ice-T is as right about some things as he is righteous about the rest. And ultimately, he's not even dangerous — least of all to the white power structure his songs condemn.

The "danger" implicit in all the uproar is of empty-headed, suggestible black kids, crouching by their boom boxes, waiting for the word. But what Ice-T's fans know and his detractors obviously don't is that "Cop Killer" is just one more entry in pop music's long history of macho hyperbole and violent boast. Flip to the classic-rock station, and you might catch the Rolling Stones announcing "the time is right for violent revoloo-shun!" from their 1968 hit "Street Fighting Man." And where were the defenders of our law-enforcement officers when a white British group, the Clash, taunted its fans with the lyrics: "When they kick open your front door / How you gonna come / With your hands on your head / Or on the trigger of your gun?"

"Die, Die, Die Pig" is strong speech, but the Constitution protects 5 strong speech, and it's doing so this year more aggressively than ever. The Supreme Court has just downgraded cross burnings to the level of bonfires and ruled that it's no crime to throw around verbal grenades like "nigger" and "kike." Where are the defenders of decorum and social stability when prime-time demagogues like Howard Stern deride African Americans as "spear chuckers"?

More to the point, young African Americans are not so naive and suggestible that they have to depend on a compact disc for their sociology lessons. To paraphrase another song from another era, you don't need a rap song to tell which way the wind is blowing. Black youths know that the police are likely to see them through a filter of stereotypes as miscreants and potential "cop killers." They are aware that a black youth is seven times as likely to be charged with a felony as a white youth who has committed the same offense, and is much more likely to be imprisoned.

They know, too, that in a shameful number of cases, it is the police themselves who indulge in "anarchy" and violence. The U.S. Justice Department has received 47,000 complaints of police brutality in the past six years, and Amnesty International has just issued a report on police brutality in Los Angeles, documenting forty cases of "torture or cruel, inhuman, or degrading treatment."

Menacing as it sounds, the fantasy in "Cop Killer" is the fantasy of the powerless and beaten down — the black man who's been hassled once too often ("A pig stopped me for nothin'!"), spread-eagled against a police car, pushed around. It's not a "responsible" fantasy (fantasies seldom are). It's not even a very creative one. In fact, the sad thing about "Cop Killer" is that it falls for the cheapest, most conventional image of rebellion that our culture offers: the lone gunman spraying fire from his AK-47. This is not "sedition"; it's the familiar, all-American, Hollywood-style pornography of violence.

Which is why Ice-T is right to say he's no more dangerous than George Bush's pal Arnold Schwarzenegger, who wasted an army of cops in *Terminator 2.* Images of extraordinary cruelty and violence are marketed every day, many of far less artistic merit than "Cop Killer." This is our free market of ideas and images, and it shouldn't be any less free for a black man than for other purveyors of "irresponsible" sentiments, from David Duke to Andrew Dice Clay.[1]

Just, please, don't dignify Ice-T's contribution with the word 10 *sedition.* The past masters of sedition — men like George Washington, Toussaint L'Ouverture, Fidel Castro, or Mao Zedong, all of whom led and won armed insurrections — would be unimpressed by "Cop Killer" and probably saddened. They would shake their heads and mutter words like "infantile" and "adventurism." They might point out that the cops are hardly a noble target, being, for the most part, honest working stiffs who've got stuck with the job of patrolling ghettos ravaged by economic decline and official neglect.

There is a difference, the true seditionist would argue, between a revolution and a gesture of macho defiance. Gestures are cheap. They feel good, they blow off some rage. But revolutions, violent or otherwise, are made by people who have learned how to count very slowly to ten.

---

[1]David Duke, an advocate of white supremacy, was defeated in his bid for governor of Louisiana in 1991. Andrew Dice Clay is a stand-up comedian known for his use of offensive language against women and minorities.

Freedom of Speech and Holocaust Revisionism

DAVID M. OSHINSKY AND MICHAEL CURTIS

College newspapers are facing a dilemma that pits free speech against historical deception. A group calling itself the Committee for Open Debate on the Holocaust has sent an advertisement to at least a dozen leading campus dailies. The ad contends that the Holocaust never occurred.

Newspapers at Harvard, Yale, Brown, the University of Pennsylvania, and the University of Southern California have refused to run it. Those at Northwestern, Cornell, Duke, and the University of Michigan have published it amid protests from students, faculty, and members of their own editorial boards. At Rutgers, the ad was printed free of charge on December 3 as a "guest commentary," surrounded by rebuttals.

The ad attempts to prey on students' ignorance about the Holocaust. It insists, without evidence, that there were no mass killings of Jews and no "execution gas chambers in any camp in Europe that was under German control." It claims the so-called execution chambers were "fumigation chambers," used "to delouse clothing . . . and prevent disease." It is "from this life-*saving* procedure," the ad says, "that the myth of extermination gas chambers emerged."

The slickly done ad does not use the violent language common to the literature of racist and nativist groups. It wraps itself in concepts of free speech and open inquiry, arguing that all points of view deserve to be heard. Timed to exploit the controversy about political correctness, the ad says, "elitist" and "Zionist" groups have stifled debate on the Holocaust in order "to drum up world sympathy" for Jewish causes and Israel.

The ad was written by Bradley R. Smith, a political soulmate of 5 the California-based Institute for Historical Review, the principal promoter of "Holocaust revisionism." Its founder, Willis A. Carto, was described by the Anti-Defamation League last year as "perhaps the leading anti-Semite in the United States." He has been associated with the Populist Party, whose presidential candidate in 1988 was David Duke; the Liberty Lobby, a hate group; and the Noontide Press, which distributes such tracts as "The Testing of Negro Intelligence" and "The International Jew."

David M. Oshinsky is a professor of history at Rutgers University. Michael Curtis, also at Rutgers, is a professor of political science. Their article was published in the *New York Times* on December 11, 1991.

In 1980, Mr. Carto's institute offered $50,000 to anyone who could "prove" that Jews were exterminated at Auschwitz. Mel Mermelstein, a Holocaust survivor, submitted sworn declarations from people who had been in the camp. When the institute refused to pay up, he took its officers to court in Los Angeles. That Jews were gassed to death at Auschwitz "is not reasonably subject to dispute," the presiding judge declared. "It is simply a fact." In 1985, Mr. Mermelstein was awarded the $50,000, plus $40,000 for pain and suffering.

Bradley Smith's committee apparently believes that its theories will be tolerated by some on First Amendment grounds and accepted by others out of ignorance or worse. The Duke student newspaper naively repeated the committee's description of itself as a group of revisionist scholars. Duke's history department was appalled and responded with a statement that distinguished between those who revise history and those who deny it.

Most college editors seem aware of the committee's intentions. Their decision to print its ad is based on principle: an aversion to censorship or a belief that hate material should be aired and publicly refuted. Surely their right to publish such ads should not be questioned. They alone must decide what good purpose, if any, is served by printing ads that are intentionally hurtful and obviously false.

The ads should be rejected. If one group advertises that the Holocaust never happened, another can buy space to insist that American blacks were never enslaved. The stakes are high because college newspapers may soon be flooded with ads that present discredited assertions as if they were part of normal historical debate. If the Holocaust is not a fact, then nothing is a fact, and truth itself will be diminished.

Free Speech on the Internet: Opinion on the Constitutionality of the Communications Decency Act

STEWART DALZELL

The Internet is a far more speech-enhancing medium than print, the village green, or the mails. Because it would necessarily affect the Internet itself, the CDA would necessarily reduce the speech available for adults on the medium. This is a constitutionally intolerable result.

Some of the dialogue on the Internet surely tests the limits of conventional discourse. Speech on the Internet can be unfiltered, unpolished, and unconventional, even emotionally charged, sexually explicit, and vulgar — in a word, "indecent" in many communities. But we should expect such speech to occur in a medium in which citizens from all walks of life have a voice. We should also protect the autonomy that such a medium confers to ordinary people as well as media magnates.

Moreover, the CDA will almost certainly fail to accomplish the government's interest in shielding children from pornography on the Internet. Nearly half of Internet communications originate outside the United States, and some percentage of that figure represents pornography. Pornography from, say, Amsterdam will be no less appealing to a child on the Internet than pornography from New York City, and residents of Amsterdam have little incentive to comply with the CDA.

My analysis does not deprive the government of all means of protecting children from the dangers of Internet communication. The government can continue to protect children from pornography on the Internet through vigorous enforcement of existing laws criminalizing obscenity. . . . As we learned at the hearing, there is also a compelling need for public education about the benefits and dangers of this new medium, and the government can fill that role as well. In my view, our action today should only mean that the government's permissible supervision of Internet content stops at the traditional line of unprotected speech.

Parents, too, have options available to them. As we learned at 5 the hearing, parents can install blocking software on their home

---

Stewart Dalzell is a judge for the United States Court of Appeals for the Third Circuit. Reprinted here are excerpts from his opinion in striking down major parts of the Communications Decency Act (CDA). The excerpts were published in the *New York Times* on June 13, 1996.

computers or they can subscribe to commercial online services that provide parental controls. It is quite clear that powerful market forces are at work to expand parental options to deal with these legitimate concerns. More fundamentally, parents can supervise their children's use of the Internet or deny their children the opportunity to participate in the medium until they reach an appropriate age. . . .

Cutting through the acronyms and argot that littered the hearing testimony, the Internet may fairly be regarded as a never-ending worldwide conversation. The government may not, through the CDA, interrupt that conversation. As the most participatory form of mass speech yet developed, the Internet deserves the highest protection from governmental intrusion.

True it is that many find some of the speech on the Internet to be offensive, and amid the din of cyberspace many hear discordant voices that they regard as indecent. The absence of governmental regulation of Internet content has unquestionably produced a kind of chaos, but as one of the plaintiffs' experts put it with such resonance at the hearing: "What achieved success was the very chaos that the Internet is. The strength of the Internet is that chaos." Just as the strength of the Internet is chaos, so the strength of our liberty depends upon the chaos and cacophony of the unfettered speech the First Amendment protects.

For these reasons, I without hesitation hold that the CDA is unconstitutional on its face.

Speech in America:
Free, but Not Cheap
JONATHAN YARDLEY

The trouble with free speech is that it insists on living up to its name. This is an unpleasant reality that Americans prefer to ignore, so when the price of free speech suddenly is exacted, they invariably are surprised and resentful. Last week they took it on the chin from three different directions, each blow calculated to infuriate large numbers of people.

The most significant of the three was the ruling by a special federal court that speech must be as free on the Internet as anywhere else and that governmental attempts to limit it are "profoundly

Jonathan Yardley is a Pulitzer Prize–winning columnist for the *Washington Post Book World,* where this article appeared on June 17, 1996. His latest book is *Monday Morning Quarterback* (1998).

repugnant." This means that the various pornographers who have found in the Net a splendid vehicle for their wares are free to peddle them as they wish, including to children who have figured out how to crack the codes of cyberspace.

Then there was the decision by Joseph E. Seagram & Sons to place advertisements for Crown Royal Canadian Whiskey on a television channel in Texas. No federal law prohibits ads for hard liquor on TV or radio, but for half a century the country's distillers have eschewed such promotions as a sop to Prohibitionist sentiment — and in the hopes of avoiding federal legislation such as that banning tobacco ads from the airwaves.

Finally there was the capitulation of Marge Schott, the owner of the Cincinnati Reds, to her fellow members of Major League Baseball's inner circle. She will forfeit the management of her club's affairs for two and a half years as self-inflicted punishment for her unfortunate habit of blurting out insulting comments about ethnic, racial, and religious groups, as well as her enthusiasm for the administrative style of Adolf Hitler.

Chalk it up as two victories for free speech and one loss. The 5 smut peddlers can deal on the Internet and the booze peddlers can hawk their wares on television — at least for the moment — but poor Marge Schott has had her toy taken away from her because she can't keep her mouth shut. Given the past history of free-speech controversies, the one certainty about all three of these cases is that they haven't been closed yet.

The knottiest by far is the Internet. It may or may not be true, as the federal judges in Philadelphia declared, that the Net is "the most participatory marketplace of mass speech that this country — and indeed the world — has yet seen," but it certainly is true that it is as much a free public forum as any other. This means that anyone who goes online is free — to borrow a few words from the "Poetic License" on the wall in my office — "to write anything he jolly well pleases." Anything, Americans too often forget, means *anything.*

That is why the pornographers have seized upon the Net as yet another medium for profit, and that is why we have no choice save to let them do so. Thus the law of the land is placed in direct conflict with the best interests of the majority of its citizens, who would prefer to shield their children from premature and gratuitous exposure to material of potentially damaging import. The law aimed at controlling smut in cyberspace may be a bad one, and many of those who wrote it may have done so for cynical political motives, but its essential purpose is exemplary.

So the question becomes how to accomplish that purpose within the bounds of constitutional law. The solution is relatively simple, but this is not to say that many people will choose to adopt it. Various technical mechanisms already exist by which parents can control their children's access to all or part of the Internet; these may add a bit to the cost of having a computer, but surely concerned parents would be willing to pay a bit more for their children's well-being. Perhaps those same parents could even learn to declare certain parts of the Net off-limits to their kids, though it must ruefully be acknowledged that saying no to children has fallen far out of favor in this permissive age.

We can say no to porn and to hard liquor as well. It may be socially undesirable for booze to be promoted freely, but those who manufacture and sell it have every right to do so. Again, we have a case wherein the law and the public interest are at odds. The distilled spirits industry may have taken the politic course in keeping its ads off the airwaves, but in so doing it waived its constitutional rights. Seagram's motives in breaking away from the rest of the industry may be entirely greedy and have nothing at all to do with lofty legal principles, but the Constitution smiles on the greedy and the eleemosynary alike. We can't have both free speech and unfree advertising; we have to choose, and thus far we've chosen the former.

If we don't want liquor manufacturers promoting their goods on   10
television, the best way to get that message across is to stop buying those goods. By the same token, if we take offense at the words uttered in public by the owner of a business, we can take our own business elsewhere. That seems to be what many of the good burghers of Cincinnati have done; attendance is down at Reds' games and disenchantment with the team's owner is up. In the natural course of the marketplace, sooner or later Marge Schott would be driven out of business as a consequence of her inability to control her tongue.

But Major League Baseball operates not by the marketplace but by its own higher law. The team Schott owns is not a self-contained entity but part of a larger one known since time immemorial as Organized Baseball. It has the right to impose conditions of membership, one of which apparently is the suspension of the First Amendment. No doubt it is a sign of progress that Organized Baseball, which stayed silent while Jackie Robinson was vilified by racist players and fans, now claims to abhor language of similar import; but at least in the case of Schott, this progress has been achieved at the expense of protections the rest of us take for granted.

There is, of course, an easy way around all these nasty and often irreconcilable issues. If we dislike free speech — or, more accurately, if we dislike free speech when it expresses unpleasant opinions — then the thing to do is to get rid of it. In the course of the republic's two-plus centuries, more than a few Americans have tried to do exactly that, in some instances with temporary success. So far we have managed to understand that free speech is well worth the costs it occasionally exacts, but as last week's events reminded us, this knowledge is always in peril.

"Cultural Vandals" Hide behind Free Speech

JEFF DURSTEWITZ

In his June 11 Politics & People column "Teen Violence Spawned by Guns and Cultural Rot," Al Hunt got it half right: Teen violence is spawned by cultural rot. But the gun issue is really a red herring. Guns, by themselves, do nothing at all. And the focus on "teen" violence — as opposed to the terrible intellectual, emotional, and spiritual harm we are doing all our children in this country — is far too specific.

As Bill Bennett says, we do indeed live in a society that seems dedicated to corrupting our children and stealing their innocence. Nine-year-olds and younger are watching *South Park,* even though its Brechtian sensibility is geared toward college students. A whole sub-genre of "action" movies link and equate mayhem (i.e., body count) with humor and camaraderie. Steven Spielberg said he wouldn't take his ten-year-old to see *Jurassic Park,* yet he knew many parents would. Music, computer games, the Internet — the evidence of moral and cultural degradation is almost inescapable. Under the guise of "free speech," merchandisers are aggressively doing violence to our kids. They, in turn, are doing violence to each other. If Socrates was executed in ancient Athens for "corrupting the youth," what punishment should we contemplate for today's cultural vandals?

It's about time we all acknowledged a basic fact: The First Amendment doesn't mean that anything goes, anytime. We have the right to set standards and limits where children — who are essentially defenseless — are concerned. The Constitution should not be a ready license to rob our kids of their precious childhood, not to mention submerging their minds and souls in an endless, demoralizing, and deepening flood dreck.

Jeff Durstewitz

THINKING AND WRITING ABOUT FREEDOM OF SPEECH

Questions for Discussion and Writing

1. How does Lawrence relate *Brown v. Board of Education* to issues of free speech? What principle does he invoke in defense of restrictive speech codes on campus?

Jeff Durstewitz's letter to the editor responds to "Teen Violence Spawned by Guns and Cultural Rot" by Albert R. Hunt (see page 650). It appeared in the *Wall Street Journal* on June 29, 1998.

2. Hentoff argues for exposure of students to bad ideas as well as good ones. (See p. 6 for a quotation from *Areopagitica,* in which John Milton makes the same point.) What bad ideas does Hentoff have in mind? Spell out the educational advantages of such exposure. What is Hentoff's main criticism of university officials? Do you think it is justified?

3. Can you think of circumstances in which creative freedom should bow to social responsibility? What evidence does Ehrenreich use to prove that "Cop Killer" is not dangerous? Is it convincing?

4. Oshinsky and Curtis raise the question of media responsibility to the truth. Does a belief in freedom of speech mean that newspapers have a right to publish "discredited assertions as if they were part of normal historical debate"? Why or why not? Are "discredited assertions" the same as Hentoff's "bad ideas"? Has the college newspaper on your campus ever been guilty of publishing nontruths?

5. Dalzell acknowledges the dangers to children from pornographic material on the Internet. What is his solution? What reasons does Dalzell give for thinking it is important to protect speech on the Internet?

6. What is the high price of free speech? Yardley says, "We can't have both free speech and unfree advertising." How would he resolve this dilemma? Why does he condemn the judgment against Marge Schott?

7. Do you think Durstewitz's complaints about cultural corruption is justified? Can you give other examples of "intellectual, emotional, and spiritual harm" to which children are exposed? How would Yardley respond to Durstewitz?

8. Summarize the cartoonist's wry claim about the First Amendment. Is the same point expressed in any of the essays in this chapter?

Topics for Research

Lyrics in rock music: How dangerous are they?

Codes of speech conduct at some colleges and universities: goals and effects

Religious displays on public land

Freedom of speech on the Internet

Prayer in public schools

Free speech issues in school newspapers

TAKING THE DEBATE ONLINE

- **Academic Freedom and Campus Speech Codes** <www.american-comm.org/~aca/law/academic.html> Maintained by the American Communication Association with over sixty links to freedom of speech issues as they relate to higher education.

- **Freedom of Speech and Privacy in the Information Age** <http://qsilver.queensu.ca/law/sopinka.htm> A faculty of law from Queen's University writes about the freedom of speech and privacy in the information age.

- **American Civil Liberties Union** <www.aclu.org/issues/freespeech/hmfs.html> The ACLU's site condemning censorship in cinema, literature, and life.

- **Massachusetts Music Industry Coalition** <http://www.ultranet.com/~crowleyn/mmic.html> This site condemns the censorship of musical expression.

- **Trinity College of Vermont: Jeff Haig** <www.trinityvt.edu/jhaig/censor.htm> Useful sources in the study of censorship past, present, and future, including groups that are in favor of censorship.

- **CNN Interactive** <www.gabrielmedia.org/news/cda/forlinks.html> This page links to fifteen sites supporting the Communications Decency Act.

CHAPTER SIXTEEN

Privacy in the Information Age

Although the word *privacy* is nowhere mentioned in the Constitution, the right to privacy has been inferred from the intent of several Amendments: the First, the Third, the Ninth, and the Fourteenth. Needless to say, the makers of that document could not have foreseen the worldwide dissemination of information, private as well as public, which the development of technology would make possible at the end of the twentieth century. Today the courts, wrestling with charges that the right to privacy is being violated, must try to strike a balance between the right to privacy and the right to know and to speak freely.

Electronic purveyors of information can make our financial records, our medical history, our buying habits, and other data available to those who are interested. Television talk shows encourage people to divulge intimate secrets to millions of viewers. Employers test their employees for drug use and demand information about personal habits and life choices. On computer Web sites strangers are invited to enter our homes and share our lives. Even in the open air we are being watched. In an effort to control crime, more than two thousand surveillance cameras have been mounted in the streets and parks of Manhattan to monitor public activity.

One disturbing result of this information explosion has been the exposure of children to adult knowledge. Neil Postman, author of *The Disappearance of Childhood,* says,

> With the new technologies, television being at the forefront, there are fewer and fewer secrets, medical secrets, sexual secrets, political secrets. Adults used to reveal secrets to you, the child, in stages, in

school, in books. When you knew all the secrets, you became an adult. But now all of that is available on the Internet or TV.[1]

But the capacity of machines to provide information would not be enough to make us vulnerable to public scrutiny. Changes in the social and moral climate of the last four decades have removed many of our defenses. "Letting it all hang out" strikes millions of people as an acceptable guide to behavior. It may be hard to believe that in the not-so-distant past extramarital pregnancy, homosexuality, even a diagnosis of cancer were deeply held secrets. Now we express ourselves far more freely in our language, both in everyday speech and in literature, in our clothing, and in our sexual relationships. Births have been televised; so has a death.

Some observers, however, think that today's absence of privacy is no more serious than that experienced by earlier generations who lived in small towns and villages where everybody's activities were a matter of common knowledge. In the city people can and often do remain anonymous. Even the decline of the extended family, in which personal behavior was closely watched and evaluated by an army of relatives, has contributed to a greater sense of privacy.

Nevertheless, the questions surrounding this issue will multiply as public and private places become increasingly interchangeable. If people value the convenience of having wide access to information, services, and entertainment, as well as the right to express themselves freely, are they justified in thinking that they will also be able to guard their privacy? Do they perhaps regard the loss of privacy as a price they are willing to pay for admission to the global village? If not, how can their privacy be protected?

---

[1]Anthony Ramirez, "Lolitas Don't Shock Anymore, but *Lolita* Still Does," *New York Times,* August 2, 1998, p. Wk 5.

Privacy Is the Problem, Not the Solution

JEFFREY OBSER

I wonder what Richard Nixon would have thought of the recently concluded [June 1997] Federal Trade Commission (FTC) hearings on privacy in the datasphere. After all, Nixon suffered the most humiliating privacy loss ever. Surely he could empathize with all the people who are upset that strangers can find dossiers about them on the World Wide Web or that their personal information has become an unregulated commodity floating through distant databases. He was as shocked and confused as we are that a convenient new communications technology — in his case, audiotape — would turn around and tattle on him. And, just like us, he reacted by demanding more privacy.

It mystifies us that the man thought he could have it both ways — record everything and get away with everything. But curiously, it mystifies nobody that we all expect to talk freely and shop with convenience through electronic networks without establishing some sort of reputation for ourselves. In conditions of the utmost anonymity, living in "communities" where neighbors don't talk to one another, we expect, as Nixon did, to be trusted. And we are outraged to find that it's not possible, and they're subpoenaing our tapes on Capitol Hill. Why, we ask, does anyone need to know all this stuff about me?

Privacy May Be a Problem

The exploitation of personal data that the FTC hearings took up is plainly a serious problem. But nobody wants to admit that privacy itself may really be that problem's root cause rather than its antidote.

Modern life allows us an unprecedented level of physical privacy in real time and space. This isolated existence not only feeds our paranoia but necessitates the electronic record keeping that enables us to deal all day with total strangers. As the scale of interactions and commerce broadens across the Web, the complexity of that record keeping promises only to deepen.

Want to buy gas on credit? Easy! Even easier than the times 5 when the mechanic down the street knew you personally. The

Jeffrey Obser was an intern at *HotWired* when he published the essay excerpted here in *Salon* on June 26, 1997. As a graduate student in journalism at the University of California–Berkeley, he wrote his master's thesis on privacy in the information age.

difference is that now, the pump will know your name, a distant computer will make a record, and the fellow behind the bullet-proof glass won't give a damn. He has privacy, you have privacy. Everyone happy?

It's no coincidence that the jurist Louis Brandeis wrote his often-cited, groundbreaking "right to be let alone" privacy screed in 1890, just when the close-knit scrutiny of real villages began to give way to the anonymity of urban life. People took privacy for granted until then; in the days before databases, it was not an abstract quality. One's bedroom or backyard were either private or they weren't — and one's reputation was rarely more permanent or widespread than the memory banks of the people one dealt with personally.

Over the last fifty years, our journey into suburbs and cars and flickering TV nighttimes behind barred windows has given us extraordinary seclusion in our personal and home lives. And yet we've only felt more insecure. Only 34 percent of Americans polled by the Louis Harris firm expressed concern about personal privacy in 1970. By 1995, the figure was up to 80 percent.

What happened? This growing concern doesn't indicate a simple increase in how much we value privacy, any more than the soaring number of lawyers in the United States means we value justice more. Instead, it's a fearful reaction to the collapse of trust in our culture.

Technological Innovations and the Loss of Privacy

In *The Naked Society* (1964), Vance Packard trembled at the twentieth-century innovations that were draining American life of privacy and autonomy: social control by large, impersonal employers; pressure on companies to scrutinize customer choices in a sophisticated manner in order to compete for market share; galloping advances in electronic technology; and the McCarthy-era adoption of a pervasive top-security mentality in both government and business.

Nearly a decade later, at the dawn of computerized record keeping, James B. Rule pointed out in *Private Lives and Public Surveillance* (1973) that the transition to a society of mobile strangers didn't necessarily increase surveillance — the prying eyes of small-town neighbors are, he felt, in most cases worse. But it did lead to more *centralized* surveillance — out of sight and, for practical purposes, beyond the control of the individual.

By 1993, in the book *The Costs of Privacy,* Steven L. Nock attacked privacy itself as the problematic result of systemic social separation. "Privacy grows as the number of strangers grows," Nock wrote. "And since strangers tend to not have reputations, there will be more surveillance when there are more strangers. Privacy is one consequence, or cost, of growing numbers of strangers. Surveillance is one consequence, or cost, of privacy."

Nock called credit cards, those handy generators of much of the personal data we've lost control over, "portable reputations." In the era of the Internet, cheap computing and an increasingly global economy, those portable reputations record more and more of our activities, and more and more strangers and institutions demand them from us. The trends toward economic consolidation, less face-to-face accountability in our public lives and faster computing will exert great pressure for ever more elaborate identification and credentialing schemes. The spread of the use of the social security number to sixty government agencies is one result of this pressure. Retina and thumbprint scans, already in pilot testing, will be the next.

We can complain all we want about Big Brother, but when we wrested our reputations from human memory and turned them over to far less judgmental computer circuits and phone lines — vanquishing those nasty old village snoops who might keep us from living out our hearts' desires — reputation remained as important as ever. The difference is that even as we have downplayed its significance — whether out of honest egalitarianism or excessive individualism — we have consigned it to the banal, impersonal testing ground of supermarket checkout stands and preemployment background checks.

Are Privacy Laws Needed?

The only thing a computer ever asks is: Are you approved, or not? And everyone from medical insurers to prospective employers to creditors views us as a potential threat until our data prove otherwise. Setting up new privacy regulations isn't going to alleviate this pressure; it may only lead to more elaborate credentials and invasive identifiers for individuals and increased secrecy for the institutions that manage our reputations.

Privacy, particularly when enshrined in law, can protect the corrupt and malign as well as the good and upstanding. But the bulk of breathless newspaper reports issuing forth on this issue since 1996 have almost universally ignored this, instead focusing on the hypothetical risks of baddies out there finding out where Joe Consumer lives and (gasp!) what his children's names are. Most have taken the same grave, utterly simplistic angle: Privacy good. Stalkers bad. Internet dangerous. Call Congressman. All have invariably repeated the same shopworn Top Ten privacy-violation horror stories, mostly hypothetical and mostly based on the absurdity of having to hide out from one's health maintenance organization (HMO), spoon-fed to hungry reporters by a small group of widely quoted privacy activists. James Wheaton, senior counsel of the First Amendment Project, an Oakland, California, group trying to protect and expand the

Freedom of Information Act, laments "enormous imprecision" in the concerns raised by some of these activists.

By giving government officials the power to deny public-records access to anyone without credentials (i.e., the little guy), Wheaton says, "the privacy activists may inadvertently be helping the moneyed interests and doing nothing for greater security." Even with their good intentions and a laudable commitment to civil liberties, the professional privacy advocates have little besides fear as a selling point — fear of the stalker, the fraud perpetrator, the government agency run amok. But the fear and paranoia that have become so entrenched in the public mind are the primary cause of all this high-tech surveillance in the first place because nobody wants to deal with anybody in person any more.

Sure, there are legitimate issues of informational privacy, and at their best, the FTC hearings constructively aired them. Businesses that collect personal information from Web browsing should have some regulation against selling it, and anyone can see that companies compiling dossiers on every American are a threat to — Well, let's not bring up Hitler again. But the drumbeat of scare stories has focused too much attention on the Internet, even though nobody has explained how the Internet causes the problems in any direct or unique way. Credit-card fraud, costing literally billions of dollars in losses in recent years, was a problem as soon as credit cards were invented — and the Secret Service, which investigates computer crime, has no evidence to date that the resourceful credit-fraud rings have sought or needed help from the Internet.

Collection of Information by the Government

It's ironic that Americans are asking for privacy protection from the same government that has in the last few years expanded electronic surveillance beyond Richard Nixon's wildest dreams — always with an appeal to public fear and mistrust. Federal agencies are creating centralized databases to track every new job hire in the country (to catch illegal immigrants and deadbeat dads), to make sure that welfare recipients don't overstay their five years by changing states and to provide instant "terrorist" profiling to airport security agents. The country has not hesitated in the last few years to wipe out the civil liberties of whole swaths of the population in futile gropes for greater public security that's never attained.

But as soon as the most minute interest of upper-income people is threatened, Congress is shut down with phone calls, as it was during the Lexis-Nexis fiasco in the summer of 1995 and the Social Security Web site controversy in April 1996. Privacy is a vastly different issue to those whose names aren't on anyone's direct-mail list. Ask a homeless person what "privacy" means, and the answer might in-

volve a large appliance box. Once you're on the street, you're a reputation refugee — and no computer is ever going to approve your
e-cash transaction.

The Need to Reevaluate Trust

Simple loss of privacy is not the real problem underlying all the 20
tossing and turning we're going through over the openness the Internet has thrust upon us. The entire experience of Internet use has
total privacy as its point of departure — "meatspace" privacy, real-
time anonymity, the kind that keeps anyone from knowing you're
surfing the Web in your partner's underwear.

No, privacy is only part of the equation. The other part is the
basic question of trust, that elusive property that we've all, in our
hearts, given up on. This wide-ranging loss of our electronic virginity
was well under way twenty years ago but remained invisible until
the Web forced us to confront it. We should be grateful for that. The
arrival of the global village could be an opportunity to reevaluate
our notions of trust and strangerhood. Maybe it will force us to.

Nixon's demands for privacy were ultimately fruitless and pathetic because there was no longer any trust to base that privacy on.
He never understood that — and as privacy-loss hysteria begins to
push laws through Congress that may do more harm than good,
sadly, neither do we.

60 Minutes, *Kevorkian, and a Death for the Cameras*

CARYN JAMES

It is not a gracefully composed camera shot: Dr. Jack Kevorkian
blocks the camera's view as he injects his incurably ill patient,
Thomas Youk, with lethal drugs. Sitting upright, wearing his glasses
and a plaid shirt, Mr. Youk has been given a sedative and his head
has lolled back out of camera range; perhaps because we cannot see
his face, the off-camera voices commenting as they watch this videotape are more chilling than anything on screen.

"Is he dead now?" Mike Wallace asks.

"He's dying now," Dr. Kevorkian says.

Caryn James is a journalist for the *New York Times.* This essay appeared in her
Critic's Notebook column on November 23, 1998.

The broadcast of Mr. Youk's death, shown last night on the CBS News program *60 Minutes,* caused exactly the flurry of media attention Dr. Kevorkian and CBS were looking for. The report was denounced by everyone from George Will on the ABC News program *This Week* to John Cardinal O'Connor from the pulpit of St. Patrick's Cathedral, which simply made the critics part of the hype machine.

Mr. Youk, a fifty-two-year-old man suffering the degeneration of 5 Lou Gehrig's disease, asked Dr. Kevorkian to help him die. The doctor seized an opportunity to cross the legal line from assisted suicide, enabling patients to kill themselves, to euthanasia, actively administering a lethal injection.

But deeper boundaries were crossed as well. That this death was staged for the cameras is the most unsettling aspect of the story, a dark corollary to the growing assumption that the untelevised life is not worth living. Mr. Youk's untelevised death did not seem good enough for Dr. Kevorkian. The taping and its broadcast are, in the crudest terms, a stunt death.

The *60 Minutes* broadcast does not come in isolation, though. It is part of a climate in which many of life's most intimate areas are common grist for the media.

When President Clinton's illicit sex life made headlines, he responded in part by publicizing his meetings with spiritual advisers. If sex and religion have gone public, no wonder death has finally made an appearance on a Top Ten program, whose producers cannot be sorry this report appeared in the November sweeps period, when ratings turn into advertising dollars.

The fact that Dr. Kevorkian made the tape himself and later brought it to *60 Minutes* is beside the point. Dr. Kevorkian admits on the air that he wants the tape to lead to his arrest. By broadcasting it, CBS goes beyond reporting the news and becomes complicit, the carrier of a death played for the cameras.

It is that staged quality, evident in Mr. Youk's two taped encounters 10 with Dr. Kevorkian, that is especially troubling. The *60 Minutes* report begins with Mr. Youk's first meeting with Dr. Kevorkian, which was videotaped. That tape turns out to be even more distressing than the moment of death. Mr. Youk is barely able to lift his hand and is obviously struggling to speak and to breathe. He fears choking on his own saliva.

That tape, so painful to watch, makes it clear why Mr. Youk and his family turned to Dr. Kevorkian. Ironically, it makes the case for assisted suicide more powerfully than the death scene, which is so calm it seems anticlimactic as Dr. Kevorkian gives Mr. Youk three injections.

Watching the death adds nothing to the legitimate debate about euthanasia. Think about the equivalent: a news report about a grisly murder that goes on to show dismembered body parts. In televising his death, *60 Minutes* goes beyond reporting into lurid sensationalism. But without the death tape, no one would have noticed yet another feature on Dr. Kevorkian.

The *60 Minutes* report includes a brief attempt at balance. Dr. Mark Siegler, a medical ethicist at the University of Chicago, calls Dr. Kevorkian's action "a medicalized killing" and says it is "dangerous to patients and dangerous to society."

But the report races past its most profound and troubling issues, of free will and privacy. Dr. Kevorkian says that when he suggested euthanasia rather than assisted suicide to Mr. Youk, "I sensed a reluctance in him." Later we see Mr. Youk agreeing as Dr. Kevorkian reads aloud a statement for him to sign, stating there has been no duress, but we haven't a clue how that reluctance was overcome.

When Mr. Wallace interviews the Youk family after the death, 15 Mr. Youk's wife says of his choice to die: "Tom's very private. And also he believes it's a private issue. You should be able to do what makes sense to you." She seems unaware of the irony that this private moment would be broadcast to the world.

The media landscape that fosters such a broadcast has changed radically in the past few years.

In 1994, the ABC News program *Prime Time Live* showed part of a Dutch documentary, "Death on Request," in which a man with Lou Gehrig's disease died by his doctor's injection. Since then, the influence of the Internet has been pervasive.

As he was dying of cancer in 1996, Timothy Leary charted his last days on his Web site, where he planned to show his eventual suicide, though in the end he died off camera. This summer a baby's birth was shown on the Internet while it happened. And as the recent trajectory of political gossip has shown, a shaky bridge has been built from the Internet, with its editorial free-for-all, to the mainstream media. (Word of Representative Henry J. Hyde's decades-old adultery traveled in a flash from the online magazine *Salon* to newspapers and television.)

By showing Mr. Youk's death, *60 Minutes* creeps closer not only to the Internet but also to the lowest and literally cheapest form of television, reality programming. Whether it's *America's Funniest Home Videos* or *World's Wildest Police Videos,* reality programs foster the sense that real life is mere fodder for television; from there it is a small step to a life and now a death literally made for TV.

What is poignantly clear from the report is that Mr. Youk died 20 without his family around him. They were sent away before Dr. Kevorkian began his injections, to avoid the chance they might be implicated in any crime. The television audience eventually watched, but we are not his family, a distinction *60 Minutes* blurred in its frightening conflation of public and private.

The shabby camera work at Mr. Youk's death spared us the worst horrors. The next televised death may be less amateurish and all the more disturbing as it looks straight into the eyes of a person who has agreed to die for the camera.

What Privacy Rights?

BOB HERBERT

A recent report out of Washington tells a story about Dr. Louis Hafken, a psychiatrist in Providence, Rhode Island, who received a letter from a company that reviews prescription drug benefits for insurers and employers.

The letter contained what should have been confidential information about one of Dr. Hafken's patients, including a printout of her prescription records. It noted that she was taking Ativan, an antianxiety drug. The company wanted to know why. Was the patient depressed, or suffering from panic disorder, or experiencing alcohol withdrawal? Did the doctor plan to continue giving her Ativan?

The doctor did not provide the requested information. "Frankly," he was quoted as saying, "it's none of their business."

The patient was naturally upset to learn that her employer had examined the records of her psychiatric treatment. The implications of such snooping are obvious. Dr. Hafken said many of his patients "are afraid to be completely honest in therapy" because they fear that people other than their doctors will learn of matters that were supposed to have remained secret.

They have reason to be worried. We are very close to the day 5 when strangers will know, or will be able to know, anything they want about you.

Your financial profile and buying habits have long since been catalogued and traded like baseball cards. Your medical records, supposedly secure, are not. Your boss may well be monitoring your telephone conversations and e-mail. Hidden video cameras have been installed — sometimes legally and sometimes not — in dressing rooms and public bathrooms. Thieves armed with your social security number can actually hijack your identity.

"Nothing Sacred: The Politics of Privacy" is a report released last month by the Center for Public Integrity, a highly regarded nonpartisan research organization. The report warned that the privacy of Americans "is being compromised and invaded from many angles" and asserted that Congress has not done nearly enough to slow the assault.

"Time and again," said Charles Lewis, director of the center, "Congress has put the economic interests of various privacy invaders ahead of the privacy interests of the American public."

Bob Herbert is a columnist for the *New York Times.* This article appeared in his In America column on September 27, 1998.

According to the report, Congress first heard testimony that there were problems keeping medical records confidential in 1971. But it still has not passed legislation designed to curb the abuses.

So you still get cases like that of Mark Hudson, a former insur- 10 ance company employee who told the *Times* in 1996 that he was shocked to find during his computer training that he could call up the records of any of the company's subscribers, including information about his own psychiatric treatment and the antidepressant medication he was taking.

"I can tell you unequivocally that patient confidentiality is not eroding," he said. "It can't erode because it's simply nonexistent."

The right to privacy in the workplace is virtually nonexistent as well.

"Most people assume that Federal laws protect Americans from being spied upon in the workplace," said the report. "To the contrary, over the years Congress has rejected legislation spelling out basic privacy protections for employees."

In addition to the possible monitoring of telephone conversations and e-mail, workers are frequently subjected to the scrutiny of hidden video cameras, can be required to type at computers that monitor the number of errors they make and the number of breaks they take, and often are compelled to provide urine samples and submit to psychological exams.

For some jobs, the scrutiny is reasonable. For others, it is not. In 15 all cases it should be properly regulated, and the guidelines should be clear. That is not what is happening. As the center's report noted, Congress has gone out of its way to preserve the right of employers to eavesdrop and otherwise spy upon and collect personal data on their employees.

For decades, privacy advocates have called for legislation that would spell out and guarantee a citizen's basic right to privacy. But tremendous amounts of money are being made from the rampant transfer of the most personal types of information. The huge corporate interests and others that benefit from that gold mine do not want it sealed.

Talk Show Telling versus Authentic Telling: The Effects of the Popular Media on Secrecy and Openness

EVAN IMBER-BLACK

Well, my guests today say that they can't bear to keep their secrets locked inside of them any longer. And they've invited their spouse or lover to come on national television to let them hear the secrets for the first time.

— Montel Williams

The young woman entered my therapy room slowly, with the usual hesitation of a new client. I settled her in a chair, expecting to begin the low-key question-and-answer conversation that usually takes the entire first session. Almost before she could pronounce my name, she began telling me a deeply personal and shameful secret. In an effort to slow her down and start to build a relationship that might be strong enough to hold her enormous pain, I gently asked her what made her think it was all right to tell me things so quickly. "I see people doing it on *Oprah* all the time," she replied.

Throughout history human beings have been fascinated by other people's secrets. In great literature, theater, and films we view how people create and inhabit secrets and cope with the consequences of planned or unplanned revelation. Life-changing secrets are central to such ancient dramas such as *Oedipus* or Shakespeare's *Macbeth* as well as to twentieth-century classics such as Ibsen's *A Doll's House,* Eugene O'Neill's *Long Day's Journey into Night,* Arthur Miller's *Death of a Salesman* and *All My Sons,* or Lorraine Hansberry's *A Raisin in the Sun.* Like me, you may remember the poignancy of the sweet secrets in the O. Henry tale "Gift of the Magi," where a wife secretly cuts and sells her hair to buy her husband a watch chain for Christmas, while he, unbeknownst to her, sells his watch in order to buy silver combs for her hair. Contemporary popular films, such as *Ordinary People, The Prince of Tides,* or *The Wedding Banquet,* also illustrate the complexity of secrets and their impact on every member of a family. Literary and dramatic

Evan Imber-Black, Ph.D., is director of program development at the Ackerman Institute for the Family in New York City and a professor of psychiatry at the Albert Einstein College of Medicine. Her published work includes *Rituals for Our Times* (with Janine Roberts, Ed.D.; 1992) and *Secrets in Families and Family Therapy* (1993). Printed here is an excerpt from her book *The Secret Life of Families: Truth-Telling, Privacy, and Reconciliation in a Tell-All Society* (1998).

portrayals of perplexing secrets and their often complicated and messy resolutions help us to remember that keeping and opening secrets is not simple. Perhaps most important, they help us appreciate our own deep human connection to the dilemmas of others.

Since the advent of television, however, we have begun to learn about other people's secrets and, by implication, how to think about our own secrets in a very different way. Exploiting our hunger for missing community, both afternoon talk shows and evening magazine shows have challenged all of our previously held notions about secrecy, privacy, and openness. While such shows have been around for nearly thirty years, in the 1980s something new began to appear: celebrities began to open the secrets in their lives on national television.[1] As we heard about Jane Fonda's bulimia, Elizabeth Taylor's drug addiction, or Dick Van Dyke's alcoholism — formerly shameful secrets spoken about with aplomb — centuries of stigma seemed to be lifting. Other revelations enabled us to see the pervasiveness of wife battering and incest. The unquestioned shame and secrecy formerly attached to cancer, adoption, homosexuality, mental illness, or out-of-wedlock birth began to fall away.

This atmosphere of greater openness brought with it many benefits. In my therapy practice I experienced an important shift as the people I worked with displayed a greater ease in raising what might never have been spoken about a decade earlier. Frightening secrets lost some of their power to perpetuate intimidation. Those who had been silenced began to find their voices and stake their claim as authorities on their own lives.

But as the arena of the unmentionable became smaller and 5 smaller, a more dangerous cultural shift was also taking place: the growth of the simplistic belief that telling a secret, regardless of context, is automatically beneficial. This belief, promulgated by television talk shows and media exposés, has ripped secrecy and openness away from their necessary moorings in connected and empathic relationships. Painful personal revelations have become public entertainment, used to sell dish soap and to manufacture celebrity.

If cultural norms once made shameful secrets out of too many happenings in human life, we are now struggling with the reverse assumption: that opening secrets — no matter how, when, or to whom — is morally superior and automatically healing. The daily spectacle of strangers opening secrets in our living rooms teaches us that no distinctions need be drawn, no care need be taken, no thought given to consequences.

---

[1]For a complete discussion of the history of talk television and the wider context in which it is embedded, see J. A. Heaton and N. L. Wilson, *Tuning In Trouble: Talk TV's Destructive Impact on Mental Health* (San Francisco: Jossey-Bass, 1995).

Talk Show Telling

From a *Sally Jessy Raphael* show in 1994, we hear and see the following conversation:

> *Sally*: Let's meet David and Kelly. They're newlyweds. They got married in December. . . . As newlyweds, what would happen if he cheated on you? What would you do?
>
> *Kelly*: I don't know.
>
> *[Before David begins to speak, the print at the bottom of the screen reads, "Telling Kelly for the first time that he's cheating on her," thus informing the audience of the content of the secret before Kelly is told.]*
>
> *David*: I called Sally and told the producer of the show that I was living a double life. . . . I had a few affairs on her.
>
> *Sally (to Kelly):* Did you know about that?
>
> *[Camera zooms in on Kelly's shocked and pained expression; she is speechless and in tears, and she shakes her head while members of the audience chuckle.]*
>
> *Sally*: Kelly, how do you feel? On the one hand, listen to how awful and bad this is. On the other hand, he could have just not ever told you. He loves you so much that he wanted to come and get this out. . . .

In the late 1960s the *Phil Donahue Show* began a new media format for sharing interesting information and airing issues. This shifted in the late 1970s and 1980s to celebrity confessions and the destruction of taboos. In the 1990s talk TV brings us the deliberate opening of secrets that one person in a couple or a family has never heard before. In a cynical grab for ratings and profits, the format of such shows has changed rapidly from one where guests were told ahead of time that they were going to hear a secret "for the first time on national television" to one where guests are invited to the show under some other ruse. These programs are referred to as "ambush" shows.

According to former talk show host Jane Whitney, "Practically anyone willing to 'confront' someone — her husband's mistress, his wife's lover, their promiscuous best friend — in a televised emotional ambush could snare a free ticket to national notoriety. *Those who promised to reveal some intimate secret to an unsuspecting loved one got star treatment* " (italics added).[2] Presently there are over thirty talk shows on every weekday. Forty million Americans watch these shows, and they are syndicated in many other countries.[3] Even if you

---

[2]J. Whitney, "Why I Simply Had to Shut Up," *New York Daily News,* June 11, 1995, p. 6.

[3]Talk television is extremely profitable. A typical show costs about $200,000 a week to produce, compared to an average $1 million a week for a drama. In 1992, for instance, Oprah Winfrey's show earned $157 million, Phil Donahue's show $90 million, and Sally Jessy Raphael's show $60 million (Heaton and Wilson, *Tuning In Trouble*).

have never watched a talk show, you live in an environment where assumptions about secrets have been affected by talk show telling.

Opening painful secrets on talk TV shows promotes a distorted 10 sense of values and beliefs about secrecy and openness. While viewers are drawn into the sensational content of whatever secret is being revealed, the impact on relationships after the talk show is over is ignored. Indeed, when there has been severe relationship fallout, or even tragedy following the opening of a secret, talk show hosts and producers claim they have no responsibility, intensifying the belief that secrets can be recklessly opened without any obligation to be concerned about the aftermath. Consider the following:

- In one notorious incident in 1995, a young man named Jonathon Schmitz murdered an acquaintance, Scott Amedure, following an unwelcome revelation on the *Jenny Jones* show.[4] Schmitz had been told that he was coming on the show to meet a "secret admirer." He was *not* told that the show was about "men who have secret crushes on men."[5] When his shock and humiliation resulted in Amedure's murder, the host and producers insisted they had no responsibility.

- On the *Montel Williams* show, a woman heard for the first time that her sister had been sleeping with her boyfriend for several years. She came on the show after being told it was a show about "old boyfriends."

- Former talk show host Jane Whitney describes a show she did called "Revealing Your Double Life." A mother was invited on who had no idea why her son had cut himself off from her for two years. Whitney, of course, knew that the son was about to reveal his pending sexual reassignment surgery. When she met the mother just before the show, the woman implored her, "Do you know what's wrong? We were always so close. I don't know what's happened. Is he sick? Does he have AIDS?" Assuring the mother that "everything would be all right," Whitney lied and kept the secret in order to maximize its revelation on the show.[6]

- Ricki Lake invited on a man who had been keeping his homosexuality a secret from his family. His roommate announced that he had taken it upon himself to tell the man's family this secret.[7]

---

[4]*Newsweek*, March 20, 1995, p. 30; *New York Times*, March 12, 1995, p. A22, and March 14, 1995, pp. A1, A10.

[5]The tragedy attached to this particular show distracts our attention from an important dimension of many of these programs, which is that they commonly pander to feelings of homophobia, racism, and sexism. See Heaton and Wilson, *Tuning In Trouble*, for a full discussion of this issue.

[6]Whitney, "Why I Simply Had to Shut Up."

[7]J. A. Heaton, and N. L. Wilson, "Tuning In to Trouble," *Ms.* magazine, September/October 1995, 6(2), pp. 45–48.

When such actions occur over and over again on talk TV, we lose our capacity to ask a critical question — namely, under what circumstances do we have the right to open another person's secret?

On talk television, husbands hear for the first time that their wives want a divorce; mothers are told the secret of their daughters' sexual abuse; wives discover that their husbands tell friends about their sexual relationship. And all of this occurs in a context in which the host disingenuously denies any responsibility for what is set in motion in the complex ecology of family relationships.

Talk show telling ignores the importance of committed relationships. Telling can be anonymous and disguised. A studio audience and a viewing audience consisting of strangers hear the previously hidden details of our lives. Commercial breaks cavalierly interrupt the opening and hearing of a painful secret. Eavesdropping stands in for sincere listening. Voyeurism substitutes for witnessing. The host's pseudo-intimate hugs and caresses replace genuine healing.

When secrets are opened on television, several peculiar triangles are created. The relationship between the person telling the secret and the person hearing the secret is immediately invaded by the audience, the host, and the "expert," each with a calculated and repetitious role. These roles are imbued with arrogance: the belief that one knows what is best for other people to do about the secrets in their lives. Talk show telling involves opening secrets to a huge group of uninvolved, faultfinding listeners who have no responsibility for the relationship after the talk show ends.

When a secret is about to be revealed, captions are placed below the image of the person who has not yet heard it. The audience sees such words as "About to hear that his wife just had an abortion" or "Jim is not Ellen's biological father." Thus the audience knows the content of the secret before the person whose life the secret affects. A context of humiliation is constructed. Often the audience laughs or gasps while the camera catches a close-up of the perplexed face of the listener. The recipient of the secret is, in fact, the last to know. This structure reduces empathy and enables the audience to feel separate from and superior to the ambushed guest.

The audience encourages further revelations through applause.[8] As viewers, we get the message over and over that opening a secret, regardless of consequences, gains attention and approval. Loudly applauded, cheered, jeered, and fought over, secrets are in fact trivialized. On talk shows, a secret of sexual abuse equals a secret about family finances equals a secret about being a Nazi equals a secret of paternity.

---

[8]See R. Cialdini, *Influence: How and Why People Agree to Things* (New York: William Morrow, 1984), for a discussion regarding studies on compliance showing that once people agree to participate in something, they often go along with much more than they originally intended.

Once a secret is revealed, both the teller and the recipient are immediately vulnerable to the judgmental advice and criticism of strangers. Blaming and taking sides abound. Not a moment elapses for reflection on the magnitude and gravity of what has occurred. Every secret is instantly reduced to a one-dimensional problem that will yield to simplistic solutions.

Soon after a secret is opened, the host goes into high gear with some variation of the message that opening the secret can have only good results. Sally Jessy Raphael tells the young wife who has just discovered the secret of her husband's affairs in front of millions of unasked-for snoopers, "He loves you so much that he wanted to come and get this out." The message to all is that telling a secret, in and of itself, is curative. There is no place for ambivalence or confusion. Indeed, guests are often scolded for expressing doubt or hesitation about the wisdom of national disclosure of the intimate aspects of their lives.

The host's position as a celebrity can frame the content of a given secret and the process of telling as either normal or abnormal, good or bad. When Oprah Winfrey joins guests who are exposing secrets of sexual abuse or cocaine addiction with revelations of her own, the telling becomes hallowed. No distinctions are drawn between what a famous person with a lot of money and power might be able to speak about without consequences and what an ordinary person who is returning to their family, job, and community after the talk show might be able to express. Conversely, some hosts display initial shock, dismay, and negativity toward a particular secret, its teller, or its recipient. When a guest on the *Jerry Springer Show* who has just discovered that a woman he had a relationship with is a transsexual hides in embarrassment and asks the host what he would do, Springer responds, "Well, I certainly wouldn't be talking about it on national TV!" A context of disgrace is created, only to be transformed at the next commercial break into a context of understanding and forgiveness.

Toward the end of any talk show on which secrets have been re- 20 vealed, a mental health therapist enters. A pseudo-therapeutic context is created. The real and difficult work that is required after a secret opens disappears in the smoke and mirrors of a fleeting and unaccountable relationship with an "expert" who adopts a position of superiority and assumed knowledge about the lives of people he or she has just met.[9] While we are asked to believe that there are no

---

[9]See L. Armstrong, *Rocking the Cradle of Sexual Politics* (New York: Addison-Wesley, 1994), for a thoughtful discussion of the impact of such "experts" on talk television when the topic is incest. According to Armstrong, such a structure diminishes the issue, reducing it from one with crucial political implications to simply a matter of personal opinion.

loose ends when the talk show is over, the duplicitousness of this claim is evident in the fact that many shows now offer "aftercare," or real therapy, to deal with the impact of disclosing a secret on television.[10]

The time needed even to begin to deal adequately with any secret is powerfully misrepresented on talk television. In just under forty minutes on a single *Montel Williams* show, a man told his wife he was in a homosexual relationship; a woman told her husband she was having an affair with his boss; another woman told her boyfriend that she was a transsexual; a wife revealed to her husband that they were $20,000 in debt; and a woman told her boyfriend that she had just aborted their pregnancy. An ethos of "just blurt it out" underpins these shows.

Talk show telling also erases age-appropriate boundaries between parents and children. Children are often in the audience hearing their parents' secrets for the first time. On one show an eight-year-old boy heard his aunt reveal that he had been abandoned by his mother because she "didn't want" him. Children may also be onstage revealing a secret to one parent about the other parent, without a thought given to the guilt children experience when they are disloyal to a parent.[11] The impact on these children, their sense of shame and embarrassment, and what they might encounter when they return to school the next day is never considered.

Ultimately, talk show telling transforms our most private and intimate truths into a commodity. Shows conclude with announcements: "Do you have a secret that you've never told anyone? Call and tell us"; "Have you videotaped someone doing something they shouldn't do? Send us the tape." A juicy secret may get you a free airplane trip, a limousine ride, an overnight stay in a fancy hotel. While no one forces anyone to go on a talk show, the fact that most guests are working-class people who lack the means for such travel makes talk show telling a deal with the devil.

---

[10]Jamie Diamond, "Life after Oprah," *Self,* August 1994, pp. 122–125, 162; also see Heaton and Wilson, *Tuning In Trouble,* for a thoughtful critique of the questionable quality of such "aftercare."

[11]*Sally Jessy Raphael Show,* November 29, 1994, "We Want Mom to Leave Her Cheating Husband"; transcript by Journal Graphics.

Privacy Rights: The New Employee Relations Battlefield

WILLIAM S. HUBBARTT

Can an employee be dismissed for dating a fellow employee?

Can a manager monitor conversations in his employees' break room?

Does a drug test invade privacy, or is it a reasonable safeguard against accidents on the job?

Is e-mail private correspondence?

These and other questions strike at the heart of the conflict between an employer's concern for managing the safety and security of the workplace and an employee's privacy interest.

The news media are filled with reports of employers who routinely conduct locker searches, monitor telephone calls, mount video cameras that watch employees on the job, and monitor computers and electronic mail systems. Many of these stories emerge when a lawsuit is filed by an outraged employee seeking redress for a perceived violation of his or her privacy.

I say "perceived" because an employee's right to privacy in the private-sector workplace is *not* fundamentally guaranteed by the Constitution or federal laws, even though many employees believe this to be the case. On the other hand, employers do not have carte blanche. Some federal and state laws do afford certain limited privacy protections for employees. But in their desire to control their businesses, some employers clearly cross the boundary between reasonable management practices and outrageous personal violations.

Why are conflicts over privacy increasing?

Companies don't set out to spy on employees or break into 5 desks and lockers. But as companies have watched losses caused by theft and drug abuse soar, they have responded by instituting controls to protect their assets and interests. Such common deterrents as drug testing and workplace surveillance are extremely sensitive and can offend employees if they are not explained adequately and implemented with care.

Another "hot spot" is workplace technology. Sophisticated computer and communications technology allows managers to monitor

---

William S. Hubbartt is the founder and president of Hubbartt and Associates, a human resources consulting firm, and the author of five books, including *The New Battle over Workplace Privacy* (1998), from which this excerpt is taken.

performance by monitoring conversations or counting keystrokes. Again, if such procedures are instituted with little explanation or respect, employees will have strong negative reactions.

Their reactions are understandable. Most of us regard the right to privacy as one of the fundamental freedoms of a democratic society. Our history lessons taught us that the American colonists sought privacy protections and freedom from colonial rule of the English government. Our founding fathers sought to include privacy protections in our Constitution and our government. We grew up believing that individuals should be protected from unwanted prying into their personal lives and activities and that information about one's private life should not be subject to scrutiny by others, by the government, or by one's employer.

With these expectations, it's natural that both employers and employees wonder whether there are laws against employer spying and just what privacy rights employees are entitled to on the job. In truth, there *is* no comprehensive privacy statute. Yes, there is a constitutional provision that limits certain search and seizure actions by the government. And yes, there are laws that limit certain forms of monitoring and specify how an employer can use or release private information. But most of the constitutional protections we enjoy as private citizens vanish when we go to work. While the government, as an employer, is subject to constitutional privacy limitations, laws impose few limitations on the private employer.

Our privacy rights on the job are much more limited than most of us believe. The Constitution affords only limited privacy protections. . . . Local laws vary from state to state and, like federal laws, are subject to judicial interpretation. Many areas of privacy are new and have yet to be legislated. Other laws are so recent that cases that hinge on their interpretation are only now making their way through the court system, so it may be months or years before an employer can see the significance of a ruling. In the meantime, employers and employees find themselves clashing on privacy in a number of areas, as the following summary reveals.

Preemployment Tests

Arlene Kurtz learned that workplace privacy concerns begin at the   10
start of the employment process when she applied for a job as a clerk typist with the city of North Miami, Florida. The city had developed a policy that all job applicants must sign an affidavit stating that they had not used tobacco products for one year before seeking city employment. The city had implemented a no-smoking policy in 1990, claiming that smokers create higher health costs, as much as $4,611 per year more than nonsmokers. When Kurtz refused to sign the affidavit, she was not hired. She then filed suit against the city alleging that the no-smoking rule was an invasion of privacy.

In her suit, Kurtz claimed that the rule interfered with an aspect of her personal life in which she had a legitimate expectation of privacy. She alleged that if the city's ban against the hiring of smokers was permitted, it would allow employers to further regulate personal lives of employees on other matters, such as when to go to bed at night, what to drink on weekends, where to take vacations, or what hobbies to engage in. In evaluating the facts of the case, the courts sided with the city, indicating that the city's concern for protecting employees' health and for controlling health care costs justified the no-smoking rule.[1]

In *Kurtz,* the city was able to justify its preemployment smoking rule. But other kinds of preemployment tests also have been subject to privacy invasion or other legal claims:

Physical exams.   Many firms use physical exams in prehire placement and during employment. Improper use of this information can result in a privacy invasion or violate employment laws.

Drug/alcohol screening.   Record numbers of firms are conducting drug/alcohol screening tests. The intrusive nature of these tests prompts many privacy invasion claims.

Background checks.   Improper handling or disclosure of information gathered from education, credentials, credit, driving, or criminal records can result in privacy claims or other labor law violations.

Reference checks.   Résumé fraud and other employee relations problems have led employers to seek verification of employment information provided by job candidates. Careless use of this information can result in privacy or defamation claims.

Testing.   Employer use of psychological testing, polygraph testing, and other kinds of paper-and-pencil measuring instruments are subject to legal restrictions. Improper inquiries of handling of test results can lead to privacy invasion claims.

After-Hours Activities

What an employee does off the job is his or her business — or is it? Employer intrusions into personal lives of employees create many questions. Can an employer regulate or prevent employees from taking a second job? Can an employee be fired because he was arrested off the job? What should an employer do if an employee refuses to work because of religious beliefs? Is it lawful for an employer to

---

[1]*Kurtz v. City of North Miami,* 11 IER Cases 480, US, No. 95-545 (1996).

regulate an employee's drinking or smoking off the job? Is it a privacy invasion when the employer limits dating between employees? These kinds of issues have created many privacy invasion claims.

Consider the case of Robin Joy Brown, who applied to the State of Georgia for a position as a state's attorney.

> Brown had all the prerequisites: a Phi Beta Kappa undergraduate, she had received a law scholarship, edited the law review, received her law degree, and completed law clerk experience. After being offered a job by the Georgia state's attorney's office, she accepted. But prior to starting her employment she advised a deputy state's attorney of her plans for an upcoming wedding and that she would be changing her name from Brown to Shahar. She did not tell the deputy that she planned to marry another woman.
>
> When Georgia Attorney General Bowers learned that the planned wedding was to another woman, he withdrew the job offer stating in a letter that the purported marriage would "jeopardize the proper function of this office." Brown went ahead with her marriage plans, changed her name to Shahar, and filed suit for loss of job. In her suit, Shahar alleged that she was "fired" because of her participation in a private religious ceremony of marriage. The U.S. Court of Appeals ultimately heard the case and found that the employer's action violated the Shahars' constitutional right of intimate association.[2]

Employer involvement in off-the-job conduct usually occurs in one of the following areas:

Criminal and other off-duty misconduct. Some individuals just can't seem to stay out of trouble. Inappropriate collection or release of this information can lead to privacy claims and other liabilities.

Secondary employment. Employees may feel that secondary employment is a private affair, but when it affects the employer's business, the employer may have a say. 20

Smoking and use of other lawful products off the job. Off-the-job use of lawful products is generally the employee's business. On some issues, an employer may have justification to regulate off-duty conduct, but privacy claims frequently occur when employers try to control this kind of conduct.

Employee dating. Regulation of dating may seem beyond the employer's purview, but sexual harassment claims as well as privacy invasion claims make this a sensitive subject.

Personal beliefs and lifestyles. Employee beliefs and lifestyles may be related to religion, marital status, or sexual preference.

---

[2]*Shahar v. Bowers,* 11 IER Cases 521 (1994).

These issues are highly personal, and improper handling of them can lead to privacy invasion or other legal claims.

Conclusion

In all aspects of our lives, certain individual freedoms are given up in order to accommodate the greater needs of the public, the government, or an organization such as an employer. Because of terrorism and hijacking, our society readily submits to use of metal detector screens and searches of personal belongings when boarding commercial aircraft at the airport. Upon return from overseas trips, travelers customarily accept luggage searches because of the recognized need to control the unauthorized influx of drugs into the country.

Freedom of speech does not protect the calling out of "fire" in a crowded theater. As a society, we tolerate the increased presence of security cameras at banks, retail stores, and other places where cash is handled because we recognize that the use of these devices to deter crime is more important than the loss of certain aspects of our privacy. But privacy rights seem to be diminishing, and employer prying seems to be growing. 25

Imperial Bedroom
JONATHAN FRANZEN

Privacy, privacy, the new American obsession: espoused as the most fundamental of rights, marketed as the most desirable of commodities, and pronounced dead twice a week. Even before Linda Tripp pressed the Record button on her tape recorder, commentators were warning that "privacy is under siege," that "privacy is in a dreadful state," that "privacy as we now know it may not exist in the year 2000." Not just Big Brother but little brother, John Q. Public, too, is shadowing me through networks of computers. Security cameras no bigger than spiders watch from every shaded corner, dour feminists monitor bedroom behavior and water-cooler conversations, genetic sleuths decoct my entire being from a droplet of saliva, and voyeurs can retrofit ordinary camcorders with a filter that lets them *see through people's clothing.* Then comes the flood of

Jonathan Franzen is a frequent contributor to *Harper's Magazine* and *The New Yorker,* where this essay appeared on October 12, 1998. He has written two novels, *The Twenty-Seventh City* (1988) and *Strong Motion* (1992), and is a recipient of a Guggenheim Fellowship and a Whiting Writers' Award. This essay has been excerpted here.

dirty suds from the Office of the Independent Counsel, oozing forth through official and commercial channels to saturate the national consciousness. Lewinskygate marks, in the words of the philosopher Thomas Nagel, "the culmination of a disastrous erosion" of privacy; it represents, in the words of the author Wendy Kaminer, "the utter disregard for privacy and individual autonomy that exists in totalitarian regimes." In the person of Kenneth Starr, "the public sphere" has finally overwhelmed — shredded, gored, trampled, invaded, run roughshod over — "the private."

The panic about privacy has all the finger-pointing and paranoia of a good old American scare, but it's missing one vital ingredient: a genuinely alarmed public. Americans care about privacy mainly in the abstract. Sometimes a well-informed community unites to defend itself, as when Net users bombarded the White House with e-mails against the "clipper chip," and sometimes an especially outrageous piece of news provokes a national outcry, as when the Lotus Development Corporation tried to market a CD-ROM containing financial profiles of nearly half the people in the country. By and large, though, even in the face of wholesale infringements like the war on drugs, Americans remain curiously passive. I'm no exception. I read the editorials and try to get excited, but I can't. More often than not, I find myself feeling the opposite of what the commentators want me to. . . .

On the Saturday morning when the *Times* came carrying the complete text of the Starr report, what I felt as I sat alone in my apartment and tried to eat my breakfast was that my own privacy — not Clinton's, not Lewinsky's — was being violated. I love the distant pageant of public life, both the pageantry and the distance. Now a President was facing impeachment, and, as a good citizen, I had a duty to stay informed about the evidence; but the evidence here consisted of two people's groping, sucking, and mutual self-deception. What I felt, when this evidence landed beside my toast and coffee, wasn't a pretend revulsion to camouflage a secret interest in the dirt; I wasn't offended by the sex qua sex; I wasn't worrying about a potential future erosion of my own rights; I didn't feel the President's pain in the empathic way he'd once claimed to feel mine; I wasn't repelled by the revelation that public officials do bad things; and although I'm a registered Democrat, my disgust was of a different order from my partisan disgust at the news that the Giants have blown a fourth-quarter lead. What I felt I felt personally. I was being intruded on. . . .

So here's the problem. On the Saturday morning the Starr report came out, my privacy was, in the classic liberal view, absolute. I was alone in my home and unobserved, unbothered by neighbors, unmentioned in the news, and perfectly free, if I chose, to ignore the report and do the pleasantly *al dente* Saturday crossword; yet the report's mere existence so offended my sense of privacy that I could hardly bring myself to touch the thing. Two days later, I was disturbed in my home by a ringing phone, asked to cough up my mother's maiden name, and made aware that the digitized minutiae of my daily life were being scrutinized by strangers; and within five minutes I'd put the entire episode out of my mind. I felt encroached on when I was ostensibly safe, and I felt safe when I was ostensibly encroached on. And I didn't know why.

The right to privacy — defined by Louis Brandeis and Samuel   5
Warren, in 1890, as "the right to be let alone" — seems at first glance to be an elemental principle in American life. It's the rallying cry of activists fighting for reproductive rights, against stalkers, for the right to die, against a national health-care database, for stronger data-encryption standards, against paparazzi, for the sanctity of employee e-mail, and against employee drug testing. On closer examination, though, privacy proves to be the Cheshire cat of values: not much substance, but a very winning smile.

Legally, the concept is a mess. Privacy violation is the emotional core of many crimes, from stalking and rape to Peeping Tommery and trespass, but no criminal statute forbids it in the abstract. Civil law varies from state to state but generally follows a forty-year-old analysis by the legal scholar Dean William Prosser, who dissected the invasion of privacy into four torts: *intrusion* on my solitude; the publishing of *private facts* about me which are not of legitimate public concern; publicity that puts my character in a *false light;* and *appropriation* of my name or likeness without my consent. This is a crumbly set of torts. Intrusion looks like trespass, false light like defamation, and appropriation like theft; and the harm that remains when these extraneous offenses are subtracted is so admirably captured by the phrase "infliction of emotional distress" as to render the tort of privacy invasion all but superfluous. What really undergirds privacy is the classic liberal conception of personal autonomy. In the last few decades, many judges and scholars have chosen to speak of a "zone of privacy," rather than a "sphere of liberty," but this is a shift in emphasis, not in substance: not the making of a new doctrine but the remarketing of an old one. . . .

Even issues that legitimately touch on privacy are rarely concerned with the actual emotional harm of unwanted exposure or intrusion. A proposed national Genetic Privacy Act, for example, is premised on the idea that my DNA reveals more about my identity and my future health than other medical data do. In fact, DNA is as yet no more intimately revealing than a heart murmur, a family history of diabetes, or an inordinate fondness for Buffalo chicken wings. As with any medical records, the potential for abuse of genetic information by employers and insurers is chilling, but this is only tangentially a privacy issue; the primary harm consists of things like job discrimination and higher insurance premiums. In a similar way, the problem of online security is mainly about nuts and bolts. What American activists call "electronic privacy" their European counterparts call "data protection." Our term is exciting; theirs is accurate. If someone is out to steal your Amex number and expiration date, or if an evil ex-boyfriend is looking for your new address, or if you're plotting a leveraged buyout of Texaco, you need the kind of hard-core secrecy that encryption seeks to guarantee. If you're talking to a friend on the phone about how much you hate *The English Patient,* however, you need only a *feeling* of privacy (unless you work for Miramax).

The social drama of data protection goes something like this: a hacker or an insurance company or a telemarketer gains access to a sensitive database, public-interest watchdogs bark loudly, and new firewalls go up. Just as most people are moderately afraid of germs but leave virology to the Centers for Disease Control, most Americans take a reasonable interest in privacy issues but leave the serious custodial work to experts. Our problem now is that the custodians have started speaking a language of panic and treating privacy not as one of many competing values but as the one value that trumps all others. . . .

When Americans do genuinely sacrifice privacy, moreover, they do so for tangible gains in health or safety or efficiency. Most legalized infringements — HIV notification, airport X-rays, Megan's Law, Breathalyzer roadblocks, the drug-testing of student athletes, laws protecting fetuses, laws protecting the vegetative, remote monitoring of automobile emissions, county-jail strip searches, even Ken Starr's cleansing exposure of presidential corruption — are essentially public-health measures. I resent the security cameras in Washington Square Park, but I appreciate the ones on a subway platform. The risk that someone is abusing my E-Z Pass toll records seems to me comfortably low in comparison with my gain in convenience. Ditto the risk that someone will make me a victim of the First Amendment; with 270 million people in the country, my own chances of being nationally exposed are next to nil.

The legal scholar Lawrence Lessig has characterized Americans 10 as "bovine" for making calculations like this and for thereby acquiescing in what he calls the "Sovietization" of personal life. The curious thing about privacy, though, is that simply by expecting it we can usually achieve it. One of my neighbors in the apartment building across the street spends a lot of time at her mirror examining her pores, and I can see her doing it, just as she can undoubtedly see me sometimes. But our respective privacies remain intact as long as neither of us *feels* seen. When I send a postcard through the U.S. mail, I'm aware in the abstract that mail handlers may be reading it, may be reading it aloud, may even be laughing at it, but I'm safe from all harm, unless, by sheer bad luck, the one handler in the country whom I actually know sees the postcard and slaps his forehead and says, "Oh, jeez, I know this guy."

Our privacy panic isn't merely exaggerated. It's founded on a fallacy. Ellen Alderman and Caroline Kennedy, in *The Right to Privacy,* sum up the conventional wisdom of privacy advocates like this: "There is less privacy than there used to be." The claim has been made or implied so often, in so many books and editorials and talk-show dens, that Americans, no matter how passive they are in their behavior, now dutifully tell pollsters that they're very much worried about privacy. From almost any historical perspective, however, the claim seems bizarre.

In 1890, an American typically lived in a small town under conditions of near-panoptical surveillance. Not only did his every purchase "register," but it registered in the eyes and in the memory of shopkeepers who knew him, his parents, his wife, and his children. He couldn't so much as walk to the post office without having his movements tracked and analyzed by neighbors. Probably he grew up sleeping in a bed with his siblings and possibly with his parents, too. Unless he was well-off, his transportation — a train, a horse, his own two feet — either was communal or exposed him to the public eye.

In the suburbs and exurbs where the typical American lives today, tiny nuclear families inhabit enormous houses, in which each person has his or her own bedroom and, sometimes, bathroom. Compared even with suburbs in the sixties and seventies, when I was growing up, the contemporary condominium development or gated community offers a striking degree of anonymity. It's no longer the rule that you know your neighbors. Communities increasingly tend to be virtual, the participants either faceless or firmly in control of the faces they present. Transportation is largely private: The latest SUVs are the size of living rooms and come with onboard telephones, CD players, and TV screens; behind the tinted windows of one of these high-riding, I-see-you-but-you-can't-see-me mobile PrivacyGuard® units, a person can be wearing pajamas or a licorice bikini, for all anybody knows or cares. Maybe the government intrudes on the family a little more than it did a hundred years ago (social workers look in on the old and the poor, health officials require inoculations, the police inquire about spousal battery), but from a privacy perspective these intrusions don't begin to make up for the small-town snooping they've replaced.

"The right to be let alone"? Far from disappearing, it's exploding. It's the essence of modern American architecture, landscape, transportation, communications, and mainstream political philosophy. The real reason that Americans are passive about privacy is so big as to be almost invisible: We're flat-out *drowning* in privacy.

What's threatened isn't the private sphere. It's the public 15 sphere. Much has been made of the discouraging effect that the Starr investigation may have on future aspirants to public office (only zealots and zeros need apply), but that's just half of it. The public world of Washington, because it's public, belongs to everyone. We're all invited to participate with our votes, our patriotism, our campaigning, and our opinions. The collective weight of a population makes possible our faith in the public world as something larger and more enduring and more dignified than any messy individual can be in private. But, just as one sniper in a church tower can keep the streets of an entire town empty, one real gross-out scandal can undermine that faith.

If privacy depends upon an expectation of invisibility, the expectation of *visibility* is what defines a public space. My "sense of privacy" functions to keep the public out of the private *and* to keep the private out of the public. A kind of mental Border collie yelps in distress when I feel that the line between the two has been breached. This is why the violation of a public space is so similar, as an experience, to the violation of privacy. I walk past a man taking a leak on a sidewalk in broad daylight (delivery-truck drivers can be especially self-righteous in their "Ya gotta go, ya gotta go" philosophy of bladder management), and although the man with the yawning fly is ostensibly the one whose privacy is compromised by the leak, I'm the one who feels the impingement. Flashers and sexual harassers and fellators on the pier and self-explainers on the cross-town bus all similarly assault our sense of the public by exposing themselves. . . .

Reticence, meanwhile, has become an almost obsolete virtue. People now readily name their diseases, rents, and antidepressants. Sexual histories get spilled on first dates, Birkenstocks and cutoffs infiltrate the office on casual Fridays, telecommuting puts the boardroom in the bedroom, "softer" modern office design puts the bedroom in the boardroom, salespeople unilaterally address customers by their first names, waiters won't bring me food until I've established a personal relationship with them, voice-mail machinery stresses the "I" in "I'm sorry, but I don't understand what you dialed," and cyberenthusiasts, in a particularly grotesque misnomer, designate as "public forums" pieces of etched silicon with which a forum's unshaved "participant" may communicate while sitting cross-legged in tangled sheets and wearing gym shorts. The networked world as a threat to privacy? It's the ugly spectacle of a privacy triumphant.

A genuine public space is a place where every citizen is welcome to be present, and where the purely private is excluded or restricted. One reason that attendance at art museums has soared in recent years is that museums still feel public in this way. After those tangled sheets, how delicious the enforced decorum and the hush, the absence of in-your-face consumerism. How sweet the promenading, the seeing and being seen. Everybody needs a promenade sometimes — a place to go when you want to announce to the world (not the little world of friends and family but the big world, the real world) that you have a new suit, or are in love, or suddenly realize that you stand a full inch taller when you don't hunch your shoulders.

Unfortunately, the fully public place is a nearly extinct category. We still have courtrooms and the jury pool, commuter trains and bus stations, here and there a small-town Main Street that really is a main street rather than a strip mall, certain coffee bars, and certain city sidewalks. Otherwise, for American adults the only halfway public space is the world of work. Here, especially in the upper echelons of business, codes of dress and behavior are routinely enforced, personal disclosures are penalized, and formality is still the rule. But these rituals extend only to the employees of the firm, and even they, when they become old, disabled, obsolete, or outsourceable, are liable to be expelled and thereby relegated to the tangled sheets. . . .

In a coast-to-coast, shag-carpeted imperial bedroom, we could 20 all just be messes and save ourselves the trouble of pretending. But who wants to live in a pajama-party world? Privacy loses its value unless there's something it can be defined against. "Meanwhile the rest of us go on trying to fool each other" — and a good thing, too. The need to put on a public face is as basic as the need for the privacy in which to take it off. We need both a home that's not like a public space and a public space that's not like home. . . .

Privacy: Protections and Threats

WHITFIELD DIFFIE AND SUSAN LANDAU

Protecting the national security and enforcing the laws are basic societal values. Often they stand in competition with another basic societal value: privacy. The competition is hardly an equal contest. National security and law enforcement not only have political constituencies, they are represented by major societal organizations. Privacy has no such muscle behind it. As a result, although an attachment to privacy endures and at times grows, privacy is often violated.

The Dimensions of Privacy

Two hundred years ago, if you chose to speak to a colleague about private matters, you had to do it in person. Others might have seen the two of you walk off together, but to overhear your

Whitfield Diffie, an engineer at Sun Microsystems, Inc., is the inventor of public-key cryptography, which allows the use of a public key to create a document in codes to be decoded by the recipient with a private key. Susan Landau is a professor of computer science at the University of Massachusetts, Amherst. Excerpted here is a chapter from their book *Privacy on the Line: The Politics of Wiretapping and Encryption* (1998). [The original notes have been omitted, and bibliographic notes inserted.]

conversation an eavesdropper would have had to follow closely and would likely have been observed. Today, the very communication links that have made it possible to converse at a distance have the potential to destroy the privacy such conversations previously enjoyed.

From video cameras that record our entries into shops and buildings to supermarket checkout tapes that list every container of milk and package of cigarettes we buy, privacy is elusive in modern society. There are records of what we do, with whom we associate, where we go. Insurance companies know who our spouses are, how many children we have, how often we have our teeth cleaned. The increasing amount of transactional information — the electronic record of when you left the parking lot, the supermarket's record of your purchase — leaves a very large public footprint and presents a far more detailed portrait of the individual than those recorded at any time in the past. Furthermore, information about individuals is no longer under the control of the person to whom the information pertains; such loss of control is loss of privacy.

Privacy as a Fundamental Human Right

Privacy is at the very soul of being human. Legal rights to privacy appeared two thousand years ago in Jewish laws such as this: "[If one man builds a wall opposite his fellow's] windows, whether it is higher or lower than them . . . it may not be within four cubits [If higher, it must be four cubits higher, for privacy's sake]."[1] The Talmud explains that a person's neighbor "should not peer and look into his house."

Privacy is the right to autonomy, and it includes the right to be 5 let alone. Privacy encompasses the right to control information about ourselves, including the right to limit access to that information. The right to privacy embraces the right to keep confidences confidential and to share them in private conversation. Most important, the right to privacy means the right to enjoy solitude, intimacy, and anonymity.[2]

Not all these rights can be attained in modern society. Some losses occur out of choice. (In the United States, for example, candidates for office make public much personal information, such as tax and medical records, that private citizens are allowed to keep private.) Some losses are matters of convenience. (Almost no one pays bills in cash anymore.) But the maintenance of some seclusion is fundamental to the human soul. Accordingly, privacy is recognized

---

[1]Herbert Danby, *The Mishnah* (Oxford: Oxford UP, 1933), p. 367.

[2]David Flaherty, *Protecting Privacy in Surveillance Societies: the Federal Republic of Germany, Sweden, France, Canada, and the United States* (Chapel Hill: U of North Carolina P, 1989), p. 8.

by the international community as a basic human right. Article 12 of the 1948 Universal Declaration of Human Rights states:

> No one shall be subjected to arbitrary interference with his privacy, family, home or correspondence, nor to attacks upon his honour and reputation. Everyone has the right to the protection of the law against such interference or attacks.[3]

The 1967 International Covenant on Human Rights makes the same point.

The Soviet Union, East Germany, and other totalitarian states rarely respected the rights of individuals, and this includes the right to privacy. Those societies were permeated by informants, telephones were assumed to be tapped and hotel rooms to be bugged: life was defined by police surveillance. Democratic societies are supposed to function differently.

Privacy in American Society

Privacy is essential to political discourse. The fact is not immediately obvious because the most familiar political discourse is public. History records political speeches, broadsides, pamphlets, and manifestos, not the quiet conversations among those who wrote them. Without the opportunity to discuss politics in private, however, the finished positions that appear in public might never be formulated.

Democracy requires a free press, confidential lawyer-client relations, and the right to a fair trial. The foundations of democracy rest upon privacy, but in various democratic societies the protection of privacy is interpreted in varying ways. Britain, for example, has much looser laws regarding wiretaps than the United States. A number of European nations extend more protection to individuals' data records than the United States does.

Privacy is culture dependent. Citizens of crowded countries 10 such as India and the Netherlands hold very different views of what constitutes privacy than citizens of the United States. The American concept developed in a land with a bountiful amount of physical space and in a culture woven from many disparate nationalities.

In the 1970s, as rapid computerization brought fear of a surveillance society, some nations sought to protect individuals from the misuse of personal data. Sweden, Germany, Canada, and France established data-protection boards to protect the privacy and the integrity of records on individual citizens. When the U.S. congress passed a Privacy Act with a similar goal, President Gerald Ford objected to the creation of another federal bureaucracy, and no U.S. data-protection commission was ever established.[4] Ten states have data-protection laws,

---

[3]Academy on Human Rights, *Handbook of Human Rights* (1993), p. 3.
[4]Flaherty, p. 305.

and California includes a right to privacy in its state constitution. New York is the only state that attempts any oversight (ibid.). It would, however, be a mistake to view the lack of a major regulatory apparatus in the United States as a lack of legal protection of privacy.

Privacy Protection in the United States

Most Americans believe that privacy is a basic right guaranteed by the Constitution. The belief has some truth to it, but not nearly as much as some believe. Nowhere is the word *privacy* mentioned in the Constitution, nor is a right to privacy explicit in any amendment. Privacy is nonetheless implicit to the Constitution.

The First Amendment protects the individual's freedoms of expression, religion, and association. The Third Amendment protects the private citizen against the state's harboring an army in his home, the Fourth against unreasonable search or seizure. The Fifth Amendment ensures that an individual cannot be compelled to provide testimony against himself. The Ninth Amendment reserves to "the people" those rights that are not enumerated in the Constitution. And "the Fourteenth Amendment's guarantee that no person can be deprived of life, liberty or property without due process of law, provides an additional bulwark against governmental interference with individual privacy."[5] . . .

Why Privacy?

Despite strictures to prevent abuses, the U.S. government has invaded citizens' privacy many times over the last fifty years, in many different political situations, targeting individuals and political groups. Politicians have been wiretapped, and lawyers' confidential conversations with clients have been eavesdropped upon by FBI investigators.

Sometimes invasion of privacy has been government policy; sometimes a breach has occurred because an individual within the government misappropriated collected information. The history of the last five decades shows that attacks on privacy are not an anomaly. When government has the power to invade privacy, abuses occur.

Conflict between protecting the security of the state and the privacy of its individuals is not new, but technology has given the state much more access to private information about individuals than it once had. As Justice Louis Brandeis so presciently observed in his dissenting opinion in *Olmstead,*

> "in the application of a constitution, our contemplation cannot be only of what has been but of what may be." The progress of science in fur-

---

[5]United States Senate, Committee on the Judiciary, Subcommittee on Constitutional Rights, *Federal Data Banks and Constitutional Rights,* Vol. I (Washington, D.C.: U.S. Government Printing Office, Ninety-Third Congress, Second Session, 1974), p. ix.

nishing the government with means of espionage is not likely to stop with wiretapping. Ways may some day be developed by which the Government, without removing papers from secret drawers, can reproduce them in court, and by which it will be enabled to expose to a jury the most intimate occurrences of the home. Advances in the psychic and related sciences may bring means of exploring unexpressed beliefs, thoughts and emotions. . . . Can it be that the Constitution affords no protection against such invasions of individual security?[6]

Preservation of privacy is critical to a democratic political process. Change often begins most tentatively, and political discussion often starts in private. Journalists need to operate in private when cultivating sources. Attorneys cannot properly defend their clients if their communications are not privileged. As the Church Committee observed:

> Personal privacy is protected because it is essential to liberty and the pursuit of happiness. Our Constitution checks the power of Government for the purpose of protecting the rights of individuals, in order that all our citizens may live in a free and decent society. Unlike totalitarian states, we do not believe that any government has a monopoly on truth.
>
> When Government infringes those rights of nurturing and protecting them, the injury spreads far beyond the particular citizens targeted to untold numbers of other Americans who may be intimidated.
>
> Persons most intimidated may well not be those at the extremes of the political spectrum, but rather those nearer the middle. Yet voices of moderation are vital to balance public debate and avoid polarization of our society.[7]

What type of society does the United States seek to be? The incarceration of Japanese Americans during World War II began with an invasion of privacy and ended in the tyrannical disruption of many individual lives. Could the roundup of Japanese Americans have occurred so easily if the Census Bureau's illegal cooperation had not made the process so efficient? The purpose of the Bill of Rights is to protect the rights of the people against the power of the government. In an era when technology makes the government ever more efficient, protection of these rights becomes ever more important.

Citizens of the former Eastern Bloc countries attest to the corruption of society that occurs when no thought or utterance is private. No one suggests that people living in the United States face

---

[6]Louis Brandeis, Dissenting opinion in *Olmstead* v. *United States* (277 U.S. 438, 1928), p. 474.

[7]United States Senate, Senate Select Committee to Study Governmental Operations with Respect to Intelligence Activities, *Intelligence Activities and the Rights of Americans, Final Report, Book II,* Report 94–755, (Ninety-Fourth Congress, Second Session, April 23, 1976), pp. 290–291.

imminent governmental infringements of this type, but in 1972 congressional staffers wrote that "what separates military intelligence in the United States from its counterparts in totalitarian states, then, is not its capabilities, but its intentions."[8] Electing officials we believe to be honest, trusting them to appoint officials who will be fair, and insulating the civil service from political abuse, we hope to fill the government with people of integrity. Recent history is replete with examples of abuse of power. Relying solely on intentions is dangerous for any society, and the Founding Fathers were careful to avoid it.

The right to be let alone is not realistic in modern society. But in 20 a world that daily intrudes upon our personal space, privacy and confidentiality in discourse remain important to the human psyche. Thoughts and values still develop in the age-old traditions of talk, reflection, and argument, and trust and privacy are essential. Our conversations may be with people who are at a distance, and electronic media may transmit discussions that once might have occurred over a kitchen table or on a walk to work. But confidentiality — and the perception of confidentiality — are as necessary for the soul of mankind as bread is for the body.

THINKING AND WRITING ABOUT PRIVACY IN THE INFORMATION AGE

Questions for Discussion and Writing

1. Obser says that privacy issues are based on social and economic class. Explain his claim. How does he support it? What, according to Obser, is the real reason for our fear of loss of privacy?
2. What are James's objections to the *60 Minutes* program with Dr. Kevorkian? Why did a televised death strike people as more invasive than a televised birth? Was this program different from the programs discussed by Imber-Black? Should there be limits to "reality" programming on TV?
3. Herbert wants "legislation that would spell out and guarantee a citizen's basic right of privacy." Does he suggest what legislation he would advise? What feelings do you think Herbert is trying to evoke in his readers?
4. Do you think that talk show telling should be controlled? If so, to what extent should it be controlled and by whom?
5. How far should employers be permitted to go in acquiring information about employees? Summarize Hubbartt's views on the subject. Does

---

[8]United States Senate, Committee on the Judiciary, Staff of the Subcommittee on Constitutional Rights, *Army Surveillance of Civilians: A Documentary Analysis* (Ninety-Second Congress, Second Session, 1972), p. 96.

TWO-WAY STREET

the type of work make a difference? Make a list of reasonable and unreasonable requirements. Explain the reasons for your choices.

6. Franzen asserts that we are "*drowning* in privacy." What examples does he give of the invasion of public space by private acts? Can you think of others?

7. What, according to Diffie and Landau, are the moral and spiritual dimensions of privacy? (Many scholars have noted that the great religions that appeared in ancient and medieval times were born in the desert.) Do you feel that you have suffered from a lack of privacy in your life? If so, what were the consequences?

8. What comment is the cartoonist making about the information superhighway and its effect on privacy?

Topics for Research

Privacy in student dormitories

Surveillance in reducing crime

Privacy in Orwell's *Nineteen Eighty-Four*

Legal efforts to guarantee electronic privacy

TAKING THE DEBATE ONLINE

- **Electronic Privacy Information Center <http://www.epic.org/** EPIC, a public-interest research center in Washington, D.C., includes some of the latest developments in Internet privacy issues, links to many online resources, and policy archives.

- **The Privacy Page <http://www.privacy.org>**   This site offers more than two dozen links to privacy-related articles in several online magazines, as well as a resource archive and links to other privacy organizations.

- **Privacy Law in the USA <http://www.rbs2.com/privacy.htm>**   Created by attorney Ronald B. Standler, this essay covers the history of privacy law, modern privacy laws, the privacy of businesses, invasions of privacy by journalists, and more.

- **Privacy in the Digital Age <http://cnet.com/Content/Features/Dlife/Privacy>**   The Computer Network, a leading news media company, published this article by Susan Stellin on issues related to Internet privacy, including who might be watching you, what your rights are, and how to protect yourself.

- **The Privacy Forum <http://www.vortex.com/privacy.html>**   The Privacy Forum includes a moderated digest for the discussion and analysis of issues relating to the general topic of privacy in the information age. Topics include a wide range of telecommunications, information, and database collecting and sharing that pertains to the privacy concerns of individuals, groups, businesses, and government.

CHAPTER SEVENTEEN

Punishment

When crime (or the perception of crime) mounts in the United States, the demand for punishment also increases. But even advocates of punishment disagree about both the goals and the kinds of punishment most likely to be fair and effective.

One view holds that the goal of punishment is rehabilitation, or the return of the criminal to productive activity. Another sees the goal as retribution, a payment exacted from the criminal by an outraged society. Still another may regard punishment primarily as a deterrent, removing the criminal from activity and serving as a caution to would-be criminals. These goals are not, of course, necessarily exclusive of one another.

In recent years doubts about the success of rehabilitation and fear of revolving-door justice have resulted in support for changes in the criminal justice system. The demands for capital punishment — thirty-eight federal crimes are now punishable by death — more prisons, longer prison terms, tougher parole, trials of juveniles as adults, even the reappearance of chain gangs in at least three states, testify to the widespread belief that only harsher punishment can reduce the incidence of crime.

As a society we accept limits. These are broadly defined in the Eighth Amendment to the Constitution, which prohibits "cruel and unusual punishment." But a completely satisfactory definition of such punishment would be hard to find. The caning of Michael Fay, an eighteen-year-old American living in Singapore who was convicted of minor vandalism, occasioned a heated debate in this country between those who approved of the punishment and those who considered it barbarous.

Among those involved in the actual administration of criminal justice, including prison wardens and other correctional officials, a growing minority has begun to question the effectiveness of incarceration for nonviolent offenders. Some judges have introduced innovative penalties like public shaming — mandating a public show of remorse or posting the name of a criminal in a public place available to neighbors. But the questions to be asked about all punishments are the same. In the words of the well-known criminologist James Q. Wilson, "Is it useful? Is it just? Or is it only cruel?"

In a book first published in 1764 and considered to be the foundation of modern criminology, Italian philosopher Cesare Beccaria laid out the principles that ought to govern the administration of punishment:

> A punishment may not be an act of violence, of one, or of many against a private member of society; it should be public, immediate and necessary; the least possible in the case given; proportioned to the crime and determined by the laws.[1]

Punishment v. Rehabilitation
RICHARD WASSERSTROM

There is a view, held most prominently but by no means exclusively by persons in psychiatry, that we ought never punish persons who break the law and that we ought instead to do something much more like what we do when we treat someone who has a disease. According to this view, what we ought to do to all such persons is to do our best to bring it about that they can and will function in a satisfactory way within society. The functional equivalent to the treatment of a disease is the rehabilitation of an offender, and it is a rehabilitative system, not a punishment system, that we ought to have if we are to respond, even to criminals, in anything like a decent, morally defensible fashion.

Karl Menninger has put the proposal this way:

> If we were to follow scientific methods, the convicted offender would be detained indefinitely pending a decision as to whether and how to reintroduce him successfully into society. All the skill and knowledge of modern behavior science would be used to examine his personality as-

---

[1] Cesare Beccaria, *An Essay in Crimes and Punishment,* London, 1770.

Richard Wasserstrom, who retired in 1994, was a professor of philosophy at the University of California at Santa Cruz. This selection is from *Philosophy and Social Issues: Five Studies* (1980).

sets, his liabilities and potentialities, the environment from which he came, its effects upon him, and his effects upon it.

Having arrived at some diagnostic grasp of the offender's personality, those in charge can decide whether there is a chance that he can be redirected into a mutually satisfactory adaptation to the world. If so, the most suitable techniques in education, industrial training, group administration, and psychotherapy should be selectively applied. All this may be best done extramurally or intramurally. It may require maximum "security" or only minimum "security." If, in due time, perceptible change occurs, the process should be expedited by finding a suitable spot in society and industry for him, and getting him out of prison control and into civil status (with parole control) as quickly as possible.[1]

It is important at the outset to see that there are two very different arguments which might underlie the claim that the functional equivalent of a system of treatment is desirable and in fact always ought to be preferred to a system of punishment.

The first argument fixes upon the desirability of such a system over one of punishment in virtue of the fact that, because no offenders are responsible for their actions, no offenders are ever justifiably punished. The second argument is directed toward establishing that such a system is better than one of punishment even if some or all offenders are responsible for their actions. A good deal of the confusion present in discussion of the virtues of a system of treatment results from a failure to get clear about these two arguments and to keep the two separate. The first is superficially the more attractive and ultimately the less plausible of the two. Each, though, requires its own explication and analysis.

One way in which the first argument often gets stated is in terms 5 of the sickness of offenders. It is, so the argument begins, surely wrong to punish someone for something that he or she could not help, for something for which he or she was not responsible. No one can help being sick. No one ought, therefore, ever be punished for being sick. As the Supreme Court has observed: "Even one day in prison would be cruel and unusual punishment for the 'crime' of having a common cold."[2] Now, it happens to be the case that everyone who commits a crime is sick. Hence, it is surely wrong to punish anyone who commits a crime. What is more, when a response is appropriate, the appropriate response to sickness is treatment. For this reason what we ought to do is to treat offenders, not punish them.

One difficulty with this argument is that the relevance of sickness to the rightness or wrongness of the punishment of offenders is

---

[1]Menninger, "Therapy, Not Punishment," reprinted in Jeffrie G. Murphy, ed. *Punishment and Rehabilitation* (Belmont, Calif.: Wadsworth Publishing Co., 1973), p. 136.

[2]*Robinson v. California,* 370 U.S. 660 (1962).

anything but obvious. Indeed, it appears that the conclusion depends upon a non sequitur just because we seldom, if ever, seek to punish people for being sick. Instead we punish them for actions they perform. On the surface, at least, it would seem that even if someone is sick, and even if the person cannot help being sick, this in no way implies that none of his or her actions could have been other than what it was. Thus, if the argument against ever punishing the guilty criminal is to be at all persuasive, it must be shown that for one reason or another, the sickness which afflicts all criminals must affect their actions in such a way that they are thereby prevented ever from acting differently. Construed in this fashion, the argument is at least coherent and responsive. Unfortunately, there is now no reason to be persuaded by it.

It might be persuasive were there any reason to believe that all criminal acts were, for example, instances of compulsive behavior; if, that is, we thought it likely to be true that all criminals were in some obvious and distinguishable sense afflicted by or subjected to irresistible impulses which compelled them to break the law. For there are people who do seem to be subjected to irresistible impulses and who are thereby unable to keep themselves from, among other things, committing crimes. And it is surely troublesome if not clearly wrong to punish them for these actions. Thus, the kleptomaniac or the person who is truly already addicted to narcotics does seem to be suffering from something resembling a sickness and, moreover, to be suffering from something which makes it very difficult if not impossible for such a person to control the actions so compelled. Pity not blame seems appropriate, as does treatment rather than punishment.[3]

Now, the notion of compulsive behavior is not without difficulties of its own. How strong, for instance, does a compulsion have to be before it cannot be resisted? Would someone be a kleptomaniac only if such an individual would steal an object even though a policeman were known by the person to be present and observing every move? Is there anything more that is meant by compulsive behavior than the fact that it is behavior which is inexplicable or unaccountable in terms of the motives and purposes people generally have? More importantly, perhaps, why do we and why should we suppose that the apparently "motiveless" behavior must be the product of compulsions which are less resistible than those to which we all are at times subjected? As has been observed, " . . . it is by no means self-evident that [a wealthy] person's yearnings for valueless [items] are inevitably stronger or more nearly irresistible

---

[3] The Supreme Court has worried about this problem in, for example, the case of chronic alcoholism, in *Powell v. Texas,* 392 U.S. 514 (1968). The discussion in this and related cases is neither very clear nor very illuminating.

than the poor man's hunger for a square meal or for a pack of cigarettes."[4]

But while there are problems such as these, the more basic one
is simply that there is no reason to believe that all criminal acts are
instances of compulsive behavior. Even if there are persons who are
victims of irresistible impulses, and even if we ought always to treat
and never to punish such persons, it surely does not follow that
everyone who commits a crime is doing a compulsive act. And because this is so, it cannot be claimed that all criminals ought to be
exempted from punishment — treated instead — because they have
a sickness of this sort.

It might be argued, though, that while compulsive behavior ac- 10
counts only for some criminal acts, there are other sicknesses which
account for the remainder. At this juncture the most ready candidate to absorb the remaining cases is that of insanity. The law, for
example, has always been willing to concede that a person ought
never be punished if the person was so sick or so constituted that
he or she did not know the nature or quality of the act, or if this
were known, that the person did not know that the act was wrong.
And more recently, attempts have been made, sometimes successfully, to expand this exemption to include any person whose criminal action was substantially the product of mental defect or
disease.[5]

Once again, though, the crucial point is not the formulation of
the most appropriate test for insanity, but the fact that it is far from
evident, even under the most "liberal" test imaginable, that it would
be true that everyone who commits a crime would be found to be
sick and would be found to have been afflicted with a sickness which
in some sense rendered the action in question unavoidable. Given
all of our present knowledge, there is simply every reason to suppose that some of the people who do commit crimes are neither
subject to irresistible impulses, incapable of knowing what they
are doing, nor suffering from some other definite mental disease.
And, if this is so, then it is a mistake to suppose that the treatment of
criminals is on this ground always to be preferred to their punishment.

There is, though, one final version of the claim that every criminal action is excusable on grounds of the sickness of the actor. And
this version does succeed in bringing all the remaining instances of
criminality, not otherwise excusable, within the category of sickness. It does so only by making the defining characteristic or

---

[4] Barbara Wootton, *Social Science and Social Pathology* (London: G. Allen &
Unwin, 1959), p. 235.

[5] See, e.g., *Durham v. United States,* 214 F. 2d 862 (D.C. Cir., 1954); *United States v.
Brawner,* 471 F. 2d 969 (D.C. Cir., 1972); and Model Penal Code § 4.01.

symptom of mental illness the commission of an illegal act. All criminals, so this argument goes, who are not insane or subject to irresistible impulses are sociopaths — people afflicted with that mental illness which manifests itself exclusively through the commission of antisocial acts. This sickness, like any other sickness, should be treated rather than punished.

Once this stage of the discussion is reached, it is important to be aware of what has happened. In particular, there is no longer the evidentiary claim that all criminal acts are caused by some sickness. Instead there is the bare assertion that this must be so — an assertion, moreover, of a somewhat deceptive character. The illness which afflicts these criminals *is simply* the criminal behavior itself. The disease which is the reason for not punishing the action is identical with the action itself. At this point any attempt to substantiate or disprove the existence of a relationship between sickness and crime is ruled out of order. The presence of mental illnesses of these kinds cannot, therefore, be reasons for not punishing, or for anything else.

Thus, even if it is true that we ought never to punish and that we ought always to treat someone whose criminal action was unavoidable because the product of some mental or physical disease — even if we concede all this — it has yet to be demonstrated, without begging the question, that all persons who commit crimes are afflicted with some disease or sickness of this kind. And, therefore, if it is always wrong to punish people, or if it is always preferable to treat them, then an argument of a different sort must be forthcoming.

In general form that different argument is this: The legal system ought to abandon its attempts to assess responsibility and punish offenders and it ought instead to focus solely on the question of how most appropriately the legal system can deal with, that is, rehabilitate if possible, the person presently before the court — not, however, because everyone is sick, but because no good comes from punishing even those who are responsible.

One such proponent of this view is Lady Barbara Wootton.[6] Her position is an ostensibly simple one. What she calls for is the "elimination" of responsibility. The state of mind, or *mens rea,* of the actor at the time he or she committed the act in question is no longer to be determinative — in the way it now is — of how he or she shall be dealt with by society. Rather, she asserts, when someone has been accused of violating the law we ought to have a social mechanism that will ask and answer two distinct questions: Did the accused in fact do the act in question? If he or she did, given all that

[6] Barbara Wootton, *Crime and the Criminal Law* (London: Stevens, 1963).

we know about this person (including his or her state of mind), what is the appropriate form of social response to him or her?

Lady Wootton's proposal is for a system of social control that is thoroughly forward-looking, and in this sense, rehabilitative in perspective. With the elimination of responsibility comes the elimination of the need by the legal system to distinguish any longer between wickedness and disease. And with the eradication of this distinction comes the substitution of a forward-looking, treatment system for the backward-looking, punitive system of criminal law.

The mental state or condition of the offender will continue to be important but in a different way. "Such conditions . . . become relevant, not to the question of determining the measure of culpability but to the choice of the treatment most likely to be effective in discouraging him from offending again. . . ."[7]

> One of the most important consequences must be to obscure the present rigid distinction between the penal and the medical institution. . . . For purposes of convenience offenders for whom medical treatment is indicated will doubtless tend to be allocated to one building, and those for whom medicine has nothing to offer to another; but *the formal distinction between prison and hospital will become blurred, and, one may reasonably expect, eventually obliterated altogether. Both will be simply "places of safety" in which offenders receive the treatment which experience suggests is most likely to evoke the desired response.*[8]

Thus, on this view even if a person was responsible when he or she acted and blameworthy for having so acted, we still ought to behave toward him or her in roughly the same way that we behave toward someone who is sick — we ought, in other words, to do something very much like treating him or her. Why? Because this just makes more sense than punishment. The fact that he or she was responsible is simply not very relevant. It is wrong of course to punish people who are sick; but even with those who are well, the more humane and civilized approach is one that concerns itself solely with the question of how best to effect the most rapid and complete rehabilitation or "cure" of the offender. The argument is not that no one is responsible or blameworthy; instead, it is that these descriptions are simply irrelevant to what, on moral grounds, ought to be the only significant considerations, namely, what mode of behavior toward the offender is most apt to maximize the likelihood that he or she will not in the future commit those obnoxious or dangerous acts that are proscribed by the law. The only goal ought to be rehabilitation (in this extended sense of "rehabilitation"), the only issue how to bring about the rehabilitation of the offender.

---

[7] Ibid., p. 77.
[8] Ibid., pp. 79–80 (emphasis added).

The moral good sense of this approach can be perceived most [20] clearly, so the argument goes on, when we contrast this thoroughly forward-looking point of view with punishment. For if there is one thing which serves to differentiate any form of punishment from that of treatment, it is that punishment necessarily permits the possibility and even the desirability that punishment will be imposed upon an offender even though he or she is fully "cured"— even though there is no significant likelihood that he or she will behave improperly in the future. And, in every such case in which a person is punished — in every case in which the infliction of the punishment will help the offender not at all (and may in fact harm him or her immeasurably) — the act of punishment is, on moral grounds, seriously offensive. Even if it were true that some of the people who commit crimes are responsible and blameworthy, and even if it were the case that we had meaningful techniques at our disposal for distinguishing those who are responsible from those who are not — still, every time we inflict a punishment on someone who will not be benefited by it, we commit a seriously immoral act. This claim, or something like it, lies, I think, at the base of the case which can be made against the punishment even of the guilty. For it is true that any system of punishment does require that some people will be made to suffer even though the suffering will help them not at all. It is this which the analogue to a system of treatment, a rehabilitative system such as Lady Wootton's, expressly prevents, and it is in virtue of this that such a system might be thought preferable.[9]

---

[9] There are some additional, more practical arguments that might be offered in support of such a proposal.

To begin with, by making irrelevant the question of whether the actor was responsible when he or she acted, the operation of the criminal law could be greatly simplified. More specifically, by "eliminating" the issue of responsibility we thereby necessarily eliminate the requirement that the law continue to attempt to make those terribly difficult judgments of legal responsibility which our system of punishment requires to be made. And, as a practical matter, at least, this is no small consideration. For surely there is no area in which the techniques of legal adjudication have functioned less satisfactorily than in that of determining the actor's legal responsibility as of the time he violated the law. The attempts to formulate and articulate satisfactory and meaningful criteria of responsibility; the struggles to develop and then isolate specialists who can meaningfully and impartially relate these criteria to the relevant medical concepts and evidence; and the difficulties encountered in requiring the traditional legal fact-finding mechanism — the jury — ultimately to resolve these issues — all of these bear impressive witness, it could plausibly be claimed, for the case for ceasing to make the effort.

In addition, it is no doubt fair to say that most people do not like to punish others. They may, indeed, have no objection to the punishment of others; but the actual task of inflicting and overseeing the infliction of an organized set of punishments is distasteful to most. It is all too easy, therefore, and all too typical, for society to entrust the administration of punishments to those who, if they do not actually enjoy it,

There are, I think, both practical and theoretical objections to a proposal such as this. The practical objections concern, first, the possibility that certain "effective" treatments may themselves be morally objectionable, and, second, the possibility that this way of viewing offenders may create a world in which we all become indifferent to the characteristics that distinguish those who are responsible from those who are not. The ease, for example, with which someone like Menninger tends to see the criminal not as an adult but as a "grown-up child"[10] says something about the ease with which a kind of paternalistic manipulativeness could readily pervade a system composed of "places of safety."[11]

These are, though, contingent rather than necessary worries. A system organized in accordance with this rehabilitative ideal could have a view that certain therapies were impermissible on moral grounds, just as it could also treat all of the persons involved with all of the respect they deserved as persons. Indeed, it is important when comparing and contrasting proposals for rehabilitative systems with punishment to make certain that the comparisons are of things that are comparable. There are abuses present in most if not all institutional therapeutic systems in existence today, but there are also abuses present in most if not all institutional penal systems in existence today. And the practical likelihood of the different abuses is certainly worth taking seriously in trying to evaluate the alternatives. What is not appropriate, however, is to contrast either an ideal of the sort proposed by Wootton or Menninger with an existing penal one, or an ideal, just penal system with an existing therapeutic one.[12]

These matters to one side, one of the chief theoretical objections to a proposal of the sort just described is that it ignores the

---

at least do not find it unpleasant. Just as there is no necessary reason for punishments ever to be needlessly severe, so there is no necessary reason for those who are charged with the duty of punishing to be brutal or unkind. Nonetheless, it is simply a fact that it is difficult, if not impossible, to attract sensitive, kindly or compassionate persons to assume this charge. No such analogous problem, it might be argued, attends the call for treatment.

[10] "What might deter the reader from conduct which his neighbors would not like does not necessarily deter the grown-up child of vastly different background. . . .

"It is not the successful criminal upon whom we inflict our antiquated penal system. It is the unsuccessful criminal, the criminal who really doesn't know how to commit crimes, and who gets caught. . . . The clumsy, the desperate, the obscure, the friendless, the defective, the diseased — these men who commit crimes that do not come off — are bad actors, indeed. But they are not the professional criminals, many of whom occupy high places." Menninger, "Therapy, Not Punishment," supra note 1.

[11] These are discussed persuasively and in detail by Morris in his important article, "Persons and Punishment," *The Monist* 52 (1968): 476–490.

[12] I think that Morris at times indulges in an improper comparison of the two. Ibid.

whole question of general deterrence. Were we to have a system such as that envisioned by Lady Wootton or Menninger, we would ask one and only one question of each person who violated the law: What is the best, most efficacious thing to do to this individual to diminish substantially the likelihood that he or she will misbehave in this, or similar fashion, again? If there is nothing at all that need be done in order for us to be quite confident that he or she will not misbehave again (perhaps because the person is extremely contrite, or because we are convinced it was an impulsive, or otherwise unlikely-to-be-repeated act), then the logic of this system requires that the individual be released forthwith. For in this system it is the future conduct of the actor, and it alone, that is the only relevant consideration. There is simply no room within this way of thinking to take into account the achievement of general deterrence. H. L. A. Hart has put the matter this way in explaining why the *reform* (when any might be called for) of the prisoner cannot be the general justifying aim of a system of punishment.

> The objection of assigning to Reform this place in punishment is not merely that punishment entails suffering and reform does not; but that Reform is essentially a remedial step for which ex hypothesi there is an opportunity only at the point where the criminal law has failed in its primary task of securing society from the evil which breach of the law involves. Society is divisible at any moment into two classes: (i) those who have actually broken a given law and (ii) those who have not yet broken it but may. *To take Reform as the dominant objective would be to forgo the hope of influencing the second — and in relation to the more serious offenses — numerically much greater class. We should thus subordinate the prevention of first offenses to the prevention of recidivism.*[13]

A system of punishment will on this view find its justification in the fact that the announcement of penalties and their infliction upon those who break the laws induces others to obey the laws. The question why punish anyone at all *is* answered by Hart. We punish because we thereby deter potential offenders from becoming actual offenders. For Hart, the case for punishment as a general social practice or institution rests on the prevention of crime; it is not to be found either in the inherent appropriateness of punishing offenders or in the contingently "corrective" or rehabilitative powers of fines or imprisonments on some criminals.

Yet, despite appearances, the appeal to general deterrence is not as different as might be supposed from the appeal to a rehabilitative ideal. In both cases, the justification for doing something (or nothing) to the offender rests upon the good consequences that will

---

[13] H. L. A. Hart, *The Concept of Law* (Oxford: Clarendon Press, 1961), p. 181 (emphasis added).

ensue. General deterrence just as much as rehabilitation views what should be done to offenders as a question of *social control.* It is a way of inducing those who can control their behavior to regulate it in such a way that it will conform to the dictates of the law. The disagreement with those who focus upon rehabilitation is only over the question of whose behavioral modification justifies the imposition of deprivations upon the criminals. Proponents of general deterrence say it is the modification of the behavior of the noncriminals that matters; proponents of rehabilitation say it is the modification of the behavior of the criminals that is decisive. Thus, a view such as Hart's is less a justification of punishment than of a system of threats of punishment. For if the rest of society could be convinced that offenders would be made to undergo deprivations that persons would not wish to undergo we would accomplish all that the deterrent theory would have us achieve through our somewhat more visible applications of these deprivations to offenders. This is so because it is the belief that punishment will follow the commission of an offense that deters potential offenders. The actual punishment of persons is on this view necessary in order to keep the threat of punishment credible. . . .

Justice Served or Medieval Sadism?

GREGORY P. HETTER AND ALAN BUEL KENNADY

I was pleased to see an American, Jonathan Holburt, writing on your March 28 editorial page to defend the "Strong Arm of Singapore Law," in which "a young American who confessed to a ten-day spree of vandalism here has been sentenced to six strokes of the [bamboo] cane, a $1,400 fine, and four months in jail."

I have followed this story in the newspapers with progressively greater astonishment. Our State Department's charge d'affaires wastes America's good will and my tax dollars protesting the punishment of a young American vandal.

As America slides into social chaos at the hands of the lawyers, Singapore is an interesting lesson. In the span of the same fifty years that America has slipped into crime and disorder under an ever-more incoherent set of legal manipulations that have deprived society of the right to protect itself, Singapore has risen from a seamy,

---

These letters appeared in the *Wall Street Journal* on April 12, 1994.

corrupt seaport to an astonishingly productive, orderly multicultural society that lives in peace because of respect for and enforcement of high standards of civil behavior.

The lessons are clear. In America, the lawyers have control of the judiciary, the presidency, and the Congress. The hour is very late for America. Certainly no one in Washington seems aware, nor do the cultural radicals at the indoctrination centers which we still call universities.

I suspect if this vandal is caned it will turn out to be a seminal 5
moment in his life and may well save him from further destructive behavior. After having given Dr. Spock's teachings fifty years of trial and having seen the error, I feel we need to give caning a chance.

Gregory P. Hetter, M.D.

The apologia Mr. Holburt offered for Singapore's use of the rattan (a bamboo shaft) on a young American convicted of vandalism is casuistic in the extreme. He neglects to mention that the rattan is used for only three classes of offense: vandalism, murder, and rape.

No matter how traumatized a Singaporean may be to find his or her car spray-painted, no one who has not entirely lost touch with Western standards of justice would argue that vandalism is comparable to murder or rape, and merits a punishment normally accorded to these. In fact, the strokes of the rattan result in severe injury — it is no mere spanking. Anyone who has ever handled bamboo will know that, once snapped, it breaks into numerous longitudinal slats that splay when pressed against something and that pinch when retracted. Each stroke of the rattan will splay against the victim's buttocks, and with each recoil will lift off long, bloody strips of the victim's flesh. That is the reason the rattan is normally saved for murder and rape: After sixteen strokes (the maximum), the victim is not only scarred for life, but without prompt medical attention could die from shock or loss of blood.

I was in Singapore twice as a member of the U.S. Marines. We were all carefully briefed about this bizarre penalty when we took liberty there. And I have no sympathy for willful vandals. But this punishment is nothing less than a sadistic punishment that has no more place in the modern world than the Islamic practice of maiming thieves or the medieval European practice of frying religious and political dissidents on an enormous skillet. Indeed, Singapore uses the rattan as a punishment for vandalism, and equates it with murder or rape, primarily to suppress political dissent.

Alan Buel Kennady

Pain: The Forgotten Punishment

GRAEME NEWMAN

It is said that Brunelleschi, the great Italian artist, architect, and engineer of the Renaissance, had to reexamine Rome's Pantheon in order to learn how to build the great *Duomo* of Florence. The Pantheon was built in the second century A.D. Western civilization had forgotten over a period of about one thousand years how to build a dome.

The same may be said of criminal punishment today. We have forgotten how to punish — although we are perhaps more fortunate in that our amnesia is only a couple of hundred years old.

If there is any doubt that we are in some kind of punishment crisis — perhaps confusion is a better word — the following examples, one from the everyday world of the criminal court, the other from the highest court in the land, easily illustrate the point.

> In a park at Hillside Avenue and 20th Street in the Queens Village section of New York, a radio plays rock music and nineteen-year-old Robert Loftman relaxes, tapping out the rhythm on the grass.
>
> Clifford Smith comes by. He's only sixteen, but he acts tough. He objects to Loftman playing the radio. "Get the . . . out of the park," he orders.
>
> Loftman stands up. Smith warns:
>
> "If you take another step, I'll blow you away."
>
> Loftman takes another step.
>
> Clifford Smith produces a .38 caliber handgun and pulls the trigger crazily. Twice the gun fails to fire. The third time it finds its mark, and Loftman is struck in the stomach.
>
> Loftman subsequently dies.
>
> Smith is found guilty of manslaughter and sentenced to five years probation by Justice Kenneth N. Browne of State Supreme Court.
>
> D.A. John Santucci of Queens complains that the judge should have given a prison sentence.
>
> Loftman's mother, on hearing the sentence, cries:
>
> "There's no justice! He snuffed out my son's life for no reason. Why shouldn't he be made to suffer?"[1]

> William James Rummel was convicted of theft for a third time, and was prosecuted under the Texas recidivist statute which mandates life imprisonment for anyone upon his third conviction of a felony. The

---

Graeme Newman, a professor of criminal justice at the State University of New York, Albany, is the author of *The Punishment Response* (1978), *Understanding Violence* (1979), and *Just and Painful* (1983), from which this excerpt is taken.

[1] Reported in the *New York Times*, April 14, 1981.

total amount of goods and services Rummel stole came to $229.11. He appealed the conviction all the way to the United States Supreme Court on the grounds that the sentence amounted to cruel and unusual punishment. The court refused to rule that this punishment was grossly disproportionate to the offense. So, Mr. Rummel continues to serve his life sentence. (Decided March 18, 1980.)[2]

One can see that the sentences of probation for the murderer and life imprisonment for the three minor thefts are, to put it mildly, unjust. Judges are supposed to be among our more wise and well-informed people. How can they — especially in the highest court of the land — affirm punishments of such bizarre proportions?

The answer is that our legislators, our judges, our prosecutors 5 have been thoroughly confused by the twentieth-century penologists, who have advocated one reform after another, each reform successively recognized as a failure.

The reformers have tried to water down criminal punishment into nonpunitive alternatives such as probation, halfway houses, or conjugal visits in prison. Or they have insisted that prison should be a "treatment" rather than a punishment. Indeed the more vocal of them, such as Dr. Karl Menninger in his book *The Crime of Punishment,* have argued that criminals are "sick," not bad.

There is now a virtual clamor of consensus that these "reforms" have been absolute failures. Prisons have failed to rehabilitate. Offenders have often been worse off "treated" rather than "punished."[3]

In the 1970s the prestigious Committee on Incarceration, chaired by Senator Charles Goodell, led a new wave of reform. This was to be a return to retribution and a strict reorientation of criminal punishment away from treatment and back to punishment.

But these reformers are now drowning in their own solution. Longer and more prison terms have been the logical result of their reforms which now face us with one of the most terrible social problems of today: a veritable archipelago of prisons overflowing with inmates. And they have produced a fiscal bind of considerable magnitude.

The Attorney General's Task Force on Violent Crime, chaired by 10 former Attorney General Griffin Bell and Governor James Thompson (August 17, 1981), noted that as of January 1981:

> Approximately 315,000 were incarcerated in all state and 51 federal correctional institutions. On any given day, an additional 158,000 persons are being held in over 3,000 jails.[4]

---

[2] *Rummel v. Estelle,* 63 L. Ed. 2d, 382 (1980).

[3] See D. Rothman, *Conscience and Convenience* (Boston: Little, Brown, 1980); also Willard Gaylin et al., *Doing Good: The Limits of Benevolence* (New York: Pantheon, 1978).

[4] These statistics are reported annually in U.S. Department of Justice. *Prisoners in State and Federal Institutions.* Washington, D.C.: GPO, SD-NPS-PSF-5.

At a cost of roughly $20,000 per inmate per year, this amounts to a colossal annual expenditure of $10 billion. The *Task Force Report* adds that to accommodate the existing inmate population according to nationally recognized standards of square footage, it would cost an additional $10 billion.

A number of states have tried to address this problem by floating prison bond issues. In the November 1981 election in New York State, a $500 million bond issue was narrowly defeated. Perhaps this is a sign to the experts that the people are not prepared to spend so much money on this form of punishment.

Yet it is undoubtedly clear, when one reads of the many cases like that of Mrs. Loftman's son, that a punishment must be found that can meet with the philosophical challenge of just punishment and that can also go much of the way to solving the fiscal problem of criminal punishment.

The solution lies in the rediscovery of punishment in all its variety, for there are many punishments that do not need the expensive apparatus of prison and which will do the job of administering pain so much better than prison. The answer is really so simple, yet in this century has been lost. We must take seriously what the advocates of retribution have been saying for a long time, but not truly understanding:

Punishment must, above all else, be painful.   15

Indeed, pain is part of the definition of punishment. The origin of the word pain is the Latin *poena,* which meant in Roman times, punishment or penalty. Its meaning as a localized and acute sense experience is of relatively recent origin, probably of seventeenth-century England.[5]

In those days punishment was there for all to see. It was publicly intimate and largely physical. Ears were cut off, the whip was applied, and so was the death penalty. These were clear and concrete punishments; there could be no doubt that they were painful.

This is not the case today. We are simply told that so-and-so received "five years," another "two years." What do *these* punishments mean? What is the concrete difference between two years' and five years' punishment of prison? We shall see in this book that these

---

[5] See H. Fabregga and S. Tyma, "Culture, Language and the Shaping of Illness: An Illustration Based on Pain," *Journal of Psychosomatic Research* 20 (1976): 323–337. Scholars have traced the word back to about 400 B.C. when it referred to a penalty, specifically a fine. Around 500 A.D. it meant to inflict suffering, and in another sense the opposite of pleasure. Not until 1100 did it come to mean suffering in a general sense (that is, the suffering in hell) and eventually in 1400 to mean suffering of mental as well as physical pain (this no doubt, coinciding with the mental tortures of the Inquisition). The modern meaning of any mental or physical suffering, or that one specifically "had a pain," did not arise until after 1600.

sentences have no concrete meaning whatsoever either to the public or to the criminal who is punished.[6]

In other words, the punishment is *symbolic,* and the great problem is that the powerful need for punishment will not be adequately satisfied with symbolic punishments. They must be concrete. That is, they must clearly inflict pain. This means that we must return to truly painful punishment for crimes.

Does this mean: Bring back the whip and the lash? Let's start 20 cutting off the hand of a thief, the tongue of a blasphemer? Or turning back the clock to the tortures of two hundred years ago when criminals were whipped till blood gushed out of their backs and until they collapsed and died? How could any civilized person or society even contemplate such punishments?

If we are to rediscover the significance of pain in punishment we must be prepared to consider all kinds of punishment which clearly inflict pain. Yes, we must reconsider corporal punishment. We must reconsider the infliction of all punishments regardless of the kind of pain, whether mental or physical, that they produce.

Many of these kinds of pain already occur in our prisons. However, they occur by default rather than by design, and this is essentially what is wrong with them. The eminent historian David Rothman of Columbia University has claimed in his book *Conscience and Convenience* that this state of affairs exists because of lack of money to deal with them. But, while an important factor, this explanation fails to penetrate the veneer of excuses we have invented during the course of this century, for the failures of our correctional system.

The fundamental reason for the mess we are in is that there is no clear purpose to our use of punishment.[7] This is because we have lost the art of matching crimes to their punishments which our forefathers were most adept at doing. The reason we have lost this art is that the prime ingredient in translating the crime into its punishment has been cast aside.

That ingredient is pain.

We must see that pain is not only the prime ingredient of punish- 25 ment but it is also a necessary condition of justice. For without it there can be no punishment. And there can be no justice without punishment — which was the source of Mrs. Loftman's complaint.

It is also true that too much pain may make a particular punishment unjust. But we shall see that the cases in which too much of it

---

[6] Indeed, in this monograph, Professor Wilkins noted that it was not possible for his staff to agree upon what the difference between these sentences really meant. See L. T. Wilkins, *Principles of Guidelines for Sentencing: Methodological and Philosophical Issues* (Washington, D.C.: National Institute of Criminal Justice, 1981).

[7] See G. Newman, review of Rothman's *Conscience and Convenience* in *Crime and Delinquency* (July 1981): 422–428.

is used result from our failure to comprehend pain in a concrete way, a result, paradoxically, of our having "civilized" our punishments. Today these unjust punishments occur mostly in our irresponsible use of prison, without any clear idea of what kind of pain we wish to administer. The Supreme Court case of Mr. Rummel is a prime example.

This confusion about the use of pain in criminal punishment is well demonstrated by the following quotation from the 1976 Report of the Committee on Incarceration, *Doing Justice,* a committee comprised of a prestigious body of clerics, laymen, social scientists, and lawyers:

> One reason for preferring incarceration is simply that we have not found another satisfactory severe punishment. Historically, the alternative was corporal punishment, but that is worse. Incarceration at least can be divided into weeks, months, and years — and its duration prescribed by standards. Given the numerous possibilities that modern technology affords for inflicting pain and the difficulty of measuring degrees of subjective distress, effectively controlling the use of corporal punishment is virtually an impossible task.
>
> Beyond the question of effective control, corporal punishment poses disturbing ethical problems. Besides any physical pain involved, intentional corporal maltreatment evokes in its victim intense feelings of humiliation and terror. . . . Ought a civilized state ever to visit such mortifications? Might there not exist a right to the integrity of one's own body, that not even the state's interests in punishing may override?[8]

The confusion is clear. They call corporal punishment "maltreatment," but they do not call prison "maltreatment." They claim that corporal punishment causes humiliation and terror — yet we will see in this book that none of the research substantiates this claim. But it is well established that prison rests on a platform of humiliation and terror. Some criminals may deserve such punishment. Unfortunately, humiliation and terror in prisons occur by default not by design and therefore subject all inmates to such punishments regardless of their crimes.

Not one of the committee's factual claims is true. Corporal punishment *can* be controlled because of the very fact that it can be technologically and scientifically administered. It is prison that is out of control, not corporal punishment.

As for the claim that a criminal has the right of integrity over his own body: Who are they trying to fool? Such a right is worthless if

---

[8] A. Von Hirsch, *Doing Justice: The Choice of Punishments,* Report of the Committee for the Study of Incarceration. Preface by Charles Goodell, Chairman (New York: Hill and Wang, 1976).

that body is enclosed in a prison cell, especially if that cell contains other violent inmates who may attack each other at will.

Given this confusion of our experts about criminal punishment it seems perfectly reasonable for a civilized society to reconsider the painful possibilities of criminal punishment — *all* the possibilities, including various ways of inflicting pain. . . .

1. Acute corporal punishment should be introduced to fill the gap between the severe punishment of prison and the nonpunishment of probation.

2. For the majority of property crimes, the preferred corporal punishment is that of electric shock because it can be scientifically controlled and calibrated, and is less violent in its application when compared with other corporal punishments such as whipping.

3. For violent crimes in which the victim was terrified and humiliated, and for which a local community does not wish to incarcerate, a violent corporal punishment should be considered, such as whipping. In these cases, humiliation of the offender is seen as justifiably deserved.

4. Every effort should be made to develop a split system of criminal justice: one system for the punishment of *crimes,* and one for the punishment of *criminals.* 35

5. After an offender has committed a number of repeated offenses, or when the combined injury and damage of his crimes reach a certain amount, he will be treated as a criminal deserving of incarceration.

6. Only criminals should receive prison as a punishment, and only two prison sentences should be allowed: fifteen years for the first incarceration, and life if the individual recommits after his release. The fifteen-year term is the "warning" that the offender is close to the point of no return. There is no more getting off lightly with corporal punishment.

7. The decision to incarcerate will depend on many factors, but should especially depend on how much money the community is prepared to spend on incarcerating repeat offenders.

8. Before pronouncing either a fifteen-year or a life sentence, the judge should be required to seek a budgetary assessment of the cost of keeping this offender for the respective period. If such money is not approved beforehand by the Division of Budget, the sentence should be disallowed, and corporal punishment substituted.

9. A life sentence means life. If we truly believe that treatment or 40 rehabilitation no longer works, then there is no sense at all, especially from the point of view of incapacitation, in ever letting the "dangerous" criminal out.

10. The measure of the effectiveness of prison as a punishment should not be whether the offender recommits after release. Rather,

the notion of prison as retributive considers it entirely possible that a truly terrible offender may not have sufficient time in one life to work through the guilt of his crimes. Furthermore, even if he does work off his guilt, there is no expectation at all, according to the retributive philosophy, that the offender should have learned not to repeat his crime. What he *has* learned is that his crimes have a reciprocal cost to him in suffering. Thus, we do not speak of "rehabilitation" of the criminal, but of "redemption."

11. When corporal punishment is used, offenders should receive the same punishment for the same crime, whether it is their first offense or not. The only time an offender's entire record should be taken into account is when we decide to incarcerate. At that point an assessment of the dollar cost of the criminal's offenses may be considered, along with other individual background factors.

12. Because corporal punishment does not discriminate according to the offender's background, no distinction should be made according to age, sex, race, or any other social or psychological characteristic when deciding on the amount of deserved corporal punishment. Of course a medical examination will be required to establish the offender's fitness to receive punishment.

13. The scaling of corporal punishment will be tied to (1) the comparative seriousness of offense categories, and (2) the amount of injury and damage of the offense.

14. Corporal punishment may be applied according to intensity, frequency, and time, but should never exceed an eight-hour period.

15. Corporal punishment should be immediate: applied as soon as possible after the sentence (and preferably upon the finding of guilt).

16. All punishment should be public: Corporal punishment should be conducted in the presence of community representatives, including the press, and a description of the offender's crime or crimes should be graphically portrayed to the public at the time of the punishment. Prisons should also be opened to public tours.

17. Corporal punishment should never be used either in combination with prison or in order to "correct" the offender, because in these uses it comes too close to torture, which is barbaric and destructive.

18. Judges must be given more discretion not less. Corporal punishment, along with a "guidelines" model, is merely a first transitional step toward breaking down sentencing practices which at present are rigid and narrow. By using creative punishments judges will help free the higher courts to break with the purely quantitative notion of crime and punishment, and to begin thinking in terms of *appropriateness.*

19. Fines should be eliminated from the range of punishment alternatives unless they are part of a punishment that tries to reflect a particular offense.

20. When prisons are used as a chronic punishment we must take full responsibility for their harshness and put them to a clear retributive purpose. This means getting rid of the watered down versions of prisons, and making those few prisons that will exist extremely harsh places, reserved only for the terrible few.

21. A prison-intensive system will deemphasize prison as a form of punishment. The advantages of this strategy are obvious: a decrease in the number of people in prison, and a great savings in cost.

But by far the greatest consequence of this deemphasis in prisons is that fewer persons will come under the direct control of the State (which is what we mean by prisons), and that the major portion of criminal punishment (that is, corporal punishment) will be conducted with the view that it is not criminals per se who are being punished at all, but free citizens who have exercised their right to break the law.

In this way the most basic of all freedoms in a society is preserved: the freedom to break the law.

Distinguishing between Felons and Truants

GIL GARCETTI

The juvenile justice system is failing to protect us from the surge in violent crimes committed by young people.

The patchwork of laws put on the books over the past thirty years isn't working. One problem is that the system was designed to help troubled youths who committed minor offenses, but 75 percent of the current cases in juvenile court are felonies. We need to act immediately to replace it with a coherent program that protects society from violent juvenile criminals, efficiently rehabilitates youths who can be saved — and also knows how to tell the difference.

Core Principles

Here are some principles that could form the core of a revision:

Remove many violent offenders from the juvenile system. Violent youths who are seventeen years old should be sent directly to adult court. In 1993, about 50 percent of the juveniles referred to the Pro-

---

Gil Garcetti is the district attorney for Los Angeles County. This essay originally appeared in the *Los Angeles Times* on February 7, 1994.

bation Department for possible criminal offenses were seventeen years old. So were many juveniles charged with the most serious crimes.

Prosecutors should have discretion to transfer even much 5 younger juveniles accused of the most serious crimes to adult courts. State legislators have proposed lowering the age at which a youth can be tried as an adult from sixteen to fourteen, but the numbers matter less than letting prosecutors use their own judgment. For instance, a fifteen-year-old is in juvenile court, accused of a double murder. If the murders had occurred nine days later, on his sixteenth birthday, he could have been tried as an adult and, if convicted, sentenced to life without the possibility of parole. Convicted juvenile offenders must be freed by age twenty-five.

Limit juvenile confidentiality. Society needs to identify juveniles who commit serious crimes and know what happens to them in court. Improvements have been made over the years, but there are still instances where agencies charged with providing services to children are not aware of criminal proceedings involving a child. School officials, for instance, concerned about violating confidentiality laws, have often not told teachers about students who had been convicted of crimes.

Deliver real rehabilitation. Juvenile justice has to efficiently deliver rehabilitative services to juveniles who commit minor offenses. The first step is coordination among all the agencies that assist young people at risk. We need to identify and help the growing number of children who have never had structure or hope in their lives. Government can also offer parents help with parenting skills and intervention before the family structure falls apart.

The present juvenile system puts truants and murderers through the same procedures, including the appointment of attorneys at public expense and long judicial hearings. We need laws that allow better choices between punishment and guidance, and that use resources more wisely.

Accountability

Make juveniles — and their parents — accountable. Punishment that fits the crime must be meted out fairly and with certainty. Currently, juvenile burglars are often sent straight home on probation while adults who commit the same offense get a mandatory prison sentence; this sort of thing makes juvenile offenders believe they can get away with almost anything.

Parents must be held responsible for keeping their children in 10
school. We can enforce violations of the Education Code and at the
same time assist parents with "stay in school" programs. Parents must
also pay for the damage their children cause, including the cost of graffiti cleanups. Current law provides for restitution of up to $10,000 to vic-
tims of juvenile crime. New laws should simplify this recovery and reinforce parental responsibility, while also offering parenting assistance.

Intervene early to prevent violence later. This is the most important step we can take to stop juvenile crime. Legislators need to
change the laws that prohibit and punish as well as provide programs and funding to give children the skills and motivation to stay
in school and away from gangs, drugs and crime.

Keep juveniles away from guns. We must substantially stiffen
laws and penalties for juveniles in possession of guns and for adults
who make guns available to juveniles. No loopholes, no exceptions.

A new juvenile justice system would quickly reduce the level of
fear we all feel. Over the long term, it would reduce the number of juvenile and adult violent criminals. We need to put reformers to work
right away and give them a time limit, no more than 180 days, to produce a framework for a new juvenile justice system. I offer one of my
senior prosecutors to this effort.

The reformers should be nonpartisan; this is not about politics.
It is about making California a safe, desirable place to live.

Justice for Young Criminals: Emphasize Punishment

BRADLEY S. O'LEARY

Society has a primary duty to punish juvenile offenders, not to
rehabilitate them.

The punishment of boot camp, life imprisonment, or execution
should fit the viciousness of the crime, not the age of the violent offender. As a society, we cannot show any sympathy for, or accept
any excuses from, the young thugs, perverts, and psychopaths who
are destroying our schools and neighborhoods.

Thousands of young violent offenders have no moral compass
and no fear of punishment. Worst of all, many have no sense of right

Bradley S. O'Leary is copublisher of the *O'Leary/Kamber Report.* This essay appeared in *USA Weekend* on May 13–15, 1994.

and wrong. The statistics are shocking and grim. According to *Uniform Crime Reports for the United States,* in 1992, 2,829 juveniles were arrested for murder, 5,369 for forcible rape, 40,434 for robbery and 63,777 for aggravated assault. The National Crime Victimization Survey conducted a few years ago by the federal Justice Department estimated that some 430,000 children had been the victims of rape, robbery, or assault at school. *These* are the children we must protect — not those who lack religious beliefs, eat the wrong diet, were abused by a family member, or were driven to violence by television or music. Those are not valid reasons for our citizens to live in perpetual fear of evil kids and violent juvenile offenders.

Do the Crime, Serve the Time

What can we do? Curfews for young people in shopping malls and other public areas should be instituted. And all of the estimated 270,000 children who bring a gun or a knife to school each day should be sent to boot camp for six months. Any juvenile who uses a deadly weapon in committing a crime should be given a mandatory one-year prison sentence.

Juveniles arrested for crimes like 1993's rape and murder of two   5
girls in Houston, or the heartless murder of three innocent boys in Arkansas, should not be let off by too-lenient courts or age-mandated early-release programs. They should serve time like adults and even face the prospect of society's ultimate solution for violent offenders — no matter what their age. Juveniles fourteen or older must be tried as adults for violent crimes involving rape, murder, armed robbery, and aggravated assault.

The first lesson that should be taught in school is: You do the crime, you serve the time. Parents, teachers, and society as a whole will not enjoy peace of mind until our schools and streets are free of violent juveniles.

Just Revenge

MARK COSTANZO

The Bible Tells Me So

In their final appeals to jurors, prosecutors in capital murder trials are fond of quoting scripture to lend authority to their arguments. And there are many verses to choose from. In particular, the Old Testament seems to suggest killing as a response to a variety of crimes. The most popular quotation is from Deuteronomy (19:21): "Life for life, eye for eye, tooth for tooth, hand for hand, foot for foot." Moreover, the Old Testament recommends death for an assortment of crimes, including murder, contempt for parental authority, defiling sacred places or objects, kidnapping for ransom, sorcery, bestiality, worshiping false gods, profaning the Sabbath, adultery, incest, homosexuality, blasphemy, bearing false witness in court, harlotry, negligence that results in a death, and false prophesy.

Yet, despite the apparent biblical endorsement of executions, there is much even in the Old Testament to suggest that killing may not be the appropriate penalty for murder. God did not kill Cain for the murder of Abel, and several cities of refuge were established so that wrongdoers could escape vengeance at the hands of the victims' families. The idea that "vengeance belongs to the Lord" and that we should "love our neighbor as ourselves" are major themes of the Old Testament. Even the often misinterpreted "eye for an eye" passage was meant to *restrain* rather than to *require* vengeance. Religious scholars point out that, taken in context, the passage does not tell us that we must exact proportional revenge, but that we may not take from others more than has been taken from us, that we must resist the urge to retaliate with ever greater violence. *Lex talionis,* the doctrine of legal retaliation, represented an advance, a movement away from unrestrained retaliation.

Though the Old Testament authorizes executions in principle, in practice "there were such extensive procedural requirements for the imposition of the death penalty that, by design, it was nearly impossible to secure a death verdict." Mosaic law and, later, the rabbinic tradition established a nearly unreachable standard of proof.

Mark Costanzo is the chair of the Department of Social Psychology at Claremont McKenna College and a faculty member at the Center for Organizational and Behavioral Sciences at Claremont Graduate University. His work on the death penalty includes several scholarly articles, testimony as an expert witness, and appearances on national radio and television. This excerpt is taken from his book *Just Revenge: Costs and Consequences of the Death Penalty* (1997). [Footnotes have been omitted.]

In the Talmudic courts (called Sanhedrins) two witnesses judged to be competent had to testify that they saw the accused commit the crime after being forewarned that the act was illegal and punishable by death. Confessions were inadmissible. So was testimony against the defendant by family members of the victim or persons with a preexisting grievance against the defendant. If any aspect of the evidence or testimony was found to be unreliable, the defendant could not be killed. Such restrictions served to make capital punishment extremely rare under Talmudic law.

For Christians, the Old Testament must be interpreted in light of the New Testament, which goes much farther in repudiating revenge: "You have heard that it was said, 'An eye for an eye and a tooth for a tooth.' But I say to you, do not resist one who is evil. But if any one strikes you on the right cheek, turn to him the other also" (Matthew 5:38–41). The New Testament emphasizes love, compassion, mercy, charity, forgiveness. And, if we are to follow the example of Christ, forgiveness and compassion are especially important when dealing with criminals and outcasts. When Christ was confronted with a woman convicted of adultery (a capital crime at the time), the crowd who had assembled to stone her asked, "Teacher, this woman hath been taken in adultery, in the very act. Now the law of Moses commanded us to stone such: What then sayest thou of her?" In response, Jesus "lifted up himself and said unto them, 'He that is without sin among you, let him cast the first stone'" (John 8:3–11). The same message can be found in Luke: "Judge not and you will not be judged; condemn not, and you will not be condemned; forgive, and you will be forgiven" (6:37). The entire life and teachings of Jesus argue against killing as a form of punishment. Though not a theologian, Charles Dickens made the point well:

> Though every other man who wields a pen should turn himself into a commentator on the scriptures — not all their united efforts could persuade me that executions are a Christian law. . . . If any text appeared to justify the claim, I would reject that limited appeal, and rest upon the character of the Redeemer and the great scheme of His religion.

Although the Bible can be read to support the death penalty, 5 this support is subject to severe restrictions. Specifically, guilt must be certain and execution must be necessary to serve the interests of justice (e.g., to protect others or to instill respect for moral authority). Indeed, no less an authority than Pope John Paul II has observed that the necessary requirements for the death penalty are seldom, if ever, met. In "Evangelium Vitae" (The Gospel of Life) the pope argues that "as explicitly formulated, the precept 'You shall not kill' is strongly negative: it indicates the extreme limit which can never be exceeded." John Paul II goes on to note that punishment ought not go to the extreme of executing the offender except in cases of absolute necessity: in other words, when it would not be possible otherwise to defend society. Today, however, as a result of steady improvements in the organization of the penal system, such cases are very rare, if not practically nonexistent. . . . If bloodless means are sufficient to defend human lives against an aggressor and to protect public order and the safety of persons, public authority must limit itself to such means.

The pope is not a lone voice among religious leaders. Religious organizations are nearly unanimous in their condemnation of capital punishment. More than forty such organizations (including American Baptists, Catholics, Episcopalians, Jews, Lutherans, Mennonites, Methodists, Presbyterians, Quakers, and Unitarians) have issued statements calling for the abolition of capital punishment.

Moral Philosophy and the Functions of Punishment

When measured against the usual standards for evaluating punishment, the death penalty doesn't make much sense. Obviously, killing a prisoner eliminates the possibility of rehabilitation; a corpse cannot go on to lead a more virtuous life. The goal of incapacitation is not advanced: the condemned man is already safely behind prison walls, unable to commit further crimes in free society. The supposed deterrent effect is illusory: as we have seen, executions appear actually to *increase* the level of violence in society. And since incapacitation and protection of society are just as effectively — and more cheaply — achieved through life imprisonment, killing the prisoner is simply unnecessary.

Moreover, how does the notion of killing murderers square with the cherished principle of "the sanctity of human life"? This idea is central to the world's great religions as well as the ancient Greek, Egyptian, Persian, and Babylonian moral philosophers. If life is sacred, it means that every person has the right to live simply by virtue of the fact that he or she is a living, breathing human being. This right is unearned and inalienable, in part because we are created "in the image of God." This basic principle certainly implies that the death penalty is morally wrong. However, three centuries ago, John Locke offered a classic defense of the death penalty on moral grounds. He argued that although the right to life is inherent and absolute, it is possible to "forfeit" one's right to life by committing a crime that "deserves death." His arguments have provided ammunition for supporters of capital punishment ever since. Locke also argued for severe punishment on the grounds of deterrence. He believed that we should punish "to the degree and with as much severity, as will suffice to make it an ill bargain to the offender, give him cause to repent, and terrify others from doing the like."

Another influential moral argument is usually traced to Immanuel Kant. He believed that murderers must be killed based on the principle of "equal" or "just" retribution:

> What kind and what degree of punishment does public legal justice adopt as its principle and standard? None other than the principle of equality . . . any undeserved evil that you inflict on someone else among the people is one that you do to yourself. . . . Only the law of retribution can determine exactly the kind and degree of punishment.

This idea has an elegant and appealing simplicity. It is an elaboration of the idea of *lex talionis* and is similar to the argument that murderers must be "paid back" in kind for their crimes. The principle of equality introduced by Kant seems to provide a standard that is independent of religious or political authority. And whereas Locke linked his notion of retribution to deterrence, Kant apparently felt that such practical considerations were not important enough to discuss.

Another argument offered in defense of the idea that justice requires the killing of murderers might be called the "moral solidarity" argument. If societies are held together, in part, by a shared consensus of what constitutes immoral behavior, then those who violate the moral order must be punished to restore moral balance in society. Further, for murderers, any punishment less than death is too weak to convey the strong sense of outrage and condemnation felt by the community. Only by killing the murderer can we repair the moral integrity of the larger community. In his book *For Capital Punishment,* Walter Berns puts it like this: 10

> [The death penalty] serves to remind us of the majesty of the moral order that is embodied in our law and of the terrible consequences of its breach. . . . The criminal law must be made awful, by which I mean awe-inspiring, or commanding "profound respect or reverential fear." It must remind us of the moral order by which alone we can live as human beings.

These arguments raise several questions. If by killing, murderers forfeit their right to live, does that mean that we are, in turn, *obliged* to kill them? Or will other forms of severe punishment suffice? If someone *deserves* to die, does it mean that we have the right to kill him? Should we try to induce in prisoners the equivalent amount of suffering they induced in their victims? Do executions really strengthen the moral solidarity of the community, or do they demean and corrupt the collective morality? Should executions be bloody, excruciating, and public to fully inspire awe and "reverential fear"? Is it necessary to kill in order to show that killing is wrong? And given the varied backgrounds and capacities of defendants, the diverse types of murder, and the limits of human understanding, is it even possible to decide fairly which murderers deserve to die?

The simplest counterargument is that, if killing is morally wrong, it is wrong for both the individual and the state. To be sure, there are circumstances where killing may be necessary, for example, when a police officer shoots a robber who is about to kill a clerk, when a soldier kills an enemy soldier during a time of war, when a woman shoots a violently abusive husband who is coming toward her brandishing a knife. These situations involve imminent danger, split-second decisions, and self-defense or defense of innocent others. Unlike police officers, who occasionally kill to protect their own lives or the lives of innocent people, the executioner performs an unnecessary killing, a killing that has nothing to do with self-defense, imminent danger, or the protection of society. The murderer has already been captured and waits in a prison cell safely isolated from the community.

The law of equal retribution proposed by Kant and others cannot be a literal prescription for how to punish violent criminals. We would find it morally repugnant to torture torturers, rape rapists, or terrorize terrorists. We do not try to kill murderers using the same method they used to kill their victims. Instead, we imprison them. Our efforts to mitigate punishments arise out of the recognition that we must not sink to the level of the criminal; raping a rapist would debase us, weaken our moral solidarity, and undermine the moral authority of the state. We cannot simply respond to cruelty with our own acts of cruelty. Acts of brutality committed by the state in the name of justice never ennoble us. There must be severe punishment for horrible crimes, but that does not oblige us to kill those who have killed.

Try as we might, we can never sever the ties between moral concerns and practical realities. *Morality can only be assessed in practice.* Even if we accept the morality of the death penalty in the abstract, we must always look at how it is administered in the real world. Is the death penalty still moral if innocent people are sometimes convicted or executed? Is it still moral if the race of the murderer or the victim play a substantial role in determining which defendants will be sentenced to die? Is it still moral if the ultimate penalty squanders money that could be more productively spent on preventing crime? Is it still moral if executions provoke, rather than deter, violent criminals? These questions must be answered before any final judgment can be made about the morality of the death penalty. Moral theory must give way to moral practice, and abstract benefits must be balanced against tangible costs. Defenders of capital punishment must defend this punishment *as it exists* in the real world.

Moral Responsibility and Free Will

Suppose a man has been convicted of a murder. In a jealous 15
rage, he rapes his ex-wife and then stabs her to death. Clearly, he
must be severely punished for his horrible crime. He has shown that
he is violent and society must be protected from him. His actions —
rape and murder — legally qualify him for the death penalty. But before deciding whether he should die in the execution chamber or
live out the rest of his life in prison, we must understand not only
the crime, but also the criminal.

Here are four possibilities. First, suppose that he is a young man
from a wealthy family who has enjoyed most of life's advantages: loving parents, material comfort, good schools, travel, and interesting
experiences. Next, suppose that he is a young man with a brutal past:
He and his mother suffered routine beatings from an abusive father
throughout his childhood and into his adolescence. He grew up in a
poverty-ridden, gang-infested neighborhood and received very little
in the way of parental guidance or supervision. Third, suppose that he
had an unremarkable middle-class background. He achieved his life's
dream of becoming a police officer and was honored several times for
his bravery. More than once he saved the lives of innocent by-
standers. Or, finally, suppose that the killer is indisputably psychotic
and that he had spent much of his life in mental institutions.

The striking differences in the backgrounds of these men raise
some disturbing questions. Are all four men equally deserving of
death? Are all four equally responsible for their crimes? If not
equally responsible, is one of them, say, 90 percent responsible, another 80 percent, 70 percent, or 60 percent responsible? Should
background even matter? Does the good service of the police officer
count for anything or should all four men be treated the same?
Would you be more inclined to show mercy if murderer number one
was brain damaged? If murderer number two was a heroin addict?
Any assessment of moral blameworthiness must go beyond the act
for which a person is on trial. All systems of justice recognize this.
That is not to say that the person's crime must be excused or that
the person must not be severely punished. He must be held accountable and he must be punished harshly. It is merely to say that even
identical crimes may have very different causes and may be the
product of very different life circumstances. We judge, convict, and
punish a person. And a person — even a person who has committed
a hideous crime — is more than the worst thing he or she has ever
done. We are obligated to look not only at the vicious act, but also to
struggle to understand the circumstances that produced the act, the
reasons and motives that lie beneath it.

Supporters of capital punishment would argue that this is precisely the kind of information jurors are instructed to take into

account when making the life-or-death decision. But the fact that jurors are told to take such information into account obscures the issue of our limited ability to understand the reasons behind someone else's actions. Imagine that you are a juror in a capital case. You have already decided that the defendant is guilty, and now you must decide whether he should be killed or sent to prison for the rest of his life. To decide whether to show mercy, you must make a full and fair assessment of the multitude of factors that led to the murder. To make this assessment, it is first necessary to have the defendant's important life events and experiences laid out before you: his upbringing, family environment, education, formative experiences, the things that shaped his character and behavior. You would also need to know something of his innate, inherited talents, abilities, and predilections. You would also need to have some understanding of how he responded to the events in his life, the impact of his experiences. Of course, it is impossible to know all of this. It is difficult enough to understand the behavior of people we have known for years. Even if we could manage to shut off our feelings of rage and revulsion, it would still be exceedingly difficult to find and consider enough information to allow us to fathom the reasons for a brutal murder. And, as a practical matter, no defendant or public defender can afford to present all the necessary information, and no set of jury instructions can adequately guide jurors in making this morally profound decision. Few defense attorneys even attempt to present sufficient information to make such an assessment.

Despite scientific advances in behavioral genetics and psychology, we are still a very long way from completely mapping out the motives, intentions, habits, interpretations, and situational pressures that propel a particular act of violence. The process is still mysterious. Perhaps if we had complete information and a year or two to sift through the information, we could arrive at a definitive answer to the question, Why did this person commit this terrible crime? But a thorough evaluation of moral culpability is clearly impossible within the constraints of the American courtroom. Some defenders present little information to help the jurors, and even the most careful defenders and prosecutors cannot uncover and present all of the reasons for the violent act. It is simply beyond human understanding. To believe that we can make such judgments is misguided hubris.

At the heart of the matter is an ancient and unresolvable philo- 20 sophical debate: free will versus determinism. Without at least an assumption of free will there can be no discussion of ethical behavior or criminal responsibility. Nearly all of us believe in some measure of free will, but we are all partly determinists too. Do you or do you not believe that you are a product of your genetic endowment and your life experiences? If you believe that your behavior is a function of inheritance and experience, you are, at least, a limited determinist, what William James, the great philosopher and psychologist, might have called a "soft determinist." Whereas the "hard determinist" insists that our actions are entirely determined, that no one is free to act differently from the way he or she does act, the soft determinist believes that we possess free will within the constraints imposed by heredity and environment. That, although our actions are not fully determined, our actions are strongly influenced by our conditioning, our values and habits, and the situations we find ourselves in.

In discussing the reasons behind criminal behavior, Stephen Nathanson argues that we must take into account the effort required by a criminal to resist criminal actions and the obstacles to moral behavior encountered by the criminal:

> A person's degree of moral desert is determined by considerations of what could reasonably be expected of him. If a person faces such powerful obstacles to moral behavior that it would require extraordinary amounts of effort to act well, then, though he acts badly, he is not morally to blame . . . different behavior could not reasonably be expected. The causes of difficulty need not be environmental. They could be physical, psychological, or of any sort, but if they make alternative actions extremely difficult or impossible, a person is not fully blameworthy for his deeds, even if they were wrong acts triggered by bad motives.

The philosopher Jeffrey Reiman takes an even broader view suggesting that the larger society must bear some responsibility for the actions of murderers. America spawns more vicious murderers than any other "civilized" country on earth. The social conditions that predictably produce violent offenders (e.g., poverty, routine exposure to violence as a child, access to lethal weapons) are at least partly to blame. It has been said that each nation gets the criminals it deserves. Put differently, a society bears responsibility for violent criminals to the extent that it tolerates social conditions that predictably lead to violence. Until these conditions are remediated, some of the blame rests with the larger community.

Let me be clear: The argument is not that murderers should be excused for their crimes. They must be held accountable and punished severely. The argument is that we cannot possibly fathom the multiple and subtle influences that cause a particular behavior. Instead of pretending omniscience, we should be more humble about our capacity to understand fully why someone commits a horrible crime. We can and should send a dangerous criminal to prison for the rest of his or her life, but we should not presume to judge which people deserve to live and which deserve to die. Our judgments are bound to be faulty.

Just Revenge

Beneath the usual justifications for punishing criminals lurks a more visceral and potent motive for the death penalty: revenge. The desire to lash back at those who have harmed us has deep roots in our evolutionary past. It is a powerful human motive that must be taken seriously, but it is not a sufficient justification for killing. Although individually we all feel the primitive urge to exact revenge against those who harm us, collectively we must strive to be more rational, fair, moral, and humane than the criminals who commit the acts of violence or cruelty that we condemn. We all sympathize with a bereaved father who attempts to kill the man who murdered his child. But a group's craving for revenge is far less innocent and immediate, and far less justifiable. A victim's relative who attempts to kill a murderer commits a crime of passion motivated by rage and grief. In contrast, the process leading up to a state-sponsored killing is slow, deliberate, methodical, and largely stripped of human emotion. The anger of families of victims is understandable, but anger should not be the basis of social policy. A community's angry cry for killing a murderer is far uglier than the anger felt by an individual who has been wronged by another.

We have all felt wronged and we have all experienced the power- 25
ful emotions that drive the hunger for revenge. The urge to see a murderer killed is rooted in the rage and revulsion that most Americans feel when they hear about a horrible, inexplicable murder. We empathize with the victim and the family of the victim, and we want to see the murderer pay dearly for his or her crime. In movies, operas, plays, and novels, exacting revenge on those who offend us is often portrayed as emotionally satisfying. But just because the appetite for revenge is real and powerful, that does not mean we should indulge our appetite or build it into our legal system. Justice must take precedence over revenge. Arthur Koestler made this point vividly: "Deep inside every civilized being there lurks a tiny Stone Age man, dangling a club to rob and rape, and screaming 'an eye for an eye.' But we would rather not have that little fur-clad figure dictate the law of the land." Feelings of anger and revulsion at a horrible crime are understandably human and may be even a healthy indication of concern for the welfare of others. However, even if we accept the legitimacy of anger, anger does not outweigh all other considerations. Feelings of outrage and the quest for revenge do not guarantee that punishments will be fairly or rationally imposed. Anger does not ensure justice; it is an obstacle to justice.

It would be immoral to execute everyone who kills another human being. Every legal system on earth recognizes this. Consequently, every nation with capital punishment must create some method of selecting out those killers who truly "deserve" to die. Because no selection process is perfect, bias, prejudice, and error

creep into every system of capital punishment. If the morality of revenge and the morality of the death penalty are to be defended, the
defense must be of the death penalty as it is administered in the real
world. Too often, defenders of the death penalty argue for its morality in a theoretical, idealized world. The claim that killing is morally
justified must be reconciled with disquieting facts: the inevitability
of wrongful convictions, the reality of discrimination on the basis of
wealth and race, the likelihood that executions increase the murder
rate, the reality that millions of dollars must be squandered to bring
about a single execution.

Killing is a morally acceptable penalty only if it is essential, and
only if it provides substantial benefits that cannot be gained by any
other means. Capital punishment is not just a moral abstraction. It is
a reality that must be evaluated on the basis of benefits and costs.

For the Death Penalty

ERNEST VAN DEN HAAG

There are two basic arguments for the death penalty; they are
independent of, yet consistent with, one another.

The first argument is moral: The death penalty is just; it is deserved for certain crimes. One can explain why one feels that certain
crimes deserve the death penalty. But as usual with moral arguments, one cannot show this conviction to be *factually* correct (or,
for that matter, incorrect) since moral arguments rest not on facts
but on our evaluation of them. My evaluation leads me to believe
that, e.g., premeditated murder or treason (a fact) is so grave and
horrible a crime (an evaluation) as to deserve nothing less than the
death penalty, that only the death penalty (a fact) is proportionate
to the gravity of the crime (an evaluation).

My widely shared view is opposed by abolitionists, who claim
that the death penalty is unjust for any crime, and inconsistent with
human dignity. Professor Conrad's arguments in favor of this position seem unconvincing to me. Since most abolitionists believe, as I
do, that punishments should be proportionate to the perceived
gravity of crimes, the abolitionist claim seems to me logically pre-
carious. It implies either that murder is not so horrible after all —

Ernest van den Haag is the retired John M. Olin Professor of Jurisprudence and
Public Policy at Fordham University. This essay is from *The Death Penalty Pro and
Con: A Debate* (1983). The negative side of this debate was defended by John P. Con-
rad, who has served as chief of the U.S. Bureau of Prisons.

not horrible enough, at any rate to deserve death — or that the death penalty is too harsh a punishment for it, and indeed for any conceivable crime. I find it hard to believe that one can hold either view seriously, let alone both. But I am wrong: Professor Conrad does, and he is by no means alone in the academic world.

I must confess that I have never understood the assorted arguments claiming that the death penalty is inconsistent with human dignity or that, somehow, society has no right to impose it. One might as well claim that death generally, or at least death from illness, is inconsistent with human dignity, or that birth is, or any suffering or any undesirable social condition. Most of these are unavoidable. At least death by execution can be avoided by not killing someone else, by not committing murder. One can preserve one's dignity in this respect if one values it. Incidentally, execution may be physically less humiliating and painful than death in a hospital. It is, however, morally more humiliating and meant to be: It indicates the extreme blame we attach to the crime of murder by deliberately expelling the murderer from among the living.

As for the dignity of society, it seems to me that by executing 5 murderers it tries to keep its promise to secure the lives of innocents, to vindicate the law, and to impose retribution on those who so horribly violate it. To do anything less would be inconsistent with the dignity of society.

I see no evidence for society somehow not having "the right" to execute murderers. It has always done so. Traditional laws and Scriptures have always supported the death penalty. I know of no reasoning, even in a religious (theocratic) state, that denies the right of secular courts to impose it. We in America have a secular republic, of course, and therefore, the suggestion that the right to punish belongs only to God, or that the right to impose capital punishment does, is clearly out of place. It is not a religious but a secular task to put murderers to death. Our Constitution does provide for it (Amendments V and XIV). However much we believe in divine justice, it is to occur after, not in, this life. As for justice here and now, it is done by the courts, which are authorized in certain cases to impose the death penalty. A secular state cannot leave it to God. And incidentally, no theocratic state ever has. If they make mistakes, one can hope that God will correct the courts hereafter — but this is no ground for depriving courts of their duty to impose the penalties provided by law where required, nor is it a ground for depriving the law of the ability to prescribe the punishments felt to be just, including the death penalty.

The second argument in favor of capital punishment is material, grounded on empirical facts. They are contested, as readers of this book know, but no one would deny that what is contested are facts. The factual question is: Does the death penalty deter murder more than life imprisonment, or does it make no difference?

I do not agree with Professor Conrad's wishful idea that the work of Professor Isaac Ehrlich has been discredited. I believe that Ehrlich's findings — that the death penalty does indeed deter more than any other penalty currently inflicted, so that each execution saves between seven and nine innocent lives, the lives of victims who will not be murdered in the year of execution because of the deterrent effects of executions — have been confirmed by subsequent studies and have stood up sturdily under criticism competent and incompetent, which Ehrlich has convincingly refuted. However, Ehrlich's work is controversial. Anything is, if a sufficient number of people attack it. It is fair, therefore, to say that although the preponderance of evidence is now supporting the hypothesis that capital punishment deters more than any other punishment, the statistical demonstration has not been conclusive enough to convince everybody. Certainly not Professor Conrad and his friends. They have not changed their pre-Ehrlich convictions, and indeed tend to dismiss his work.

But Conrad's fellow abolitionists have admitted that they would want to abolish the death penalty even if it were shown statistically that each execution does reduce the homicide rate by 500 murders per year. Why then worry about statistical proof? And why take seriously people so irrational that they would sacrifice the lives of 500 innocents to preserve the life of one convicted murderer?

Statistics have their place. But here I think they scarcely are 10 needed. Harsher penalties are more deterrent than milder ones. Not only does our whole criminal justice system accept this view; we all do to the extent to which deterrence is aimed at in our everyday life. All other things equal, we penalize our children, our friends, or our business partners the more harshly the more we feel we must deter them and others in the future from a wrong they have done. Social life would not be possible if we did not believe that we can attract people to actions we desire by giving them incentives, and deter them from actions we do not desire by disincentives. The incentives and disincentives are usually proportionate to the felt desirability or undesirability of what we want to attract to or deter from. Why should murder be an exception? Why should we not believe that the greatest disincentive — the threat of death — is most likely to be the greatest deterrent?

Where there is life there is hope. This certainly is one major argument in favor of the death penalty. The murderer who premeditates his crime — and crimes of passion are not subject to capital punishment — if he contemplates the risk of life imprisonment is not likely to believe that, if convicted, he will remain in prison for life. He knows, however inchoately, about parole, pardons, commutations — he believes above all that he, a smart and superior fellow, will find a way to escape. Few prisoners actually do escape. But practically all "lifers" believe that they will, at least when they start their sentence. So believing, they do not greatly fear a sentence of life imprisonment and are not deterred by it. This is why the rate of stranger-murders — murders in which victim and murderer do not know one another and to which the threat of the death penalty should apply — as a proportion of all murders has steadily climbed in the last twenty years. The murderers knew that in practice they would get away with life imprisonment, from which they would be paroled after a few years. Or they hoped they would escape. After all, we executed all of five prisoners in 1981, only one of whom was executed against his wishes. (All of them were white, to the great disappointment of the civil liberties lobby.) At this rate no murderer can foresee execution or be deterred by it.

I find it hard to believe, as Professor Conrad does, that most men are incapable of murder. I admire his optimism. But I find it hard to share. I do not see how he can cling to his faith after Stalin and Hitler, in the presence of assorted tyrants and murderers in power from Albania to Iran to China. But faith obviously is not subject to empirical verification. I am optimistic, however, in my own way, which seems more realistic to me: I believe that most men can be deterred from murder by the threat of the death penalty.

Even if Conrad were right, even if his claim that only a few men would ever become murderers in the absence of the threat of punishment were correct, I should continue to advocate the death penalty to deter these few men. And even if only some of these men need the threat of capital punishment to be deterred, while others would be deterred by the threat of life imprisonment, I should advocate the death penalty to deter the very few who, according to Conrad, do, or even just may, require it to be deterred. The lives of the innocents that will or may be spared because of the death penalty are more valuable to me, and to any civilized society, than the lives of murderers. I do not want to risk their lives for the sake of the lives of murderers.

The reader will have to decide for himself on which side he wants to be.

Even Prisoners Must Have Hope

RICHARD STRATTON

I did eight years in federal prison for smuggling marijuana. I was punished, I was demeaned, and I was scared. I waded through sewage backed up from toilets. I lived in overcrowded cells. I saw men brutally beaten. It could have been worse: It could have been pointless. I wasn't condemned to idleness. I wasn't denied a place to exercise, a television to watch, an education to embrace. By the time I left prison, I had earned a bachelor's degree, written a novel, mastered enough law to get out early. Now I have a wife, two sons, a job, and a message: Don't make prisons more miserable than they already are.

For all the lip service once paid to rehabilitation in this country, imprisonment in America is about nothing but punishment, and punishment is the intentional infliction of pain by those in power upon the less powerful. In the United States we equate justice with vengeance; we embrace the theory of "just deserts" for criminals and deviants. Instead of improving the harsh conditions that create crime and violence, which might restore peace and harmony to our society, we inflict more pain, more punishment, thus creating more crime and more violence.

The get-tough-on-crime attitudes of the 1980s have given us rampant, desperate inner-city crime and violence in the 1990s. If we continue with our vengeful attitude toward criminals (poor minorities, the mentally ill, those who have nothing to lose), the violence will only get worse until there is an all-out war between the haves and the have-nots. Do I overstate? Maybe. For the moment, most violent felons attack people who live near them, who look like them, who share the same social class. Will the crime stay confined? I saw that hate festering in the American gulag all during the 1980s. Now I am watching it spill into the streets.

Today's politically motivated campaigns to make prison conditions even harsher are so wrongheaded it scares me — not because I fear the conditions but because I fear the rage and violence that will ricochet back at society. The only prison programs that have consistently been proven to reduce recidivism and temper violence are the education and counseling programs designed to help prisoners make positive changes in their lives. Prisoners who seek out some

---

Richard Stratton is the editor of *Prison Life*. This editorial appeared in *Newsweek* on October 17, 1994.

sort of education while in prison have a very low recidivism rate. Yet we have eliminated Pell grants for prisoners and have cut back or discontinued other highly effective programs.

To do justice, to break the cycle of violence, to make America 5 safer, prisons need to offer inmates a chance to heal like a human, not merely to heel like a dog. Society is right to expect that prisons will promote respect for the dominant culture and our laws. But how? To paraphrase Malcolm X, a man who has nothing to lose is a dangerous man. Take away what rights prisoners have and no one will be safe — not the guards, not the police, not even the other prisoners.

Prisoners, no matter how heinous their crime, have a right to our compassion and understanding, just as their victims have a right to restitution and to healing, just as society has a right to be protected. Prisoners have a right to hope, they have a right to opportunities that will enable them to change the behavior that led them to crime, and they have a right to reenter society after they've done their time. Prisoners have a right to become welcome members of society instead of brutalized and brutal outcasts.

The Law and Shame

JAMES B. TWITCHELL

The word *stigma* means blot or blemish and is a signifier of inflicted shame. The word comes to us from Latin, as the Romans literally branded unruly slaves and criminals. These brands were lightly burnt onto the skin and disappeared within a few years. Many of those branded were Christians. In a provocative bit of cultural jujitsu, early Christianity picked up the concept and applied it retroactively to the wounds of Christ. His wounds received on the cross would miraculously appear on the hands of a true penitent: the stigmata.

A stigma is different from a "mark," which is deep within the body. The mark of Cain, for instance, is forever embedded in an entire race. Or a witch's mark is impossible to remove. You should temporarily shun someone with a stigma. But you should avoid forever someone with a mark. What stigma is to mark, humiliation is to banishment.

James B. Twitchell is Alumni Professor of English at the University of Florida and the author of seven nonfiction books. Reprinted here is an excerpt from his book *For Shame: The Loss of Common Decency in American Culture* (1997).

All cultures apply stigmas. In many parts of the world some kind of face or body paint is used. The system used to allocate stigmas is called the law. Stigmas have to be applied with great caution lest they become subverted, as the Romans learned. The key to their effective use is not their application, but the willingness of those who see them to respond by shunning. Wrongly applied, they become "badges."

In American history the best-known use of stigmas was by the Puritans. Who does not know of Hester Prynne's scarlet letter? What we don't realize is that an entire alphabet was used. So in Maryland, for instance, county justices could brand *H* for hog stealer, *R* for runaway slave, or *T* for thief. Colonial America was an ideal culture for such shaming. Here was an isolated community with real danger around the edges. Being cast out, if only temporarily, meant confronting genuine peril. There was great safety in conformity, in circling the wagons, in living close. In addition, being incarcerated meant social and financial expense for the group. How much more efficient to use the pillory, dunking stools, stocks, or even branding, and let public opprobrium bring the miscreant back into line. Tar and a few feathers did the work of jail.

Oh mercy! we say. How cruel and heartless were our colonial ancestors. We prefer to use small, costly iron boxes far from public view. We forget that the rise of imprisonment was an aspect of the great social transformation of Romanticism. Assuming man to be naturally good (Rousseau's noble savage, Wordsworth's "Mighty Prophet! Seer Blest!" and all that), putting misfits in jail was thought to literally give them a chance to re-form. Like liquids of different density shaken up, the natural goodness would float to the top. *Penitentiary* originally meant a place to do penance, to get "in touch" with your better self. That sentimental view is long past. Today many people seem to spend their entire lives going into and out of the cages. In fact, a considerable percentage of our population now believes that a little prison time is part of standard maturation. Many of the rest of us seem willing to let this occur. So when the demand for boxes outstrips the supply, we just build more of them. What an irony! The less effective prisons are in reducing crime, the higher the demand for still more imprisonment.

Not everyone, however, agrees. In recent years the dispensers of the law are finally realizing that shame has a place in punishment. Stigma, judiciously applied, can be a far more efficient method of behavioral modification than cage time. In one of the best overviews of the legal situation, Dan Kahan, a professor in the University of Chicago Law School, concludes "What Do Alternative Sanctions Mean?" by contending that shaming can be an equitable method of punishment. Properly administered, degradation ceremonies are inexpensive, efficient, fair, and an effective deterrent.

So we find judges in Florida insisting that, after repeated offenses, drunk drivers apply a neon sticker or special license plates to their cars, alerting all of danger. A slumlord is sentenced to house arrest in one of his rat-infested tenements. He is greeted with this sign: Welcome Reptile! In other cases, this time in Rhode Island, child molesters have been forced to pay for their pictures inserted in a local newspaper with the caption "I was convicted for child molestation. If you are a child molester, get professional help immediately, or you may find your picture and name in the paper and your life under control of the state." "Megan's Law" in New Jersey gives county prosecutors the right to inform neighbors of a relocating offender. A repeat offender has been required to post signs with letters at least three inches high around his residence and car: DANGEROUS SEX OFFENDER — NO CHILDREN ALLOWED.

Shaming works best in a population sensitive to social degradation. Ask an adolescent male which he prefers — suspension from school for a week or having to wear a frilly bonnet for an hour in gym class — and you'll find out. A purse snatcher in high school is forced to put taps in his shoes. In the *New York Times* of March 24, 1996, is a photograph of a young man whose punishment was to stand for a weekend in front of the gas station where he had skimmed cash, holding a sign saying "I am a thief."

In my estimation, ten minutes under the dunce cap may have done more than vials of Ritalin for those suffering from attention deficit disorder, dysrationalia, or whatever affliction du jour is conjured up by counselors and drug companies, accepted by gullible parents, and haltingly paid for by insurance companies.

One of the most efficient ways of collecting unpaid student loans 10 has been for the collection agency to send a list of truants to the local newspapers. This has worked wonders, especially with doctors and lawyers. The most efficient way to collect past-due land taxes is often to insert a flyer in the newspaper with the names of debtors. So, too, in Miami and other cities, the posting of the names of "johns" on freeway billboards seems to deter prostitution.

One of the more interesting uses of shaming is the "perp walk" performed daily in many big cities. It is a standard scene on the evening news, captured every day in the city's papers, the brief moment when the alleged perpetrator of whatever latest atrocity is walked by police out the door of a station house. We watch as an accused murderer or mobster, helplessly handcuffed, is dragged through a horde of screaming reporters and jostling photographers. You naturally assume you're seeing a barbaric mob wreaking random havoc. What we don't see is that this is a choreographed ritual for shaming, all parties participating for the camera.

In New York, for instance, the perp walk is a vital part of the criminal justice system, with its own etiquette and traditions. It depends on the collusion of police, photographers, and editors. When time is short, the walk is from one door of the courthouse to another, just long enough for the pictures to be taken. This is called "perp parade" and it has to be done well before the evening news deadlines. In the old days, the perp was allowed a coat to hide behind, but in the modern version he has only his hands. Sometimes the perp refuses to cooperate, as with John Gotti, who was unfailingly polite and chatted up the reporters.

The most recent revival of a shaming ritual long out of fashion is the chain gang. The once common sight of felons in chains breaking rocks, or road crews in groups of five linked with eight-foot chains, disappeared about thirty years ago. After the 1932 film classic *I Am a Fugitive from a Chain Gang* portrayed brutal conditions for prisoners, states removed leg irons from work crews. Now public opinion has changed again. *Cool Hand Luke* is already a generation old, long forgotten. When revoking an inmate's television privileges is the commonest form of discipline (or so the public believes), something else must be done. So the chain gangs are now reappearing, and with much hoopla.

First in Alabama (which prides itself on this kind of thing), then Florida, and then in southwestern states like Arizona, men in specially colored garb (not the broad black-and-white stripes of yore) are linked together to pound pebbles out of rocks. This is occurring in full public view; in fact, the press is encouraged to cover it. Although the prisoners voluntarily choose the work details, the predictable criticism has resulted, along with the expected euphemisms. In press releases the Florida Department of Corrections, confusing purpose with its own PR, calls it the Restricted Labor Squad.

In the *New York Times Magazine* of September 17, 1995, under a two-page full-color photo showing just the legs of inmates (all African Americans, incidentally and most unfortunately; the article later went on to point out that the five-man groups are usually "racially correct" — three blacks and two whites apiece), is this caption: 15

> Roadside Attraction — The fiction is that chain-gang work is rehabilitating. The reality is that it is pure spectacle. Above: An eyeful for motorists on Interstate 65 near Huntsville, Ala. Opposite: Handcuffs are removed so a prisoner can perform the useless task of breaking rocks.

Brent Staples, who usually writes for the editorial page, continues the caption's sentiment in the text below:

> Any animal with teeth enough will chew off its leg to escape a trap. Human beings behaved similarly when chain gang imprisonment — a successor to slavery — swept through the labor-starved South during Reconstruction. Beaten and driven like maltreated beasts, shackled to

one another around the clock, prisoners turned to self-mutilation to make themselves useless for work. They slashed their bodies, broke their own legs, crippled themselves by cutting their tendons.

Staples goes on to reiterate that the work the gangs do is value-less, that this represents a resurgence of spectacle into American life, that "the men in shackles and white suits are medium-security prisoners — not quite the ax murderers, assassins, and sundry death-row candidates that onlookers might wish to imagine. The gangs are made up of nonviolent criminals only — check forgers, deadbeat dads, safe crackers, parole violators," and that people pass by the carful to gawk.

All this that Mr. Staples condemns is, of course, exactly the point. Public punishment, something long lost in our culture, should be directed to work of no value. What you did in the stocks is just sit there. You lost face. You were degraded. The act is a "spectacle" on purpose. It needs to be watched by others if it is to have the desired effect. And, perhaps most important, shame will not affect ax mur-derers and "sundry death-row candidates." Who wants to shame them? Check forgers, deadbeat dads, all manner of bullies, and pa-role violators are another matter.

How degenerate, how Southern, and how barbaric, says the ever urbane Mr. Staples, mindful of the world view of his more usual habi-tat. Do a Nexis search of the use of shame on the editorial page of the *Times* and you will see it is one of their favorite invocations. Shame on this, shame on that, they say about once a month. How much of *their* shaming sticks?

Often modern shaming depends on the proper use of media. A generation ago the editorial page might have worked. Shame worked in preelectronic cultures wherever people couldn't get away from their communications environment — a neighborhood, a town, a village. Once people began to wander away, shame didn't work as well. The malfeasant could escape the hot blush by ducking into a corner for a while. You need to know that you are known to be shamed.

For most of us, the speed of communication has changed to 186,000 miles a second. So it means that you can reach anyone any-where in the country in less than a sixtieth of a second. Everyone, everywhere. But alas, not in your backyard. This makes shame one of the most powerful means of social control again — if you know how to use it.

Advertisers have become especially susceptible to countrywide shaming. Large corporations that produce essentially interchange-able products like toothpaste or automobiles know that an annoyed customer is often far more potent than a satisfied one. You may not switch brands because one is better than another (rarely the case),

20

but you may switch because you don't like something the company is doing elsewhere. Even worse than a dissatisfied customer is an outraged one who complains not about the product but about your entire way of doing business. Sears Roebuck and Unilever reduced their advertising budgets for trash TV as the direct result of bad press and fears of alienating customers.

Avoiding public shaming is one reason why cigarette companies like RJR-Nabisco and Philip Morris attempt to keep their nasty products away from their other brands. This is also why they are so skittish about what entertainment they sponsor lest they disturb a small, vociferous audience. It is also why they are finally willing to 'fess up to their past subterfuges. For instance, the shaming of large corporations that sponsor violence on television such as General Motors and the U.S. Army has proven one of the few predictable ways to temper content. Calvin Klein pulled ads featuring pubescents in their underwear because of public outrage. Time Warner got rid of its highly profitable interest in gangsta rap because it was publicly humiliated by the unlikely team of William Bennett of Empower America, C. Delores Tucker of the National Congress of Black Women, and countless editorial writers.

Many cities are finding that their local-access television station, made possible by the coaxial cable, is also a powerful tool. So in Seattle a list of those convicted of soliciting prostitution and of repeated drunk driving is regularly scrolled down the screen. For six months the city of Miami flashed names and addresses of sex buyers on the city's cable channel, Met 9. Cable officials said the program attracts a big audience, but legal problems put an end to the practice as the names of some innocent people were accidentally included. Although prostitutes continue to ply their trade, officials say that embarrassing sex customers has worked.

There is no doubt that using shame as punishment is dangerous. Shaming is very volatile and must be used with extreme caution. True, we may not be the ideal culture in which shaming can function. Island communities are most sensitive. We are not the Japanese, Eskimos, Easter Islanders, or the colonial Puritans. But even so, we are filled with social islands. Internet users, for instance, are susceptible to "flaming" or criticism on the screen. Why not use it to shame virus-spreading hackers? Adolescents, who cause much of modern crime, are island dwellers. Gangs, football teams, and fraternities depend on shame, often brutally delivered. Why not try to leach some of that power in the name of social harmony?

To many of the have-nots in our culture, the threat of social degra- 25 dation as currently delivered is hollow. But to conclude that inhabitants of the inner cities can't respond to shame is as ridiculous as the nineteenth-century idea that nonwhites could not blush and hence were shameless. Quite the opposite, as Sheldon Zhang has argued in "Measuring Shame in an Ethnic Context." As with other discriminated-against groups like Gypsies, blacks are probably more susceptible to shame than their white inner-city counterparts. The thesis of Fox Butterfield's recent *All God's Children* is that the roots of black violence lie in the internalizing of antebellum white codes of honor and shame.

Much of ghetto organization is based on boundaries drawn by shaming. The power of being disrespected, of being "dissed," shows the shame fields are indeed electrified. The law should work with that community to find out what is appropriate. We may need to be equal *before* the law, but not necessarily punished in exactly the same way. Punishments need to fit the crime, the criminal, and the community.

In my state of Florida, for instance, the police have protected marchers who chant at drug dealers, "Drug dealer, drug dealer, you ain't cool — you're just acting like a fool" and "If you keep selling that crack, we'll be back." The police have stepped aside while the marchers have drawn chalk arrows in the street pointing at a drug dealer's house. The best part of such shaming is that residents see themselves as enforcing their own standards. They chant to their neighbors, "Neighbor, neighbor, don't you hide — come on out and join our side" and "If you can't join the fight, turn on your porch light." The lights, as Mireya Navarro reports for the *New York Times* of August 30, 1996, flicker on.

The main problem with shame is that, once applied, it can't be controlled. In the science of modern punishment, perhaps too much has been made of maintaining control. Classical penology isolated four ends of punishment: retribution, rehabilitation, deterrence, and incapacitation. Only incapacitation can be controlled with any predictability. Even that is hardly precise. At least three million people now pass through state and federal cages each year, costing billions of dollars (at $20,000 per young prisoner and $69,000 for those over age sixty) and doing untold damage (8 to 16 percent are victims of sexual assault while in prison). Our current incarceration rate of 519 per 100,000 is five times greater than most industrial nations. The figures for Mexico and Japan are 97 and 36 respectively. If the rates of recidivism are correct, many of these dollars are being inefficiently spent. Rehabilitation has not occurred; it is often not even attempted. The risk/reward ratios may be moving in favor of shaming, if only because other methods have proven so wasteful, so spiteful, and so — dare I say it? — racist. Does anyone really doubt that the high percentage of blacks in the prison population mutes the public reaction to an unsatisfactory penal situation?

In addition, we need to restore shaming as a legitimate topic of cultural conversation. Although it is not politically correct or easy to discuss, stigmatizing behavior is not always so dangerous as its alternatives. Not demeaning certain behavior is sometimes worse. Look at it in reverse. Behavior once stigmatized as deviant is now tolerated and even sanctioned. Divorce and illegitimacy, once seen as betokening the breakdown of the family, are now viewed benignly. Illegitimacy has been officially rebaptised as "nonmarital childbearing," and divorced and unmarried mothers and fathers are lumped together in the category of "single-parent families." Addiction has become not a function of willpower but of genetic determinism. Violence is often considered an economic strategy, not a reckless disregard for the rights of others. Are we better off for having removed the stigma that surrounded these events? While it may be comforting to think the stifling oppression of Victorian shame is lifting, what is underneath may be worse.

THINKING AND WRITING ABOUT PUNISHMENT

Questions for Discussion and Writing

1. Why does Wasserstrom favor punishment even if the criminal will never commit another crime? What are his objections to Lady Wootton's proposal for "a system of social control"? Do they seem valid?
2. How do you respond to the arguments about the caning of Michael Fay? Do you think that corporal punishment would be effective in reducing juvenile crime in the United States?
3. What does Newman mean by symbolic punishment? Do his twenty-one rules for punishment fulfill the criteria for fairness and effectiveness for punishment? Are there portions of Newman's argument with which you disagree? Defend your point of view.
4. Which of Garcetti's proposals seems easiest to implement? Which most difficult to implement? Give reasons for your answer. Does O'Leary's attitude seem appropriate to the problem or too harsh? Can you think of other solutions to the problem of juvenile criminality?
5. Summarize the arguments of Van den Haag and Costanzo for and against capital punishment. On what issues do they disagree? Do some important questions remain unanswered? Which argument seems stronger? Explain the reasons for your answer.
6. Stratton's article appeared in 1994. Since then crime has decreased, in part, some experts think, because of longer and more frequent prison terms. Does this information influence your evaluation of Stratton's argument? Why or why not?
7. Twitchell mentions a number of activities, both legal and illegal, in which shaming has produced results. Do you agree that all the activities he names justify shaming?
8. What is the cartoonist saying about prison terms as deterrents to crime?

"LAST SPRING YOU ROBBED ME AND GOT 3 YEARS. LAST MONTH YOU NAILED ME AGAIN AND GOT 5 TO 10 ... HAVEN'T YOU LEARNED YOUR LESSON YET?"

Topics for Research

Alternatives to incarceration for petty crime

The reality of prison life

History of corporal punishment in the schools

Rehabilitation programs: What works?

TAKING THE DEBATE ONLINE

- **Steve's Criminal Justice Corner <http://web2.airmail.net/tosca/Steves .html>** This exhaustive site created by a criminal justice student provides scores of links to correction and prison resources around the country, crime statistics and theories, courts and criminal law sites, and much more.

- **Juvenile Punishment <http://crime.miningco.com/library/blfiles/ bljuvp.htm>** Some of the topics covered in this long list of links compiled by miningco.com include alternatives to imprisonment, the death penalty and minors, and juvenile justice versus adult justice.

- **Angel on Death Row <http://www2.pbs.org/wgbh/pages/frontline/ angel>** Part of the PBS online website, this *Frontline* special focuses on the real-life cases in the movie *Dead Man Walking* and includes interviews with some of the principal people involved in the case. It also presents opposing views on the death penalty from two U.S. Supreme Court justices, two legal scholars, U.S. Roman Catholic bishops, and Pope John Paul II.

- **Death Penalty Information and Resources** **<http://sun.soci.niu.edu/ ~critcrim/dp/dp.html>** Some of the many links compiled at this exhaustive site on the death penalty include general information, statistics, papers, fact sheets, litigation and legislation, information on religion and the death penalty, and arguments in support of the death penalty.

- **Death Penalty Information Center** **<http://www.essential.org/dpic>** Selected as the *Legal Times'* Site of the Week, this site provides extensive statistical information on more than a dozen topics, including women and juveniles on death row, race factors, costs of execution, the question of deterrence, and state-by-state information.

- **Wesley Lowe's Pro Death Penalty Web Page** **<http://www.rit.edu/ ~wwl2461/cp.html>** Wesley Lowe, a student at the Rochester Institute of Technology, dedicated his page to murder victims. Some of the topics he covers are the historical evidence of deterrence, capital punishment versus life without parole, racism issues, the risk of executing innocent people, and more.

CHAPTER EIGHTEEN

Sexual Harassment

Sexual harassment, like affirmative action, has traveled a winding path from its original source. In 1964, when the Civil Rights Act accepted anti-discrimination provisions on sex, the term *sexual harassment* had not yet been coined. In 1977, however, the courts ruled on a violation of the act, called *quid pro quo,* in which an employee was punished by a supervisor for rejecting a sexual advance. A second kind of harassment, which emerged in a U.S. Supreme Court ruling in 1986, introduced the term *hostile environment,* a far looser definition, in which speech or conduct alone, even if not accompanied by a demotion or discharge from employment or a reduction in pay, is discriminatory and punishable by law.

Quid pro quo cases are hard to prove, and most sexual harassment cases now accuse a defendant of creating a hostile environment in a workplace or a school that prevents the plaintiff from performing effectively. Because *hostile environment* is so broadly defined, it has been increasingly difficult for employers to know exactly what rules to impose or for employees to know exactly when they have violated a rule. Some critics think that the rules governing conduct in the workplace have gone too far. Judith Vladeck, a New York employment lawyer, objects that by "so sanitizing the workplace . . . you're removing any pleasure in the relationships among people who work together."[1]

Court cases on sexual harassment sometimes collide with the right to free speech. For example, Florida shipyard workers were barred from bringing in "reading material deemed sexually suggestive — like novels."[2] Colleges and universities have not been im-

---

[1]*New York Times,* March 22, 1998, p. Wk 4.

[2]Walter Olson, "The Long Arm of Harassment Law," *New York Times,* July 7, 1996, p. E7.

mune from such controversies. At one New England college a professor was suspended after being accused by a student of using sexual metaphors in a writing class. But he returned to work after a judge ruled that his First Amendment rights had been violated.

The lawyer quoted above emphasizes that, despite some frivolous lawsuits and setbacks in court, a real problem exists. "What I think is getting lost, now that the issue has become so sensational, is that sexual harassment is a serious, significant problem to working women." Recent Supreme Court rulings have clarified some issues and identified new kinds of harassment complaints "from people who turned down sexual advances or felt threatened in the workplace but did not suffer professional harm, and from men and women intimidated by the behavior of people of the same sex."

In the late 1990s accusations of sexual harassment moved to the elementary school. The Clinton administration, joined by a number of organizations, urged the courts "to recognize peer harassment for children," claiming that "our schools, in many respects, are training grounds for sexual harassment."[3] Not all observers applauded such intervention. One critic argued that "lawsuits force schools to treat normal boys as sexual culprits."[4]

Despite the confusion, advocates on both sides agree that the crucial word in any definition of acceptable conduct in the workplace or at school is *reasonable.* As one of the following articles makes clear, however, reasonable people don't always agree on what constitutes reasonable conduct. One problem is that harassment is often a matter of subjective interpretation, and creating policies that can accommodate conflicting interpretations of behavior has proved difficult.

---

[3]Margot Slade, "Tales from the Front Line of Sexual Harassment," *New York Times,* July 19, 1998, p. Wk 3.

[4]Christina Hoff Sommers, "The Pre-teen Sexual Harasser," *New York Times,* January 9, 1999, p. A19.

What Sexual Harassment Is — and Is Not

ELLEN BRAVO AND ELLEN CASSEDY

Louette Colombano was one of the first female police officers in her San Francisco district. While listening to the watch commander, she and the other officers stood at attention with their hands behind their backs. The officer behind her unzipped his fly and rubbed his penis against her hands.

Diane, a buyer, was preparing to meet an out-of-town client for dinner when she received a message: her boss had informed the client that she would spend the night with him. Diane sent word that she couldn't make it to dinner. The next day she was fired.

Few people would disagree that these are clear-cut examples of sexual harassment. Touching someone in a deliberately sexual way, demanding that an employee engage in sex or lose her job — such behavior is clearly out of bounds. (It's also *illegal*. . . .) But in less obvious cases, many people are confused about where to draw the line.

Is It Harassment?

Is all sexual conversation inappropriate at work? Is every kind of touching off limits? Consider the following examples. In your opinion, which, if any, constitute sexual harassment?

- A male manager asks a female subordinate to lunch to discuss a new project.
- A man puts his arm around a woman at work.
- A woman tells an off-color joke.
- These comments are made at the workplace:

  "Your hair looks terrific."

  "That outfit's a knockout."

  "Did you get any last night?"

The answer in each of these cases is, "It depends." Each one 5 *could* be an example of sexual harassment — or it could be acceptable behavior.

Ellen Bravo is the codirector of 9to5, an organization for working women. Ellen Cassedy, a founder of 9to5, is a writer based in Washington, D.C. This article is excerpted from their book, *The 9 to 5 Guide to Combating Sexual Harassment* (New York: John Wiley & Sons, 1992). Reprinted by permission of John Wiley & Sons, Inc.

Take the case of the manager asking a female subordinate to lunch to discuss a new project. Suppose this manager often has such lunchtime meetings with his employees, male and female. Everyone is aware that he likes to get out of the office environment in order to get to know the associates a little better and to learn how they function — for example, whether they prefer frequent meetings or written reports, detailed instructions or more delegation of responsibility. The female subordinate in this case may feel she's being treated just like other colleagues and be glad to receive the individual attention.

On the other hand, suppose this subordinate has been trying for some time, unsuccessfully, to be assigned to an interesting project. The only woman who does get plum assignments spends a lot of time out of the office with the boss; the two of them are rumored to be sleeping together. The lunch may represent an opportunity to move ahead, but it could mean that the manager expects a physical relationship in return. In this case, an invitation to lunch with the boss is laden with unwelcome sexual overtones.

An arm around the shoulder, an off-color joke, comments about someone's appearance, or even sexual remarks may or may not be offensive. What matters is the relationship between the two parties and how each of them feels.

"Your hair looks terrific," for instance, could be an innocuous compliment if it were tossed off by one co-worker to another as they passed in the hall. But imagine this same phrase coming from a male boss bending down next to his secretary's ear and speaking in a suggestive whisper. Suddenly, these innocent-sounding words take on a different meaning. The body language and tone of voice signify something sexual. While the comment itself may not amount to much, the secretary is left to wonder *what else the boss has in mind.*

On the other hand, even words that may seem grossly inappropriate — "Did you get any last night?" — can be harmless in certain work situations. One group of male and female assembly-line workers talked like this all the time. What made it okay? They were friends and equals — no one in the group had power over any of the others. They were all comfortable with the banter. They hadn't drawn up a list specifying which words were acceptable to the group and which were not. But they had worked together for some time and knew one another well. Their remarks were made with affection and accepted as good-natured. No one intended to offend — and no one was offended. The assembly-line area was relatively isolated, so the workers weren't in danger of bothering anyone outside their group. Had a new person joined the group who wasn't comfortable with this kind of talk, the others would have stopped it. They might have thought the new person uptight, they might not have liked the new atmosphere, but they would have respected and honored any request to eliminate the remarks.

This is the essence of combating sexual harassment — creating a workplace that is built on mutual respect.

Looking at Harassment

Try assessing whether each of the following scenarios constitutes sexual harassment. Then consider the analysis that follows.

Scenario 1: Justine works in a predominantly male department. She has tried to fit in, even laughing on occasion at the frequent sexual jokes. The truth is, though, that she gets more irritated by the jokes each day. It is well known in the department that Justine has an out-of-town boyfriend whom she sees most weekends. Nonetheless, Franklin, one of Justine's co-workers, has said he has the "hots" for her and that — boyfriend or not — he's willing to do almost anything to get a date with her. One day, Sarah, another of Justine's co-workers, overheard their boss talking to Franklin in the hallway. "If you can get her to go to bed with you," the boss said, "I'll take you out to dinner. Good luck." They chuckled and went their separate ways. (From the consulting firm of Jane C. Edmonds & Associates, Inc., *Boston Globe,* 10/24/91.)

The boss is out of line. True, he probably didn't intend anyone to overhear him. But why was he having this conversation in the hallway? What was he doing having the conversation at all? The boss is responsible for keeping the workplace free of harassment. Instead, he's giving Franklin an incentive to make sexual advances to a co-worker and then to brag about it.

The conversation may constitute harassment not only of Justine but also of Sarah, who overheard the conversation. A reasonable woman might easily wonder, "Who's he going to encourage to go after *me*?" Ideally, Sarah should tell the two men she was offended by their remarks. But given that one of them is her boss, it would be understandable if she were reluctant to criticize his behavior.

Franklin isn't just romantically interested in Justine; he "has the hots" for her and is willing to "do almost anything" to get a date with her. Justine could well be interested in a "fling" with Franklin. But she's irritated by the sexual remarks and innuendoes in the workplace. It's unlikely that she would be flattered by attention from one of the men responsible for this atmosphere.

Justine can just say no to Franklin. But she may well object to having to say no over and over. And most women are not pleased to be the brunt of jokes and boasts. Some may argue that whether Franklin and Justine get together is a personal matter between the two of them. The moment it becomes the subject of public boasting, however, Franklin's interest in Justine ceases to be just a private interaction.

The law doesn't say Justine should be tough enough to speak up on her own — it says the company is responsible for providing an environment free of offensive or hostile behavior. As the person in charge, the boss ought to know what kind of remarks are being made in the workplace and whether employees are offended by them. Instead of making Franklin think the way to win favor with him is to pressure a co-worker into bed, the manager might want to arrange for some training on sexual harassment.

Scenario 2: Freda has been working for Bruce for three years. He believes they have a good working relationship. Freda has never complained to Bruce about anything and appears to be happy in her job. Bruce regularly compliments Freda on her clothing; in his opinion, she has excellent taste and a good figure. Typically, he'll make a remark like "You sure look good today." Last week, Freda was having a bad day and told Bruce that she was "sick and tired of being treated like a sex object." Bruce was stunned. (From the consulting firm of Jane C. Edmonds & Associates, Inc., *Boston Globe,* 10/24/91.)

There's really not enough information to come to any conclusion in this case. The scenario explains how Bruce feels, but not Freda. In the past, when he said, "Hey, you look good today," did Freda usually answer, "So do you"? Or did he murmur, "Mmm, you look go-o-o-o-d," and stare at her chest while she crossed her arms and said, "Thank you, sir"? In addition to complimenting Freda's appearance, did Bruce ever praise her work? Did he compliment other women? Men?

It is plausible that Freda might have been upset earlier. She probably wouldn't say she was tired of being treated like a sex object unless she'd felt that way before. Why didn't she speak up sooner? It's not uncommon for someone in Freda's situation to be reluctant to say anything for fear of looking foolish or appearing to be a "bad sport." Remember, Bruce is her boss.

Bruce states that he was stunned when Freda blew up at him. He needs to consider whether Freda might have given him any signals he ignored. He should ask himself how his compliments fit in with the way he treats other employees. Has he really given Freda an opening to object to his remarks?

The most comfortable solution might be for Bruce and Freda to sit down and talk. Perhaps Freda doesn't really mind the compliments themselves but wants more attention paid to her work. If Freda has been upset about the compliments all along, Bruce is probably guilty only of not paying close attention to her feelings. He should let her know that he values her work *and* her feelings, listen carefully to what she has to say, and encourage her to speak up promptly about issues that may arise in the future.

Scenario 3: Barbara is a receptionist for a printing company. Surrounding her desk are five versions of ads printed by the company for a beer distributor. The posters feature women provocatively posed with a can of beer and the slogan, "What'll you have?" On numerous occasions, male customers have walked in, looked at the posters, and commented, "I'll have you, baby." When Barbara tells her boss she wants the posters removed, he responds by saying they represent the company's work and he's proud to display them. He claims no one but Barbara is bothered by the posters.

The legal standard in this case is not how the boss feels, but whether a "reasonable woman" might object to being surrounded by such posters. The company has other products it could display. Barbara has not insisted that the company refuse this account or exclude these posters from the company portfolio. She has merely said she doesn't want the posters displayed around *her* desk. Barbara's view is substantiated by how she's been treated; the posters seem to give customers license to make suggestive remarks to her.

Scenario 4: Therese tells Andrew, her subordinate, that she needs him to escort her to a party. She says she's selecting him because he's the most handsome guy on her staff. Andrew says he's busy. Therese responds that she expects people on her staff to be team players.

Therese may have wanted Andrew merely to accompany her to the party, not to have a sexual relationship with her. And Andrew might have been willing to go along if he hadn't been busy. Nevertheless, a reasonable employee may worry about what the boss means by such a request, particularly when it's coupled with remarks about personal appearance.

Andrew might not mind that Therese finds him handsome. But most people would object to having their job tied to their willingness to make a social appearance with the boss outside of work. The implicit threat also makes Therese's request unacceptable. The company should prohibit managers from requiring subordinates to escort them to social engagements.

Scenario 5: Darlene invites her co-worker Dan for a date. They begin a relationship that lasts several months. Then Darlene decides she is no longer interested and breaks up with Dan. He wants the relationship to continue. During the workday, he frequently calls her on the interoffice phone and stops by her desk to talk. Darlene tries to brush him off, but with no success. She asks her manager to intervene. The manager says he doesn't get involved in personal matters.

Most managers are rightly reluctant to involve themselves in 30
employees' personal relationships. Had Darlene asked for help dealing with Dan outside of work, the manager would have been justified
in staying out of it. He could have referred her to the employee assistance program, if the company had one.

Once Dan starts interfering with Darlene's work, however, it's a
different story. The company has an obligation to make sure the
work environment is free from harassment. If Darlene finds herself
less able to do her job or uncomfortable at work because of Dan and
if her own efforts have failed, the manager has both the right and the
responsibility to step in and tell Dan to back off.

*Scenario 6:   Susan likes to tell bawdy jokes. Bob objects. Although
he doesn't mind when men use such language in the office, he doesn't
think it's appropriate for women to do so.*

An employee who objects to off-color jokes shouldn't have to listen to them at work, and management should back him up. Bob's
problem, however, is restricted to jokes told by women. If he doesn't
have the same problem when men tell such jokes, it's his problem —
not the company's. Management can't enforce Bob's double standard.

*Scenario 7:   Janet is wearing a low-cut blouse and short shorts.
John, her co-worker, says, "Now that I can see it, you gotta let me have
some." Janet tells him to buzz off. All day, despite Janet's objections,
John continues to make similar remarks. When Janet calls her supervisor over to complain, John says, "Hey, can you blame me?"*

The company has a right to expect clothing appropriate to the 35
job. If Janet's clothes are inappropriate, management should tell her
so. But Janet's outfit doesn't give John license to say or do whatever
he likes. Once she tells him she doesn't like his comments, he
should stop — or be made to do so.

Scenario 8:   Someone posts a Hustler *magazine centerfold in the
employee men's room. No women use this room.*

Some would say that if the women aren't aware of the pinups in
the men's room, they can't be offensive. But when men walk out of the
restroom with such images in their mind's eye, how do they view their
female co-workers? And when the women find out about the pinups — as they will — how will they feel? As the judge ruled in a
1991 Florida case involving nude posters at a shipyard, the presence
of such pictures, even if they aren't intended to offend women, "sexu-
alizes the work environment to the detriment of all female employees."

A Common-Sense Definition

Sexual harassment is not complicated to define. To harass some-one is to bother him or her. Sexual harassment is bothering some-one in a sexual way. The harasser offers sexual attention to someone who didn't ask for it and doesn't welcome it. The unwelcome behav-ior might or might not involve touching. It could just as well be spo-ken words, graphics, gestures, or even looks (not any look — but the kind of leer or stare that says, "I want to undress you").

Who decides what behavior is offensive at the workplace? The recipient does. As long as the recipient is "reasonable" and not un-duly sensitive, sexual conduct that offends him or her should be changed.

That doesn't mean there's a blueprint for defining sexual harass- 40
ment. "Reasonable" people don't always agree. Society celebrates pluralism. Not everyone is expected to have the same standards of morality or the same sense of humor. Still, reasonable people will agree *much of the time* about what constitutes offensive behavior or will recognize that certain behavior or language can be expected to offend some others. Most people make distinctions between how they talk to their best friends, to their children, and to their elderly relatives. Out of respect, they avoid certain behavior in the presence of certain people. The same distinctions must be applied at work.

Sexual harassment is different from the innocent mistake — that is, when someone tells an off-color joke, not realizing the listener will be offended, or gives what is meant as a friendly squeeze of the arm to a co-worker who doesn't like to be touched. Such behavior may repre-sent insensitivity, and that may be a serious problem, but it's usually not sexual harassment. In many cases, the person who tells the joke that misfires or who pats an unreceptive arm *knows right away* that he or she has made a mistake. Once aware or made aware, this individual will usually apologize and try not to do it again.

Do They Mean It?

Some offensive behavior stems from what University of Illinois psychologist Louise Fitzgerald calls "cultural lag." "Many men en-tered the workplace at a time when sexual teasing and innuendo were commonplace," Fitzgerald told the *New York Times.* "They have no idea there's anything wrong with it." Education will help such men change their behavior.

True harassers, on the other hand, *mean* to offend. Even when they know their talk or action is offensive, they continue. Sexual ha-rassment is defined as behavior that is not only unwelcome but *re-peated.* (Some kinds of behavior are *always* inappropriate, however, even if they occur only once. Grabbing someone's breast or crotch, for example, or threatening to fire a subordinate who won't engage in sexual activity does not need repetition to be deemed illegal.)

The true harasser acts not out of insensitivity but precisely because of the knowledge that the behavior will make the recipient uncomfortable. The harasser derives pleasure from the momentary or continuing powerlessness of the other individual. In some cases, the harasser presses the victim to have sex, but sexual pleasure itself is not the goal. Instead, the harasser's point is to dominate, to gain power over another. As University of Washington psychologist John Gottman puts it, "Harassment is a way for a man to make a woman vulnerable."

Some harassers target the people they consider the most likely 45 to be embarrassed and the least likely to file a charge. Male harassers are sometimes attempting to put "uppity women" in their place. In certain previously all-male workplaces, a woman who's simply attempting to do her job may be considered uppity. In this instance, the harassment is designed to make the woman feel out of place, if not to pressure her out of the job. Such harassment often takes place in front of an audience or is recounted to others afterwards ("pinch and tell").

Dr. Frances Conley, the renowned neurosurgeon who quit her job at Stanford Medical School after nearly twenty-five years of harassment, told legislators at a sexual harassment hearing in San Diego, California, that the "unsolicited touching, caressing, comments about my physical attributes" she experienced "were always for effect in front of an audience. . . ."

Part of the Job

Some harassers who don't consciously set out to offend are nevertheless unwilling to curb their behavior even after they're told it's offensive. If a woman doesn't like it, they figure that's her problem. And some harassers consider sexual favors from subordinates to be a "perk," as much a part of the job as a big mahogany desk and a private executive bathroom. A young woman on President Lyndon Johnson's staff, according to *A Sexual Profile of Men in Power* (Prentice-Hall, 1977), by Sam Janus and others, "was awakened in her bedroom on his Texas ranch in the middle of the night by a searching flashlight. Before she could scream, she heard a familiar voice: 'Move over. This is your president.'"

Men can be harassed by women, or both harasser and victim can be of the same sex. Overwhelmingly, however, sexual harassment is an injury inflicted on women by men. While the number of hard-core harassers is small, their presence is widely felt. Sexual harassment is ugly. And it's damaging — to the victims, to business, and to society as a whole.

DEFINING SEXUAL HARASSMENT

Sexual harassment means bothering someone in a sexual way.

Sexual harassment is behavior that is not only unwelcome but in most cases *repeated.*

The goal of sexual harassment is not sexual pleasure but gaining power over another.

Some male harassers want to put "uppity women" in their place.

The essence of combating sexual harassment is fostering mutual respect in the workplace.

Flirting with Dangerous Precedents
ELIZABETH LARSON

Since Anita Hill made her accusations against Clarence Thomas five years ago, the number of sexual harassment charges filed with the Equal Employment Opportunity Commission has more than doubled, from 6,127 cases in 1990 to 14,420 in 1994. Even before Ms. Hill, the number of complaints filed with the EEOC had been steadily rising, from just 3,661 cases in 1981.

In response to this alarming trend, American corporations are spending hundreds of millions of dollars on seminars to educate their employees about sexual harassment and hiring executives to deal with complaints before they get filed. The truth, though, is that these armies of experts may be fueling the problem rather than containing it. Like the college students persuaded by their feminist sisters that an unwanted kiss is really rape, today's businesswomen are being taught that behavior they once would have considered boorish or inappropriate constitutes actionable sexual harassment. Employers may think they are hiring consultants to protect them from

---

Elizabeth Larson is a Los Angeles–based policy analyst on women's business issues for the Independent Women's Forum. This is adapted from the spring issue of the *Women's Quarterly,* published by the IWF.

lawsuits, but what is actually being taught is a very different lesson: A wink or a leer can be money in the bank.

In what is believed to be the first sexual harassment case, *Barnes v. Train,* in 1974, a woman working at the Environmental Protection Agency alleged that her job was abolished after she refused to engage in an affair with her boss. A federal district court dismissed the case, finding that although Ms. Barnes had suffered discrimination, this discrimination was based not on the fact that she was a woman but on her refusal to have sex with the director of the agency. The decision was reversed on appeal, and Ms. Barnes was eventually awarded $18,000 in back pay as damages.

Move forward twenty-one years. Wal-Mart Stores is now appealing a 1995 jury verdict that awarded $50 million in punitive damages to a worker in its receiving department who charged that her supervisor liked to joke about her figure. How did the courts come to regard a tasteless remark as nearly 3,000 times more serious than a woman losing her job for refusing sex with her boss?

Like the concept of *date rape,* the term *sexual harassment* didn't 5 even exist two decades ago. It joined the American lexicon in the late 1970s with the publication of Lin Farley's *Sexual Shakedown: The Sexual Harassment of Women on the Job* and Catharine MacKinnon's *Sexual Harassment of Working Women.* In the 1986 case *Meritor Savings Bank v. Vinson,* a court upheld Ms. MacKinnon's "hostile environment" argument for the first time. This dramatically increased an employer's potential liability because the plaintiff was no longer required to prove she had been subject to a threat (e.g., "Have sex with me or you're fired") — only that she found herself uncomfortable at work, whether because of male comments (e.g., "Nice blouse you have on") or — as in the 1991 Jacksonville Shipyards case in Florida — because of sexy pinups on the wall.

Our legal system has gone from punishing behavior that is objectively wrong to that which is subjectively offensive. As the courts' sympathy toward acutely sensitive women has expanded, the average amount awarded in sexual harassment cases has multiplied to some $250,000 today, according to the trade journal *Business Insurance.*

While relatively few women filing complaints actually get a shot at this legal jackpot (the EEOC ended up litigating only fifty cases in 1990), the cost to businesses attempting to avoid harassment charges is huge. Sexual harassment seminars run by professional consultants and legal advisers range in length from four hours to two days and can cost several thousand dollars each. And that's just the beginning. As the *9 to 5 Guide to Combating Sexual Harassment* (published by a feminist lobbying group) suggests, "Training should be ongoing, not a onetime session, and presented on paid time."

In some areas of the country, these voluntary efforts are required by law. Since 1993, California has required all companies, regardless of size, to notify their employees that sexual harassment is unlawful. Employers must provide examples of what constitutes sexual harassment and make sure they have explained how employees can get in touch with government agencies to deal with their complaints. Connecticut companies with more than fifty workers have been required since 1991 to conduct at least two hours of sexual harassment awareness training for all managers. No wonder that businesses are now purchasing expensive "sexual harassment liability insurance," with premiums ranging from $1,500 to $25,000 annually per company, depending on its size and history of lawsuits.

You could say that the rapid growth of the sexual harassment industry is a huge tax liberalism imposes on business. The culture of victimization is becoming so embedded in the courts and legislatures that a handful of sexual harassment lawsuits are now seen as representative of the average working woman's lot.

Yet this zeal to punish employers will also punish working 10 women. If women are going to continue to make inroads into the work force, they will have to deal with office cranks and curmudgeons, louts and Lotharios, backstabbers and boors — just as men have always had to do. It's hard to legislate away unpleasant personalities. In the end, the true backlash against women will not stem from lewd, sexist male bosses but from something far more threatening to the achievements of women: an employer's silent rejection of a woman's job application for fear of trouble.

Female Chauvinist Pigs?

MARGARET CARLSON

It's got sex, power, and — as an extra added attraction — that other American obsession, dieting. It's the reverse-discrimination suit filed by eight men from Boston who found the Jenny Craig weight-loss organization too full of, well, female chauvinist pigs. The girl talk in the office, says plaintiff Joseph Egan, about "who to marry, who is pregnant, how to get pregnant" was offensive, and it was sexist to ask his male colleagues to shovel the snow and insensitive to tell another he was "sensitive for a guy." These men found themselves on a slower track than their female colleagues, and so some of them quit, others were laid off, and all of them filed complaints. Last week three of the plaintiffs cleared the first hurdle: the

Margaret Carlson is a columnist for *Time* magazine. This essay, which appeared in the magazine on December 12, 1994, is from her column, Public Eye.

Massachusetts Commission Against Discrimination determined that there was probable cause of gender bias and ordered mediation. The other five are awaiting action.

All are in great demand, however, and not by accident. The first thing they did, after hiring an all-female team of lawyers, was hire a public-relations firm, which alerted the press about the case before the commission ruling. Although last year, according to the Equal Employment Opportunity Commission, women filed 11,000 sexual-harassment complaints and men fewer than 1,000, this case made the front page of the *Wall Street Journal* the next day. And before you could say sweeps week, the *Today* show, *Entertainment Tonight, A Current Affair,* and *CBS This Morning,* among others, were on the phone to the men's Boston publicist, Paul Dugan. There was much debate among the advisers about how high or low to go on the media food chain — should the guys go for a slam dunk with a supersensitive host like Maury Povich or risk potentially tough questions on network programs? But not to worry. After accepting airfare and hotel accommodations to appear on *Today,* three of the Jenny Craig Eight, prepped like witnesses at the Simpson trial, came off like a bunch of wounded Alan Aldas, shocked — shocked — to be exposed to off-color comments.

Now, there should be nothing wrong with this picture: as women gain power, they may misuse it and sex, as badly as some men. In fact, sexual harassment won't really be taken seriously until it affects men. But the sheer inequality of attention to this case — as opposed to the other 91 percent of cases filed by women that do not happen to involve a sitting president or a U.S. Supreme Court nominee — can also be seen as one more example of the inequality that made antidiscrimination laws necessary in the first place. All this attention also suggests a man who is sexually harassed has a greater claim on our sympathies — a notion coming this week to a Multiplex near you in *Disclosure,* a movie in which predatory executive Demi Moore accosts sweet, sensitive Michael Douglas. Jenny Craig plaintiff Tracy Tinkham looks more like Joey Buttafuoco than Michael Douglas, but never mind. Perhaps he was succeeding handsomely at counseling overweight women and should have been promoted instead of being let go for breaking a trivial rule. We are asked to believe that these men's having to listen to jokes about push-up bras or being asked to lift a heavy box makes for a winning case and worldwide media attention, when women have been listening to penis jokes and making coffee for decades. Sure, complaints about failing to be promoted simply because they were men in a woman's world are serious. But before the Jenny Craig Eight pour their hearts out to Sally Jessy Raphael, they should check with all the women who have looked up the corporate ladder and seen ten men for every woman and wondered how they could prove their lack of success was due to some failure in the corporate culture, and not in themselves.

Misreading Sexual
Harassment Law

GWENDOLYN MINK

In the debate surrounding the investigation of President Clinton, some feminists have painted the rest of us into a corner. Defending the President, they have argued that what he is accused of doing is not sexual harassment. This distorts the law and trivializes women's experiences.

Kathleen Willey has described herself as a volunteer worker seeking paid employment at the time she says she was groped by the President. Yet according to Gloria Steinem, she was just "a supporter" at whom Bill Clinton made a "reckless pass." Feminism is supposed to be about taking seriously what women say about themselves. But here is a leading feminist rewriting another woman's experience — to protect a man — and in effect compromising twenty years of sexual harassment jurisprudence.

Ms. Steinem is not alone among feminists in this retreat from sexual harassment law. Though Patricia Ireland, the president of the National Organization for Women, defended Ms. Willey after her *60 Minutes* interview, Ms. Ireland has drawn troubling distinctions between the cases of Ms. Willey and Monica Lewinsky.

Ms. Ireland has said that the alleged relationship between Ms. Lewinsky and the President did not involve sexual harassment because, as reported, it was consensual and violated only private marital vows, not public prohibitions against sex discrimination.

But how do we know that? The legal inquiry has not been completed. If there was a relationship, how do we know that it was welcomed or that it didn't contaminate the White House as a workplace? The relationship is properly the subject of a legal discovery process in cases like Paula Jones's. That process includes investigating a possible pattern of behavior on the part of the alleged perpetrator.

Demonstrating pattern and practice is often the only way a plaintiff in a sexual harassment suit can get a hearing. After all, sexual harassment is less often about a boss's inappropriate obsession with one woman than about bosses who behave inappropriately toward many women, but with each one only once.

Even if it turns out that Ms. Lewinsky had a consensual relationship with the President, Mr. Clinton would not be exempt from in-

Gwendolyn Mink is a professor of politics at the University of California at Santa Cruz. This article appeared in the *New York Times* on March 30, 1998.

vestigation. When power differences between the two people involved are extreme, consent counts for little.

So the Supreme Court said in 1986, when it ruled that the primary factor in determining sexual harassment is unwelcomeness, not consent. Many women feel pressured to meet the sexual requests of their bosses — technically, give their "consent" — even though they may not welcome the requests or liaisons, may not solicit them, and may also be offended by them.

That so many feminists don't appreciate the distinction between welcomeness and consent bodes ill for sexual harassment law. Similarly, when some feminists claim that what Paula Jones and Kathleen Willey have accused the President of doing isn't really sexual harassment because it happened only once and because the President took no for an answer, they are forgetting something important: there is no numerical threshold for harassment.

Nor does the law say each boss gets to ask each female worker   10
for oral sex once as long as he doesn't force her when she says no. There would be precious little protection for women if all male bosses were entitled to one free hit.

We must affirm the distinction drawn by the Supreme Court between welcomeness and consent. Otherwise no woman who unwillingly succumbs to her boss will have any legal recourse.

We must also insist that even one unwelcome sexual advance is too many: if what Ms. Jones and Ms. Willey say is true, the fact that the President didn't force them to have sex would not exonerate him from harassment charges.

Many people, including some feminists, construe this President's alleged misconduct as being "just about sex." To the defendant in any sexual harassment case, discovery and cross-examination are indeed "just about sex," since sex is, after all, one goal of the harasser.

If we permit the President to escape his obligation to tell the truth because the subject is "only" sex, then defendants in future harassment cases may claim the same exemption.

In a he-said-she-said situation where "he" has power and "she"   15
does not — which is common in harassment cases — the defendant's stonewalling will always deprive the plaintiff of a fair hearing.

Who's Harassing Whom?

MARIANNE M. JENNINGS

Nearly thirty years in the workplace, and not once have I been sexually harassed. I suppose I'm grateful, but given the action other working women seem to be getting, part of me wonders: exactly what's wrong with me? It's not as if I haven't been in high-risk environments. I began my legal career as an intern for the federal government. Yet I haven't had so much as a compliment from a male coworker since the Reagan administration. After the Anita Hill spectacle in 1991, I noticed men averting their eyes.

But what I resent more than the lack of attention is the assumption underlying the rules and court decisions governing sexual harassment: that I am incapable of handling unwanted sexual suggestion. My employer trusts me with budgeting, lobbying, fundraising, and shaping the minds of the next generation but is forced by the Equal Employment Opportunity Commission and the courts to conclude that I can't handle the advances of knuckleheads.

I resent the women who bring sexual harassment suits and convince courts that we are as helpless and victimized as Melanie Wilkes in *Gone with the Wind*. I come from a long line of unharassed women who taught me that the best defense against offensive male behavior is a good offense. The female arm has an appendage created for dealing with cads. Women in the 1940s used said appendage quite effectively to administer a slap in the face and thereby deter drunken sailors. And yet working women today can't handle a boor in wing tips and bifocals without the help of the Supreme Court?

The court's recent rulings on harassment make it easier to win damages against a company even if it is unaware that a supervisor is harassing an employee and even if the plaintiff suffered no career damage. The likely result: companies will redouble their already vigorous efforts aimed at preventing harassment.

But who's harassing whom when I'm forced to attend "sensitiv- 5 ity training" seminars and reveal my personal feelings to coworkers with whom I don't even exchange recipes? At one Fortune 500 company, a sensitivity consultant instructed employees to conduct the following "group exercise": "I want all of the men to sit down on the floor in the center of the room. You are not allowed to speak while sitting down. The women are to stand around the men in a circle and begin to whistle and make sexist comments about the appearance

---

Marianne M. Jennings is a professor of legal and ethical studies in the College of Business at Arizona State University. This article appeared in the *Wall Street Journal* on July 6, 1998.

and anatomy of the men." What if I don't *want* to talk about my colleagues' anatomy?

How innocent are the victims of harassment anyway? *Dateline NBC* recently ran a story on women who claimed they were harassed while working on the production lines at a Ford plant in Chicago. They tearfully told of sleeping with supervisors to keep their jobs and of being hospitalized for stress. These women defined their ethical dilemma as most people who make poor decisions do: either I stay here and get harassed, or I leave and take another job for less pay but keep my sanity and virtue. To put it another way, the supervisors' brutish behavior was awful, but for $22 an hour the employees were willing to put up with it. Similarly, if you believe Anita Hill's story, she tolerated Clarence Thomas's misbehavior for years because riding to a career pinnacle on the tails of a shooting star was worth it.

Like tenants who claim "constructive eviction" due to horrible living conditions yet remain on the leased premises, the legal claim of women that their working environment is hostile doesn't jibe with their own decision to remain. Women define what's repulsive, stay in it, and then file and win multimillion-dollar verdicts, which in many cases exceed the amounts awarded to children crippled in horrific accidents. The courtroom playing field reflects academic theories such as the following, touted in the *Journal of Business Ethics:* "Sexual harassment signifies to women that their presence is threatening to the dominant patriarchal order, that they are unwelcome, and works to maintain gender stratification." The guys at the Ford plant were interested in "gender stratification"? Sounds to me like they were just after a roll in the hay.

The most damaging result of sexual harassment law is the chilling effect it has on men in the workplace. Mentoring, which I had from decent and honorable men and without which I would not have survived thirty years ago, is a lost art. Men who hold the keys and skills for advancement hesitate to involve themselves in one-on-one counseling of female employees. Men fear closing the office door during meetings with women. At the University of Nebraska, a graduate student was even ordered to remove a picture of his bikini-clad wife from his desk after two colleagues complained.

I see a fear in my male colleagues' eyes that they will unwittingly offend someone and will be the subject of a career-derailing investigation. The fear is justified. An accused rapist, after all, receives better treatment than an accused harasser. The rape defendant is entitled to due process, the presumption of innocence, and his day in court. When a man is charged with sexual harassment, the employer's response will be swift, decisive, and one-sided.

I resent that men in my office feel they must cast their eyes 10 downward. It's not their sexual appetites they're holding back. It's candor. It's friendliness. It's lunch together. They're certainly not harassers, but they can no longer risk being my friends or mentors. Feminists claimed victory with these latest decisions because liability for sexual harassment now rests squarely with those responsible — employers. That's wrong. Employers don't cause sexual harassment. Women have defined it, capitalized on it, and exacerbated it. We also possess the tools for handling it, without a federal judge or bureaucracy. Dear sisters, we have met the enemy and she is us.

Sexual Harassment Is a Power Play

DONNA HENRY AND CATHY GOODWIN

In response to "Who's Harassing Whom," editorial page, July 6, by Marianne Jennings: I'm glad Ms. Jennings has never been the victim of sexual harassment and hope that she never knows the indignity and horror that accompanies this form of power abuse. She asks, "What's wrong with me? . . . I haven't had so much as a compliment from a male worker. . . ." The implication is that harassment can be equated with an innocent compliment. She goes on to equate sexual harassment with "the advances of knuckleheads" and minimizes such behavior by saying, "Sounds to me like they were just after a roll in the hay." Make no mistake: Sexual harassment is about power — a power play by people who have power against people who have none.

Ms. Jennings characterizes the victim's plight as poor decision making on their part. "Either I stay here and get harassed, or I leave and take another job for less pay but keep my sanity and virtue." She misses the point: everyone has the right to work in an environment that is not hostile or abusive. To keep running from the source of sexual harassment is to allow the system to perpetuate itself on other victims.

I am a consultant in gender relations in the workplace, and I wholeheartedly agree with Ms. Jennings that men and women no longer know how to relate to one another at work in a manner which creates a dignified and productive quality of life in the workplace. Building bridges between the sexes is key to dialogue, not the polarizing "sensitivity training" as described by Ms. Jennings: "Women are to stand around the men . . . and make sexist comments." Substi-

These letters in response to Marianne M. Jennings's article "Who's Harassing Whom?" (page 632) appeared on the editorial page of the *Wall Street Journal* on July 14, 1998.

tuting one form of abuse for another, a male target for a female target, is clearly unprofessional and causes further damage to a work force in need of healing, not further abuse.

Donna Henry

I agree with Ms. Jennings that a lot of consulting firms are milking a sensitive situation. I wouldn't like to lie on the floor and share my secrets or make fun of male bodies either. But here's where I'm confused. Ms. Jennings wonders why women making $22 an hour don't walk out. That works two ways: Why don't some of those unwilling participants in corporate workshops just walk out? Why doesn't the graduate student transfer to a school where he can display photos of his bikini-clad wife? I wonder how Ms. Jennings would feel if a woman or a gay man chose to display beefcake photos of a bikini-clad boyfriend.

So she's never been harassed? Great. I've never been mugged. 5 Should I argue that people who get mugged are asking for it, or perhaps they should just find another place to walk? Maybe both, but, last time I checked, mugging was still a crime.

Cathy Goodwin

A Call for Lustiness

CAMILLE PAGLIA

Liberal Democrats, who supported Anita Hill against Clarence Thomas in 1991, are waking up to the police state that their rigid rules have created. Now, as allegations fly about presidential sex, we can finally distinguish between genuine sexual coercion and free expression of sexual thought.

As a college teacher, I've long held that no person in power should demand sexual favors in return for a high grade or promotion. Nor should subordinates sexually involved with teachers or managers enjoy an unfair advantage over their peers. Those principles are a genuine contribution to feminist history.

But the secondary "hostile environment" policy, which allows employees to file lawsuits on nebulous grounds of psychological distress, is grotesquely totalitarian. It offends free-speech rights and is predicated on a reactionary female archetype: the prudish Victorian lady who faints at a sexual innuendo. This isn't feminism; it's Puritanism.

Camille Paglia is professor of humanities at the University of the Arts in Philadelphia and the author of *Sexual Personae* (1990), *Sex, Art, and American Culture* (1992), and *The Birds (BFI Film Classics)* (1998). This article appeared in *Time* magazine on March 3, 1998.

The Anita Hill case, far from expanding women's rights, was a disaster for civil liberties. That Hill, an articulate graduate of the Yale Law School, could find no job-preserving way to communicate to her employer her discomfort with mild off-color banter strained credulity. That Thomas could be publicly grilled about trivial lunchtime conversations that occurred ten years earlier was an outrage worthy of Stalinist Russia.

An antiseptically sex-free workplace is impossible and unnatural. 5 We want a sophisticated art of seduction. Feminist excesses have paralyzed and neutered white, upper-middle-class young men, as should be obvious to any visitor to the campuses of the elite schools. I want a society of lusty men and lusty women whose physical and mental energies are in exuberant free flow. While men must behave honorably (governors and presidents should not be dropping their pants in front of female employees or secretly preying on buxom young interns), women must also watch how they dress and behave. For every gross male harasser, there are ten female sycophants who shamelessly use their sexual attractions to get ahead. We don't want a society of surveillance by old maids and snitches. The proper mission of feminism is to encourage women to take personal responsibility without running to parental authority figures for help.

The fanatic overprotection of women is fast making us an infantile nation. We need to treat sex with greater realism and imagination. Women should be taught not that they are passive wards of the state but that sex is a great human comedy where the joke is always on us.

THINKING AND WRITING ABOUT SEXUAL HARASSMENT

Questions for Discussion and Writing

1. Bravo and Cassedy make outstanding use of examples to clarify their definition of sexual harassment. Are there any conclusions with which you disagree? If so, explain your objections. Is there any part of the definition in the box that ought to be defined more clearly or that might be hard to prove in an official complaint?
2. The main thrust of Larson's article is an attack on the growing sexual-awareness training industry. What are her objections? How does she make the transition to adverse results for women? If you have ever attended a sexual awareness workshop or course, compare your reactions to Larson's.
3. What is the tone of Carlson's article on sex discrimination against men? Point out places that make her attitude clear. Do you think the men's objections should be taken seriously? Why or why not?
4. What is Mink's main point? What is the difference between "welcomeness and consent"? Why does Mink think it dangerous to insist that some cases are "just about sex"?

5. What is the meaning of the title of Jennings's article? Do you think she is being fair to the victims of harassment? Do you agree with her conclusion about "the most dangerous results of sexual harassment law"? With which other writer in this section does she seem most compatible?

6. The letters that respond to Jennings argue different points. Summarize their objections. Have all of Jennings's issues been adequately addressed? Notice that both letter writers agree with Jennings at some point. Is this an effective strategy?

7. Paglia seems to be advising both men and women to lighten up. Do you think she is unfair to women who claim sexual harassment? What warrant about women underlies her call for lustiness?

8. The cartoon figures represent justices of the Supreme Court, one of whom is identified as Clarence Thomas. Before his confirmation in November 1991, an aide accused him of sexual harassment. In *Facts on File* and other sources you can find reports of the hearings held by the Senate Judiciary Committee in October 1991 to evaluate the charges. Do you think that the cartoonist is trivializing the alleged offense?

Topics for Research

Sexual harassment policies and programs at your school

Selected sexual harassment cases at colleges and universities

The Paula Jones case

Sexual harassment in women's sports (*New York Times,* March 7, 1999, p. 1)

TAKING THE DEBATE ONLINE

- **Dr. Sara Feldman-Schorrig's Sexual Harassment Pages** <http://pw2 .netcom.com/%7Eschorrig/psych.html> A psychologist provides information designed to help judges, juries, and the general public distinguish between valid and grossly exaggerated or fabricated sexual harassment claims. She offers a list of links on recent sexual harassment cases, links to her reviews on plays and movies about harassment, and an extensive section called diverse opinions that offers commentary by men and women on harassment issues.

- **Defining Sexual Harassment** <http://www.pbs.org/newshour/bb/law/ jan-june98/harassment 4-22a.html> This transcript of a *PBS Online News Hour* report discusses a sexual harassment case involving a female employee of Burlington Industries and provides links to other *Online News Hour* sexual harassment reports, such as harassment in the U.S. army, same-sex harassment, and a debate on the terms of sexual harassment.

- **Sexual Assault Information Page** <http://www.cs.utk.edu/~bartley/ index/sexualHarassment> The Sexual Assault Information Page provides links to information concerning acquaintance rape, child sexual abuse/assault, incest, rape, ritual abuse, sexual assault, and sexual harassment, as well as links to harassment resources at many universities throughout Canada and the United States.

- **Sexual Harassment: It's Not Academic** <http://165.224.220.66/offices/ OCR/ocrshpam.html> This pamphlet from the Office for Civil Rights articulates different types of sexual harassment situations that can occur in a school environment and offers ways for school officials to combat it.

- **The A-Team** <http://www.a-team.org> Comprised of lawyers, trial consultants, psychologists, and medical doctors, the A-Team is an organization whose mission is to help those wrongly accused of child abuse, domestic violence, date rape, sexual harassment, and other gender crimes. Some of their links include articles on science and the law, what to do if you've been falsely accused, and opinions on men's organizations.

CHAPTER NINETEEN

Sex and Violence in Popular Culture

The ongoing controversy about explicit sex and violence in movies, television, and rap music has surfaced again with particular urgency. A 1995 *New York Times* article found that "nine out of ten of those polled could think of something bad to say about popular culture, with a large proportion mentioning too much sex, violence, and vulgar language."[1] The reasons for the renewed attacks are not hard to find. Crime and sexual activity among the young have energized the search for a cause, and popular culture is a perennial target. But the extraordinary accessibility of this culture raises new alarms. Never has commercial entertainment been so widely and easily available to the young, the population thought to be most susceptible to its influence.

The debate begins with claims about the nature and extent of that influence. Are some forms of popular entertainment necessarily dangerous and immoral? How much are viewers affected by continued exposure to depictions of explicit sex and violence? Researchers have argued the point for years, but today a majority consensus believes that long-term viewing does, in fact, alter the behavior of certain audiences. In recent years what appear to be copycat crimes have followed the showing of particularly violent films. Experts also debate the relative effects of fictional and real-life images: Which are more corrupting — the graphic creations in movies or the daily reports of real-life horrors in the news?

Not surprisingly, even where agreement exists on the nature of the problem, there is disagreement about solutions. However

---

[1] Elizabeth Kolbert, "Americans Despair of Popular Culture," *New York Times,* August 20, 1995, sec. H, p. 1.

strongly some critics feel about the dangers of exposure, they argue that the dangers of government censorship may, in the long run, be greater. But if government intervention is rejected, can other solutions — a rating system for television shows and music albums, a V-chip in the TV set allowing parents to block undesirable programs, respect by producers for the so-called family hour, and above all, closer monitoring by parents — guarantee that young people will be insulated from exposure to sex and violence in the media? Most Americans are not optimistic. The *New York Times* poll shows that 63 percent of those questioned believe that ratings alone, for example, will not "keep children from seeing or listening to inappropriate material."

Of course, popular culture is not the only source of exposure. Movies, television, and music reflect the activities, tastes, fantasies, and prejudices of a larger society. Reducing the amount of sex and violence in the media is certainly easier than reforming a whole society. Still, the question remains: To what extent can any reform in popular entertainment successfully address the problems of teenage crime and sexual activity?

Sex, Violence, and Videotape
IRVING KRISTOL

On March 31, Britain experienced an unexpected cultural shock. That was when Professor Elizabeth Newson, head of the child development unit at Nottingham University, issued a report on violence-rich videos (known in the United Kingdom as "video nasties") and their effect on children. The report was signed by twenty-five psychologists and pediatricians, all known to be of the liberal persuasion. Its gist is summed up by the following quotations:

"Many of us hold our liberal ideals of freedom of expression dear, but now begin to feel that we were naive in our failure to predict the extent of damaging material and its all-too-free availability to children."

It then went on: "By restricting such material from home viewing, society must take on a necessary responsibility in protecting children from this, as from other forms of child abuse."

A storm of controversy ensued, which the American press largely ignored. A Labour member of Parliament introduced legislation to limit the availability of such "video nasties." The movie in-

Irving Kristol, a fellow of the American Enterprise Institute, coedits *The Public Interest.* This essay appeared in the May 31, 1994, issue of the *Wall Street Journal.*

dustry was naturally outraged, since so much of their profits come from the subsequent sale of videotapes, and they cried "Censorship!"— which, of course, is what was being advocated. More surprising was the reaction of the Tory Home Minister, Michael Howard, who turned out to be "wet" (we would say "soft") on this whole issue. He was very worried about all those households without children, whose freedom to watch "video nasties" would be circumscribed.

Both True and False

And then, inevitably, there were the unreconstructed liberal aca- 5
demics, who kept insisting that no one had ever proved a causal relation between TV violence and aggressive behavior by the young. This was both true and false. It was true in the sense that such clearcut, causal relations are beyond the reach of social science — there are simply too many other factors that influence youthful behavior. It was false because there is an abundance of circumstantial evidence that points to the existence of such a relation — circumstantial evidence so strong as to raise no reasonable doubt in the minds of ordinary people, and of parents especially.

In the Spring 1993 issue of *The Public Interest,* Brandon Centerwall, a professor of epidemiology at the University of Washington, summarizes much of this circumstantial evidence. He focuses on research findings on the effect of television when it was introduced to rural, isolated communities in Canada and when English-language TV came to South Africa in 1975, having previously been banned by the Afrikaans-speaking government. In all such instances there was a spectacular increase in violent crime, most especially among the young.

Professor Centerwall also notes that when TV was introduced in the United States after World War II, the homicide rate among whites, who were the first to buy sets, began to rise, while the black homicide rate didn't show any such increase until four years later.

Statistical studies of the relation between youthful aggressiveness and TV can be deceptive, Professor Centerwall explains, if they focus on the overall, average response — which, indeed, seems weak. But aggressive impulses, like most human phenomena, are distributed along a bell-shaped curve, and it is at the margin where the significant effect is to be observed: "It is an intrinsic property of such 'bell curve' distributions that small changes in the average imply major changes at the extremes. Thus, if an exposure to television causes 8 percent of the population to shift from below-average aggression to above-average aggression, it follows that the homicide rate will double."

Professor Centerwall concludes that "the evidence indicates that if, hypothetically, television technology had never been developed, there would today be 10,000 fewer homicides each year in the United States, 70,000 fewer rapes, and 700,000 fewer injurious assaults. Violent crime would be half what it is."

So the evidence for some kind of controls over television (and tapes) is strong enough to provoke popular and political concern. It is certainly true that any such controls will involve some limitations on the freedom of adults to enjoy the kind of entertainment they might prefer. But modest limits on adult liberties ought to be perfectly acceptable if they prevent tens of thousands of our children from growing up into criminal adults. And it is the children we should be focusing on. The violence-prone adults, especially at the pathological fringe, are beyond our reach and, in most cases, beyond all possibility of redemption. It is the young people — especially those who have not yet reached adolescence — who are most affected by television, as all the studies agree.

Something will surely be done about this problem, despite the American Civil Liberties Union and other extreme interpreters of the First Amendment. In Britain, Mr. Howard has reluctantly agreed to propose appropriate legislation, propelled by a powerful consensus among Tories, the Labour Party, the Liberal Party, the media, and popular opinion. There is little doubt that, in the United States, a momentum for similar action is building up. How politicians will respond to it remains to be seen. But the idea that our popular culture can have malignant effects upon our young, and upon our society in its entirety, seems to be an idea whose coming cannot be long delayed.

And if there is a connection between our popular culture and the plague of criminal violence we are suffering from, then is it not reasonable to think that there may also be such a connection between our popular culture and the plagues of sexual promiscuity among teenagers, teenage illegitimacy, and, yes, the increasing number of rapes committed by teenagers? Here again, we don't really need social science to confirm what common sense and common observations tell us to be the case.

Can anyone really believe that soft porn in our Hollywood movies, hard porn in our cable movies, and violent porn in our "rap" music is without effect? Here, the average, overall impact is quite discernible to the naked eye. And at the margin, the effects, in terms most notably of illegitimacy and rape, are shockingly visible.

Clearly, something must be done to lower the temperature of the sexual climate in which we live. And whatever is done, it will of necessity limit the freedoms of adults to indulge their sexual fantasies. Most of us will not mourn the loss of such freedoms, but — as with violence — there are those who will loudly protest any such rude "violation" of our "civil liberties."

Censorship, we will be told, is immoral — though no moral code of any society that has ever existed has ever deemed it so. Besides, we will be told further, it is ineffectual. Well, those of us who have lived in a slightly chillier sexual climate have survived as witnesses to the fact that it is not so ineffectual after all. True, censorship makes a difference only at the margin. But, and this cannot be repeated too often, it is at the margin where the crucial action is. This is as true for sexual activity as it is for economic activity.

Invitation to Promiscuity

The most common (hypocritical and politically cowardly) response to the problems generated by our overheated sexual climate is that these are something parents have to do something about. But parents cannot do it on their own. They never have been able to do it on their own. Parents have always relied on churches, schools, and the popular culture for help. Today, no such reliance is possible.

The mainline churches, still intoxicated with a vulgarized Freudianism, have discovered that sex is good and repression is bad. The schools hand out condoms to adolescents while timidly suggesting that they ought to limit their activity to "responsible sex." This is nothing less than an official invitation to promiscuity. The culture, meanwhile, is busy making as much money as possible out of as much sex as possible.

No, the government, at various levels, will have to step in to help the parents. And it will do so despite the anticipated cries of outrage from libertarians, liberal or conservative. The question, and it is no easy question, is just how to intervene. That is the issue that is now up for serious discussion.

The Myth of Television Depravity
MICHAEL HIRSCHORN

A nationwide *New York Times* poll two Sundays ago reported that 21 percent of those surveyed blame television for teenage violence, compared with only 8 percent who believe the breakdown of the family is the cause of the trouble. To solve this putative problem, the Senate has passed legislation requiring violence-screening technology in all new television sets, and conservatives would like to see prime time declared a violence-and-sex free zone. As best I can tell, the effect of this radical change would be about . . . zero.

Michael Hirschorn was the executive editor of *New York* magazine when the essay from which this excerpt is taken appeared on September 4, 1995.

It is remarkable, in fact, how consistently prime-time television dwells on the very issues the conservatives complain are being ignored by Hollywood: how to raise children, how to keep families together, what to do with aging parents, how to construct a meaningful life when money is short and both parents must work. Have you seen MTV recently? The network considered literally satanic by many conservatives is now almost completely devoid of the T&A that made it so controversial a few years ago.

Watched as a block, prime-time TV shows yield a remarkably consistent message: They are dramas and comedies of coping, far from the merry subversion of families that top conservative media critic L. Brent Bozell III says is "all the rage" now. The harried Roseanne and husband Dan making do with little money and a touchingly infirm grasp on how best to be parents; Grace from *Grace under Fire* finding her way as a single mother; the cops on *NYPD Blue* (those butt shots are pretty much a thing of the past) earnestly dramatizing the conflicting demands of family and work, competence and ethics — *these are among the most popular shows in America,* and to accuse television of subverting family values without considering this mainstream programming means someone is either not doing his homework or just doesn't care.

Consider *ER,* the runaway hit of last season. In a single episode the following happens: overworked boyfriend worrying how to show a girlfriend's son that he cares; two doctors debating whether a patient should be given an expensive medical test; a brother and sister, amid many tears, telling their mother she must go into an old-age home; a doctor telling a poor mom without health insurance that he'll treat the daughter anyway; an illegal immigrant worrying about being treated because she fears being deported; the poor mom watching her daughter almost die; a married fortyish woman desperately trying to get pregnant; a character taking in her troubled pregnant sister. At show's end, the black actor Eriq La Salle, playing the son who has put his mother in a home, is shown massaging her feet and looking over the family photo album. The old lady tells her doctor son: "Your talent is God's gift to you. What you do with it is your gift back to God." Could there be a purer family-values moment?

Family values make their way even into the single–New Yorker 5 sitcoms. On *Seinfeld,* where much of the comic frisson comes from the fact that every character on the show is venal, solipsistic Jerry helps his grandmother open a bottle of ketchup, then helps his mother get back $50 his bad uncle Leo has owed her for fifty years.

Ellen, a kind of distaff *Seinfeld,* opens with a fur protest that's played for anti-PETA ridicule. "Everyone here is passionately dedicated to the cause," Ellen says. "Could one of you introduce me to the girl without the bra?" counters the Arye Gross character. *Ba-dum*

dum. One guy has made sandwiches for the protest — "lettuce, tomato, and seal pup. I call 'em my club sandwiches." The self-righteous organizer slaps him. He retorts: "There's one thing I love about you political extremists. It's your ability to laugh at yourselves." Ellen gets arrested at the protest. Her friend never comes to help her because, she says, "I was on my way to the fur department, then I saw these great little shoes." After several wacky plot twists, thirtysomething Ellen ends up in the custody of her silly suburban parents, and there are jokes about eating your vegetables. It's a nightmare, and Ellen tries to sneak out with her parents' car. They call the police and have her arrested again. The judge is astonished. "You called the police on your own daughter?" he asks. Ellen stands up for her parents, and this time they all end up in jail. It turns out to be something of a bonding experience: They may quarrel, but they're all willing to go to jail for one another. Out the next day, they drive home singing Steppenwolf's "Born to be Wild" together.

On *Mad about You,* a popular (but not top ten) show about a prosperous, happily married Manhattan couple, Jamie learns that her mom was briefly on television and that her aunt Lolly consorted with a number of famous fifties comedians up in the Catskills. On *Grace under Fire,* Grace's father-in-law has a heart-bypass operation, and Grace must get the whole family, including her terrifying mother-in-law, through the ordeal. She promises Dad-in-law that if he dies, she'll let Mom-in-law live with her — even though Grace is no longer married to his son. Son and daughter-in-law exchange tearful professions of love. Meanwhile, the couple who are Grace's best friends decide whether to keep trying to have a baby or to adopt.

Is there a more wholesome group of kids than the cute boys and girls on *Friends?* They are all white and hetero; dress well; have nice haircuts; work hard; and rarely smoke, drink, or have sex. They are, as Michael Kinsley once said of Al Gore, an old person's idea of young people.

Dole Depravity Score

Casual sex — None; discussion on *Roseanne* of what to do about the fifteen-year-old D.J., whose trouble in school is caused, it turns out, by the fact that he gets spontaneous erections. *Gratuitous violence* — No violence of any sort. *Mainstreaming deviancy* — None; except for the singles on *Seinfeld* and *Friends,* virtually everyone else on the top ten is either conspicuously married or in a family (and Disney hasn't even taken over ABC yet). *Slurs against religion* — None. *E.T. syndrome (subverting parental authority)* — None. Kids do what Mama and Papa say in *Grace, Roseanne,* and *Home Improvement,* where zestily insensitive dad Tim Allen is clearly hipper than his three generi-boys. *Attacks on the free-enterprise system* — The

Roseanne episode ends postmodernistically with her talking to an actor playing the network censor, proposing a number of names for erections ("raising the drawbridge," "standing up for democracy") while the increasingly exasperated network official keeps repeating "No." She finally points to a camera, revealing to him that all her lines in fact are already being broadcast. He looks over his shoulder in shock and says, "Is that on? Aw, shit!" The expletive is beeped out and his mouth is pixelated. It's the funniest moment on prime time.

TV Isn't Violent Enough

MIKE OPPENHEIM

Caught in an ambush, there's no way our hero (Matt Dillon, Eliot Ness, Kojak, Hoss Cartwright . . .) can survive. Yet, visibly weakening, he blazes away, and we suspect he'll pull through. Sure enough, he's around for the final clinch wearing the traditional badge of the honorable but harmless wound: a sling.

As a teenager with a budding interest in medicine, I knew this was nonsense and loved to annoy my friends with the facts.

"Aw, the poor guy! He's crippled for life!"

"What do you mean? He's just shot in the shoulder."

"That's the worst place! Vital structures everywhere. There's the 5 blood supply for the arm: axillary artery and vein. One nick and you can bleed to death on the spot."

"So he was lucky."

"OK. If it missed the vessels it hit the brachial plexus: the nerve supply. Paralyzes his arm for life. He's gotta turn in his badge and apply for disability."

"So he's *really* lucky."

"OK. Missed the artery. Missed the vein. Missed the nerves. Just went through the shoulder joint. But joint cartilage doesn't heal so well. A little crease in the bone leaves him with traumatic arthritis. He's in pain the rest of his life — stuffing himself with codeine, spending his money on acupuncture and chiropractors, losing all his friends because he complains all the time. . . . Don't ever get shot in the shoulder. It's the end. . . ."

Today, as a physician, I still sneer at TV violence, though not be- 10 cause of any moral objection. I enjoy a well-done scene of gore and slaughter as well as the next viewer, but "well-done" is something I

When this essay was published in the February 11, 1984, issue of *TV Guide,* Mike Oppenheim was a freelance writer and physician practicing medicine in California.

rarely see on a typical evening in spite of the plethora of shootings, stabbings, muggings, and brawls. Who can believe the stuff they show? Anyone who remembers high-school biology knows the human body can't possibly respond to violent trauma as it's usually portrayed.

On a recent episode, Matt Houston is at a fancy resort, on the trail of a vicious killer who specializes in knifing beautiful women in their hotel rooms in broad daylight. The only actual murder sequence was in the best of taste: all the action off screen, the flash of a knife, moans on the sound track.

In two scenes, Matt arrives only minutes too late. The hotel is alerted, but the killer's identity remains a mystery. Absurd! It's impossible to kill someone instantly with a knife thrust — or even render him unconscious. Several minutes of strenuous work are required to cut enough blood vessels so the victim bleeds to death. Tony Perkins in *Psycho* gave an accurate, though abbreviated, demonstration. Furthermore, anyone who has watched an inexperienced farmhand slaughter a pig knows that the resulting mess must be seen to be believed.

If consulted by Matt Houston, I'd have suggested a clue: "Keep your eyes peeled for someone panting with exhaustion and covered with blood. That might be your man."

Many Americans were puzzled at the films of the assassination attempt on President Reagan. Shot in the chest, he did not behave as TV had taught us to expect ("clutch chest, stagger backward, collapse"). Only after he complained of a vague chest pain and was taken to the hospital did he discover his wound. Many viewers assumed Mr. Reagan is some sort of superman. In fact, there was nothing extraordinary about his behavior. A pistol is certainly a deadly weapon, but not predictably so. Unlike a knife wound, one bullet can kill instantly — provided it strikes a small area at the base of the brain. Otherwise, it's no different: a matter of ripping and tearing enough tissue to cause death by bleeding. Professional gangland killers understand the problem. They prefer a shotgun at close range.

The trail of quiet corpses left by TV's good guys, bad guys, and   15 assorted ill-tempered gun owners is ridiculously unreal. Firearms reliably produce pain, bleeding, and permanent, crippling injury (witness Mr. Reagan's press secretary, James Brady: shot directly in the brain but very much alive). For a quick, clean death, they are no match for Luke Skywalker's light saber.

No less unreal is what happens when T. J. Hooker, Magnum, or a Simon brother meets a bad guy in manly combat. Pow! Our hero's fist crashes into the villain's head. Villain reels backward, tipping over chairs and lamps, finally falling to the floor, unconscious.

Handshakes all around. . . . Sheer fantasy! After hitting the villain, our hero would shake no one's hand. He'd be too busy waving his own about wildly, screaming with the pain of a shattered fifth metacarpal (the bone behind the fifth knuckle), an injury so predictable it's called the "boxer's fracture." The human fist is far more delicate than the human skull. In any contest between the two, the fist will lose.

The human skull is tougher than TV writers give it credit. Clunked with a blunt object, such as the traditional pistol butt, most victims would not fall conveniently unconscious for a few minutes. More likely, they'd suffer a nasty scalp laceration, be stunned for a second or two, then be extremely upset. I've sewn up many. A real-life, no-nonsense criminal with a blackjack (a piece of iron weighing several pounds) has a much better success rate. The result is a large number of deaths and permanent damage from brain hemorrhage.

Critics of TV violence claim it teaches children sadism and cruelty. I honestly don't know whether or not TV violence is harmful, but if so the critics have it backward. Children can't learn to enjoy cruelty from the neat, sanitized mayhem on the average series. There isn't any! What they learn is far more malignant: that guns or fists are clean, efficient, exciting ways to deal with a difficult situation. Bang! — you're dead! Bop! — you're unconscious (temporarily)!

"Truth-in-advertising" laws eliminated many absurd commercial claims. I often daydream about what would happen if we had "truth in violence"— if every show had to pass scrutiny by a board of doctors who had no power to censor but could insist that any action scene have at least a vague resemblance to medical reality ("Stop the projector! . . . You have your hero waylaid by three Mafia thugs who beat him brutally before he struggles free. The next day he shows up with this cute little Band-aid over his eyebrow. We can't pass that. You'll have to add one eye swollen shut, three missing front teeth, at least twenty stitches over the lips and eyes, and a wired jaw. Got that? Roll 'em . . .").

Seriously, real-life violence is dirty, painful, bloody, disgusting. It [20] causes mutilation and misery, and it doesn't solve problems. It makes them worse. If we're genuinely interested in protecting our children, we should stop campaigning to "clean up" TV violence. It's already too antiseptic. Ironically, the problem with TV violence is: It's not violent enough.

TV Causes Violence?
Try Again

IRA GLASSER

To the Editor:

In "Look to Television's Role in Youth Violence" (letter, June 1), Paul Kettl, a professor of psychiatry, cites research that shows a statistical correlation between the rise in the rate of homicide in the United States and the onset of television. He cites his own research, which shows, he states, that "Children who watch more than two hours of television a day are especially at risk" of having "behavioral problems."

He doesn't say if this finding applies to all children or what else may be going on in the lives of those children with behavioral problems. Nor does he say whether the research implicates all television watching or only certain programs or perhaps the news. Although never said explicitly, the implication is there to draw: Watching too much television may turn your kid into a killer. And indeed your headline draws that conclusion.

But such conclusions misuse and misunderstand the nature of such research. The kind of research Dr. Kettl cites is called epidemiological research. This consists of observing groups of people and then showing statistical associations between their life-styles or behavior and what happens to them later. Scientists know, as the public often does not, that such epidemiological research tells us nothing about cause and effect.

For example, some early epidemiologic research showed a statistical association between heart disease and the number of television sets a person owned. But this did not mean that owning more than one television set caused heart disease. Clinical trials demonstrated that cholesterol, but not the number of television sets one owned, was causally related.

Similarly, one could show that the rate at which grass grows correlates with the number of drownings. As one increases, so does the other. But that's because both are caused by warm weather. One would not seek to reduce the number of drownings by buying lawn mowers. 5

Yet that is precisely what is being suggested to curb violence. "Television is the cause," many people will falsely conclude after reading about such statistical associations.

This letter from Ira Glasser, executive director of the American Civil Liberties Union since 1978, appeared in the *New York Times* on June 15, 1994.

Television? Not drug prohibition, or the easy availability of guns or the loss of hope or relentless deprivation? No, we don't want to address those intractable problems. But dealing with television is easy. We can censor it. We can threaten to pass laws regulating when certain programs can be shown. We can decide, as a Florida hotel chain did for its rooms, to block reception of local television news that covers crime zealously (news article, June 3).

Finding scapegoats and diverting our attention from real and difficult problems is not new. But as we are not so gullible as to believe that we can reduce drownings by cutting the grass or have healthier hearts by limiting ourselves to owning one television, let us also not leap to the conclusion that watching too much television makes people killers. No studies show such a cause-and-effect connection. Homicide is a tad more complicated.

Ira Glasser

Teen Violence Spawned by Guns and Cultural Rot
ALBERT R. HUNT

There has been a predictable political response after the rash of tragic killings by children at schools from Springfield, Oregon, to Jonesboro, Arkansas.

Liberals cry for tougher gun-control laws: if only these deranged youths didn't have easy access to guns, many of these atrocities wouldn't happen, they say.

Conservatives place much of the blame on popular culture; Hollywood and television are overwhelmingly violence-oriented, the argument goes, and the music industry is a real villain for pandering to the worst instincts of kids by glorifying sexual obscenities and bestial brutality.

Both arguments are exaggerations. Some of these teenage perpetrators don't fit into any stereotypes. *Slate,* Microsoft's always interesting online magazine, noted that Kip Kinkel, the teenager in Springfield who killed his parents and two schoolmates, came from a good family that tried to teach him how to use guns safely and didn't give him easy access. His only known entertainment vices were cartoons. Others are simply mentally unbalanced kids, a type that has

Albert R. Hunt has worked at the *Wall Street Journal* for more than thirty years as a reporter, a bureau chief, and most recently as the executive Washington editor. This article appeared in the *Wall Street Journal* on June 11, 1998.

always existed: Luke Woodham, the seventeen-year-old Pearl, Mississippi, kid who killed his mother and a classmate, testified that demons instructed him to do it.

More importantly, however, both sides also make important points. There is room for common cause, say some diverse but very smart people who worry a lot about violence: politicians like Senator Joe Lieberman (Democrat, Connecticut) and Bill Bennett, a prominent Republican, and scholars like criminologist John Dilulio and psychiatrist Alvin Poussaint.

"The music pounds and pounds with messages of violence and degradation of women; if you talk to people on the streets, they will tell you this is public-enemy number one," says Mr. Dilulio of Princeton University. But he also suggests that for any antiviolence program to work, "You have to make it impossible for kids to get easy access to guns."

Similarly, Dr. Poussaint, who teaches at Harvard, notes that easy access to guns "makes the problems much worse. Gun defenders say you could still murder with a knife but one kid I was interviewing pointed out that you can't have a drive-by shooting with a knife." But he also believes the culture's romanticization of violence — in movies, television, and music — "certainly contributes to a general disregard for authority; children see or hear this over and over again and they become a little bit more numb to violence."

Messrs. Lieberman and Bennett have teamed up to try to focus public scrutiny on what they term "cultural rot," ranging from gangster-rap music to Jerry Springer's television show. They have embarrassed some major corporations, like Seagram's, by spotlighting how they reap big profits from these obscenities. Mr. Bennett, the conservative icon, says, "It's just dumb not to recognize how dangerous it is to so easily put guns in kids' hands."

Of course there are larger societal problems. But while violence in general has declined over the last several years, it is rising among teenagers, and certainly any short-term efforts to address this should focus on both guns and popular culture.

Movie actor Charlton Heston, the new president of the National Rifle Association, insisted this week that the school shootings were "a child issue, not a gun issue." Does Mr. Heston think that the people killed in Jonesboro would have been just as vulnerable to a bow and arrow? Or does he believe the four-year-old in Greensboro, North Carolina, who shot and killed his six-year-old neighbor in April is a "child problem"?

Next week the most important antigun legislation of this session will be offered by Democratic Representative Carolyn McCarthy, a suburban New York nurse and mother who got into politics after her husband was killed by a crazed gunman on a commuter train. The measure would crack down on dealers who sell to kids, require manufacturers to make safer guns, and penalize adults who allow children easy access to a firearm that is then used to kill or injure someone.

The gun lobby, with its huge campaign contributions, is convinced Republican congressional leaders will thwart this initiative. They probably are right, but some politicians may pay a price, as did Ms. McCarthy's NRA-backing predecessor. Polls indicate strong support for such measures.

There's also a growing public backlash against the plethora of violent movies, television, video games, and music. David Walsh, director of the National Institute on Media and the Family, notes that it's estimated the average American kid has seen 200,000 acts of violence on television by the time he or she graduates from high school. Try to take your kids to a movie that is devoid of violence or sex. Or just look at some of the graphic violence in the best-selling video games.

Nothing is more offensive than some of the music. After Mitchell Johnson, thirteen, and Drew Golden, eleven, killed five people and injured ten at Westside Middle School in Jonesboro, one of the teachers conducted an exhaustive survey. The results showed that Mitchell Johnson was a fanatical devotee of two gangster-rap artists, the late TuPac Shakur and Bone Thugs & Harmony. Both are full of vulgarity, degrading to women, and advocate blasting people with guns. In the three-school survey, a majority of kids listened to these groups and said their parents didn't have a clue as to their lyrics.

Bill Bennett and Joe Lieberman know there are clear First 15 Amendment issues here and wisely don't advocate any bans. But they want to embarrass those who produce this trash. "The weapon of choice for our side is shame," says Mr. Bennett. "We have to be ashamed instead of this anything goes crap."

Defenders of this rot insist there is no reliable data that links violence to culture. That flies in the face of common sense. If Frank Sinatra songs make people feel romantic and John Phillips Sousa makes people feel patriotic, then the obscene violence of shock rocker Marilyn Manson or gangsta-rapper Snoop Doggy Dogg might encourage impressionable and troubled teenagers to feel perverted or violent.

Violence Never Solved
Anything, but It's Entertaining

HOLMAN W. JENKINS JR.

The stock market is jittery. Poverty stares us in the face. At least we still have violent programming on TV, but some would take even this solace away from us.

A debatable sociological wisdom crept into the law with the 1996 Telecommunications Act. Children who watch violent television are at risk of becoming aggressive and violent themselves. Adults who steep themselves in the local news develop an exaggerated fear of the world, the so-called mean world syndrome.

As one of the many scholars plying this vein has noted approvingly, "policymakers are taking the position that television programmers should provide warnings to make viewers aware of the risks of watching certain shows." Because we are programmed by TV, we need the V-chip to reprogram our programmer.

Certainly television has wrought changes in the world, but before asking how it has reshaped human nature, how has human nature shaped television?

Since it became popular to denounce the "wasteland" in the 5 early 1950s, surprisingly few have asked basic questions about the supply and demand for violent programming. The standard critique assumes supply without demand: The audience is dumbly trapped before the show, which is calculated to lift them to a higher state of "arousal" in order to become more receptive to the messages of advertisers.

Now we have the benefit of an economist looking at all this, James Hamilton of Duke, whose new book is *Channeling Violence: The Economic Market for Violent Television Programming.*

It turns out that broadcasters are neither as dumb nor as smart as the standard critique paints them. Pollsters constantly reiterate that Americans find TV "too violent," but combing more finely through the data one finds a substantial minority of dissenters, the people who actually watch violent TV. In Nielsen speak, these are males age eighteen to thirty-four, females age eighteen to thirty-four, and then males age thirty-five to forty-nine. There is demand after all, and it comes from young adults of both sexes.

That broadcasters are prepared to oblige them is no mystery. These viewers are advertisers' most valuable and elusive

---

Holman W. Jenkins Jr. writes the Business World column for the *Wall Street Journal.* This column appeared on October 28, 1998.

demographic group. Young adults are out building lives and careers. They are just developing the brand attachments that will last a lifetime but are seldom to be found in front of a TV where marketers can reach them.

Advertisers pay richly to reach youthful consumers. Ted Turner, who can often be heard denouncing television violence from a podium, has given us Saturday Night Nitro on TNT — whole evenings of delicious violence aimed at young adult viewers. Even when competing against *Monday Night Football,* 65 percent of the movies on TNT contained violence. The rest of the year 92 percent contained violence.

Mr. Hamilton says broadcasters don't aim their violence at 10 younger children, and advertisers don't reward broadcasters for young children in the audience. Their viewing is an "externality," like pollution. But someone might have said the same about adult viewers back when the Big Three networks forced everyone to sit through the same programs.

Thanks to technology and the proliferation of channels, audiences have been freed to go their separate ways. Cable, especially premium cable, has become the violence medium, while violence has dropped steeply on the major networks.

The action-adventure genre has all but disappeared, with the sorry exceptions of CBS's *Walker, Texas Ranger* and ABC's new *Vengeance Unlimited.* The networks base their survival hopes on compiling the last large audiences in television-land, so they fill up our evenings with newsmagazines and sitcoms — shows that attract young people without driving other viewers out of the room.

Why does the younger demographic have a special taste for violent programming? We can at least speculate.

Dolf Zillmann, a psychologist at the University of Alabama, has been one of the few paying attention to the viewer's perspective. Among his several contributions, he has shown that teenagers swarm to horror flicks so the boys can demonstrate their manly unflappability and girls can demonstrate their vulnerable desirability. Boys and girls who fulfill these roles are rated as more sexually desirable by their peers.

Young people, as they set about making room for themselves in 15 the world, are especially full of anxiety about whether good guys or bad guys triumph in the end. Nor are they burdened unduly by a sense of proportionality. Mr. Zillmann points to a program in which a lawyer cheats an old lady out of her savings. The audience's sense of poetic justice is no less fulfilled by "seeing him burn and die in a crash" than seeing him receive a fine and disbarment.

Mr. Hamilton, the economist, supplies buttressing evidence when you consider that the young are less discriminating in matters of taste. Unsurprisingly, the more stars *TV Guide* awards a film, the less violent the film is likely to be. Violent shows are often bad shows. A lousy producer working with a bunch of mediocre writers and actors is going to resort to cloddish violence to dramatize what would otherwise have to be rendered by more literary means.

Criminologists have long noted that homicide becomes rarer among elite social groups as those groups make greater use of lawyers. TV seems to be evolving in the same direction. Lawyer shows are proliferating on the networks. Boilerplate courtroom drama may be replacing shoot-em-up as the preferred formula for resolving conflict.

Those who worry about television may sincerely dream of society becoming a nicer, less competitive place. Children do sometimes mow down their school chums, acting out a scene they may have seen on cable. But claiming we have to reprogram the media watched by 99.99 percent of us to influence the behavior of 0.01 percent is to be rendered helpless by a much smaller problem.

Only sick minds are interested in plotless violence. A British censor once explained his methods by saying he made certain cuts "because we were worried about a very few people who might be vulnerable to being influenced by playing one particular scene in that video repeatedly in their home."

These "very few people" surely exist in the audience, but making 20 television the issue only avoids the question of how we could be doing a better job of identifying the homicidally mentally ill before someone gets hurt.

A Desensitized Society Drenched in Sleaze

JEFF JACOBY

I was seventeen years old when I first saw an X-rated movie. It was Thanksgiving in Washington, D.C. My college dorm had all but emptied out for the holiday weekend. With no classes, no tests, and nobody around, I decided to scratch an itch that had long been tormenting me.

I used to see these movies advertised in the old *Washington Star,* and — like any seventeen-year-old boy whose sex life is mostly theoretical — I burned with curiosity. I wondered what such films might be like, what awful, thrilling secrets they might expose.

Jeff Jacoby is a columnist for the *Boston Globe,* where this essay appeared on June 8, 1995.

And so that weekend I took myself to see one. Full of anticipation, nervous and embarrassed, I walked to the Casino Royale at 14th Street and New York Avenue. At the top of a long flight of stairs, a cashier sat behind a cage. "Five dollars," he demanded — steep for my budget, especially since a ticket to the movies in the late seventies usually cost $3.50. But I'd come this far and couldn't turn back. I paid, I entered, I watched.

For about twenty minutes. The movie, I still remember, was called *Cry for Cindy,* and what I saw on the screen I'd never seen — I'd never even imagined — before. A man and a woman, oral sex, extreme close-ups. The sheer gynecological explicitness of it jolted me. Was *this* the forbidden delight hinted at by those ads? This wasn't arousing, it was repellent. I was shocked. More than that: I was ashamed.

I literally couldn't take it. I bolted the theater and tumbled down   5
the steps. My heart was pounding and my face was burning. I felt dirty. Guilty. I was conscience-stricken.

All that — over a dirty movie.

Well, I was an innocent at seventeen. I was naive and inexperienced, shy with girls, the product of a parochial-school education and a strict upbringing. Explicit sex — in the movies, music, my social life — was foreign to me. Coming from such an environment, who *wouldn't* recoil from *Cry for Cindy* or feel repelled by what it put up on that screen?

But here's the rub: Dirty movies don't have that effect on me anymore. I don't make a practice of seeking out skin flicks or films with explicit nudity, but in the years since I was seventeen, I've certainly seen my share. Today another sex scene is just another sex scene. Not shocking, not appalling, nothing I feel ashamed to look at. Writhing bodies on the screen? Raunchy lyrics in a song? They may entertain me or they may bore me, but one thing they no longer do is make me blush.

I've become jaded. And if a decade and a half of being exposed to this stuff can leave *me* jaded — with my background, my religious schooling, my disciplined origins — what impact does it have on kids and young adults who have never been sheltered from anything? What impact does it have on a generation growing up amid dysfunctional families, broken-down schools, and a culture of values-free secularism?

If sex- and violence-drenched entertainment can desensitize me,   10
it can desensitize anyone. It can desensitize a whole society. It can drag us to the point where nothing is revolting. Where nothing makes us blush.

And what happens to an unblushing society? Why, everything. Central Park joggers get raped and beaten into comas. Sixth-graders sleep around. Los Angeles rioters burn down their neighborhood and murder dozens of their neighbors. The Menendez boys blow off their parents' heads. Lorena Bobbitt mutilates her husband in his sleep. "Artists" sell photographs of crucifixes dunked in urine. Pro-life fanatics open fire on abortion clinics. Daytime TV fills up with deviants. The U.S. Naval Academy fills up with cheaters. The teen suicide rate goes through the roof.

And we get used to all of it. We don't blush.

The point isn't that moviegoers walk out of Oliver Stone's latest grotesquerie primed to kill. Or that Geto Boys' sociopathic lyrics ("Leavin' out her house, grabbed the bitch by her mouth / Drug her back in, slam her down on the couch. / Whipped out my knife, said, 'If you scream I'm cutting,' / Open her legs and . . .") cause rape. The point is that when blood and mayhem and sleazy sex drench our popular culture, we get accustomed to blood and mayhem and sleazy sex. We grow jaded. Depravity becomes more and more tolerable because less and less scandalizes us.

Of course, the entertainment industry accepts no responsibility for any of this. Time Warner and Hollywood indignantly reject the criticisms heaped on them in recent days. We don't cause society's ills, they say, we only reflect them. "If an artist wants to deal with violence or sexuality or images of darkness and horror," said film director Clive Barker, "those are legitimate subjects for artists."

They are, true. Artists have dealt with violence and sexuality 15 and horror since time immemorial. But debauchery is not art. There is nothing ennobling about a two-hour paean to bloodlust. To suggest that Snoop Doggy Dogg's barbaric gang-rape fantasies somehow follow in the tradition of Sophocles' tragic drama, Chaucer's romantic poetry, or Solzhenitsyn's moral testimony is to suggest that there is no difference between meaning and meaninglessness.

For Hollywood and Time Warner, perhaps there no longer is. The question before the house is, what about the rest of us?

THINKING AND WRITING ABOUT SEX AND VIOLENCE IN POPULAR CULTURE

Questions for Discussion and Writing

1. Kristol defends a limited censorship of popular culture. Summarize his reasons. Would any of the writers in Chapter 15, Freedom of Speech, agree with him?
2. Hirschorn claims that prime-time TV shows reflect sound moral values. Do you agree, or do you think his examples are too selective? Can you think of popular TV shows that do not reflect sound values? If so, what *do* they reflect?

3. Although Oppenheim is writing about violence and Jacoby is writing about sex both their claims are based on a shared assumption. Explain it, and decide whether it is valid.

4. What evidence do you find in these essays that establishes a cause-and-effect relationship between TV violence and youthful crime? What fallacy does Glasser see in the arguments attempting to prove a relationship?

5. What examples of "cultural rot" does Hunt provide? Can you give more examples? Or do you think he is exaggerating?

6. Why does Jenkins think we should resist trying to "reprogram the media"? Do you agree with his explanation for teenage attraction to violent films? If not, do you have other explanations?

7. Several authors contend that TV or movie violence is not to blame for youthful crime. What causes do they suggest?

8. What ironic comment is the cartoonist making about studies of TV violence?

Topics for Research

Violence in selected TV shows: justified or unjustified?

Sex on TV: what message?

The significance of Gangsta Rap

Survey of studies on the effect of TV and movie violence

Influence of music videos and sports events on youthful behavior

TAKING THE DEBATE ONLINE

- **Legal Issues Surrounding Violence in the Media** <http://www-honors.ucdavis.edu/html/violence/web.html>   This site, created by a University of California–Davis honors student, explores some of the legal issues surrounding media violence. It includes an interview with the director of the television crime series *Profiler,* a mock trial debate, a First Amendment handbook, media violence handouts, and more.

- **Parental Choice in Television Programming** <http://www.fcc.gov/vchip/legislation.html>   These excerpts of the V-chip legislation are provided by the Federal Communications Commission, an independent government agency whose mission is to encourage competition in all communications markets and to protect the public interest.

- **Profits or Prestige: Sex and Violence in Feature Films** <http://web.syr.edu/~jlmcquiv/film_sv.html>   This thoroughly researched essay by James McQuivey at Syracuse University explores some of the reasons that film producers in Hollywood rely on sexual and violent content. It ends with a series of charts and graphs that try to track and analyze box office receipts, Academy Award nominations, and violent content.

- **Media Scope: Media Policy Clearinghouse** <http://mediascope.org/mediascope/clearing.htm>   This site contains an extensive collection of resources about media, including film, television, the Internet, electronic interactive games, and music.

- **Media Watch** <http://www.mediawatch.com/main.html>   Media Watch, an organization whose goal is to challenge abusive stereotypes and other biased images commonly found in the media, provides these links to media-related news stories, videos, and an archive of past content.

- **NCTV: National Coalition on Television Violence** <http://www.nctvv.org/NCTV%20Images/Contents.html>   The National Coalition on Television Violence provides information on blocking devices, community action, recent news briefs, and a list of links to other organizations whose mission is to end TV violence.

PART FOUR

Classic Arguments

From Crito

PLATO

*Plato, who died in 347 B.C., was one of the greatest Greek
philosophers. He was a student of the Greek philosopher Socrates,
whose teachings he recorded in the form of dialogues between
Socrates and his pupils. In the dialogue below, Crito visits Socrates —
who is in prison, condemned to death for corrupting the youth of
Athens — and tries to persuade him to escape. Socrates, however, refuses, basing his decision on his definition of justice and virtue.*

Socrates: . . . Ought a man to do what he admits to be right, or
ought he to betray the right?

Crito: He ought to do what he thinks right.

Socrates: But if this is true, what is the application? In leaving the
prison against the will of the Athenians, do I wrong any? Or rather
do I not wrong those whom I ought least to wrong? Do I not desert
the principles which are acknowledged by us to be just — what do
you say?

Crito: I cannot tell, Socrates; for I do not know.

Socrates: Then consider the matter in this way: — Imagine that I   5
am about to play truant (you may call the proceeding by any name
which you like), and the laws of the government come and interro-
gate me: "Tell us, Socrates," they say: "what are you about? Are you
not going by an act of yours to overturn us — the laws, and the
whole state, as far as in you lies? Do you imagine that a state can
subsist and not be overthrown, in which the decisions of law have
no power, but are set aside and trampled upon by individuals?"
What will be our answer, Crito, to these and the like words? Any one,
and especially a rhetorician, will have a good deal to say on behalf of
the law which requires a sentence to be carried out. He will argue
that this law should not be set aside; and shall we reply, "Yes, but
the state has injured us and given an unjust sentence." Suppose I say
that?

Crito: Very good, Socrates.

Socrates: "And was that our agreement with you?" the law would
answer; "or were you to abide by the sentence of the state?" And if I
were to express my astonishment at their words, the law would
probably add: "Answer, Socrates, instead of opening your eyes —
you are in the habit of asking and answering questions. Tell us, —
What complaint have you to make against us which justifies you in
attempting to destroy us and the state? In the first place did we not

From Plato's *Crito*, trans. Benjamin Jowett, 3rd ed. (New York: Dial Press, 1982).

bring you into existence? Your father married your mother by our aid and begat you. Say whether you have any objection to urge against those of us who regulate marriage?" None, I should reply. "Or against those of us who after birth regulate the nurture and education of children, in which you also were trained? Were not the laws, which have the charge of education, right in commanding your father to train you in music and gymnastics?" Right, I should reply. "Well then, since you were brought into the world and nurtured and educated by us, can you deny in the first place that you are our child and slave, as your fathers were before you? And if this is true you are not on equal terms with us; nor can you think that you have a right to do to us what we are doing to you. Would you have any right to strike or revile or do any other evil to your father or your master, if you had one, because you have been struck or reviled by him, or received some other evil at his hands? — you would not say this? And because we think right to destroy you, do you think that you have any right to destroy us in return, and your country as far as in you lies? Will you, O professor of true virtue, pretend that you are justified in this? Has a philosopher like you failed to discover that our country is more to be valued and higher and holier far than mother or father or any ancestor, and more to be regarded in the eyes of the gods and of men of understanding? Also to be soothed, and gently and reverently entreated when angry, even more than a father, and either to be persuaded, or if not persuaded, to be obeyed? And when we are punished by her, whether with imprisonment or stripes, the punishment is to be endured in silence, and if she leads us to wounds or death in battle, thither we follow as is right; neither may any one yield or retreat or leave his rank, but whether in battle or in a court of law, or in any other place, he must do what his city and his country order him; or he must change their view of what is just: and if he may do no violence to his father or mother, much less may he do violence to his country." What answer shall we make to this, Crito? Do the laws speak truly, or do they not?

Crito: I think that they do.

Socrates: Then the laws will say, "Consider, Socrates, if we are speaking truly that in your present attempt you are going to do us an injury. For, having brought you into the world, and nurtured and educated you, and given you and every other citizen a share in every good which we had to give, we further proclaim to any Athenian by the liberty which we allow him, that if he does not like us when he has become of age and has seen the ways of the city, and made our acquaintance, he may go where he pleases and take his goods with him. None of us laws will forbid him or interfere with him. Any one who does not like us and the city, and who wants to emigrate to a colony or to any other city, may go where he likes, retaining his property. But he who has experience of the manner in which we order justice and administer the state, and still remains, has entered into an implied contract that he will do as we command him. And he who disobeys us is, as we maintain, thrice wrong; first, because in disobeying us he is disobeying his parents; secondly, because we are the authors of his education; thirdly, because he has made an agreement with us that he will duly obey our commands; and he neither obeys them nor convinces us that our commands are unjust; and we do not rudely impose them, but give him the alternative of obeying or convincing us; — that is what we offer, and he does neither.

"These are the sort of accusations to which, as we were saying, 10 you, Socrates, will be exposed if you accomplish your intentions; you, above all other Athenians." Suppose now I ask, why I rather than anybody else? They will justly retort upon me that I above all other men have acknowledged the agreement. "There is clear proof," they will say, "Socrates, that we and the city were not displeasing to you. Of all Athenians you have been the most constant resident in the city, which, as you never leave, you may be supposed to love. For you never went out of the city either to see the games, except once when you went to the Isthmus, or to any other place unless when you were on military service; nor did you travel as other men do. Nor had you any curiosity to know other states or their laws: your affections did not go beyond us and our state; we were your special favorites, and you acquiesced in our government of you; and here in this city you begat your children, which is a proof of your satisfaction. Moreover, you might in the course of the trial, if you had liked, have fixed the penalty at banishment; the state which refuses to let you go now would have let you go then. But you pretended that you preferred death to exile, and that you were not unwilling to die. And now you have forgotten these fine sentiments, and pay no respect to us the laws, of whom you are the destroyer; and are doing what only a miserable slave would do, running away and turning your back upon the compacts and agreements which you made as a citizen. And first of all answer this very question: Are we right in saying that you agreed to be governed according to us in deed, and not in word only? Is that true or not?" How shall we answer, Crito? Must we not assent?

Crito: We cannot help it, Socrates.

Socrates: Then will they not say: "You, Socrates, are breaking the covenants and agreements which you made with us at your leisure, not in any haste or under any compulsion or deception, but after you have had seventy years to think of them, during which time you were at liberty to leave the city, if we were not to your mind, or if our covenants appeared to you to be unfair. You had your choice, and might have gone either to Lacedaemon or Crete, both which states are often praised by you for their good government, or to some other Hellenic or foreign state. Whereas you, above all our Athenians, seemed to be so fond of the state, or, in other words, of us her laws (and who would care about a state which has no laws?), that you never stirred out of her; the halt, the blind, the maimed were not more stationary in her than you were. And now you run away and forsake your agreements. Not so, Socrates, if you will take our advice; do not make yourself ridiculous by escaping out of the city.

"For just consider, if you transgress and err in this sort of way, what good will you do either to yourself or to your friends? That your friends will be driven into exile and deprived of citizenship, or will lose their property, is tolerably certain; and you yourself, if you fly to one of the neighboring cities, as, for example, Thebes or Megara, both of which are well governed, will come to them as an enemy, Socrates, and their government will be against you, and all patriotic citizens will cast an evil eye upon you as a subverter of the laws, and you will confirm in the minds of the judges the justice of their own condemnation of you. For he who is a corrupter of the laws is more than likely to be a corrupter of the young and foolish portion of mankind. Will you then flee from well-ordered citizens and virtuous men? and is existence worth having on these terms? Or will you go to them without shame, and talk to them, Socrates? And what will you say to them? What you say here about virtue and justice and institutions and laws being the best things among men? Would that be decent of you? Surely not. But if you go away from well-governed states to Crito's friends in Thessaly, where there is a great disorder and licence, they will be charmed to hear the tale of your escape from prison, set off with ludicrous particulars of the manner in which you were wrapped in a goatskin or some other disguise, and metamorphosed as the manner is of runaways; but will there be no one to remind you that in your old age you were ashamed to violate the most sacred laws from a miserable desire of a little more life? Perhaps not, if you keep them in a good temper; but if they are out of temper you will hear many degrading things; you will live, but how? — as the flatterer of all men, and the servant of all men; and doing what? — eating and drinking in Thessaly, having gone abroad in order that you may get a dinner. And where will be your fine sentiments about justice and virtue? Say that you wish to live for the sake of your children — you want to bring them up and educate them — will you take them into Thessaly and deprive them of Athenian citizenship? Is this the benefit which you will confer upon them? Or are you under the impression that they will be better cared for and educated here if you are still alive, although absent from them; for your friends will take care of them? Do you fancy that if you are an inhabitant of Thessaly they will take care of them, and if you are an inhabitant of the other world that they will not take care of them? Nay: but if they who call themselves friends are good for anything, they will — to be sure they will.

"Listen, then, Socrates, to us who have brought you up. Think not of life and children first, and of justice afterwards, but of justice first, that you may be justified before the princes of the world below. For neither will you nor any that belong to you be happier or holier or juster in this life, or happier in another, if you do as Crito bids. Now you depart in innocence, a sufferer and not a doer of evil; a victim, not of the laws of men. But if you go forth, returning evil for evil, and injury for injury, breaking the covenants and agreements which you have made with us, and wronging those whom you ought least of all to wrong, that is to say, yourself, your friends, your country, and us, we shall be angry with you while you live, and our brethren, the laws in the world below, will receive you as an enemy; for they will know that you have done your best to destroy us. Listen, then, to us and not to Crito."

This, dear Crito, is the voice which I seem to hear murmuring in 15
my ears, like the sound of the flute in the ears of the mystic; that voice, I say, is humming in my ears, and prevents me from hearing any other. And I know that anything more which you may say will be vain. Yet speak, if you have anything to say.

Crito: I have nothing to say, Socrates.

Socrates: Leave me then, Crito, to fulfill the will of God, and to follow whither he leads.

Discussion Questions

1. What debt to the law and his country does Socrates acknowledge? Mention the specific reasons for which he owes obedience. Is the analogy of the country to parents a plausible one? Why or why not?
2. Explain the nature of the "implied contract" that exists between Socrates and the state. According to the state, how has Socrates forfeited his right to object to punishment?
3. What appeal does that state make to Socrates' sense of justice and virtue?

Writing Suggestions

4. Socrates bases his refusal to escape the death penalty on his definition of justice and virtue. Basing your own argument on other criteria, make a claim for the right of Socrates to try to escape his punishment. Would some good be served by his escape?
5. The analogy between one's country and one's parents is illustrated at great length in Socrates' argument. In the light of modern ideas about the relationship between the state and the individual in a democracy, write a refutation of the analogy. Perhaps you can think of a different and more fitting one.

A Modest Proposal

JONATHAN SWIFT

*This essay is acknowledged by almost all critics to be the most power-
ful example of irony in the English language. (Irony means saying
one thing but meaning another.) In 1729 Jonathan Swift, prolific
satirist and dean of St. Patrick's Cathedral in Dublin, was moved to
write in protest against the terrible poverty in which the Irish were
forced to live under British rule. Notice that the essay is organized according to one of the patterns outlined in Part Two of this book (see
Presenting the Stock Issues, Chapter 9, p. 346). First, Swift establishes
the need for a change, then he offers his proposal, and finally, he lists
its advantages.*

It is a melancholy object to those who walk through this great
town[1] or travel in the country, when they see the streets, the roads,
and cabin doors, crowded with beggars of the female sex, followed
by three, four, or six children, all in rags and importuning every passenger for an alms. These mothers, instead of being able to work for
their honest livelihood, are forced to employ all their time in
strolling to beg sustenance for their helpless infants, who, as they
grow up, either turn thieves for want of work, or leave their dear native country to fight for the Pretender in Spain, or sell themselves to
the Barbados.[2]

I think it is agreed by all parties that this prodigious number of
children in the arms, or on the backs, or at the heels of their mothers, and frequently of their fathers, is in the present deplorable state
of the kingdom a very great additional grievance; and therefore who-
ever could find out a fair, cheap, and easy method of making these
children sound, useful members of the commonwealth would deserve so well of the public as to have his statue set up for a pre-
server of the nation.

But my intention is very far from being confined to provide only
for the children of professed beggars; it is of a much greater extent,
and shall take in the whole number of infants at a certain age who
are born of parents in effect as little able to support them as those
who demand our charity in the streets.

As to my own part, having turned my thoughts for many years
upon this important subject, and maturely weighed the several

---

[1] Dublin. — ED.

[2] The Pretender was James Stuart, who was exiled to Spain. Many Irish men had
joined an army attempting to return him to the English throne in 1715. Others had become indentured servants, agreeing to work for a set number of years in Barbados or
other British colonies in exchange for their transportation out of Ireland. — ED.

668

schemes of other projectors,[3] I have always found them grossly mistaken in their computation. It is true, a child just dropped from its dam may be supported by her milk for a solar year, with little other nourishment; at most not above the value of two shillings, which the mother may certainly get, or the value in scraps, by her lawful occupation of begging; and it is exactly at one year that I propose to provide for them in such a manner as instead of being a charge upon their parents or the parish, or wanting food and raiment for the rest of their lives, they shall on the contrary contribute to the feeding, and partly to the clothing, of many thousands.

There is likewise another great advantage in my scheme, that it 5 will prevent those voluntary abortions, and that horrid practice of women murdering their bastard children, alas, too frequent among us, sacrificing the poor innocent babes, I doubt, more to avoid the expense than the shame, which would move tears and pity in the most savage and inhuman breast.

The number of souls in this kingdom being usually reckoned one million and a half, of these I calculate there may be about two hundred thousand couples whose wives are breeders; from which number I subtract thirty thousand couples who are able to maintain their own children, although I apprehend there cannot be so many under the present distress of the kingdom; but this being granted, there will remain an hundred and seventy thousand breeders. I again subtract fifty thousand for those women who miscarry, or whose children die by accident or disease within the year. There only remain an hundred and twenty thousand children of poor parents annually born. The question therefore is, how this number shall be reared and provided for, which, as I have already said, under the present situation of affairs, is utterly impossible by all the methods hitherto proposed. For we can neither employ them in handicraft or agriculture; we neither build houses (I mean in the country) nor cultivate land. They can very seldom pick up a livelihood by stealing till they arrive at six years old, except where they are of towardly parts;[4] although I confess they learn the rudiments much earlier, during which time they can however be looked upon only as probationers, as I have been informed by a principal gentleman in the county of Cavan, who protested to me that he never knew above one or two instances under the age of six, even in a part of the kingdom so renowned for the quickest proficiency in that art.

I am assured by our merchants that a boy or a girl before twelve years old is no salable commodity; and even when they come to this age they will not yield above three pounds, or three pounds and a half a crown at most on the Exchange; which cannot turn to account

---

[3] Planners. — ED.
[4] Innate talents. — ED.

either to the parents or the kingdom, the charge of nutriment and rags having been at least four times that value.

I shall now therefore humbly propose my own thoughts, which I hope will not be liable to the least objection.

I have been assured by a very knowing American of my acquaintance in London, that a young healthy child well nursed is at a year old a most delicious, nourishing, and wholesome food, whether stewed, roasted, baked, or boiled; and I make no doubt that it will equally serve in a fricassee or a ragout.[5]

I do therefore humbly offer it to public consideration that of the 10 hundred and twenty thousand children, already computed, twenty thousand may be reserved for breed, whereof only one fourth part to be males, which is more than we allow to sheep, black cattle, or swine; and my reason is that these children are seldom the fruits of marriage, a circumstance not much regarded by our savages, therefore one male will be sufficient to serve four females. That the remaining hundred thousand may at a year old be offered in sale to the persons of quality and fortune through the kingdom, always advising the mother to let them suck plentifully in the last month, so as to render them plump and fat for a good table. A child will make two dishes at an entertainment for friends; and when the family dines alone, the fore or hind quarter will make a reasonable dish, and seasoned with a little pepper or salt will be very good boiled on the fourth day, especially in winter.

I have reckoned upon a medium that a child just born will weigh twelve pounds, and in a solar year if tolerably nursed increaseth to twenty-eight pounds.

I grant this food will be somewhat dear, and therefore very proper for landlords, who, as they have already devoured most of the parents, seem to have the best title to the children.

Infant's flesh will be in season throughout the year, but more plentiful in March, and a little before and after. For we are told by a grave author, an eminent French physician,[6] that fish being a prolific diet, there are more children born in Roman Catholic countries about nine months after Lent than at any other season; therefore, reckoning a year after Lent, the markets will be more glutted than usual, because the number of popish infants is at least three to one in this kingdom; and therefore it will have one other collateral advantage, by lessening the number of Papists among us.

I have already computed the charge of nursing a beggar's child (in which list I reckon all cottagers, laborers, and four-fifths of the farmers) to be about two shillings per annum, rags included; and I

---

[5] Stew. — ED.

[6] A reference to Swift's favorite French writer, François Rabelais (1494?–1553), who was actually a broad satirist known for his coarse humor. — ED.

believe no gentleman would repine to give ten shillings for the carcass of a good fat child, which, as I have said, will make four dishes of excellent nutritive meat, when he hath only some particular friend or his own family to dine with him. Thus the squire will learn to be a good landlord, and grow popular among the tenants; the mother will have eight shillings net profit, and be fit for work till she produces another child.

Those who are more thrifty (as I must confess the times require) may flay the carcass; the skin of which artificially[7] dressed will make admirable gloves for ladies, and summer boots for fine gentlemen.

As to our city of Dublin, shambles[8] may be appointed for this purpose in the most convenient parts of it, and butchers we may be assured will not be wanting; although I rather recommend buying the children alive, and dressing them hot from the knife as we do roasting pigs.

A very worthy person, a true lover of his country, and whose virtues I highly esteem, was lately pleased in discoursing on this matter to offer a refinement upon my scheme. He said that many gentlemen of his kingdom, having of late destroyed their deer, he conceived that the want of venison might be well supplied by the bodies of young lads and maidens, not exceeding fourteen years of age nor under twelve, so great a number of both sexes in every county being now ready to starve for want of work and service; and these to be disposed of by their parents, if alive, or otherwise by their nearest relations. But with due deference to so excellent a friend and so deserving a patriot, I cannot be altogether in his sentiments; for as to the males, my American acquaintance assured me from frequent experience that their flesh was generally tough and lean, like that of our schoolboys, by continual exercise, and their taste disagreeable; and to fatten them would not answer the charge. Then as to the females, it would, I think with humble submission, be a loss to the public, because they soon would become breeders themselves; and besides, it is not improbable that some scrupulous people might be apt to censure such a practice (although indeed very unjustly) as a little bordering upon cruelty; which, I confess, hath always been with me the strongest objection against any project, how well soever intended.

But in order to justify my friend, he confessed that this expedient was put into his head by the famous Psalmanazar,[9] a native of the island Formosa, who came from thence to London above twenty

---

[7] With art or craft. — ED.

[8] Butcher shops or slaughterhouses. — ED.

[9] Georges Psalmanazar was a Frenchman who pretended to be Japanese and wrote an entirely imaginary *Description of the Isle Formosa*. He had become well known in gullible London society. — ED.

years ago, and in conversation told my friend that in his country when any young person happened to be put to death, the executioner sold the carcass to persons of quality as a prime dainty; and that in his time the body of a plump girl of fifteen, who was crucified for an attempt to poison the emperor, was sold to his Imperial Majesty's prime minister of state, and other great mandarins of the court, in joints from the gibbet, at four hundred crowns. Neither indeed can I deny that if the same use were made of several plump young girls in this town, who without one single groat to their fortunes cannot stir abroad without a chair, and appear at the playhouse and assemblies in foreign fineries which they never will pay for, the kingdom would not be the worse.

Some persons of a desponding spirit are in great concern about that vast number of poor people who are aged, diseased, or maimed, and I have been desired to employ my thoughts what course may be taken to ease the nation of so grievous an encumbrance. But I am not in the least pain upon that matter, because it is very well known that they are every day dying and rotting by cold and famine, and filth and vermin, as fast as can be reasonably expected. And as to the younger laborers, they are now in almost as hopeful a condition. They cannot get work, and consequently pine away for want of nourishment to a degree that if any time they are accidentally hired to common labor, they have not strength to perform it; and thus the country and themselves are happily delivered from the evils to come.

I have too long digressed, and therefore shall return to my subject. I think the advantages by the proposal which I have made are obvious and many, as well as of the highest importance. 20

For first, as I have already observed, it would greatly lessen the number of Papists, with whom we are yearly overrun, being the principal breeders of the nation as well as our most dangerous enemies; and who stay at home on purpose to deliver the kingdom to the Pretender, hoping to take their advantage by the absence of so many good Protestants, who have chosen rather to leave their country than to stay at home and pay tithes against their conscience to an Episcopal curate.

Secondly, the poorer tenants will have something valuable of their own, which by law may be made liable to distress,[10] and help to pay their landlord's rent, their corn and cattle being already seized and money a thing unknown.

Thirdly, whereas the maintenance of an hundred thousand children, from two years old and upwards, cannot be computed at less than ten shillings a piece per annum, the nation's stock will be thereby increased fifty thousand pounds per annum, besides the profit of a new dish introduced to the tables of all gentlemen of for-

---

[10] Subject to possession by lenders. — ED.

tune in the kingdom who have any refinement in taste. And the money will circulate among ourselves, the goods being entirely of our own growth and manufacture.

Fourthly, the constant breeders, besides the gain of eight shillings sterling per annum by the sale of their children, will be rid of the charge of maintaining them after the first year.

Fifthly, this food would likewise bring great custom to taverns, where the vintners will certainly be so prudent as to procure the best receipts for dressing it to perfection, and consequently have their houses frequented by all the fine gentlemen, who justly value themselves upon their knowledge in good eating; and a skillful cook, who understands how to oblige his guests, will contrive to make it as expensive as they please.

Sixthly, this would be a great inducement to marriage, which all wise nations have either encouraged by rewards or enforced by laws and penalties. It would increase the care and tenderness of mothers toward their children, when they were sure of a settlement for life to the poor babes, provided in some sort by the public, to their annual profit instead of expense. We should see an honest emulation among the married women, which of them could bring the fattest child to the market. Men would become as fond of their wives during the time of their pregnancy as they are now of their mares in foal, their cows in calf, or sows when they are ready to farrow; nor offer to beat or kick them (as is too frequent a practice) for fear of a miscarriage.

Many other advantages might be enumerated. For instance, the addition of some thousand carcasses in our exportation of barreled beef, the propagation of swine's flesh, and improvements in the art of making good bacon, so much wanted among us by the great destruction of pigs, too frequent at our tables, which are no way comparable in taste or magnificence to a well-grown, fat, yearling child, which roasted whole will make a considerable figure at a lord mayor's feast or any other public entertainment. But this and many others I omit, being studious of brevity.

Supposing that one thousand families in this city would be constant customers for infants' flesh, besides others who might have it at merry meetings, particularly weddings and christenings, I compute that Dublin would take off annually about twenty thousand carcasses, and the rest of the kingdom (where probably they will be sold somewhat cheaper) the remaining eighty thousand.

I can think of no one objection that will possibly be raised against this proposal, unless it should be urged that the number of people will be thereby much lessened in the kingdom. This I freely own, and it was indeed one principal design in offering it to the world. I desire the reader will observe, that I calculate my remedy for this one individual kingdom of Ireland and for no other that ever was, is, or I think ever can be upon earth. Therefore let no man talk to me of other expedients: of taxing our absentees at five shillings a pound: of using neither clothes nor household furniture except what is of our own growth and manufacture: of utterly rejecting the materials and instruments that promote foreign luxury: of curing the expensiveness of pride, vanity, idleness, and gaming in our women: of introducing a vein of parsimony, prudence, and temperance: of learning to love our country, in the want of which we differ even from Laplanders and the inhabitants of Topinamboo:[11] of quitting our animosities and factions, nor acting any longer like the Jews, who were murdering one another at the very moment their city was taken:[12] of being a little cautious not to sell our country and conscience for nothing: of teaching landlords to have at least one degree of mercy toward their tenants: lastly, of putting a spirit of honesty, industry, and skill into our shopkeepers; who, if a resolution could now be taken to buy only our native goods, would immediately unite to cheat and exact upon us in the price, the measure, and the goodness, nor could ever yet be brought to make one fair proposal of just dealing, though often and earnestly invited to it.

Therefore I repeat, let no man talk to me of these and the like expedients, till he hath at least some glimpse of hope that there will ever be some hearty and sincere attempt to put them in practice. 30

But as to myself, having been wearied out for many years with offering vain, idle, visionary thoughts, and at length utterly despairing of success, I fortunately fell upon this proposal, which, as it is wholly new, so it hath something solid and real, of no expense and little trouble, full in our own power, and whereby we can incur no danger in disobliging England. For this kind of commodity will not bear exportation, the flesh being of too tender a consistence to admit a long continuance in salt, although perhaps I could name a country which would be glad to eat up our whole nation without it.

After all, I am not so violently bent upon my own opinion as to reject any offer proposed by wise men, which shall be found equally innocent, cheap, easy, and effectual. But before something of that kind shall be advanced in contradiction to my scheme, and offering a better, I desire the author or authors will be pleased maturely to consider two points. First, as things now stand, how they will be able to find food and raiment for an hundred thousand useless mouths and backs. And secondly, there being a round million of creatures in human figure throughout this kingdom, whose sole subsistence put into a common stock would leave them in debt two millions of pounds sterling, adding those who are beggars by profession to the bulk of farmers, cottagers, and laborers, with their wives and children who are beggars in effect; I desire those politi-

---

[11] District of Brazil. — ED.

[12] During the Roman siege of Jerusalem (A.D. 70), prominent Jews were charged with collaborating with the enemy and put to death. — ED.

cians who dislike my overture, and may perhaps be so bold to attempt an answer, that they will first ask the parents of these mortals whether they would not at this day think it a great happiness to have been sold for food at a year old in this manner I prescribe, and thereby have avoided such a perpetual scene of misfortunes as they have since gone through by the oppression of landlords, the impossibility of paying rent without money or trade, the want of common sustenance, with neither house nor clothes to cover them from the inclemencies of the weather, and the most inevitable prospect of entailing the like of greater miseries upon their breed forever.

I profess, in the sincerity of my heart, that I have not the least personal interest in endeavoring to promote this necessary work, having no other motive than the public good of my country, by advancing our trade, providing for infants, relieving the poor, and giving some pleasure to the rich. I have no children by which I can propose to get a single penny; the youngest being nine years old, and my wife past childbearing.

Discussion Questions

1. What implicit assumption about the treatment of the Irish underlies Swift's proposal? Do expressions such as "just dropped from its dam" and "whose wives are breeders" give the reader a clue?
2. In this essay Swift assumes a persona; that is, for the purposes of the proposal he makes, he pretends to be a different person. Describe the characteristics of that person. Point out the places in the essay that reveal them.
3. In several places, however, Swift reveals himself as the outraged witness of English cruelty and indifference. Note the language that seems to reflect his own feelings.
4. Throughout the essay Swift recites lists of facts, many of them in the form of statistics. How do these facts contribute to the persuasiveness of his argument? How do they affect the reader?
5. What social practices and attitudes of both the Irish and the English does Swift condemn?
6. Does Swift offer any solutions for the problems he attacks? How do you know?
7. When this essay first appeared in 1729, some readers took it seriously and accused Swift of monstrous cruelty. Can you think of reasons that these readers failed to recognize the ironic intent?

Writing Suggestions

8. Try an ironical essay of your own. Choose a subject that clearly lends itself to such treatment. As Swift did, use logic and restraint in your language.
9. Choose a problem for which you think you have a solution. Defend your solution by using the stock issues as your pattern of organization.

Civil Disobedience

HENRY DAVID THOREAU

Henry David Thoreau (1817–1862), philosopher and writer, is best known for Walden, *an account of his solitary retreat to Walden Pond, near Concord, Massachusetts. Here he remained for more than two years in an effort to "live deliberately, to front only the essential facts of life." "Civil Disobedience" was first given as a lecture in 1848 and published in 1849. It was widely read and influenced both Mahatma Gandhi in the passive-resistance campaign he led against the British in India and Martin Luther King Jr. in the U.S. civil rights movement.*

I heartily accept the motto, — "That government is best which governs least"; and I should like to see it acted up to more rapidly and systematically. Carried out, it finally amounts to this, which also I believe, — "That government is best which governs not at all"; and when men are prepared for it, that will be the kind of government which they will have. Government is at best but an expedient; but most governments are usually, and all governments are sometimes, inexpedient. The objections which have been brought against a standing army, and they are many and weighty, and deserve to prevail, may also at last be brought against a standing government. The standing army is only an arm of the standing government. The government itself, which is only the mode which the people have chosen to execute their will, is equally liable to be abused and perverted before the people can act through it. Witness the present Mexican war, the work of comparatively a few individuals using the standing government as their tool; for, in the outset, the people would not have consented to this measure.

This American government, — what is it but a tradition, though a recent one, endeavoring to transmit itself unimpaired to posterity, but each instant losing some of its integrity? It has not the vitality and force of a single living man; for a single man can bend it to his will. It is a sort of wooden gun to the people themselves. But it is not the less necessary for this; for the people must have some complicated machinery or other, and hear its din, to satisfy that idea of government which they have. Governments show thus how successfully men can be imposed on, even impose on themselves, for their own advantage. It is excellent, we must all allow. Yet this government never of itself furthered any enterprise, but by the alacrity with which it got out of its way. *It* does not keep the country free. *It* does not settle the West. *It* does not educate. The character inherent in the American people has done all that has been accomplished; and it would have done somewhat more, if the government had not sometimes got in its way. For government is an expedient by which men would fain succeed in letting one another alone; and, as has been said, when it is most expedient, the governed are most let alone by it. Trade and commerce, if they were not made of India-rubber, would never manage to bounce over the obstacles which legislators are continually putting in their way; and, if one were to judge these men wholly by the effects of their actions, and not partly by their intentions, they would deserve to be classed and punished with those mischievous persons who put obstructions on the rail-roads.

But, to speak practically and as a citizen, unlike those who call themselves no-government men, I ask for, not at once no government, but *at once* a better government. Let every man make known what kind of government would command his respect, and that will be one step toward obtaining it.

After all, the practical reason why, when the power is once in the hands of the people, a majority are permitted, and for a long period continue, to rule, is not because they are most likely to be in the right, nor because this seems fairest to the minority, but because they are physically the strongest. But a government in which the majority rule in all cases cannot be based on justice, even as far as men understand it. Can there not be a government in which majorities do not virtually decide right and wrong, but conscience? — in which majorities decide only those questions to which the rule of expediency is applicable? Must the citizen ever for a moment, or in the least degree, resign his conscience to the legislator? Why has every man a conscience, then? I think that we should be men first, and subjects afterward. It is not desirable to cultivate a respect for the law, so much as for the right. The only obligation which I have a right to assume, is to do at any time what I think right. It is truly enough said, that a corporation has no conscience; but a corporation of conscientious men is a corporation *with* a conscience. Law never made men a whit more just; and, by means of their respect for it, even the well-disposed are daily made the agents of injustice. A common and natural result of an undue respect for law is, that you may see a file of soldiers, colonel, captain, corporal, privates, powder-monkeys, and all, marching in admirable order over hill and dale to the wars, against their wills, aye, against their common sense and consciences, which makes it very steep marching indeed, and produces a palpitation of the heart. They have no doubt that it is a damnable business in which they are concerned; they are all peaceably inclined. Now, what are they? Men at all? or small moveable forts and magazines, at the service of some unscrupulous man in power? Visit the Navy-Yard, and behold a marine, such a man as an American government can make, or such as it can make a man with its black arts, — a mere shadow and reminiscence of humanity, a man laid out alive and standing, and already, as one may say, buried under arms with funeral accompaniments, though it may be, —

Not a drum was heard, nor a funeral note,
As his corse to the rampart we hurried;
Not a soldier discharged his farewell shot
O'er the grave where our hero we buried.

The mass of men serve the state thus, not as men mainly, but as 5 machines, with their bodies. They are the standing army, and the militia, jailers, constables, posse comitatus, &c. In most cases there is no free exercise whatever of the judgment or of the moral sense; but they put themselves on a level with wood and earth and stones; and wooden men can perhaps be manufactured that will serve the purpose as well. Such command no more respect than men of straw, or a lump of dirt. They have the same sort of worth only as horses and dogs. Yet such as these even are commonly esteemed good citizens. Others, — as most legislators, politicians, lawyers, ministers, and office-holders, — serve the State chiefly with their heads; and, as they rarely make any moral distinctions, they are as likely to serve the Devil, without *intending* it, as God. A very few, as heroes, patriots, martyrs, reformers in the great sense, and *men*, serve the state with their consciences also, and so necessarily resist it for the most part, and they are commonly treated as enemies by it. A wise man will only be useful as a man, and will not submit to be "clay," and "stop a hole to keep the wind away," but leave that office to his dust at least: —

I am too high-born to be propertied,
To be a secondary at control,
Or useful serving-man and instrument
To any sovereign state throughout the world.

He who gives himself entirely to his fellow-men appears to them useless and selfish; but he who gives himself partially to them is pronounced a benefactor and philanthropist.

How does it become a man to behave toward this American government today? I answer that he cannot without disgrace be associated with it. I cannot for an instant recognize that political organization as *my* government which is the *slave's* government also.

All men recognize the right of revolution; that is, the right to refuse allegiance to, and to resist, the government, when its tyranny or its inefficiency are great and unendurable. But almost all say that such is not the case now. But such was the case, they think, in the Revolution of '75. If one were to tell me that this was a bad government because it taxed certain foreign commodities brought to its ports, it is most probable that I should not make an ado about it, for I can do without them. All machines have their friction; and possibly this does enough good to counterbalance the evil. At any rate, it is a great evil to make a stir about it. But when the friction comes to have its machine, and oppression and robbery are organized, I say, let us not have such a machine any longer. In other words, when a sixth of the population of a nation which has undertaken to be the refuge of liberty are slaves, and a whole country is unjustly overrun and conquered by a foreign army, and subjected to military law, I think that it is not too soon for honest men to rebel and revolutionize. What makes this duty the more urgent is the fact, that the country so overrun is not our own, but ours is the invading army.

Paley, a common authority with many on moral questions, in his chapter on the "Duty of Submission to Civil Government," resolves all civil obligation into expediency; and he proceeds to say, "that so long as the interest of the whole society requires it, that is, so long as the established government cannot be resisted or changed without public inconveniency, it is the will of God that the established government be obeyed, and no longer. . . . This principle being admitted, the justice of every particular case of resistance is reduced to a computation of the quantity of the danger and grievance on the one side, and of the probability and expense of redressing it on the other." Of this, he says, every man shall judge for himself. But Paley appears never to have contemplated those cases to which the rule of expediency does not apply, in which a people, as well as an individual, must do justice, cost what it may. If I have unjustly wrested a plank from a drowning man, I must restore it to him though I drown myself. This, according to Paley, would be inconvenient. But he that would save his life, in such a case, shall lose it. This people must cease to hold slaves, and to make war on Mexico, though it cost them their existence as a people.

In their practice, nations agree with Paley; but does any one think that Massachusetts does exactly what is right at the present crisis? 10

> A drab of state, a cloth-'o-silver slut,
> To have her train borne up, and her soul trail in the dirt.

Practically speaking, the opponents to a reform in Massachusetts are not a hundred thousand politicians at the South, but a hundred thousand merchants and farmers here, who are more interested in commerce and agriculture than they are in humanity, and are not prepared to do justice to the slave and to Mexico, *cost what it may.* I quarrel not with far-off foes, but with those who, near at home, cooperate with, and do the bidding of, those far away, and without whom the latter would be harmless. We are accustomed to say, that the mass of men are unprepared; but improvement is slow, because the few are not materially wiser or better than the many. It is not so important that many should be as good as you, as that there be some absolute goodness somewhere; for that will leaven the whole lump. There are thousands who are *in opinion* opposed to slavery and to the war, who yet in effect do nothing to put an end to them; who, esteeming themselves children of Washington and Franklin, sit down with their hands in their pockets, and say that they know not what to do, and do nothing; who even postpone the question of freedom to the question of free-trade, and quietly read the prices-current along with the latest advice from Mexico, after dinner, and, it may be, fall asleep over them both. What is the price-current of an honest man and patriot today? They hesitate, and they regret, and sometimes they petition; but they do nothing in earnest and with effect. They will wait, well disposed, for others to remedy the evil, that they may no longer have it to regret. At most, they give only a cheap vote, and a feeble countenance and God-speed, to the right, as it goes by them. There are nine hundred and ninety-nine patrons of virtue to one virtuous man; but it is easier to deal with the real possessor of a thing than with the temporary guardian of it.

All voting is a sort of gaming, like checkers or backgammon, with a slight moral tinge to it, a playing with right and wrong, with moral questions; and betting naturally accompanies it. The character of the voters is not staked. I cast my vote, perchance, as I think right; but I am not vitally concerned that that right should prevail. I am willing to leave it to the majority. Its obligation, therefore, never exceeds that of expediency. Even voting *for the right* is *doing* nothing for it. It is only expressing to men feebly your desire that it should prevail. A wise man will not leave the right to the mercy of chance, nor wish it to prevail through the power of the majority. There is but little virtue in the action of masses of men. When the majority shall at length vote for the abolition of slavery, it will be because they are indifferent to slavery, or because there is but little slavery left to be abolished by their vote. *They* will then be the only slaves. Only *his* vote can hasten the abolition of slavery who asserts his own freedom by his vote.

I hear of a convention to be held at Baltimore, or elsewhere, for the selection of a candidate for the presidency, made up chiefly of editors, and men who are politicians by profession; but I think, what is it to any independent, intelligent, and respectable man what decision they may come to? Shall we not have the advantage of his wisdom and honesty, nevertheless? Can we not count upon some independent votes? Are there not many individuals in the country who do not attend conventions? But no: I find that the respectable man, so called, has immediately drifted from his position, and despairs of his country, when his country has more reason to despair of him. He forthwith adopts one of the candidates thus selected as the only *available* one, thus providing that he is himself *available* for any purposes of the demagogue. His vote is of no more worth than that of any unprincipled foreigner or hireling native, who may have been bought. O for a man who is *a man,* and, as my neighbor says, has a bone in his back which you cannot pass your hand through! Our statistics are at fault: The population has been returned too large. How many *men* are there to a square thousand miles in this country? Hardly one. Does not America offer any inducement for men to settle here? The American has dwindled into an Odd Fellow, — one who may be known by the development of his organ of gregariousness, and a manifest lack of intellect and cheerful self-reliance; whose first and chief concern, on coming into the world, is to see that the Almshouses are in good repair; and, before yet he has lawfully donned the virile garb, to collect a fund for the support of the widows and orphans that may be; who, in short, ventures to live only by the aid of the Mutual Insurance company, which has promised to bury him decently.

It is not a man's duty, as a matter of course, to devote himself to the eradication of any, even the most enormous wrong; he may still properly have other concerns to engage him; but it is his duty, at least, to wash his hands of it, and, if he gives it no thought longer, not to give it practically his support. If I devote myself to other pursuits and contemplations, I must first see, at least, that I do not pursue them sitting upon another man's shoulders. I must get off him first, that he may pursue his contemplations too. See what gross inconsistency is tolerated. I have heard some of my townsmen say, "I should like to have them order me out to help put down an insurrection of the slaves, or to march to Mexico; — see if I would go"; and yet these very men have each, directly by their allegiance, and so indirectly, at least, by their money, furnished a substitute. The soldier is applauded who refuses to serve in an unjust war by those who do not refuse to sustain the unjust government which makes the war; is applauded by those whose own act and authority he disregards and sets at nought; as if the State were penitent to that degree that it hired one to scourge it while it sinned, but not to that degree that it left off sinning for a moment. Thus, under the name of Order and Civil Government, we are all made at last to pay homage to and support our own meanness. After the first blush of sin, comes its indifference; and from immoral it becomes, as it were, *un*moral, and not quite unnecessary to that life which we have made.

The broadest and most prevalent error requires the most disinterested virtue to sustain it. The slight reproach to which the virtue of patriotism is commonly liable, the noble are most likely to incur. Those who, while they disapprove of the character and measures of a government, yield to it their allegiance and support, are undoubtedly its most conscientious supporters, and so frequently the most serious obstacles to reform. Some are petitioning the State to dissolve the Union, to disregard the requisitions of the President. Why

do they not dissolve it themselves, — the union between themselves
and the State, — and refuse to pay their quota into its treasury? Do
not they stand in the same relation to the State, that the State does
to the Union? And have not the same reasons prevented the State
from resisting the Union which have prevented them from resisting
the State?

How can a man be satisfied to entertain an opinion merely, and 15
enjoy *it*? Is there any enjoyment in it, if his opinion is that he is aggrieved? If you are cheated out of a single dollar by your neighbor,
you do not rest satisfied with knowing that you are cheated, or with
saying that you are cheated, or even with petitioning him to pay you
your due; but you take effectual steps at once to obtain the full
amount, and see that you are never cheated again. Action from principle, the perception and the performance of right, changes things
and relations; it is essentially revolutionary, and does not consist
wholly with anything which was. It not only divides states and
churches, it divides families; ay, it divides the *individual,* separating
the diabolical in him from the divine.

Unjust laws exist: Shall we be content to obey them, or shall we
endeavor to amend them, and obey them until we have succeeded,
or shall we transgress them at once? Men generally, under such a
government as this, think that they ought to wait until they have persuaded the majority to alter them. They think that, if they should
resist, the remedy would be worse than the evil. But it is the fault of
the government itself that the remedy *is* worse than the evil. *It*
makes it worse. Why is it not more apt to anticipate and provide for
reform? Why does it not cherish its wise minority? Why does it cry
and resist before it is hurt? Why does it not encourage its citizens to
be on the alert to point out its faults, and *do* better than it would
have them? Why does it always crucify Christ, and excommunicate
Copernicus and Luther, and pronounce Washington and Franklin
rebels?

One would think, that a deliberate and practical denial of its authority was the only offence never contemplated by government;
else, why has it not assigned its definite, its suitable and proportionate penalty? If a man who has no property refuses but once to earn
nine shillings for the State, he is put in prison for a period unlimited
by any law that I know, and determined only by the discretion of
those who placed him there; but if he should steal ninety times nine
shillings from the State, he is soon permitted to go at large again.

If the injustice is part of the necessary friction of the machine of
government, let it go, let it go: Perchance it will wear smooth, — certainly the machine will wear out. If the injustice has a spring, or a
pulley, or a rope, or a crank, exclusively for itself, then perhaps you
may consider whether the remedy will not be worse than the evil;
but if it is of such a nature that it requires you to be the agent of in-

justice to another, then, I say, break the law. Let your life be a counter friction to stop the machine. What I have to do is to see, at any rate, that I do not lend myself to the wrong which I condemn.

As for adopting the ways which the State has provided for remedying the evil, I know not of such ways. They take too much time, and a man's life will be gone. I have other affairs to attend to. I came into this world, not chiefly to make this a good place to live in, but to live in it, be it good or bad. A man has not everything to do, but something; and because he cannot do *everything,* it is not necessary that he should do *something* wrong. It is not my business to be petitioning the Governor or the Legislature any more than it is theirs to petition me; and, if they should not hear my petition, what should I do then? But in this case the State has provided no way: Its very Constitution is the evil. This may seem to be harsh and stubborn and unconciliatory; but it is to treat with the utmost kindness and consideration the only spirit that can appreciate or deserves it. So is all change for the better, like birth and death, which convulse the body.

I do not hesitate to say, that those who call themselves Abolition- 20 ists should at once effectually withdraw their support, both in person and property, from the government of Massachusetts, and not wait till they constitute a majority of one, before they suffer the right to prevail through them. I think that it is enough if they have God on their side, without waiting for that other one. Moreover, any man more right than his neighbors, constitutes a majority of one already.

I meet this American government, or its representative, the State government, directly, and face to face, once a year — no more — in the person of its tax-gatherer; this is the only mode in which a man situated as I am necessarily meets it; and it then says distinctly, Recognize me; and the simplest, the most effectual, and, in the present posture of affairs, the indispensablest mode of treating with it on this head, of expressing your little satisfaction with and love for it, is to deny it then. My civil neighbor, the tax-gatherer, is the very man I have to deal with, — for it is, after all, with men and not with parchment that I quarrel, — and he has voluntarily chosen to be an agent of the government. How shall he ever know well what he is and does as an officer of the government, or as a man, until he is obliged to consider whether he shall treat me, his neighbor, for whom he has respect, as a neighbor and well-disposed man, or as a maniac and disturber of the peace, and see if he can get over this obstruction to his neighborliness without a ruder and more impetuous thought or speech corresponding with his action? I know this well, that if one thousand, if one hundred, if ten men whom I could name, — if ten *honest* men only, — aye, if *one* HONEST man, in this State of Massachusetts, *ceasing to hold slaves,* were actually to withdraw from this copartnership, and be locked up in the county jail therefor, it would be the abolition of slavery in America. For it matters not how small the beginning may seem to be: What is once well done is done forever. But we love better to talk about it: That we say is our mission. Reform keeps many scores of newspapers in its service, but not one man. If my esteemed neighbor, the State's ambassador, who will devote his days to the settlement of the question of human rights in the Council Chamber, instead of being threatened with the prisons of Carolina, were to sit down the prisoner of Massachusetts, that State which is so anxious to foist the sin of slavery upon her sister, — though at present she can discover only an act of inhospitality to be the ground of a quarrel with her, — the Legislature would not wholly waive the subject the following winter.

Under a government which imprisons any unjustly, the true place for a just man is also a prison. The proper place today, the only place which Massachusetts has provided for her freer and less desponding spirits, is in her prisons, to be put out and locked out of the State by her own act, as they have already put themselves out by their principles. It is there that the fugitive slave, and the Mexican prisoner on parole, and the Indian come to plead the wrongs of his race, should find them; on that separate, but more free and honorable ground, where the State places those who are not *with* her, but *against* her, — the only house in a slave State in which a free man can abide with honor. If any think that their influence would be lost there, and their voices no longer afflict the ear of the State, that they would not be as an enemy within its walls, they do not know by how much truth is stronger than error, nor how much more eloquently and effectively he can combat injustice who has experienced a little in his own person. Cast your whole vote, not a strip of paper merely, but your whole influence. A minority is powerless while it conforms to the majority; it is not even a minority then; but it is irresistible when it clogs by its whole weight. If the alternative is to keep all just men in prison, or give up war and slavery, the State will not hesitate which to choose. If a thousand men were not to pay their tax-bills this year, that would not be a violent and bloody measure, as it would be to pay them, and enable the State to commit violence and shed innocent blood. This is, in fact, the definition of a peaceable revolution, if any such is possible. If the tax-gatherer, or any other public officer, asks me, as one has done, "But what shall I do?" my answer is, "If you really wish to do any thing, resign your office." When the subject has refused allegiance, and the officer has resigned his office, then the revolution is accomplished. But even suppose blood should flow. Is there not a sort of blood shed when the conscience is wounded? Through this wound a man's real manhood and immortality flow out, and he bleeds to an everlasting death. I see this blood flowing now.

I have contemplated the imprisonment of the offender, rather than the seizure of his goods, — though both will serve the same purpose, — because they who assert the purest right, and consequently are most dangerous to a corrupt State, commonly have not spent much time in accumulating property. To such the State renders comparatively small service, and a slight tax is wont to appear exorbitant, particularly if they are obliged to earn it by special labor with their hands. If there were one who lived wholly without the use of money, the State itself would hesitate to demand it of him. But the rich man, — not to make any invidious comparison, — is always sold to the institution which makes him rich. Absolutely speaking, the more money, the less virtue; for money comes between a man and his objects, and obtains them for him; and it was certainly no great virtue to obtain it. It puts to rest many questions which he would otherwise be taxed to answer; while the only new question which it puts is the hard but superfluous one, how to spend it. Thus his moral ground is taken from under his feet. The opportunities of living are diminished in proportion as what are called the "means" are increased. The best thing a man can do for his culture when he is rich is to endeavor to carry out those schemes which he entertained when he was poor. Christ answered the Herodians according to their condition. "Show me the tribute-money," said he; — and one took a penny out of his pocket; — if you use money which has the image of Cæsar on it, and which he has made current and valuable, that is, *if you are men of the State,* and gladly enjoy the advantages of Cæsar's government, then pay him back some of his own when he demands it; "Render therefore to Cæsar that which is Cæsar's, and to God those things which are God's," — leaving them no wiser than before as to which was which; for they did not wish to know.

When I converse with the freest of my neighbors, I perceive that, whatever they may say about the magnitude and seriousness of the question, and their regard for the public tranquility, the long and the short of the matter is, that they cannot spare the protection of the existing government, and they dread the consequences to their property and families of disobedience to it. For my own part, I should not like to think that I ever rely on the protection of the State. But, if I deny the authority of the State when it presents its tax-bill, it will soon take and waste all my property, and so harass me and my children without end. This is hard. This makes it impossible for a man to live honestly, and at the same time comfortably, in outward respects. It will not be worth the while to accumulate property; that would be sure to go again. You must hire or squat somewhere, and raise but a small crop, and eat that soon. You must live within yourself, and depend upon yourself always tucked up and ready for a start, and not have many affairs. A man may grow rich in Turkey even, if he will be in all respects a good subject of the Turkish government. Confucius said: "If a state is governed by the principles of reason, poverty and misery are subjects of shame; if a state is not

governed by the principles of reason, riches and honors are the subjects of shame." No: Until I want the protection of Massachusetts to
be extended to me in some distant southern port, where my liberty
is endangered, or until I am bent solely on building up an estate at
home by peaceful enterprise, I can afford to refuse allegiance to
Massachusetts, and her right to my property and life. It costs me
less in every sense to incur the penalty of disobedience to the State,
than it would to obey. I should feel as if I were worth less in that
case.

Some years ago, the State met me in behalf of the Church, and   25
commanded me to pay a certain sum toward the support of a clergyman whose preaching my father attended, but never I myself. "Pay,"
it said, "or be locked up in the jail." I declined to pay. But, unfortunately, another man saw fit to pay it. I did not see why the schoolmaster should be taxed to support the priest, and not the priest the
schoolmaster; for I was not the State's schoolmaster, but I supported myself by voluntary subscription. I did not see why the
lyceum should not present its tax-bill, and have the State to back its
demand, as well as the Church. However, at the request of the se-
lectmen, I condescended to make some such statement as this in
writing: — "Know all men by these presents, that I, Henry Thoreau,
do not wish to be regarded as a member of any incorporated society
which I have not joined." This I gave to the town clerk; and he has it.
The State, having thus learned that I did not wish to be regarded as a
member of that church, has never made a like demand on me since;
though it said that it must adhere to its original presumption that
time. If I had known how to name them, I should then have signed off
in detail from all the societies which I never signed on to; but I did
not know where to find a complete list.

I have paid no poll-tax for six years. I was put into a jail once on
this account, for one night; and, as I stood considering the walls of
solid stone, two or three feet thick, the door of wood and iron, a foot
thick, and the iron grating which strained the light, I could not help
being struck with the foolishness of that institution which treated
me as if I were mere flesh and blood and bones, to be locked up. I
wondered that it should have concluded at length that this was the
best use it could put me to, and had never thought to avail itself of
my services in some way. I saw that, if there was a wall of stone between me and my townsmen, there was a still more difficult one to
climb or break through, before they could get to be as free as I was. I
did not for a moment feel confined, and the walls seemed a great
waste of stone and mortar. I felt as if I alone of all my townsmen had
paid my tax. They plainly did not know how to treat me, but be-
haved like persons who are underbred. In every threat and in every
compliment there was a blunder; for they thought that my chief desire was to stand the other side of that stone wall. I could not but

smile to see how industriously they locked the door on my meditations, which followed them out again without let or hindrance, and *they* were really all that was dangerous. As they could not reach me, they had resolved to punish my body; just as boys, if they cannot come at some person against whom they have a spite, will abuse his dog. I saw that the State was half-witted, and it was timid as a lone woman with her silver spoons, and that it did not know its friends from its foes, and I lost all my remaining respect for it, and pitied it.

Thus the State never intentionally confronts a man's sense, intellectual or moral, but only his body, his senses. It is not armed with superior wit or honesty, but with superior physical strength. I was not born to be forced. I will breathe after my own fashion. Let us see who is the strongest. What force has a multitude? They only can force me who obey a higher law than I. They force me to become like themselves. I do not hear of *men* being *forced* to live this way or that by masses of men. What sort of life were that to live? When I meet a government which says to me, "Your money or your life," why should I be in haste to give it my money? It may be in a great strait, and not know what to do: I cannot help that. It must help itself; do as I do. It is not worth the while to snivel about it. I am not responsible for the successful working of the machinery of society. I am not the son of the engineer. I perceive that, when an acorn and a chestnut fall side by side, the one does not remain inert to make way for the other, but both obey their own laws, and spring and grow and flourish as best they can, till one, perchance, overshadows and destroys the other. If a plant cannot live according to its nature, it dies; and so a man.

The night in prison was novel and interesting enough. The prisoners in their shirt-sleeves were enjoying a chat and the evening air in the doorway, when I entered. But the jailer said, "Come, boys, it is time to lock up"; and so they dispersed, and I heard the sound of their steps returning into the hollow apartments. My roommate was introduced to me by the jailer, as "a first-rate fellow and a clever man." When the door was locked, he showed me where to hang my hat, and how he managed matters there. The rooms were whitewashed once a month; and this one, at least, was the whitest, most simply furnished, and probably the neatest apartment in the town. He naturally wanted to know where I came from, and what brought me there; and, when I had told him, I asked him in my turn how he came there, presuming him to be an honest man, of course; and, as the world goes, I believe he was. "Why," said he, "they accuse me of burning a barn; but I never did it." As near as I could discover, he had probably gone to bed in a barn when drunk, and smoked his pipe there; and so a barn was burnt. He had the reputation of being a clever man, had been there some three months waiting for his trial to come on, and would have to wait as much longer; but he was quite domesticated and contented, since he got his board for nothing, and thought that he was well-treated.

He occupied one window, and I the other; and I saw, that if one stayed there long, his principal business would be to look out the window. I had soon read all the tracts that were left there, and examined where former prisoners had broken out, and where a grate had been sawed off, and heard the history of the various occupants of that room; for I found that even here there was a history and a gossip which never circulated beyond the walls of the jail. Probably this is the only house in the town where verses are composed, which are afterward printed in a circular form, but not published. I was shown quite a long list of verses which were composed by some young men who had been detected in an attempt to escape, who avenged themselves by singing them.

I pumped my fellow-prisoner as dry as I could, for fear I should 30 never see him again; but at length he showed me which was my bed, and left me to blow out the lamp.

It was like travelling into a far country, such as I had never expected to behold, to lie there for one night. It seemed to me that I never had heard the town-clock strike before, nor the evening sounds of the village; for we slept with the windows open, which were inside the grating. It was to see my native village in the light of the Middle Ages, and our Concord was turned into a Rhine stream, and visions of knights and castles passed before me. They were the voices of old burghers that I heard in the streets. I was an involuntary spectator and auditor of whatever was done and said in the kitchen of the adjacent village-inn, — a wholly new and rare experience to me. It was a closer view of my native town. I was fairly inside of it. I never had seen its institutions before. This is one of its peculiar institutions; for it is a shire town. I began to comprehend what its inhabitants were about.

In the morning, our breakfasts were put through the hole in the door, in small oblong-square tin pans, made to fit, and holding a pint of chocolate, with brown bread, and an iron spoon. When they called for the vessels again, I was green enough to return what bread I had left; but my comrade seized it, and said that I should lay that up for lunch or dinner. Soon after, he was let out to work at haying in a neighboring field, whither he went every day, and would not be back till noon; so he bade me good-day, saying that he doubted if he should see me again.

When I came out of prison, — for some one interfered, and paid that tax, — I did not perceive that great changes had taken place on the common, such as he observed who went in a youth, and emerged a tottering and gray-headed man; and yet a change had to my eyes come over the scene, — the town, and State, and country, — greater than any that mere time could effect. I saw yet more distinctly the State in which I lived. I saw to what extent the people among whom I lived could be trusted as good neighbors and friends; that their friendship was for summer weather only; that they did not greatly propose to do right; that they were a distinct race from me by their prejudices and superstitions, as the Chinamen and Malays are; that, in their sacrifices to humanity, they ran no risks, not even to their property; that, after all, they were not so noble but they treated the thief as he had treated them, and hoped, by a certain outward observance and a few prayers, and by walking in a particular straight though useless path from time to time, to save their souls. This may be to judge my neighbors harshly; for I believe that many of them are not aware that they have such an institution as the jail in their village.

It was formerly the custom in our village, when a poor debtor came out of jail, for his acquaintances to salute him, looking through their fingers, which were crossed to represent the grating of a jail window, "How do ye do?" My neighbors did not thus salute me, but first looked at me, and then at one another, as if I had returned from a long journey. I was put into jail as I was going to the shoemaker's to get a shoe which was mended. When I was let out the next morning, I proceeded to finish my errand, and having put on my mended shoe, joined a huckleberry party, who were impatient to put themselves under my conduct; and in half an hour, — for the horse was soon tackled, — was in the midst of a huckleberry field, on one of our highest hills, two miles off, and then the State was nowhere to be seen.

This is the whole story of "My Prisons."   35

I have never declined paying the highway tax, because I am as desirous of being a good neighbor as I am of being a bad subject; and, as for supporting schools, I am doing my part to educate my fellow-countrymen now. It is for no particular item in the tax-bill that I refuse to pay it. I simply wish to refuse allegiance to the State, to withdraw and stand aloof from it effectually. I do not care to trace the course of my dollar, if I could, till it buys a man, or a musket to shoot one with, — the dollar is innocent, — but I am concerned to trace the effects of my allegiance. In fact, I quietly declare war with the State, after my fashion, though I will still make what use and get what advantage of her I can, as is usual in such cases.

If others pay the tax which is demanded of me, from a sympathy with the State, they do but what they have already done in their own case, or rather they abet injustice to a greater extent than the State requires. If they pay the tax from a mistaken interest in the individual taxed, to save his property or prevent his going to jail, it is because they have not considered wisely how far they let their private feelings interfere with the public good.

This, then, is my position at present. But one cannot be too much on his guard in such a case, lest his action be biased by obstinacy, or an undue regard for the opinions of men. Let him see that he does only what belongs to himself and to the hour.

I think sometimes, Why, this people mean well; they are only ignorant; they would do better if they knew how: why give your neighbors this pain to treat you as they are inclined to? But I think again, this is no reason why I should do as they do, or permit others to suffer much greater pain of a different kind. Again, I sometimes say to myself, When many millions of men, without heat, without ill will, without personal feelings of any kind, demand of you a few shillings only, without the possibility, such is their constitution, of retracing or altering their present demand, and without the possibility, on your side, of appeal to any other millions, why expose yourself to this overwhelming brute force? You do not resist cold and hunger, the winds and the waves, thus obstinately; you quietly submit to a thousand similar necessities. You do not put your head into the fire. But just in proportion as I regard this as not wholly a brute force, partly a human force, and consider that I have relations to those millions as to so many millions of men, and not of mere brute or inanimate things, I see that appeal is possible, first and instantaneously, from them to the Maker of them, and, secondly, from them to themselves. But, if I put my head deliberately into the fire, there is no appeal to fire or to the Maker of fire, and I have only myself to blame. If I could convince myself that I have any right to be satisfied with men as they are, and to treat them according, and not according, in some respects, to my requisitions and expectations of what they and I ought to be, then, like a good Mussulman and fatalist, I should endeavor to be satisfied with things as they are, and say it is the will of God. And, above all, there is this difference between resisting this and a purely brute or natural force, that I can resist this with some effect; but I cannot expect, like Orpheus, to change the nature of the rocks and trees and beasts.

I do not wish to quarrel with any man or nation. I do not wish to 40
split hairs, to make fine distinctions, or set myself up as better than my neighbors. I seek rather, I may say, even an excuse for conforming to the laws of the land. I am but too ready to conform to them. Indeed, I have reason to suspect myself on this head; and each year, as the tax-gatherer comes round, I find myself disposed to review the acts and position of the general and State governments, and the spirit of the people, to discover a pretext for conformity.

> We must affect our country as our parents;
> And if at any time we alienate
> Our love or industry from doing it honor,
> We must respect effects and teach the soul
> Matter of conscience and religion,
> And not desire of rule or benefit.

I believe that the State will soon be able to take all my work of this sort out of my hands, and then I shall be no better a patriot than my fellow-countrymen. Seen from a lower point of view, the Constitution, with all its faults, is very good; the law and the courts are very respectable; even this State and this American government are, in many respects, very admirable and rare things, to be thankful for, such as a great many have described them; but seen from a point of view a little higher, they are what I have described them; seen from a higher still, and the highest, who shall say what they are, or that they are worth looking at or thinking of at all?

However, the government does not concern me much, and I shall bestow the fewest possible thoughts on it. It is not many moments that I live under a government, even in this world. If a man is thought-free, fancy-free, imagination-free, that which *is not* never for a long time appearing *to be* to him, unwise rulers or reformers cannot fatally interrupt him.

I know that most men think differently from myself; but those whose lives are by profession devoted to the study of these or kindred subjects, content me as little as any. Statesmen and legislators, standing so completely within the institution, never distinctly and nakedly behold it. They speak of moving society, but have no resting-place without it. They may be men of a certain experience and discrimination, and have no doubt invented ingenious and even useful systems, for which we sincerely thank them; but all their wit and usefulness lie within certain not very wide limits. They are wont to forget that the world is not governed by policy and expediency. Webster never goes behind government, and so cannot speak with authority about it. His words are wisdom to those legislators who contemplate no essential reform in the existing government; but for thinkers, and those who legislate for all time, he never once glances at the subject. I know of those whose serene and wise speculations on this theme would soon reveal the limits of his mind's range and hospitality. Yet, compared with the cheap professions of most reformers, and the still cheaper wisdom and eloquence of politicians in general, his are almost the only sensible and valuable words, and we thank Heaven for him. Comparatively, he is always strong, original, and, above all, practical. Still his quality is not wisdom, but prudence. The lawyer's truth is not Truth, but consistency, or a consistent expediency. Truth is always in harmony with herself, and is not concerned chiefly to reveal the justice that may consist with wrong-doing. He well deserves to be called, as he has been called, the Defender of the Constitution. There are really no blows to be given by him but defensive ones. He is not a leader, but a follower. His leaders are the men of '87. "I have never made an effort," he says, "and never propose to make an effort; I have never countenanced an effort, and never mean to countenance an effort, to disturb the arrangement as originally made, by which the various States came into the Union." Still thinking of the sanction which the Constitution gives to slavery, he says, "Because it was a part of the original compact, — let it stand." Notwithstanding his special acuteness and ability, he is unable to take a fact out of its merely political relations, and behold it as it lies absolutely to be disposed of by the intellect, — what, for instance, it behooves a man to do here in America today with regard to slavery, but ventures, or is driven, to make some such desperate answer as the following, while professing to speak absolutely, and as a private man, — from which what new and singular code of social duties might be inferred? "The manner," says he, "in which the governments of those States where slavery exists are to regulate it, is for their own consideration, under their responsibility to their constituents, to the general laws of propriety, humanity, and justice, and to God. Associations formed elsewhere, springing from a feeling of humanity, or any other cause, have nothing whatever to do with it. They have never received any encouragement from me, and they never will."[1]

They who know of no purer sources of truth, who have traced up its stream no higher, stand, and wisely stand, by the Bible and the Constitution, and drink at it there with reverence and humility; but they who behold where it comes trickling into this lake or that pool, gird up their loins once more, and continue their pilgrimage toward its fountainhead.

No man with a genius for legislation has appeared in America. They are rare in the history of the world. There are orators, politicians, and eloquent men, by the thousand; but the speaker has not yet opened his mouth to speak, who is capable of settling the much-vexed questions of the day. We love eloquence for its own sake, and not for any truth which it may utter, or any heroism it may inspire. Our legislators have not yet learned the comparative value of free-trade and of freedom, of union, and of rectitude, to a nation. They have no genius or talent for comparatively humble questions of taxation and finance, commerce and manufactures and agriculture. If we were left solely to the wordy wit of legislators in Congress for our guidance, uncorrected by the seasonable experience and the effectual complaints of the people, America would not long retain her rank among the nations. For eighteen hundred years, though perchance I have no right to say it, the New Testament has been written; yet where is the legislator who has wisdom and practical talent enough to avail himself of the light which it sheds on the science of legislation?

The authority of government, even such as I am willing to submit to, — for I will cheerfully obey those who know and can do bet- 45

---

[1] These extracts have been inserted since the Lecture was read.

ter than I, and in many things even those who neither know nor can do so well, — is still an impure one: To be strictly just, it must have the sanction and consent of the governed. It can have no pure right over my person and property but what I concede to it. The progress from an absolute to a limited monarchy, from a limited monarchy to a democracy, is a progress toward a true respect for the individual. Even the Chinese philosopher was wise enough to regard the individual as the basis of the empire. Is a democracy, such as we know it, the last improvement possible in government? Is it not possible to take a step further towards recognizing and organizing the rights of man? There will never be a really free and enlightened State, until the State comes to recognize the individual as a higher and independent power, from which all its own power and authority are derived, and treats him accordingly. I please myself with imagining a State at last which can afford to be just to all men, and to treat the individual with respect as a neighbor; which even would not think it inconsistent with its own repose, if a few were to live aloof from it, not meddling with it, nor embraced by it, who fulfilled all the duties of neighbors and fellowmen. A State which bore this kind of fruit, and suffered it to drop off as fast as it ripened, would prepare the way for a still more perfect and glorious State, which also I have imagined, but not yet anywhere seen.

Discussion Questions

1. Summarize briefly Thoreau's reasons for arguing that civil disobedience is sometimes a *duty*.
2. Thoreau, like Martin Luther King Jr. in "Letter from Birmingham Jail" (p. 719), speaks of "unjust laws." Do they agree on the positions that citizens should take in response to these laws? Are Thoreau and King guided by the same principles? In Plato's "Crito" (p. 663), what does Socrates say about obedience to unjust laws?
3. What examples of government policy and action does Thoreau use to prove that civil disobedience is a duty? Explain why they are — or are not — effective.
4. Why do you think Thoreau provides such a detailed account of one day in prison? (Notice that King does not give a description of his confinement.) What observation about the community struck Thoreau when he emerged from jail?

Writing Suggestions

5. Argue that civil disobedience to a school policy or action is justified. (Examples might include failure to establish an ethnic studies department, refusal to allow ROTC on campus, refusal to suspend a professor accused of sexual harassment.) Be specific about the injustice of the policy or action and the values that underlie the resistance.

6. Under what circumstances might civil disobedience prove to be dangerous and immoral? Can you think of cases of disobedience when *conscience*, as Thoreau uses the term, did not appear to be the guiding principle? Try to identify what you think is the true motivation for the resistance.

Declaration of Sentiments
and Resolutions, Seneca Falls

ELIZABETH CADY STANTON

Elizabeth Cady Stanton (1815–1902) was an early activist in the movement for women's rights, including the right to vote and the freedom to enroll in college and to enter professions that were closed to women. She was also active in the campaign to abolish slavery. In 1848 the first women's rights convention was held in her home in Seneca Falls, New York, where the "Declaration of Sentiments and Resolutions" was issued.

When, in the course of human events, it becomes necessary for one portion of the family of man to assume among the people of the earth a position different from that which they have hitherto occupied, but one to which the laws of nature and of nature's God entitle them, a decent respect to the opinions of mankind requires that they should declare the causes that impel them to such a course.

We hold these truths to be self-evident: that all men and women are created equal; that they are endowed by their Creator with certain inalienable rights; that among these are life, liberty, and the pursuit of happiness; that to secure these rights governments are instituted, deriving their just powers from the consent of the governed. Whenever any form of government becomes destructive of these ends, it is the right of those who suffer from it to refuse allegiance to it, and to insist upon the institution of a new government, laying its foundation on such principles, and organizing its powers in such form, as to them shall seem most likely to effect their safety and happiness. Prudence, indeed, will dictate that governments long established should not be changed for light and transient causes; and accordingly all experience hath shown that mankind are more disposed to suffer, while evils are sufferable, than to right themselves by abolishing the forms to which they were accustomed. But when a long train of abuses and usurpations, pursuing invariably the same object evinces a design to reduce them under absolute despotism, it is their duty to throw off such government, and to provide new guards for their future security. Such has been the patient sufferance of the women under this government, and such is now the necessity which constrains them to demand the equal station to which they are entitled.

The history of mankind is a history of repeated injuries and usurpations on the part of man toward woman, having in direct object the establishment of an absolute tyranny over her. To prove this, let facts be submitted to a candid world.

He has never permitted her to exercise her inalienable right to the elective franchise.

He has compelled her to submit to laws, in the formation of 5 which she had no voice.

He has withheld from her rights which are given to the most ignorant and degraded men — both natives and foreigners.

Having deprived her of this first right of a citizen, the elective franchise, thereby leaving her without representation in the halls of legislation, he has oppressed her on all sides.

He has made her, if married, in the eye of the law, civilly dead.

He has taken from her all right in property, even to the wages she earns.

He has made her, morally, an irresponsible being, as she can 10 commit many crimes with impunity, provided they be done in the presence of her husband. In the covenant of marriage, she is compelled to promise obedience to her husband, he becoming, to all intents and purposes, her master — the law giving him power to deprive her of her liberty, and to administer chastisement.

He has so framed the laws of divorce, as to what shall be the proper causes, and in case of separation, to whom the guardianship of the children shall be given, as to be wholly regardless of the happiness of women — the law, in all cases, going upon a false supposition of the supremacy of man, and giving all power into his hands.

After depriving her of all rights as a married woman, if single, and the owner of property, he has taxed her to support a government which recognizes her only when her property can be made profitable to it.

He has monopolized nearly all the profitable employments, and from those she is permitted to follow, she receives but a scanty remuneration. He closes against her all the avenues to wealth and distinction which he considers most honorable to himself. As a teacher of theology, medicine, or law, she is not known.

He has denied her the facilities for obtaining a thorough education, all colleges being closed against her.

He allows her in Church, as well as State, but a subordinate posi- 15 tion, claiming Apostolic authority for her exclusion from the ministry, and, with some exceptions, from any public participation in the affairs of the Church.

He has created a false public sentiment by giving to the world a different code of morals for men and women, by which moral delinquencies which exclude women from society, are not only tolerated, but deemed of little account in man.

He has usurped the prerogative of Jehovah himself, claiming it as his right to assign for her a sphere of action, when that belongs to her conscience and to her God.

He has endeavored, in every way that he could, to destroy her confidence in her own powers, to lessen her self-respect, and to make her willing to lead a dependent and abject life.

Now, in view of this entire disfranchisement of one-half the people of this country, their social and religious degradation — in view of the unjust laws above mentioned, and because women do feel themselves aggrieved, oppressed, and fraudulently deprived of their most sacred rights, we insist that they have immediate admission to all the rights and privileges which belong to them as citizens of the United States.

In entering upon the great work before us, we anticipate 20 no small amount of misconception, misrepresentation, and ridicule; but we shall use every instrumentality within our power to effect our object. We shall employ agents, circulate tracts, petition the State and National legislatures, and endeavor to enlist the pulpit and the press in our behalf. We hope this Convention will be followed by a series of Conventions embracing every part of the country.

Resolutions

WHEREAS, The great precept of nature is conceded to be, that "man shall pursue his own true and substantial happiness." Blackstone in his Commentaries remarks, that this law of Nature being coeval with mankind, and dictated by God himself, is of course superior in obligation to any other. It is binding over all the globe, in all countries and at all times; no human laws are of any validity if contrary to this, and such of them as are valid, derive all their force, and all their validity, and all their authority, mediately and immediately, from this original; therefore,

Resolved, That such laws as conflict, in any way, with the true and substantial happiness of woman, are contrary to the great precept of nature and of no validity, for this is "superior in obligation to any other."

Resolved, That all laws which prevent woman from occupying such a station in society as her conscience shall dictate, or which place her in a position inferior to that of man, are contrary to the great precept of nature, and therefore of no force or authority.

Resolved, That woman is man's equal — was intended to be so by the Creator, and the highest good of the race demands that she should be recognized as such.

Resolved, That the women of this country ought to be enlight- 25 ened in regard to the laws under which they live, that they may no longer publish their degradation by declaring themselves satisfied with their present position, nor their ignorance, by asserting that they have all the rights they want.

Resolved, That inasmuch as man, while claiming for himself intellectual superiority, does accord to woman moral superiority, it is preeminently his duty to encourage her to speak and teach, as she has an opportunity, in all religious assemblies.

Resolved, That the same amount of virtue, delicacy, and refinement of behavior that is required of woman in the social state, should also be required of man, and the same transgressions should be visited with equal severity on both man and woman.

Resolved, That the objection of indelicacy and impropriety, which is so often brought against woman when she addresses a public audience, comes with a very ill-grace from those who encourage, by their attendance, her appearance on the stage, in the concert, or in feats of the circus.

Resolved, That woman has too long rested satisfied in the circumscribed limits which corrupt customs and a perverted application of the Scriptures have marked out for her, and that it is time she should move in the enlarged sphere which her great Creator has assigned her.

Resolved, That it is the duty of the women of this country to secure to themselves their sacred right to the elective franchise.

Resolved, That the equality of human rights results necessarily from the fact of the identity of the race in capabilities and responsibilities.

Resolved, therefore, That, being invested by the Creator with the same capabilities, and the same consciousness of responsibility for their exercise, it is demonstrably the right and duty of woman, equally with man, to promote every righteous cause by every righteous means; and especially in regard to the great subjects of morals and religion, it is self-evidently her right to participate with her brother in teaching them, both in private and in public, by writing and by speaking, by any instrumentalities proper to be used, and in any assemblies proper to be held; and this being a self-evident truth growing out of the divinely implanted principles of human nature, any custom or authority adverse to it, whether modern or wearing the hoary sanction of antiquity, is to be regarded as a self-evident falsehood, and at war with mankind.

[At the last session Lucretia Mott offered and spoke to the following resolution:]

Resolved, That the speedy success of our cause depends upon the zealous and untiring efforts of both men and women, for the overthrow of the monopoly of the pulpit, and for the securing to woman an equal participation with men in the various trades, professions, and commerce.

Discussion Questions

1. Are all the grievances listed in the document of equal importance? If not, which seem the most important? Why?

2. What is "the great precept of nature" on which the resolutions are based? How does this compare to the motivating principle of the Declaration of Independence?
3. What characteristics of male thinking and behavior are attacked in the Declaration at Seneca Falls?
4. Does the Declaration at Seneca Falls anywhere suggest that women have gifts superior to those of men? Does it suggest that equal rights for women bestow benefits on others as well?

Writing Suggestions

5. Is it necessary today to call attention to some of the old grievances or to suggest new ones? Pick out one or two old issues, and offer examples to show that such a need no longer exists. Or argue that women are still being deprived of their right to their own "true and substantial happiness."
6. Most newspapers and journals treated the Declaration at Seneca Falls with contempt and ridicule. What attitudes and convictions in the mid-nineteenth century could have caused such a reaction?

Warfare: An Invention — Not a Biological Necessity

MARGARET MEAD

Margaret Mead (1901–1978) was the first American anthropologist to study childhood, adolescence, and gender. Her work focused primarily on culture rather than biology or race as the primary factor in determining variations in human behavior and personality. As a graduate student, she conducted field research on adolescence and sexuality in Samoa. Her resulting work, the best-selling Coming of Age in Samoa *(1928), made her a household name in the United States. She went on to publish forty-four books, including* Growing Up in New Guinea *(1930) and* Sex and Temperament *(1935), and hundreds of articles. In the past fifteen years, her early research in Samoa has been challenged by Derek Freeman, an anthropologist who characterizes Mead's work as being antievolutionary and fundamentally flawed in its portrayal of sexuality in the South Seas. Freeman's accusations, however, have been discredited by many scholars who recognize Mead's important contributions to the field. The following article, in which Mead argues that warfare is a cultural invention not a biological necessity, was published in* Asia *in 1940.*

Is war a biological necessity, a sociological inevitability, or just a bad invention? Those who argue for the first view endow man with such pugnacious instincts that some outlet in aggressive behavior is necessary if man is to reach full human stature. It was this point of view which lay back of William James's famous essay, "The Moral Equivalent of War," in which he tried to retain the warlike virtues and channel them in new directions. A similar point of view has lain back of the Soviet Union's attempt to make competition between groups rather than between individuals. A basic, competitive, aggressive, warring human nature is assumed, and those who wish to outlaw war or outlaw competitiveness merely try to find new and less socially destructive ways in which these biologically given aspects of man's nature can find expression. Then there are those who take the second view: warfare is the inevitable concomitant of the development of the state, the struggle for land and natural resources of class societies springing, not from the nature of man, but from the nature of history. War is nevertheless inevitable unless we change our social system and outlaw classes, the struggle for power, and possessions; and in the event of our success warfare would disappear, as a symptom vanishes when the disease is cured.

One may hold a compromise position between these two extremes; one may claim that all aggression springs from the frustration of man's biologically determined drives and that, since all forms of culture are frustrating, it is certain each new generation will be aggressive and the aggression will find its natural and inevitable expression in race war, class war, nationalistic war, and so on.

All three positions are very popular today among those who think seriously about the problems of war and its possible prevention, but I wish to urge another point of view, less defeatist perhaps than the first and third, and more accurate than the second: that is, that warfare, by which I mean organized conflict between two groups as *groups,* in which each group puts an army (even if the army is only fifteen Pygmies) into the field to fight and kill, if possible, some of the members of the army of the other group — that warfare of this sort is an invention like any other of the inventions in terms of which we order our lives, such as writing, marriage, cooking our food instead of eating it raw, trial by jury, or burial of the dead, and so on. Some of this list any one will grant are inventions: trial by jury is confined to very limited portions of the globe; we know that there are tribes that do not bury their dead but instead expose or cremate them; and we know that only part of the human race has had a knowledge of writing as its cultural inheritance. But, whenever a way of doing things is found universally, such as the use of fire or the practice of some form of marriage, we tend to think at once that it is not an invention at all but an attribute of humanity itself. And yet even such universals as marriage and the use of fire are inventions like the rest, very basic ones, inventions which were perhaps necessary if human history was to take the turn it has taken, but nevertheless inventions. At some point in his social development man was undoubtedly without the institution of marriage or the knowledge of the use of fire.

The case for warfare is much clearer because there are peoples even today who have no warfare. Of these the Eskimo are perhaps the most conspicuous example, but the Lepchas of Sikkim are an equally good one. Neither of these peoples understands war, not even the defensive warfare. The idea of warfare is lacking, and this lack is as essential to carrying on war as an alphabet or a syllabary is to writing. But whereas the Lepchas are a gentle, unquarrelsome people, and the advocates of other points of view might argue that they are not full human beings or that they had never been frustrated and so had no aggression to expend in warfare, the Eskimo case gives no such possibility of interpretation. The Eskimo are not a mild and meek people; many of them are turbulent and troublesome. Fights, theft of wives, murder, cannibalism occur among them — all outbursts of passionate men goaded by desire or intolerable circumstance. Here are men faced with hunger, men faced with loss of their wives, men faced with the threat of extermination by other men, and here are orphan children, growing up miserably with no one to care for them, mocked and neglected by those about them. The personality necessary for war, the circumstances necessary to goad men to desperation are present, but there is no war. When a traveling Eskimo entered a settlement he might have to fight the strongest man in the settlement to establish his position among them, but this was a test of strength and bravery, not war. The idea of warfare, of one *group* organizing against another *group* to maim and wound and kill them, was absent. And without that idea passions might rage but there was no war.

But, it may be argued, isn't this because the Eskimo have such a   5
low and undeveloped form of social organization? They own no land, they move from place to place, camping, it is true, season after season on the same site, but this is not something to fight for as the modern nations of the world fight for land and raw materials. They have no permanent possessions that can be looted, no towns that can be burned. They have no social classes to produce stress and strains within the society which might force it to go to war outside. Doesn't the absence of war among the Eskimo, while disproving the biological necessity of war, just go to confirm the point that it is the state of development of the society which accounts for war, and nothing else?

We find the answer among the Pygmy peoples of the Andaman Islands in the Bay of Bengal. The Andamans also represent an exceedingly low level of society: they are a hunting and food-gathering people; they live in tiny hordes without any class stratification; their houses are simpler than the snow houses of the Eskimo. But they knew about warfare. The army might contain only fifteen determined Pygmies marching in a straight line, but it was the real thing none the less. Tiny army met tiny army in open battle, blows were exchanged, casualties suffered, and the state of warfare could only be concluded by a peacemaking ceremony.

Similarly, among the Australian aborigines, who built no permanent dwellings but wandered from water hole to water hole over their almost desert country, warfare — and rules of "international law" — were highly developed. The student of social evolution will seek in vain for his obvious causes of war, struggle for lands, struggle for power of one group over another, expansion of population, need to divert the minds of a populace restive under tyranny, or even the ambition of a successful leader to enhance his own prestige. All are absent, but warfare as a practice remained, and men engaged in it and killed one another in the course of a war because killing is what is done in wars.

From instances like these it becomes apparent that an inquiry into the causes of war misses the fundamental point as completely as does an insistence upon the biological necessity of war. If a people have an idea of going to war and the idea that war is the way in which certain situations, defined within their society, are to be handled, they will sometimes go to war. If they are a mild and unaggressive people, like the Pueblo Indians, they may limit themselves to defensive warfare; but they will be forced to think in terms of war because there are peoples near them who have warfare as a pattern, and offensive, raiding, pillaging warfare at that. When the pattern of warfare is known, people like the Pueblo Indians will defend themselves, taking advantage of their natural defenses, the *mesa* village site, and people like the Lepchas, having no natural defenses and no idea of warfare, will merely submit to the invader. But the essential point remains the same. There is a way of behaving which is known to a given people and labeled as an appropriate form of behavior. A bold and warlike people like the Sioux or the Maori may label warfare as desirable as well as possible; a mild people like the Pueblo Indians may label warfare as undesirable; but to the minds of both peoples the possibility of warfare is present. Their thoughts, their hopes, their plans are oriented about this idea, that warfare may be selected as the way to meet some situation.

So simple peoples and civilized peoples, mild peoples and violent, assertive peoples, will all go to war if they have the invention, just as those peoples who have the custom of dueling will have duels and peoples who have the pattern of vendetta will indulge in vendetta. And, conversely, peoples who do not know of dueling will not fight duels, even though their wives are seduced and their daughters ravished; they may on occasion commit murder but they will not fight duels. Cultures which lack the idea of the vendetta will not meet every quarrel in this way. A people can use only the forms it has. So the Balinese have their special way of dealing with a quarrel between two individuals; if the two feel that the causes of quarrel are heavy, they may go and register their quarrel in the temple before the gods, and, making offerings, they may swear never to have anything to do with each other again. Under the Dutch government they registered such mutual "not-speaking" with the Dutch government officials. But in other societies, although individuals might feel as full of animosity and as unwilling to have any further contact as do the Balinese, they cannot register their quarrel with the gods and go on quietly about their business because registering quarrels with the gods is not an invention of which they know.

Yet, if it be granted that warfare is after all an invention, it may 10 nevertheless be an invention that lends itself to certain types of personality, to the exigent needs of autocrats, to the expansionist desires of crowded peoples, to the desire for plunder and rape and loot which is engendered by a dull and frustrating life. What, then, can we say of this congruence between warfare and its uses? If it is a form which fits so well, is not this congruence the essential point? But even here the primitive material causes us to wonder, because there are tribes who go to war merely for glory, having no quarrel with the enemy, suffering from no tyrant within their boundaries, anxious neither for land nor loot nor women, but merely anxious to win prestige which within that tribe has been declared obtainable only by war and without which no young man can hope to win his sweetheart's smile of approval. But if, as was the case with the Bush Negroes of Dutch Guiana, it is artistic ability which is necessary to win a girl's approval, the same young man would have to be carving rather than going out on a war party.

In many parts of the world, war is a game in which the individual can win counters — counters which bring him prestige in the eyes of his own sex or of the opposite sex; he plays for these counters as he might, in our society, strive for a tennis championship. Warfare is a frame for such prestige-seeking merely because it calls for the display of certain skills and certain virtues; all of these skills — riding straight, shooting straight, dodging the missiles of the enemy, and sending one's own straight to the mark — can be equally well exercised in some other framework and, equally, the virtues — endurance, bravery, loyalty, steadfastness — can be displayed in other contexts. The tie-up between proving oneself a man and proving this by a success in organized killing is due to a definition which many societies have made of manliness. And often, even in those societies which counted success in warfare a proof of human worth, strange turns were given to the idea, as when the Plains Indians gave their highest awards to the man who touched a live enemy rather than to the man who brought in a scalp — from a dead enemy — because killing a man was less risky. Warfare is just an invention known to the majority of human societies by which they permit their young men either to accumulate prestige or avenge their honor or acquire loot or wives or slaves or sago lands or cattle or appease the blood lust of their gods or the restless souls of the recently dead. It is just an invention, older and more widespread than the jury system, but none the less an invention.

But, once we have said this, have we said anything at all? Despite a few instances, dear to the hearts of controversialists, of the loss of the useful arts, once an invention is made which proves congruent with human needs or social forms, it tends to persist. Grant that war is an invention, that it is not a biological necessity nor the outcome of certain special types of social forms, still, once the invention is made, what are we to do about it? The Indian who had been subsisting on the buffalo for generations because with his primitive weapons he could slaughter only a limited number of buffalo did not return to his primitive weapons when he saw that the white man's more efficient weapons were exterminating the buffalo. A desire for the white man's cloth may mortgage the South Sea Islander to the white man's plantation, but he does not return to making bark cloth, which would have left him free. Once an invention is known and accepted, men do not easily relinquish it. The skilled workers may smash the first steam looms which they feel are to be their undoing, but they accept them in the end, and no movement which has insisted upon the mere abandonment of usable inventions has ever had much success. Warfare is here, as part of our thought; the deeds of warriors are immortalized in the words of our poets; the toys of our children are modeled upon the weapons of the soldier; the frame of reference within which our statesmen and our diplomats work always contains war. If we know that it is not inevitable, that it is due to historical accident that warfare is one of the ways in which we think of behaving, are we given any hope by that? What hope is there of persuading nations to abandon war, nations so thoroughly imbued with the idea that resort to war is, if not actually desirable and noble, at least inevitable whenever certain defined circumstances arise?

In answer to this question I think we might turn to the history of other social inventions, inventions which must once have seemed as firmly entrenched as warfare. Take the methods of trial which preceded the jury system: ordeal and trial by combat. Unfair, capricious, alien as they are to our feeling today, they were once the only methods open to individuals accused of some offense. The invention of trial by jury gradually replaced these methods until only witches, and finally not even witches, had to resort to the ordeal. And for a long time the jury system seemed the one best and finest method of settling legal disputes, but today new inventions, trial before judges only or before commissions, are replacing the jury system. In each case the old method was replaced by a new social invention; the ordeal did not go out because people thought it unjust or wrong, it went out because a method more congruent with the institutions and feelings of the period was invented. And, if we despair over the way in which war seems such an ingrained habit of most of the human race, we can take comfort from the fact that a poor invention will usually give place to a better invention.

For this, two conditions at least are necessary. The people must recognize the defects of the old invention, and some one must make a new one. Propaganda against warfare, documentation of its terrible cost in human suffering and social waste, these prepare the ground by teaching people to feel that warfare is a defective social institution. There is further needed a belief that social invention is possible and the invention of new methods which will render warfare as out-of-date as the tractor is making the plow, or the motor car the horse and buggy. A form of behavior becomes out-of-date only when something else takes its place, and in order to invent forms of behavior which will make war obsolete, it is a first requirement to believe that an invention is possible.

Discussion Questions

1. Mead uses a common organizational strategy — refuting the opposing view. (See an extended discussion of this on page 344.) In this essay she refutes several theories about the origin of warfare. Summarize these theories. Where does she state her own thesis?
2. Mead supports her argument with examples and analogies. Are they all equally convincing? How can a reader assess the strengths and weaknesses of her examples?
3. In the last part of her essay Mead acknowledges that war is a "usable invention." How does she answer this apparent weakness in her argument?
4. What solution to the problem of warfare does Mead propose? Do you find any flaws in her proposal? Explain your agreement or disagreement with the plausibility of her solution.

Writing Suggestions

5. In an article entitled "Where Have All the Young Men Gone? The Perfect Substitute for War," the author marvels at the significance of a gathering in 1998 of more than a million people to celebrate France's victory in the World Cup, a soccer game. "The vast majority of Europeans," he writes, "have found a way to hate one another without hacking one another to pieces."[1] (In a tragic irony, this article appeared in 1999 during the brutal "ethnic cleansing" of ethnic Albanians in Kosovo and the bombing of Serbia by NATO forces.)

   Argue that sporting events do or do not represent a substitute for war. Develop two or three issues — similarities or differences — that support your claim.
6. Pacifism is defined by *Webster's New International Dictionary* as "opposition to war or the use of military force for any purpose." If you consider yourself to be a pacifist, write a defense of your belief, using examples and analogies to make your position clear. But if you believe with Bertrand Russell, the British mathematician and philosopher, that "Absolute pacifism, as a method of gaining your ends, is subject to very severe limitations,"[2] defend your point of view, again using examples, as Mead does.

---

[1]Paul Auster, the *New York Times Magazine,* April 4, 1999, p. 144.
[2]*Dictionary of the Mind* (New York: Philosophical Library, 1952), p. 162.

Politics and the English Language

GEORGE ORWELL

This essay, written after World War II, develops George Orwell's claim that careless and dishonest use of language contributes to careless and dishonest thought and political corruption. Political language, he argues, is "largely the defense of the indefensible." But Orwell, novelist, critic, and political satirist — best known for his book Nineteen Eighty-Four — *believes that bad language habits can be reversed, and he lists rules for getting rid of some of the most offensive.*

Most people who bother with the matter at all would admit that the English language is in a bad way, but it is generally assumed that we cannot by conscious action do anything about it. Our civilization is decadent and our language — so the argument runs — must inevitably share in the general collapse. It follows that any struggle against the abuse of language is a sentimental archaism, like preferring candles to electric light or hansom cabs to aeroplanes. Underneath this lies the half-conscious belief that language is a natural growth and not an instrument which we shape for our own purposes.

Now, it is clear that the decline of a language must ultimately have political and economic causes: It is not due simply to the bad influence of this or that individual writer. But an effect can become a cause, reinforcing the original cause and producing the same effect in an intensified form, and so on indefinitely. A man may take to drink because he feels himself to be a failure, and then fail all the more completely because he drinks. It is rather the same thing that is happening to the English language. It becomes ugly and inaccurate because our thoughts are foolish, but the slovenliness of our language makes it easier for us to have foolish thoughts. The point is that the process is reversible. Modern English, especially written English, is full of bad habits which spread by imitation and which can be avoided if one is willing to take the necessary trouble. If one gets rid of these habits one can think more clearly, and to think clearly is a necessary first step towards political regeneration: So that the fight against bad English is not frivolous and is not the exclusive concern of professional writers. I will come back to this presently, and I hope that by that time the meaning of what I have said here will have become clearer. Meanwhile, here are five specimens of the English language as it is now habitually written.

From *Horizon,* April 1946.

These five passages have not been picked out because they are especially bad — I could have quoted far worse if I had chosen — but because they illustrate various of the mental vices from which we now suffer. They are a little below the average, but are fairly representative samples. I number them so that I can refer back to them when necessary:

(1) I am not, indeed, sure whether it is not true to say that the Milton who once seemed not unlike a seventeenth-century Shelley had not become out of an experience ever more bitter in each year, more alien *[sic]* to the founder of that Jesuit sect which nothing could induce him to tolerate.

Professor Harold Laski (Essay in *Freedom of Expression*)

(2) Above all, we cannot play ducks and drakes with a native battery of idioms which prescribes such egregious collocations of vocables as the Basic *put up with* for *tolerate* or *put at a loss* for *bewilder.*

Professor Lancelot Hogben *(Interglossa)*

(3) On the one side we have the free personality: By definition it is not neurotic, for it has neither conflict nor dream. Its desires, such as they are, are transparent, for they are just what institutional approval keeps in the forefront of consciousness; another institutional pattern would alter their number and intensity; there is little in them that is natural, irreducible, or culturally dangerous. But *on the other side,* the social bond itself is nothing but the mutual reflection of these self-secure integrities. Recall the definition of love. Is not this the very picture of a small academic? Where is there a place in this hall of mirrors for either personality or fraternity?

Essay on psychology in *Politics* (New York)

(4) All the "best people" from the gentlemen's clubs, and all the frantic fascist captains, united in common hatred of Socialism and bestial horror of the rising tide of the mass revolutionary movement, have turned to acts of provocation, to foul incendiarism, to medieval legends of poisoned wells, to legalize their own destruction of proletarian organizations, and rouse the agitated petty-bourgeoisie to chauvinistic fervor on behalf of the fight against the revolutionary way out of the crisis.

Communist pamphlet

(5) If a new spirit *is* to be infused into this old country, there is one thorny and contentious reform which must be tackled, and that is the humanization and galvanization of the BBC. Timidity here will bespeak cancer and atrophy of the soul. The heart of Britain may be sound and of strong beat, for instance, but the British lion's roar at present is like that of Bottom in Shakespeare's *Midsummer Night's Dream* — as gentle as any sucking dove. A virile new Britain cannot continue indefinitely to be traduced in the eyes or rather ears, of the world by the effete languors of Langham Place, brazenly masquerading as "standard English." When the Voice of Britain is heard at nine o'clock, better far and infinitely less ludicrous to hear aitches honestly dropped than the present priggish, inflated, inhibited, school-ma'amish arch braying of blameless bashful mewing maidens!

Letter in *Tribune*

Each of these passages has faults of its own, but, quite apart from avoidable ugliness, two qualities are common to all of them. The first is staleness of imagery: The other is lack of precision. The writer either has a meaning and cannot express it, or he inadvertently says something else, or he is almost indifferent as to whether his words mean anything or not. The mixture of vagueness and sheer incompetence is the most marked characteristic of modern English prose, and especially of any kind of political writing. As soon as certain topics are raised, the concrete melts into the abstract and no one seems to think of turns of speech that are not hackneyed: Prose consists less and less of *words* chosen for the sake of their meaning, and more and more of *phrases* tacked together like the sections of a prefabricated hen-house. I list below, with notes and examples, various of the tricks by means of which the work of prose-construction is habitually dodged:

Dying metaphors. A newly invented metaphor assists thought 5 by evoking a visual image, while on the other hand a metaphor which is technically "dead" (e.g., *iron resolution*) has in effect reverted to being an ordinary word and can generally be used without loss of vividness. But in between these two classes there is a huge dump of worn-out metaphors which have lost all evocative power and are merely used because they save people the trouble of inventing phrases for themselves. Examples are: *ring the changes on, take up the cudgels for, toe the line, ride roughshod over, stand shoulder to shoulder with, play into the hands of, no axe to grind, grist to the mill, fishing in troubled waters, rift within the lute, on the order of the day, Achilles' heel, swan song, hotbed.* Many of these are used without knowledge of their meaning (what is a "rift," for instance?), and incompatible metaphors are frequently mixed, a sure sign that the writer is not interested in what he is saying. Some metaphors now current have been twisted out of their original meaning without those who use them even being aware of the fact. For example, *toe the line* is sometimes written *tow the line.* Another example is *the hammer and the anvil*, now always used with the implication that the anvil gets the worst of it. In real life it is always the anvil that breaks the hammer, never the other way about: A writer who stopped to think what he was saying would be aware of this, and would avoid perverting the original phrase.

Operators or verbal false limbs. These save the trouble of picking out appropriate verbs and nouns, and at the same time pad each sentence with extra syllables which give it an appearance of symmetry. Characteristic phrases are: *render inoperative, militate against, make contact with, be subjected to, give rise to, give grounds for, have the effect of, play a leading part (role) in, make itself felt, take effect, exhibit a tendency to, serve the purpose of,* etc., etc. The keynote is the elimination of simple verbs. Instead of being a single word, such as *break, stop, spoil, mend, kill,* a verb becomes a *phrase,* made up of a noun or adjective tacked on to some general-purpose verb such as *prove, serve, form, play, render.* In addition, the passive voice is wherever possible used in preference to the active, and noun constructions are used instead of gerunds (*by examination of* instead of *by examining*). The range of verbs is further cut down by means of the *-ize* and *de-* formation, and the banal statements are given an appearance of profundity by means of the *not un-* formation. Simple conjunctions and prepositions are replaced by such phrases as *with respect to, having regard to, the fact that, by dint of, in view of, in the interests of, on the hypothesis that;* and the ends of sentences are saved from anticlimax by such resounding commonplaces as *greatly to be desired, cannot be left out of account, a development to be expected in the near future, deserving of serious consideration, brought to a satisfactory conclusion,* and so on and so forth.

Pretentious diction. Words like *phenomenon, element, individual* (as noun), *objective, categorical, effective, virtual, basic, primary, promote, constitute, exhibit, exploit, utilize, eliminate, liquidate,* are used to dress up simple statements and give an air of scientific impartiality to biased judgments. Adjectives like *epoch-making, epic, historic, unforgettable, triumphant, age-old, inevitable, inexorable, veritable,* are used to dignify the sordid processes of international politics, while writing that aims at glorifying war usually takes on an archaic color, its characteristic words being: *realm, throne, chariot, mailed fist, trident, sword, shield, buckler, banner, jackboot, clarion.* Foreign words and expressions such as *cul de sac, ancien régime, deus ex machina, mutatis mutandis, status quo, gleichshaltung, weltanschauung,* are used to give an air of culture and elegance. Except for the useful abbreviations *i.e., e.g.,* and *etc.,* there is no real need for any of the hundreds of foreign phrases now current in English. Bad writers, and especially scientific, political, and sociological writers, are nearly always haunted by the notion that Latin or Greek words are grander than Saxon ones, and unnecessary words like *expedite, ameliorate, predict, extraneous, deracinated, clandestine, subaqueous,* and hundreds of others constantly gain ground from their Anglo-Saxon opposite numbers.[1] The jargon peculiar to Marxist writing (*hyena, hangman, cannibal, petty bourgeois, these gentry, lackey, flunkey, mad*

---

[1] An interesting illustration of this is the way in which the English flower names which were in use till very recently are being ousted by Greek ones, *snapdragon* becoming *antirrhinum, forget-me-not* becoming *myosotis,* etc. It is hard to see any practical reason for this change of fashion: It is probably due to an instinctive turning-away from the more homely word and a vague feeling that the Greek word is scientific. [All notes are Orwell's.]

dog, White Guard, etc.) consists largely of words and phrases translated from Russian, German, or French; but the normal way of coining a new word is to use a Latin or Greek root with the appropriate affix and, where necessary, the *-ize* formation. It is often easier to make up words of this kind (*deregionalize, impermissible, extramarital, nonfragmentatory,* and so forth) than to think up the English words that will cover one's meaning. The result, in general, is an increase in slovenliness and vagueness.

Meaningless words.   In certain kinds of writing, particularly in art criticism and literary criticism, it is normal to come across long passages which are almost completely lacking in meaning.[2] Words like *romantic, plastic, values, human, dead, sentimental, natural, vitality,* as used in art criticism, are strictly meaningless in the sense that they not only do not point to any discoverable object, but are hardly ever expected to do so by the reader. When one critic writes, "The outstanding feature of Mr. X's work is its living quality," while another writes, "The immediately striking thing about Mr. X's work is its peculiar deadness," the reader accepts this as a simple difference of opinion. If words like *black* and *white* were involved, instead of the jargon words *dead* and *living,* he would see at once that language was being used in an improper way. Many political words are similarly abused. The word *fascism* has now no meaning except insofar as it signifies "something not desirable." The words *democracy, socialism, freedom, patriotic, realistic, justice,* have each of them several different meanings which cannot be reconciled with one another. In the case of a word like *democracy,* not only is there no agreed definition, but the attempt to make one is resisted from all sides. It is almost universally felt that when we call a country democratic we are praising it: Consequently the defenders of every kind of regime claim that it is a democracy, and fear that they might have to stop using the word if it were tied down to any one meaning. Words of this kind are often used in a consciously dishonest way. That is, the person who uses them has his own private definition, but allows his hearer to think he means something quite different. Statements like *Marshal Pétain was a true patriot, The Soviet Press is the freest in the world, The Catholic Church is opposed to persecution,* are almost always made with intent to deceive. Other words used in variable meanings, in most cases more or less dishonestly, are: *class, totalitarian, science, progressive, reactionary, bourgeois, equality.*

---

[2] Example: "Comfort's catholicity of perception and image, strangely Whitmanesque in range, almost the exact opposite in aesthetic compulsion, continues to evoke that trembling atmospheric accumulative hinting at a cruel, an inexorably serene timelessness . . . Wrey Gardiner scores by aiming at simple bull's-eyes with precision. Only they are not so simple, and through this contended sadness runs more than the surface bittersweet of resignation" (*Poetry Quarterly*).

Now that I have made this catalog of swindles and perversions, let me give another example of the kind of writing that they lead to. This time it must of its nature be an imaginary one. I am going to translate a passage of good English into modern English of the worst sort. Here is a well-known verse from Ecclesiastes:

> I returned and saw under the sun, that the race is not to the swift, nor the battle to the strong, neither yet bread to the wise, nor yet riches to men of understanding, nor yet favor to men of skill; but time and chance happeneth to them all.

Here it is in modern English:

> Objective consideration of contemporary phenomena compels the conclusion that success or failure in competitive activities exhibits no tendency to be commensurate with innate capacity, but that a considerable element of the unpredictable must invariably be taken into account.

This is a parody, but not a very gross one. Exhibit (3), above, for 10 instance, contains several patches of the same kind of English. It will be seen that I have not made a full translation. The beginning and ending of the sentence follow the original meaning fairly closely, but in the middle the concrete illustrations — race, battle, bread — dissolve into the vague phrase "success or failure in competitive activities." This had to be so, because no modern writer of the kind I am discussing — no one capable of using phrases like "objective consideration of contemporary phenomena"— would ever tabulate his thoughts in that precise and detailed way. The whole tendency of modern prose is away from concreteness. Now analyze these two sentences a little more closely. The first contains forty-nine words but only sixty syllables, and all its words are those of everyday life. The second contains thirty-eight words of ninety syllables: Eighteen of its words are from Latin roots, and one from Greek. The first sentence contains six vivid images, and only one phrase ("time and chance") that could be called vague. The second contains not a single fresh, arresting phrase, and in spite of its ninety syllables it gives only a shortened version of the meaning contained in the first. Yet without a doubt it is the second kind of sentence that is gaining ground in modern English. I do not want to exaggerate. This kind of writing is not yet universal, and outcrops of simplicity will occur here and there in the worst-written page. Still, if you or I were told to write a few lines on the uncertainty of human fortunes, we should probably come much nearer to my imaginary sentence than to the one from Ecclesiastes.

As I have tried to show, modern writing at its worst does not consist in picking out words for the sake of their meaning and inventing images in order to make the meaning clearer. It consists in gumming together long strips of words which have already been set in order by someone else, and making the results presentable by sheer humbug. The attraction of this way of writing is that it is easy. It is easier — even quicker once you have the habit — to say *In my opinion it is a not unjustifiable assumption that* than to say *I think*. If you use ready-made phrases, you not only don't have to hunt about for words; you also don't have to bother with the rhythms of your sentences, since these phrases are generally so arranged as to be more or less euphonious. When you are composing in a hurry — when you are dictating to a stenographer, for instance, or making a public speech — it is natural to fall into a pretentious, Latinized style. Tags like *a consideration which we should do well to bear in mind* or *a conclusion to which all of us would readily assent* will save many a sentence from coming down with a bump. By using stale metaphors, similes, and idioms, you save much mental effort, at the cost of leaving your meaning vague, not only for your reader but for yourself. This is the significance of mixed metaphors. The sole aim of a metaphor is to call up a visual image. When these images clash — as in *The Fascist octopus has sung its swan song, the jackboot is thrown into the melting pot* — it can be taken as certain that the writer is not seeing a mental image of the objects he is naming; in other words he is not really thinking. Look again at the examples I gave at the beginning of this essay. Professor Laski (1) uses five negatives in fifty-three words. One of these is superfluous, making nonsense of the whole passage, and in addition there is the slip *alien* for akin, making further nonsense, and several avoidable pieces of clumsiness which increase the general vagueness. Professor Hogben (2) plays ducks and drakes with a battery which is able to write prescriptions, and, while disapproving of the everyday phrase *put up with*, is unwilling to look *egregious* up in the dictionary and see what it means. (3), if one takes an uncharitable attitude towards it, is simply meaningless: Probably one could work out its intended meaning by reading the whole of the article in which it occurs. In (4), the writer knows more or less what he wants to say, but an accumulation of stale phrases chokes him like tea leaves blocking a sink. In (5), words and meaning have almost parted company. People who write in this manner usually have a general emotional meaning — they dislike one thing and want to express solidarity with another — but they are not interested in the detail of what they are saying. A scrupulous writer, in every sentence that he writes, will ask himself at least four questions, thus: What am I trying to say? What words will express it? What image or idiom will make it clearer? Is this image fresh enough to have an effect? And he will probably ask himself two more: Could I put it more shortly? Have I said anything that is avoidably ugly? But you are not obliged to go to all this trouble. You can shirk it by simply throwing your mind open and letting the ready-made phrases come crowding in. They will construct your sentences for you — even think your thoughts for you, to a certain extent — and at need they will perform the important service of partially concealing your meaning even from yourself. It is at this point that the special connection between politics and the debasement of language becomes clear.

In our time it is broadly true that political writing is bad writing. Where it is not true, it will generally be found that the writer is some kind of rebel, expressing his private opinions and not a "party line." Orthodoxy, of whatever color, seems to demand a lifeless, imitative style. The political dialects to be found in pamphlets, leading articles, manifestos, White Papers, and the speeches of undersecretaries do, of course, vary from party to party, but they are all alike in that one almost never finds in them a fresh, vivid, home-made turn of speech. When one watches some tired hack on the platform mechanically repeating the familiar phrases — *bestial atrocities, iron heel, bloodstained tyranny, free peoples of the world, stand shoulder to shoulder* — one often has a curious feeling that one is not watching a live human being but some kind of dummy; a feeling which suddenly becomes stronger at moments when the light catches the speaker's spectacles and turns them into blank discs which seem to have no eyes behind them. And this is not altogether fanciful. A speaker who uses that kind of phraseology has gone some distance towards turning himself into a machine. The appropriate noises are coming out of his larynx, but his brain is not involved as it would be if he were choosing his words for himself. If the speech he is making is one that he is accustomed to make over and over again, he may be almost unconscious of what he is saying, as one is when one utters the responses in church. And this reduced state of consciousness, if not indispensable, is at any rate favorable to political conformity.

In our time, political speech and writing are largely the defense of the indefensible. Things like the continuance of British rule in India, the Russian purges and deportations, the dropping of the atom bombs on Japan, can indeed be defended, but only by arguments which are too brutal for most people to face, and which do not square with the professed aims of political parties. Thus political language has to consist largely of euphemism, question-begging, and sheer cloudy vagueness. Defenseless villages are bombarded from the air, the inhabitants driven out into the countryside, the cattle machine-gunned, the huts set on fire with incendiary bullets: This is called *pacification*. Millions of peasants are robbed of their farms and sent trudging along the roads with no more than they can carry; this is called *transfer of population* or *rectification of frontiers*. People are imprisoned for years without trial, or shot in the back of the neck, or sent to die of scurvy in Arctic lumber camps: This is called *elimination of unreliable elements*. Such phraseology is needed if one wants to name things without calling up mental pictures of them. Consider for instance some comfortable English professor defending Russian totalitarianism. He cannot say outright, "I believe in killing off your opponents when you can get good results by doing so." Probably, therefore, he will say something like this:

> While freely conceding that the Soviet régime exhibits certain features which the humanitarian may be inclined to deplore, we must, I think, agree that a certain curtailment of the right to political opposition is an unavoidable concomitant of transitional periods, and that the rigors which the Russian people have been called upon to undergo have been amply justified in the sphere of concrete achievement.

The inflated style is itself a kind of euphemism. A mass of Latin words fall upon the facts like soft snow, blurring the outlines and covering up all the details. The great enemy of clear language is insincerity. When there is a gap between one's real and one's declared aims, one turns as it were instinctively to long words and exhausted idioms, like a cuttlefish squirting out ink. In our age there is no such thing as "keeping out of politics." All issues are political issues, and politics itself is a mass of lies, evasions, folly, hatred, and schizophrenia. When the general atmosphere is bad, language must suffer. I should expect to find — this is a guess which I have not sufficient knowledge to verify — that the German, Russian, and Italian languages have all deteriorated in the last ten or fifteen years, as a result of dictatorship.

But if thought corrupts language, language can also corrupt 15 thought. A bad usage can spread by tradition and imitation, even among people who should and do know better. The debased language that I have been discussing is in some ways very convenient. Phrases like *a not unjustifiable assumption, leaves much to be desired, would serve no good purpose, a consideration which we should do well to bear in mind,* are a continuous temptation, a packet of aspirins always at one's elbow. Look back through this essay, and for certain you will find that I have again and again committed the very faults I am protesting against. By this morning's post I have received a pamphlet dealing with conditions in Germany. The author tells me that he "felt impelled" to write it. I open it at random, and here is almost the first sentence that I see: "(The Allies) have an opportunity not only of achieving a radical transformation of Germany's social and political structure in such a way as to avoid a nationalistic reaction in Germany itself, but at the same time of laying the foundations of a cooperative and unified Europe." You see, he "feels impelled" to write — feels, presumably, that he has something new to say — and yet his words, like cavalry horses answering the bugle, group themselves automatically into the familiar dreary pattern. This invasion of one's mind by ready-made phrases *(lay the foundations, achieve a radical transformation)* can only be prevented if one is constantly on guard against them, and every such phrase anesthetizes a portion of one's brain.

I said earlier that the decadence of our language is probably curable. Those who deny this would argue, if they produced an argument at all, that language merely reflects existing social conditions, and that we cannot influence its development by any direct tinkering with words and constructions. So far as the general tone or spirit of a language goes, this may be true, but it is not true in detail. Silly words and expressions have often disappeared, not through any evolutionary process but owing to the conscious action of a minority. Two recent examples were *explore every avenue* and *leave no stone unturned,* which were killed by the jeers of a few journalists. There is a long list of flyblown metaphors which could similarly be got rid of if enough people would interest themselves in the job; and it should also be possible to laugh the *not un-* formation out of existence,[3] to reduce the amount of Latin and Greek in the average sentence, to drive out foreign phrases and strayed scientific words, and, in general, to make pretentiousness unfashionable. But all these are minor points. The defense of the English language implies more than this, and perhaps it is best to start by saying what it does *not* imply.

To begin with it has nothing to do with archaism, with the salvaging of obsolete words and turns of speech, or with the setting up of a "standard English" which must never be departed from. On the contrary, it is especially concerned with the scrapping of every word or idiom which has outworn its usefulness. It has nothing to do with correct grammar and syntax, which are of no importance so long as one makes one's meaning clear, or with the avoidance of Americanisms, or with having what is called a "good prose style." On the other hand it is not concerned with fake simplicity and the attempt to make written English colloquial. Nor does it even imply in every case preferring the Saxon word to the Latin one, though it does imply using the fewest and shortest words that will cover one's meaning. What is above all needed is to let the meaning choose the word, and not the other way about. In prose, the worst thing one can do with words is to surrender to them. When you think of a concrete object, you think wordlessly, and then, if you want to describe the thing you have been visualizing you probably hunt about till you find the exact words that seem to fit. When you think of something abstract you are more inclined to use words from the start, and unless you make a conscious effort to prevent it, the existing dialect will come rushing in and do the job for you, at the expense of blurring or even changing your meaning. Probably it is better to put off

---

[3] One can cure oneself of the *not un-* formation by memorizing this sentence: *A not unblack dog was chasing a not unsmall rabbit across a not ungreen field.*

using words as long as possible and get one's meaning as clear as one can through pictures or sensations. Afterwards one can choose — not simply *accept* — the phrases that will best cover the meaning, and then switch round and decide what impression one's words are likely to make on another person. This last effort of the mind cuts out all stale or mixed images, all prefabricated phrases, needless repetitions, and humbug and vagueness generally. But one can often be in doubt about the effect of a word or a phrase, and one needs rules that one can rely on when instinct fails. I think the following rules will cover most cases:

(i)   Never use a metaphor, simile, or other figure of speech which you are used to seeing in print.

(ii) Never use a long word where a short one will do.

(iii) If it is possible to cut a word out, always cut it out.

(iv) Never use the passive where you can use the active.

(v)   Never use a foreign phrase, a scientific word, or a jargon word if you can think of an everyday English equivalent.

(vi) Break any of these rules sooner than say anything outright barbarous.

These rules sound elementary, and so they are, but they demand a deep change in attitude in anyone who has grown used to writing in the style now fashionable. One could keep all of them and still write bad English, but one could not write the kind of stuff that I quoted in those five specimens at the beginning of this article.

I have not here been considering the literary use of language, but merely language as an instrument for expressing and not for concealing or preventing thought. Stuart Chase and others have come near to claiming that all abstract words are meaningless, and have used this as a pretext for advocating a kind of political quietism. Since you don't know what Fascism is, how can you struggle against Fascism? One need not swallow such absurdities as this, but one ought to recognize that the present political chaos is connected with the decay of language, and that one can probably bring about some improvement by starting at the verbal end. If you simplify your English, you are freed from the worst follies of orthodoxy. You cannot speak any of the necessary dialects, and when you make a stupid remark its stupidity will be obvious, even to yourself. Political language — and with variations this is true of all political parties, from Conservatives to Anarchists — is designed to make lies sound truthful and murder respectable, and to give an appearance of solidity to pure wind. One cannot change this all in a moment, but one can at least change one's own habits, and from time to time one can even, if one jeers loudly enough, send some worn-out and useless phrase — some *jackboot, Achilles' heel, hotbed, melting pot, acid test, veritable inferno,* or other lump of verbal refuse — into the dustbin where it belongs.

Discussion Questions

1. Orwell disagrees with a common assumption about language. What is it? Where in the essay does he attack this assumption directly?
2. What faults do his five samples of bad language have in common? Select examples of these faults in each passage.
3. What "tricks" for avoiding good prose does Orwell list? Do you think that some are more dangerous or misleading than others? Explain the reasons for your answer.
4. What different reasons does Orwell suggest for the slovenliness of much political writing and speaking? What examples does he give to support these reasons? Are they persuasive?
5. How does Orwell propose that we get rid of our bad language habits? Do you think his recommendations are realistic? Can the teaching of writing in school assist in the remedy?
6. Why does Orwell urge the reader to "look back through this essay" to find "the very faults I am protesting against"? Can you, in fact, find any?

Writing Suggestions

7. Choose a speech or an editorial whose meaning seems to be obscured by pretentious diction, meaningless words, euphemism, or "sheer cloudy vagueness." Point out the real meaning of the piece. If you think that its purpose is deceptive, expose the unpleasant truth that the author is concealing. Use Orwell's device, giving concrete meaning to any abstractions. (One source of speeches is a publication called *Vital Speeches of the Day.* Another is the *New York Times,* which often prints in full, or excerpts major portions of, speeches by leading figures in public life.)
8. Orwell's essay appeared before the widespread use of television. Do you think that TV makes it harder for politicians to be dishonest? Choose a particular public event — a war, a street riot, a terrorist activity, a campaign stop — and argue either for or against the claim that televised coverage makes it harder for a politician to engage in "sheer cloudy vagueness." Or does it make no difference at all? Be specific in your use of evidence.

Letter from Birmingham Jail

MARTIN LUTHER KING JR.

Martin Luther King Jr. (1929–1968) was a clergyman, author, distinguished civil rights leader, and winner of the Nobel Prize for peace in 1964 for his contributions to racial harmony and his advocacy of nonviolent response to aggression. He was assassinated in 1968. In the following selections we meet King in two of his various roles. In "Letter from Birmingham Jail," he appears as historian and philosopher. He wrote the letter from a jail cell on April 16, 1963, after his arrest for participation in a demonstration for civil rights for African Americans. The letter was a reply to eight Alabama clergymen who, in a public statement, had condemned demonstrations in the streets.

My dear Fellow Clergymen,

While confined here in the Birmingham city jail, I came across your recent statement calling our present activities "unwise and untimely." Seldom, if ever, do I pause to answer criticism of my work and ideas. If I sought to answer all of the criticisms that cross my desk, my secretaries would be engaged in little else in the course of the day, and I would have no time for constructive work. But since I feel that you are men of genuine good will and your criticisms are sincerely set forth, I would like to answer your statement in what I hope will be patient and reasonable terms.

I think I should give the reason for my being in Birmingham, since you have been influenced by the argument of "outsiders coming in." I have the honor of serving as president of the Southern Christian Leadership Conference, an organization operating in every southern state, with headquarters in Atlanta, Georgia. We have some eighty-five affiliate organizations all across the South — one being the Alabama Christian Movement for Human Rights. Whenever necessary and possible we share staff, educational, and financial resources with our affiliates. Several months ago our local affiliate here in Birmingham invited us to be on call to engage in a nonviolent direct-action program if such were deemed necessary. We readily consented and when the hour came we lived up to our promises. So I am here, along with several members of my staff, because we were invited here. I am here because I have basic organizational ties here.

Beyond this, I am in Birmingham because injustice is here. Just as the eighth-century prophets left their little villages and carried

From *A Testament of Hope* (1986).

their "thus saith the Lord" far beyond the boundaries of their home-towns; and just as the Apostle Paul left his little village of Tarsus and carried the gospel of Jesus Christ to practically every hamlet and city of the Graeco-Roman world, I too am compelled to carry the gospel of freedom beyond my particular hometown. Like Paul, I must constantly respond to the Macedonian call for aid.

Moreover, I am cognizant of the interrelatedness of all communities and states. I cannot sit idly by in Atlanta and not be concerned about what happens in Birmingham. Injustice anywhere is a threat to justice everywhere. We are caught in an inescapable network of mutuality, tied in a single garment of destiny. Whatever affects one directly affects all indirectly. Never again can we afford to live with the narrow, provincial "outside agitator" idea. Anyone who lives in the United States can never be considered an outsider anywhere in this country.

You deplore the demonstrations that are presently taking place 5 in Birmingham. But I am sorry that your statement did not express a similar concern for the conditions that brought the demonstrations into being. I am sure that each of you would want to go beyond the superficial social analyst who looks merely at effects, and does not grapple with underlying causes. I would not hesitate to say that it is unfortunate that so-called demonstrations are taking place in Birmingham at this time, but I would say in more emphatic terms that it is even more unfortunate that the white power structure of this city left the Negro community with no other alternative.

In any nonviolent campaign there are four basic steps: (1) collection of the facts to determine whether injustices are alive, (2) negotiation, (3) self-purification, and (4) direct action. We have gone through all of these steps in Birmingham. There can be no gainsaying of the fact that racial injustice engulfs this community.

Birmingham is probably the most thoroughly segregated city in the United States. Its ugly record of police brutality is known in every section of this country. Its unjust treatment of Negroes in the courts is a notorious reality. There have been more unsolved bombings of Negro homes and churches in Birmingham than any city in this nation. These are the hard, brutal, and unbelievable facts. On the basis of these conditions Negro leaders sought to negotiate with the city fathers. But the political leaders consistently refused to engage in good faith negotiation.

Then came the opportunity last September to talk with some of the leaders of the economic community. In these negotiating sessions certain promises were made by the merchants — such as the promise to remove the humiliating racial signs from the stores. On the basis of these promises Reverend Shuttlesworth and the leaders of the Alabama Christian Movement for Human Rights agreed to call a moratorium on any type of demonstrations. As the weeks and months unfolded we realized that we were the victims of a broken promise. The signs remained. Like so many experiences of the past we were confronted with blasted hopes, and the dark shadow of a deep disappointment settled upon us. So we had no alternative except that of preparing for direct action, whereby we would present our very bodies as a means of laying our case before the conscience of the local and national community. We were not unmindful of the difficulties involved. So we decided to go through a process of self-purification. We started having workshops on nonviolence and repeatedly asking ourselves the questions, "Are you able to accept blows without retaliating?" "Are you able to endure the ordeals of jail?" We decided to set our direct-action program around the Easter season, realizing that with the exception of Christmas, this was the largest shopping period of the year. Knowing that a strong economic withdrawal program would be the by-product of direct action, we felt that this was the best time to bring pressure on the merchants for the needed changes. Then it occurred to us that the March election was ahead and so we speedily decided to postpone action until after election day. When we discovered that Mr. Connor was in the run-off, we decided again to postpone action so that the demonstrations could not be used to cloud the issues. At this time we agreed to begin our nonviolent witness the day after the run-off.

This reveals that we did not move irresponsibly into direct actions. We too wanted to see Mr. Connor defeated; so we went through postponement after postponement to aid in this community need. After this we felt that direct action could be delayed no longer.

You may well ask, "Why direct action? Why sit-ins, marches, etc.? Isn't negotiation a better path?" You are exactly right in your call for negotiation. Indeed, this is the purpose of direct action. Nonviolent direct action seeks to create such a crisis and establish such creative tension that a community that has constantly refused to negotiate is forced to confront the issue. It seeks so to dramatize the issue that it can no longer be ignored. I just referred to the creation of tension as a part of the work of the nonviolent resister. This may sound rather shocking. But I must confess that I am not afraid of the word tension. I have earnestly worked and preached against violent tension, but there is a type of constructive nonviolent tension that is necessary for growth. Just as Socrates felt that it was necessary to create a tension in the mind so that individuals could rise from the bondage of myths and half-truths to the unfettered realm of creative analysis and objective appraisal, we must see the need of having nonviolent gadflies to create the kind of tension in society that will help men to rise from the dark depths of prejudice and racism to the majestic heights of understanding and brotherhood. So the purpose of the direct action is to create a situation so crisis-packed that it

10

will inevitably open the door to negotiation. We, therefore, concur with you in your call for negotiation. Too long has our beloved Southland been bogged down in the tragic attempt to live in monologue rather than dialogue.

One of the basic points in your statement is that our acts are untimely. Some have asked, "Why didn't you give the new administration time to act?" The only answer that I can give to this inquiry is that the new administration must be prodded about as much as the outgoing one before it acts. We will be sadly mistaken if we feel that the election of Mr. Boutwell will bring the millennium to Birmingham. While Mr. Boutwell is much more articulate and gentle than Mr. Connor, they are both segregationists, dedicated to the task of maintaining the status quo. The hope I see in Mr. Boutwell is that he will be reasonable enough to see the futility of massive resistance to desegregation. But he will not see this without pressure from the devotees of civil rights. My friends, I must say to you that we have not made a single gain in civil rights without determined legal and nonviolent pressure. History is the long and tragic story of the fact that privileged groups seldom give up their privileges voluntarily. Individuals may see the moral light and voluntarily give up their unjust posture; but as Reinhold Niebuhr has reminded us, groups are more immoral than individuals.

We know through painful experience that freedom is never voluntarily given by the oppressor; it must be demanded by the oppressed. Frankly, I have never yet engaged in a direct-action movement that was "well-timed," according to the timetable of those who have not suffered unduly from the disease of segregation. For years now I have heard the words "Wait!" It rings in the ear of every Negro with a piercing familiarity. This "Wait" has almost always meant "Never." It has been a tranquilizing thalidomide, relieving the emotional stress for a moment, only to give birth to an ill-formed infant of frustration. We must come to see with the distinguished jurist of yesterday that "justice too long delayed is justice denied." We have waited for more than 340 years for our constitutional and God-given rights. The nations of Asia and Africa are moving with jetlike speed toward the goal of political independence, and we still creep at horse and buggy pace toward the gaining of a cup of coffee at a lunch counter. I guess it is easy for those who have never felt the stinging darts of segregation to say, "Wait." But when you have seen vicious mobs lynch your mothers and fathers at will and drown your sisters and brothers at whim; when you see hate-filled policemen curse, kick, brutalize, and even kill your black brothers and sisters with impunity; when you see the vast majority of your 20 million Negro brothers smothering in an airtight cage of poverty in the midst of an affluent society; when you suddenly find your tongue twisted and your speech stammering as you seek to explain to your six-year-old daughter why she can't go to the public amusement park that has just been advertised on television, and see tears welling up in her little eyes when she is told that Funtown is closed to colored children, and see the depressing clouds of inferiority begin to form in her little mental sky, and see her begin to distort her little personality by unconsciously developing a bitterness toward white people; when you have to concoct an answer for a five-year-old son asking in agonizing pathos: "Daddy, why do white people treat colored people so mean?"; when you take a cross-country drive and find it necessary to sleep night after night in the uncomfortable corners of your automobile because no motel will accept you; when you are humiliated day in and day out by nagging signs reading "white" and "colored"; when your first name becomes "nigger" and your middle name becomes "boy" (however old you are) and your last name becomes "John," and when your wife and mother are never given the respected title "Mrs."; when you are harried by day and haunted by night by the fact that you are a Negro, living constantly at tiptoe stance never quite knowing what to expect next, and plagued with inner fears and outer resentments; when you are forever fighting a degenerating sense of "nobodiness"; then you will understand why we find it difficult to wait. There comes a time when the cup of endurance runs over, and men are no longer willing to be plunged into an abyss of injustice where they experience the blackness of corroding despair. I hope, sirs, you can understand our legitimate and unavoidable impatience.

You express a great deal of anxiety over our willingness to break laws. This is certainly a legitimate concern. Since we so diligently urge people to obey the Supreme Court's decision of 1954 outlawing segregation in the public schools, it is rather strange and paradoxical to find us consciously breaking laws. One may well ask, "How can you advocate breaking some laws and obeying others?" The answer is found in the fact that there are two types of laws: There are *just* and there are *unjust* laws. I would agree with Saint Augustine that "An unjust law is no law at all."

Now what is the difference between the two? How does one determine when a law is just or unjust? A just law is a man-made code that squares with the moral law or the law of God. An unjust law is a code that is out of harmony with the moral law. To put it in the terms of Saint Thomas Aquinas, an unjust law is a human law that is not rooted in eternal and natural law. Any law that uplifts human personality is just. Any law that degrades human personality is unjust. All segregation statutes are unjust because segregation distorts the soul and damages the personality. It gives the segregator a false sense of superiority, and the segregated a false sense of inferiority. To use the words of Martin Buber, the great Jewish philosopher, segregation substitutes an "I-it" relationship for the "I-thou" relationship, and ends up relegating persons to the status of things. So segregation is not only politically, economically, and sociologically unsound, but it is morally wrong and sinful. Paul Tillich has said that sin is separation. Isn't segregation an existential expression of man's tragic separation, an expression of his awful estrangement, his terrible sinfulness? So I can urge men to disobey segregation ordinances because they are morally wrong.

Let us turn to a more concrete example of just and unjust laws. 15 An unjust law is a code that a majority inflicts on a minority that is not binding on itself. This is difference made legal. On the other hand, a just law is a code that a majority compels a minority to follow that it is willing to follow itself. This is sameness made legal.

Let me give another explanation. An unjust law is a code inflicted upon a minority which that minority had no part in enacting or creating because they did not have the unhampered right to vote. Who can say that the legislature of Alabama which set up the segregation laws was democratically elected? Throughout the state of Alabama all types of conniving methods are used to prevent Negroes from becoming registered voters, and there are some counties without a single Negro registered to vote despite the fact that the Negro constitutes a majority of the population. Can any law set up in such a state be considered democratically structured?

These are just a few examples of unjust and just laws. There are some instances when a law is just on its face and unjust in its application. For instance, I was arrested Friday on a charge of parading without a permit. Now there is nothing wrong with an ordinance which requires a permit for a parade, but when the ordinance is used to preserve segregation and to deny citizens the First Amendment privilege of peaceful assembly and peaceful protest, then it becomes unjust.

I hope you can see the distinction I am trying to point out. In no sense do I advocate evading or defying the law as the rabid segregationist would do. This would lead to anarchy. One who breaks an unjust law must do it *openly, lovingly* (not hatefully as the white mothers did in New Orleans when they were seen on television screaming, "nigger, nigger, nigger"), and with a willingness to accept the penalty. I submit that an individual who breaks a law that conscience tells him is unjust, and willingly accepts the penalty by staying in jail to arouse the conscience of the community over its injustice, is in reality expressing the very highest respect for law.

Of course, there is nothing new about this kind of civil disobedience. It was seen sublimely in the refusal of Shadrach, Meshach, and Abednego to obey the laws of Nebuchadnezzar because a higher moral law was involved. It was practiced superbly by the early Christians who were willing to face hungry lions and the excruciating pain of chopping blocks, before submitting to certain unjust laws of the Roman Empire. To a degree academic freedom is a reality today because Socrates practiced civil disobedience.

We can never forget that everything Hitler did in Germany was   20 "legal" and everything the Hungarian freedom fighters did in Hungary was "illegal." It was "illegal" to aid and comfort a Jew in Hitler's Germany. But I am sure that if I had lived in Germany during that time I would have aided and comforted my Jewish brothers even though it was illegal. If I lived in a Communist country today where certain principles dear to the Christian faith are suppressed, I believe I would openly advocate disobeying these antireligious laws. I must make two honest confessions to you, my Christian and Jewish brothers. First, I must confess that over the last few years I have been gravely disappointed with the white moderate. I have almost reached the regrettable conclusion that the Negro's great stumbling block in the stride toward freedom is not the White Citizen's Councilor or the Ku Klux Klanner, but the white moderate who is more devoted to "order" than to justice; who prefers a negative peace which is the absence of tension to a positive peace which is the presence of justice; who constantly says, "I agree with you in the goal you seek, but I can't agree with your methods of direct action"; who paternalistically feels that he can set the timetable for another man's freedom; who lives by the myth of time and who constantly advises the Negro to wait until a "more convenient season." Shallow understanding from people of good will is more frustrating than absolute misunderstanding from people of ill will. Lukewarm acceptance is much more bewildering than outright rejection.

I had hoped that the white moderate would understand that law and order exist for the purpose of establishing justice, and that when they fail to do this they become dangerously structured dams that block the flow of social progress. I had hoped that the white moderate would understand that the present tension of the South is merely a necessary phase of the transition from an obnoxious negative peace, where the Negro passively accepted his unjust plight, to a substance-filled positive peace, where all men will respect the dignity and worth of human personality. Actually, we who engage in nonviolent direct action are not the creators of tension. We merely bring to the surface the hidden tension that is already alive. We bring it out in the open where it can be seen and dealt with. Like a boil that can never be cured as long as it is covered up but must be opened with all its pus-flowing ugliness to the natural medicines of air and light, injustice must likewise be exposed, with all of the tension its exposing creates, to the light of human conscience and the air of national opinion before it can be cured.

In your statement you asserted that our actions, even though peaceful, must be condemned because they precipitate violence. But can this assertion be logically made? Isn't this like condemning the robbed man because his possession of money precipitated the evil act of robbery? Isn't this like condemning Socrates because his unswerving commitment to truth and his philosophical delvings precipitated the misguided popular mind to make him drink the hemlock? Isn't this like condemning Jesus because His unique God-consciousness and never-ceasing devotion to His will precipitated the evil act of crucifixion? We must come to see, as federal courts have consistently affirmed, that it is immoral to urge an individual to withdraw his efforts to gain his basic constitutional rights because the quest precipitates violence. Society must protect the robbed and punish the robber.

I had also hoped that the white moderate would reject the myth of time. I received a letter this morning from a white brother in Texas which said: "All Christians know that the colored people will receive equal rights eventually, but it is possible that you are in too great of a religious hurry. It has taken Christianity almost two thousand years to accomplish what it has. The teachings of Christ take time to come to earth." All that is said here grows out of a tragic misconception of time. It is the strangely irrational notion that there is something in the very flow of time that will inevitably cure all ills. Actually time is neutral. It can be used either destructively or constructively. I am coming to feel that the people of ill will have used time much more effectively than the people of good will. We will have to repent in this generation not merely for the vitriolic words and actions of the bad people, but for the appalling silence of the good people. We must come to see that human progress never rolls in on wheels of inevitability. It comes through the tireless efforts and persistent work of men willing to be co-workers with God, and without this hard work time itself becomes an ally of the forces of social stagnation. We must use time creatively, and forever realize that the time is always ripe to do right. Now is the time to make real the promise of democracy, and transform our pending national elegy into a creative psalm of brotherhood. Now is the time to lift our national policy from the quicksand of racial injustice to the solid rock of human dignity.

You spoke of our activity in Birmingham as extreme. At first I was rather disappointed that fellow clergymen would see my nonviolent efforts as those of the extremist. I started thinking about the fact that I stand in the middle of two opposing forces in the Negro community. One is a force of complacency made up of Negroes who, as a result of long years of oppression, have been so completely drained of self-respect and a sense of "somebodiness" that they have adjusted to segregation, and of a few Negroes in the middle class who, because of a degree of academic and economic security, and because at points they profit by segregation, have unconsciously become insensitive to the problems of the masses. The other force is one of bitterness and hatred, and comes perilously close to advocating violence. It is expressed in the various black nationalist groups that are springing up over the nation, the largest and best known being Elijah Muhammad's Muslim movement. This movement is nourished by the contemporary frustration over the continued existence of racial discrimination. It is made up of people who have lost faith in America, who have absolutely repudiated Christianity, and who have concluded that the white man is an incurable "devil." I have tried to stand between these two forces, saying that we need not follow the "do-nothingism" of the complacent or the hatred and despair of the black nationalist. There is the more excellent way of love and nonviolent protest. I'm grateful to God that, through the Negro church, the dimension of nonviolence entered our struggle. If this philosophy had not emerged, I am convinced that by now many streets of the South would be flowing with floods of blood. And I am further convinced that if our white brothers dismiss us as "rabble-rousers" and "outside agitators" those of us who are working through the channels of nonviolent direct action and refuse to support our nonviolent efforts, millions of Negroes, out of frustration and despair, will seek solace and security in black nationalist ideologies, a development that will lead inevitably to a frightening racial nightmare.

Oppressed people cannot remain oppressed forever. The urge 25 for freedom will eventually come. This is what happened to the American Negro. Something within has reminded him of his birthright of freedom; something without has reminded him that he can gain it. Consciously and unconsciously, he has been swept in by what the Germans call the *Zeitgeist,* and with his black brothers of Africa, and his brown and yellow brothers of Asia, South America, and the Caribbean, he is moving with a sense of cosmic urgency toward the promised land of racial justice. Recognizing this vital urge that has engulfed the Negro community, one should readily understand public demonstrations. The Negro has many pent-up resentments and latent frustrations. He has to get them out. So let him march sometime; let him have his prayer pilgrimages to the city hall; understand why he must have sit-ins and freedom rides. If his repressed emotions do not come out in these nonviolent ways, they will come out in ominous expressions of violence. This is not a threat; it is a fact of history. So I have not said to my people "get rid of your discontent." But I have tried to say that this normal and healthy discontent can be channelized through the creative outlet of nonviolent direct action. Now this approach is being dismissed as extremist. I must admit that I was initially disappointed in being so categorized.

But as I continued to think about the matter I gradually gained a bit of satisfaction from being considered an extremist. Was not Jesus an extremist in love — "Love your enemies, bless them that curse you, pray for them that despitefully use you." Was not Amos an extremist for justice — "Let justice roll down like waters and righteousness like a mighty stream." Was not Paul an extremist for the gospel of Jesus Christ — "I bear in my body the marks of the Lord Jesus." Was not Martin Luther an extremist — "Here I stand; I can do none other so help me God." Was not John Bunyan an extremist — "I will stay in jail to the end of my days before I make a butchery of my conscience." Was not Abraham Lincoln an extremist — "This nation cannot survive half slave and half free." Was not Thomas Jefferson an extremist — "We hold these truths to be self-evident, that all men are created equal." So the question is not whether we will be extremist but what kind of extremist will we be. Will we be extremists for hate or will we be extremists for love? Will we be extremists for the preservation of injustice — or will we be extremists for the cause of justice? In that dramatic scene on Calvary's hill, three men were crucified. We must not forget that all three were crucified for the same crime — the crime of extremism. Two were extremists for immorality, and thusly fell below their environment. The other, Jesus Christ, was an extremist for love, truth, and goodness, and thereby rose above his environment. So, after all, maybe the South, the nation, and the world are in dire need of creative extremists.

I had hoped that the white moderate would see this. Maybe I was too optimistic. Maybe I expected too much. I guess I should have realized that few members of a race that has oppressed another race can understand or appreciate the deep groans and passionate yearnings of those that have been oppressed and still fewer have the vision to see that injustice must be rooted out by strong, persistent, and determined action. I am thankful, however, that some of our white brothers have grasped the meaning of this social revolution and committed themselves to it. They are still all too small in quantity, but they are big in quality. Some like Ralph McGill, Lillian Smith, Harry Golden, and James Dabbs have written about our struggle in eloquent, prophetic, and understanding terms. Others have marched with us down nameless streets of the South. They have languished in filthy roach-infested jails, suffering the abuse and brutality of angry policemen who see them as "dirty nigger-lovers." They, unlike so many of their moderate brothers and sisters, have recognized the urgency of the moment and sensed the need for powerful "action" antidotes to combat the disease of segregation.

Let me rush on to mention my other disappointment. I have been so greatly disappointed with the white church and its leadership. Of course, there are some notable exceptions. I am not unmindful of the fact that each of you has taken some significant stands on this issue. I commend you, Reverend Stallings, for your Christian stance on this past Sunday, in welcoming Negroes to your worship service on a nonsegregated basis. I commend the Catholic leaders of this state for integrating Springhill College several years ago.

But despite these notable exceptions I must honestly reiterate that I have been disappointed with the church. I do not say that as one of the negative critics who can always find something wrong with the church. I say it as a minister of the gospel, who loves the church; who was nurtured in its bosom; who has been sustained by its spiritual blessings, and who will remain true to it as long as the cord of life shall lengthen.

I had the strange feeling when I was suddenly catapulted into 30 the leadership of the bus protest in Montgomery several years ago that we would have the support of the white church. I felt that the white ministers, priests, and rabbis of the South would be some of our strongest allies. Instead, some have been outright opponents, refusing to understand the freedom movement and misrepresenting its leaders; all too many others have been more cautious than courageous and have remained silent behind the anesthetizing security of the stained-glass windows.

In spite of my shattered dreams of the past, I came to Birmingham with the hope that the white religious leadership of this community would see the justice of our cause, and with deep moral concern, serve as the channel through which our just grievances would get to the power structure. I had hoped that each of you would understand. But again I have been disappointed. I have heard numerous religious leaders of the South call upon their worshipers to comply with a desegregation decision because it is the *law,* but I have longed to hear white ministers say, "Follow this decree because integration is morally *right* and the Negro is your brother." In the midst of blatant injustices inflicted upon the Negro, I have watched white churches stand on the sideline and merely mouth pious irrelevancies and sanctimonious trivialities. In the midst of a mighty struggle to rid our nation of racial and economic injustice, I have heard so many ministers say, "Those are social issues with which the gospel has no real concern," and I have watched so many churches commit themselves to a completely otherworldly religion which made a strange distinction between body and soul, the sacred and the secular.

So here we are moving toward the exit of the twentieth century with a religious community largely adjusted to the status quo, standing as a taillight behind other community agencies rather than a headlight leading men to higher levels of justice.

I have traveled the length and breadth of Alabama, Mississippi, and all the other southern states. On sweltering summer days and crisp autumn mornings I have looked at her beautiful churches with their lofty spires pointing heavenward. I have beheld the impressive outlay of her massive religious education buildings. Over and over again I have found myself asking: "What kind of people worship here? Who is their God? Where were their voices when the lips of Governor Barnett dripped with words of interposition and nullification? Where were they when Governor Wallace gave the clarion call for defiance and hatred? Where were their voices of support when tired, bruised, and weary Negro men and women decided to rise from the dark dungeons of complacency to the bright hills of creative protest?"

Yes, these questions are still in my mind. In deep disappointment, I have wept over the laxity of the church. But be assured that my tears have been tears of love. There can be no deep disappointment where there is not deep love. Yes, I love the church; I love her sacred walls. How could I do otherwise? I am in the rather unique position of being the son, the grandson, and the great-grandson of preachers. Yes, I see the church as the body of Christ. But, oh! How we have blemished and scarred that body through social neglect and fear of being nonconformists.

There was a time when the church was very powerful. It was 35 during that period when the early Christians rejoiced when they were deemed worthy to suffer for what they believed. In those days the church was not merely a thermometer that recorded the ideas and principles of popular opinion; it was a thermostat that transformed the mores of society. Wherever the early Christians entered a town the power structure got disturbed and immediately sought to convict them for being "disturbers of the peace" and "outside agitators." But they went on with the conviction that they were "a colony of heaven," and had to obey God rather than man. They were small in number but big in commitment. They were too God-intoxicated to be "astronomically intimidated." They brought an end to such ancient evils as infanticide and gladiatorial contest.

Things are different now. The contemporary church is often a weak, ineffectual voice with an uncertain sound. It is so often the archsupporter of the status quo. Far from being disturbed by the presence of the church, the power structure of the average community is consoled by the church's silent and often vocal sanction of things as they are.

But the judgment of God is upon the church as never before. If the church of today does not recapture the sacrificial spirit of the early church, it will lose its authentic ring, forfeit the loyalty of millions, and be dismissed as an irrelevant social club with no meaning for the twentieth century. I am meeting young people every day whose disappointment with the church has risen to outright disgust.

Maybe again, I have been too optimistic. Is organized religion too inextricably bound to the status quo to save our nation and the world? Maybe I must turn my faith to the inner spiritual church, the church within the church, as the true *ecclesia* and the hope of the world. But again I am thankful to God that some noble souls from the ranks of organized religion have broken loose from the paralyzing chains of conformity and joined us as active partners in the struggle for freedom. They have left their secure congregations and walked the streets of Albany, Georgia, with us. They have gone through the highways of the South on tortuous rides for freedom. Yes, they have gone to jail with us. Some have been kicked out of their churches, and lost support of their bishops and fellow ministers. But they have gone with the faith that right defeated is stronger than evil triumphant. These men have been the leaven in the lump of the race. Their witness has been the spiritual salt that has preserved the true meaning of the gospel in these troubled times. They have carved a tunnel of hope through the dark mountain of disappointment.

I hope the church as a whole will meet the challenge of this decisive hour. But even if the church does not come to the aid of justice, I have no despair about the future. I have no fear about the outcome of our struggle in Birmingham, even if our motives are presently misunderstood. We will reach the goal of freedom in Birmingham and all over the nation, because the goal of America is freedom. Abused and scorned though we may be, our destiny is tied up with the destiny of America. Before the Pilgrims landed at Plymouth we were here. Before the pen of Jefferson etched across the pages of history the majestic words of the Declaration of Independence, we were here. For more than two centuries our foreparents labored in this country without wages; they made cotton king; and they built the homes of their masters in the midst of brutal injustice and shameful humiliation — and yet out of a bottomless vitality they continued to thrive and develop. If the inexpressible cruelties of slavery could not stop us, the opposition we now face will surely fail. We will win our freedom because the sacred heritage of our nation and the eternal will of God are embodied in our echoing demands.

I must close now. But before closing I am impelled to mention 40 one other point in your statement that troubled me profoundly. You warmly commended the Birmingham police force for keeping "order" and "preventing violence." I don't believe you would have so warmly commended the police force if you had seen its angry violent dogs literally biting six unarmed, nonviolent Negroes. I don't believe you would so quickly commend the policemen if you would observe their ugly and inhuman treatment of Negroes here in the city jail; if you would watch them push and curse old Negro women and young Negro girls; if you would see them slap and kick old Negro men and young boys; if you will observe them, as they did on two occasions, refuse to give us food because we wanted to sing our grace together. I'm sorry that I can't join you in your praise for the police department.

It is true that they have been rather disciplined in their public handling of the demonstrators. In this sense they have been rather publicly "nonviolent." But for what purpose? To preserve the evil system of segregation. Over the last few years I have consistently preached that nonviolence demands that the means we use must be as pure as the ends we seek. So I have tried to make it clear that it is wrong to use immoral means to attain moral ends. But now I must affirm that it is just as wrong, or even more so, to use moral means to preserve immoral ends. Maybe Mr. Connor and his policemen have been rather publicly nonviolent, as Chief Pritchett was in Albany, Georgia, but they have used the moral means of nonviolence to maintain the immoral end of flagrant racial injustice. T. S. Eliot has said that there is no greater treason than to do the right deed for the wrong reason.

I wish you had commended the Negro sit-inners and demonstrators of Birmingham for their sublime courage, their willingness to suffer, and their amazing discipline in the midst of the most inhuman provocation. One day the South will recognize its real heroes. They will be the James Merediths, courageously and with a majestic sense of purpose facing jeering and hostile mobs and the agonizing loneliness that characterizes the life of the pioneer. They will be old, oppressed, battered Negro women, symbolized in a seventy-two-year-old woman of Montgomery, Alabama, who rose up with a sense of dignity and with her people decided not to ride the segregated buses, and responded to one who inquired about her tiredness with ungrammatical profundity: "My feet is tired, but my soul is rested." They will be the young high school and college students, young ministers of the gospel, and a host of their elders courageously and nonviolently sitting-in at lunch counters and willingly going to jail for conscience's sake. One day the South will know that when these disinherited children of God sat down at lunch counters they were in reality standing up for the best in the American dream and the most sacred values in our Judeo-Christian heritage, and thusly, carrying our whole nation back to those great wells of democracy which were dug deep by the Founding Fathers in the formulation of the Constitution and the Declaration of Independence.

Never before have I written a letter this long (or should I say a book?). I'm afraid that it is much too long to take your precious time. I can assure you that it would have been much shorter if I had been writing from a comfortable desk, but what else is there to do when you are alone for days in the dull monotony of a narrow jail cell other than write long letters, think strange thoughts, and pray long prayers?

If I have said anything in this letter that is an overstatement of the truth and is indicative of an unreasonable impatience, I beg you to forgive me. If I have said anything in this letter that is an understatement of the truth and is indicative of my having a patience that makes me patient with anything less than brotherhood, I beg God to forgive me.

I hope this letter finds you strong in the faith. I also hope that 45 circumstances will soon make it possible for me to meet each of you, not as an integrationist or a civil rights leader, but as a fellow clergyman and a Christian brother. Let us all hope that the dark clouds of racial prejudice will soon pass away and the deep fog of misunderstanding will be lifted from our fear-drenched communities and in some not too distant tomorrow the radiant stars of love and brotherhood will shine over our great nation with all of their scintillating beauty.

Yours for the cause of Peace and Brotherhood,
Martin Luther King Jr.

Discussion Questions

1. As in "I Have a Dream" (p. 734), King uses figurative language in his letter. Find some particularly vivid passages, and evaluate their effect in the context of this letter.
2. Explain King's distinction between just and unjust laws. Are there dangers in attempting to make such a distinction?
3. What characteristics of mind and behavior does King exhibit in the letter? Select the specific passages that provide proof.
4. Why does King say that "the white moderate" is a greater threat to African American progress than the outspoken racist? Is his explanation convincing?
5. How does King justify his philosophy of nonviolence in the face of continued aggression against Americans who are of African descent?

Writing Suggestions

6. Can you think of a law against which defiance would be justified? Explain why the law is unjust and why refusal to obey is morally defensible.
7. In paragraph 12 King lists the grievances of African Americans in this country. King's catalog is similar to the lists in the Declaration of Independence. Can you think of any other group that might compile a list of grievances? If so, choose a group and draw up such a list making sure that your list is as clear and specific as those you have read.

I Have a Dream

MARTIN LUTHER KING JR.

In the widely reprinted "I Have a Dream" speech, Martin Luther King Jr. appears as the charismatic leader of the civil rights movement. This inspirational address was delivered on August 28, 1963, in Washington, D.C., at a demonstration by two hundred thousand people for civil rights for African Americans.

Five score years ago, a great American, in whose symbolic shadow we stand, signed the Emancipation Proclamation. This momentous decree came as a great beacon light of hope to millions of Negro slaves who had been seared in the flames of withering injustice. It came as a joyous daybreak to end the long night of captivity.

But one hundred years later, we must face the tragic fact that the Negro is still not free. One hundred years later, the life of the Negro is still sadly crippled by the manacles of segregation and the chains of discrimination. One hundred years later, the Negro lives on a lonely island of poverty in the midst of a vast ocean of material prosperity. One hundred years later, the Negro is still languishing in the corners of American society and finds himself an exile in his own land. So we have come here today to dramatize an appalling condition.

In a sense we have come to our nation's capital to cash a check. When the architects of our republic wrote the magnificent words of the Constitution and the Declaration of Independence, they were signing a promissory note to which every American was to fall heir. This note was a promise that all men would be guaranteed the unalienable rights of life, liberty, and the pursuit of happiness.

It is obvious today that America has defaulted on this promissory note insofar as her citizens of color are concerned. Instead of honoring this sacred obligation, America has given the Negro people a bad check; a check which has come back marked "insufficient funds." But we refuse to believe that the bank of justice is bankrupt. We refuse to believe that there are insufficient funds in the great vaults of opportunity of this nation. So we have come to cash this check — a check that will give us upon demand the riches of freedom and the security of justice. We have also come to this hallowed spot to remind America of the fierce urgency of *now.* This is no time to engage in the luxury of cooling off or to take the tranquilizing drugs of gradualism. *Now* is the time to make real the promises of

From *A Testament of Hope* (1986).

Democracy. *Now* is the time to rise from the dark and desolate valley of segregation to the sunlit path of racial justice. *Now* is the time to open the doors of opportunity to all of God's children. *Now* is the time to lift our nation from the quicksands of racial injustice to the solid rock of brotherhood.

It would be fatal for the nation to overlook the urgency of the moment and to underestimate the determination of the Negro. This sweltering summer of the Negro's legitimate discontent will not pass until there is an invigorating autumn of freedom and equality. Nineteen sixty-three is not an end, but a beginning. Those who hope that the Negro needed to blow off steam and will now be content will have a rude awakening if the nation returns to business as usual. There will be neither rest nor tranquillity in America until the Negro is granted his citizenship rights. The whirlwinds of revolt will continue to shake the foundations of our nation until the bright day of justice emerges.

But there is something that I must say to my people who stand on the warm threshold which leads into the palace of justice. In the process of gaining our rightful place we must not be guilty of wrongful deeds. Let us not seek to satisfy our thirst for freedom by drinking from the cup of bitterness and hatred. We must forever conduct our struggle on the high plane of dignity and discipline. We must not allow our creative protest to degenerate into physical violence. Again and again we must rise to the majestic heights of meeting physical force with soul force. The marvelous new militancy which has engulfed the Negro community must not lead us to a distrust of all white people, for many of our white brothers, as evidenced by their presence here today, have come to realize that their destiny is tied up with our destiny and their freedom is inextricably bound to our freedom. We cannot walk alone.

And as we walk, we must make the pledge that we shall march ahead. We cannot turn back. There are those who are asking the devotees of civil rights, "When will you be satisfied?" We can never be satisfied as long as the Negro is the victim of the unspeakable horrors of police brutality. We can never be satisfied as long as our bodies, heavy with the fatigue of travel, cannot gain lodging in the motels of the highways and the hotels of the cities. We cannot be satisfied as long as the Negro's basic mobility is from a smaller ghetto to a larger one. We can never be satisfied as long as a Negro in Mississippi cannot vote and a Negro in New York believes he has nothing for which to vote. No, no, we are not satisfied, and we will not be satisfied until justice rolls down like waters and righteousness like a mighty stream.

I am not unmindful that some of you have come here out of great trials and tribulations. Some of you have come fresh from narrow jail cells. Some of you have come from areas where your quest for freedom left you battered by the storms of persecution and staggered by the winds of police brutality. You have been the veterans of creative suffering. Continue to work with the faith that unearned suffering is redemptive.

Go back to Mississippi, go back to Alabama, go back to South Carolina, go back to Georgia, go back to Louisiana, go back to the slums and ghettos of our northern cities, knowing that somehow this situation can and will be changed. Let us not wallow in the valley of despair.

I say to you today, my friends, that in spite of the difficulties and 10 frustrations of the moment I still have a dream. It is a dream deeply rooted in the American dream.

I have a dream that one day this nation will rise up and live out the true meaning of its creed: "We hold these truths to be self-evident; that all men are created equal."

I have a dream that one day on the red hills of Georgia the sons of former slaves and the sons of former slaveowners will be able to sit down together at the table of brotherhood.

I have a dream that one day even the state of Mississippi, a desert state sweltering with the heat of injustice and oppression, will be transformed into an oasis of freedom and justice.

I have a dream that my four little children will one day live in a nation where they will not be judged by the color of their skin but by the content of their character.

I have a dream today. 15

I have a dream that one day the state of Alabama, whose governor's lips are presently dripping with the words of interposition and nullification, will be transformed into a situation where little black boys and black girls will be able to join hands with little white boys and white girls and walk together as sisters and brothers.

I have a dream today.

I have a dream that one day every valley shall be exalted, every hill and mountain shall be made low, the rough places will be made plain, and the crooked places will be made straight, and the glory of the Lord shall be revealed, and all flesh shall see it together.

This is our hope. This is the faith with which I return to the South. With this faith we will be able to hew out of the mountain of despair a stone of hope. With this faith we will be able to transform the jangling discords of our nation into a beautiful symphony of brotherhood. With this faith we will be able to work together, to pray together, to struggle together, to go to jail together, to stand up for freedom together, knowing that we will be free one day.

This will be the day when all of God's children will be able to 20 sing with new meaning

My country, 'tis of thee,
Sweet land of liberty,
  Of thee I sing:
Land where my fathers died,
Land of the pilgrims' pride,
From every mountain-side
  Let freedom ring.

And if America is to be a great nation this must become true. So let freedom ring from the prodigious hilltops of New Hampshire. Let freedom ring from the mighty mountains of New York. Let freedom ring from the heightening Alleghenies of Pennsylvania!

Let freedom ring from the snowcapped Rockies of Colorado!

Let freedom ring from the curvaceous peaks of California!

But not only that; let freedom ring from Stone Mountain of Georgia!

Let freedom ring from Lookout Mountain of Tennessee!   25

Let freedom ring from every hill and molehill of Mississippi. From every mountainside, let freedom ring.

When we let freedom ring, when we let it ring from every village and every hamlet, from every state and every city, we will be able to speed up that day when all of God's children, black men and white men, Jews and Gentiles, Protestants and Catholics, will be able to join hands and sing in the words of the old Negro spiritual, "Free at last! free at last! thank God almighty, we are free at last!"

Discussion Questions

1. King's style alternates between the abstract and the concrete, between the grandiloquent and the simple, with abundant use of metaphors. Find examples of these qualities. Are all the stylistic strategies equally effective? Explain your answer.

2. What specific injustices suffered by African Americans does King mention? Why does he interrupt his series of "Let freedom ring" imperatives at the end with the statement, "But not only that"?

3. What values does the speech stress? Would these values be equally appealing to both blacks and whites? Why or why not?

4. More than thirty-five years later, how much of King's indictment of conditions remains true? Mention specific changes or lack of changes. If conditions have improved, does that make his speech less meaningful today?

Writing Suggestions

5. Using the same material as the original, rewrite this speech for an audience that is not impressed with the inspirational style. Think carefully about the changes in language you would make to convince this audience that, despite your dispassionate treatment, injustices exist and should be rectified.

6. Choose another highly emotional subject — for example, women's rights, child pornography, nuclear power — and write an inspirational speech or advertisement urging your audience to change their views. Be passionate, but try to avoid sentimentality or corniness. (You may want to look at other examples of the inspirational or hortatory style in a collection of speeches, among them speeches made in favor of the abolition of slavery and women's suffrage, declarations of war, and inaugural addresses.)

Arguing about Literature

Writing a paper about a work of literature — a novel, a short story, a poem, or a play — is not so different from writing about matters of public policy. In both cases you make a claim about something you have read and demonstrate the validity of that claim by providing support. In papers about literature, support consists primarily of evidence from examples and details in the work itself and your own interpretation of the language, the events, and the characters. In addition, you can introduce expert scholarly opinion and history and biography where they are relevant.

First, a note about the differences between imaginative literature and argumentative essays. Although the strategies for writing papers about them may be similar, strategies for reading and understanding the works under review will be different. Suppose you read an essay by a psychologist who wants to prove that lying to children, even with the best intentions, can have tragic consequences. The claim of the essay will be directly stated, perhaps even in the first sentence. But if an author writes a short story or a play about the same subject, he or she will probably not state the central idea directly but will *show* rather than *tell*. The theme will emerge through a narrative of dramatic events, expressions of thoughts and feelings by the characters, a depiction of relationships, descriptions of a specific setting, and other elements of fiction. In other words, you will derive the idea or the theme indirectly. This is one reason that a work of fiction can lend itself to multiple interpretations. But it is also the reason that literature, with its evocation of the mysteries of real life, exerts a perpetual fascination.

Different kinds of literary works emphasize different elements. In the following discussion the elements of fiction, poetry, and drama are briefly summarized. The discussion will suggest ways of reading imaginative literature for both pleasure and critical analysis.

THE ELEMENTS OF FICTION

The basic elements of imaginative prose — a short story, a novel, or a play — are *theme, conflict,* and *character.* Other elements such as language, plot, point of view, and setting also influence the effectiveness of any work, but without a central idea, a struggle between opposing forces, and interesting people, it's unlikely that the work will hold our attention. (On the other hand, literature is full of exceptions, and you will certainly find examples that defy the rules.)

The theme is the central idea. It answers the question, What is the point of this story or play? Does the author give us some insight into a personal dilemma? Does he or she show how social conditions shape human behavior? Do we learn how certain traits of character can influence a human life? The answers to these questions apply not only to the specific situation and invented characters in a particular story. In the most memorable works the theme — the lesson to be drawn, the truth to be learned — embodies an idea that is much larger than the form the story assumes. For example, in "The Use of Force," the short story by William Carlos Williams at the end of this appendix, the title refers to the *subject* but not the theme. The author wanted to say something *about* the use of force. His theme is a complicated and unwelcome insight into human nature, with implications for all of us, not just the doctor who is the principal actor in the story.

Conflict is present in some form in almost all imaginative writing. It creates suspense and introduces moral dilemmas. External conflicts occur between individuals and between individuals and natural forces. Internal conflicts take place in the minds and hearts of the characters who must make difficult choices between competing goals and values — between right and wrong, pleasure and duty, freedom and responsibility. These two kinds of conflict are not exclusive of each other. A story of war, for example, will include suspenseful physical encounters between opposing forces, but the characters may also be compelled to make painful choices about their actions. In the best works, conflicts are important, not trivial. They may reveal uncommon virtues or shortcomings in the characters, alter their relationships with other people, and even change the course of their lives.

Conflicts exist only because characters — human beings, or in some satires, animals — engage in them. In contests with forces of nature, as in Hemingway's *The Old Man and the Sea,* it is the courage and persistence of a human being that gives meaning to the story.

Memorable fictional characters are not easy to create. As readers we demand that characters be interesting, plausible, consistent, and active, physically and mentally. We must care about them, which is not the same as liking them. To care about characters means retaining enough curiosity about them to keep reading and to regret their departure when the story has come to an end. However different and unfamiliar their activities, we should feel that the characters are real. Even in science fiction we insist that the creatures exhibit human characteristics that we can recognize and identify with. But fictional characters should also be distinguishable from one another. Stereotypes are tiresome and unconvincing.

We learn about characters primarily from their speech and their actions but also from what the author and other characters reveal about them. Remembering that characters often withhold information or conceal their motives, even from themselves, we must often depend on our own knowledge and experience to interpret their behavior and judge their plausibility.

THE ELEMENTS OF DRAMA

Drama shares with fiction the elements we have discussed earlier — theme, conflict, and character. But because a play is meant to be performed, it differs from a written story in significant ways. These differences impose limits on the drama, as opposed to the novel, which can do almost anything.

First, stage action is restricted. Violent action — a war scene, for example — must usually take place offstage, and certain situations — such as the hunt for Moby Dick in Melville's novel — would be hard to reproduce in a theater. This means that a play emphasizes internal rather than external conflict.

Second, the author of a play, unlike the author of a short story or a novel, cannot comment on the action, the characters, or the significance of the setting. (It is true that a narrator sometimes appears on stage as a kind of Greek chorus to offer observation on the action, but this is uncommon.) A much greater burden must therefore rest on what the characters say. They must reveal background, explain offstage events, interpret themselves and others, and move the plot forward largely through speech. If the author of a novel lacks skill in reproducing plausible speech, he can find ways to avoid dialogue, but the playwright has no such privilege. She must have an ear for the rhythms and idioms of language that identify particular characters.

Another element which assumes more importance in a play than in a novel is plot. The dramatist must confine an often complicated and event-filled story to two or three hours on the stage. And, as in any listening experience, the audience must be able to follow the plot without the luxury of going back to review.

As you read a long play, you may find it helpful to keep in mind a simple diagram that explains the development of the plot, whether comedy or tragedy. The Freytag pyramid, created in 1863 by a German critic, shows that almost every three- or five-act play begins in a problem or conflict which sets in motion a series of events, called *the rising action*. At some point there is a *climax*, or turning point, followed by *the falling action*, which reverses the fortunes of the main characters and leads to a conclusion that may be happy or unhappy.

Shakespeare's *Macbeth* is an almost perfect example of the pyramid. The rising action in this tragedy is one of continued success for the main characters. The climax is a crisis on the battlefield, after which the fortunes of Macbeth and Lady Macbeth decline, ending in failure and death. In a comedy, the developments are reversed. The rising action is a series of stumbles and mishaps; then in the climax the hero finds the money or rescues the heroine and the falling action ushers in a number of welcome surprises that culminate in a happy ending. (Think of a Jim Carrey adventure.) Typically the rising action in any play takes longer and thus creates suspense.

Reading a play is not the same as seeing one on stage. Many playwrights, like novelists, describe their settings and their characters in elaborate detail. In *Long Day's Journey Into Night,* Eugene O'Neill's autobiographical play, descriptions of the living-room in which the action occurs and of the mother and father, who appear in the first act, cover more than three pages in small print. When you read, you fill the imaginary stage with your own interpretations of the playwright's descriptions, derived perhaps from places or persons in your own experience. You may forget that the playwright is dependent on directors, set designers, and actors, with other philosophies and approaches to stagecraft, to interpret his or her work. It can come as a surprise to see the stage version of the play you have read and interpreted very differently.

All playwrights want their plays to be performed. Still, the best plays are read far more frequently than they are produced on stage. Fortunately, reading them is a literary experience with its own rewards.

THE ELEMENTS OF POETRY

There are several kinds of poetry, among them epic, dramatic, and lyric. Epic poetry celebrates the heroic adventures of a human or superhuman character in a long, event-filled narrative. Milton's *Paradise Lost* is the preeminent example in English, but you may also be familiar with *The Iliad, The Odyssey,* and *The Aeneid,* the epics of ancient Greece and Rome. Dramatic poetry also tells a story, sometimes through monologue, as in Robert Browning's "My Last Duchess," where the Duke recounts the reasons why he murdered his wife; sometimes through dialogue, as in Robert Frost's "The Death of the Hired Man." These stories are often told in blank verse, unrhymed five-beat lines. Playwrights of the past, Shakespeare among others, adopted this poetic form.

Modern poems are much more likely to be lyrics — poetry derived from song. (The term *lyric* comes from the word for an ancient musical instrument, the lyre.) The lyric is most frequently an expression of the poet's feeling rather than an account of events. The characteristics that make poetry harder to read than prose are the very characteristics that define it: compression and metaphor. A lyric poem is highly concentrated. It focuses on what is essential in an experience, the details that illuminate it vividly against the background of our ordinary lives. Metaphor is a form of figurative language, a way of saying one thing to mean something else. It is a simile which omits the "like" or "as": for example, "A mighty fortress is our God." The poet chooses metaphoric images that appeal to our senses in order to reinforce the literal meaning. In a famous poem Thomas Campion compared the beauty of his sweetheart's face to that of a garden.

> There is a garden in her face
> Where roses and white lilies grow,
> A heavenly paradise is that place,
> Wherein all pleasant fruits do flow.

A poem, like an essay, tries to prove something. Like a short story, its message is indirect, expressed in the language of metaphor. It seldom urges a practical course of action. What it tries to prove is that a feeling or a perception — a response to love or death, or the sight of a snowy field on a dark night — is true and real.

The lyric poet's subjects are common ones — love, joy, sorrow, nature, death — but he or she makes uncommon use of words, imagery, and rhythm. These are the elements you examine as evidence of the poet's theme and depth of feeling.

Precisely because the poem will condense her experience, the poet must choose words with immediate impact. For example, in a poem about an encounter with a snake, Emily Dickinson writes,

> But never met this Fellow
> Attended, or alone
> Without a tighter breathing
> And Zero at the bone —

Although we have never seen this use of "zero" before, it strikes us at once as the perfect choice to suggest a kind of chilling fear.

In the best poems images transform the most commonplace experiences. Here is the first quatrain of Shakespeare's sonnet number 73, about loving deeply what will not live forever.

> That time of year thou mayest in me behold
> When yellow leaves or none or few do hang
> Upon those boughs which shake against the cold
> Bare ruined choirs where late the sweet birds sang.

Nowhere does Shakespeare mention that he is growing old. Instead, here and in subsequent stanzas he creates images of dead or dying things — autumn trees, the coming of night, dying fires — that convey feelings of cold and desolation. The final couplet expresses the theme directly:

> Thus thou perceivs't, which makes thy love more strong,
> To love that well which thou must leave ere long.

It is the imagery, however, that brings the theme to life and enables us to understand and share the poet's feeling.

Rhythm, defined as measured and balanced movement, is almost as important as language. As children, even before we fully understand all the words, we derive pleasure from the sounds of Mother Goose and the Dr. Seuss rhymes. Their sound patterns reflect the musical origin of poetry and the fact that poetry was meant to be chanted rather than read. Listen to the rhythm of these opening lines from Andrew Marvell's "To His Coy Mistress" — "Had we but world enough and time, / This coyness, lady, were no crime" — and hear the lilting four-beat meter that suggests song. If you look through an anthology of poetry written before the twentieth century, you will see even from the appearance of the poems on the page that the cadence or rhythm of most poems creates an orderly pattern. Edgar Allan Poe's "The Raven" is a familiar example of poems in which rhyme and rhythm come together to produce a harmonious design.

Measured movement in poetry is less common today. Free verse breaks with this ancient convention. (The very regularity of "The Raven" is now a subject for parody.) The poet of free verse invents his own rhythms, governed by meaning, free association, and a belief in poetry as a democratic art, one capable of reaching all people. In "Song of Myself," Walt Whitman (1819–1892), one of America's most influential poets, writes in a new voice that resembles the sound of spoken language:

> A child said *What is the grass?* fetching it to me with
>   full hands,

How could I answer the child? I do not know what it is
    any more than he.
I guess it must be the flag of my disposition, out of hopeful
    green stuff woven.

Notice, however, that the phrase "out of hopeful green stuff woven" is the language of poetry, not prose.

Much twentieth-century poetry dispenses altogether with both rhyme and formal rhythms, but the lyric remains unmistakably alive. Perhaps you have read poems by William Carlos Williams or e. e. cummings, who have used new rhythms to create their own distinctive versions of the lyric.

THE CULTURAL CONTEXT

Even those works that are presumed to be immortal and universal are products of a particular time in history and a particular social and political context. These works may therefore represent points of view with which we are unsympathetic. Today, for example, some women are uncomfortable with Shakespeare's *The Taming of the Shrew,* which finds comic possibilities in the subjugation of a woman to her husband's will. Jews may be offended by the characterization of Shylock in *The Merchant of Venice* as a Jewish money-lender who shows little mercy to his debtor. Some African Americans have resented the portrayal of Jim, the slave in *Huckleberry Finn.* Even *Peter Pan* has provoked criticism for its depiction of American Indians. In your own reading you may find fault with an author's attitude toward his subject; defending your own point of view against that of the author can be a satisfying literary exercise. To bring fresh, perhaps controversial, interpretations into an analysis may, indeed, enliven discussion and even revive interest in older works that no longer move us. But remember that the evidence will be largely external, based on social and political views that will themselves need explanation.

There is, after all, a danger in allowing our ideas about social and political correctness to take over and in imposing our values on those of another time, place, or culture. Literature, like great historical writing, enables us to enter worlds very different from our own. The worlds we read about in novels and plays may be governed by different moral codes, different social conventions, different religious values, many of which we reject or don't understand. Characters in these stories, even those cast as heroes and heroines, sometimes behave in ways we consider ignorant or self-serving. (Russell Baker, the humorist, observed that it was unfortunate that the writers of the past were not so enlightened as we are.) But reading has always offered an experience otherwise unavailable, a ready escape from our own lives into the lives of others, whose ways, however strange, we try to understand, whether or not we approve.

CHOOSING WHAT TO WRITE ABOUT

Your paper can take one of several different approaches. It is worth emphasizing that comedy and tragedy generally share the same literary elements. A tragedy, of course, ends in misfortune or death. A comedy typically ends with a happy resolution of all problems.

1. You may analyze or explain the meaning or theme of a work that is subject to different interpretations. For example, a famous interpretation of *Hamlet* in 1910[1] suggested that Hamlet was unable to avenge his father's murder because of guilt over his own Oedipal love for his mother. Or, having seen a distorted movie version of a familiar book (unfortunately, there are plenty of examples) you can explain what you think is the real theme of the book and how the movie departs from it.

Some stories and plays, although based in reality, seem largely symbolic. "The Lottery," a widely read short story by Shirley Jackson, describes a ritual that hints at other meanings than those usually attributed to lotteries. *Waiting for Godot*, a play by Samuel Beckett, is a work that has inspired a dozen interpretations; the name *Godot*, with the embedded word *God*, suggests several. But exercise caution in writing about symbols. Saul Bellow, the Nobel Prize–winning novelist, has written an essay, "Deep Readers of the World, Beware!" that explains the dangers. He reminds us that "a true symbol is substantial, not accidental. You cannot avoid it, you cannot remove it."

2. You may analyze the conflicts in a story or play. The conflicts that make interesting papers are those that not only challenge our understanding (as with Iago's villainy in *Othello*) but encourage us to reflect on profound moral issues. For example, how does Mark Twain develop the struggle in Huckleberry Finn between his southern prejudices and his respect for Jim's humanity? How does John Proctor, the hero of Arthur Miller's *The Crucible*, resolve the moral dilemmas that lead him to choose death rather than a freedom secured by lies?

3. You may choose to write about an especially vivid or contradictory character, describing his traits in such a way as to make clear why he is worth a detailed examination. The protagonist of *The Stranger* by Albert Camus, for example, is a murderer who, although

---

[1] Ernest Jones, *Hamlet and Oedipus* (New York: Norton, 1949).

he tells us little or nothing about himself and is therefore difficult to understand, eventually earns our sympathy.

4. You may concentrate on the setting if it has special significance for the lives of the characters and what they do, as in Joseph Conrad's *Heart of Darkness* and Tennessee Williams's *A Streetcar Named Desire*. Setting may include time or historical period as well as place. Ask if the story or play would have taken shape in quite the same way in another time and place.

5. You may examine the language or style. No analysis of a poem would be complete without attention to the language, but the style of a prose work can also contribute to the impact on the reader. Hemingway's clean, economical style has often been studied, as has Faulkner's dense, complicated prose, equally powerful but very different. But you should probably not attempt an analysis of style unless you are sure you can discuss the uses of diction, grammar, syntax, and rhythm.

GUIDELINES FOR WRITING THE PAPER

1. Decide on a limited topic as the subject for your paper. The most interesting topics, of course, are those that are not so obvious: original interpretations, for example, that arise from a genuine personal response. Don't be afraid to disagree with a conventional reading of the literary work, but be sure you can find sufficient evidence for your point of view.

2. Before you begin to write, make a brief outline of the points that will support your thesis. You may find that you don't have enough evidence to make a good case to a skeptical reader. Or you may find that you have too much for a short paper and that your thesis, therefore, is too broad.

3. The evidence that you provide can be both internal and external. Internal evidence is found in the work itself: an action that reveals motives and consequences, statements by the characters about themselves and others, comments by the author about her characters, and interpretation of the language. External evidence comes from outside the work: a comment by a literary critic, information about the historical period or the geographical location of the work, or data about the author's life and other works he has written.

If possible, use more than one kind of evidence. The most important proof, however, will come from a careful selection of material from the work itself.

4. One temptation to avoid is using quotations from the work or from a critic so abundantly that your paper consists of a string of quotations and little else. Remember that the importance of your

paper rests on *your* interpretations of the evidence. Your *own* analysis should constitute the major part of the paper. The quotations should be introduced only to support important points.

5. Organize your essay according to the guidelines you have followed for an argumentative essay on a public issue (see Chapter 9, pp. 337–57). Two of the organizational plans that work best are defending the main idea and refuting the opposing view — that is, a literary interpretation with which you disagree. In both cases the simplest method is to state your claim — the thesis you are going to defend — in the first paragraph and then line up evidence point by point in order of importance. If you feel comfortable beginning your paper in a different way, you may start with a paragraph of background: the reasons that you have chosen to explore a particular topic or a description of your personal response to the work — for example, where you first saw a play performed, how a story or poem affected you. (H. L. Mencken, the great American social critic, said discovering *Huckleberry Finn* was "the most stupendous event of my whole life!" What a beginning for an essay!)

It is always useful to look at book or movie reviews in good newspapers and magazines for models of organization and development that suggest a wide range of choices for your own paper.

SAMPLE STORY AND ANALYSIS

Read the following short story, and reflect on it for a few moments. Then turn back to the following questions. Were you surprised at the actions of the doctor? What is the author saying about the use of force? Do you agree? What kinds of conflicts has he dramatized? Are some more important than others? How do the characterizations of the people in the story contribute to the theme?

Thinking about the answers to these questions will give you a clearer perspective on the essay written by a student that follows the story. After reading the essay, you may see other elements of fiction that might have been analyzed in a critical paper.

The Use of Force

WILLIAM CARLOS WILLIAMS

They were new patients to me, all I had was the name, Olson. Please come down as soon as you can, my daughter is very sick.

When I arrived I was met by the mother, a big startled looking woman, very clean and apologetic who merely said, Is this the doctor? and let me in. In the back, she added, You must excuse us, doctor, we have her in the kitchen where it is warm. It is very damp here sometimes.

The child was fully dressed and sitting on her father's lap near the kitchen table. He tried to get up, but I motioned for him not to bother, took off my overcoat and started to look things over. I could see that they were all very nervous, eyeing me up and down distrustfully. As often, in such cases, they weren't telling me more than they had to, it was up to me to tell them; that's why they were spending three dollars on me.

The child was fairly eating me up with her cold, steady eyes, and no expression to her face whatever. She did not move and seemed, inwardly, quiet; an unusually attractive little thing, and as strong as a heifer in appearance. But her face was flushed, she was breathing rapidly, and I realized that she had a high fever. She had magnificent blonde hair, in profusion. One of those picture children often reproduced in advertising leaflets and the photogravure sections of the Sunday papers.

She's had a fever for three days, began the father and we don't 5 know what it comes from. My wife has given her things, you know, like people do, but it don't do no good. And there's been a lot of sickness around. So we tho't you'd better look her over and tell us what is the matter.

As doctors often do I took a trial shot at it as a point of departure. Has she had a sore throat?

Both parents answered me together, No . . . No, she says her throat don't hurt her.

Does your throat hurt you? added the mother to the child. But the little girl's expression didn't change nor did she move her eyes from my face.

Have you looked?

I tried to, said the mother, but I couldn't see.   10

William Carlos Williams (1883–1963) wrote poems, novels, plays, and short stories. A pediatrician in the industrial city of Rutherford, New Jersey, much of his work, including "The Use of Force" (*The Farmers' Daughters,* 1938), depicts the daily hardships of his impoverished patients.

As it happens we had been having a number of cases of diphtheria in the school to which this child went during that month and we were all, quite apparently, thinking of that, though no one had as yet spoken of the thing.

Well, I said, suppose we take a look at the throat first. I smiled in my best professional manner and asking for the child's first name I said, come on, Mathilda, open your mouth and let's take a look at your throat.

Nothing doing.

Aw, come on, I coaxed, just open your mouth wide and let me take a look. Look, I said opening both hands wide. I haven't anything in my hands. Just open up and let me see.

Such a nice man, put in the mother. Look how kind he is to you. 15 Come on, do what he tells you to. He won't hurt you.

At that I ground my teeth in disgust. If only they wouldn't use the word "hurt" I might be able to get somewhere. But I did not allow myself to be hurried or disturbed but speaking quietly and slowly I approached the child again.

As I moved my chair a little nearer suddenly with one cat-like movement both her hands clawed instinctively for my eyes and she almost reached them too. In fact she knocked my glasses flying and they fell, though unbroken, several feet away from me on the kitchen floor.

Both the mother and father almost turned themselves inside out in embarrassment and apology. You bad girl, said the mother, taking her and shaking her by one arm. Look what you've done. The nice man . . .

For heaven's sake, I broke in. Don't call me a nice man to her. I'm here to look at her throat on the chance that she might have diphtheria and possibly die of it. But that's nothing to her. Look here, I said to the child, we're going to look at your throat. You're old enough to understand what I'm saying. Will you open it now by yourself or shall we have to open it for you?

Not a move. Even her expression hadn't changed. Her breaths 20 however were coming faster and faster. Then the battle began. I had to do it. I had to have a throat culture for her own protection. But first I told the parents that it was entirely up to them. I explained the danger but said that I would not insist on a throat examination so long as they would take the responsibility.

If you don't do what the doctor says you'll have to go to the hospital, the mother admonished her severely.

Oh yeah? I had to smile to myself. After all, I had already fallen in love with the savage brat, the parents were contemptible to me. In the ensuing struggle they grew more and more abject, crushed, exhausted while she surely rose to magnificent heights of insane fury of effort bred of her terror of me.

The father tried his best, and he was a big man but the fact that she was his daughter, his shame at her behavior and his dread of hurting her made him release her just at the critical moment several times when I had almost achieved success, till I wanted to kill him. But his dread also that she might have diphtheria made him tell me to go on, go on though he himself was almost fainting, while the mother moved back and forth behind us raising and lowering her hands in an agony of apprehension.

Put her in front of you on your lap, I ordered, and hold both her wrists.

But as soon as he did the child let out a scream. Don't, you're 25 hurting me. Let go of my hands. Let them go I tell you. Then she shrieked terrifyingly, hysterically. Stop it! Stop it! You're killing me!

Do you think she can stand it, doctor! said the mother.

You get out, said the husband to his wife. Do you want her to die of diphtheria?

Come on now, hold her, I said.

Then I grasped the child's head with my left hand and tried to get the wooden tongue depressor between her teeth. She fought, with clenched teeth, desperately! But now I also had grown furious — at a child. I tried to hold myself down but I couldn't. I know how to expose a throat for inspection. And I did my best. When finally I got the wooden spatula behind the last teeth and just the point of it into the mouth cavity, she opened up for an instant, but before I could see anything she came down again and gripping the wooden blade between her molars she reduced it to splinters before I could get it out again.

Aren't you ashamed, the mother yelled at her. Aren't you 30 ashamed to act like that in front of the doctor?

Get me a smooth-handled spoon of some sort, I told the mother. We're going through with this. The child's mouth was already bleeding. Her tongue was cut and she was screaming in wild hysterical shrieks. Perhaps I should have desisted and come back in an hour or more. No doubt it would have been better. But I have seen at least two children lying dead in bed of neglect in such cases, and feeling that I must get a diagnosis now or never I went at it again. But the worst of it was that I too had got beyond reason. I could have torn the child apart in my own fury and enjoyed it. It was a pleasure to attack her. My face was burning with it.

The damned little brat must be protected against her own idiocy, one says to one's self at such times. Others must be protected against her. It is social necessity. And all these things are true. But a blind fury, a feeling of adult shame, bred of a longing for muscular release are the operatives. One goes on to the end.

In a final unreasoning assault I overpowered the child's neck and jaws. I forced the heavy silver spoon back of her teeth and down her throat till she gagged. And there it was — both tonsils covered with membrane. She had fought valiantly to keep me from knowing her secret. She had been hiding that sore throat for three days at least and lying to her parents in order to escape just such an outcome as this.

Now truly she *was* furious. She had been on the defensive before but now she attacked. Tried to get off her father's lap and fly at me while tears of defeat blinded her eyes.

Rampolla   1

Jennifer Rampolla

Professor Harrington

English 102-C

May 2, 20--

Title indicates
subject

Conflicts in "The Use of Force"

Introduction

"The Use of Force" tells us something about human nature that probably comes as no surprise: The impulse to

The theme

use violence against a helpless but defiant opponent can be
thrilling and irresistible. But the conflict which produces
this insight is not a shoot-out between cops and robbers,

Theme emerges
through conflicts

not a fight for survival against a dangerous enemy, but a
struggle between a grown man and a sick child.

In this story two major conflicts are dramatized, one
external or physical, the other internal or psychological.
The conflicts seem obvious. Even the blunt, unadorned

Naming the
major conflicts
(external and
internal)

language means to persuade us that nothing is concealed.
But below the surface, some motives remain unacknowledged, and we guess at them only because we know how

A concealed
conflict (to be
explained later)

easily people deceive themselves.

The external conflict is vividly depicted, a physical

Body

struggle between doctor and child, complete with weapon--
a metal spoon. The outcome is hardly in doubt; the doctor

External conflict
developed

will win. One critic calls this story primarily "an
accomplishment (external conflict) story" (Madden 16). But

Evidence: com-
ment from a
critic

the internal conflict that accompanies a difficult choice is
the real heart of the story. The doctor must decide between

Internal conflict
developed

waiting for a more opportune time to examine the child or
exercising brute force to subdue her now. When he decides
on brute force, he seems aware of his motives.

But the worst of it was that I too had got beyond
reason. I could have torn the child apart in
my own fury and enjoyed it. It was a pleasure
to attack her.

Evidence:
Quotation

This shocking revelation is not, however, the whole
story. <u>Why</u> has he got beyond reason? Why does he take
pleasure in attacking a child? The answer lies not only in

Concealed con-
flict, based on the
characters and
their relationship

what we know about the antagonists but in what we can assume about their relationship to each other.

Rampolla   2

Description
of the child

The child is brilliantly portrayed in a few grim
encounters with the doctor. She is strong, stubborn,
secretive, and violent. Despite her size and age, she is a
match for the doctor, a challenge that at first excites him.

Evidence:
Quotation

I had to smile to myself. After all, I had already
fallen in love with the savage brat. . . . In the
ensuing struggle . . . she surely rose to magnificent heights of insane fury. . . .

Description
of the doctor

The picture of the doctor is somewhat harder to read.
Sixty years ago (when this story was written) the doctor in
a working-class community occupied a position of unusual
power and authority. He would not be accustomed to

Unexpressed
social conflict

challenges at any level. Clearly the differences in social and
economic status between the doctor and his clients are
another source of conflict that influences his use of force.

Evidence: Exter-
nal, from history

Like many people in positions of power, the doctor is torn
by contradictory emotions toward those below him. On the
one hand, he despises those who are deferential to him, in
this case the child's parents. On the other hand, it is
unthinkable that a child should dare to oppose him, not
only in refusing to obey his instructions but in trying, like
a desperate small animal, to attack him. It is even more

Evidence:
Quotation

unthinkable that she should prevail in any contest. He
confesses to "a feeling of adult shame." If we look for it,
there is also a hint of sexual conflict. The child is blond and

Perhaps another
concealed
conflict?

beautiful; the doctor says he is in love with her. (Would
this story have worked in quite the same way if the child
had been a boy?) The doctor attempts to rationalize his use

The doctor's
real motivation

of force, but he knows that it is not the child's welfare that
finally compels him to overcome her resistance. In the end,
reason gives way to pride and vanity.

Conclusion

Most of us respond to this story with a mixture of
feelings--anger at the pleasure the doctor takes in his use of

The reader's
mixed reaction

force, confusion and even fear at the realization that
doctors may not always behave like gentle and loving
helpers, and pity for the little girl with whom it is easy to
identify. The author doesn't spell out the moral implications
of the doctor's internal conflict. But perhaps it is significant

Rampolla   3

that the author gives the last words to the little girl: "Tears   Sympathy for
of defeat blinded her eyes." I think he has chosen this   the child
ending in order to direct our sympathy to the victim, an
unhappy child who struggled hopelessly to protect herself.
Although we know that the doctor has performed a   Reaction to
necessary and merciful act, we are left to wonder if it   the theme
matters that he has done it for the wrong reason.

Rampolla   4

Works Cited

Madden, David. <u>Studies in the Short Story</u>. New York: Holt,
    1980.

Trifles

SUSAN GLASPELL

CHARACTERS

GEORGE HENDERSON, *county attorney*
HENRY PETERS, *sheriff*
LEWIS HALE, *a neighboring farmer*
MRS. PETERS
MRS. HALE

SCENE: *The kitchen in the now abandoned farmhouse of John Wright, a gloomy kitchen, and left without having been put in order — the walls covered with a faded wall paper. Down right is a door leading to the parlor. On the right wall above this door is a built-in kitchen cupboard with shelves in the upper portion and drawers below. In the rear wall at right, up two steps is a door opening onto stairs leading to the second floor. In the rear wall at left is a door to the shed and from there to the outside. Between these two doors is an old-fashioned black iron stove. Running along the left wall from the shed door is an old iron sink and sink shelf, in which is set a hand pump. Downstage of the sink is an uncurtained window. Near the window is an old wooden rocker. Center stage is an unpainted wooden kitchen table with straight chairs on either side. There is a small chair down right. Unwashed pans under the sink, a loaf of bread outside the breadbox, a dish towel on the table — other signs of incompleted work. At the rear the shed door opens and the Sheriff comes in followed by the County Attorney and Hale. The Sheriff and Hale are men in middle life, the County Attorney is a young man; all are much bundled up and go at once to the stove. They are followed by the two women — the Sheriff's wife, Mrs. Peters, first; she is a slight wiry woman, a thin nervous face. Mrs. Hale is larger and would ordinarily be called more comfortable looking, but she is disturbed now and looks fearfully about as she enters. The women have come in slowly, and stand close together near the door.*

COUNTY ATTORNEY (*at stove rubbing his hands*): This feels good. Come up to the fire, ladies.

MRS. PETERS (*after taking a step forward*): I'm not — cold.

Susan Glaspell (1876–1948) was an American playwright and novelist. In 1916 she wrote *Trifles* for the Provincetown Players, a Provincetown, Massachusetts, theater troupe founded by Glaspell and her husband. Based on her recollection of a real murder case that she covered as a journalist in Iowa, *Trifles* was so successful that Glaspell decided to rewrite it as a short story, "A Jury of Her Peers."

756

SHERIFF (*unbuttoning his overcoat and stepping away from the stove to right of table as if to mark the beginning of official business*): Now, Mr. Hale, before we move things about, you explain to Mr. Henderson just what you saw when you came here yesterday morning.

COUNTY ATTORNEY (*crossing down to left of the table*): By the way, has anything been moved? Are things just as you left them yesterday?

SHERIFF (*looking about*): It's just about the same. When it dropped below zero last night I thought I'd better send Frank out this morning to make a fire for us — (*sits right of center table*) no use getting pneumonia with a big case on, but I told him not to touch anything except the stove — and you know Frank.

COUNTY ATTORNEY: Somebody should have been left here yesterday.

SHERIFF: Oh — yesterday. When I had to send Frank to Morris Center for that man who went crazy — I want you to know I had my hands full yesterday. I knew you could get back from Omaha by today and as long as I went over everything here myself ———

COUNTY ATTORNEY: Well, Mr. Hale, tell just what happened when you came here yesterday morning.

HALE (*crossing down to above table*): Harry and I had started to town with a load of potatoes. We came along the road from my place and as I got here I said, "I'm going to see if I can't get John Wright to go in with me on a party telephone." I spoke to Wright about it once before and he put me off, saying folks talked too much anyway, and all he asked was peace and quiet — I guess you know about how much he talked himself; but I thought maybe if I went to the house and talked about it before his wife, though I said to Harry that I didn't know as what his wife wanted made much difference to John ———

COUNTY ATTORNEY: Let's talk about that later, Mr. Hale. I do want to talk about that, but tell now just what happened when you got to the house.

HALE: I didn't hear or see anything; I knocked at the door, and still it was all quiet inside. I knew they must be up, it was past eight o'clock. So I knocked again, and I thought I heard somebody say, "Come in." I wasn't sure, I'm not sure yet, but I opened the door — this door (*indicating the door by which the two women are still standing*) and there in that rocker — (*pointing to it*) sat Mrs. Wright. (*They all look at the rocker down left.*)

COUNTY ATTORNEY: What — was she doing?

HALE: She was rockin' back and forth. She had her apron in her hand and was kind of — pleating it.

COUNTY ATTORNEY: And how did she — look?

HALE: Well, she looked queer.

COUNTY ATTORNEY: How do you mean — queer?

HALE: Well, as if she didn't know what she was going to do next. And kind of done up.

COUNTY ATTORNEY (*takes out notebook and pencil and sits left of center table*): How did she seem to feel about your coming?

HALE: Why, I don't think she minded — one way or other. She didn't pay much attention. I said, "How do, Mrs. Wright, it's cold, ain't it?" And she said, "Is it?" — and went on kind of pleating at her apron. Well, I was surprised; she didn't ask me to come up to the stove, or to set down, but just sat there, not even looking at me, so I said, "I want to see John." And then she — laughed. I guess you would call it a laugh. I thought of Harry and the team outside, so I said a little sharp: "Can't I see John?" "No," she says, kind o' dull like. "Ain't he home?" says I. "Yes," says she, "he's home." "Then why can't I see him?" I asked her, out of patience. "'Cause he's dead," says she. "*Dead?*" says I. She just nodded her head, not getting a bit excited, but rockin' back and forth. "Why — where is he?" says I, not knowing what to say. She just pointed upstairs — like that. (*Himself pointing to the room above.*) I started for the stairs, with the idea of going up there. I walked from there to here — then I says, "Why, what did he die of?" "He died of a rope round his neck," says she, and just went on pleatin' at her apron. Well, I went out and called Harry. I thought I might — need help. We went upstairs and there he was lyin' ———

COUNTY ATTORNEY: I think I'd rather have you go into that upstairs, where you can point it all out. Just go on now with the rest of the story.

HALE: Well, my first thought was to get that rope off. It looked . . . (*stops; his face twitches*) . . . but Harry, he went up to him, and he said, "No, he's dead all right, and we'd better not touch anything." So we went back downstairs. She was still sitting that same way. "Has anybody been notified?" I asked. "No," says she, unconcerned. "Who did this, Mrs. Wright?" said Harry. He said it businesslike — and she stopped pleatin' of her apron. "I don't know," she says. "You don't *know*?" says Harry. "No," says she. "Weren't you sleepin' in the bed with him?" says Harry. "Yes," says she, "but I was on the inside." "Somebody slipped a rope round his neck and strangled him and you didn't wake up?" says Harry. "I didn't wake up," she said after him. We must 'a' looked as if we didn't see how that could be, for after a minute she said, "I sleep sound." Harry was going to ask her more questions but I said maybe we ought to let her tell her story first to the coroner, or the sheriff, so Harry went fast as he could to Rivers' place, where there's a telephone.

COUNTY ATTORNEY: And what did Mrs. Wright do when she knew that you had gone for the coroner?

HALE: She moved from the rocker to that chair over there (*pointing to a small chair in the down right corner*) and just sat there with her hands held together and looking down. I got a feeling that I ought to make some conversation, so I said I had come in to see if John wanted to put in a telephone, and at that she started to laugh, and then she stopped and looked at me — scared. (*The County Attorney, who has had his notebook out, makes a note.*) I dunno, maybe it wasn't scared. I wouldn't like to say it was. Soon Harry got back, and then Dr. Lloyd came and you, Mr. Peters, and so I guess that's all I know that you don't.

COUNTY ATTORNEY (*rising and looking around*): I guess we'll go upstairs first — and then out to the barn and around there. (*To the Sheriff.*) You're convinced that there was nothing important here — nothing that would point to any motive?

SHERIFF: Nothing here but kitchen things. (*The County Attorney, after again looking around the kitchen, opens the door of a cupboard closet in right wall. He brings a small chair from right — gets on it and looks on a shelf. Pulls his hand away, sticky.*)

COUNTY ATTORNEY: Here's a nice mess. (*The women draw nearer up center.*)

MRS. PETERS (*to the other woman*): Oh, her fruit; it did freeze. (*To the Lawyer.*) She worried about that when it turned so cold. She said the fire'd go out and her jars would break.

SHERIFF (*rises*): Well, can you beat the woman! Held for murder and worryin' about her preserves.

COUNTY ATTORNEY (*getting down from chair*): I guess before we're through she may have something more serious than preserves to worry about. (*Crosses down right center.*)

HALE: Well, women are used to worrying over trifles. (*The two women move a little closer together.*)

COUNTY ATTORNEY (*with the gallantry of a young politician*): And yet, for all their worries, what would we do without the ladies? (*The women do not unbend. He goes below the center table to the sink, takes a dipperful of water from the pail, and pouring it into a basin, washes his hands. While he is doing this the Sheriff and Hale cross to cupboard, which they inspect. The County Attorney starts to wipe his hands on the roller towel, turns it for a cleaner place.*) Dirty towels! (*Kicks his foot against the pans under the sink.*) Not much of a housekeeper, would you say, ladies?

MRS. HALE (*stiffly*): There's a great deal of work to be done on a farm.

COUNTY ATTORNEY: To be sure. And yet (*with a little bow to her*) I know there are some Dickson County farmhouses which do not have such roller towels. (*He gives it a pull to expose its full-length again.*)

MRS. HALE: Those towels get dirty awful quick. Men's hands aren't always as clean as they might be.

COUNTY ATTORNEY: Ah, loyal to your sex, I see. But you and Mrs. Wright were neighbors. I suppose you were friends, too.

MRS. HALE (*shaking her head*): I've not seen much of her of late years. I've not been in this house — it's more than a year.

COUNTY ATTORNEY (*crossing to women up center*): And why was that? You didn't like her?

MRS. HALE: I liked her all well enough. Farmers' wives have their hands full, Mr. Henderson. And then ——

COUNTY ATTORNEY: Yes —— ?

MRS. HALE (*looking about*): It never seemed a very cheerful place.

COUNTY ATTORNEY: No — it's not cheerful. I shouldn't say she had the homemaking instinct.

MRS. HALE: Well, I don't know as Wright had, either.

COUNTY ATTORNEY: You mean that they didn't get on very well?

MRS. HALE: No, I don't mean anything. But I don't think a place'd be any cheerfuller for John Wright's being in it.

COUNTY ATTORNEY: I'd like to talk more of that a little later. I want to get the lay of things upstairs now. (*He goes past the women to up right where steps lead to a stair door.*)

SHERIFF: I suppose anything Mrs. Peters does'll be all right. She was to take in some clothes for her, you know, and a few little things. We left in such a hurry yesterday.

COUNTY ATTORNEY: Yes, but I would like to see what you take, Mrs. Peters, and keep an eye out for anything that might be of use to us.

MRS. PETERS: Yes, Mr. Henderson. (*The men leave by up right door to stairs. The women listen to the men's steps on the stairs, then look about the kitchen.*)

MRS. HALE (*crossing left to sink*): I'd hate to have men coming into my kitchen, snooping around and criticizing. (*She arranges the pans under sink which the lawyer had shoved out of place.*)

MRS. PETERS: Of course it's no more than their duty. (*Crosses to cupboard up right.*)

MRS. HALE: Duty's all right, but I guess that deputy sheriff that came out to make the fire might have got a little of this on. (*Gives the roller towel a pull.*) Wish I'd thought of that sooner. Seems mean to talk about her for not having things slicked up when she had to come away in such a hurry. (*Crosses right to Mrs. Peters at cupboard.*)

MRS. PETERS (*who has been looking through cupboard, lifts one end of towel that covers a pan*): She had bread set. (*Stands still.*)

MRS. HALE (*eyes fixed on a loaf of bread beside the breadbox, which is on a low shelf of the cupboard*). She was going to put this in there. (*Picks up loaf, abruptly drops it. In a manner of returning to familiar things.*) It's a shame about her fruit. I wonder if it's all gone. (*Gets up on the chair and looks.*) I think there's some here that's all right, Mrs. Peters. Yes — here; (*holding it toward the window*) this is cherries, too. (*Looking again.*) I declare I believe that's the only one. (*Gets down, jar in her hand. Goes to the sink and wipes it off on the outside.*) She'll feel awful bad after all her hard work in the hot weather. I remember the afternoon I put up my cherries last summer. (*She puts the jar on the big kitchen table, center of the room. With a sigh, is about to sit down in the rocking chair. Before she is seated realizes what chair it is; with a slow look at it, steps back. The chair which she has touched rocks back and forth. Mrs. Peters moves to center table and they both watch the chair rock for a moment or two.*)

MRS. PETERS (*shaking off the mood which the empty rocking chair has evoked. Now in a businesslike manner she speaks*): Well I must get those things from the front room closet. (*She goes to the door at the right but, after looking into the other room, steps back.*) You coming with me, Mrs. Hale? You could help me carry them. (*They go in the other room; reappear, Mrs. Peters carrying a dress, petticoat, and skirt, Mrs. Hale following with a pair of shoes.*) My, it's cold in there. (*She puts the clothes on the big table and hurries to the stove.*)

MRS. HALE (*right of center table examining the skirt*): Wright was close. I think maybe that's why she kept so much to herself. She didn't even belong to the Ladies' Aid. I suppose she felt she couldn't do her part, and then you don't enjoy things when you feel shabby. I heard she used to wear pretty clothes and be lively, when she was Minnie Foster, one of the town girls singing in the choir. But that — oh, that was thirty years ago. This all you want to take in?

MRS. PETERS: She said she wanted an apron. Funny thing to want, for there isn't much to get you dirty in jail, goodness knows. But I suppose just to make her feel more natural. (*Crosses to cupboard*). She said they was in the top drawer in this cupboard. Yes, here. And then her little shawl that always hung behind the door. (*Opens stair door and looks.*) Yes, here it is. (*Quickly shuts door leading upstairs.*)

MRS. HALE (*abruptly moving toward her*): Mrs. Peters?

MRS. PETERS: Yes, Mrs. Hale? (*At up right door.*)

MRS. HALE: Do you think she did it?

MRS. PETERS (*in a frightened voice*): Oh, I don't know.

MRS. HALE: Well, I don't think she did. Asking for an apron and her little shawl. Worrying about her fruit.

MRS. PETERS (*starts to speak, glances up, where footsteps are heard in the room above. In a low voice*): Mr. Peters says it looks bad for her. Mr. Henderson is awful sarcastic in a speech and he'll make fun of her sayin' she didn't wake up.

MRS. HALE: Well, I guess John Wright didn't wake when they was slipping that rope under his neck.

MRS. PETERS (*crossing slowly to table and placing shawl and apron on table with other clothing*): No, it's strange. It must have been done awful crafty and still. They say it was such a — funny way to kill a man, rigging it all up like that.

MRS. HALE (*crossing to left of Mrs. Peters at table*): That's just what Mr. Hale said. There was a gun in the house. He says that's what he can't understand.

MRS. PETERS: Mr. Henderson said coming out that what was needed for the case was a motive; something to show anger, or — sudden feeling.

MRS. HALE (*who is standing by the table*): Well, I don't see any signs of anger around here. (*She puts her hand on the dish towel, which lies on the table, stands looking down at table, one-half of which is clean, the other half messy.*) It's wiped to here. (*Makes a move as if to finish work, then turns and looks at loaf of bread outside the breadbox. Drops towel. In that voice of coming back to familiar things.*) Wonder how they are finding things upstairs. (*Crossing below table to down right.*) I hope she had it a little more red-up up there. You know, it seems kind of *sneaking.* Locking her up in town and then coming out here and trying to get her own house to turn against her!

MRS. PETERS: But, Mrs. Hale, the law is the law.

MRS. HALE: I s'pose 'tis. (*Unbuttoning her coat.*) Better loosen up your things, Mrs. Peters. You won't feel them when you go out. (*Mrs. Peters takes off her fur tippet, goes to hang it on chair back left of table, stands looking at the work basket on floor near down left window.*)

MRS. PETERS: She was piecing a quilt. (*She brings the large sewing basket to the center table and they look at the bright pieces, Mrs. Hale above the table and Mrs. Peters left of it.*)

MRS. HALE: It's a log cabin pattern. Pretty, isn't it? I wonder if she was goin' to quilt it or just knot it? (*Footsteps have been heard coming down the stairs. The Sheriff enters followed by Hale and the County Attorney.*)

SHERIFF: They wonder if she was going to quilt it or just knot it! (*The men laugh, the women look abashed.*)

COUNTY ATTORNEY (*rubbing his hands over the stove*): Frank's fire didn't do much up there, did it? Well, let's go out to the barn and get that cleared up. (*The men go outside by up left door.*)

MRS. HALE (*resentfully*): I don't know as there's anything so strange, our takin' up our time with little things while we're waiting for them to get the evidence. (*She sits in chair right of table smoothing out a block with decision.*) I don't see as it's anything to laugh about.

MRS. PETERS (*apologetically*): Of course they've got awful important things on their minds. (*Pulls up a chair and joins Mrs. Hale at the left of the table.*)

MRS. HALE (*examining another block*): Mrs. Peters, look at this one. Here, this is the one she was working on, and look at the sewing! All the rest of it has been so nice and even. And look at this! It's all over the place! Why, it looks as if she didn't know what she was about! (*After she has said this they look at each other, then start to glance back at the door. After an instant Mrs. Hale has pulled at a knot and ripped the sewing.*)

MRS. PETERS: Oh, what are you doing, Mrs. Hale?

MRS. HALE (*mildly*): Just pulling out a stitch or two that's not sewed very good. (*Threading a needle.*) Bad sewing always made me fidgety.

MRS. PETERS (*with a glance at door, nervously*): I don't think we ought to touch things.

MRS. HALE: I'll just finish up this end. (*Suddenly stopping and leaning forward.*) Mrs. Peters?

MRS. PETERS: Yes, Mrs. Hale?

MRS. HALE: What do you suppose she was so nervous about?

MRS. PETERS: Oh — I don't know. I don't know as she was nervous. I sometimes sew awful queer when I'm just tired. (*Mrs. Hale starts to say something, looks at Mrs. Peters, then goes on sewing.*) Well, I must get these things wrapped up. They may be through sooner than we think. (*Putting apron and other things together.*) I wonder where I can find a piece of paper, and string. (*Rises.*)

MRS. HALE: In that cupboard, maybe.

MRS. PETERS (*crosses right looking in cupboard*): Why, here's a bird-cage. (*Holds it up.*) Did she have a bird, Mrs. Hale?

MRS. HALE: Why, I don't know whether she did or not — I've not been here for so long. There was a man around last year selling canaries cheap, but I don't know as she took one; maybe she did. She used to sing real pretty herself.

MRS. PETERS (*glancing around*): Seems funny to think of a bird here. But she must have had one, or why would she have a cage? I wonder what happened to it?

MRS. HALE: I s'pose maybe the cat got it.

MRS. PETERS: No, she didn't have a cat. She's got that feeling some people have about cats — being afraid of them. My cat got in her room and she was real upset and asked me to take it out.

MRS. HALE: My sister Bessie was like that. Queer, ain't it?

MRS. PETERS (*examining the cage*): Why, look at this door. It's broke. One hinge is pulled apart. (*Takes a step down to Mrs. Hale's right.*)

MRS. HALE (*looking too*): Looks as if someone must have been rough with it.

MRS. PETERS: Why, yes. (*She brings the cage forward and puts it on the table.*)

MRS. HALE (*glancing toward up left door*): I wish if they're going to find any evidence they'd be about it. I don't like this place.

MRS. PETERS: But I'm awful glad you came with me, Mrs. Hale. It would be lonesome for me sitting here alone.

MRS. HALE: It would, wouldn't it? (*Dropping her sewing.*) But I tell you what I do wish, Mrs. Peters. I wish I had come over sometimes when *she* was here. I — (*looking around the room*) — wish I had.

MRS. PETERS: But of course you were awful busy, Mrs. Hale — your house and your children.

MRS. HALE (*rises and crosses left*): I could've come. I stayed away because it weren't cheerful — and that's why I ought to have come. I — (*looking out left window*) — I've never liked this place. Maybe because it's down in a hollow and you don't see the road. I dunno what it is, but it's a lonesome place and always was. I wish I had come over to see Minnie Foster sometimes. I can see now — (*Shakes her head.*)

MRS. PETERS (*left of table and above it*): Well, you mustn't reproach yourself, Mrs. Hale. Somehow we just don't see how it is with other folks until — something turns up.

MRS. HALE: Not having children makes less work — but it makes a quiet house, and Wright out to work all day, and no company when he did come in. (*Turning from window.*) Did you know John Wright, Mrs. Peters?

MRS. PETERS: Not to know him; I've seen him in town. They say he was a good man.

MRS. HALE: Yes — good; he didn't drink, and kept his word as well as most, I guess, and paid his debts. But he was a hard man, Mrs. Peters. Just to pass the time of day with him — (*Shivers.*) Like a raw wind that gets to the bone. (*Pauses, her eye falling on the cage.*) I should think she would 'a' wanted a bird. But what do you suppose went with it?

MRS. PETERS: I don't know, unless it got sick and died. (*She reaches over and swings the broken door, swings it again, both women watch it.*)

MRS. HALE: You weren't raised round here, were you? (*Mrs. Peters shakes her head.*) You didn't know — her?

MRS. PETERS: Not till they brought her yesterday.

MRS. HALE: She — come to think of it, she was kind of like a bird herself — real sweet and pretty, but kind of timid and — fluttery. How — she — did — change. (*Silence: then as if struck by a happy thought and relieved to get back to everyday things. Crosses right above Mrs. Peters to cupboard, replaces small chair used to stand on to its original place down right.*) Tell you what, Mrs. Peters, why don't you take the quilt in with you? It might take up her mind.

MRS. PETERS: Why, I think that's a real nice idea, Mrs. Hale. There couldn't possibly be any objection to it could there? Now, just what would I take? I wonder if her patches are in here — and her things. (*They look in the sewing basket.*)

MRS. HALE (*crosses to right of table*): Here's some red. I expect this has got sewing things in it. (*Brings out a fancy box.*) What a pretty box. Looks like something somebody would give you. Maybe her scissors are in here. (*Opens box. Suddenly puts her hand to her nose.*) Why ——— (*Mrs. Peters bends nearer, then turns her face away.*) There's something wrapped up in this piece of silk.

MRS. PETERS: Why, this isn't her scissors.

MRS. HALE (*lifting the silk*): Oh, Mrs. Peters — it's ——— (*Mrs. Peters bends closer.*)

MRS. PETERS: It's the bird.

MRS. HALE: But, Mrs. Peters — look at it! Its neck! Look at its neck! It's all — other side *to.*

MRS. PETERS: Somebody — wrung — its — neck. (*Their eyes meet. A look of growing comprehension, of horror. Steps are heard outside. Mrs. Hale slips box under quilt pieces, and sinks into her chair.*

Enter Sheriff and County Attorney. Mrs. Peters steps down left and stands looking out of window.)

COUNTY ATTORNEY (*as one turning from serious things to little pleasantries*): Well, ladies, have you decided whether she was going to quilt it or knot it? (*Crosses to center above table.*)

MRS. PETERS: We think she was going to — knot it. (*Sheriff crosses to right of stove, lifts stove lid, and glances at fire, then stands warming hands at stove.*)

COUNTY ATTORNEY: Well, that's interesting, I'm sure. (*Seeing the bird-cage.*) Has the bird flown?

MRS. HALE (*putting more quilt pieces over the box*): We think the — cat got it.

COUNTY ATTORNEY (*preoccupied*): Is there a cat? (*Mrs. Hale glances in a quick covert way at Mrs. Peters.*)

MRS. PETERS (*turning from window takes a step in*): Well, not *now*. They're superstitious, you know. They leave.

COUNTY ATTORNEY (*to Sheriff Peters, continuing an interrupted conversation*): No sign at all of anyone having come from the outside. Their own rope. Now let's go up again and go over it piece by piece. (*They start upstairs.*) It would have to have been someone who knew just the ——— (*Mrs. Peters sits down left of table. The two women sit there not looking at one another, but as if peering into something and at the same time holding back. When they talk now it is in the manner of feeling their way over strange ground, as if afraid of what they are saying, but as if they cannot help saying it.*)

MRS. HALE (*hesitatively and in hushed voice*): She liked the bird. She was going to bury it in that pretty box.

MRS. PETERS (*in a whisper*): When I was a girl — my kitten — there was a boy took a hatchet, and before my eyes — and before I could get there ——— (*Covers her face an instant.*) If they hadn't held me back I would have — (*catches herself, looks upstairs where steps are heard, falters weakly*) — hurt him.

MRS. HALE (*with a slow look around her*): I wonder how it would seem never to have had any children around. (*Pause.*) No, Wright wouldn't like the bird — a thing that sang. She used to sing. He killed that, too.

MRS. PETERS (*moving uneasily*): We don't know who killed the bird.

MRS. HALE: I knew John Wright.

MRS. PETERS: It was an awful thing was done in this house that night, Mrs. Hale. Killing a man while he slept, slipping a rope around his neck that choked the life out of him.

MRS. HALE: His neck. Choked the life out of him. (*Her hand goes out and rests on the bird-cage.*)

MRS. PETERS (*with rising voice*): We don't know who killed him. We don't *know.*

MRS. HALE (*her own feeling not interrupted*): If there'd been years and years of nothing, then a bird to sing to you, it would be awful — still, after the bird was still.

MRS. PETERS (*something within her speaking*): I know what stillness is. When we homesteaded in Dakota, and my first baby died — after he was two years old, and me with no other then ———

MRS. HALE (*moving*): How soon do you suppose they'll be through looking for the evidence?

MRS. PETERS: I know what stillness is. (*Pulling herself back.*) The law has got to punish crime, Mrs. Hale.

MRS. HALE (*not as if answering that*): I wish you'd seen Minnie Foster when she wore a white dress with blue ribbons and stood up there in the choir and sang. (*A look around the room.*) Oh, I *wish* I'd come over here once in a while! That was a crime! That was a crime! Who's going to punish that?

MRS. PETERS (*looking upstairs*): We mustn't — take on.

MRS. HALE: I might have known she needed help! I know how things can be — for women. I tell you, it's queer, Mrs. Peters. We live close together and we live far apart. We all go through the same things — it's all just a different kind of the same thing. (*Brushes her eyes, noticing the jar of fruit, reaches out for it.*) If I was you I wouldn't tell her her fruit was gone. Tell her it *ain't.* Tell her it's all right. Take this in to prove it to her. She — she may never know whether it was broke or not.

MRS. PETERS (*takes the jar, looks about for something to wrap it in; takes petticoat from the clothes brought from the other room, very nervously begins winding this around the jar. In a false voice*): My, it's a good thing the men couldn't hear us. Wouldn't they just laugh! Getting all stirred up over a little thing like a — dead canary. As if that could have anything to do with — with — wouldn't they *laugh!* (*The men are heard coming downstairs.*)

MRS. HALE (*under her breath*): Maybe they would — maybe they wouldn't.

COUNTY ATTORNEY: No, Peters, it's all perfectly clear except a reason for doing it. But you know juries when it comes to women. If there was some definite thing. (*Crosses slowly to above table. Sheriff crosses down right. Mrs. Hale and Mrs. Peters remain seated at either side of table.*) Something to show — something to make a story about — a thing that would connect up with this strange

way of doing it ———— (*The women's eyes meet for an instant.
Enter Hale from outer door.*)

HALE (*remaining by door*): Well, I've got the team around. Pretty cold
out there.

COUNTY ATTORNEY: I'm going to stay awhile by myself. (*To the Sheriff.*)
You can send Frank out for me, can't you? I want to go over
everything. I'm not satisfied that we can't do better.

SHERIFF: Do you want to see what Mrs. Peters is going to take in? (*The
Lawyer picks up the apron, laughs.*)

COUNTY ATTORNEY: Oh, I guess they're not very dangerous things the
ladies have picked out. (*Moves a few things about, disturbing the
quilt pieces which cover the box. Steps back.*) No, Mrs. Peters
doesn't need supervising. For that matter a sheriff's wife is married to the law. Ever think of it that way, Mrs. Peters?

MRS. PETERS: Not — just that way.

SHERIFF (*chuckling*): Married to the law. (*Moves to down right door to
the other room.*) I just want you to come in here a minute,
George. We ought to take a look at these windows.

COUNTY ATTORNEY (*scoffingly*): Oh, windows!

SHERIFF: We'll be right out, Mr. Hale. (*Hale goes outside. The Sheriff follows the County Attorney into the room. Then Mrs. Hale rises,
hands tight together, looking intensely at Mrs. Peters, whose eyes
make a slow turn, finally meeting Mrs. Hale's. A moment Mrs. Hale
holds her, then her own eyes point the way to where the box is concealed. Suddenly Mrs. Peters throws back quilt pieces and tries to
put the box in the bag she is carrying. It is too big. She opens box,
starts to take bird out, cannot touch it, goes to pieces, stands there
helpless. Sound of a knob turning in the other room. Mrs. Hale
snatches the box and puts it in the pocket of her big coat. Enter
County Attorney and Sheriff, who remains down right.*)

COUNTY ATTORNEY (*crosses to up left door facetiously*): Well, Henry, at
least we found out that she was not going to quilt it. She was
going to — what is it you call it, ladies?

MRS. HALE (*standing center below table facing front, her hand against
her pocket*): We call it — knot it, Mr. Henderson.

CURTAIN.

To His Coy Mistress
ANDREW MARVELL

Had we but world enough, and time,
This coyness, lady, were no crime.
We would sit down, and think which way
To walk, and pass our long love's day.
Thou by the Indian Ganges' side   5
Should'st rubies find; I by the tide
Of Humber[1] would complain. I would
Love you ten years before the Flood;
And you should, if you please, refuse
Till the conversion of the Jews.   10
My vegetable love should grow
Vaster than empires, and more slow.
An hundred years should go to praise
Thine eyes, and on thy forehead gaze;
Two hundred to adore each breast;   15
But thirty thousand to the rest:
An age at least to every part,
And the last age should show your heart.
For, lady, you deserve this state,
Nor would I love at lower rate.   20
    But at my back I always hear
Time's wingèd chariot hurrying near;
And yonder all before us lie
Deserts of vast eternity.
Thy beauty shall no more be found,   25
Nor in thy marble vault shall sound
My echoing song; then worms shall try
That long-preserved virginity;
And your quaint honor turn to dust,

Andrew Marvell (1621–1678) was a long-time member of the British Parliament and a writer of political satires. Today, however, he is remembered for two splendid poems, "The Garden" and the one that appears here. "To His Coy Mistress" is a noteworthy expression of an idea familiar in the love poems of many languages — *carpe diem,* Latin for "seize the day," the idea that life is fleeting and love and other pleasures should be enjoyed while the lovers are still young and beautiful.

[1]An estuary in England. — ED.

And into ashes all my lust.   30
The grave's a fine and private place,
But none, I think, do there embrace.
   Now, therefore, while thy youthful hue
Sits on thy skin like morning dew,
And while thy willing soul transpires   35
At every pore with instant fires,
Now let us sport us while we may;
And now, like amorous birds of prey,
Rather at once our time devour,
Than languish in his slow-chapped[2] power.   40
Let us roll all our strength and all
Our sweetness up into one ball;
And tear our pleasures with rough strife
Thorough[3] the iron gates of life.
Thus, though we cannot make our sun   45
Stand still, yet we will make him run.

---

[2] Slow-jawed. — ED.
[3] Through. — ED.

ACKNOWLEDGMENTS (continued from page iv)

Julia Álvarez. "A White Woman of Color." Copyright © 1998 by Julia Álvarez. From *Half and Half* by Claudine Chiawei O'Hearn. Copyright © 1998 by Claudine Chiawei O'Hearn. Reprinted by permission of Pantheon Books, a division of Random House, Inc.

Amtrak® advertisement. "There's something about a train that's magic." Reprinted by permission of Amtrak®. Amtrak® is a registered service mark of the National Railroad Passenger Corporation.

Marcia Angell. "The Supreme Court and Physician-Assisted Suicide — The Ultimate Right." From *The New England Journal of Medicine,* January 2, 1997 (v. 336, no. 1). Copyright © 1997 by the Massachusetts Medical Society. All Rights Reserved. Reprinted by permission.

Barbara Allen Babcock. "Protect the Jury System, Judge Was the Problem." The *Los Angeles Times,* October 8, 1995. Reprinted by permission.

Russell Baker. "Taking the Saps." From the Observer column in the *New York Times,* June 15, 1996. Copyright © 1996 by The New York Times. Reprinted by permission.

Jim Borgman. "Two-Way Street" cartoon. © 1997 Cincinnati Enquirer. Reprinted with special permission of King Features Syndicate.

Bostongas advertisement. "Perhaps the most beautiful thing about using energy more efficiently isn't the fuel it can save." Illustrator: Suzanne Barnes. Reprinted by permission of Bostongas and the illustrator.

Ellen Bravo and Ellen Cassedy. "What Sexual Harassment Is — and Is Not." From *The 9 to 5 Guide to Combating Sexual Harassment: Candid Advice from 9to5, the National Association of Working Women.* © 1992 John Wiley & Sons, Inc. Reprinted by permission of John Wiley & Sons, Inc.

Stephen P. Breen. "I'm into comfortable footwear" cartoon. © 1997 Asbury Park Press. Reprinted by permission of Stephen P. Breen and Asbury Park Press.

Armin A. Brott. "Not All Men Are Sly Foxes." From *Newsweek,* June 1, 1992. Copyright © 1992 by Armin A. Brott. Reprinted by permission of the author.

Timothy C. Brown. "Women Unfit for Combat? Au Contraire!" From the *Wall Street Journal,* September 30, 1997, A22. Copyright © 1992 Dow Jones & Company, Inc. Reprinted with permission of the *Wall Street Journal* and the author. All rights reserved.

Warren E. Burger. "The Right to Bear Arms." From *Parade,* January 14, 1990. Reprinted with permission from Parade, copyright © 1990, and the author.

Arthur Caplan. "Euthanasia for Kids." Excerpt from *Due Consideration: Controversy in the Age of Medical Miracles* by Arthur Caplan. Copyright © 1998 John Wiley & Sons, Inc. Reprinted by permission of John Wiley & Sons.

Margaret Carlson. "Female Chauvinist Pigs?" From *Time,* December 12, 1994, v. 144, no. 24, p. 62. © 1994 Time, Inc. Reprinted by permission.

Peggy Carlson. "Why We Don't Need Animal Experimentation." From the *Wall Street Journal,* November 7, 1995, p. A23. © 1995 Dow Jones & Company, Inc. Reprinted with permission of the *Wall Street Journal.* All rights reserved.

Stephen L. Carter. "Racial Justice on the Cheap." From *Reflections of an Affirmative Action Baby* by Stephen L. Carter. © 1991 by Stephen L. Carter. Reprinted by permission of HarperCollins Publishers, Inc.

Cease Fire advertisement. "A gun in the home is much more likely to kill a family member than to kill an intruder." Reprinted courtesy of Cease Fire, Inc.

Chef Boyardee advertisement. "An after-school lesson *in* simple mathematics." © International Home Foods, Inc. Reprinted by permission.

Carl Cohen. Testimony before a Congressional Committee. From *Measure,* January/February 1996. Reprinted by permission.

James Collins, Paul L. Hackett, and Bill Norton. "Women Are Not a Warrior Class" [letters to the editor]. The *Wall Street Journal,* October 9, 1997, A20. Copyright ©

Glossary and
Index of Terms

Hasty generalization: drawing conclusions from insufficient evidence   *302–03*

Induction: reasoning by which a general statement is reached on the basis of particular examples   *284–85*

Inference: an interpretation of the *facts*   *11, 54–55*

Major premise: see *syllogism*

Minor premise: see *syllogism*

Motivational appeal: an attempt to reach an *audience* by recognizing their *needs* and *values* and how these contribute to their decision making   *11*

Motivational warrant: a type of *warrant* based on the *needs* and *values* of an *audience*   *206–07*

Need: in the hierarchy of Abraham Maslow, whatever is required, whether psychological, or physiological, for the survival and welfare of a human being   *169–71*

Non sequitur: "it does not follow"; using irrelevant proof to buttress a *claim*   *309*

Picturesque language: words that produce images in the minds of the *audience*   *247–49*

Policy: a course of action recommended or taken to solve a problem or guide decisions   *11, 71–73*

Post hoc: mistakenly inferring that because one event follows another they have a causal relation; from *post hoc ergo propter hoc* ("after this, therefore because of this"); also called "doubtful cause"   *303–04*

Proposition: see *claim*

Qualifier: a restriction placed on the *claim* may not always be true as stated   *52, 202*

Refutation: an attack on an opposing view to weaken it, invalidate it, or make it less credible   *344–45*

Reservation: a restriction placed on the *warrant* to indicate that unless certain conditions are met, the warrant may not establish a connection between the *support* and the *claim*   *202*

Slanting: selecting *facts* or words with *connotations* that favor the arguer's bias and discredit alternatives   *244–47*

Slippery slope: predicting without justification that one step in a process will lead unavoidably to a second, generally undesirable step   *307*

Slogan: an attention-getting expression used largely in politics or advertising to promote support of a cause or product   *256–60*

Statistics: information expressed in numerical form   *155–56, 162–64*

Stipulative definition: a *definition* that makes clear that it will explore a particular area of meaning of a term or issue   *111–12*

Straw man: disputing a view similar to, but not the same as, that of the arguer's opponent   *308–09*

Style: choices in words and sentence structure that make a writer's language distinctive   *352*

Substantive warrant: a *warrant* based on beliefs about the reliability of *factual evidence*   *206–07*

Support: any material that serves to prove an issue or *claim;* in addition to *evidence,* it includes appeals to the *needs* and *values* of the *audience*   *11, 152–74*

Syllogism: a formula of deductive *argument* consisting of three propositions: a major premise, a minor premise, and a conclusion   *290–94*

Thesis: the main idea of an essay   *300–02*

Toulmin model: a conceptual system of argument devised by the philosopher Stephen Toulmin; the terms *claim, support, warrant, backing, qualifier,* and *reservation* are adapted from this system   *300–02*

Two wrongs make a right: diverting attention from the issue by introducing a new point, e.g., by responding to an accusation with a counteraccusation that makes no attempt to refute the first accusation   *309*

Values: conceptions or ideas that act as standards for judging what is right or wrong, worthwhile or worthless, beautiful or ugly, good or bad   *172–74*

Warrant: a general principle or assumption that establishes a connection between the *support* and the *claim*   *11–13, 199–207*

Index of Authors and Titles

SIXTH EDITION

ELEMENTS of ARGUMENT

A Text and Reader

ANNETTE T. ROTTENBERG

RESOURCES FOR TEACHING

ELEMENTS OF ARGUMENT

A Text and Reader

SIXTH EDITION

RESOURCES FOR TEACHING

ELEMENTS OF ARGUMENT
A Text and Reader
SIXTH EDITION

PREPARED BY

Annette T. Rottenberg

With an essay by
Gail Stygall
University of Washington

BEDFORD / ST. MARTIN'S   BOSTON   ◆   NEW YORK

Preface

In these notes I have assembled some of the assignments and classroom activities that have proved successful over the years in illuminating the elements of argument and eliciting thoughtful student response. Every teacher will have a collection of favorite devices, and I claim no superiority for mine. If some of the materials are not suitable, they may, however, suggest other kinds that are. Together with the writing suggestions in the text and the "Classic Arguments" they should provide an ample repertory of things to do for every day of the course. Clearly there will be more material than any single class can profitably use. But I keep in mind what a wise supervising teacher long ago gave me as one of her secrets for confidence in the classroom: "Always be overprepared."

The text is flexible. Students usually need or want more practice in some areas than others. If the use of support, for example, is one element in which the majority of students are weak, you may want to spend more time on the material in Chapter 5 and omit an extended discussion of language and fallacies. The heart of the text is, of course, Chapters 3, 4, 5, and 6. Remaining Chapters 7 and 8 can be handled less intensively.

Part Two treats the writing process itself, analyzing its parts and providing guidelines for organizing, developing, and researching. It builds on Part One's five Writer's Guides, which give instructions for writing particular kinds of essays. New to Part Two and this edition is Chapter 11 on the presentation of oral argument, an increasingly important instrument for both laypeople and professionals. We hope to enable students to become not only more proficient public speakers but more knowledgeable members of an audience.

Part Three, "Opposing Viewpoints," lends itself to formal and informal classroom debate and longer papers that incorporate research. A short unit on debate is included in the *Resources for Teaching*. This chapter-by-chapter section can also be used throughout the course as a reference guide for papers that fulfill different kinds of writing assignments, especially those that call for in-depth analysis of opposing arguments. Part Four, "Classic Arguments," is another source of material for study and reference.

The most ambitious use of "Opposing Viewpoints" is as a source of information and opinion for the research paper. An enlarged section on research and use of the library and two documented research papers appear in Chapter 10. Suggestions for research paper subjects appear at the end of each section in "Opposing Viewpoints." For shorter papers students can limit their reading to material in the text. For longer papers they can look for additional material in the library or on the Internet. "Taking the Debate Online" provides students with Web links for the controversial topics in the book. I have included a new appendix on Rogerian argument for instructors who would like to introduce the theories of Carl Rogers to their students.

The linear organization of the course should pose no problems. It is true that from the first assignment students will be writing arguments — before they have completed the study of the elements of argument. This practice, however, is the same as that of any other composition course where the process is one of deepening, widening, and enriching a first draft or a series of undeveloped generalizations. Many teachers of composition, myself among them, believe that students should begin to write whole essays from the beginning of the course. Attention to the components of argument follows when students attempt to make their essays stronger by concentrating on the particular areas that need development and revision.

The essay at the beginning of this manual provides an overview of some of the special concerns and problems instructors should anticipate when teaching a course in argument, as well as practical general suggestions that might be useful in dealing with these concerns and problems.

Finally, teachers and students will find additional resources, including links, syllabi, assignment ideas, and online debates, at the book's website: <www.bedfordstmartins.com/rottenberg>.

Contents

PART THREE
Opposing Viewpoints   60

PART FOUR
Classic Arguments   78

Strategies for
Teaching Argumentation:
An Overview

INTRODUCTION

One of the joys we experience in teaching argumentation is seeing our students take a step into the real world of rhetoric and argument. Instructors who have taught many semesters of introductory freshman composition without including argument notice an immediate difference in the papers they read and evaluate when they do opt for a semester of argumentation. After a semester in the argumentation classroom, students often find they now have a means for articulating the opinions, views, and knowledge that they feel belong in the public discussion. Moreover, the informal logic model, once understood, may be taken into other classrooms as a means for analyzing readings and writing. With the flexibility of *Elements of Argument* and with the dialogue of argument in the classroom, students have access to a practical, everyday logic, so often missing in public discussions of issues.

Although teaching argument is different from teaching the purely expository freshman writing course, it is, in many ways, easier for the instructor. Many freshman composition instructors have struggled to create a real purpose for students when the students have to produce brief explanatory or illustrative essays. Not yet knowledgeable enough to join the essayists who populate their readers, students may not see the point of practicing consistency within forms. Even in the studio classroom, with a peer audience available, students in the expository course may reason that writing is just another form of exercise, not something they might ever need to do in the real world. Argument, on the other hand, diminishes the instructor's struggle to create a real audience. Students may participate immediately, whether the forum is the classroom, campuswide issues, or national elections, and they can see that their writing can make a difference with a real audience.

If you are new to teaching written argumentation, this shift into active argument need not mean you have to reject what you already know. Many of us now teaching English were ourselves taught composition by the modes approach. The various ways in which we articulate arguments make use of those very same patternings — process, cause and effect, classification, comparison, definition. What changes is that we teach our students how to use those structures to serve as support for their arguments.

STUDENTS' EXPERIENCE WITH ARGUMENT

Students arriving in the freshman composition classroom that is focused on argument have rarely been asked to take a stand before in writing contexts. Our nation's comparatively unimpressive performance in the persuasive essay category for seventeen-year-olds participating in the International Education Association writing project indicates how little our students may know about argument and persuasion when they begin college (Purves and Takala). Although many aspects of a process writing curriculum have been developed in the elementary and high schools, we still may not take it for granted that our students have had prior practice in argument. A related problem is that students doubt that we really want their opinions; in high school, they probably experienced institutional constraints on their views. Even if they had offered their opinions, they may have had those opinions rejected and may now hesitate to trust us. Moreover, prior to college their basic belief systems have probably gone unchallenged. They may offer what appears to them to be the wisdom of a community, but they have not yet had to maintain that wisdom in the face of a decidedly different community, such as the college classroom.

SETTING THE TONE FOR THE CLASSROOM

Because students have often had so little practice in oral or written argument, we must try to maintain a classroom in which open discussion and debate are the standard procedure. Many instructors use intercollegiate debate as a model to set the necessary atmosphere. Instructors may tape sessions of *Firing Line, Meet the Press,* or *The McLaughlin Group* for classroom discussion. Other instructors arrange for their classes to hear a full intercollegiate debate.

Setting the tone, however, goes beyond having students observe impersonal or distanced third-person demonstrations of debate and argumentation. Students need to hear one another assert and defend arguments, and they must have the opportunity to respond to one another face to face. Scheduling discussion time is a useful strategy, following selected reading assignments. Students may be asked to come to class with brief responses to a particular essay, responses that include the students' own arguments about the topic at issue. Arranging for these reaction discussions places tolerance at a premium in the argumentative writing classroom, and the instructor often becomes the immediate arbiter of conflicting views and opinions. You should expect students to ask for your opinion on the various topics, as they invariably will, and prepare your own reactions and responses accordingly.

MAINTAINING THE FORUM: DEBATES ON PAPER

Many instructors continue the open forum by shifting their focus to actual writing assignments, arranging assignments so that one student is graded for responding directly to another student's paper. Argument becomes quite real when a student sees that his or her reasoning does not convince a classmate. Even a skilled writer learns from this assignment that a good argument acknowledges alternative views. Students who quote out of context, don't order their arguments well, or use logical fallacies without understanding what they represent often see during the refutation process what effect these practices have on the audience. Some instructors extend the dialogue even further by requiring a rebuttal paper in response to the refutation paper. For instructors who have been using a process approach to writing, this paper exchange is a means of helping students recognize the value of audience. In a direct exchange of papers, students cannot help being reminded of the dialogic nature of argumentation.

USING PEER RESPONSES

Process approaches can be further adapted for the argumentation classroom through the use of the audience questionnaire, as suggested by Professor Rottenberg in Chapter 1 of this manual. Instructors, instead of distributing generic peer-response forms, may ask students to evaluate one another's work in terms of the results of class opinions, requiring students to write briefly about which segments of the class a particular essay will convince, harden, or fail to move. These same peer responders can explore in writing why they think the paper will succeed or fail by pointing to specific parts of the argument and evaluating the strategies informing its delivery. Peer responders may also list and develop counterarguments and offer counterevidence, keeping the focus on the dialogue between writer and reader.

Peer response exercises can also be used effectively with Part One of *Elements of Argument*. In conjunction with specific chapters, instructors can design peer-response forms for assigned student essays that direct the student responders to the important aspects of argument covered in those chapters. Instructors need to know that students who are inexperienced at focused response may need support in the form of a guided response sheet. Early in the semester, an instructor might ask both the student writer and the peer responder to answer the following questions about the student's essay:

What is the claim being made here? Write several sentences explaining your answer. You may want to quote from the text of the essay.

Is this an argument? Use evidence from Chapter 1 of your text to support your answer.

What type of claim is being made? Explain your answer based on what is said about claims in Chapter 3.

As writer, describe the purpose or effect you believe your claim will have on the reader.

As reader, describe the actual effect of the claim. Do you agree? Did you agree before you started reading? Did your opinion change? Why or why not?

Describe the representative person who you believe would be convinced by this essay. Include several characteristics such as age, sex, education, and family background.

Later in the semester, instructors can include further questions that ask students to evaluate the writer's use of definitions or to provide counterdefinitions in response to inadequately developed definitions. Chapter 5 on support and Chapter 6 on warrants also provide opportunities for students to integrate the material of the text with what they are attempting in their own writing.

PROVIDING BACKGROUND INFORMATION
TO AID CRITICAL READING

Although peer response exercises, discussion, and debate can promote critical reading, instructors should expect students to lack knowledge about the issues presented in the readings in the text. Instructors should anticipate that some or all of the students will know little about the issues involved. This cannot be attributed, in my view, to cultural "illiteracy," but rather to reasons of age or development. For example, the first time many people think about euthanasia (one of the topics in "Opposing Viewpoints," Part Three) is either when they become parents or when they find themselves caring for aged or infirm parents. This issue may simply be one that we do not seek out until it affects us. That is not to say, however, that in an argumentation class we exempt our students from that issue because of their lack of experience. Instead, we simply need to be prepared to support their reading. For example, students may need contextual information to understand James Rachels's discussion of a baby born with Down's syndrome.

If you have chosen to make "Opposing Viewpoints" the core of your course, you may find it useful before you begin assigning the sections to survey your students on the knowledge they have about the particular issue. Often gaps in knowledge revealed by the survey can be filled with very little discussion. But without the knowledge necessary to evaluate fully the arguments in question, students can have more difficulty than is necessary in discerning even the structure or main points of the essays.

TEACHING WARRANTS AND ASSUMPTIONS

At least partly because our students have had so little practice in argument, they may have problems understanding what we mean by warrants and assumptions. Conflating the terms *assumption* and *warrant* for the purposes of an introductory class, I have often chosen to illustrate the terms by beginning with an exercise such as "Who Should Survive?" suggested by Professor Rottenberg in Chapter 6 of this manual. A further step in that exercise would be to ask students to rank survivors in order of their correspondence with students' value systems. Invariably, students are unable to reach a consensus, revealing underlying assumptions that they hold about human behavior.

Instructors can also begin teaching warrants by asking students to complete statements beginning with the following leads: All lawyers . . . ; All English teachers . . . ; All students. . . . Such statements allow students to begin to see the kinds of assumptions they use implicitly every day. What they say in a discussion about what all lawyers do often reveals what they believe about the criminal justice system or about the civil recovery system. The beliefs about English teachers are interesting, and sometimes disheartening. Students report that they speak more carefully in front of an off-duty English teacher, reveal less about whether they read "popular" fiction, think we value grammar above everything, or believe we are the classic ivory tower type of teacher. Inevitably, students begin to recognize warrants and assumptions. Students realize that they have operating warrants about English teachers: that English teachers are always and on every occasion English teachers; that English teachers read only canonical literature; that grammar is all that counts in an English class; and that English classes have little to do with real life.

These discussions, however time-consuming, are a necessary part of introducing warrants to students. While the terminology may be foreign to students, the process of using warrants is not, and with very little practice students can learn the appropriate questions to ask themselves as they try to discern warrants in their own work and the work of others.

Students can also practice adding a series of "because" clauses to the main points of their papers as a way of clarifying their assumptions. For example, a student writing a paper about how television viewing negatively affects children cited passivity, exposure to violence, and fear as her main points. When in

4

an in-class exercise she was asked to identify her warrants with a "because" clause for each, she wrote, "because interaction, not passivity, is a better learning experience" in response to her first point and "because violence and fear are poor standards for society" to the second and third. Not only did the student gain valuable experience in identifying the warrants behind her claims, she also learned a powerful revision strategy. As her peers pointed out to her, she had grouped two of the points together, with the third being entirely separate. In revising her paper, she concentrated on the last two points, eliminated the first, and turned in a more coherent paper, which included a now-explicit discussion of her warrant.

DIFFERENT WORDINGS OF CLAIMS AND WARRANTS

Students will often propose several versions of claim and warrant for the same essay. Often one group of students will select as claim a very narrow assertion, while another group will select a generalization, perhaps an inference from the text. Likewise, students will show variation in their wording of warrants. As long as students do not go beyond what claims and warrants a particular author might make, some variation in wording not only is acceptable, but also is helpful to students working in an argumentative setting. They will learn that the rhetorical effect of different wording is intrinsic to assessing and addressing their audience.

TEACHING FALLACIES: THE EDITORIAL JOURNAL

Another tool for generating material for argument is the editorial journal. Instructors can require students to maintain a weekly folder containing several examples of what they think are successful and unsuccessful editorials and letters from local or campus newspapers and to record their responses to those editorials and letters in an editorial journal. Students assigned this exercise soon develop a standard against which they judge effective and ineffective arguments. It is then often useful to have students use their developing standard in combination with logical fallacies from Chapter 8. Students can submit for group discussion the most effective and least effective examples they've culled from editorial pages. Asking students to respond to the most troubling and fallacious letters and editorials often bridges the gap between classroom writing and the "real world" of discourse. Many students take the additional step of sending their responses to the local or campus newspaper and sometimes experience the delight of seeing their names in print in those pages.

A variation on this same exercise is an in-class letter-writing task in which students select the most troubling problem on campus and attempt to persuade the appropriate administrator to respond. The instructor may ask different groups to vary their approaches by assigning, for example, one group to argue a claim of fact, another a claim of value. Groups may assess the effectiveness of the arguments of other groups, with the entire class selecting the best letter for the particular audience.

DISTINGUISHING BETWEEN INDUCTION
AND DEDUCTION: RESEARCH ASSIGNMENTS

One other aspect of teaching an informal logic model in the writing classroom bears discussion. Many traditional argumentative writing courses have assigned induction and deduction separately. In teaching with an informal Toulmin model, the differences between the traditional and informal approaches often become blurred. Students who have become adept in using the informal model complain vigorously that there is no such thing as a truly inductive paper. Arguing that the Toulmin model requires that warrants be acknowledged, whether the paper is inductive or deductive, students assert that the differences are minimal. For the standard student paper, in which a thesis appears early in the essay, students are indeed correct, and the distinction is difficult to make. A so-called inductive paper with a thesis indicates that the writer has already drawn a conclusion, thus making it less than purely inductive in nature.

If the course you are teaching requires separate inductive and deductive papers, consider making the distinction on the basis of the style of research supporting the paper. For example, I have assigned one essay that focuses on an inductive style of research as a primary research project. These projects, chosen in collaborative groups, have included student-designed surveys of their classmates, observations of behavior on campus, in parking lots, and in shopping malls, and interviews. I have received essays that developed from student observations of people's behavior while standing in line, from student interviews with hard-core video game players, and from student surveys addressing the necessity of improving the food available in campus vending machines. Because inferencing and the "inductive leap" are highlighted with this approach, students can more easily see the differences between induction and deduction. For a deductive paper, on the other hand, I have stressed a secondary research approach, having students begin from basic assumptions about a subject and then examine a particular instance.

Many philosophers and historians of science have made the same point: that observations are always guided by a particular framework. The informal Toulmin model makes this point quite clear to students. What counts as a fact or as an observation is already warranted before the search for facts and observations begin.

CONCLUSION

I hope my suggestions will be useful for planning a forum on issues in your writing classroom. It is probable that many of your students will have only the composition classroom in which to engage in written debates on public policy issues. Becoming engaged in the consideration, analysis, and argument of various positions, students truly prepare to take their place in civic discussions. As instructors in written argument, we hold a unique position by virtue of our providing the forum in which this process takes place. Few students leave the argumentation classroom without having experienced a change of some kind, and few teachers can resist that kind of opportunity. By providing a model of analysis of argument useful both inside and outside the classroom and by providing the forum for an exchange of views, we can emphasize the uses of writing in unexpectedly productive ways.

Works Cited

Purves, Alan C., and Sauli Takala, eds. *An International Perspective on the Evaluation of Written Composition.* Oxford: Pergamon Press, 1982.

— Gail Stygall
University of Washington

Bibliography on the Toulmin Model

Listed below are articles by teachers of composition, rhetoric, speech, and debate that explain and apply the Toulmin model for use in the classroom

Brockriede, Wayne, and Douglas Ehninger. "Toulmin on Argument: An Interpretation and Application." *The Quarterly Journal of Speech,* 46 (1960), 44–53. The authors interpret the Toulmin model as presented in Toulmin's *The Uses of Argument.* They clearly define each element of the model and explain its advantages over traditional systems of logic.

Christenson, Thomas, and Paul R. Nelson. "The Toulmin Model: Asset and Millstone." In David A. Thomas (ed.), *Advanced Debate: Readings in Theory, Practice and Teaching.* Skokie, IL: National Textbook, 1975, 228–234. The authors provide a clear summary of Toulmin, distinguishing between the "basic" model — claim, data, and warrant — and the "expanded" model, which introduces the other elements of backing, reservation, and qualifier.

Kaufer, David S., and Christine M. Neuwirth. "Integrating Formal Logic and the New Rhetoric: A Four-Stage Heuristic." *College English,* 45 (1983), 380–389. The authors argue that formal logic can be used to supplement insights from the new rhetoric (as put forth by Toulmin and others), believing that an argument should be tested for its deductive certainty as well as for the plausibility of its premises. They provide a four-stage model for teaching students how to integrate logical and probabilistic reasoning in arguments.

Kneupper, Charles W. "Teaching Argument: An Introduction to the Toulmin Model." *College Composition and Communication,* 29 (1978), 237–241. Kneupper begins with an attack on the use of logic and fallacies as a means of teaching argumentative composition. He offers a brief summary of Toulmin's model as a superior method, then applies the model to the first paragraph of Thoreau's *Civil Disobedience,* diagramming the argument in simplified form. He emphasizes that for students "how they are arguing will be clearer," and they will be able to see relationships between parts of the argument.

Stratman, James F. "Teaching Written Argument: The Significance of Toulmin's Layout for Sentence-Combining." *College English,* 48 (1982), 718–733. The author believes that in using Toulmin's "layout" for argument in sentence-combining, students can learn new syntactic patterns. They can learn "skills appropriate to argument — estimating the relevance of acts, assessing validity, and planning refutations based on premises shared with an opponent." For example, one way of helping students to learn the function and importance of warrants is to have them adapt such warrants explicitly in a sentence-combining exercise.

"Toulmin's layout can reveal how syntactic transformations strengthen or weaken the structure implicit in argumentative exercises by revealing changes in the underlying relations between 'claim' and 'evidence' that these transformations may entail." A complicated analysis but thought-provoking.

Trent, Jimmie D. "Toulmin's Model of an Argument: An Examination and Extension." *The Quarterly Journal of Speech,* 54 (1968), 252–259. Trent views Toulmin's model as a supplement to syllogistic reasoning. He nevertheless argues that Toulmin presents arguments more clearly and accurately than the classical syllogism.

Several textbooks on writing, speech, and debate explain and apply the Toulmin model. A few are listed below.

Ehninger, Douglas. *Influence, Belief, and Argument: An Introduction to Responsible Persuasion.* Glenview, IL: Scott, Foresman, 1974. This book explains the Toulmin model and includes suggestions after each chapter for additional reading.

Ehninger, Douglas, and Wayne Brockriede. *Decision by Debate.* 2d ed. New York: Harper & Row, 1978. This text includes a comprehensive summary of the Toulmin model along with suggestions after each chapter for further reading.

Makay, John J. *Speaking with an Audience: Communicating Ideas and Attitudes.* New York: Harper & Row, 1977.

McCroskey, James C. *An Introduction to Rhetorical Communication.* 4th ed. Englewood Cliffs, NJ: Prentice-Hall, 1982.

Rieke, Richard D., and Malcolm O. Sillars. *Argumentation and the Decision-Making Process.* New York: Wiley, 1975.

Sproule, J. Michael. *Argument: Language and Its Influence.* New York: McGraw-Hill, 1980. This book includes a list of references on argument.

Toulmin, Steven, Richard Rieke, and Allan Janik. *An Introduction to Reasoning.* 2d ed. New York: Macmillan, 1984.

Zacharis, John C., and Coleman C. Bender. *Speech Communications: A Rational Approach.* New York: Wiley, 1976. This book includes additional readings after each chapter.

PART ONE

THE STRUCTURE OF ARGUMENT

CHAPTER 1
Understanding Argument
(text pages 3–24)

1. For years, ever since I began to teach argumentation, I have collected articles from every available source on the subjects that we are likely to discuss in class or use as assignment topics. I invite students and colleagues to contribute to the collection, which now numbers about forty different subjects. The materials in these files also serve as a backup resource for students who are unable to find articles in the library on popular subjects such as abortion, euthanasia, gun control, etc., because the materials have been removed by overzealous researchers.

   I also use the clippings to introduce a unit, displaying articles that point to problems connected with definitions or hidden assumptions or fallacious reasonings. Students always show a good deal of interest in the clippings, which represent "real life" and report recent research findings of which they may be unaware.

2. After discussion of the exercises at the end of the chapter, assign a brief search through newspapers and magazines (beginning perhaps with the school newspaper) for arguments about current affairs. Such a search enables students to arrive at several important conclusions.

   a. The most obvious one is that arguments of the kind they will be reading and writing in class are to be found everywhere and that they are the foundation of the democratic process. Students will also discover that a good deal of the factual reporting about political events is reporting of controversies or arguments.

   b. Without much familiarity with formal arguments, students may at first regard them all as vehicles of reasoned analysis. As they reflect on their examples, they will recognize that passion and ideology are formidable — sometimes the only — components of many arguments.

   c. Many, perhaps most, freshman students believe that hard-core problems in our society remain unsolved because at best we lack the will to solve them, or at worst evil people conspire to frustrate attempts at solution. One other explanation of our failures may not readily occur to them: lack of knowledge. We may ask: What kind of knowledge — that is, data and interpretation of data — do we need in order to solve apparently intractable problems of poverty, war, prejudice, crime, mental illness? When we introduce this question, we may find that some students think that these problems are new and peculiar to American society. Much of the information needed will turn out to be psychological, the kind most difficult to discover or verify. I use this discussion to encourage a reflective caution when evaluating and advocating solutions.

    d. Not all arguments have two equally valid sides. Some have multiple sides. Others may be said to have only one morally acceptable side. Ask students to suggest subjects that exemplify these conclusions.

3. Students may be asked to keep informal journals that list controversial subjects appearing in newspapers and magazines, on TV and radio, on the campus and in town. For each subject they may set down some of the important facts, values, and general principles underlying the claims. The journal entries can then serve as a source of subjects for assignments or discussion in class and in conferences with the instructor. A worthwhile dividend of such journal keeping is an increase in the practice of reading and listening, of becoming familiar with the sources and subjects of public controversies.

4. I would leave discussion and analysis of the three major elements of argument — claim, support, and warrant — to the subsequent chapters. At this point I would require only that students show understanding of the definitions.

5. In speech classes students sometimes analyze their audience, i.e., their classmates, before making a proposal that might be unpopular. They distribute questionnaires that they themselves have constructed in an effort to discover the social and political preferences of their classmates. The results of the questionnaire help them to choose an argumentative strategy that will persuade this audience to look more favorably on the proposition being argued.

    An application of this procedure for a writing class might work as follows: At the beginning of the semester, after having read about audience, a small group of students, perhaps four or five, makes up an informal questionnaire that is filled out by the members of the class. The results of the questionnaire are tabulated and distributed to the class. Later in the semester, for selected papers (for example, arguments of policy) the writers are encouraged to examine the results and add a note describing how and why they have adapted their arguments to the values of this particular audience.

CHAPTER 2
Responding to Argument
(text pages 25–50)

This chapter emphasizes that critical reading, listening, and looking are all essential to the mastery of the elements of argument. Most of us are familiar with the problems encountered by students in reading and responding to a difficult text. The problems are multiple: unfamiliarity with the subject, limited vocabulary, weak sense of metaphor, inability to recognize clues of organization and development. Many of these problems are clearly the result of too little practice — not enough careful attention to hard texts, not enough instruction in the mechanics of reading such material. It's also possible, as Sven Birkerts suggests in *The Gutenberg Elegies,* that reading is becoming more tedious as electronic communication effects a radical change in consciousness and literacy. But so far, there is no real substitute for reading in the print media. (Even Bill Gates and Nicholas Negroponte write books to tell us about computers.) Diagnosing the reading difficulties at the beginning of the course — through short quizzes and discussions — can tell us where to offer help.

If the amount of reading many of us do has declined, the amount of listening has greatly increased. But instruction in listening has not kept pace. Jay Heinrichs, author of "How Harvard Destroyed Rhetoric" (*Harvard Magazine,* July–August 1995) deplores the scarcity of serious academic interest in public speech. Rhetoric at Harvard was once, of course, the study of persuasive oratory. And rhetorical theory, whether or not we use the vocabulary of Aristotle or the Sophists, still animates any study of formal argument. Today the proliferation of "undisciplined argument" has convinced Mr. Heinrichs that the study of public speech should be restored. "Too few citizens," he says, "know how to listen critically."

READING CRITICALLY

1. Elsewhere in this manual I've suggested calling attention to the vocabulary of an assigned reading *before* students read it. Pointing out the clues that reveal the organization and development of a long, complex argument, again before students read the whole piece, can help them read it more effectively and with greater confidence. Most students find outlining tiresome and unenlightening, partly because they don't do it well, partly because many long articles defy conventional outlining. But early in the course, outlining one or two pieces on the board as students follow the text of an assigned essay can give a sense of what organization means and how it controls the development of the argument. Whether or not they outline their assignments, almost all students will find it useful to write a brief summary of an argument as a means of review. I consider practice in précis writing an essential part of any course that requires critical reading.

2. The primary goals of critical reading, of course, are, first, understanding the argument and, then, determining how effectively the arguer supported his claim. But there are additional benefits to be derived from careful reading, benefits that can directly affect the student's writing. Critical reading, which often means over-reading, invites an appreciation of language. Winston Churchill spoke of the advantages of having been a relatively slow learner who had to repeat his lessons: "I got into my bones the essential structure of the ordinary British sentence — which is a noble thing."

    This is where annotation pays off for the prospective writer. Students who must respond physically as well as mentally, by writing in the margins, should become more careful readers — more sensitive to diction and to the rhythms of a variety of styles and modes of organization that can be adapted for their own papers.

11

LISTENING CRITICALLY

1. Many school libraries have collections of recorded speeches and debates. Tapes allow replay of portions for class analysis. Just as students gloss a written text, they can annotate an oral presentation, expressing approval or disapproval, asking questions when they hear a doubtful statement. The instructor can model critical listening by stopping the tape at relevant intervals and offering a running commentary. She explains the reasons for her judgments and encourages additional response from the class. Students can listen for examples of logical argument and persuasive language. They can also learn to recognize clichés, slogans, short cuts, and other departures from clear thinking. (See Chapter 7.) With relatively little practice, students can become adept at the art of listening.

2. Deborah Tannen, professor of linguistics at Georgetown University, has written several books that interpret the conversational styles of different cultures as well as of men and women, among them *You Just Don't Understand: Women and Men in Conversation* (Ballantine, 1991) and *The Argument Culture: Moving from Debate to Dialogue* (Random House, 1998). Tannen's discussions emphasize the failure to listen attentively and with a will to understand as a major impediment to fruitful communication.

3. Careful listening plays a significant role in jury trials and formal investigations. In some celebrated cases, jurors seemed to have listened selectively. Students may be surprised to learn that jurors are not permitted to take notes during a trial or to ask questions of witnesses. A lawyer who has proposed changes in the jury system says, "Jurors often ignore the instructions or misapply them." We can ask students to be alert to televised trials or congressional committee hearings as sources of exercises in careful listening. Courtrooms, as Toulmin observed, are model venues of argumentation.

4. In learning to listen with attention to the speech of others, students may also improve their ability to hear their own language in writing. Because many students are able to hear errors in grammar and usage that escape the eye, I often ask them to read their papers aloud before submitting them.

Bibliography

Atwan, Robert, Donald McQuade, and John W. Wright. *Edsels, Luckies, and Frigidaires.* New York: Delta Publishing Co., 1979.

"The Content of Television Talk Shows: Topics, Guests, and Interactions." Michigan State U. study, 1995. Commissioned by the Henry J. Kaiser Family Foundation.

Corbett, Edward P. J. *Classical Rhetoric for the Modern Student.* New York: Oxford U. Press, 1971.

Kurtz, Howard. *Hot Air: All Talk All the Time. An Inside Look at the Performers and the Pundits.* New York: New York Times Book, 1996.

LOOKING CRITICALLY

1. This new section examines the visual arguments in commercial advertisements, cartoons, and photojournalism. (See Chapter 3, "Claims of Fact,"

question 5, for more discussion about ads.) Students are often unaware of the messages that even the simplest landscape or interior is capable of delivering — claims of fact, value, and policy. The great Hungarian photographer, André Kertesz, whose reception in New York was less than friendly, was told, "Your pictures talk too much." And, in fact, his photographs of people reading (*On Reading*, Penguin, 1982) are exquisite examples of value claims.

2. At this writing the TV films that document the suffering of ethnic Albanians expelled from Kosovo are powerful arguments that seem to need no verbal text. Students can profitably explore the impact of the claims underlying such visual imagery and ask whether pictures alone can be sufficient to justify a conclusion. If so, why? Or are words necessary to give additional, perhaps conflicting, evidence? What warrants underlie these implied claims?

3. Students in the class who know something about photography can be asked to explain the way in which composition, color, and other attributes work to convey a point of view. Or a member of the school art department can be invited to speak on the subject of visual argumentation in ads and photojournalism.

4. Explaining the implicit argument in an ad that relies largely on visual imagery is an obvious subject for oral presentation in which visual aids can be used to good effect.

5. Some students may be interested in examining the implied claims in movie posters, such as those they see at the video store. Several critics have suggested interpretations that are not so obvious to the untrained eye. They are entertainingly summarized in *Civilization*, April/May 1999, pp. 35 ff.

6. Another accessible subject is fashion advertising, which has come under fire in recent years. Some of the most provocative ads, by Calvin Klein, are directed at young people of college age who will probably recognize the implied claims.

RESPONDING ONLINE

Few instructional methods bring home to the student writer the nature of critical reading and revising better than online peer responding. But many teachers have become frustrated when they first attempt to use computer networks for peer responding, sometimes to the extent that they eventually reject online responding altogether, and this in spite of the many exciting successes reported by instructors who use networked computers in writing instruction.

1. The principal rule for instructors who wish to bring their students into the networked writing environment is not to expect too much too soon. Most groups of students respond amazingly well to the requirement to work online, but some resist, probably responding more to their own sense of inadequacy with computers than from any inherent antipathy toward technology.

As should happen any time people are introduced to a new environment, especially one as potentially intimidating as networked computers, the instructor should allow considerable time for the students to explore the terrain on their own. There are a number of ways of doing this; perhaps the most straightforward is to have students send each other brief online autobiographies and respond to them uncritically, or exchange online reactions to a local event or important happening.

The instructor should not feel that this acclimatizing is a poor use of time. Most writing done in the industrialized world is done on computers, and an increasing amount of that writing is being done over computer networks. The time may be approaching when "writing" will become synonymous with "writing online"; the writing instructor will more and more come to see the student's ease and dexterity with online writing to be as important as the student's ease and dexterity with language itself.

2. One of the well-documented benefits of online responding is that students write much more than they do in non-networked classrooms, but this benefit can also mean an intimidating increase in the presumed need to evaluate student writing. Instructors experienced in online peer work, however, have developed means by which students can be held accountable for their online assignments and yet the instructor can avoid being overwhelmed by a barrage of electronic text. Although methods vary, the instructor should pay attention to the way student e-mail accounts are assigned, the nature of the text editors the students will be using, the particular characteristics of how a local "mailer" manages e-mail traffic, and the way e-mail client software (such as Eudora or Pegasus) can direct, file, and collate student messages. All of these elements of the online peer environment contribute to managing student work in responsible ways.

3. Using computer networks for peer online responding to student drafts encourages students to develop greater critical reading and revising skills independently of the kind of continual teacher monitoring found in the traditional writing classroom. But occasions arise that require the specific guidance and intervention of the instructor. Generally, there are two kinds of these requirements for intervention: pedagogical and behavioral.

   a. The instructor intervenes pedagogically online when review of the students' drafting or online responding indicates a need for information or advice.

   b. The instructor intervenes for behavioral reasons when students take advantage of the freedoms of online writing to engage in disruptive or illegal behavior. Such behavior may include harassment of various kinds, provocative statements that extend beyond the boundaries of academic discourse, or illegal use of electronic resources. Occasionally (but very rarely) students will engage in "flame wars," or heated verbal exchanges serving no academic purpose.

   In these cases, the instructor sends mail to one or more parties emphasizing that online communication within the classroom context must remain within the terms of the class's policies and that otherwise sanctions may be imposed.

CHAPTER 3
Claims
(text pages 51–105)

CLAIMS OF FACT

1. Students have little difficulty understanding claims of fact. But before giving an assignment, I offer a dozen or more examples of such claims to make clear what kinds of arguments they produce. These are in addition to examples in the book.

2. If students have already elected a major or are about to do so, they can find subjects in their areas of specialization. At this point library research need not be emphasized. Students are often able to find sufficient factual data in their memories or their notes. (Wherever possible, they should, of course, give credit to their sources, even to a lecturer in an academic course.)

   I point out that the reports they may be asked to make on the job are often claims of fact, in which the students provide proof that a condition exists or that something has been found to be true as a result of research. The claims, or thesis statements of their essays, correspond to the conclusions of their reports, which, like the claims, may appear first. *Example* (in an article about food colorants): "The development of organic chemistry produced a series of compounds that are well suited to coloring food. Today most of the food colorants are chemicals produced by synthesis from simple basic materials." (*A Progress Report,* Massachusetts Agricultural Station, July–August 1974.)

   Such straightforward factual reports are not likely to be models of creativity, but they emphasize other important qualities of good writing: adequate support, a direct, unadorned style, and clear transitions between ideas. They offer practice in the kind of clear exposition that all writers are well advised to master before they go further.

3. More challenging are factual claims that are clearly controversial. Some will require only reflection on personal observation as support; others will need objective data. *Examples:* "The students on this campus are increasingly conservative." "Teaching writing on the word processor will not produce better writers." "Children are now judged to be reliable witnesses in child-abuse cases." "Attractive people are regarded by others as more intelligent and sensitive than unattractive people."

   Encourage students to stick to the facts and avoid direct expression of value judgments (although, of course, these may be implicit).

4. Another source of assignments may be the materials in Part One's short debates and Part Three's, "Opposing Viewpoints." Ask students to choose one of the subjects and, after reading all or most of the selections, derive a limited factual claim. *Example:* "Animal experimentation has provided enormous medical benefits for human beings."

   The supporting materials will not be original. This assignment tests the writer's ability to extract relevant data in support of a thesis, express the facts in his or her own language, and organize them logically.

15

5. In this edition we continue to include advertisements that represent all the elements of argument. In our culture ads are the most prominent examples of abbreviated arguments that often conceal as much as they reveal, and students enjoy uncovering the missing elements. One caution: Although students may have studied ads in high school and can analyze them with some sophistication, they are disposed to treat all advertisement as untruthful. Ads that conceal or distort are usually the most interesting to examine, but I try to get students to make careful distinctions between the ads that support their claims, or seem to, and those that don't.

6. Inevitably, controversial claims will move student writers to ascribe causes. (A discussion of causal argument has been added to Chapter 3.)

   A number of tragic school shootings occurred in 1998 and 1999, both in the United States — Arkansas, Kentucky, Colorado — and abroad, in Scotland and Canada. They occasioned an outpouring of analyses, impassioned attempts to discover the *causes* of such aberrant behavior in children.

   Students probably have discussed these events in their high school classes. They have also expressed their opinions about the causes to newspaper and television viewers. The social and psychological conditions that may have contributed to these tragedies are subjects for written assignments. So are suggested solutions as claims of policy.

7. Students must be cautioned to avoid assuming that explanations imply justification. For example, according to psychology professor Erwin Staub, the atrocities that occurred in Kosovo province can be explained: " [E]ven violent leaders often express and even share needs of their people. The needs of the Serbs for a feeling of security and for identity as a people are intense." But, he goes on to say, although these needs help to explain Serb behavior, "they cannot justify it."[1]

Classic Arguments

The selections in Part Four, "Classic Arguments," provide more examples of the elements of argument. For comments on the use of these essays, please see the discussions under "Classic Arguments" in these notes.

CLAIMS OF VALUE

1. As they begin to write, students will discover that the line between claims of fact and claims of value is often blurred, but in real-life arguments outside the classroom, these distinctions are not crucial. We make them in the classroom largely because they allow us to examine the elements more closely. Before beginning to write a claim of value, students should consult the "Writer's Guide to the Evaluation Paper," which summarizes the process.

2. Claims of value are more demanding than claims of fact. Facts remain important, but now students must express an attitude toward them. Despite the fact that values are a part of almost every argument — even in claims of fact they may be implicit in the choices of subjects and data —

[1] *The Campus Chronicle,* University of Massachusetts, Amherst, April 23, 1999, p. 1.

16

students are sometimes unclear about how to uncover and express them. These approaches may be helpful:

a. *Ask personal questions.* What do you want out of life? Do you dislike anything about yourself? Do you have religious beliefs? If so, how do they influence your behavior? What are the good things about your family? What are the most valuable things you own? What kind of country do you want the United States to be? And so on. (Of course, for purposes of the exercise the answers need not be true, and it should be clear to students that they are under no obligation to bare their souls. On the other hand, most students, like the rest of us, enjoy talking about themselves.)

The answers that emerge can be written on the board, listed as positive and negative values. You will probably have to change the language, finding more precise terms than the ones that the students offer. This exercise defines values and value systems in a readily understandable way. Values as a form of support will be discussed more fully in Chapter 5, but this discussion should assist students to find the values that can be defended in their value claims.

b. *Analyze one or two essays in the text to discover the values of the author.* Look at "From *Crito*," in which Socrates argues against his right to avoid punishment. What character traits does Socrates reveal about himself, both explicitly and implicitly? What traits in the citizen does Socrates admire? What traits does he condemn? How would you define his value system?

I ask students to answer such questions in short, in-class assignments — fifteen minutes — for which they must produce a well-organized paragraph: clear topic sentence and sufficient supporting material. Because they stress economy and directness, such assignments are useful for teaching some elements of style.

3. As with claims of fact, students can draw on campus experience for subjects that lend themselves to class discussion, outlining, and reinforcing the ways in which claims of value differ from claims of fact. *Examples:* "Student evaluations of teachers are worthless." "Funds for Gay Awareness Week are unjustified."

4. In this unit, too, I point out that claims of value are often required on the job in the form of personnel reports or reports that evaluate marketing strategies and campaigns. If students are interested, topics for such papers can be obtained from books on technical writing or from the business departments of the school.

5. A ready-to-use anthology of material for claims of value appears in a special supplement of the *Wall Street Journal*, March 5, 1998, called "Divining the American Character." It includes more than a dozen articles on how "the bedrock morals co-exist uneasily with a desire 'to live and let live.'" Needless to say, several of the articles deal with President Clinton and public approval–disapproval of his public and private performance.

CLAIMS OF POLICY

1. Since claims of policy assert that something should or should not be done, they presuppose the existence of a problem needing solution. I emphasize that both facts and values are indispensable to defense of a policy claim,

17

because in many arguments students will first have to establish that a problem exists, then underscore how the desired values will be served by adoption of the proposed solution.

2. As an introduction to this unit, short problems, either real or hypothetical, can test the ability of students to find solutions — that is, to defend claims of policy. The facts are clearly laid out in the summary of the problem. In order to justify the solution, students will need to expose the values that underlie their claims. *Example of a real problem:*

The Plagiarism Problem

John Jones, a senior at U____ M____, was enrolled in a second-semester writing course, *Writing about Film.* A few weeks before the end of the semester he suffered a crisis in his love life. The woman who had been his inseparable companion suddenly informed him that she was no longer interested in continuing their friendship. John lost control of himself for a few weeks; he stayed in his room brooding, drank heavily every night, and stopped going to classes. Three days before the end of the semester, he found out that in order to pass the film course and then to graduate, he had to fulfill a final assignment — attend a film and write a review of it. Frantic, John went to the library, copied out a review of a film by a professional critic, and submitted it to the instructor. The instructor recognized the plagiarism and failed John for the course. The failure meant that John could not graduate despite the fact that he had a job waiting for him in Seattle. He argued with the instructor to no avail. The instructor said that he had made it very clear from the beginning of the semester that any plagiarism would result in a failure for the course. John appealed to the provost, who had the authority to grant a Pass for the course.

Question: Should the provost rule that John need not do anything more to fulfill the writing course and allow him to graduate?

3. I have called attention to this problem in the text, but perhaps it bears repeating. In defending claims of policy, students must guard against offering solutions for enormous problems that have defied solution for decades or even centuries. Their ambitions may be laudable, but nevertheless they should be urged to confine themselves to solutions that can be defended in 750 words.

4. "Opposing Viewpoints" is a collection of problems in search of solutions. Assign readings in any of the subjects and ask students to propose solutions based on their evaluations of the arguments.

In defending their claims of policy students should try to use the pattern of organization we call *defending the stock issues* — need, plan, and advantage (see "Writing an Argumentative Paper"). This pattern permits them to be exhaustive without becoming confused by a multitude of details and a variety of possible approaches.

5. Policy claims are, of course, inherent in any business or professional activity. Ask students who have job experience to write out short summaries of specific problems they remember having encountered on the job, either their own or someone else's. The problems should be substantive, and the facts should be clearly stated. Then ask other students to suggest solutions. Students may also ask for examples of problems from the business departments of the school.

These short writing exercises emphasize clarity, accuracy, and a sensitivity to the audience — the employer, supervisor, or other employees — who will act on the decision.

If the solutions differ, students may discuss the differences and try to uncover the reasons for them. Do the differences derive from lack of sufficient data or from conflicting values? Can the differences be reconciled?

6. After reading "The Right to Bear Arms," students may be interested in pursuing the anti–gun-control arguments based on the Second Amendment to the Constitution. If there is time they can write to The Second Amendment Foundation, 12500 N.E. 10th Place, Bellevue, WA 98005 for material. This foundation, which "defends our constitutional heritage to privately own and possess firearms," has published a series of monographs with such titles as *The Great American Gun War* and *Of Arms and the Law.*

7. Not surprisingly, gun control reemerges as an issue of intense controversy after a mass shooting, such as the massacre in Littleton, Colorado, on April 20, 1999. A TV news report pointed out that the recent episodes of murder and injury in schools have all occurred in rural or small-town institutions. The report argues that big urban schools in poor neighborhoods have remained relatively unscathed, in large part because of strict inspection and surveillance of weapons. A comparison-and-contrast paper might document the differences between gun control measures in small-town and urban schools.

8. The bibliography on gun-control policy is very large. A few items of interest are:

Kenneth T. Lyons, president of the International Brotherhood of Police Officers, before the Senate Judiciary Committee on August 3, 1993. An argument for banning assault weapons.

Jacob Sullum, "Weapon Assault," *Reason*, July 1994.

9. See also Chapter 13, "Corporate Responsibility." Gun manufacturers may be the next defendants in lawsuits charging corporate irresponsibility.

DEBATE: WHICH REMEDY FOR DRUG ADDICTION PROMISES GREATER BENEFITS FOR SOCIETY — LEGALIZATION OR FORCED TREATMENT?

1. The debate over legalization of drugs thrives on analogies. One side likens criminalization of drugs to prohibition of alcohol from 1919 to 1933 under the Eighteenth Amendment, which it terms a disaster. The other side points to modest success in the widening prohibition of tobacco, another potent drug. In addition, drug policies in other countries, notably Switzerland and the Netherlands, are invoked to prove that models exist for our own failed programs. Students should consider the reasons that analogies can offer slippery support in claims of policy.

2. *Advertising.* Data provided by recent studies from the University of Michigan Institute for Social Research and the U.S. Justice Department show an alarming rise in drug use among the young, including junior high schoolers. Thirteen percent of eighth graders used marijuana in 1994, double the number of 1991. According to the director, the Michigan study should remind us of the 1960s, when drug use emerged from the shadows.

An organization called Partnership for Responsible Drug Information accuses Partnership for a Drug-Free America of advertising that contributes to the problem. (Students have surely seen these ads on TV.) The message is criticized for "exaggerating the dangers of illegal drugs, especially marijuana, in order to scare young people from trying them." But, the argument goes, when young people discover that the dangers are not real, they "jump to the opposite conclusion, that drugs are less dangerous than the reality." How do students evaluate the antidrug appeals? Which kinds of appeals are most effective? Ask students to try their hands at creating antidrug ads that would make a strong impression on teenagers. Perhaps they can find a way to test them outside the classroom.

3. A short debate in the *New York Times*, November 17, 1998, p. D9, argues the question: "Marijuana Votes: Bane or Benefit? Voters in Alaska, Arizona, Nevada, Oregon and Washington have approved initiatives to legalize marijuana for medical use. Does this application encourage marijuana abuse?" Jim McDonough, Director of Strategy for the White House Drug Control Office, says yes. Sam Vagenas, Executive Director, National Council for Drug Control, says no.

Bibliography

DiIulio, John J. "Two Million Prisoners are Enough." *Wall Street Journal*, March 12, 1999, p. A19. Argues that too many nonviolent drug offenders are in prison.

Friedman, Milton. "There's No Justice in the War on Drugs." *New York Times*, January 11, 1998, p. A19. Emphasizes "disproportionate imprisonment of blacks" and "destruction of inner cities."

Miron, Jeffrey A. "The Case for Making Drugs Legal." *The Boston Globe*, June 21, 1996, p. E1.

Stares, Paul B. *Global Habit: The Drug Problem in a Borderless World.* Washington, DC: Brookings Institution, 1996. Argues for continuing negative controls like sanctions against drug trafficking but says that "positive controls, including treatment and prevention must become the dominant means of reducing production and consumption."

CHAPTER 4
Definition
(text pages 106–51)

1. I often begin this unit by dividing the class into four or five groups and assigning to each group the definition of a common object — book, bed, chair, cup, shoe. The definitions that emerge from the group are then compared to those in the dictionary. (The definitions by students are often remarkably close.)

After this exercise I ask students to describe the process of definition they have just engaged in. As the discussion proceeds, students discover, first of all, that in matters of definition we know more than we can tell. (See Michael Polanyi's fascinating examination of this in *The Tacit Dimen-*

sion.) Apart from this philosophical dilemma, the attempt to define these familiar objects gives practice in distinguishing the properties that separate similar objects or objects belonging to the same genres. Equally important, students must think of examples if they are to make useful distinctions — between a shoe and a boot, between a chair and a stool, between a book and a magazine. The same necessity to resort to examples will become even clearer when they define abstract terms.

2. You may assign a single vague or ambiguous term, on which there is sure to be disagreement, for an extended discussion by each member of the class: success; the good life; normal sexuality; maturity; heroism; necessities, comforts and luxuries.

   Some or all of the completed papers may be duplicated and distributed to the whole class. Through a discussion or written assignment the class may examine the criteria governing the different definitions. Can we reach a consensus? Why or why not? What are the implications of success or failure in reaching consensus about these particular terms?

3. I ask students to tackle the definitions of words that have acquired several, sometimes contradictory, meanings. *Example:* discrimination. For most students, this word carries a negative connotation. I sometimes offer the following example:

   > A young woman who knows nothing about the mechanics of a car finds herself stranded in a parking lot because the engine of her car will not start. Passing near her are two people — a young man and a young woman. The car owner ignores the young woman and turns to the young man, asking him if he can identify and perhaps solve the problem of the stalled car.

   Does this action represent *discrimination* in the negative sense? Students must explain their answers in such a way as to make clear how they define the term.

   They might also be directed to examine the use of the word in aesthetic criticism. Why has the word taken on negative connotations in other areas of discourse? Before writing on the conflicting meanings of a term, students should consult "A Note on Comparison and Contrast."

4. Students can find examples of implicit definitions even in their popular songs. *Example:* Pink Floyd in "The Wall": "We don't need no education. We don't need no thought control. . . . Teachers, leave us kids alone." How is education defined in this song?

   Stereotype has suffered the same fate as *discrimination.* I've discussed with students a different perception of a word almost always treated nowadays as a reflection of prejudice. From *The Biosexual Factor* by Richard Hagen:

   > Stereotypes are the stuff of prediction. Used correctly, they can save us a great deal of grief. If ignored, they may exact a price. The teenage girl who hitchhikes alone because she doesn't accept stereotypic warnings about male sexual behavior is likely to learn a lot about stereotypes.

5. In recent years the definition of *disability* has received critical attention from the medical and legal professions. The American Psychiatric Association lists more than three hundred illnesses, among them "road rage" and

"jury duty disorder." (*New York Times,* Week In Review, September 28, 1997.) Students can look up rulings on the Americans with Disabilities Act in *Facts on File* for June 27, 1998. It provides information on cases that broaden the definition.

DEBATE: DOES THE AMERICAN JURY SYSTEM DELIVER JUSTICE?

1. Toulmin compared arguments to lawsuits. Jury trials, in which the adversarial process is so clearly exhibited, can be a rich source for examination of the elements of the Toulmin model. Fortunately, noteworthy jury trials are reported in all the media and are readily available to students.

   The right to a trial by a jury of one's peers, guaranteed by the Constitution, rejects justice dispensed by despots and those of a different class. But judgments by juries of one's peers may also be flawed. Would the process be fairer if each juror voted without talking to fellow jurors? Not necessarily. Michael Walzer, in *Spheres of Justice* (Basic Books, 1988, p. 308) defends the use of power by some jurors in the jury room:

   > The jury room is one more setting for the unequal exercise of power. Some of the members have more rhetorical skill, or personal charm, or moral force, or simple stubbornness than others, and they are more likely to determine the verdict. We might think of such people as "natural leaders" in the sense that their leadership doesn't hang on their wealth or birth or even their education; it is intrinsic to the political process. If the jurors never met or talked with one another but simply listened to the arguments of the lawyers, thought their own thoughts, and then voted, natural leaders would never appear. The power of the more passive jurors would certainly be enhanced by such a procedure; whether verdicts would be better or worse, I don't know. But I suspect that the jury system as a whole would be devalued, and that individual jurors would value their own roles less. For we commonly think of truth emerging from discussion — much as we think of policies emerging from the give-and-take of political debate. And it is better, more satisfying, to share in the discussions and debates, even if unequally, than to abolish them for the sake of simple equality.

2. In recent years, most strikingly in the notorious O. J. Simpson case, we have observed a new dynamic at work to influence a verdict: jury nullification. In such an action the jurors reject (or nullify) the evidence presented by the prosecution and in the words of Alan Dershowitz (*Contrary to Popular Opinion*, Pharos Books, 1992, p. 28):

   > [They] view the evidence through the prism of their own experience. Jurors are more likely to sympathize with the arguments of those with whom they most closely identify. And many jurors identify on the basis of race, class, religion, gender and ethnicity.

   Another defense of jury nullification: "When a clear conflict between our conceptions of justice and the rule of law is irreconcilable . . . I think justice must be given priority." (Randy E. Barnett, *The Structure of Liberty: Justice and the Rule of Law*, Clarendon Press, 1998, p. 130.)

   Some students may want to argue for or against jury nullification. It's a daunting assignment, but there are always a few prospective lawyers in the class who would be glad to take it on. The paper should be at least 1000 words.

3. Part I in the Dershowitz book is titled "Judges, Justices, Juries and the Courts." Of special interest here are "Street Justice Ruled in the Rodney King Case" and "Juries Answer Only to Conscience."

4. Ask students to evaluate the appeals to values in some famous speeches to juries, among others, by Clarence Darrow on the death penalty in the Loeb–Leopold case in 1924, Bartolomeo Vanzetti in the Sacco–Vanzetti trial in 1921 (see Chapter 5, "Evidence," item 5), and by both the defense and the prosecution of the Catonsville nine in 1968.

CHAPTER 5
Support
(text pages 152–98)

FACTS AND INFERENCES

1. Students seem to subscribe to the belief that a knowledge of the facts is sufficient to induce a change in our habits and attitudes, but there is plenty of expert evidence that the plain truth is not enough. Robert Sternberg, a Yale University psychologist, says, "People will go to great lengths to avoid information that contradicts their original stories. There's a lot of research that shows that people seek to confirm what they think, rather than disconfirm what they think." (*Boston Globe,* August 21, 1993, p. 7.)

   An interesting area for research by students is the relationship between facts about food and the choices people make. Several studies over the years suggest that the facts don't cause most people to alter their eating habits. Students can survey classmates to determine if their behavior confirms the results of these studies.

2. Ask students to create a set of facts, then request that their classmates derive inferences about the actions or people involved. *Examples:* the contents of a grocery cart in the checkout line; an accident; a crime.

3. Assign reading of the following passage. Ask students to write either a short or a long essay that summarizes some of the inferences we draw from observing what people wear. Since the subject is so large (this excerpt is part of a book about clothing), this exercise gives students practice in narrowing the subject of discussion and choosing a thesis statement or paragraph that can be adequately developed in the number of words assigned.

   For thousands of years human beings have communicated with one another first in the language of dress. Long before I am near enough to talk to you on the street, in a meeting, or at a party, you announce your sex, age, and class to me through what you are wearing — and possibly give me important information (or disinformation) as to your occupation, origin, personality, opinions, tastes, sexual desires, and current mood. I may not be able to put what I observe into words, but

I register the information unconsciously, and you simultaneously do the same for me.

By the time we meet and converse we have already spoken to each other in an older and more universal tongue.

—Alison Lurie
The Language of Clothing

4. On September 15, 1995, the *New York Times* published a report giving several different versions of an alleged crime: the shooting of a black police officer by a white police officer (p. B1). The white officer argued that he had mistaken the victim for a criminal. The *Times* summarized the disputed accounts in a chart labeled "Sorting It Out." The chart included three different views of the shooting by witnesses and participants and three different opinions of the wound by medical examiners.

A written assignment on this story calls for a clear thesis statement or paragraph, extraction of the most important data, and arrangement of materials, in an orderly and emphatic way. Above all, it calls for an acknowledgment of the distinctions between facts and inferences in the testimony reported in the article and in the students' interpretations of the testimony. Not least, the students find this assignment interesting and provocative.

5. Ask students to look up information by advocates on both sides of the controversies surrounding one of the popular natural mysteries: the Loch Ness monster, the Bermuda Triangle, Findhorn, Bigfoot, or Sasquatch, etc. Then assign a paper, short or long, that reviews the data on both sides and tries to come to a conclusion regarding the validity of the respective claims. Have students justify their conclusions by defending the evidence. If students find that they cannot make up their minds, this is also a conclusion, but they should be prepared to say why the evidence on both sides proved equally strong or equally weak.

The sighting of UFOs and stories of abduction by aliens continue to be reported and, like a belief in astrology, are hard to put down. Some polls reveal that a majority of Americans believe in UFOs and are certain that they have seen them. Students can examine the reports as they appear in the supermarket tabloids and then read explanations by scientists as a way of distinguishing between spurious and sound evidence and reasoning.

The article by Curtis Peebles can lead students to *The Skeptical Inquirer* of May/June 1998, which includes a special section entitled "The Alien Files." The articles in this section examine several phenomena associated with a belief in alien abduction and visitation. One article by a psychologist says that "a study of 126 schoolchildren and 224 undergraduates shows knowledge of aliens is related more to watching television than to having the relevant experiences." Three articles demystify the origins of the crashed "saucer" in Roswell, New Mexico. One article that students might find of special interest reveals the myth-making behind the movie, *Men in Black*.

6. Most students will have opinions about the television program *The X-Files*. Ask them how they respond to the absence of support for the mysteries they dramatize.

EVIDENCE

1. From the first paper students have been required to use evidence. Having now read the more elaborate explanations of both factual and opinion evidence in Chapter 5, students can return to their claims of fact, value, and policy and reevaluate the facts and opinions in their essays. Would more data strengthen their claim? If so, what kind? Where can it be found? Would additional expert opinion make their arguments more convincing? If so, whose opinions? Where can they be found?

   If the students show some interest in revising their papers to include more data, encourage them to do so.

2. A popular exercise calls on students to look up the *New York Times* edition that appeared on their birthdays and write a paper that emphasizes straightforward presentation of data to support their claims. Students must find a thesis around which the information can be organized — about the kinds of films being shown, the nature of women's fashion, advertisements for jobs, scientific discoveries of the day, crimes, etc.

3. Advertisements again. This time students choose ads that offer information about the products. They then evaluate the data. In some cases, of course, they will be unequipped to decide whether the data are accurate or sufficient, but if the ads are directed to a lay audience, readers have a right to ask questions about the sufficiency, relevance, and recency of the data. In other words, if readers think that evidence for the virtues of the product is inadequate, what else would they want to know?

4. Students sometimes approach the subject of information in ads with the preconception that ads do not offer information — only slogans. Students may therefore be asked to contrast two or more ads that offer different amounts and qualities of information. Is information more important in some kinds of ads than others — for example, in automobile advertisements, which are often dense with facts?

5. If there is time for lengthier papers, ask students to examine the evidence in the following cases (or any others that remain controversial):

   a. the Sacco–Vanzetti case, 1921
   b. the kidnapping and murder of the Lindbergh baby, 1932
   c. the assassination of President John F. Kennedy, 1963
   d. the kidnapping of Patty Hearst, 1974
   e. the Bernhard Goetz case, 1987
   f. the Rodney King case, 1991
   g. the O. J. Simpson case, 1994
   h. The Louise Woodward case, 1998

6. In leading students to examine the credentials of experts, ask them to consider the authors in the text and the "Opposing Viewpoints" as "experts." It will be easy enough to identify such writers as Gordon Allport, a psychologist, and Barbara Allen Babcock, a law professor, as authorities in their fields. Even in more problematic disciplines, such as education, we recognize the authority of Paul Goodman, for example, who spent a lifetime studying and writing about the meaning of education and whose opinions are regarded by other experts as authoritative.

But what are we to say of writers who reflect on their personal experience or expound their philosophies? Why do we think Elisha Dov Hack's views are worth reading? After all, he is no more an "expert" on sexual mores than many of his readers. It might come as a small revelation to students, and pertinent to their participation in a writing course, to recognize that the credibility of Hack and other nonprofessional "experts" is based largely on their excellence as writers. They can discover interesting propositions, and organize, develop, and express them in spirited and highly readable prose. They are intelligent, of course, but also curious about most subjects and well informed about many.

STATISTICS

1. Students usually need practice in reporting statistics — extracting them from news stories and arranging them in interesting and readable form. Students can research the following subjects and report the information as data that might support a claim. They should, of course, limit the time period for the data. Have them submit their prose summaries to their classmates. Are the data clear and accessible to these readers?

   a. world population growth

   b. teenage pregnancies

   c. women in the labor market

   d. growth of ethnic populations in the United States

   e. American marriage patterns

   f. dimensions of poverty

   g. voting patterns in the 1996 elections

2. The three books and one article mentioned below are entertaining and informative references for both teachers and students. They are full of useful examples that should help students avoid some of the common pitfalls in interpreting and reporting statistical evidence.

   Stephen K. Campbell, *Flaws and Fallacies in Statistical Thinking* (Englewood Cliffs, NJ: Prentice-Hall, 1974)

   Darrell Huff, *How to Lie with Statistics* (New York: W. W. Norton, 1954)

   John Allen Paulos, *Innumeracy: Mathematical Illiteracy and Its Consequences.* (New York: Hill and Wang, 1988). Students will discover that six degrees of Kevin Bacon is not so fanciful after all.

   An article in the *Wall Street Journal,* April 12, 1996, p. B1, "Fright by the Numbers: Alarming Disease Data Are Frequently Flawed," calls attention to the need for caution in reading medical statistics.

   > Most of the numbers are extrapolations or estimates — at best. Yet as the media report them, often uncritically and without context, these conjectures assume the mantle of quantifiable fact.

3. Some students may be interested in and sufficiently informed about polling techniques to evaluate some of the famous polling gaffes: the *Literary Digest* poll of 1936 that predicted that Alfred Landon would defeat Franklin D. Roosevelt or the 1948 Gallup poll that predicted Thomas E. Dewey would defeat Harry S. Truman. Students might want to infer the reasons that such mistakes probably will not recur.

APPEALS TO NEEDS AND VALUES

1. A lively and immediate source of appeals to needs and values is found in speeches — students may be directed to *Vital Speeches of the Day,* which publishes speeches from a variety of speechmakers.

   In "Classic Arguments," Part Four of this book, the speech of Martin Luther King Jr., "I Have a Dream," is an outstanding example of spoken discourse that makes a profoundly emotional appeal. Other famous speeches for the purposes of this unit include:

   a. Clarence Darrow's "Address to the Prisoners of Cook County Jail" in 1902
   b. Vice President Richard Nixon's "Checkers" speech in 1952
   c. President John F. Kennedy's Inaugural Address in 1961
   d. Senator Edward Kennedy's TV address explaining to the people of Massachusetts his behavior during and after the accident at Chappaquiddick in 1969

   For example, Darrow's speech is remarkable for the inconsistency of his argument and its numerous fallacies, both of which have been overlooked by textbooks that reprint the address. Edward Kennedy's speech makes a personal appeal, arousing sympathy for his suffering and inducing guilt in the listener for having accused him unjustly.

   Since 1980, the *New York Times* has published "Basic Speeches," delivered by the major candidates in presidential campaigns. These appear in October of the campaign year. All the speeches contain copious and specific references to the values held by the candidates and, presumably, their audiences. The inaugural speeches are also revealing of the attention to values. President Clinton's second Inaugural Address on January 23, 1997, referred to "peace and freedom," "strength and decency of the human spirit," "faith and courage," "patience and a grateful heart," "challenge strengthened by achievement."

2. Advertisements by large corporations (Mobil, United Technologies, Exxon) appearing frequently in newspapers and magazines comment on political and social issues rather than the merits of their products. As short essays they can be useful for examination of values based on what is perceived to be common consent.

   a. What values do the advertisers assume that we share?
   b. What evidence (examples, facts, statistics) do they offer to convince the reader that their proposals will support our values?
   c. What is the tone of the essay (reasonable, generous, angry, sarcastic, humorous)?

3. Also useful are the ads that promise power, riches, great beauty, etc. Many of the most outrageous ones appear in *The National Enquirer* and other gossip sheets.

   a. Can you infer to what audience they make a strong appeal?
   b. What fears, needs, desires do they appeal to?
   c. What attempts are made to provide credibility?

DEBATE: IS ANIMAL RESEARCH NECESSARY
TO SAVE HUMAN LIVES?

1. Peter Singer, a leading advocate of animal rights, has asked why students are so indifferent to discrimination against animals in campus laboratories. If such laboratories exist in your campus, ask students to interview workers responsible for the experiments and then write an evaluative report that explains the nature of the experiments and the justification for them.

2. One justification for medical use of animals is "self-preservation" of the human species, species preservation being a primary instinct of all members of the animal kingdom. Whether this is a moral defense is something students should be prepared to discuss. Students should be alerted to follow news stories about the harvesting of animal organs for transplant to humans.

Bibliography

Langley, Gill, ed. *Animal Experimentation: The Consensus Changes.* New York: Chapman and Hall, 1989.

CHAPTER 6
Warrants

(text pages 199–238)

1. Although the definition of the warrant in Toulmin's *The Uses of Argument* is more complicated than we have made it appear, for the purposes of a freshman composition course, those of us who have used the Toulmin model with some success believe that the model works best if we define the warrant as synonymous with assumption, a belief we take for granted, or a general principle underlying other beliefs and attitudes. If students raise questions, we can always widen the definition.

    For obvious reasons the concept of the warrant is more difficult for students to assimilate than that of support, in part because they have seldom been required to make their assumptions explicit. Fortunately for teaching purposes, the examples that we can use are so numerous and so varied that we may call attention to the warrant repeatedly without losing student interest.

2. Advertisements offer a rich and accessible source of material. Students may choose their own ads for analysis and write or speak about them to the class. The exercise should emphasize discussion of a controversial warrant. For an oral presentation, an ad that contains more than a paragraph of text can be duplicated for distribution, and the whole class can participate in a discussion of the validity of the warrant.

3. Subjects for examination of warrants appear almost every day in school newspapers. Sometimes the subjects are about education or other matters relevant to the function and management of the school; sometimes they

respond to the world outside. Below are some current issues on college campuses today:

a. A proposal to introduce a core requirement designed to change attitudes on race and sex. (What assumptions about education underlie this proposal?)

b. A demand that faculty appointments reflect the percentage of women and minorities in the general population. (What assumptions about education and the social and political functions of the university are at work in this affirmative action proposal?)

c. A demand that Native Americans be allowed to live in a separate dormitory and be given their own student center. (What warrants about ethnic diversity and the goals of an academic institution can be uncovered?)

4. Other sources of analysis of warrants:

a. *Etiquette books.* An interesting assignment would compare etiquette books of a generation or more ago with contemporary ones. (Judith Martin's books are valuable and amusing sources of comment about present-day manners.) Have there been large changes? Small changes? In what areas? On what assumptions about social relationships and freedom have these changes been based?

A new book, *Multicultural Manners: New Rules for a Changing Society* by Norine Dresser (Wiley, 1996) gives rules of etiquette that recognize cultural and ethnic differences in this country. One reviewer of the book said, "For all its value, this book can push cultural tolerance to the breaking point."

b. *Advice columns in newspapers and magazines.* What assumptions about marriage, sexual problems, child rearing, religion, etc. underlie the advice of the columnists?

c. *Magazines for teenagers.* Have they changed in the last fifteen or twenty years? On what assumptions about the lives and values of teenagers have the publishers based their changes?

5. Go back to the earlier papers of definition and defense of value and policy claims and examine the warrants, expressed or unexpressed. *Example:* In defending his decision never to marry, a student writes that he values his freedom. What does he assume about marriage, love, individuality, commitment, etc.?

6. Students enjoy the familiar game in which a disaster has left a small number of people alive, and the players must choose an even smaller number to survive. The choices of the players reflect their assumptions about an ideal world. Whenever classes engage in this exercise, they discover how difficult it is for even a class of twenty fairly similar students to arrive at a consensus. Of course, the players must defend their selection of particular people and the order in which they rank them.

Who Should Survive?

Task: Choose seven of the following people to survive. List them in the order in which you would choose them and indicate the reasons for your selection, i.e., why you chose these particular persons and why you placed them in this particular order.

People:

a. Dr. Dane — thirty-seven, white, no religious affiliation, Ph.D. in history, college professor, in good health (jogs daily), hobby is botany, enjoys politics, married with one child (Bobby).

b. Mrs. Dane — thirty-eight, white, Jewish, rather obese, diabetic, M.A. in psychology, counselor in a mental health clinic, married to Dr. Dane, has one child.

c. Bobby Dane — ten, white, Jewish, mentally retarded with IQ of 70, healthy and strong for his age.

d. Mrs. Garcia — twenty-three, Spanish-American, Catholic, ninth-grade education, cocktail waitress, worked as a prostitute, married at age sixteen, divorced at age eighteen.

e. Jean Garcia — three months old, Spanish-American, healthy.

f. Mary Evans — eighteen, black, Protestant, trade school education, wears glasses, artistic.

g. Mr. Newton — twenty-five, black power advocate, starting last year of medical school, suspected homosexual activity, music as a hobby, physical fitness buff.

h. Mrs. Clark — twenty-eight, black, Protestant, daughter of a minister, college graduate, electronics engineer, single now after a brief marriage, member of Zero Population Growth.

i. Mr. Blake — fifty-one, white, Mormon, B.S. in mechanics, married with four children, enjoys outdoors, much experience in construction, quite handy, sympathizes with antiblack views.

j. Father Frans — thirty-seven, white, Catholic, priest, active in civil rights, former college athlete, farming background, often criticized for liberal views.

k. Dr. Gonzales — sixty-six, Spanish-American, Catholic, doctor in general practice, two heart attacks in the past five years, loves literature and quotes extensively.

ADDITIONAL TYPES OF WARRANTS

In Chapter 6 (199–238) I discuss three main categories of warrants, derived from Ehninger and Brockriede (1953): *authoritative, substantive,* and *motivational* warrants. If you would like to introduce your students to a more complex range of warrants, all of which are subtypes of the three main categories, I have provided discussions of each of seven types below: *authority, generalization, sign, cause and effect, comparison, analogy,* and *values.* A warrants chart on pp. 36–37 shows in schematic form the types of warrants, with examples and critical questions that may help students detect them in arguments. If you do choose to teach these additional types of warrants to your students, you may wish to photocopy and distribute the chart.

Authority

Arguments from authority depend on the credibility of their sources, as in this example.

> [Benjamin] Bloom maintains that most children can learn everything that is taught them with complete competence.[1]

[1]Michael Alper, "All Our Children Can Learn," *University of Chicago Magazine,* summer 1982, p. 3.

Because Benjamin Bloom is a professor of education at the University of Chicago and a widely respected authority on educational psychology, his statement about the educability of children carries considerable weight. Notice that Professor Bloom has qualified his claim by asserting that "most" children, but not all, can learn everything. The reader might also recognize the limits of the warrant — the authority could be mistaken, or there could be disagreement among authorities.

CLAIM:	Most children can learn everything that is taught them with complete competence.
SUPPORT:	Professor Bloom attests that this is so.
WARRANT:	Professor Bloom's testimony is sufficient because he is an accepted authority on educational achievement.
RESERVATIONS:	Unless the data for his studies were inaccurate, unless his criteria for evaluation were flawed, and so on.

Generalization

Arguments from generalization are based on the belief that a general principle can be derived from a series of examples. But these warrants are credible only if the examples are representative of the whole group being described and not too many contradictory examples have been ignored. In the following excerpt the author documents the tragic effects for children born "unnaturally" (outside the mother's womb) or without knowledge of their fathers.

> For years I've collected bits of data about certain unfortunate people in the news: Son of Sam, the Hillside strangler, the Pennsylvania shoemaker who raped and brutalized several women, a Florida man who killed at least thirty-four women, the man sought in connection with the Tylenol scare. All of them grew up not knowing at least one of their natural parents; most knew neither.[2]

In outline the argument takes this form:

CLAIM:	People brought up without a sense of identity with their natural parents will respond to the world with rage and violence.
SUPPORT:	Son of Sam, the Hillside strangler, the Pennsylvania shoemaker, the Florida murderer, the man in the Tylenol scare responded to the world with rage and violence.
WARRANT:	What is true of this sample is true for others in this class.
RESERVATIONS:	Unless this sample is too small or exceptions have been ignored.

Sign

As the name suggests, in arguments based on sign the arguer offers an observable datum as an indicator of a condition. The warrant that a sign is convincing can be accepted only if the sign is appropriate, if it is sufficient, and if other indicators do not dispute it (for example, an argument in which the

---

[2]Lorraine Dusky, "Brave New Babies?" *Newsweek,* December 6, 1982, p. 30.

enjoyment of Virginia Slims is presented as a sign of female liberation). In the following example the warrant is stated:

> There are other signs of a gradual demoting of the professions to the level of ordinary trades and businesses. The right of lawyers and physicians to advertise, so as to reintroduce money competition and break down the "standard practices," is being granted. Architects are being allowed to act as contractors. Teachers have been unionized.[3]

Here, too, a reservation is in order.

CLAIM:	Professions are being demoted to the level of ordinary trades and businesses.
SUPPORT:	Lawyers and physicians advertise, architects act a contractors, teachers have been unionized.
WARRANT:	These business practices are signs of the demotion of the professions.
RESERVATION:	Unless these practices are not widespread.

Cause and Effect

Causal reasoning assumes that one event or condition can bring about another. One can reason from the cause to the effect or from the effect to the cause. The following is an example of reasoning from effect (the claim) to cause (the warrant). The quotation is taken from the famous Supreme Court decision of 1954, *Brown v. Board of Education,* which mandated the desegregation of public school throughout the United States.

> Segregation of white and colored children in public schools has a detrimental effect upon the colored children. The impact is greater when it has the sanction of the law; for the policy of separating the races is usually interpreted as denoting the inferiority of the Negro group. A sense of inferiority affects the motivation of a child to learn. Segregation with the sanction of law, therefore, has a tendency to [retard] the educational and mental development of Negro children and to deprive them of some of the benefits they would receive in a racial[ly] integrated school system.[4]

The outline of the argument would take this form:

CLAIM (EFFECT):	Colored children have suffered mental and emotional damage in legally segregated schools.
SUPPORT:	They suffer from feelings of inferiority, which retard their ability to learn. They are being deprived of important social and educational benefits.
WARRANT (CAUSE):	Legal segregation has a tendency to retard the emotional and mental development of Negro children.

In cause-effect arguments the reasoning may be more complicated than an outline suggests. For one thing, events and conditions in the world are not always the result of single causes, nor does a cause necessarily produce a single result. It is probably more realistic to speak of chains of causes as well as chains of effects. A recent headline emphasizes this form of reasoning: "Ex-

---

[3]Jacques Barzun, "The Professions under Siege," *Harper's,* October 1978, p. 66.
[4]*Brown v. Board of Education of Topeka,* 347 U.S. 487–96 (May 17, 1954).

perts Fear That Unpredictable Chain of Events Could Bring Nuclear War." The article points to the shooting of the Archduke Francis Ferdinand of Austria-Hungary in the Bosnian city of Sarajevo in 1914, which "set in motion a series of events that the world's most powerful leaders could not stop" — that is, World War I.

Or, as another example, opinion polls a few years ago indicated Americans' unwillingness to "approve any bellicose activity, unless U.S. interests are seen as truly vital and are clearly defined."[5] The immediate cause of this isolationism is usually attributed to the "Vietnam syndrome," the relic of a bitter experience in an unpopular war. But this single cause, according to some students of the problem, is insufficient to explain the current mood. History, they say, reveals "decades of similar American resistance to foreign involvements."

Causes can also be either *necessary* or *sufficient.* That is, to contract tuberculosis, it is necessary to be exposed to the bacillus, but this exposure in itself may not be sufficient to bring on the disease. However, if the victim's immune system is depressed for some reason, exposure to the bacillus will be sufficient to cause the illness. Or, to make an example from law and politics: To reduce the incidence of drunk driving, it would be necessary to enact legislation that penalized the drunk driver. But that would not be sufficient unless the police and the courts were diligent in making arrests and imposing sentences.

Comparison

In some arguments characteristics and circumstances in two or more cases are compared to prove that what is true in one case ought to be true in another. Unlike the elements in analogies the things being matched in comparison belong to the same class. The following is a familiar argument based on a comparison of similar activities in different countries at different times. On the basis of these apparent similarities the author makes a judgment about America's future.

> Perhaps I'm wrong, but the auguries seem to me threatening. Like the bourgeoisie of pre–World War I in Europe, we are retreating into our well-furnished houses, hoping the storm, when it comes, will strike someone else, preferably the poor. Our narcissistic passion for sports and fitness reminds me of Germany in the twenties and early thirties, when the entire nation turned to hiking, sun-bathing, and the worship of the body beautiful, in part so as not to see what was happening to German politics — not to speak of the family next door. The belief that gold in the garden is more important than government helped to bring France to defeat in 1940 and near civil war in the 1950s. When the middle class stops believing in government or in the future, it's all over, time truly to sew the diamonds in the lining of your coat and make a run for it.[6]

This is the argument in outline form:

CLAIM: The behavior of many middle-class Americans today threatens our future.

SUPPORT: The same kind of behavior by the Germans in the twenties and thirties and by the French in the thirties and forties led to disaster.

[5]*Public Opinion,* April–May 1982, p. 16.
[6]Michael Korda, "The New Pessimism," *Newsweek,* June 14, 1982, p. 10.

WARRANT: Because such behavior brought disaster to Germany and France, it will bring disaster to America.

But is this warrant believable? Are the dissimilarities between the United States now and these European countries in earlier decades greater than the similarities? For example, if the present American passion for sport and fitness is caused by very different social forces than those that operated in Germany in the twenties and thirties, then the comparison warrant is too weak to support the author's claim.

Analogy

An analogy warrant assumes a resemblance in some characteristics between dissimilar things. Analogies differ in their power to persuade. Some are explanatory; others are merely descriptive. Those that describe are less likely to be useful in a serious argument. In conversation human beings are often likened to other animals — cows, pigs, rats, chickens. Or life and happiness are compared to a variety of objects: "Life is a cabaret," "Life is just a bowl of cherries," "Happiness is a warm puppy." But such metaphorical uses are more colorful than precise. In those examples one quality is abstracted from all the others, leaving us with two objects that remain essentially dissimilar. Descriptive analogies promise immediate access to the reader, as do paintings or photographs. Such short cuts are tempting, but descriptive analogies are seldom enough to support a claim. Consider the following example, which appears in a speech by Malcolm X, the black civil rights leader, criticizing the participation by whites in the march on Washington in 1962 for black rights and employment:

> It's just like when you've got some coffee that's too black, which means it's too strong. What do you do? You integrate it with cream, you make it weak. But if you pour too much cream in it, you won't even know you ever had coffee.[7]

This is the outline of the argument:

CLAIM: Integration of black and white people in the march on Washington weakened the black movement for rights and jobs.

SUPPORT: Putting white cream into black coffee weakens the coffee.

WARRANT: Weakening coffee with cream is analogous to weakening the black rights movement by allowing white people to participate.

The imagery is vivid, but the analogy does not represent convincing proof. The dissimilarities between whitening coffee with cream and integrating a political movement are too great to convince the reader of the damaging effects of integration. Moreover, words like *strong* and *weak* as they apply to a civil rights movement need careful definition. To make a convincing case, the author would have to offer not imagery but facts and authoritative opinion.

The following analogy is more successful because it is explanatory rather than descriptive. The elements on both sides of the analogy are failing or sick human beings and less than productive tests. This excerpt appears in an ar-

---

[7]"Message to the Grass Roots," *Roots of Rebellion,* edited by Richard P. Young (New York: Harper & Row, 1970), p. 357.

ticle by Albert Shanker, president of the American Federation of Teachers, deploring the low scores of American students in national tests.

It's not the first time we've heard about the dismal performance of U.S. students in math: NAEP [National Assessment of Educational Progress] has been giving us the same bad news for twenty years. So it should come as no surprise that our kids are nowhere near "first in the world." What can we expect now? Only, I'm afraid, that another test will be administered two years from now to see if we're doing any better.

Suppose you were feeling terrible and went to a doctor who tested you, said you had a fever, and asked you to come back in two weeks. And suppose you returned every couple of weeks for a year or so to be tested, and every time, you got the same bad news but still no diagnosis and no advice. Few of us would think much of a doctor who did nothing but test us and give us bad news. But that's what's been going on in education for twenty years.[8]

Shanker's argument may be outlined like this:

CLAIM: Testing students in math year after year without proposing remedies is fruitless.

SUPPORT: Testing a sick person again and again without offering a diagnosis or treatment would be considered unacceptable medical practice.

WARRANT: Math tests which fail to diagnose the problem and propose remedies are analogous to medical tests which offer no diagnosis or treatment for the patient.

This analogy, however, suffers from the weakness of all analogies — dissimilarities between the objects being compared. Many physical illnesses may be easier to diagnose and cure than deficiencies in math. The latter are certainly due to a variety of social, economic, and personal problems that are difficult or impossible for the educational system to treat.

Values

Warrants may also reflect needs and values, and readers accept or reject the claim to the extent that they find the warrants relevant to their own goals and standards. In Chapter 6 (199–238), Mrs. Walkup and others based their opposition to development of the Eastern Shore on a value warrant: Rural life is superior to the way of life being introduced by developers. Clearly, numbers of outsiders who valued a more sophisticated way of life did not agree.

The persuasive appeal of advertisements, as we know, leans heavily on value warrants, which are often unstated. Sometime they include almost no printed message except the name of the product accompanied by a picture. The advertisers expect us to assume that if we use their product, we can acquire the desirable characteristics of the attractive people shown using it.

Value warrants are indispensable in arguments on public policy. In the following excerpt from a radio debate, a professor of statistics at Berkeley argues in favor of affirmative action policies to promote the hiring of women faculty. Her claim has been made earlier, but her warrant and any reservations remain unstated. This is her supporting material.

[8]"Testing Is Not Enough," *New York Times,* October 20, 1991, p. E7.

WARRANTS CHART

Type of Warrant	Subtype	Example
Authoritative Warrants are based on the credibility of a source		**Claim:** Cigarette smoking is harmful.
Substantive Warrants are based on beliefs about the reliability of factual evidence	A **Generalization Warrant** is a substantive warrant based on the belief that it is possible to derive a general principle from a series of examples.	**Claim:** Marijuana is a potent medicine for relief of pain in seriously ill patients.
	A **Sign Warrant** is a substantive warrant based on the belief that an observable datum is an indicator of a particular condition.	**Claim:** Press reports and TV news programs deal in lies and deception.
	A **Cause-and-Effect Warrant** is a substantive warrant that assumes that one event or condition can bring about another.	**Claim:** Giving free food to poor countries can be counter-productive.
	A **Comparison Warrant** is a substantive warrant that assumes that what is true in one case ought to be true in another.	**Claim:** The United States should set an annual budget for physician spending, then let doctors do their work.
	An **Analogy Warrant** is a substantive warrant that assumes a resemblance in some characteristics between dissimilar things.	**Claim:** Sports have become the secular religion of America. (Harry Edwards)
Motivational Warrants are based on the values of the arguer and the audience.		**Claim:** People in this country work too hard to enjoy God and family.

SUPPORT:	WARRANT:	CRITICAL QUESTIONS
The surgeon general has determined that cigarette smoking is hazardous to your health.	The surgeon general is a reliable medical authority.	Could the authority be mistaken in this case? Do other reputable authorities disagree?
In controlled experiments marijuana has reduced severe side effects and pain of illness and cancer therapy in several patients.	What was true for the patients in the experiments will undoubtedly be true for many more.	Are the examples representative of the whole group being described? Have contradictory examples been ignored?
In 1992, NBC faked exploding gas tanks in an expose of GM trucks. In the past journalists greatly exaggerated the dangers of dioxin and radon.	Such fakery is a sign of the deceptive practices of the media.	Is the sign appropriate? Is the sign sufficient? Do other indicators dispute the sign?
Poor farmers plant fewer crops if farming becomes unprofitable.	People will lack incentive to provide for themselves if others provide for them.	Is the cited cause sufficient to bring about the effect? Have other possible causes been overlooked?
This practice has enabled Canada to save money without reducing the pay of doctors.	Because this practice is successful in Canada, it should be successful in the United States.	Are the dissimilarities between the things being compared greater than the similarities? Have all or only a few of the important characteristics been compared?
Both sports and religion have gods, saints, houses of worship, and "true believers."	The feelings of veneration for the spectacle and values of sports are analogous to the feelings of adherents of formal religion.	Is the analogy explanatory or merely descriptive? Are there sufficient similarities between the two elements to make the analogy appropriate?
Americans work 20 percent more today than in 1973 and have 32 percent less free time per week.	Work should not be an end in itself but a means to enjoyment of "mental culture, moral and social progress, and the Arts of Living." (J. S. Mill)	Might some people disagree with the arguer's values? Is the value relevant to the claim?

6.9 percent is [a] very tiny proportion of the faculty. You still have to go a long ways to see a woman teaching in this university. Most all of the students go to this university and never, ever have a woman professor, a woman associate professor, even a woman assistant professor teaching them. There's a lack of role models, there's a lack of teaching, and it brings a lack of breadth into the teaching.[9]

The Berkeley professor's argument may be outlined like this:

CLAIM:	The proportion of women on the Berkeley faculty should be increased.
SUPPORT:	Because women are only 6.9 percent of the faculty, most students never have a woman teacher.
WARRANT:	Exposure of students to women faculty is a desirable educational goal.
RESERVATION:	Unless individual women faculty members are significantly less competent than men.

DEBATE: SHOULD WE FEAR THE CLONING OF HUMAN BEINGS?

1. A helpful introduction to this complicated subject: One or two students can provide an oral overview, complete with diagrams and other visual apparatus, to ensure that students understand the process, however roughly. In the *New York Times*, March 3, 1997, there is an exceptionally clear report of Dolly's creation, accompanied by explanatory diagrams.

2. Even this introduction may not be sufficient to guarantee well-informed argument. I would ask students to submit a small, lightly annotated bibliography — three or four articles that cover both sides of the debate — before they try to support their claims.

   Despite the outpouring of books and articles on cloning, the debate is confined essentially to two major issues: predictions of the consequences for humankind and "the unresolved moral and ethical questions surrounding the creation of a human being who is the genetic duplicate of another." (Meredith Wadman, *Wall Street Journal*, January 20, 1998, p. A20. The author covers biomedical research for the British journal *Nature*.)

   "Will Cloning Beget Disaster?" A long debate in the *Wall Street Journal*, May 2, 1997, p. A11, asks a theologian and six members of the sciences and humanities — among them, David Baltimore, Robert Coles, Edmund Teller, and Robert Silverberg — to answer the question.

3. One issue that students will encounter in their reading is the relationship between cloning and abortion. "In efforts to clone humans, would human embryos be destroyed or discarded? If so, there's an ethical issue." (See Ted Peters in the bibliography.)

4. Cloning, of course, lends itself to the dark side of science fiction. In Aldous Huxley's *Brave New World* (1932), with which students may be familiar, one egg arrested in its growth can produce from eight to ninety-six human

---

[9]Elizabeth Scott, quoted in "Affirmative Action: Not a Black and White Issue," National Public Radio, week of April 25, 1977, p. 7

beings, all identical and programmed to perform identical tasks. In 1958 Huxley wrote an essay, "Brave New World Revisited," in which he pointed out that many of his predictions had come true. But had they? Students who know these works can try a paper of comparison and contrast, proving that the predictions of a dehumanized Brave New World did or did not materialize.

Bibliography

Kass, Leon. "The Wisdom of Repugnance." *The New Republic*, June 2, 1997, pp. 17–26.

Krauthammer, Charles. "Of Headless Mice . . . and Men." *Time*, January 91, 1998, p. 76.

Pence, Gregory E. *Who's Afraid of Human Cloning?* New York: Rowman and Littlefield, 1998.

Peters, Ted. *Playing God? Genetic Determination and Human Freedom.* New York: Routledge, 1977. Dr. Peters is a professor of systematic theology at Pacific Lutheran Theological Seminary in Berkeley.

CHAPTER 7
Language and Thought
(text pages 239–82)

1. Again we turn to advertisements for their use of slogans, clichés, and emotive language. Advertising claims in airline ads, we are told by a national advertising group, "promise great buys and then dissolve into airline jargon filled with restrictions." Ask students to examine some airline ads for jargon and code words that are meaningless or slippery.

   A paperback entitled *I Can Sell You Anything* by Carl P. Wrighter (Ballantine, 1972) offers a popular attack on techniques of advertising. Wrighter supports his claims by offering dozens of examples of "weasel words" in specific commercial advertisements. The claims of each ad are clearly stated. Often the argument is exaggerated, and some of the ads will no longer be familiar to students, but they can use Wrighter's formulas as a model, choosing their own ads and substituting their own weasel words.

   An article in the *New York Times,* November 26, 1998, "A Name So Smooth, the Product Glides In," by J. C. Herz, describes in fascinating detail how products are named, that is, how the sounds of letters like z, "one of the fastest sounds in the alphabet," can influence the choice of name for the product. "Orwell was dead wrong," says the author. "The language isn't being crushed under the weight of oppression. It is experiencing an algal bloom of new vocabulary." Students need not be linguists to try to uncover — or imagine — the origins of product names which seem to come out of nowhere — Advil, Nuon, Zima.

2. Have students collect literature from various politically active groups on campus. Assign a study of the language based on some of the categories in

the text: connotations, euphemisms, clichés, slogans, slanted language, picturesque language.

    a. Is the message persuasive? How much of the persuasive effect is due to the way that language is used?

    b. Identify terms that you consider effective and tell why.

    c. Identify terms that you consider ineffective and tell why.

3. Students can find slogans everywhere. The slogans of course, will, differ from year to year and from place to place, depending on the emergence of new issues. In 1996, an election year, some slogans were generated, though not so many as we might have expected. Ask students to compose their own political slogans and defend them. To whom does the slogan appeal? What short cuts have been taken; that is, what questions about your abbreviated argument might be asked by an unfriendly reader?

4. Although slogans were scarce in 1996, there were plenty of clichés — statements of obvious ideas. Students can examine the "Basic Speeches" referred to in assignments for Chapter 5. They might consider answers to the following questions: Can the use of clichés be justified? What would be the effect of substituting unusual ideas, even a surprising and perhaps unpleasant truth?

5. Have students examine some of the classic speeches of the past: Patrick Henry's *Speech before the Virginia Convention of 1775,* Abraham Lincoln's *Gettysburg Address,* Winston Churchill's address to the Congress of the United States of America on December 26, 1941. Students will notice that all of these speeches contain memorable phrases. Ask whether they think that the language in these speeches differs in any significant way from the language of the "Basic Speeches" of 1996. Have them explain any differences and describe how they contribute to the success or failure of particular speeches.

6. Students might try writing their own high school commencement addresses, avoiding both the congratulatory clichés of most graduation addresses and the bitter invective of Jacob Neusner.

7. I have used an excerpt describing the actions of Henry VIII to demonstrate the use of partisan language by a Catholic historian. Below is a passage from a Protestant historian, G. M. Trevelyan, about the same events of the English Reformation, but exhibiting, through the use of selective language, an entirely different point of view. Students may be asked to pick out the words and phrases that indicate slanting.

> It is often falsely asserted that the [Protestant] Reformation was a plunder of the poor; that it dispossessed them of their heritage in favor of a squirearchy [landed proprietor class]. The fact is that the medieval Church, on its financial side, was a squirearchy richer and more jealous of its possessions than any which had existed since the Reformation. What the revolution did was to transfer enormous wealth from one squirearchy to another; from a squirearchy which, in its very nature, was intensely conservative and seldom let go of anything in its possessions, to another which lived far more among the people, and whose extravagances often led to the division of the land, so that there grew up in Elizabethan and Jacobean times a whole class of small yeoman farmers.

The medieval Church was, no doubt, more friendly to the poor than any State Institution of those days would have been. But it was far from that Christian fraternity and generous beneficence which is often claimed for it, and which the earliest Christianity had actually displaced. It was deeply feudalized; it was no longer a really democratic institution in any strict sense of the word. Popes were the most absolute sovereigns of their day, and sometimes the most luxurious and most directly responsible for those wars which were chronic in Christendom.

I have tried to encourage students to uncover other examples in their own texts, but they find this difficult to do. The exercise above will at least induce a healthy caution about the objectivity of textbook writers, even distinguished historians.

DEBATE: SHOULD EBONICS (BLACK ENGLISH) BE TAUGHT IN SCHOOL AS A LANGUAGE IN ITS OWN RIGHT?

1. Although the controversy that erupted in 1996 when the Oakland school board approved black English as a formal language has subsided with a retraction of the resolution, it seems clear that the issues giving rise to the policy remain and will probably reemerge in the future.

    Ebonics as a bridge to the wider use of standard English is one form of bilingual education. Many of our students may not be familiar with Ebonics, but they probably will be aware of the controversy which still rages around the issue of bilingual programs for Spanish-speaking immigrants. The bibliography is extensive. Discussion of bilingual education lends itself to claims of fact, value, and policy.

2. Suppose a white student expresses himself, even in written composition, in street language. Ask students to what extent his teachers should use this language to teach standard English. Ask whether they feel that street language is fully expressive, capable of responding to all kinds of arguments, like those a student will encounter in his reading.

3. Explaining the grammar and syntax of Ebonics and its theoretical origins in West African languages can be an unusually interesting oral presentation.

4. Some instructors of Ebonics have used "parallel texts" of literary works to introduce students to the meanings expressed in more formal prose or poetry. But such instructional strategies are not unique. Most students are not conscious of the force or the weakness of particular language constructions unless they confront a comparison. Some "translations" of Shakespeare in parallel text editions are worth examining. The Perfection Form Company has issued "lite verse counterparts" of several plays. For example "But soft! What light through yonder window breaks?" becomes "But wait! What light is coming from that window?"

    Other examples from *Hamlet, King Lear,* and *Macbeth* can be found in an article in the *New York Times,* April 28, 1996, PE7, "Translations of the Bard: Perorations Devoutly to Be Missed." Ask students to what extent such translations may be helpful to readers who have difficulty with the original. Some students should be encouraged to try their hands at an essay that analyzes the emotional and aesthetic effects of such translations.

Bibliography

"The Bilingual Bog." *Newsweek*, October 23, 1995. "Students learn English faster in quality bilingual classes than they do in English-only settings."

De Witt, Karen. "Ebonics, Language of Richard Nixon." *New York Times*, December 29, 1996, sec. 4, p. 3. "Whether or not it's a unique language, black English has been appropriated by other Americans, including Presidents."

Menaud, Louis. "Johnny Be Good: Ebonics and the Language of Cultural Separation." *The New Yorker*, January 13, 1997, p. 4.

Perry, Theresa, and Lisa Delpit, eds. *The Real Ebonics Debate: Power, Language, and the Education of African-American Children*. Boston: Beacon Press, 1998. Contains eighteen articles defending Ebonics.

Porter, Rosalie Pedalino. "The Case Against Bilingual Education." *The Atlantic Monthly*, May 1998, pp. 28 ff.

Traub, James. "The Bilingual Barrier." *New York Times Magazine*, January 31, 1999.

CHAPTER 8

Induction, Deduction, and Logical Fallacies

(text pages 283–333)

1. I have expressed elsewhere my reluctance to use exercises in induction and deduction. Because they have only a tenuous connection with the actual process of composing an argument, we may spend our limited time more profitably in attention to the other elements of argument.

2. The teaching of fallacies poses special, though not insuperable, problems. Some fallacious statements by public figures are obvious, like those in the list of exercises in the text. But arguments by professional writers often contain concealed fallacies or fallacies that uninformed students are unable to identify. I have remarked on what I consider to be faulty reasoning in speeches and articles by Clarence Darrow — in fact, I am surprised at the generosity accorded by editors to some clearly deficient arguments. One example that comes immediately to mind is Ashley Montagu's "Man, the Ignoble Savage?" (from *The Nature of Human Aggression*). This essay, reprinted in several readers, purports to be an attack on the use of examples by others, but Montagu offers only one example in rebuttal, and this example is a scarcely credible rumor that remains unsubstantiated. (An interesting assignment would ask students to look for more convincing research to support Montagu's claim.)

   The rule for all of us, I think — teachers and students alike — is to cultivate fearlessness in our criticism of articles by putative experts. Since freshman students are naturally disinclined to be critical of their mentors (publicly, at least), we may risk overzealousness in uncovering faulty arguments in textbooks, newspapers, and magazines. Advertisers are not the only arguers guilty of concealment or distorted reasoning.

3. I ask students to be on the alert for dubious arguments in what they read and hear and to bring them in for examination by the class. If they are keeping journals, they may record these fallacies or what they interpret as fallacies in their journals. The nomenclature is not important. Some of their entries will turn out to be examples of sound reasoning after all, but no matter. The objective of the exercise is increased alertness. Sensitive discrimination will, we hope, come later.

In some cases, students will be lucky to find explicit references to fallacies, as in the beginning of this letter (*Wall Street Journal,* November 15, 1983): "Your editorial is an illustration of the slippery slope argument." Less explicitly, the writer will say (*Wall Street Journal,* December 7, 1983): "Your editorial was critical of Surgeon General C. Everett Koop for 'citing particularly egregious magazine articles and medical cases as proof that the United States could easily slip into some Nazi-like approval of general euthanasia.' I, for one, would not dismiss Dr. Koop's concern quite so readily."

4. In my experience at half a dozen campuses, I have found that school newspapers are rife with weak and fallacious arguments in the editorials and letters to the editor. As a source of fallacies, they have two advantages: They are easily available, and students probably feel fewer inhibitions in attacking their peers.

5. The excerpt from *A Reasonable Life* may be difficult for students to challenge. Its communitarian appeal is one that speaks directly to many young people, however strongly they may reject its basic premises. A thoughtful analysis of the Utopian vision, accessible to students, is *Utopia, the Perennial Heresy,* by Thomas Molnar. (New York: Sheed and Ward, 1967).

EXERCISES FOR CRITICAL THINKING: ANSWERS

In compiling this list of fallacies, I faced a dilemma. Some of the examples, which I didn't want to omit, did not fit neatly into the categories I had chosen to discuss in the chapter. Nevertheless, in order to avoid confusion, I decided to limit the discussion of specific fallacies, of which there are several dozens, and retain the examples. As it turned out, students had no difficulty recognizing and explaining these fallacies even when they could not find the names for them.

1. *Begging the question.* The judge is assuming the answer to the very question that a trial is supposed to answer.

2. *Non sequitur.* It doesn't follow that because something is good for us the government should enforce compliance.

3. *Post hoc fallacy.* There is no proof that watching these particular TV shows is the cause of high or low school grades. It's more reasonable to suppose that children who do well or poorly in school select one show or the other because of its appeal to their level of intelligence and achievement.

4. *Hasty generalization or small sample.* A faulty prediction for one month is not enough for an accusation of unreliability.

5. *Two wrongs don't make a right.* The writer thinks that death and danger are unacceptable for men in combat, but subjecting women to death and danger doesn't make these "wrongs" more acceptable.

6. *Faulty use of authority.* Taste is a matter of individual preference. It would be hard to prove that Cher, however gifted an actress, is superior to any-body else in her choice of a sweetener. (Of course, we also know that she is only posing for a paid advertisement.)

7. *Two wrongs don't make a right.* The arguer seems to infer that gambling is wrong, but legalizing it won't make it morally right. (This is what Norman Cousins calls "cop-out realism," or "If you can't beat 'em, join 'em.")

8. *Unknown fact or faulty comparison.* What was money spent for in the past? Have conditions changed that may make the expenditure of more money appropriate now?

9. *Non sequitur.* It doesn't follow that campus newspapers select the best or even good writers. They usually have to settle for those who make them-selves available.

10. *Begging the question.* The arguer assumes that standard English is neces-sary only for certain kinds of employment, but that remains to be proved. Standard English has other uses unrelated to employment.

11. *Faulty definition.* In this case discrimination means making judicious choices. It should not be considered pejorative. To perform their duties, which may involve physical exertion, police officers should be required to fulfill cer-tain physical standards.

12. *Faulty comparison or begging the question.* Qualified doctors and medical students are different. By definition a medical student is still being tested, and access to information in books during the testing process may defeat the purposes of testing.

13. *Faulty definition.* Chemicals are the building blocks of nature. Some may be unsafe, but they are not all synonymous with poisons by any means.

14. *Begging the question.* The arguer assumes that the only relevant criterion for choosing courses is payment of tuition. But a student enters into an implicit contract when he or she enrolls in the college or university and accepts the criteria laid down by the institution for the granting of a diploma.

15. *False dilemma.* The writer assumes that there are only two alternatives available to those who want to marry. But there is at least one more — marriages freely chosen that are not based on romantic love. Besides, we have no way of knowing how well arranged marriages worked. Staying married when divorce is difficult or unavailable doesn't prove the success of the marriage.

16. *Hasty generalization or small sample.* Three examples are not sufficient to support a generalization about a population of hundreds of thousands or millions.

17. *Hasty generalization or small sample.* One example of a highly intelligent athlete is not enough to prove the intelligence of a large population.

18. *Unknown fact.* There is insufficient evidence in this quotation to prove the reasons for Sasway's failure to register, which may or may not be based on moral principles.

19. *Post hoc fallacy.* We have no way of knowing if the exercise videos are the cause of Jane Fonda's great shape.

20. *Faulty analogy.* Harris is making an analogy between inanimate objects — buildings, cars, ham — and animate objects or students. Students, after all, have choices and some control over their education.

21. *Post hoc fallacy.* There is no evidence here that doctrines of feminism have caused women to turn to crime. Anyway, crime is usually the result of many factors that are difficult to separate.

22. *Non sequitur.* It doesn't follow that just because an activity is healthful the university should require it. (There are numbers of things that are good for us that a center of academic learning does not choose to introduce into its curriculum.)

23. *Ad hominem.* Meany is attacking the habits of the younger generation, not their views, which remain unknown.

24. *Non sequitur.* It doesn't follow that early poverty makes a candidate sympathetic to the problems of the poor. In fact, the opposite may be true.

25. *Faulty comparison.* In the European cases troops were engaged in crushing freedom; in the Little Rock case they were engaged in extending it.

26. *Post hoc fallacy.* There is no evidence that the election of Governor Jones is the cause of the corruption. His election and government corruption may be coincidental.

27. *False dilemma.* These may not be the only alternatives for the voters. There may be ways to improve education without a pay increase.

28. *Post hoc fallacy.* It would be hard to prove a cause-effect relation.

29. *Faulty comparison.* The dissimilarities between the two states are probably much greater than the similarities.

30. *Post hoc fallacy.* Self-explanatory.

31. *Faulty use of authority.* Even Galileo should have asked for stricter evidence than the great Aristotle could provide on the subject of natural science.

32. *Slippery slope fallacy.* The progression projected by Brustein — from Congress curtailing grants to artists whose work is controversial to Congress ordering the execution of artists whose work is deemed blasphemous — is hardly inevitable.

DEBATE: CAN WOMEN SERVE SUCCESSFULLY IN MILITARY COMBAT?

1. A female anthropologist argues that women in combat units will prevent men from bonding, a condition which men achieve through talk about sex. (Anna Simons, "In War, Let Men Be Men," *Wall Street Journal,* April 23, 1997, p. A31.) Male students ought to be able to respond to this. (Many men, in fact, did object in subsequent letters to the editor.)

2. In *G. I. Jane,* a 1997 movie, Demi Moore plays the first woman selected to become a Seal in the navy's elite commando unit. The U.S. Navy refused to cooperate with the filmmakers. Suggest to students who have seen the film that they analyze the portrayal of the navy and the behavior of male officers. Does the movie seem to favor women in combat?

3. Clearly this is an ideal subject for a short two-person debate. The debate might be more provocative if a man argued in favor of women in combat and a woman against it.

Bibliography

Francke, Linda Bird. *Ground Zero: The Gender Wars in the Military.* New York: Simon and Schuster, 1997. "[T]here is no moral or practical difference if women do substantial amounts of the killing and dying."

Merserau, Adam G. "'Diversity' May Prove Deadly on the Battlefield." *Wall Street Journal*, November 14, 1996, p. A18.

WRITING, RESEARCHING, AND PRESENTING ARGUMENTS

INTRODUCTION

Part Two is meant to accompany all writing assignments throughout the semester, from Part One through Parts Three and Four. It is one thing for students to grasp the concept of a claim of fact, for example, but writing an essay in which they demonstrate their ability to communicate that understanding is quite another. Chapter 9, then, instructs students in the process of preparing a paper from the very beginning: finding a topic, defining the issues, organizing the material, considering the audience, revising, and preparing the manuscript. The discussion of each step is illuminated with examples from good writers.

In introducing a new textbook, especially a handbook or a composition text, I always review its contents with the students before we begin to use it. This strategy is based on the sound premise that students don't read instruction manuals without judicious coaxing. With all books open to Chapter 9, I go through the material, turning the pages and pointing out the discussions that students ought to find helpful in the process of writing a paper. Most students will recognize the problems this chapter is designed to solve. The purpose of the exercise of course, is to encourage students to use the material themselves as a reference if they are not sure how to proceed at some point in an essay.

Chapter 10 presents the research paper as a culmination of a course in argumentative writing. Although students in all their papers so far have been demonstrating their mastery of the elements of argument and the process of composition, the research paper will put their skills to a more demanding test. In this chapter we discuss the purposes of the research paper and the procedures for helping students to produce interesting and authoritative documents: preparing a schedule, conferring with the instructor, using the library, taking notes, organizing the paper, using a style sheet. In this chapter, too, we've provided two student research papers, one in the humanities, "When a Fairy Tale Is Not Just a Fairy Tale," and one in the sciences, "Why Zoos Should Be Eliminated." They have been annotated to show students exactly how the authors proceed in defending a claim of policy and a claim of fact.

Chapter 11 is a new unit providing guidelines for oral argument. In a course that emphasizes written discourse, defending a claim before a live audience encourages awareness of the differences between speech and writing. Students must learn to accommodate both language and organization to the differing needs of listeners and readers. They already know the importance of acquiring proficiency in speech, and, despite some initial misgivings, find the speech assignments a useful and enlightening experience.

CHAPTER 9

Writing an Argumentative Paper

(text pages 337–57)

Success in teaching composition, like success in parenting, has its mysteries. Good writers and good children emerge from all kinds of environments — authoritarian, permissive, and unlikely combinations of the two. The suggestions that follow have been tested in a wide variety of programs — from some in which an activity and an assignment were designated for each day of the semester to others in which no structure was provided and floundering was a rite of passage.

When I supervise new teaching assistants, I always advise them to teach from their strengths, which might not be the same as mine, and if necessary to adapt any suggestions for assignments and classroom management to ones with which they felt more secure. New teachers who read these ideas will, I hope, be able to make similar adjustments.

ASSIGNMENTS

Three things deserve comment: choosing a topic, preparing students for the assignment, and above all making sure that students understand the *purpose* of the assignment.

1. In helping students to choose a subject, I try to mediate between structure and flexibility. Students are constrained by the objectives of the assignment, but they have plenty of choices: the suggestions in the text, new topics I might want to add to those in the text, and still others that the students themselves have chosen, based on their own interests or events that are taking place around them. It's no small dividend for us teachers that papers on many different subjects can make reading them a pleasure rather than a chore.

2. Both as teacher and as grievance officer of a large program, I have learned that a surprising number of the writing problems students wrestle with are a result of teacher failure to prepare them for the assignment. I don't assume that reading the material is the same as mastering it. I always spend at least fifteen minutes discussing the purposes of the assignment and reviewing the strategies for fulfilling them. For a definition paper, let us say, I review with students the suggestions at the end of Chapter 4, making sure that they understand the distinctions between controversial terms, asking for examples of soap operas, science fiction films, and slang terms that have recently gained popularity. Sometimes I distribute for critical discussion a faulty definition essay from a previous semester. Then we go over the guidelines for writing an essay of definition. I encourage questions, solicit examples, and otherwise try to ensure that the material has been assimilated.

    At the risk of boring this captive audience, I continue to emphasize the objectives of the assignment — the importance of clarifying words and ideas that people don't understand or about which they may disagree. I want students to feel motivated to write not only because they have found something they want to say but because they recognize that in fulfilling the assignment, they are also fulfilling an intellectual function that serves *their* purposes as learners.

3. Early in the semester, students should be introduced to the library. See the discussion on the use of the library on pages 57–58 in these notes.

COMPOSITION: STYLE, ORGANIZATION, AND DEVELOPMENT

Not surprisingly, these are the three elements of composition where student arguments are most likely to falter. Weaknesses here can, of course, cripple the most promising ideas. The bad news is that in one semester we can do little to produce polished stylists. The good news, however, is that we *can* teach organization and development.

1. Precision and grace in writing almost always depend on a good ear, long familiarity with good writing, and association with family and friends who know how to use language — conditions over which teachers of college freshmen have little control. We have tried and sometimes seen an improvement in style as a result of sentence-combining exercises, imitation of accessible prose stylists like George Orwell, and rewriting of clumsy passages by the instructor. Our goals should be modest — clarity would be enough — but our successes will also be modest.

   One of the obstacles for some students on the way to clear and straightforward expression is their adoption of an artificial written style that has little resemblance to their own voices. The style is inflated and slightly pompous, but it seems to these writers that a language closer to colloquial speech would be inappropriate and even frivolous. I encourage these students to look closely at the prose of writers who often use one-syllable words and short sentences with strong rhetorical effect. I want to convince students that simple prose is not merely an instructor's idiosyncratic preference.

   A limited vocabulary, needless to say, is a serious impediment to the reading and writing of arguments. I teach use of a full-size desk dictionary; many college students have never consulted anything but a small paperback dictionary and are at a loss to interpret the symbols in a larger one. I ask questions about the words in the assigned essays and insist that students look them up. I emphasize words that student writers can usefully introduce into their own essays. And I've been surprised and pleased to notice how often students will use these new words in subsequent essays.

2. Organization for argumentative papers can be taught by formula, to both freshman writers and upper classmen alike, and we need not apologize for a lack of invention. Invention resides in the choice of topic and the modes of development. Unlike the arrangement of ideas in description, which may be spatial, or in narration, which may be chronological, the arrangement of ideas in argument is logical, and has, therefore, wide application. I try to make clear to students that the modes of organization outlined in the text are exactly the same as those they will be expected to use in their writing in the workplace or in any activities which call for reports, evaluations, and recommendations.

   If students have trouble arranging the materials of an argument, I ask them first to establish the nature of their claims, then to examine essays in the book that exemplify an appropriate organization (defending the main idea: Watts, Townsend, Kramer; refuting the opposing view: Levin, Goodman, Schiffren, Simon, and Brott; presenting the stock issues: Shanker, Satel). Often the first paragraph of an essay serves as an introduction to the kind of organization. Most beginning writers are glad to learn that these forms exist and are ready for use in any argument. As they gain power in using these conventional forms, they will be free to modify them — for example, withholding the main idea until the end, as Allport does.

3. As for development and support, I stress this throughout the semester in every piece students read and write, pointing out varied strategies that good writers use to convince readers of the soundness of their claims.

    In introducing or summarizing the concepts of organization and development, I often use the blackboard. I write down the claim or thesis statement for an argument suggested by a student — for example, "Schools should remove vending machines of unhealthful snack food" — then ask students to suggest topic sentences for three paragraphs and the means of supporting the ideas summarized in the topic sentences. I can use this device for the three ways of organizing a claim, and I can make ample reference to the forms of support that are treated in Chapter 5.

    From time to time I duplicate good student papers, sometimes from a previous semester, for distribution to the class, and we discuss the successful use of the different ways of organizing and supporting a particular argument. Duplication of less successful papers — without names — can also work if the problems are not severe and the instructor can call attention to some strengths as well.

AVOIDING PLAGIARISM

There is no foolproof way of preventing plagiarism. But a few precautions can reduce the number of incidents.

1. Make sure that students understand the nature of the offense. Many students are genuinely ignorant of the necessity for crediting sources. Review the examples in the text. Some instructors warn students at the beginning of the semester that a finding of plagiarism will result in an F for the course. Urge students to ask questions about citation if they are in doubt.

2. Keep an impromptu paper, one written on the first or second day of class, as a sample of the student's style and thinking. (I assign a short essay in class on a subject that allows students to develop a simple argument.) This paper serves primarily as a test of the skills — or lack of skills — that students bring with them. However, if a subsequent paper exhibits a radical departure in vocabulary, syntax, and development of ideas, the instructor should inquire about the differences. A few judicious questions, starting perhaps with vocabulary, will lead to an acknowledgment of help. This works best, of course, when the source is a professional writer with clearly superior skills.

3. Avoid "free" assignments. Whatever their merits, they may tempt students who have difficulty finding subjects to "borrow" papers from friends or the library.

4. Vary assignments from year to year. It's time-consuming to think of variations on previous assignments, but it should go without saying that if the

same assignment is peddled year after year, some student papers will also make the rounds.

5. If your program calls for reviewing several drafts of a paper, you should be able to notice any abrupt changes in the final draft. But be prepared to find that some ambitious plagiarists aren't daunted and will manufacture drafts of another student's essay.

EVALUATION AND GRADING

1. Before assigning the first paper, I discuss with students the criteria for grading. As an introduction, I sometimes ask them to list in order of importance the elements of composition which ought to enter into an evaluation. In some classes half of the students will head their lists with spelling, punctuation, or grammar. What is probably already obvious to them but what they are afraid to say, knowing how perverse English teachers can be, usually comes as a relief—that nobody reads an essay merely for spelling or punctuation. I suggest that the criteria ought to be (1) an interesting and important idea; (2) clarity of expression; (3) adequate development; (4) clear organization; (5) correct spelling, grammar, and punctuation. In class discussion I try to elicit the reasons for this list and the order in which the items appear. Students need to see how these criteria are justified by their claims on the reader. (If the reader of an essay can't understand what the writer is trying to say, a good outline and lots of data will be powerless to save the argument.)

2. I put a letter grade on each paper to be returned. I make no distinction between evaluation and grading. I've discovered that if we omit letter grades from a paper — in a vain attempt to make students less grade-conscious — they will supply the grades themselves. And grading each paper makes it easier to explain, and defend, the unavoidable final grade. I must add that I never put the letter F on a paper, and sometimes I even withhold the D. If the paper really lacks any redeeming strength, I speak to the writer in conference.

3. Although the emphasis in evaluation rests on the elements of argument, I don't ignore grammar and mechanics in considering the grade. For many students, accuracy will be a hallmark of their professions. In a class of mechanical engineers to whom I taught writing, students were told by the engineer who directed the course that sloppy letters of application were routinely discarded by most companies. Employers would infer that an engineer who was careless about spelling and punctuation might also be careless about specifications for a machine. In a real sense, then, matters of spelling, grammar, and punctuation are an integral part of the argument, and not only for engineers.

4. What students do read with high interest is the paragraph or two that instructors write in summing up their evaluation of the whole paper. Comments and questions in the margin are helpful but no substitute for this final evaluation, which for students represents part of the ongoing dialogue initiated by their arguments.

As an example, I reproduce here a student paper followed by the sort of evaluation I would write. The essay is above average in style, freedom from mechanical errors, organization, and attention to development. But it is weakened by flaws that are typical of many good student arguments. Here is the essay:

The New Drinking Laws: A Sour Taste

All I wanted was an Amaretto sour. To get it, I had to have the little black stamp on the back of my hand that told the bartender I was at least twenty-one. I was only twenty and a half. So there I sat at a North Carolina nightspot with my brother and his girlfriend Debbie, sipping a soda. Six months made the difference between a watery Coke and a taste of liquor.

Debbie had a solution. She led me back to the ladies' room, licked the black stamp on the back of her hand, and pressed it onto my hand. It was light, so I darkened it with black eyeliner.

"It's backwards, but they won't notice," Debbie assured me. "It's dark in here."

Well, the bartender did notice, and I didn't get the Amaretto sour. "This is a fake," he said. "You have to come with me." He walked around to my side of the bar, grabbed my arm, and led me to a small office at the front of the bar. There, he took a bottle of rubbing alcohol out of the desk, wet a piece of cotton with it, and wiped the stamp from my hand. "Now get out of here," he said.

At first, I wanted to cry. But as I walked to the car with Debbie and Grant, I became angry. I was a responsible person, and I had never taken a drink and gotten behind the wheel. I rarely had more than two drinks at a time. Sure, I had skirted the law, but the law was unfair.

Now young people across the country are getting a taste of that unfairness. Under pressure from special-interest groups and a federal government that has threatened to take away their highway funds, every state in the country has raised the legal age for buying and drinking alcohol to twenty-one. I argue that, in raising the drinking age, states have violated the rights of a large group of people. Further, I believe that increasing the age is not the best way to deter drunken driving and reduce traffic fatalities.

Supporters of the current drinking laws question the ability of eighteen-year-olds to drink responsibly. These people need to take a look at the other responsibilities that rest with eighteen-year-olds now. Under United States law, an eighteen-year-old can vote, go to war, get married, and have a family, but cannot legally enjoy a beer. The implication is that people who are under the age of twenty-one are mature enough to assume the responsibilities of adulthood but are not responsible enough to enjoy its pleasures. I find this judgment arbitrary and unfair. Once we have decided what the age of majority should be (and we seem to have decided on the age of eighteen for most activities) we should apply that standard uniformly.

Other supporters of new laws argue that when drinking ages go up, traffic fatalities go down. In fact, studies *have* indicated that in states where the drinking age has been increased, fatalities have dropped by as much as 10 percent. This is good news, but it does not prove that the new drinking laws are entirely responsible for the drop in traffic fatalities. Tougher drunk driving laws and stepped-up efforts to educate the public about the dangers of drinking and driving could also have been major factors in the drop in fatalities.

In the last several years, drunk driving laws and penalties have been made tougher throughout the nation. That is good: Rigorous enforcement of these laws is what we need. Also, education is always a positive force. The better the general public understands the damage that irresponsible drinking can do to individuals and society, the better off everyone will be. There are problem drinkers in all age groups. The law should go after them instead of using an arbitrary age limit that restricts the rights of citizens.

Finally, I do not believe that the higher drinking age will deter people under the age of twenty-one from drinking. Those under the legal age have always found ways to skirt the law and get their hands on alcohol, and they will continue to do so. The quest for the pleasure of intoxication is part of our nature. Restricting the supply of alcohol might make it harder for eighteen-year-olds to get, but it will not make it less desirable.

I wasn't deterred from drinking the night that I got kicked out of that bar in North Carolina. After leaving there, we drove a few miles down the road to another bar, and my brother bought me my Amaretto sour. It might have been more satisfying had it been legal.

My written evaluation would say:

I think this is a hard claim to defend, but you've handled several things very well. The organization is tight, and you make excellent transitions between ideas. I liked the introduction; it's a lively, well-told personal anecdote, and your reference to it at the end makes clear that it was an integral part of your argument. Even more important, in the body of your argument you offer other kinds of support: an appeal to fairness and data about drinking and driving.

But some changes and additions might have made your argument even stronger. (1) You are probably right that the laws alone have not been responsible for the big drop in alcohol-related deaths — among fifteen- to nineteen-year-olds they have plunged from a peak of 6,281 in 1982 to 2,170 in 1988 — but most experts agree that the laws are at least partly responsible. So you would have to argue that the death rate won't rise if the drinking age is lowered. Can you find data and expert opinion to support that view? You say you are a responsible driver — good point — but are you typical? (2) The analogy with other rights granted to eighteen-year-olds is somewhat shaky. Couldn't someone argue that granting those rights to teenagers was a mistake and that we should raise the ages for all the activities you cite? There's nothing special about age eighteen that guarantees maturity. After all, most eighteen-year-olds don't vote, most marriages at eighteen aren't notably successful, and as soldiers in the army, eighteen-year-olds are under strict supervision. (3) Finally, I wonder who your audience is. Are you writing for adults who might be persuaded to change the laws? I'm not sure that your attempts to evade the law would convince them that you are mature and responsible, or that pleading for the "pleasure of intoxication" — at a time when drinking by young people is declining, for good reasons — will be very persuasive. If you like, we can talk more about this in conference, and I can show you the sources of my data.

B

PEER EVALUATION

Peer review is less useful in argumentation courses than in courses that emphasize other modes of discourse. That is because the student reviewer often lacks sufficient knowledge of the subject of the argument to make informed comment. An example: A student writing about prisons had taken all his data from a *Time* magazine article of about fifteen years ago. The paper was well written, but the student reading it had no way of knowing that the data had changed so greatly that the claims were no longer valid. If instructors want to give students practice in evaluating arguments of classmates — a potentially valuable exercise — they are well advised, I think, to limit the areas on which the critic is asked to comment.

It's true, of course, that instructors can also be ignorant of areas of knowledge investigated by a student writer. But most of us have sufficient experience as laborers in various fields of scholarship to know which questions to ask.

CONFERENCES

Some programs mandate a specific number of conferences during the semester. Some even prescribe the amount of time to be spent. One guide for teachers calls for an initial conference of two minutes! Other syllabi leave the number of conferences to the instructor. But why conferences at all?

1. One teacher of composition in a prestigious university says frankly that his function in a conference is to rewrite the student's paper, explaining the point of his revision as he goes. In fact, such an extreme strategy may work in some cases — if the student is alive to nuances of vocabulary and tone and can understand and accept the changes, if he or she learns by imitation, and if he or she has sufficient confidence to take issue with some of the teacher's revisions. Most of us, however, see the conference at its best as a dialogue or a conversation which either the teacher or the student may initiate.

   Arguments, we have told our students, are implicit dialogues, and a conference represents not only our opportunity to respond at greater length to the student's argument but the student's opportunity to respond to *us* — to the written comments, for example — and to talk about the process of composition. As the student articulates his thesis, answering our questions and explaining what he tried to do and why he chose to do it this way, some things may become clear that remained opaque when he was engaged in a monologue. Conferences can also function as mini-workshops for two, three, or four students who share a composition problem or have argued the same subject with varying degrees of success.

2. I schedule a mandatory conference during the second week of classes, and at this meeting we discuss both the strengths and the weaknesses of the diagnostic essay, which is not graded. It is gratifying to be able to tell students who have never been confident about their writing that in fact their in-class papers show promise. I am specific about the things they have done well and encourage them to build on these strengths. Other students need to know that their papers reveal problems to be worked on throughout the semester. At this point I concentrate on the big things, organization and development, and touch only lightly on style, grammar, and punctuation. (I should add that impromptu papers, although written

under imperfect conditions, can nevertheless predict real and continuing weaknesses.)

3. In part, conferences also function as a kinder, gentler substitute for written comments. One instructor wrote, "Think More!" across the top of a student paper. Am I wrong in suspecting that it might be harder to give such peremptory and humiliating advice in person?

    Poor writers, although they may come reluctantly to conference, may profit most from these sessions. They may be unwilling to pay the necessary attention to largely negative written comments, but in conference they must confront them, and the comments can be prefaced, softened, and modified to accommodate a vulnerable human presence. These students may also be more articulate in speech than in writing and better able to assist the instructor by giving a clearer sense of what they really wanted to argue.

4. Some programs require meetings for review of a mid-process paper. I require only a final paper. I will gladly look over any number of drafts and encourage students to come to me with problems they are having difficulty solving, but I don't insist on submission of papers in progress. The difference between a draft and a final paper is not so clear to me. Even a final draft — or one that the writer takes to be final — can and sometimes should be revised, and my preference is to allow as many revisions and as many conferences as a student thinks necessary or desirable. In practice, students seldom make more than one major revision of their "final" paper, and they understand that for administrative reasons, deadlines, however arbitrary, must be met. But the freedom to go on writing and conferring is available.

5. Finally, conferences allow student and teacher to look at mechanical errors and their corrections in a different way. Corrections on the student essay of spelling, grammar, and punctuation errors don't always produce improvement; many students won't — or can't — read them. And a multitude of correction results in a trail of red ink that signifies a disaster. A conference has the virtue of allowing you to ask questions, listen to answers, offer explanations, and, most of all, point out with pencil and finger the things that need change. For such problems a small physical demonstration has an impact that the written correction does not.

CHAPTER 10
Researching an Argumentative Paper
(text pages 358–416)

The objectives of the freshman research paper should be limited. The paper should be relatively short (no more than eight pages or two thousand words), it should constitute only one-fifth or less of the final grade, and the preparation for it should not consume more than a week of class time. Conferences with the students can take care of individual problems that arise during the research and the writing.

Unlike many courses in the upper classes, in which the only writing may be an examination and a research paper, our course requires papers from the very first week of class, and students practice research skills at some level throughout the semester. The research paper serves not to introduce but to bring together in a more ambitious exercise the principal elements of argument. But it is only one among many papers.

The purposes of the research paper are twofold: (1) mastering a long paper — perhaps three times longer than any of the weekly papers students have done so far — with its special and more demanding problems of organization; (2) learning how to substantiate more extensive claims of fact, value, and policy that require the data and authoritative opinion the writer cannot supply — in other words, more practice in organization and development.

I don't make the accuracy of footnoting and bibliography a major issue. Students seldom see the necessity for it, and, in fact, they are right to regard the forms as arbitrary and time-consuming. And they do change. The time for rigorous adherence to the style sheets will come when students write research papers in their major disciplines, many of which specify guidelines that professional writers in the field *must* follow. I direct students to copy the appropriate forms provided in the chapter on research, but I don't exact big penalties for the inevitable lapses.

New teachers who are introducing the research paper for the first time may find suggestions in the following outline that can be adapted to their particular programs.

1. Assign a fast reading of Chapter 10. Take ten or fifteen minutes to turn pages with students, pointing out what they will find and which parts deserve a slightly longer glance. For example, they should read the sample papers with care; for this reading, however, they can skip the MLA and APA style sheets.

   At the next class go over the important parts of the chapter. Concentrate on the tasks that must be accomplished first. Encourage questions. Reassure students that the assignment is not so daunting as they think it is. It might even be fun, and you are ready to help.

2. In class discuss finding a topic. The commonly quoted advice to graduate students about to embark on a dissertation still holds good: Choose something that really interests you, because you'll have to live with it for a while.

   The first and most obvious source of subjects will be in "Opposing Viewpoints," Part Three of the text. At least five topics are suggested for each chapter, but students may think of others that interest them more. Other subjects may be found in personal experience, at home and at school, and in the neighborhood, in town, or on campus.

3. Work out a schedule for the project. Freshman students need help in managing time, and they are grateful for a structure that defines their responsibilities. I favor making the time available for the research paper no longer than a month. (I've found that allowing more time for research and writing doesn't produce better papers.) Set deadlines for specific stages of the project:

   a. The choice of topic
   b. A briefly annotated list of five sources examined in the first week or ten days. Two of the items may be taken from "Opposing Viewpoints,"

the other three from other sources. (All of these may not appear in the final bibliography, but they represent a start.)

c. The final paper

4. Announce the availability of conferences with the instructor at any point during the research and writing. Early in the project I schedule one conference with each student. Later conferences can be based on individual need. Some students will have trouble refining and narrowing the topic. Others will need help finding sources. (If I'm familiar with the subject, I offer suggestions. Students also have access to my files with thousands of clippings.) And still others will encounter problems in organizing and in using the sources appropriately.

5. While students work on their research papers outside of class, I ask for short papers, sometimes in class, which introduce an idea or present a piece of evidence that is part of the longer paper. Some papers will suggest the need for conference. If not, papers should be returned promptly with comments relevant to the research paper. Needless to say, attention to the ongoing process of the paper should also make plagiarism more difficult.

6. Most of us are prepared for evidence of a scanty research effort. But we should also be prepared for evidence of another kind of failure. Drunk with their newly acquired knowledge of the research tool, some students produce a series of quotations, sometimes as many as twenty in a six-page paper, tightly strung together like a well-made necklace, with nothing visible between the pearls. This is *not* a research paper. We need to make clear to students that *they* are the authors and that the materials derived from other sources must be used *only* to support their claims. We should emphasize that too much research material can be as fatal as too little. "When a Fairy Tale Is Not Just a Fairy Tale" and "Why Zoos Should Be Eliminated" give students models for the intelligent use of quotations.

USE OF THE LIBRARY

At schools with large libraries it's not uncommon to discover that even by the end of the first semester, freshman students will not have visited the library unless assigned to do so. Big libraries can be intimidating, but a guided tour can reinforce the idea that the library is a friend, not an enemy. *The library tour should take place early in the semester, not at research paper time.* In this course students should begin to use the resources of the library at once, as they tackle the very first paper on defending a claim of fact.

Librarians are usually more than willing to cooperate in helping students to become familiar with library resources, and they can offer helpful experience to new instructors. I would turn to the librarians first and try to accommodate their recommendations to the purposes of the course. I make a few suggestions here based on trial and error with my own classes.

1. A tour in which twenty students follow the librarian as he or she points out library services seldom works. The students in the back can't hear, and they lose interest. Even those near the speaker will not remember a couple of weeks later exactly what they learned. At most the librarian or the instructor can walk the students through some of the areas where they are likely to be busiest — the card catalog or computerized catalog, the indexes, the major reference works, the microfiche collection.

2. Prepare students for the visit. Go over the material in the book, offering additional information about the sources. Anecdotes about your own experience with research can enliven an apparently lifeless subject.

3. Students will remember much more about the library if they arrive with specific questions. One way to produce questions that will lead to a wide range of answers is to divide the class into three sections: humanities, social sciences, and natural and physical sciences. Each section meets and arrives at a research paper topic in its field; each student in that section then prepares a specific question on the topic. (Some of the questions will be weak, but the librarian can often ask the right questions of the student and elicit a nice rephrasing.) The students assemble with the librarian in a room with a blackboard — an overhead projector is also a useful tool — where he or she can answer students' questions by writing down the names of the materials and their locations.

4. Use student resources. Some students in the class will be more proficient than others in unraveling the mysteries of the library, and they are often pleased and proud to be asked to accompany the others and point out how and where to look.

CHAPTER 11
Presenting an Argument Orally
(text pages 417–32)

1. An introduction to speeches by the class might include a student guest speaker whose argument can be evaluated in a class discussion following the speech. Criticism should be based on criteria laid out in Chapter 11. The speaker need not be perfect but should demonstrate abilities against which students in the class can measure their own. An outside speaker allows students to offer a frank evaluation, which they are sometimes reluctant to do openly for a classmate. In many schools with debate clubs and speech or drama departments, instructors can find willing candidates for the role of guest speaker. The instructor should suggest the kind of speech that fulfills the objectives of the speech unit, preferably a claim of policy that will include both facts and values.

2. In my classes students fill out an evaluation form for each speech, briefly commenting on the main elements. (I make copies of a simple form with spaces for comment.) Before I turn the evaluations over to the speakers, I read them to make sure that they are serious and respectful and then remove the names of the critics.

3. When guest speakers appear to address either the whole school or an organization on campus, I sometimes assign attendance for the class. As with the speeches in their own class, students fill out evaluation forms. The objectives of any speech unit should, of course, include not only proficiency in delivering a speech, but the critical ability to evaluate an oral argument.

4. "Words Go Right to the Brain, But Can They Stir the Heart: Some Say Popular Software Debases Public Speaking," discusses the influence of software on oral presentation, especially in business. (*New York Times,* April

17, 1999, p. A17.) Some critics think that Powerpoint and other software presentation aids "contribute to the debasement of rhetoric." A professor of communication asks us to imagine Martin Luther King Jr.'s "I Have a Dream" speech with Powerpoint.

But Stephen Pinker, professor of cognitive science and the author of *The Language Instinct*, argues that human beings are visual creatures. "If anything," he says, "Powerpoint, if used well, would ideally reflect the way we think." Pinker is on a committee at Massachusetts Institute of Technology that "is updating the traditional writing requirement to include both speech and graphic communication."

PART THREE
OPPOSING VIEWPOINTS

INTRODUCTION (text pages 433–34)

1. The debates, articles, and letters in this section represent the argumentative process in its clearest and most understandable form. If throughout the semester we have emphasized that arguments are dialogues, the selections given here will show students how the dialogues work, that is, how people on opposing sides actually respond to each other, whether well or poorly. Where it is clear that the response is not direct, that there is no clash, the debates can be equally instructive.

2. "Opposing Viewpoints" may be used as a discrete unit or as a source of materials for assignments in the text.

   a. If it is used as a self-contained unit, the introduction and the questions that precede it suggest a number of ways of examining the material and writing about it. The debate instructions that follow give, I hope, sufficient details for the organization of a classroom debate, oral or written.

   b. "Opposing Viewpoints" also lends itself to use as a source of data, expert opinion, motivational appeals, warrants, and ethical and unethical use of language. In fulfilling assignments that call for supporting materials students may find material here, either as a substitute for or in addition to library research. In several places in these notes I have suggested assignments that give students the opportunity to look for support for their claims among the selections in "Opposing Viewpoints."

   c. In addition, as pointed out earlier, "Opposing Viewpoints" can furnish the material for a research paper. Longer papers may require supplementary library research, but there is probably sufficient material in each section for a paper of six to seven pages.

3. Some of these subjects will be more effective than others for a given group of students, depending on their experience with and knowledge of the subject. "Freedom of Speech," for example, may be more interesting for students in schools where a speech code is being debated or where it has resulted in punishment for infraction. "Euthanasia" may strike a chord in a place where the fate of a handicapped infant is being publicly debated.

   When time does not permit using all the subjects, I choose the most provocative ones, those that will produce, as far as I can tell, the liveliest feelings, both for and against.

4. Given the timeliness of these subjects, research to discover whether changes that have occurred since the articles and letters in the book were written

will be indispensable. Students must be encouraged to read at least one full-coverage daily newspaper, watch TV newscasts and special reports, and listen to radio programs like *Talk of the Nation* (NPR). *Talk of the Nation* has covered every topic in Part Three of this book and a good many other subjects as well. Surveys show that most college students don't read newspapers or listen to TV newscasts. Some of them do, however, read *Time* or *Newsweek* or *U.S. News & World Report.* These students can be asked to report to the class on the ways in which the same stories are treated in different news magazines.

5. An enormously productive unit may be organized around formal classroom debate. Although debate is almost always an oral exercise, there is plenty of opportunity in a writing class for students to commit their outlines to paper, develop major points that cannot be adequately treated in the five minutes allotted to oral presentation, and make extended critiques of the debates of their classmates.

Each debate usually requires four people, two on the affirmative side, two on the negative, although the Lincoln–Douglas format — one debater on each side — is also possible. If time does not permit a round of formal debates, the class may choose four or five debate subjects, with each team producing an argument that will be duplicated or read aloud for consideration by the whole class. This organization reduces the arguments to one on each side and eliminates rebuttal time. After reading or hearing the arguments, the class may write evaluations based on answers to the questions on the debate sheet.

For supporting materials students should confine themselves to the data in this section. Their efforts will involve extracting the relevant issues and organizing them in a succinct and understandable way. They may also, of course, need to do further research for more recent data.

DEBATE

Debate may be considered an extension of the problem-solving analysis. The debaters are considering the merits of a solution to some problem, for example, a plan to restrict government agencies in their investigations of private citizens.

The debate proposition is always a two-sided question; it can be answered yes or no.

The proposition is worded so that the affirmative (yes) side will be arguing for a change in policy, or, in the case of value questions, a new idea. (The argument that violence is justified in civil rights cases is an example of the latter.) Because the affirmative is arguing for a change, they are said to have the *burden of proof,* while the negative has only to defend the status quo.

The affirmative argument usually centers around three *stock issues* that grow out of the problem-solving analysis. The affirmative will argue

1. that there is a need for a change;

2. that their proposal will meet the need;

3. that their proposal is the best solution to the problem. These stock issues are referred to as need, plan, and advantages.

The negative may answer the affirmative case in a number of ways.

1. They may *debate* every issue. "There is no problem, and even if there were, your plan is expensive, inefficient, and undesirable."

2. They may *waive* an issue. "Yes, indeed, we agree there is a serious problem, but your proposed solution is useless."

3. They may propose a *counterplan*. "Things are bad all right, but I have a better idea for improving them than yours." Tournament debaters do not do this too often for strategic reasons: It means the negative must assume part of the burden of proof.

Following are some questions you might consider as you listen to a debate:

1. How important is definition of terms? Does it become an issue in the debate?

2. Does the negative attack the affirmative argument on every point, or does the debate narrow to one or two issues?

3. Do the speakers base their arguments on any generally accepted principles or values, such as justice, individual freedom, constitutional guarantees?

4. Do you find examples of causal argument, argument from example, or argument from analogy?

5. How important is evidence in the debate? Do the speakers question the credibility of each other's sources? To what extent, if any, does the argument center around evidence?

6. What comments would you make on the speakers' oral presentation (delivery)?

7. Which side do you think won, and why?

CHAPTER 12
Affirmative Action
(text pages 435–61)

1. Affirmative action is a bewildering complex of issues involving race and sex that change from month to month and place to place as both state and federal governments enact legislation to reform or dismantle existing programs. The fundamental issues have not been resolved. Even the goals remain controversial. Equality is a key term in all the debates, but its definition as a goal of a democratic society is by no means absolute. Is equality of opportunity — which the original programs were meant to guarantee — enough? Or is equality of result the real objective?

The chancellor of the University of California at Berkeley says that the goal of affirmative action in schools should be diversity, a means of ensuring a wide-ranging population of races and cultures that can offer students an experience in multicultural living. Still, we've learned that diversity, expressed in dormitories and cultural centers that cater to strictly defined constituencies, can also emphasize differences and create dissension. Students who are familiar with such problems on their campuses may be able to think of compromises that promote both diversity and community of interests. In 1996 the University of California inaugurated a race-blind admissions policy after voters repealed affirmative action laws. In the following year minority admissions declined, but in 1998 they rebounded, although minorities did not regain their former class share.

2. Students can engage in an informal classroom debate on a claim of fact: Resolved, that women or African Americans have derived economic benefit from affirmative action programs. There are plenty of statistics on both sides.

3. It's much harder, of course, to debate a claim of value, grounded as it must be in subjective elements that are difficult to define. But student essays about personal experiences with affirmative action, based on family histories as well as their own, should be encouraged. Students have examples in the text of personal essays — Carter, Steele, del Barco — that treat the subject as more than a matter of "politically correct bean counting" (in the words of one supporter of affirmative action).

4. Debaters or discussants can also be brought in from other parts of the school — women's centers, African-American studies, law courses — where affirmative action issues are always of interest. Students are always attentive to invited speakers who seem to bring with them a breath of the so-called real world.

5. One of the unexpected consequences of equal opportunity policies is the impact on black colleges. In April 1996 the Supreme Court let stand a Mississippi law mandating equal admission standards for all state universities, both black and white. Three historically black institutions "in the past had required lower standardized test scores for admission, reflecting the low-income backgrounds and the educationally limited high schools that most of their students come from." (*New York Times,* April 24, 1996, p. A14.) Although equal opportunities policies were originally designed to enable black students to enroll in traditionally white colleges, the effect of the Mississippi law, said Elias Blake, Jr., former president of Clark College in Atlanta, will be to "close the door for the mass of blacks at the bottom." Blake concluded that the University of Texas ruling — that race cannot be a factor in admissions — and the Mississippi ruling — that admission must be determined by test scores — are "opposite sides of the same coin, one of the declining access to higher education for minorities."

Bibliography

Bergman, Barbara. *In Defense of Affirmative Action.* New York: Basic Books, 1995.

Bok, Derek, and William G. Bowen. *The Shape of the River: Long-Term Consequences of Considering Race in College and University Admissions.* New Haven: Princeton U. Press, 1998. Evidence that affirmative action has contributed to an emergent black middle class.

Bolick, Clint. *The Affirmative Action Fraud: Can We Restore the American Civil Rights Vision?* Cato Institute, 1995.

Gingrich, Newt, and Ward Connerly. "Face the Failure of Racial Preference." *New York Times,* June 15, 1997, p. E15.

Guinier, Lani. "The Real Bias in Higher Education." *New York Times*, June 24, 1997, p. A29.

"Is Affirmative Action on the Way Out?" Should It Be? A Symposium." *Commentary*, March 1998. Twenty-one scholars debate the subject. One of them is Randall Kennedy, whose article appears in this chapter.

Katzenbach, Nicholas deB., and Burke Marshall. "Not Color Blind: Just Blind." *New York Times Magazine*, February 22, 1998, pp. 42 ff. "Society uses many standards to choose some people over others. . . . To forbid using race as one such standard is to act as though discrimination had disappeared."

Traub, James. "The Class of Prop. 209." *New York Times Magazine*, May 2, 1999, pp. 44 ff. "In the wake of affirmative action, campuses in California are managing to maintain diversity without racial set-asides. This will satisfy neither liberals nor conservatives but it's a lot like the future."

CHAPTER 13

Corporate Responsibility

(text pages 462–80)

1. In this chapter students will confront an important and recurring question: Under what circumstances is the corporation responsible for harm to the user of its products? After years of trials in which the tobacco companies were acquitted, they have now agreed to pay $246 billion in reparations to the states over a period of 25 years. The money is to be spent on anti-smoking education and medical treatment for the victims of smoking. Apparently the gun manufacturers are next. An article in the *New York Times,* March 21, 1999, reports that the settlement by the tobacco companies has encouraged lawsuits against the gun industry by at least five cities — Atlanta, Chicago, Miami, New Orleans, and Bridgeport, CT. Among other things, gun manufacturers have been charged with failing both to make guns safer (although the technology exists), and to market guns more responsibly. No doubt, other cities will follow.

   Although the tobacco companies have settled, controversies about responsibility are still alive. To what extent were smokers responsible for the habits which caused disease and death? Students can argue cause and effect for this and other cases that surface regularly in the news. They may remember the suit against McDonald's for injury by hot coffee.

   These events also suggest essays of comparison and contrast: If guns and tobacco, why not automobiles? Or are there differences in the nature of the products? (Students can probably think of other products that cause harm.) John Lott Jr., professor of law at the University of Chicago, argues that "every product has illegitimate uses." (*Wall Street Journal*, June 23, 1998, p. A28.)

2. Most students will not know the origins of the sweatshop (sometimes called "sweating system"). Articles and books abound on the early twentieth-century garment and cigar workrooms. The dramatic, sometimes tragic

history of the sweatshop lends itself to oral presentation as well as to research papers.

3. More challenging — in part because the arguer may be accused of sympathy for the manufacturer — is an argument that low-paid workers in some third-world countries enjoy certain advantages. (See bibliography.)

Bibliography

"Corporations and Conscience." *New York Times*, December 6, 1998, p. A18. "Corporate officials are not only businessmen, they are citizens of the world."

Kaufman-Rosen, Leslie. "Being Cruel to Be Kind." *Newsweek*, October 17, 1994, p. 51. "How 'socially responsible' businesses such as Ben and Jerry's and the Body Shop found they couldn't stay pure and still make a profit."

Kluger, Richard. "Is It Really a Good Deal?" *Time*, June 30, 1997, p. 30. "Forget the money. The key is FDA control."

"Santa's Sweatshop." *U.S. News & World Report*, December 16, 1996. Instances of unsavory conditions abroad and steps that consumers can take.

"Stretching Federal Labor Law Far into South Pacific." *New York Times*, February 20, 1999, p. A4. "Where lawyers and Federal officials see a flagrant violation of law, many Chinese [laborers] see an opportunity to make money."

Sullum, Jacob. "Whose Risk Is It, Anyway?" *New York Times*, February 19, 1999, p. A21.

CHAPTER 14
Euthanasia
(text pages 481–510)

1. Some students may regard euthanasia as a problem of marginal interest far removed from their own lives. But apart from the mental and emotional conflict that people of all ages might experience when confronting reports of right-to-die cases in the media, students are or can be voters, and if they exercise their franchise, they will find themselves asked to vote for or against euthanasia initiatives that will surely appear more and more frequently on state ballots.

One interesting fact about the ballot initiatives is worth discussing. Eileen Doyle, in a letter to the editor in the *New York Times* (March 18, 1993), asks why "voluntary euthanasia is supported in opinion polls but rejected in voting booths." New initiatives in 1996 appear to reflect a change in public attitudes. Ask students to infer the possible reasons.

2. James Rachels's "Active and Passive Euthanasia" is a brilliant and provocative example of a definition essay. Among its other virtues two stand out as models for students: (1) clear organization, with signposts for readers such as "In what follows I will set out . . ." (Students are sometimes advised to avoid summarizing introductions — I cannot imagine why), "To begin with,"

"My second argument is . . .," "I have argued," and "Finally,"; and (2) vivid and compelling examples that lead students toward "real" decisions.

3. Some students may be more interested in the subject of euthanasia for newborn infants. It seems that severely disabled infants are not infrequently the victims of "passive" euthanasia in the hospital, but their cases seldom become public unless doctors and parents disagree and a decision is referred to the courts.

4. At the end of her article Eileen Doyle employs a risky rhetorical device: predicting the consequences of a "quality-of-life" ethic. This article appeared in 1985. Students can try to decide whether any of Doyle's predictions have been or are likely to be realized. Or are they examples of slippery slope fallacies? And if so, do they invalidate her argument?

5. Hardly a week passes that the media do not report a case in which death for a terminally ill or severely disabled person is being debated by the family, the physicians, or the state. Students are sometimes able to contribute experiences about such patients in their own families. An assignment requires them to select a recent case, one still undecided, and come to a decision about the proper treatment, basing their argument on some of the assumptions raised by the writers in this section.

Religious beliefs play a significant role in euthanasia debates. Eileen Doyle expresses the Catholic view. Ask students if they are aware of other religious positions on euthanasia — Judaic, Islamic, Buddhist, and others.

6. Sidney Hook provides an eloquent introduction to the subject of suicide for the elderly. In asking that his life-support system be removed, he is invoking passive euthanasia. His case can be viewed as a validation of Rachels's assumption that "euthanasia — even passive euthanasia — is desirable in a given case."

Hook's essay is also worth examining as an example of the use of personal experience in an argument. Does this account of his suffering make the argument for passive euthanasia more persuasive? We caution students not to assume that one or even several personal experiences can be offered as sound proof of a claim. Students will see that Hook qualifies the evidence. "Apparently those who cling to life no matter what, think so [that life is worth living even for an 'infirm octogenarian']. I do not." His essay makes clear that personal experience as evidence works best (1) when it is enriched by details and explanations, and (2) when the claim is limited. ("Each one must be permitted to make his own choice.")

The Hippocratic oath is no longer what it was. In several medical schools graduating students are not required to say, "I will give no deadly drug if asked for it, neither will I make a suggestion to this effect." Some medical ethicists regard this as a dangerous departure.

7. As the population ages, new organizations arise that provide information to those who are interested in the right to die. One is *Society for the Right to Die,* 250 West 57th Street, New York, NY 10107. The organization distributes free a copy of a living will and offers about twenty-five books and pamphlets, free or at low cost, on the legal and medical issues in choosing one's death. For a research paper, students may be interested in learning about "natural death" laws in the United States from material printed by the society.

8. Hospitals around the country are beginning to establish ethics committees to deal with the problems raised by the new medical technologies. Medical

schools also have introduced training in the ethics of decision making for terminally ill patients.

If a hospital, medical school, or philosophy department in your school — or another easily accessible facility — has established an ethics committee or a course that revolves around problems of euthanasia, students may interview one or more of the people connected with the committee or course and analyze the issues that emerge.

9. In the days following Dr. Jack Kevorkian's conviction for murder (March 26, 1999), letters and editorials both attacked and defended the verdict. The comments are worth reading for a wide spectrum of opinions on euthanasia. The judge's statement before she sentenced Dr. Kevorkian appeared in full in the *New York Times,* April 14, 1999, p. A21.

10. Peter Singer, a Princeton University bioethicist, whose extreme advocacy for animal rights has made him highly controversial, is also prominent in the euthanasia debate — and controversial here, too. His views on merciful death are based on respect not for the sanctity of life but for the quality of life. Thus, it is right to kill a severely disabled infant who is neither rational nor self-conscious. His book, *Practical Ethics* (Cambridge University Press, 1993) sets forth his views.

Students should contrast Singer's views with those of Arthur Caplan in this chapter.

Bibliography

Belkin, Lisa. *First, Do No Harm.* New York: Simon and Schuster, 1993. Details the work of the Institutional Ethics Committee at Hermann Hospital in Houston, Texas, as it debates decisions of life and death for its patients.

Delbanco, Nicholas. *In the Name of Mercy.* New York: Warner Books, 1995. A thriller about euthanasia that also includes arguments about health care and statistics on insurance.

Guidelines for the Oregon Death with Dignity Act. Available for 15 dollars from the Center for Ethics in Health Care at the Oregon Health Sciences University, Portland, Oregon. A guide for health practitioners who might assist patients to die.

Hendin, Herbert. *Seduced by Death: Doctors, Patients, and the Dutch Cure.* New York: W. W. Norton, 1997. Attacks the Dutch system as "a slippery slope" which has moved "from voluntary euthanasia to involuntary euthanasia."

Humphrey, Derek. *Final Exit.* Eugene, OR: Hemlock Society, 1992. Indicative of the mounting interest in the right to die, this book was on the best-seller list for several weeks.

Kevorkian, Jack, M.D. *Prescription: Medicine — the Goodness of Planned Death.* New York: Prometheus Books, 1991. Kevorkian is the Michigan "suicide doctor."

Rosenblatt, Stanley M. *Murder and Mercy.* New York: Prometheus Books, 1993. About a physician accused of murdering his terminally ill wife.

Shapiro, Joseph P. "Euthanasia's Home." *U.S. News & World Report,* January 13, 1997, p. 24. "What the Dutch experience can teach Americans about assisted suicide."

CHAPTER 15
Freedom of Speech
(text pages 511–32)

1. Freedom of speech on campus and on the Internet may be of most relevance to students, especially if there have been incidents of abusive language at their own schools and censorship of material on school-based websites. Students ought to examine any policy statements on their own campuses that define *racism, sexism,* or *homophobia* and threaten punishment for their expression. If examples don't exist or are difficult to find, students can be encouraged to supply them. As they do so, they should keep in mind that some schools have been forced to modify their guidelines after courts have ruled that strict speech codes violated the First Amendment.

    Arguers may find themselves walking a narrow line between truth and offense. Students should consider this question: If the truth is offensive to some groups, should it nevertheless be expressed? The issue is complicated by the very nature of the academic purpose, which is usually defined as freedom in the search for truth. And there is another question: Do people have a right to express their feelings even if the expression is morally repugnant? Nat Hentoff's article, defending the right even of "racist assholes," provides a rich catalog of examples from schools around the country, many of which will test student opinion on this subject. Charles R. Lawrence III's argument may be treated as a direct reply to Hentoff. But the two essays are also very different in style, tone, and degree of generality. If students find one article more convincing, ask them to explain why.

    Lawrence has the hard task of offering solutions for an intolerable condition. He suggests legal remedies against racial harassment, but the specific forms that these remedies will take are left to civil rights lawyers to determine. So far the remedies imposed by college administrations have not been demonstrably successful. Bans on obnoxious speech sometimes work to reduce incivility and tension; more often they do not. The president of the College of William and Mary, explaining why his school overwhelmingly rejected regulation of speech on campus, wrote, "It is almost impossible to define precisely the types of speech that qualify for regulation as discriminatory harassment." In the meantime the incidence of abusive speech — to say nothing of behavior — continues to rise. Perhaps students have ideas on the subject of remedies, based on their own experiences in the residence halls and the classroom. Courses in other cultures? Courses in human relations? Severe penalties for those guilty of offensive speech? Can students prove that any of these proposed solutions would work?

    At the University of Massachusetts a new speech code proposal ensured freedom from harassment based on race, color, national or ethnic origin, gender, sexual orientation, age, religion, marital status, military service status, and disability. The Graduate Employees Organization wanted the policy extended to include citizenship, culture, HIV status, language, parental status, political affiliation or belief, and pregnancy status. A number of faculty members protested the expansion of "protected categories" as a serious impediment to free discussion of social issues in the classroom.

2. Is freedom of speech on campus different from freedom of speech on the street? The president of Emory University argues that free speech doesn't protect "vicious epithets," because universities are places where "the habits and manners of our civil society" are passed on to the next generation. But on the street there may be different rules. In New York State the highest court ruled that abusive speech was protected under federal and state constitutional guarantees of free speech. The case arose when a woman and her son, both mentally retarded, were verbally harassed by a neighbor.

In February 1998 nine teenagers in a Miami high school went to jail for publishing and circulating a pamphlet, "First Amendment Rights," which included a veiled death threat to the black principal, racist comments, and obscene cartoons. (*New York Times*, March 4, 1998, p. A25.) The Miami American Civil Liberties Union defended the students, terming the pamphlet "a satire . . . in terms you hear on late-night stand-up comedy." The deputy superintendent of schools argued that "free speech doesn't give anyone the right to use a word that would inflame."

The newspaper article points out: "While the U.S. Supreme Court has upheld students' right to political expression, it has also permitted school officials to censor student newspapers and to discipline a student who made suggestive comments in a speech."

Discuss with the class the limits to free speech in publications written and distributed by students.

Revisionist history has emerged as a new and troubling issue. It expresses itself not only in denial of the Holocaust but in new interpretations of ancient history. Students, of course, will not find it easy to marshal and examine all the facts in these debates, but they can attempt to assess the advantages and disadvantages of an academic freedom which gives college instructors the right to espouse *any* theory. (This freedom might also encompass the right to teach creationism.) Are there just and reasonable limits to such freedom?

3. The reference to lyrics in rock music should be of special interest to students. They will almost certainly know some of the offensive lyrics that have provoked their parents. Is labeling of albums a denial of free speech, a form of censorship? A distinction can be made between censure and censorship, a distinction often ignored in the debate over works of art considered offensive. Students can offer examples that clarify the definitions of these terms.

The cover story of *Time* magazine, May 7, 1990, is "Dirty Words: America's Foul-Mouthed Pop Culture." Following the report, an essay by Charles P. Alexander, "A Parent's View of Pop Sex and Violence," argues for protests against the language but not censorship.

4. In 1996 Congress passed the Communications Decency Act, which forbade distribution of indecent material to minors on the Internet. But in 1999 the ban was ruled unconstitutional by the Supreme Court. Senator John McCain sponsored a bill to require antipornography filters on computers in schools and libraries that might receive federal funds for Internet hookups.

Ask students how they would respond to this kind of censorship. Is it feasible? Is there a better way to control children's access to obscene material on the Internet?

5. What about terrorists on the Web? Guerrilla groups now use the Internet to disseminate propaganda and plan attacks. Should they be controlled or censored? Or would this violate their rights to freedom of speech? See "Terrorists on the Web: Electronic 'Safe Haven,'" *U.S. News & World Report,* June 22, 1998, p. 46.

Bibliography

Coles, Robert. "Safety Lessons for the Internet." *New York Times,* October 11, 1997, p. A23. Asks for some legal protection for children from pornography on the Internet.

Collins, Ronald K. L., and David M. Skover. *The Death of Discourse.* New York: HarperCollins, 1996.

Fish, Stanley. *There's No Such Thing as Free Speech.* New York: Oxford U. Press, 1995.

Hentoff, Nat. *Living the Bill of Rights: How to Be an Authentic American.* New York: HarperCollins, 1998.

Levy, Steven. "Did the Net Kill Eddie?" *Newsweek,* October 13, 1997, p. 63. "A murder raises questions about whether we're doing enough to protect kids online."

MacKinnon, Catharine A. *Only Words.* Cambridge, MA: Harvard U. Press, 1995.

Strossen, Nadine. *Defending Pornography: Free Speech, Sex, and the Fight for Women's Rights.* New York: Anchor/Doubleday, 1995.

Sunstein, Cass. *Democracy and the Problem of Free Speech.* New York: Free Press, 1995.

Tribe, Laurence H. "The Internet vs. The First Amendment." *New York Times,* April 28, 1999, p. A27. The lessons of Littleton, Colorado: "It would be a mistake to think that good surveillance or control [of the Internet] can play an important role in preventing violent crimes."

CHAPTER 16
Privacy in the Information Age
(text pages 533–68)

1. Students and other adolescents are passionately protective of some private matters and just as passionately dismissive of others — eager, in fact, to share them. Ask students to examine their own hierarchies of privacy: personal health, family conflicts, ambitions, secret loves, wealth, sorrows, etc. We know that many people choose to reveal these things and more to millions of television viewers. How would students characterize the needs and values that determine whether we divulge our secrets?

2. A clinical social worker, author of *Private Matters: In Defense of the Personal Life,* writes about the expressions of grief in Littleton, Colorado:

> By far the most upsetting current manifestations of television as witness are the news and talk shows that for the past few days have encouraged Columbine students to describe their traumas on the air.

What are we to make of these public de-briefings of heart-rending sorrow?

Ask students to write an analysis of the reasons for the confessions. Should the grief-stricken survivors think of TV as a loving friend? (See Janna Malamud Smith, "Telling Our Terrible Stories to the Tube," *New York Times*, April 25, 1999, p. Wk. 17.)

3. From the *New York Times*, April 21, 1999, p. A20:

   A study by the Federal Trade Commission concluded last June that 89 percent of children's [Web] sites surveyed collected personal information from children and that few of the sites had tried to provide for meaningful parental involvement in the process. The study found that only 23 percent of the sites even tell children to seek parental permission before providing personal information. . . .

   Ask if students have ever responded to such requests. If so, do they feel that some confidence was abused? Should government attempt to regulate these exchanges?

4. One writer thinks that a telephone call has become an intrusion. After all, e-mail, he says, "would be so much neater, more considerate, more respectful of privacy." A question for students that might lead to an evaluative essay: What different purposes are served by different forms of communication, such as the letter, personal contact, the telephone, and e-mail?

5. What about gossip? Is it good or bad? S. T. Karnick thinks gossip is a benign form of social control that helps to enforce proper behavior. "Thus a person who wants to be well-regarded must watch everything he does, lest his friends, relatives, co-workers or neighbors decide to seek other company." ("In Praise of Gossip," *American Outlook*, Summer 1998, pp. 2ff.) What about gossip on the Internet? Is that different from the way in which information used to travel on the old-fashioned grapevine?

Bibliography

"The End of Privacy." *The Economist*, May 1, 1999, pp. 21–23.

Etzioni, Amitai. "Privacy Isn't Dead Yet." *New York Times*, April 6, 1999, p. A27. "We should have laws that protect all personal data, not just some."

Karaim, Reed. "The Invasion of Privacy." *Civilization*, October/November 1996.

Naik, Gautam. "Do I Have Privacy On-Line?" *Wall Street Journal*, December 9, 1996, p. R12.

Powers, Richard. "Losing Our Souls, Bit by Bit." *New York Times*, July 15, 1998, p. A23.

Shapiro, Andrew L. "Privacy for Sale: Peddling 'The Internet.'" *The Nation*, June 23, 1997.

CHAPTER 17
Punishment
(text pages 569–615)

1. With its immediate and somewhat frightening implications for teenagers, the caning of Michael Fay in Singapore is a good place to start the discussion of punishment and, more specifically, of punishment as deterrence. In California, Texas, Missouri, and elsewhere, elected officials have proposed corporal punishment for juvenile vandalism. Many students have probably suffered some form of corporal punishment when very young. Ask students to evaluate such punishment according to the criteria mentioned in the text: Is it fair? Is it effective? Or is it only cruel?

2. Court cases over the years (*Weems v. United States,* 1910; *Troy v. Dulles,* 1958; *Delaware v. Cannon,* 1963) have reflected changing attitudes toward corporal punishment. The constitutional prohibition against "cruel and unusual punishment" remains, however, the strongest obstacle to implementation of corporal punishment. Supreme Court Justice Antonin Scalia doubts whether "any federal judge . . . would uphold a new law providing public lashing, or branding of the right hand, a punishment for certain criminal offenses."

3. At least twenty states have abolished corporal punishment in their schools. In several other states, while it is seldom practiced, its legality has not been challenged. Students may want to look up the statutes which allow or prohibit corporal punishment in their states. A long letter to the *New York Times* on September 13, 1990 (p. A26), develops all the reasons that child beating is both cruel and ineffective.

4. The arrival in this country of immigrants with different ideas about discipline of errant children has renewed the debate about corporal punishment. In February 1996 a Nigerian living in New York was charged with assaulting his ten-year-old son, who suffered various injuries, including a broken wrist. The father defended his actions by alleging that he had followed the traditional ways of disciplining a child in his country. A Nigerian official denied, however, that such practices were acceptable. "A Cultural Reluctance to Spare the Rod" (*New York Times,* February 29, 1996, p. B1) says that a prime issue for many immigrant families is the belief that "Americans don't discipline their children well," and that disciplining children must include hitting them. This is a subject full of material for a variety of assignments. For example, to what extent should other cultures' practices, including the disciplining of children, be respected if they collide with American culture and law?

5. Parents increasingly are being held accountable for the misbehavior of their children. About twenty-five states have passed laws that punish parents with fines and even imprisonment if their children are found guilty of such violations of the law as vandalism, drug dealing, consorting with felons, alcohol abuse, curfew and weapons violations, shoplifting, and truancy. Here the questions of fairness and effectiveness come into especially sharp relief.

6. A short debate on capital punishment, can serve as an introduction to this enormous subject. Perhaps owing to the popularity of the movie *Dead Man*

Walking, the views of the Catholic Church on capital punishment have been widely publicized. All religions, however, incorporate references to death as punishment for some crimes, and a study of such references can be enlightening.

Many opponents of capital punishment advocate public viewing of executions. They are convinced that the sight of the killing would persuade a public in favor of the death penalty that a terrible truth has been concealed. A number of articles have appeared that describe the death watch and the death itself in hideous detail. Ask students who read such descriptions to evaluate their reactions and to defend their positions. See the bibliography for some of these articles.

7. Violent crime rates have dropped in several large cities with the highest crime rates — San Francisco, New York, Los Angeles, Philadelphia, Houston, San Antonio. Students can profitably examine the studies of experts attempting to establish cause-and-effect relations. To what extent does the prospect of punishment contribute to the decline in violent crime?

8. "In Praise of Punishment," by Stanley Brubaker, a professor of government at Colgate University, appeared in *The Public Interest,* Fall 1989. "We should understand punishment as a kind of mirror of praise. If praise expresses gratitude and approbation, punishment expresses resentment and reprobation." Brubaker's essay is, in part, an attack on legal and political philosopher John Rawls's theory of justice. A reply to Brubaker, defending Rawls, appeared in *The Public Interest,* Spring 1990.

9. Shame has resurfaced as a form of punishment in many communities. As one headline puts it: "Forget Prisons. Americans Cry for the Pillory." (*New York Times,* October 4, 1998, p. E6.) The author, Pam Belluck, points out that "President Clinton's opera of embarrassment has brought public shaming to a new high. More than ever, it appears, people are in the mood for good old red-faced humiliation."

But as this article and others make clear, public exposure of wrongdoing is not always regarded as punishment. The people on TV talk shows apparently revel in public chastisement by their hosts. Is shaming in front of a huge unfamiliar audience who will never be seen again different from one's name appearing on a billboard in a small community where the wrongdoer is known? We can ask students, who still remember being shamed in childhood by parents and peers, to assess the effects of this kind of punishment.

Some critics argue that the shaming penalty is "extrajudicial and illegal." Perhaps students can think of an attack on shaming that would be grounded in legal precedent.

Bibliography

Alter, Jonathan, and Pat Wingert. "The Return of Shame," *Newsweek,* February 6, 1995, p. 21. "Americans are fed up with everything from teen pregnancy to drunk drivers. How do we restore a sense of right and wrong?"

Anderson, David C. *Sensible Justice: Alternatives to Prison.* New York: The New Press, 1997.

Currie, Elliott. *Crime and Punishment in America.* New York: Henry Holt, 1997.

de Waal, Frans. *Good Natured: The Origins of Right and Wrong in Humans and Other Animals.* Cambridge, MA: Harvard U. Press, 1996. Argues that "obedience to certain rules, being good and being punished for being bad, have a place in the evolutionary continuum linking humans and other animals."

"Death-Watch Logs, Banality, Nausea, Triple Execution: Guards on Inmates' Final Hours." *New York Times,* January 12, 1997, p. E8.

"Executing Justice. Tightening the Nuts and Bolts of Death by Electric Chair." *New York Times,* August 3, 1997, p. E7. Changes in the execution procedure that were mandated after one convict caught on fire as electricity shot through his body.

Fox, James Alan. "Dead Man Walking." *The Boston Globe,* January 2, 1997, p. A15.

Garland, David, and Antony Duff. *A Reader of Punishment.* New York: Oxford U. Press, 1996.

Humes, Edward. *No Matter How Loud I Shout: A Year in the Life of Juvenile Court.* New York: Simon and Schuster, 1996.

Pooley, Eric. "Death or Life." *Time,* June 16, 1997.

Prejean, Helen. *Dead Man Walking: An Eyewitness Account of the Death Penalty in the United States.* New York: Vintage, 1995.

Rothwax, Harold. *Guilty.* New York: Random House, 1996.

Simmons, John, Marshall Cohen, Joshua Cohen, and Charles Beitz, eds. *Punishment: A Philosophy and Public Affairs Reader.* Princeton, NJ: Princeton U. Press, 1996.

Trombley, Stephen. *Execution Protocol: Inside America's Capital Punishment Industry.* New York: Anchor/Doubleday, 1995.

CHAPTER 18
Sexual Harassment
(text pages 616–38)

1. A few editions ago some teachers and students found it embarrassing to discuss the selections in a chapter on pornography. Now that the most explicit details of sexual misconduct appear in major newspapers — to say nothing of the proliferation of sexually explicit movies and TV shows — students probably are inured to discussions of highly suggestive material. Needless to say, teachers will need to be sensitive to issues — and vocabulary — that may cause offense.

2. Sexual harassment is a transgression absolutely dependent on clear definition. The problem of a meaning on which everybody can agree, of course, remains unresolved. The NCTE's July 1998 *Quarterly Review of Doublespeak* reported this item:

> One female student at the University of Pennsylvania lodged a sexual harassment complaint because a male student made the comment "nice legs" to her when she was wearing a miniskirt. The plaintiff called the comment a "mini-rape."

74

Ask students how much words should count. What kinds of limits would they impose on speech?

3. "A growing list of female athletes . . . say they have been sexually harassed by their male coaches." (See bibliography.) A very long article reports on many cases around the country, some of which have become highly publicized lawsuits. In the article the authors of a study on sexual harassment by male coaches make a familiar accusation: "There's no such thing as consensual anything when one person has that much control over another."

Perhaps some students know of cases that have never reached the newspapers. They may know of affairs involving teachers and students who are not athletes, affairs which pose problems of definition. No real names should be used, of course.

4. Richard Dooling blames President Clinton's troubles on sexual harassment laws that prohibit even private behavior. ("Making Criminals of Us All," *New York Times*, December 30, 1998, p. A22.) Ellen Bravo objects and defines sexual harassment more narrowly. (*New York Times*, February 6, 1999.) Other letter writers on January 4, 1999, reproached Dooling for blaming the Clinton scandal on the law.

Bibliography

Cloud, John. "Sex and the Law." *Time*, March 23, 1998, pp. 49 ff. "Sexual harassment can mean firing victims who don't give in or merely telling a dirty joke. Clinton's fate rests on laws that tie even lawyers in knots."

Elshtain, Jean Bethke. "Beyond Consent." *The New Republic*, May 4, 1998, p. 8. "It is worth reminding ourselves that there are all sorts of things we do not permit people to consent to."

Finn, Robin. "Growth in Women's Sports Stirs Harassment Issue." *New York Times*, March 7, 1999, p. A16.

Hill, Anita. "A Matter of Definition." *New York Times*, March 19, 1998, p. A25.

Olson, Walter. "Have the Harassment Rules Changed?" *Wall Street Journal*, April 6, 1998, p. A25. "The lesson of *Jones vs. Clinton* is that even cases too weak to make it to a jury can inflict ruin on defendants' reputations."

CHAPTER 19

Sex and Violence in Popular Culture

(text pages 639–59)

1. Students can serve as expert witnesses in cases for or against the censorship of sex and violence. Many of them have been immersed in television culture since early childhood. This doesn't mean, however, that they can be certain of general conclusions based only on personal experience. An analysis of this subject rests on all the important elements of argument.

   a. *Definition.* What constitutes "too much" attention to sex in TV, movies, and music? Can we distinguish "good" and "bad" violence?

b. *Support.* Students should notice that in many discussions about this subject — including several articles in the text — evidence to support a point of view is *selective.* Students can probably uncover other examples that encourage questions about the strength of an author's conclusions.

c. *Warrants.* Perhaps the most important issue is the cause-effect relationship between viewing and behavior. Although most experts seem to agree that a relationship exists, one prominent skeptic, Jonathan Freedman of the University of Toronto, continues to argue the weakness of causality: The fact that aggressive children like to watch violent shows hardly proves that the violent shows *cause* aggression. An English study found that it was "the chaos and change that [juvenile offenders] were living in" that promoted violent behavior and that "TV and movies played a relatively small part in their lives."

It's often been pointed out that Japanese movies, TV programs, and cartoons are at least as violent and pornographic as ours. Yet the rate of crime in Japan is far lower than in the United States. Ask students to find reasons that might account for the difference.

d. From *The Economist* (August 13, 1994, p. 74):

Ron Slaby of Harvard University identifies four ways in which media violence can lay itself out in a child's personality: the aggressor effect, an increase in meanness; the victim effect, an increase in fearfulness and mistrust; the bystander effect, an increase in callousness; and the appetite effect, an increase in the desire to see or commit violence. Simple imitation may also play a part.

2. TV violence has been a target for criticism almost from the inception of television itself. The first congressional hearings on this issue took place in 1954. To date, there have been more than three thousand studies of the effects of TV violence. Students might consult some of these earlier attacks and try to determine first, if the violence on TV has changed, and second, if the nature of the criticism has changed. (A special issue of *TV Guide* on June 14, 1975, was titled "Violence! On TV — Does It Affect Our Society?")

3. Biblical stories, fairy tales, even nursery rhymes and lullabies — think of "London Bridge" and "Rockabye Baby" — contain images of cruelty and violence. Students can look for the ways, if any, in which those images are different from the representations in popular culture. The research paper in the book, "When a Fairy Tale Is Not Just a Fairy Tale," is a useful introduction to the analysis.

4. Someone has said, only half in jest, that liberals are worried about too much violence, conservatives about too much sex. If students agree that this judgment is true, ask them to examine the cultural assumptions that govern these preferences.

5. Sexual talk and activity are today far more prevalent than violence on prime-time TV. In the October 1995 *Journal of Youth and Adolescence,* Monique Ward examines the sexual content of several popular TV shows. Among other things she points out that physical appearance plays an inordinate role in sexual attraction. Students might be asked to evaluate her conclusion that looks are everything. (In fact, it is easy to find characters who play romantic roles but hardly qualify as sex gods or goddesses.)

6. Do students agree with the following assessment of sexual content in TV shows and movies?

The down side is that however much good the entertainment media's sexual liberation has done or may do, it also burdens the audience with additional anxiety by holding up images, over and over, of beauty, nonstop pleasure and excitement that most lives cannot match. (*New York Times,* October 29, 1995, p. H40.)

7. Barbara Ehrenreich's discussion of gangsta rap in Chapter 15, "Freedom of Speech," is relevant to this chapter, too.

8. Ann Powers's "The Stresses of Youth, The Strains of Its Music" interprets the massacre in Littleton, Colorado, as an example of "the meanings and effects of youth culture." (*New York Times,* April 25, 1999, p. W18.) The author offers a penetrating analysis, with abundant support, of the violent extremes of music, fashion, and lifestyle which the murderers embraced. "Teachers," she says, "have long showed students how to grasp the nuances of literature and history. But instead of actually exploring youth culture in the company of young people, many adults debate its legality among themselves."

How would students respond to explorations of youth culture in class with their teachers? Would they resent it as an intrusion — or a joke? Could students speak frankly about its appeal? After all, as the author points out, "Popular art aimed at adolescents often trades on alienation."

Surely there will be some students who are not moved by Marilyn Manson or Rammstein — both favorites of Eric Harris, one of the Littleton killers — and who can write an evaluation essay rejecting or condemning the appeal of these entertainers and others.

9. What about comic books and video games? Believe it or not, there is a Comics Code Authority. It was created in 1954 to control the violence content in comic books after Frederick Wertham's celebrated attack on comic and horror books in *Seduction of the Innocent* (Rinehart, 1954). Obviously, the code has relaxed its rules in recent years.

The video games *Doom* and *Quake* were mentioned as favorites of the Littleton killers. Can students find research proving that the influence of violent games and books can also be benign? Has their own experience with such entertainment suggested that there are valuable lessons about life to be learned from those contacts?

Bibliography

Kakutani, Michiko. "To Hell with Him." *New York Times,* December 7, 1997, p. 36. The Devil downgraded, glamorizing evil and cruelty.

Keating, Frank. "Mayhem Culture." *Wall Street Journal,* December 20, 1997, p. A23. How the worlds of music and movies have changed since 1955 when the author was eleven.

The Third Annual UCLA Television Violence Report. Financed by the four major networks, this report offers "synopses of video gore oozing across the collective national psyche." Included are *Walker, Texas Ranger, The X-Files, Buffy the Vampire Slayer,* and documentaries. Internet at <http://ccp.ucla.edu/1996-97.htm>

PART FOUR

CLASSIC ARGUMENTS

INTRODUCTION

"Reading requires more than words." This observation serves as a partial text for the comments that follow on the use of the "Classic Arguments" section. To understand and enjoy the selections in this section, students will need not only the ability to decode the linguistic symbols but also *information* — about historical events and figures.

There are two sources for the background information and the interpretation of that information: the library and the instructor. Use of the library needs no recommendation from me, but I should like to put in a word for the instructor as a resource. Notwithstanding the prevailing distaste for lecturing in composition courses, it seems to me perfectly legitimate for instructors to give students the information they need in a short summary *before* they proceed, and even to interpret the data if necessary, whenever such an introduction saves valuable time, enlivens the information, and arouses student interest as library research often does not.

Since each selection in "Classic Arguments" is followed by questions and writing suggestions, I have offered here only occasional questions and suggestions for classroom activities. Instead I have written about these essays largely as I myself have responded to them — sometimes in full agreement, sometimes in partial acquiescence — and as I have discussed them with students, who have often disagreed with me.

From Crito (p. 663)

PLATO

1. This is one of the three selections in "Classic Arguments" that deal with civil disobedience. Both King and Thoreau argue that civil disobedience can be justified by recourse to moral laws that supersede the laws of government. This is an argument that students will understand and recognize as integral to the development of American democracy. Socrates, however, under threat of a death sentence by the state of Athens, refuses to escape, because escape would be a violation of the loyalty the state has a right to expect. Having lived under and been protected by the laws of Athens, he asks how he can now refuse to obey them.

    In history classes ancient Greece is identified as the cradle of Western democracy. Students therefore believe erroneously that the Greek philosophy of government exalted the individual. Socrates' conviction for introducing new deities and corrupting the youth of Athens and his acquiescence in his punishment remind students of the excesses of totalitarianism. But in *Crito* Socrates interprets his willingness to die as the decision of a good citizen and a just man who is obedient to the laws that the citizens of the state, including himself, have enacted. Justice is of all things most dear to him, and he prefers to be remembered as a victim rather than a doer of evil.

(The truth is that what Socrates believed is known almost entirely through the dialogues of Plato, who was inclined to express his own views as if they were those of his master. Plato rejected the democratic state and described the perfect society in *The Republic*, which bears little resemblance to a modern democracy.)

2. It's doubtful that one student in a thousand will agree that Socrates should make no attempt to save his own life, especially in view of the questionable nature of his crime. On the other hand, if students were to think of Socrates as one who died for his faith, would they continue to regard his acceptance of death as an act of foolishness?

3. This selection will enable students to become familiar with the celebrated Socratic dialogue, a teaching strategy in which Socrates arrives at the truth through skillful questioning and prolific use of definitions and examples.

4. Character as well as intellect play a role in Socrates' decision, and the reader of the defense can find evidence of his dignity, his moderation, his serenity, and his regard for parents, children, and friends.

5. Once it is extracted, the argument of this dialogue is clear, and the language of the translation should pose no problem. Any obstacles will probably emerge in the attempt to master or even confront the long paragraphs. Since this is a dialogue, a piece of dramatic prose, it's appropriate and helpful for parts of it to be read aloud by good readers.

    I would ask students to summarize in one or two sentences the meaning of each long paragraph before asking for a précis of the whole dialogue.

6. Socrates and Thoreau stand on opposite sides of the debate over the relationship between the individual and the state. One or two students may want to play devil's advocate and defend Socrates' submission against Thoreau's lofty individualism.

A Modest Proposal (p. 668)
JONATHAN SWIFT

1. If students are reading this essay for the first time without preparation or warning, some of them will take Swift's proposal literally. But, then, so did some eighteenth-century readers with perhaps less justification. Some teachers think that the multiple horrors of organized cruelty and genocide in the twentieth century have made Swift's proposal at least marginally credible. We hope not.

2. Students should be able to describe the person ostensibly making the "modest" proposal, since the proposer himself calls attention to his characteristics: compassionate but disinterested, thoughtful, reasonable, temperate, well informed. The question is whether such a person — one who is com-

passionate and reasonable — could make a proposal to breed human infants for food. If students agree that he could not, then why has he done so? If his reasons are not those that he alleges them to be, what can they be?

There are several ways of deciding on the answers. One is to examine the language. Does the voice of the proposer — formal, detached, heavy with statistical data — suggest one who is passionately distressed by the suffering of the Irish? Why does the proposer refer to the Irish in terms descriptive of animals rather than human beings? Is there any place in which the voice and language of the author seem to change, where he offers solutions entirely different in kind from the breeding of children for food? How are we to interpret the difference in these two voices? In the next-to-last paragraph even the voice of the proposer begins to change; to urge that Irish adults would have been fortunate to die within the first year of life is a judgment that can be offered only in bitter irony.

3. It is not just the language or the disparity between the voices that can give away the ironic stance. There are also the external criteria, including the subject itself. Are there people in Swift's audience, no matter how indifferent to the fate of the Irish, who would enjoy the prospect of eating human infants? Would an Anglican dean be likely to make such a suggestion in the expectation that reasonable people would find it acceptable? Why would an essay outlining a serious proposal to breed children for food survive for more than two hundred years not as a curiosity but as a model of expository prose for readers throughout the English-speaking world? Consideration of these questions ought to lead to a suspicion, even in the most undiscerning reader, that some other interpretation than the literal one must exist.

Civil Disobedience (p. 676)
HENRY DAVID THOREAU

Thoreau's classic defense of civil disobedience is the antithesis of Socrates' defense of the rights of the state. Thoreau believes that that government is best which governs least or not at all. He denies the authority of government to command the allegiance of an individual who does not wish to concede it. Civil disobedience is justified when conscience dictates that a greater harm will result from compliance with the law than from refusal to obey.

1. Students will need information about the Mexican War of 1846–48, to which Thoreau makes a number of references. We may assume that students know something about slavery (although a recent study by the National Endowment for the Humanities revealed that 80 percent of college seniors were ignorant of what the Emancipation Proclamation did). They will also need to know that Massachusetts was not a slave state, that Thoreau was objecting to an *implicit* sanction of slavery for economic reasons.

2. Thoreau uses the term "unjust laws," but unlike King he fails to define it. Throughout the essay he speaks of "right" and "wrong," "conscience," "a higher law." In the next-to-last paragraph he mentions the New Testament. Students can profitably wrestle with a summary of Thoreau's criteria for judgment. They can uncover clues in his opinions of slavery, the

Constitution of the United States, the majority in a democracy, voting, soldiers, imprisonment, Daniel Webster.

3. Discussing the relevance of Thoreau's ideas and actions to present-day issues — civil rights, racism, U.S. foreign policy, taxation — can test and sharpen student understanding of civil disobedience. What kind of protest would Thoreau engage in today? (His own protest ended after one day in jail when an aunt bailed him out.) What specific issues would be likely to arouse him? If he were a college student today, would he resort to protests against some college rules and activities? Many student protesters who engage in unlawful activities insist on amnesty as a condition of their surrender to the authorities. What would the participants in this civil disobedience symposium — Socrates, Thoreau, and King — have said about the refusal to accept punishment?

What would Thoreau say about the growth of government since his day? Students might speculate on the state of individual rights 150 years after Thoreau. What examples can they offer of restrictions on individual rights? Can these restrictions be justified by taking into account population growth and the increasing complexity of life?

Can the acts of civil disobedience by Thoreau and King be compared or contrasted? Students should take into consideration the causes for which each was jailed and the principles on which each based his defense.

4. This essay is like a rich cake, studded with unexpected treats. Students may find it indigestible at first, but they can be helped to enjoy it. The claim will be perfectly comprehensible to anyone who is familiar with protests against unjust laws or an unjust government. It is Thoreau's discursive organization and sonorous prose that prevent average or slow readers from appreciating the force of his ideas. Since there is hardly time in one semester to read and discuss a long essay like this one with the thoroughness it deserves, we shall have to settle for an understanding of its major ideas. Fortunately, Thoreau includes homely examples of his most abstract utterances in almost every paragraph. These examples provide the key to decoding the generalizations students may find difficult.

The essay suggests opportunities for short, in-class exercises to increase student comprehension. (1) Paraphrase an important idea. (2) Offer examples for one of Thoreau's generalizations.

Declaration of Sentiments and Resolutions, Seneca Falls (p. 695)

ELIZABETH CADY STANTON

1. Like the Declaration of Independence (reprinted in Chapter 1), this is a classic example of the use of fact, value, and policy in an argument. The argument for women's rights is based on an unambiguous warrant: "Both men *and women* are endowed by the Creator with the right to 'life, liberty, and the pursuit of happiness.'" Both documents make an appeal to a universal audience. The greatest difference between them lies in the policies they espouse. While the Declaration of Independence calls for a separation from Great Britain and the institution of a new and independent government, the Declaration of Sentiments and Resolutions calls for strenuous

efforts by both men and women toward "immediate admission to all the rights and privileges which belong to [women] as citizens of the United States."

The language of that call to action reminds us that both women's rights activists of the mid–nineteenth century and abolitionists often shared the same goals. Stanton and others supported the antislavery movement, and Frederick Douglass, the celebrated black writer and orator, attended the Seneca Falls convention and argued for the elective franchise for women.

2. Does the close imitation of the Declaration of Independence weaken or enhance the impact of the Seneca Falls declaration? That is, does it suggest a parody or a failure of originality? Or is the imitation based on strong rhetorical principles?

    How do students feel about the grievances outlined by Stanton? Are they all equally compelling? Are they as important as those in the Declaration of Independence? (Some critics have argued that they are *more* important.)

3. Some grievances will need explanation, not only of the language but of the ideas and their history.

    a. "He has never permitted her to exercise her inalienable right to the elective franchise" (para. 4).

        (Students may not know that the Nineteenth Amendment to the Constitution, which granted women the right to vote in federal and state elections, was not ratified until 1921.)

    b. "He has created a false public sentiment by giving to the world a different code of morals for men and women, by which moral delinquencies which exclude women from society, are not only tolerated, but deemed of little account in man" (para. 16).

        (Students should recognize a statement of the "double standard," but examples can make it clear for those who are not sure.)

    c. "He allows her in Church, as well as State, but a subordinate position, claiming Apostolic authority for her exclusion from the ministry, and, with some exceptions, from any public participation in the affairs of the Church" (para. 15).

        (Students who know about the current conflicts in some churches over ordination of women can initiate a discussion of this grievance.)

4. Students should try to name and evaluate the changes that have occurred in women's lives (and therefore in men's lives, too) since 1848. Most of the changes will be clear; a few will be debatable. A discussion of the changes or lack of them seems especially relevant today, when influential feminists are engaged in assessing the gains and losses brought about by the women's movement. Do students think that the gains offset the losses? (There is an unexpected irony in a recent claim by Joan Ganz Cooney, chair of the Children's Television Workshop, that a majority of working mothers of young children say they would prefer to stay at home but cannot afford to do so. Women, says Cooney, had more choices forty years ago.)

5. Needless to say, male students should be brought into any discussion of women's rights, and they should feel free to express sentiments with which the female students may not agree. The instructor may have to make quick

judgments about what is acceptable in a civil discussion, but I'd be inclined to err on the side of freedom to make a rude noise.

Warfare: An Invention — Not a Biological Necessity (p. 700)
MARGARET MEAD

1. Derek Freeman's attacks on Mead have some bearing on her essay on war. Freeman was critical of her views on evolution, accusing her of indifference to its profound importance to human history. But in this essay Mead makes clear that she regards war as a primitive response which, like other early practices, can disappear as man evolves to a higher state. In an address to the American Anthropological Association in 1960, she spoke of "the whole history of evolution, in which human evolution is one part and cultural evolution a smaller one." (Paul Sankman, "Margaret Mead, Derek Freeman, and the Issue of Evolution," *The Skeptical Inquirer*, November/December 1998, p. 35.)

2. How can the reader verify the accuracy of Mead's examples, especially those of peoples who are likely to be unfamiliar to the general reader? Many arguments are enhanced by but not necessarily dependent on examples. In this argument, however, the examples seem to provide indispensable support for a controversial claim. Students should try to decide if they can accept Mead's case as proved if they remain skeptical of the examples.

3. Susan Sontag's "Why Are We in Kosovo?" is a powerful argument that may give students further food for thought — and agreement or rebuttal — after they have read Mead. Sontag says, "War is not simply a mistake, a failure to communicate. There is radical evil in the world, which is why there are just wars. And this is a just war." (*New York Times Magazine,* May 2, 1999, pp. 52 ff.)

4. Students will find it useful to examine Mead's style, especially her accessible vocabulary, transitions, use of questions, use of examples and analogies. The organization of the essay is also worth comment. Mead rebuts some opposing views before offering her own claim in the fourth paragraph, and then continues throughout the essay to anticipate and refute other objections. Have students compare the effectiveness of this kind of development with the relatively straightforward organization of Van den Haag's rebuttals in his essay on capital punishment.

Politics and the English Language (p. 707)
GEORGE ORWELL

1. I find that Orwell's great essay grows more and more difficult to teach as our students become less and less sensitive to language and style. In the chapter on language, I have included some examples of inflated language that confirm Orwell's criticism. The deficiencies of these professional writers are not, however, those of which freshmen students are guilty in their own writing. Rather, the examples represent the kinds of obscure and pretentious language that students should be alert to in the arguments that they *read*.

In order to read Orwell intelligently, students must not only understand his terms — *dying metaphors, verbal false limbs, pretentious diction* — but also be able to appreciate the awkwardness and unintelligibility in his examples.

2. The organization of the essay, fortunately, lends itself to a study of discrete parts without a loss of sense or purpose. As teachers of argument, we should give our greatest attention to those parts that have direct relevance to the way in which bad language can distort an argument. Under "Meaningless Words," for example, Orwell uses selections from politics. But the heart of the essay may fairly be said to begin with paragraph 13. I would therefore concentrate on an understanding of Orwell's claim about the relation between politics and language. For this more examples are crucial (Orwell offers only phrases). There are brief selections in the chapter on language to which students may refer. The best long examples will usually be found in the writing and speeches of partisans on the far right and the far left of the political spectrum. You may have to begin by bringing in examples you have found that show what is meant by distortion and deception in political language. Freshman students may not know enough about the history and circumstances surrounding a particular argument to detect its misuse of language. Perhaps some egregious outburst in the school paper will serve.

Letter from Birmingham Jail (p. 719)
MARTIN LUTHER KING JR.

1. An introduction to the circumstances surrounding King's imprisonment will probably be necessary. Students will have to know something about the segregation laws in the 1960s and the civil rights demonstrations against them led by King and the southern Christian Leadership conference. King's use of *Negro* and *colored* in the sixties should also be explained. King uses the word *black* only in reference to nationalist groups, whose tactics he rejects. I've used his terms in the questions in the text because I thought it would be presumptuous to change them.

2. King's letter, which was clearly addressed to a much wider audience than the white Protestant ministers in Birmingham, is a superb example of a long exposition in which students can find skillful use of all the elements of argument. King's use of support deserves special attention.

Support

a. He recounts the indignities suffered by Negroes (para. 14). This constitutes a list of grievances like the lists in The Declaration of Independence. The grievances are expressed as personal experiences. (Notice the use of the second person and the reference to his five-year-old son.) Some readers will respond to personal experience when abstractions about law and justice fail to move them.

b. He summarizes the history of attempts to gain civil rights to prove that Negroes have been patient. This is an answer to the accusation that his activities were "untimely."

c. He invokes authorities from ancient Greece, the Bible, Christian and Judaic scholarship, American statesmen. These authorities support the validity of his protest and his "extremist" approach (para. 31).

d. He refers to the struggles of other oppressed people, struggles with which the white Protestant ministers and his larger audience will sympathize and which they will recognize as analogous to the protests of Negroes.

e. Equally important are his appeals to the values of his two audiences, small and large: a sense of justice, compassion for the oppressed, a love of freedom, admiration and respect for brave, peaceful — and worthy — resistance, and the willingness of the resisters to suffer severe consequences in the service of a noble cause.

Definition

a. Like any classic, King's letter continues to reverberate. However sketchy their knowledge of specific events, students surely know that millions of people throughout the world are actively opposing "unjust" laws, often for the first time in decades and at great risk, and that King's definition of such laws is still highly relevant.

King's definition rests primarily on religious foundations (para. 14). The Declaration of Independence also invokes the Creator as the source of justice and morality. Students can study King's language and try to decide if his definition of just and unjust laws can survive without reference to "the law of God." Some readers may feel that King's definition is too broad, too vague. Is there a danger that we may define any laws that we want to support as the laws of God? (In fact, the laws of slavery were so defined by their supporters.)

Warrant

a. The warrant in "Letter" — oppressed people have the right to protest their oppression — recalls the warrant in the Declaration of Independence. This is one of several similarities between the two documents.

b. The white ministers in Birmingham argued that they disagreed with the *tactics* of the demonstrators. Does King's lengthy response suggest that he believes the ministers might also have disapproved of the *right* to protest?

Tone

a. King's tone reflects dignity, humility, and generosity to the opposition. Throughout the letter he skillfully negotiates a narrow line between criticism of his accusers and the belief that "as men of goodwill" they will understand and accept his argument. This conciliatory tone is very different from the tone adopted by more militant black leaders. Students might find it instructive to compare the two voices.

b. In college newspapers and elsewhere the tone adopted by angry writers is often abusive and self-righteous. Ask students to look for examples and comment on the effect such attitudes have on a neutral or unfriendly reader. If there are differences in the responses, how can we account for them?

Language

King's style is lofty, grave, sermonic. Several of the literary strategies he favors emphasize his role as preacher.

a. King uses rhetorical questions throughout (for example, paras. 22 and 26). What effect might such questions have on a neutral or unfriendly audience?

b. King also uses structural repetition for emphasis (para. 44). "I Have a Dream" is an even more ambitious example of this literary technique, which King employed frequently in all his writing. Some students may recognize parallels to the language of the King James version of the Bible.

Some readers have found King's long, rhythmic sentences and figurative language pretentious and overblown. (See para. 42.) Is this elevated style appropriate in the context? Or would a less decorative style have been more effective?

Students themselves are not so likely to indulge in elaborate metaphorical language when they argue social issues — they usually succumb to this temptation when they write about nature — nor should they be encouraged to do so, but they should be alert to its use in the utterances of public figures and able to evaluate its contribution to the argument.

Organization

This is a long argument with many parts, whose transitions make it seem more closely organized than it really is. The following rough outline indicates how the argument proceeds.

1. background of the march in Birmingham;
   explanation of his imprisonment .... pp. 719–22
2. definition of just and unjust laws 723–25
3. disappointment with white moderates 725–26
4. rejection of charge of extremism;
   defense of nonviolent action 726–28
5. disappointment with the white church leadership 728–30
6. optimism about the future 730
7. attack on the police use of moral means for immoral ends 731–32
8. praise for heroic demonstrators 732
9. conclusion 732–33

I Have a Dream (p. 734)

MARTIN LUTHER KING JR.

1. Someone in the class, whether instructor or student, who can muster a compelling declamatory style, should read part of this speech aloud. If you

can obtain a recording of the original speech, so much the better. There is no better way to savor the language and to gain some understanding, however limited, of the impact of this speech on its listeners. Ask students to compare, as far as possible, its effect when read and its effect when listened to. Is there a difference? (There is no doubt that the human voice, with its timbre and its capacity for emotional expression, can indicate values as effectively as words.) Students should also keep in mind that this speech was delivered before a large outdoor crowd. Would this situation influence the kind of argument King needed to make?

2. Students should be asked to consider this speech as a *written* argument. What was the purpose of this speech? How specific was King in recommending policy or actions to be undertaken by the audience? Would the speech have been more effective as argument if King had urged the enactment of specific laws and exhorted his audience to work for them?

3. Finally, students should attend to the language. Does the language enhance the impact of the argument? Or does it sometimes distract? For example, in the fourth paragraph, there is the sustained metaphor of the promissory note. But the succeeding sentences contain figures of speech involving drugs, valleys, sunlit paths, open doors, quicksand, and rocks. Are some metaphors more effective than others? If so, why?

Appendix:
Rogerian Argument

Several instructors have recently expressed an interest in teaching the theories of Carl Rogers as an adjunct to Toulmin's theory of argument. Since Rogers emphasizes the importance of establishing common ground between two or more parties, his theories can be introduced with discussion of "Finding the Middle Ground" in Chapter Nine. In addition to the information for instructors, this appendix includes a brief introduction on Carl Rogers that can be distributed to students as a handout along with an excerpt from his book *A Way of Being* (Houghton Mifflin, 1980).

For the Student

Carl Rogers (1902–1987) was one of the founders of humanistic psychology. Of himself as therapist he wrote: "I enter the relation [with the patient] not as a scientist, not as a physician who can accurately diagnose and cure, but as a person, entering into a personal relationship." He believed that the experience of two people meeting and speaking truly to each other without assuming other roles would have a healing effect.

In later years he became convinced that the same principles of nondirective, nonconfrontational therapy that emphasized attentive listening could work, not only for couples and small groups but also for large groups, even nations, to create more harmonious relationships.

Rogers was not, of course, the only psychologist who thought that a knowledge of psychological principles could offer insight into the causes and resolution of public controversies, even the violent confrontations in war, terrorism, and the taking of hostages. The passage below summarizes another humanistic psychologist's view of the causes of war, a view influenced by Rogers's belief that the failure to understand the "reality" of the enemy was a major cause of war.

> One theory holds that people's misperceptions about their enemies act as hindrances to peace. Possible distortions include an image of the enemy as diabolical, a virile self-image, an overconfident military, lack of empathy for the enemy, selective inattention to facts, and a moral self-image.[1]

Because Rogers was resolutely optimistic about the essential goodness of human nature, a study of Rogerian psychology inevitably provokes the question: Does human nature contain evil? This is the subject of a mini-debate between Carl Rogers and Rollo May, a prominent psychoanalyst and author of *Man's Search for Himself*. Rollo May answered Yes. Carl Rogers answered No.[2] The excerpt below emphasizes the warrant on which Rogers based his claim.

---

[1]Robert S. Feldman, *Understanding Psychology*. (New York: McGraw Hill, 1990), p. 734. Feldman is summarizing the view of Ralph K. White, editor of a guidebook on the ways that psychology can help to prevent a nuclear disaster.

[2]David Myers, *Psychology*. (New York: Worth, 1989), p. 428.

Rollo May: Yes

The culture admittedly has powerful effects upon us. But it could not have these effects were these tendencies not already present. Who makes up the culture except persons like you and me? The culture is evil as well as good because we, the human beings who constitute it, are evil as well as good . . . We are bundles of both evil and good potentialities . . . Life, to me, is not a requirement to live out a pre-ordained pattern of goodness, but a challenge coming down through the centuries out of the fact that each of us can throw the lever toward good or toward evil. This seems to me to require the age-old religious truths of mercy and forgiveness, and it leaves no place for self-righteousness.

Carl Rogers: No

Though I am very well aware of the incredible amount of destructive, cruel, malevolent behavior in today's world — from the threats of war to the senseless violence in the streets — I do not find that this evil is inherent in human nature. In a psychological climate which is nurturant of growth and choice, I have never known an individual to choose the cruel or destructive path . . . [So] my experience leads me to believe that it is cultural influences which are the major factor in our evil behaviors . . . I see members of the human species . . . as essentially constructive in their fundamental nature, but damaged by their experience.

In the following passage from one of his books, Rogers reveals his intellectual and emotional journey from contemplation of his own reality to recognition of the realities of others. After reading his argument, you should try to find examples of public controversies — in this book and in the media where they are reported every day — which you think lend themselves to compromise or a middle ground. Try to be specific about the strategies you would suggest for achieving the compromise. Do you think there are controversies in which agreement is not possible or desirable? Be specific here, too, about the basic principles that might limit acceptance of a different point of view. Finally, can you point to a connection between Rogers' views of human nature in the mini-debate and the proposals for educational reform that he offers in his book?

From *A Way of Being*
CARL ROGERS

I, and many others, have come to a new realization. It is this: The only reality I can possibly know is the world as *I* perceive and experience it at this moment. The only reality you can possibly know is the world as *you* perceive and experience it at this moment. And the only certainty is that those perceived realities are different. There are as many "real worlds" as there are people! This creates a most burdensome dilemma, one never before experienced in history.

From time immemorial, the tribe or the community or the nation or the culture has agreed upon what constitutes the real world. To be sure, different tribes or different cultures might have held sharply different world views, but at least there was a large, relatively unified group which felt assured in its knowledge of the world and the universe, and knew that this perception was *true.* So the community frowned upon, condemned, persecuted, even killed those who did not agree, who perceived reality differently. Copernicus, even though he kept his findings secret for many years, was eventually declared a heretic. Galileo established proof of Copernicus's views, but in his seventies he was forced to recant his teachings. Giordano Bruno was burned at the stake in 1600 for teaching that there were many worlds in our universe.

Individuals who deviated in their perception of religious reality were tortured and killed. In the mid-1800s, Ignaz Semmelweis, an intense young Hungarian physician-scientist, was driven insane by his persecutors because he made the then absurd claim that childbed fever, that dread scourge of the maternity room, was carried from one woman to another by invisible germs on the hands and instruments of the doctors. Obvious nonsense, in terms of the reality of his day. In our own American Colonies, those who were even suspected of having psychic powers were considered witches and were hanged or crushed under great stones. History offers a continuing series of examples of the awful price paid by those who perceive a reality different from the agreed-upon real world. Although society has often come around eventually to agree with its dissidents, as in the instances I have mentioned, there is no doubt that this insistence upon a known and certain universe has been part of the cement that holds a culture together.

Today we face a different situation. The ease and rapidity of worldwide communication means that every one of us is aware of a dozen "realities"; even though we may think some of them absurd (like reincarnation) or dangerous (like communism), we cannot help but be aware of them. No longer can we exist in a secure cocoon, knowing that we all see the world in the same way.

Because of this change, I want to raise a very serious question: Can we today afford the luxury of having "*a*" reality? Can we still preserve the belief that there is a "real world" upon whose definition we all agree? I am convinced that this is a luxury we *cannot* afford, a myth we dare not maintain. Only once in recent history has this been fully and successfully achieved. Millions of people were in complete agreement as to the nature of social and cultural reality — an agreement brought about by the mesmerizing influence of Hitler. This agreement about reality nearly marked the destruction of Western culture. I do not see it as something to be emulated.

In Western culture during this century — especially in the United States — there has also been an agreed-upon reality of values. This gospel can be stated very briefly: "More is better, bigger is better, faster is better, and modern technology will achieve all three of these eminently desirable goals." But now that credo is a crumbling disaster in which few believe. It is dissolving in the smog of pollution, the famine of overpopulation, the Damocles' sword of the nuclear bomb. We have so successfully achieved the goal of "a bigger bang for a buck" that we are in danger of destroying all life on this planet.

Our attempts, then, to live in the "real world" which all perceive in the same way have, in my opinion, led us to the brink of annihilation as a species. I will be so bold as to suggest an alternative.

It appears to me that the way of the future must be to base our lives and our education on the assumption that there are as many realities as there are persons, and that our highest priority is to accept that hypothesis and proceed from there. Proceed where? Proceed, each of us, to explore openmindedly the many, many perceptions of reality that exist. We would, I believe, enrich our own lives in the process. We would also become more able to cope with the reality in which each one of us exists, because we would be aware of many more options. This might well be a life full of perplexity and difficult choices, demanding greater maturity, but it would be an exciting and adventurous life.

The question may well be raised, however, whether we could have a community or a society based on this hypothesis of multiple realities. Might not such a society be a completely individualistic anarchy? That is not my opinion. Suppose my grudging tolerance of your separate world view became a full acceptance of you and your right to have such a view. Suppose that instead of shutting out the realities of others as absurd or dangerous or heretical or stupid, I was willing to explore and learn about those realities? Suppose you were willing to do the same. What would be the social result? I think that our society would be based not on a blind commitment to a cause or creed or view of reality, but on a common commitment to each other as rightfully separate persons, with separate realities. The natural human tendency to care for another would no longer be "I care for you because you are the same as I," but, instead, "I prize and treasure you because you are different from me."

Idealistic, you say? It surely is. How can I be so utterly naive and "unrealistic" as to have any hope that such a drastic change could conceivably come about? I base my hope partly on the view of world history so aptly stated by Charles Beard: "When the skies grow dark, the stars begin to shine." So we may see the emergence of leaders who are moving in this new direction.

I base my hope, even more solidly, on the view enunciated by Lancelot Whyte, the historian of ideas, in his final book before his death. It is his theory, in which he is not alone, that great steps in human history are anticipated, and probably brought about, by changes in the unconscious thinking of thousands and millions of individuals during the period preceding the change. Then, in a relatively short space of time, a new idea, a new perspective, seems to burst upon the world scene, and change occurs. He gives the example that before 1914, patriotism and nationalism were unquestioned virtues. Then began the faint unconscious questioning which built an unconscious tradition reversing a whole pattern of thought. This new perspective burst into the open between 1950 and 1970. "My country, right or wrong" is no longer a belief to live by. Nationalistic wars are out of date and out of favor, and even though they continue, world opinion is deeply opposed. Whyte (1974) points out that "at any moment the *unconscious levels are ahead of the conscious* in the task of unifying emotion, thought and action!" [*The Universe of Experience*, Harper Torchbooks, p. 107.]

For me, this line of thought is entirely congenial. I have stated that we are wiser than our intellects, that our organisms as a whole have a wisdom and purposiveness which goes well beyond our conscious thought. I believe that this idea applies to the concepts I have been presenting in this chapter. I think that men and women, individually and collectively, are inwardly and organismically rejecting the view of one single, culture-approved reality. I believe they are moving inevitably toward the acceptance of millions of separate, challenging, exciting, informative, *individual* perceptions of reality. I regard it as possible that this view — like the sudden and separate discovery of the principles of quantum mechanics by scientists in different countries — may begin to come into effective existence in many parts of the world at once. If so, we will be living in a totally new universe, different from any in history. Is it conceivable that such a change can come about?

91

Here lies the challenge to educators — probably the most insecure and frightened among any of the professions — battered by public pressures, limited by legislative restrictions, essentially conservative in their reactions. Can they possibly espouse such a view of multiple realities as I have been describing? Can they begin to bring into being the changes in attitudes, behaviors, and values that such a world view would demand? Certainly, by themselves they cannot. But with the underlying change in what Whyte calls "the unconscious tradition," and with the aid of the new person whom I and many others see emerging in our culture, it is just conceivable that they might succeed.

I conclude that if nations follow their past ways, then, because of the speed of world communication of separate views, each society will have to exert more and more coercion to bring about a forced agreement as to what constitutes the real world and its values. Those coerced agreements will differ from nation to nation, from culture to culture. The coercion will destroy individual freedom. We will bring about our own destruction through the clashes caused by differing world views.

But I have suggested an alternative. If we accept as a basic fact of all human life that we live in separate realities; if we can see those differing realities as the most promising resource for learning in all the history of the world; if we can live together in order to learn from one another without fear; if we can do all this, then a new age could be dawning. And perhaps — just perhaps — humankind's deep organic sensings are paving the way for just such a change.

To the Instructor

Most students will respond wholeheartedly to Rogers's summons, since it elicits our most generous impulses and promises a kinder, gentler world for all of us. It stands as a friendly companion piece to Mead's "Warfare: An Invention — Not a Biological Necessity." In addition, his emphasis on education can encourage students to reflect on their own experience with multiculturalism and diversity as they have observed them, or not, at school.

Rogers was not without his critics and his contradictions. However welcome his essentially optimistic view of the human capacity for change and growth, his theories can also invite a lively dialogue. Before considering Rogers's policy recommendations, students should be familiar with the history on which Rogers bases his conclusions. They should be prepared to discuss the values that underlie his claims. (See the reference to Rogers in Chapter 8's "Divorce and Our National Values.") And, of course, they should be encouraged to ask hard questions.

I would begin by asking students to consider answers to these questions: Can you think of other examples of separate realities? Do you think that all realities are equally deserving of respect and accommodation? (Be specific.) Does Rogers try to prove that they are? Does recent history — since the publication of *A Way of Being* in 1980 — confirm or deny Rogers's hopes and convictions? Do you think Rogers and King in "I Have A Dream" agree about the shape of a future world?

Some students may want to know whether the analogy between private and public reconciliations can hold. Not everyone agrees that the therapies which are successful in solving problems between individuals can be called on to resolve the profound differences in the public arena. "In the context of a marriage, say, it does seem plausible that a husband and wife may have common goals. But is this also true in public life? [I]n many cases we don't share first principles at all — just think of the fights over abortion." (Larissa MacFarquhar, "Thank You for Not Fighting," a review of Deborah Tannen's *The Argument Culture* in the *New York Times Book Review*, April 5, 1998, p. 38.)

Students may want to consult Tannen's book, which offers a Rogerian perspective. From the review quoted above, "Tannen's is a communitarian view of the world, in which we share enough first principles that we should in theory be able to agree on the right thing to do."